FPL
REF
796.357

Scott

Bot

W9-BRW-848

Purchase of this book

made possible

by the bequest of

Henry R. & Mary P. Scott

DISCARD

FRAMINGHAM PUBLIC LIBRARY

MAR 15 1990

DISCARD

THE
Dickson Baseball
Dictionary

THE
DICKSON BASEBALL
DICTIONARY

Paul Dickson

Facts On File
New York • Oxford

To Andrew and Alexander
who got me started, and helped me
field new words for the collection.

The Dickson Baseball Dictionary

Copyright © 1989 by Paul Dickson

All rights reserved. No part of this book may
be reproduced or utilized in any form or by any
means, electronic or mechanical, including
photocopying, recording, or by any information
storage and retrieval systems, without permission
in writing from the publisher.

Library of Congress Cataloging-in-Publication Data

Dickson, Paul.
    The Dickson baseball dictionary / Paul Dickson.
      p.   cm.
    Bibliography: p.
    ISBN 0-8160-1741-7 :
    1. Baseball—United States—Dictionaries.   I. Title.
GV862.3.D53 1989
796.357'0973—dc19 88-23583

Interior design by Ron Monteleone

British Cip data available on request

Printed in the United States of America

10 9 8 7 6 5 4 3 2

CONTENTS

PREFACE

People are always asking writers how they got the idea for their latest book. It is a ritual as familiar to an author as the question "What does he/she weigh?" is to the mother of a new baby.

I'm not sure whether this is just a ritual and whether others really do care exactly how an idea was hatched, just as they really only pretend to care about the exact weight of a baby. But both rituals are important for the simple reason that they express friendship for and interest in the proud parent and author.

Having said that, I will tell you how I got the idea for this book.

On Seeing a Three-Year-Old Watch Rickey Henderson Steal Second

In September of 1981, our family went to see the Oakland Athletics play the Baltimore Orioles in Memorial Stadium in Baltimore. Among other things, it was the first time our younger son, Alex, had ever been to a baseball game. He was still a few days short of turning four, and we had almost left him home with a baby-sitter.

With breathtaking suddenness he was taken with it all. You could hear it in his voice, see it in his eyes and realize it when he chose to stay in his seat rather than leave for food and souvenirs. The moment of his hooking came within minutes of our arrival. It was not when Rickey Henderson got to first base, but when he stole second. As if engineering it with the personal authority of the Commissioner's Office in order to guarantee one more diehard fan, Henderson stole again later in the game. Alex is eleven now and, needless to say, there is a big Henderson poster above his bed.

This got me thinking about the game in a new way, not because getting hooked by Henderson was novel, but because it was, perhaps, so predictable. I had seen this earlier with my older son, Andrew, whose hooking had come in the same stadium during a doubleheader. I thought back to my own hooking, which had been in 1946 when my father took me to Yankee Stadium to see what he called the whole game. His idea of the whole game meant getting there early enough to see the batting practice, the horseplay, and the preparation of the field. We had, in fact, gotten there so early that we ran into outfielder Tommy "Old Reliable" Henrich, who was still in his street clothes. Then I remembered the night three summers later when I first saw something that I had only dreamed of: Johnny Mize in a Yankees—not a Giants—uniform.

I began to realize that the old cliche of fathers taking sons to baseball games as a rite of initiation was flawed. In reality it is the child who often brings the parent back to the game. If the youngster is hooked, his father is rehooked in the process.

Part of this process, I soon learned, had to do with getting reacquainted with baseball tradition, a very specialized body of wisdom and ritual. Being able to give a perfect, yet seemingly off-the-cuff description of the infield fly rule, knowing how to keep score and how the teams got their names, being able to recite the right aphorism at the proper moment—these are all important. So is remembering the feel of the ball itself.

On Getting a New Mitt at Age 47

I have had three baseball gloves in my lifetime. The first was bought by my grandmother when I was 11. It was technically a fielder's glove, but I always called it a mitt after the custom in my neighborhood by which all gloves were called mitts. Gloves were for boxing and snowball fights.

That first mitt was a Spalding, bought on a special train trip to New York City. I still have it, a #197 Young Star. It's a mess: a laceless, lifeless, stubby-fingered pancake with padding long ago pounded into so much dust. I hang onto it because it is a source of wonder to me. It has outlasted a dozen bats, bikes, and family sedans as well as Presidents Truman, Eisenhower, Kennedy, Johnson, Nixon, Ford, Carter, and Reagan.

It was deployed for hardball, softball and countless games of catch. It baked in the sun, rotted in the rain and once fell out of a rowboat and had to be retrieved from the muck at the bottom of a lake. It was oiled, tortured into various shapes depending on the needs of the moment and, until my dog chewed off a lion's share of the lacing, had a pocket so deep it could devour a regulation hardball.

I outgrew that mitt and didn't feel the need for another until my two sons came along. My second mitt turned up at a flea market. A decent enough piece of leather, it carried the autograph of Wayne Causey, a journeyman infielder who played for the Orioles, Kansas City A's and White Sox from 1955 through 1968. It had a marvelous snap to it when a ball hit the pocket, but the pleasure diminished considerably when the padding began migrating to the outer edge of the glove. The snap then correlated so directly with pain that I found I couldn't hear anybody field a hot one without emitting a small Pavlovian wince.

I started making plaintive noises about needing a new mitt about the time my 47th birthday hove into view. I could have bought one myself, but somehow never got around to it, perhaps because it didn't seem quite right for a man who is 20 months and two weeks older than Pete Rose to walk into a store alone and buy a mitt for himself. Then my wife announced that she was buying me one for my birthday. We'd go together and pick one out.

"Spittin' Bill" Doak c. 1916. *National Baseball Library, Cooperstown, N.Y.*

Historically, there is some question as to which player was the first to wear a protective glove. It is clear, though, that it was not until the season of 1877 that gloves became commonplace. It was then that a respected player named Albert Goodwill Spalding donned a black kid glove and desissified the notion once and for all. This was the very same A. G. Spalding who had just started a sporting goods business with his brother.

Not until the season of 1920 could a player buy a glove with a laced webbing and the natural deep pocket that such a design allows. That vastly improved glove was named for and designed by pitcher Bill Doak, who threw for the Cardinals. Since then evolution has been rapid, with manufacturers working hard to come up with a design edge they can patent and promote. Rawlings designer Rollie Latina, who came up with enough new ideas to land, by his count, "11 or 12" patents during a 40-year career, says, "Today's ball-player has a lot more control because he catches with the glove itself rather than his hand."

When we went to pick out my new mitt, the choices were overwhelming and a far cry from the homely work gloves of my childhood. There were Spaldings, Wilsons, Mizunos, Rawlings and Louisville Sluggers at prices ranging from $35 to over $100. Most were signed by stars except for those priced at $100 and up. These expensive models are termed "pro" models, so if you're a pro I suspect it is "bush" to have somebody else's moniker on your mitt. I have since learned that, while a player may autograph and authorize a glove, that is not the actual model he uses.

There was much trying on, fist pummelling and posing. The reflected image is important and I'm sure is one reason why sporting goods stores, like bridal shops, always have mirrors. I wound up with a Rawlings 1445 Darryl Strawberry "fastback." I took the tan model rather than the "strawberry"-hued version. As much as I love puns, I was not ready to wear one for my baseball reentry. A number of magic words and copyrighted phrases are stamped into its surface, including the "deep well" pocket, "edge-U-cated heel," and "holD-ster" fastening band. The webbing is an immense, supple leather network large enough for trapping and comforting small furry animals.

The glory of a brand-new mitt is the glory of leather without a memory. My Darryl Strawberry "fastback" had never committed an error or a flub of any sort. It offered the new start that middle age needs, all but begging to be shaped to my hand. Add to this the fact that for pure consumer pleasure the sweet aroma of a new baseball glove ranks with the smell of a new car, and it is easy to see why I couldn't put it down the day it came home.

On its first outing it proved to be a magnet. Not once did I have to apologize for its newness or my oldness. Second time out, a very serious catch with a man my own age, I booted a couple. The first time I used its newness as an excuse—"Still breaking it in"—and the next time I just muttered, "The old back!" But despite a few gaffes here and there the magic of the new glove had become a given. Soon it was eliciting comments and compliments in words and phrases I had not heard since I was in high school. I jumped up and pulled down a high one that just barely stuck in the top of the webbing. "Nice snowcone," said my companion as I examined the proof of what had happened—I had violated the law of gravity.

All this glory did not come without a price tag. What I found, I had to admit openly and often, was that the glove, not me, was making the difference. My abilities in the field had not improved over time. I also began to understand one of the reasons why there might not be another big league .400 hitter during my lifetime. Larry McClain, vice president for baseball at Rawlings in St. Louis, puts it in perspective: "Today's gloves are not only superior to those of the 1920s but also the 1950s." He believes that men like Willie Mays and Mickey Mantle might have fared even better in the field with some of today's models. He does, however, acknowledge that Ozzie Smith, a spectacular fielder, uses what is essentially a '50s-style glove.

My last few comments on glove evolution are not a digression but are added testimonial to the power of the present I got at age 47. Simply put, the new mitt put me back in touch with the feel of the game of baseball. To describe such a gift as marvelous is to dabble in understatement.

The act of acquiring the glove also had to do with history. To buy into baseball this way is to buy into the history of the game: children born after Watergate know about the Black Sox and the Babe, but draw a blank when the Nobel Prize or Harry Truman are mentioned. Football and basketball seem to date back a couple years at most; but baseball is a realm where players of the past die but never seem to age, where records are recalled even if they were set in 1933, where Ty and Cy are household names, and where half the people who "recall" Bobby Thomson's home run of the century weren't even born when it happened. Roger Angell put it this way in *Late Innings:* "I have read so much about the old-timers and heard older players and writers and fans (including my father) talk about them so often that they are almost as visible to me as the stars I have watched on the field."

If there is an intergenerational glue that holds all of this together, it is composed of numbers, stats and records, and words—the motley vocabulary of baseball, which is a mix of slang, nicknames, metaphors and official terminology. What were the Miracle of Coogan's Bluff and Merkle's Boner? What is a "can of corn" or a "cup of coffee"

and what are they doing on the field? How come K is the scorecard symbol for strikeout? What and when was the "live ball era"? The list goes on and on, but the point is made that baseball is intensely verbal.

It is, in fact, verbal on many levels. Tom Boswell has written that for a minor leaguer, talk is the staple of sanity and that the man who cannot spin a yarn, tell a joke or create an epigram is "condemned to be an outsider." He adds, "This rich verbal tradition—the way the game has taken on the ambiance of the frontier campfire or the farmer's cracker-barrel stove and moved it into the dugout—is what marks baseball so distinctively . . ." On another occasion he wrote, "Conversation is the blood of baseball."

Paul Dickson,
Garrett Park, Maryland

INTRODUCTION

I

Baseball needs a Webster and a standing-Revision Board to keep the dictionary of the game up to date. The sport is building its own language so steadily that, unless some step soon is taken to check the inventive young men who coin the words that attach themselves to the pastime, interpreters will have to be maintained in every grand stand to translate for the benefit of those who merely love the game and do not care to master it thoroughly.

> —Hugh S. Fullerton,
> "The Baseball Primer,"
> *The American Magazine,*
> June 1912

Back in 1913 an odd movement started in Chicago. Time has obscured some of the details, but what it amounted to was a movement away from baseball slang. The *Chicago Record-American* began covering games two ways: one in the slang of the time and, next to it, a description of the game in "less boisterous" terms. A Professor McClintock of the English department at the University of Chicago brought the matter to national attention when he suggested that the Republic would be better served if baseball slang were dropped and that, for starters, the newspapers would start describing the sport in dictionary English.

This call came at a time when, for example, *The Washington Post*'s Joe Campbell, "the Chaucer of baseball," would write: "And Amie Rusie made a Svengali pass in front of Charlie Reilly's lamps and he carved three nicks in the weather," to say that Rusie had gotten Reilly to strike out.

A few managers and players actually agreed with McClintock, but there was little sympathy expressed by the press, which whipped McClintock's notion into something big. "The question has assumed the importance of a national issue," said an editorial in the *Charleston News and Courier,* "It has received editorial discussion in the columns of the most influential newspapers, and it has aroused interest from end to end of this baseball-loving land." Calling the notion the "injury which is now proposed," the paper went on to say, "It is to be hoped, and it may reasonably be expected, that the movement will not accomplish the results which its more radical advocates desire. Baseball stories told in conventional English are dull reading indeed; and it is a pertinent fact that the decadence of cricket in England is attributed by many British newspapers to the failure of the press to put brightness or 'ginger' into the descriptions of the game."

The *Washington Post* chose to make fun of McClintock by describing play using dictionary English. Sample: "Johnson gave the batter a free pass to first" becomes "Mr. Johnson pitched four balls that in immediate sequence made a detour of the plate, which, according to the rules of the game, entitled the batter to go to first base, despite the fact that he had not even aimed his bat at the baseball in any one instance." After a thorough roasting, the *Post* concluded, "Much of the English used by Professor McClintock himself was once regarded as slang."

On the other hand, *The Nation* saw the threat as a serious one and wrote about it as if it were a disease: "One of the most puzzling problems of this puzzling era is the effect wrought upon our native speech by contact with the national pastime."

All of this was, of course, a passing controversy that amounted to little; but it did

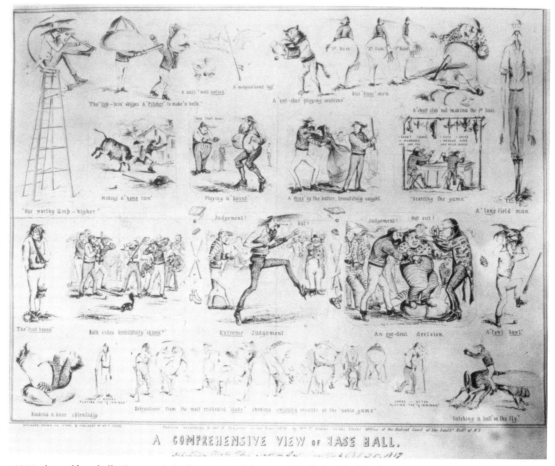

1859 view of baseball. Slang and the language of the game had already developed to the point where baseball was fit for spoofing. Among other things, the cartoon shows a very early use of the term shortstop.   *National Baseball Library, Cooperstown, N.Y.*

serve to drive home a point: Baseball had its own ever-changing language, and it was not to be meddled with. Ironically, not too many years would pass before men and women with PhDs would be making names for themselves not by decrying slang but by collecting it—not only that of the diamond, but also of the carnival, the hobo jungle, the railroad yard, the soda fountain—and publishing it in *American Speech*, the superb journal devoted to the riches of American English.

It also served to underscore another point: The baseball language of the press was different from that of the participants in the game.

Sometimes lost in all of this discussion of the propriety of slang is the fact that it was a remarkably rich and effective way of writing that could allow the drama of nine innings to be compressed into one socko, lung-straining sentence. Such sentences tend to retain their vitality for many years. An example from the *San Francisco Examiner* for April 13, 1932: "Greeting big George Ernshaw like a long lost 'cousin,' Babe Ruth and the New York Yankees fell upon the right-handed act of the Athletics this chilly afternoon, blasted him off the field in four innings and outslugged the American League champions 12 to 6."

If baseball is a game of slang, it is also a

game of heaped-on modifiers. A word like *single* seldom stands naked. Listen, as one is described in a sentence by Richard Justice of the *Washington Post:* "The only California run scored after Davis had wild-pitched rookie Wally Joyner (three for four) into scoring position and then given up a broken-bat, opposite-field bloop single to Brian Downing." (May 22, 1986)

A few conclusions derived from the study of baseball language are in order. The first is personal; the rest are general:

1. If someone had told me at the beginning of this project that I would be able to find nearly 5,000 words, terms, names and phrases to define, I would have said this was impossible. That I did is not an accomplishment to be credited to the author, but rather one to be scored to the game itself, with an assist to that rich and flexible entity known as the English language. (While I was working on the book, I occasionally thought that the game might have an entirely different tone and presence if it had evolved in, say, France or Germany. This is impossible to prove, of course.)

   It also came as a surprise to realize that a number of terms had more than one meaning in the context of this game. There are six baseball meanings of *in*, five for *option* and four for *leather*. *Chin music, pickle, flag* and *in the hole* each have three distinctly different meanings.

   The fact of the matter is that there would have been even more entries if I had used each and every item of baseball slang that I came across. For the sake of the reader (to say nothing of the writer), I chose not to use those lesser specimens. One rule of thumb used was to ignore those terms that showed up only once in the research and were not confirmed elsewhere. For instance, I was able to find only one instance of *David Harums,* the eponym

used to describe owners and managers, and it does not appear in the dictionary. A recent example of the ephemeral is the line, "Elvis has left the building," for an out-of-the-park home run. It was created, puckishly, by television comedian David Letterman who told his audience that baseball announcers needed a new means of announcing a home run. It has been used by announcers, but always explained in terms of Letterman's humor of the absurd.

   There were also a number of words that have appeared elsewhere than in lists of baseball terms and seemed so *general* to American English that I left them out. A few examples: *blunder, boo, break even, discard, edge, fast one, fluke, hoist* (to hit high), *lift one, nook, shake up, shoulder-high, shine* (to perform well) and *toss up.*

2. Baseball has a particular infatuation with what one critic of sportswriters once termed, "the incorrect use of correct words." There are hundreds of examples, but the point can be made by simply listing a selection of synonyms for the hard-hit ball or *line drive.* It is variously known as an *aspirin,* a *BB,* a *bolt,* a *clothesline,* a *frozen rope,* a *pea,* a *rocket,* and a *seed.* A player's throwing arm seems to be called everything but an arm: *gun, hose, rifle, soupbone, whip* and *wing,* to name just a few. The arm is not the only renamed body part. From top to bottom, players have *lamps* (eyes), a *pipe* (neck or throat), *hooks* (hands), *wheels* (legs) and *tires* (feet).

   So many allusions are made to food and dining—including pitches that seem to fall off the table—that a fairly well-balanced diet suggests itself in terms like *can of corn, cup of coffee, fish cakes, banana stalk, mustard, pretzel, rhubarb, green pea, juice, meat hand, grapefruit league* and *tater.* Among the many terms for the ball itself are *apple, can-*

taloupe, egg, pea, potato and *tomato.* Implements? There is the *plate* (also known as the *platter, pan* and *dish*) and, of course, the *fork ball.* Dessert? The red abrasion from a slide into base is a *strawberry* and the fan's time-honored sound of disapproval is a *raspberry.*

3. Slang, we are always being told, is ephemeral. This is not borne out by baseball slang because for every seemingly fleeting term or phrase, there seems to be one that hangs on for several generations. Many terms that began as slang have been so widely accepted and are used so routinely that they are no longer considered slang. This point was first made in an article in the *Saturday Review* in 1933 in which the author, Murray Godwin, pointed to the permanence of such "slang" as *sacrifice* and *wind up.* Compare this, for example, to the slang of popular music or the high school, which seems to change constantly.

Etymologist Peter Tamony put it much more strongly. In his essay on the term "Dick Smith" (a name assigned to a loner in baseball and horseracing slang) he wrote: "It is always amusing to be able to run down the history and origin of a real slang word. Real slang always laughs at the professors and others who hold that it is ephemeral. They mistake mere metaphor and simile for slang. To hold that slang is largely ephemeral is to say that dress is ephemeral because women's fashions change four times a year. A large part of our slang has a long, long history, but records of it are short. It is only since the advent of the modern sports page, about 1900, that this vital and human aspect, this color of our speech, has been properly recorded."

Baseball slang is in fact hard to kill, and specific terms have a way of asserting themselves after being written off as archaic. While researching this book, many articles came to light which had declared dead a term that is still very much alive today. A 1964 article in *Baseball Digest,* by Tim Horgan of the *Boston Traveler,* tells us, for example, "there are no more bleachers. They are now 'porches.'" The same article reported that home run and can of corn had become verbal antiques and, "No pitcher today . . . throws a fastball or, as our forefathers knew it, 'a high hard one.'" In 1933 Damon Runyon described a hit that "used to be called" a Texas Leaguer and in 1937 sportswriter Curley Grieve of the *San Francisco Examiner* told his readers, "A left-handed hurler is no longer a southpaw. He's a cock-eyed hurler."

Similarly, a 1982 article on baseball slang that appeared in the *USAir* inflight magazine, listed the term *wheelhouse* (for the area of the batter's greatest hitting strength) as one of a number of bygone words that had "gone down swinging." If the term is dead, no one has bothered to tell the many writers and sportscasters who use it regularly. "Frozen," as applied to a line drive, is labeled an "out-of-date cant" that "embarrasses everyone within hearing distance" in *The Old Ball Game,* Tristram Potter Coffin's 1971 work; yet it survives today as a common baseball adjective (e.g., frozen rope).

Then there is the term "can of corn," which is annually declared dead, but which comes back as surely as Opening Day. Among the recent obituaries:

1986. "For starters, one phrase that's out is can of corn," wrote Scott Ostler in the *Los Angeles Times,* ". . . several players warned me to stay away from that one."

1987. Mets catcher Gary Carter deems the term "ancient history" in an article in the *St. Petersburg Times* on the latest in baseball slang.

On the other hand, consider another vegetable. There are a number of writers who have reported the term *pea* (for a ball batted or pitched so fast that it can hardly be seen) as an example of the very latest in baseball lingo, even though it can be traced back at least to 1910. To fill out the platter, there is *rhubarb*, which never seems to have gone out of vogue since it made its baseball debut in the 1930s.

4. There is a tone to the language of the game that is remarkably pastoral. If any image dominates the language of the game it is that of rural America. Even under a dome, it is a game of *fields and fences*, where *ducks sit on the pond* and pitchers sit in the *catbird seat*. New players come out of the *farm system* and a *farmhand* who pitches may get to work in the *bullpen*.

It is also low key. Although some of the terms for whacking the ball with the bat are strong (to *crush, smash, powder*) and *base stealing* is aptly named, other actions are described in absurdly mild terms. The most glaring example takes place when the ball is thrown at the batter by the pitcher. This is done in an attempt to intimidate or injure the batter. Terms associated with this act include *bean* and *beanball, dust* and *duster, brush* and *brush back, shave* and *barber*. It is sometimes called a *purpose pitch* or *chin music* that can be used to *flip* a batter. Such behavior may lead to a noisy and sometimes violent confrontation that is called a *rhubarb*.

Compare this to a headline run over a *Washington Post* interview with New York Giants linebacker Lawrence Taylor a few days before Super Bowl XXI: "Taylor: 'Kill Shots' Make the Game." Comedian George Carlin has a routine in which he compares the pastoral game of baseball to football, which is played on a *gridiron* where there is *blitzing, red-dogging, drives* into *enemy territory* and where *bombs* are thrown. Baseball is played in a *park*, and the offensive plays include the *free pass, homer* and *sacrifice fly*. In football you *spear, march* and *score;* in baseball you *walk, stretch* and *run home*. In an op-ed piece in the *New York Times* (September 6, 1987) Steve Palay points out that the language of arms control is very close to that of football (*throw weight, end run, hammering out* an agreement, etc.) but that it would be better served if it was taken from baseball. "Arms control is not won," Palay concludes, "it is played. And going into 'extra innings' sounds so much better than 'sudden death.'"

All of this is not to say that baseball terminology is without its dark side. A letter from Jim Land of Felton, California published in the October 5, 1987 *Sporting News*, makes the point: "Baseball terminology, steeped in tradition, pays tribute to chicanery. For example, stealing bases, stealing signs, cheating toward the lines, robbing homers and hits, stabs, swipes, bluffs and suicide squeeze are all part of the game. There are hidden ball tricks, faked tags and in-the-vicinity plays."

5. For reasons that are unclear, baseball seems driven to come up with its own terms for things that are used widely in other sports. Everywhere else teams are piloted by head coaches, but baseball insists on *managers* (and with rare exception dresses them like players) and all the referees are called *umpires*. If other sports had to deal with discrimination and segregation, baseball dealt with the *color bar*. Substitutes are good enough for most sports, but not for baseball, which insists on loading its benches and bullpens with *firemen, pinch hitters, pinch runners* and *platoon players*. Baseball players never seem to turn, they always *pivot*. In realms as diverse as bowling and bombing, a strike is a hit; but in baseball alone it is a *miss*. Out of bounds works for everyone else, but baseball insists on *foul territory*. If the same facility is used for football on Sunday and baseball on

Monday, it is transformed overnight from a stadium to a *ballpark*. And the locker rooms used by the football players become *clubhouses* for the baseball players.

6. If one person had to be singled out for having had the most influence on the official language of the game, it is a pioneering Englishman named Henry Chadwick, but this may only be because he came along so early that he was essentially given the opportunity to fill in blanks. He wrote the first rule book, created the first box score and served as one of the game's first journalists. He also created many of the early baseball manuals that were used during the latter half of the 19th century.

Beyond this, there have been several attempts to give somebody the title of father of baseballese (baseball jargon). Among them is the assertion that a school of midwestern and western baseball writers appeared in the late 19th century and had a great impact in building the vocabulary needed to describe the game. The assertion is made in John Allen Krout's 1929 *Annals of American Sport* and he gives some of their names: "Shortly after 1883 Leonard Washburn, Finley Peter Dunne, who earned national fame as the creator of Mr. Dooley, and Charles Seymour began to write their entertaining stories of Anson's White Stockings for the Chicago papers."

But all of this is somewhat misleading because so many people have had a continuing impact. A very small and incomplete list would have to include Branch Rickey, Casey Stengel, Earl Weaver, Red Barber, Yogi Berra, Ring Lardner, Red Smith, Dizzy Dean, Jim Murray, Gaylord Perry, Theodore A. "TAD" Dorgan, Alexander Cartwright, Pierce Egan, Jim Brosnan, Satchel Paige, Willard Mullin, Leo Durocher and Babe Ruth.

II.

No other sport and few other occupations have introduced so many phrases, so many words, so many twists into our language as has baseball. The true test comes in the fact that old ladies who have never been to the ballpark, coquettes who don't know or care who's on first, men who think athletics begin and end with a pair of goalposts, still know and use a great deal of baseball-derived terminology. Perhaps other sports in their efforts to replace baseball as "our national pastime," have two strikes on them before they come to bat.
—Tristram Potter Coffin,
The Old Ball Game

If you don't understand the game you won't enjoy it. I'll explain it to you. The first guy gets up to take his cut. Maybe he whiffs, maybe he gets on. Let's say he gets on. So then there is a guy on first. Then the second guy comes up to take his cut. Maybe he whiffs, maybe he gets on. Let's say . . .
—Cab driver explaining the game
in a Nunnally Johnson story retold
in Fred Schwed's
How to Watch a Baseball Game

Why is baseball terminology so dominant an influence in the language? Does it suggest that the situations that develop as the game is played are comparable to the patterns of our daily work? Does the sport imitate the fundamentals of the national life or is the national life shaped to an extent by the character of the sport? In any case, here is an opportunity to reflect on the meaning of what I think I heard Reggie Jackson say in his spot on a national network in the last World Series: "The country is as American as baseball."
—Elting E. Morison in
American Heritage,
August/September 1986

The influence of baseball on American English at large is stunning and strong. Perhaps the best way to drive this home is to present a partial list of terms and phrases that started in baseball (or, at least, were given a major boost by it) but that have much wider application, to wit: "A" team, ace, Alibi Ike, Annie Oakley, back to back, ballpark figure, bat a thousand, batting average, bean, bench, benchwarmer, Black Sox, bleacher, the breaks, breeze/breeze through, Bronx cheer, bush, bush league(r), boner, bonehead, box score, bunt, butter-fingers, "call 'em as I see 'em," catch flat-footed, caught in a squeeze play, charley horse, choke, circus catch, clutch, clutch hitter, curveball, doubleheader, double play, extra innings, fan, fouled out, gate money, get one's innings in, get to first base, go to bat for, grandstand play, grandstander, ground rules, hardball, heads up, hit and run, "hit 'em where they ain't," hit the dirt, home run, hot stove league, hustle, in the ballpark, in a pinch, in there pitching, "it ain't over 'til it's over," "it's a (whole) new ballgame," jinx, keep your eye on the ball, ladies' day, Louisville Slugger, minor league, muff, "nice guys finish last," ninth-inning rally, off base, on-deck, one's licks, on the ball, on the bench, out in left field, out of my league, phenom, pinch hitter, play ball with, play the field, play-by-play, pop up, rain check, rhubarb, right off the bat, rookie, rooter, Ruthian, safe by a mile, "say it ain't so, Joe," screwball, seventh-inning stretch, showboat, shut out, smash hit, southpaw, spitball, squeeze play, Stengalese, strawberry, strike out, sucker, switch hitter, team play, Tinker-to-Evers-to-Chance, touch all bases, two strikes against him, "wait 'til next year," warm up, whitewash, "Who's on first?" windup, "you can't win 'em all," "you could look it up"

You *could* look it up! That is the exact point of this book.

ACKNOWLEDGMENTS

The writer wishes to acknowledge his indebtedness to the Mayo brothers, Ringling Brothers, Smith brothers, Rath brothers, the Dolly sisters, and former President Buchanan for their aid in instructing him in the technical terms of baseball, such as "bat," "ball," "pitcher," "foul," "sleeping car," and "sore arm."
—Ring Lardner,
from his Preface to
You Know Me Al

Four sources of help and information were absolutely essential to the researching of this book. Collectively, their influence and inspiration are felt on practically every page. These are:

David Shulman of New York City who allowed me to use his collection of unpublished citations on the earliest use of certain terms. His generosity and guidance are acknowledged with great admiration.

Charles D. Poe of Houston, who spent many, many hours finding examples of baseballese and player nicknames. His influence is felt on almost every page of this book.

The late Peter Tamony of San Francisco and the people at the University of Missouri who now administer his one-of-a-kind collection on the American language. Tamony spent most of his life collecting and writing about slang. One of his particular passions was the language of sport and the information he collected on baseball terms is without parallel. I am especially indebted to Randy Roberts who is cataloging the Tamony Collection for the organization that administers it under the full name of the Joint Collection University of Missouri Western Historical Manuscript Collection—Columbia and State Historical Society of Missouri Manuscripts.

The staff of the National Baseball Library at Cooperstown, New York, who really know how to help a guy.

Robert "Skip" McAfee of the Society for American Baseball Research, Columbia, Maryland, was kind enough to come in the late innings to spot missing entries and help with last-minute corrections.

I also must express my special indebtedness to one Edward J. Nichols, whose 1939 Pennsylvania State thesis, "An Historical Dictionary of Baseball Terminology," has proven to be invaluable.

Ever since I first thought about starting this project, Joseph C. Goulden has been feeding me a steady diet of clippings, with examples of baseballese carefully marked and annotated. Thanks.

Other people who have made important contributions to this work are listed here. I thank them all for their help and enthusiasm:

Lane Akers; Dr. Reinhold A. Aman, Maledicta; Russell Ash; Q. David Bowers; Gerald Cohen; Bob Davids; Jay Davis, the *Waldo Independent;* Percy Dean; Bill Deane, National Baseball Library; Charles F. Dery; Alex, Andrew and Nancy Dickson; Ross Eckler of *Word Ways;* Steve Fiffer; Martin Gardner; Tom Gill; Robert Greenman; Thomas R. Heitz, librarian, National Baseball Library; Robert Hendrickson; George S. Hobart, curator, documentary photographs, Library of Congress; Truxton Hulbert, Belfast Free Library; Bob Ingraham; W. Lloyd Johnson, executive director, SABR; Cliff Kachline, who helped get the project started; Dave Kelly, Library of Congress sports specialist; Pat Kelly, National Baseball Library; Norbert Kraich; Richard Lederer; Matthew E. Lieff; Christopher Mead; William Mead; Ron Menchine; Rick Minch, the Cleveland Indians; Bill Plummer, Amateur Softball Association of America; Frank Potter; Pam Silva, the Merriam-Webster Co., Springfield, Mass.; Bob Skole; Michael A. Stackpole; John Sullivan, the Library of Congress; and Bill Tammeus.

HOW TO USE THE DICTIONARY

Having long thought that *I* needed a baseball dictionary, I imagined what one would look and feel like well before the first word of this one was put down on paper. From the outset the idea was that it had to be useful to a nine-year-old looking for a clear definition of the infield fly rule, but it also had to be a book that would appeal to two of the toughest audiences for the printed word: the baseball fanatic and the lover of language.

First and foremost, this is a dictionary meant for these three users. But it is also a book for browsing, and for that reason, there will be a flexibility in the presentation of entries. If, for example, a good story begs to be told as a digression, it gets told.

Nonetheless, a general format has been adopted, which is as follows:

> **entry 1.** *part of speech/usage* first definition.
> **2.** *part of speech/usage* second definition.
> **3.** SYNONYM.

Following the part of speech, either *arch.* for archaic or *obs.* for obsolete may be indicated. Great restraint has been exercised in using the archaic label because, as was pointed out in the Introduction, certain terms have had a way of making a comeback at the very moment they are deemed to be dead. (I had been convinced that *yakker* [for curveball] was archaic until I heard Jim Palmer use the term twice during a baseball telecast. I had already labeled *twirler* [for pitcher] as archaic when I read this line in the July 1, 1987, *Lewiston* [Maine] *Daily Sun* in an account of a game in Jay, Maine: "The Litchfield twirler had a shutout until the seventh inning.")

A term is labeled obsolete only when it refers to a rule, practice or element of the game that is no longer a part of it and that seems unlikely ever to stage a comeback.

A word appearing in capital letters within a definition indicates a synonymous cross-reference. If the synonym appears as a term's first definition, the reader should turn to that term's entry for a full definition.

When it appears useful to the reader, the term is illustrated as it appears in the context of an attributed, dated quotation. I have also included, as part of the definition, the historic background of the concept or object in question.

Following each definition, any or all of the following elements are likely to appear.

1st Rookie Appearance A dated reference often accompanied by a display of a term as it appears in that reference. In most cases it is, of course, impossible to cite the very earliest example that appears in print, so this feature is really meant to give the reader a feel for the relative antiquity and early use of the word or phrase. Lest there be any question, the citation given will be the earliest found.

Most of these citations are marked with the initials of the researcher who found them—EJN for Edward J. Nichols, PT for Peter Tamony, DS for David Shulman or CDP for Charles D. Poe.

For reasons of space, not every citation will be followed by the actual reference. Most of those without the actual quote are from Nichols' 1939 doctoral thesis, "An Historical Dictionary of Baseball Terminology." These were omitted as they have been known through the Nichols thesis for some years.

ETY Origin and Etymology When possible, the history of the word is given. If there are a number of theories about the origin of a word, all will be given and often they will be followed by a discussion of their relative merit. Such explanations are not attempted when the term itself appears to suggest its origin, as is the case with terms like *out* and *fly ball*.

Some terms will have more than one etymology and these may be in conflict with one another. The principle at work in this dictionary is that *all* the claims should be presented. If there is a bias lurking in this book, it is that words and phrases can have a motley assortment of etymologies that have acted corroboratively to give the term momentum and popularity. One of them may, in fact, be the original, but that does not mean the others did not have important influence. This is at odds with the belief that all terms have a single "story" behind them.

EXT External Use Use of the term in the language at large as it is used outside baseball. It is through these sub-entries that one gets to see the immense influence of baseball on the American language. Interestingly, there are a number of terms, which no longer sound like baseball terms, that appear to have first sprung from the diamond.

USE Usage Note Comment on a special context in which a term may be used.

SEE Cross-reference Words in italics at the end of an entry may be consulted as separate entries.

The Jargon of the Diamond

The diamond has a language all its own;
If a player makes an error, it's a "bone";
    If he attempts the "squeeze"
    And strikes out, it's a "breeze";
A play at which the fans belch forth a groan.

A safe drive to the field is called a "bingle";
If good for one base only, it's a "single";
    If the hurler throws a "cripple"
    And the batter clouts a "triple,"
The swat will put the nerves of fans a-tingle.

When a runner's left on base, 'tis said he "died."
If he goes out on a high fly, he has "skied";
    A one-hand stop's a "stab";
    The pitcher's mound, the "slab";
Successful plays are certainly "inside."

When a player's making good his work is "grand."
But let him boot just one and he's "panned";
    If he comes up in a "pinch"
    And he "whiffs"—well, it's a cinch,
The fickle fans will yell, "He should be 'canned.' "

—John H. Miller,
Baseball magazine,
October 1916

A

A   1. The third level of minor league baseball, following AAA and AA. It is usually referred to as "single A" or "class A."
2. Scorecard abbreviation for assist.
3. Box score abbreviation for attendance.

AA   Second tier of minor league classification.

AAA   The highest minor league classification, just below the Majors.
USE   Written AAA, it is almost always "Triple A" when spoken.

AB   Standard scorecard and box score abbreviation for at bat.

abbreviations   There are a number of abbreviations used in baseball that are used most commonly when scoring a game and in box scores that appear in the newspapers. Although some of these terms are used only on scorecards or in box scores, others are used in both and are therefore listed together.

Abbreviation	Term
A	Assist, Attendance
"A"	First Team
AB	Official At Bat
AL	Active List, American League
B	Bunt
'B'	Second Team
BA	Batting Average
BB	Base on Balls (Walk)
BK	Balk
CG	Complete Game
CS	Caught Stealing
DP	Double Play
DH	Designated Hitter, Doubleheader
DL	Disabled List
E	Error
ER	Earned Run
ERA	Earned Run Average
F	Foul Out
FC	Fielder's Choice
FO	Force Out
FP	Fielding Percentage
G	Game
GS	Games Started

H	Hit
HB	Hit Batter
HBP	Hit by Pitcher
HR	Home Run
IP	Innings Pitched
IW	Intentional Walk
K	Strikeout
(K reversed)	Strikeout, called
KC	Strikeout, called
KS	Strikeout, swinging
L	Line Drive
LOB	Left on Base
LP	Losing Pitcher
OF	Outfield
OS	Official Scorer
PB	Passed Ball
PO	Put Out
R	Run
RBI	Run(s) Batted In
S	Sacrifice
SF	Sacrifice Fly
SB	Stolen Base
SH	Sacrifice Hit
SHO	Shutout
SO	Strikeout
SS	Split Squad; Shortstop
T	Time taken to play game
2B	Double
3B	Triple
TP	Triple Play
WP	Wild Pitch/Winning Pitcher
X	Something out of the ordinary (used rarely, when a boxscore compiler feels compelled to append a note to the summary of a game)

Term	Abbreviation
Active List	AL
American League	AL
Assist	A
At Bat, Official	AB
Attendance	A
Balk	BK
Base on Balls	BB
Batting Average	BA
Bunt	B
Called Out on Strikes	KC

Caught Stealing	CS
Complete Game	CG
Designated Hitter	DH
Disabled List	DL
Double	2B
Doubleheader	DH
Double Play	DP
Earned Run	ER
Earned Run Average	ERA
Error	E
Fielder's Choice	FC
Fielding Percentage	FP
First Team	'A'
Force Out	FO
Foul Fly	F
Game	G
Games Started	GS
Hit	H
Hit Batter	HB
Hit by Pitcher	HP
Home Run	HR
Infield	IF
Innings Pitched	IP
Intentional Walk	IW
Left on Base	LOB
Line Drive	L
Losing Pitcher	LP
Outfield	OF
Passed Ball	PB
Put Out	PO
Run	R
Run Batted In	RBI
Sacrifice	S
Sacrifice Fly	SF
Sacrifice Hit	SH
Second Team	'B'
Shortstop	SS
Shutout	SHO
Something out of the ordinary	X
Split Squad	SS
Stolen Base	SB
Strikeout	K, SO
Strikeout Swinging	KS
Time taken to play game	T
Triple	3B
Triple Play	TR
Official At Bat	AB
Walk	BB
Wild Pitch	WP
Winning Pitcher	WP

SEE *box score, scorecard, scoring*

able *v.* Often used to describe a batter awarded first base upon receiving a base on balls.

Abner Doubleday Field Small ball park (capacity 10,000) near the National Baseball Hall of Fame in Cooperstown, New York. It has been used since 1940 as the site for the annual Hall of Fame Game. It is named for Abner Doubleday, who, according to the traditional but erroneous story, invented baseball in Cooperstown in 1839.

aboard *adv.* On base. If two men are on base, there are "two aboard."
1ST 1907. (*McClure's Magazine*, April; EJN)
USE Aboard is one of several long-standing nautical allusions in baseball terminology. See also around the horn, and at bat, on deck, in the hold.

abroad *adv.* Playing away from one's home grounds.

accept the offering *v.* To swing at a pitch.

ace **1.** *n/obs.* A run or score in the earliest era of baseball, so called in the rules of the original Knickerbocker Club in 1845. In that original version, the first team to score 21 aces was the winner regardless of the number of innings played. Aces were also called counts.

Ace. The original Red Stocking Club (1869), with a mutton-chopped Asa Brainard appearing in the upper right-hand corner. *Prints and Photographs Division, the Library of Congress*

Abner Doubleday Field. Located on the site of the former Elihu Phinney cow pasture, where Doubleday and his pals were thought to have first played the game, it now hosts the annual Hall of Fame game. *National Baseball Library, Cooperstown, N.Y.*

2. *n.* A team's top pitcher.
1ST 1902. "The work of McCreedie has been watched closely too, and he gives promise of being an Ace." (*TSN*, November 15; PT)
ETY In 1869, pitcher Asa Brainard won 56 out of 57 games played by the Cincinnati Red Stockings, baseball's first professional team. From then on, any pitcher with a dazzling string of wins was called an "Asa," which later became ace. The fact that the ace is the most valuable card in a deck of cards certainly helped the term evolve. Lexicographer Eric Partridge and others have traced the term "flying ace," an outstanding fighter pilot of World War I, to cards.
3. *adj.* Best, or foremost, such as "his ace fastball."

across the body *adj.* Said of a fielding play when a player either catches a ball by extending the gloved hand to the opposite side of the body, or when a player expeditiously throws the ball over or across his body rather than with his arm extended straight away from the body.

across the letters *adj.* A pitched ball that passes across the batter's chest at the approximate location on the uniform of the letters spelling out the team name.

across the shirt *adj.* Pitched ball that is close to the batter, chest high.
1ST 1937. (*Pittsburgh Press*, January 11; EJN)

action pitch *n.* The pitch thrown when the count is full—three balls and two strikes—with two outs and men on base. The situation calls for the base runners to start running just before the ball is delivered.

activate *v.* To return a player to the team's active roster after injury, illness or suspension.

active list *n.* Those players on a team's playing roster, excluding those inactive due to illness, injury or some other factor.

activity *n.* A relief pitcher or pitchers warming up, as in, "There's activity in the Cardinals' bull pen."

adios *v.* To hit a home run, as in "He adiosed that one." Adios is Spanish for goodbye and this bit of "Span-glish" is in keeping with the traditional penchant of sportscasters to say goodbye to a baseball as it is heading into home-run territory.

Adirondack Bat Co. A manufacturer of baseball bats located in New York State.

adjudge *v.* For an umpire to make a decision.

admire a third strike *v.* To be called out on strikes while watching the third one.

advance *v.* To gain one or more bases.

advance sale *n.* The number of tickets sold before the actual day of the game.

afterpiece *n./arch.* The second game of a double header.

agate *n.* BASEBALL.
ETY This very well may derive from another name for the ball—marble. Agates (or aggies) were popular forms of marbles.

agent *n.* Person who negotiates a player's salary with a professional ball club and also makes other business arrangements in the player's interest, such as commercial endorsements. It was not until 1970 that the team owners agreed to let agents represent players in contract negotiations.

aggregation *n.* A team.
1ST 1898. (*New York Tribune,* June 17; EJN)

aggressive hitter *n.* Term often used for a batter who habitually swings at pitches delivered out of the strike zone.

Agreement, National *n.* Baseball's constitution. Defined most directly and given historical perspective by Hugh S. Fullerton in his "Baseball Primer" of 1912: "The contract entered into by the American and National leagues and later subscribed to by the minor leagues, numbering about forty, to insure peace, protect property rights and assign territory as well as to prevent competitive bidding for the services of players."

ahead *adj.* To be winning.

ahead of the count. *adj.* Said of the pitcher when there are more strikes than balls on the batter. Also, describing the batter when there are more balls than strikes. Conversely, the batter and pitcher in these two situations are, respectively, behind in the count.

AILC Abbreviation for All-Important Loss Column.

aim *v.* Pitchers are said to do this when, in working too hard to put the ball over the strike zone, they deviate from their natural motion.

air ball *n./arch.* FLY BALL.
1ST 1862. (*New York Sunday Mercury,* July 13; EJN)

airhead *n.* Zany or spacey player; one with little brainpower.

air it out *v.* To hit the ball a long distance.

air mail *v.* To throw the ball over another player's head. "A catcher who throws one into center field on an attempted steal air mails the second baseman," according to Joe Falleta in the December 1983 *Baseball Digest.*

air pocket *n.* What a dropped fly ball is accused of having hit.

airtight *adj.* Said of the best of defenses.
1ST 1910. (*Baseball* magazine, September; EJN)

airtight infield *n.* Said of defensive unit that rarely lets a batted ball get past the infield.

AK's *n.* Short for ant-killer, a term for hard hit ground balls.

AL Standard abbreviation for American League and active list.

a la carte *adj.* Fielding the ball with one hand.
USE Sometimes corrupted to *aly carte,* which is how it appears, for instance, in *Dizzy's Definitions,* a collection of terms and definitions published by Dizzy Dean.

ALCS Abbreviation for American League Championship Series. This intialism, along with the counterpart NLCS, has come into common use in radio and television broadcasts during the playoffs and World Series.

Alibi Ike *n.* Player who has an excuse for every fault and mistake.
1ST ETY 1914. From Ring Lardner's short story "Alibi Ike." In the story the nickname is

All-American team. A rare composite photograph showing a touring All-American team. Despite the fact that most All-American teams have been honorary, this one went on the road.   *Prints and Photographs Division, the Library of Congress*

given to a baseball player named Frank X. ("I guess the X stands for 'excuse me.' ") Farrell. The name gained further recognition in the 1932 movie *Alibi Ike* starring Joe E. Brown. Traced back to 1743, the word alibi took on a new life with Lardner's characterization.
EXT One who excuses all of his faults and mistakes. A condition: "Alibi Ikes Can Be Cured" ("Teen-Age Date Line," *San Francisco Examiner*, March 19, 1966; PT)

In his book *Good Words to You,* John Ciardi notes that after Lardner created the term, "It became an established Am. slang idiom almost at once and remains so."

alive   *adj.* Describing a fastball that seems to have its own animation; one that appears to speed up and take a sudden hop or rise as it nears the plate. Such a ball is often said to "move."

All-America   *n./adj:* High school or college player voted as the best player in the country in his position at his level.

All-American Amateur Baseball Assoc-iation   Group based in Johnstown, Pennsylvania, which helps advance, develop and regulate baseball at the amateur level.

All-American out   *n.* A poor hitter.

All-American team   *n.* An honorary team composed of the best players from the two major leagues. Based on his research in this area, Edward J. Nichols noted, "All Star teams may actually play, whereas all-American teams are mere honorary selections."
1ST 1905. (*Sporting Life,* September 2; EJN)

alleged flinger   *n./arch.* Derogatory term for pitcher; one who does not measure up to expectations.

alley 1. *n.* In the outfield, the areas between the center fielder and the right fielder and the center fielder and the left fielder. "Rickey Henderson's average continues to dwindle as he swings for the fences instead of the alleys . . ."

(*St. Petersburg Times,* April 3, 1987) See also hole.

2. *n.* The center of home plate; the "heart" of the plate.

3. *n./arch.* The dirt path between the pitcher's box and home plate that was common to most ballparks in the first half of the 20th century.

all groups   *n.* Designation that is used in amateur baseball for all-star teams that are selected from teams playing at different levels and in different leagues. An area all-group team may include high school players from various levels of public and parochial school competition, e.g., the All-South Jersey All-Groups All-Star Team.

alligator mouth   *n./arch.* Loudmouth.

all-important loss column   *n.* Phrase used to point to the fact that there is more to a club's standing than the column in which wins are counted. This is because standings are based on the number of wins and losses, not on the winning percentage. Also, because teams will have played different numbers of games at any given point, the true measure of a team's performance is the number of losses it has posted. The loss column is also "all-important" because the losses cannot be "made up" or overcome.

all over the plate   *adj.* Wild; describing a pitcher who cannot deliver the ball in the strike zone.

allow   *v.* To give up runs.

all runners breaking   When those on base run (break) for the next base. This occurs when there are two outs and the count on the batter is three balls and two strikes. The base runners break during the pitcher's windup because the pitch must result in a hit, walk, foul ball or the final out of the inning. In other words, there is no risk in running at this point.

all-star   *adj.* A title awarded at almost every level of baseball with the annual selection of a team comprising the best players from a league or a geographic area.

All-Star balloting   Throughout the history of the All-Star Game, various methods have been used to determine the major league All-Star Teams. Beginning in 1933 and 1934, fans voted for the players through ballots printed in the *Chicago Tribune.* From 1935 through 1946, the managers voted; fans voted from 1947

All-Star balloting. The ballot and ballot box as it appeared in 1973 when the election was sponsored by Gillette. Posing with the "king-sized" ballot replica are two Cleveland Indian ballgirls.   *Courtesy of the Cleveland Indians*

through 1957 and the players, managers and coaches voted from 1958 to 1969. Since 1970 the fans have voted. The decision to turn the balloting over to the fans has, according to the critics of non-professional voting, turned selection of the game's starting players into more of a popularity contest than a true contest based on merit.

Even with spaces for write-ins, the number of names on the ballot has risen regularly. In 1979 the number went up from 128 to 144. On the 1986 ballot, 208 names appeared.

Balloting has been an activity sponsored by a company willing to put up a million dollars a year for the privilege. The Gillette Safety Razor Company conducted the voting from 1970 to 1986 and *USA Today* and its parent, Gannett Co., Inc., picked it up beginning in 1987.

All-Star break   The three-day, mid-July break in the schedule of major league baseball to accommodate the All-Star Game. It represents the mid-point in the season and is an important point of reference when charting a team's fortunes. For instance, a manager may say that his team will be in fine shape if his club is within

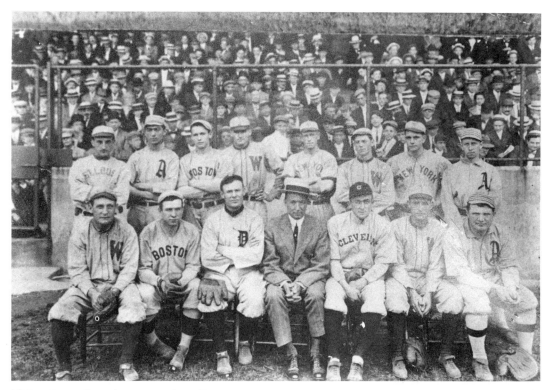

All-Star Game. Photo from 1911 of an All-Star team that played Cleveland in a special exhibition game for the benefit of the widow of Cleveland pitcher Addie Joss, who had died that spring. In the front row (left to right) are: Germany Schaefer, Tris Speaker, Sam Crawford, Jimmy McAleer (manager), Ty Cobb (in a borrowed Cleveland uniform), Gabby Street and Paddy Livingston. Standing in the back row (l. to r.) are: Bobby Wallace, Frank "Home Run" Baker, Joe Wood, Walter Johnson, Hal Chase, Clyde Milan, Russell Ford and Eddie Collins. The All-Stars beat Cleveland by a score of 7 to 2. *National Baseball Library, Cooperstown, N.Y.*

three games of first place by the time of the All-Star break.

All-Star Game 1. *n.* Annual interleague game played each July between players selected as the best at their position in their league. The starting players are selected by fan balloting, while the pitchers, coaches and substitutes are selected by the respective managers. At least one player must be picked from each team.

The All-Star Game was first played in 1933 in Chicago. It was the brainchild of *Chicago Tribune* sports editor Arch Ward who saw it as a one-shot "Dream Game" to go along with the 1933 Century of Progress Exposition going on in the city. Though opposed by some owners, the idea appealed to the presidents of the two leagues and the Commissioner of Baseball, Kenesaw Mountain Landis. In the game, played in Chicago's Comiskey Park on July 6, 1933, a

third-inning home run hit by Babe Ruth led the American League to a 4-2 win.

Because of World War II, the game was not played in 1945. Between 1959 and 1963, there were two All-Star Games, but this idea was scrapped as it became clear that two games lacked the impact of one. The only game to be postponed was the one scheduled for July 14, 1981, which was moved to August 9 because of a players' strike.
2. *n.* Any similar contest at other levels of play and in softball.

All-Star team   *n.* Either participant in an All-Star Game.
1ST   1905. (*Sporting Life*, September 2; EJN)

all-time   *adj.* Describing a player past or present who is considered the best or one of the best in baseball history. The term is sometimes applied to an event. "Whereas sports fans everywhere are celebrating the outstanding accomplishment of Roger Clemens as one of the all-time great individual performances in the history of baseball." (Senator Edward Kennedy, [D-Mass.] in a resolution commending Roger Clemens of the Boston Red Sox for striking out a record 20 batters in a single, nine-inning game; *Congressional Record,* May 1, 1986)

all to the mustard   In good physical condition.
1ST   1907. (*New York Evening Journal,* April 18; EJN)

Alphonse and Gaston act/Alphonse and Gaston play   Fielding situation in which one or more players defer to another, often allowing dropping the ball in the process.
ETY   Alphonse and Gaston were two cartoon characters created by Frederick B. Opper, also the creator of Happy Hooligan. The two comic characters defered to one another to the point where they were unable to get anything done: "After you, my dear Alphonse." "No, after you, my dear Gaston." They have become symbolic of exaggerated politeness.

altered bat   *n.* A bat that does not conform to the rules. The term is more likely to be used in softball than in baseball, where it is more likely to be termed a *doctored bat.* In the playing rules of the Amateur Softball Association, a player coming to the plate with an altered bat will be called out. An altered bat is a legal bat, one marked "Official Softball" by the manufacturer, that has been changed. Examples would include the replacement of a metal handle with a wooden one, inserting something into the bat or adding a foreign substance such as paint. One is, however, allowed to replace one legal safety grip with another.

alternative pitch   *n.* An illegal pitch of any sort.
USE   This is an obvious euphemism and tends to be used with tongue firmly in cheek.

alto queso *[Spanish]*   *n.* High cheese Spanish style. Often used to describe a high fast ball delivered by a pitcher from Latin America.

aluminum bat   *n.* Metal bat used by college players since 1972 and at virtually all levels of amateur baseball, but not in the professional leagues, where they are prohibited. It is also widely used in softball.

Although initially more expensive than wooden bats, they never break so they are appealing in terms of cost. Generally speaking, they are said to help weak hitters drive the ball farther and given an extra edge to sluggers. However, these metal bats are opposed by the professional baseball establishment for a number of reasons ranging from their potentially devastating effect on batting records to the fact that they ping rather than crack when coming in contact with a ball.

amass   *v.* To score a large number of runs.

amateur   *n.* Any player who is not a professional.

Amateur Softball Association of America   This group first met in 1933 in conjunction with the Century of Progress Exposition in Chicago. Its purpose was to establish a standard set of rules for a game to be played at the exposition. This rules committee eventually became known as the International Joint Rules Committee on Softball.

The ASA is recognized as the governing body of American softball and is headquartered in Oklahoma City, Oklahoma. With 105 local associations with 5,000 local administrators situated throughout the United States, the ASA directs programs for male, female and coed leagues with players aged 9 through 65.

Amazing Mets   Description that has been used for New York's National League team from its beginning in 1962 to the present. In *The Amazing Mets,* published after the Mets' amazing 1969 season, sportswriter Jerry Mitchell recalls how the label was affixed after the team's very first outing:

"It made its first appearance that first spring in the club's St. Petersburg training camp, in fact, when Stengel, the man who was to make so much of so little, i.e. the Mets, watched them win their first exhibition game. The Professor, beginning with his post-game oration before the writers and a large fringe of old gaffer tourists, exclaimed:

" 'They're amazing!'

"Before long, Stengel had turned that sentiment into a lament: 'They're amazing. Can't anybody here play this game?' "

No matter how good or bad they have been in the intervening years, they have been amazing, albeit for different reasons. To quote Mitchell again, "In their infant days they were

Amazing Mets. Mets skipper Casey Stengel, who also called his club the "Amazin's." *Courtesy of the New York Mets*

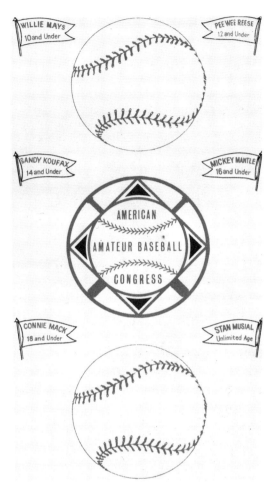

American Amateur Baseball Congress. The cover of an AABC information card that identifies its six leagues. *Courtesy of the American Amateur Baseball Congress*

amazing, perhaps, because they somehow escaped being condemned by the city of New York, chased out of town or sentenced to Outer Mongolia by a magistrate used to long years of success by the rich, powerful Yankees."

The term shows up in book titles, newspaper headlines and even a record album, *The Amazing Mets*, made by members of the team in 1968 and featuring such selections as "We're Gonna Win" and "Green Grass of Shea."

Amazin's *n.* Variation on the Amazing Mets and the term that Casey Stengel himself often used to refer to the Mets. "The Amazin's amazed us so often that almost every one of the 2,175,373 fans who saw them at home this year . . . must be convinced that he was there on that one special afternoon or crucial evening when the Mets won the big game that fused them as contenders and future champions." (Roger Angell in *The Summer Game;* CDP)
SEE *Stengelese.*

ambish *n.* Ambition on the part of a player or team.
1ST 1908. (*New York Evening Journal,* April 13; EJN)

American Amateur Baseball Congress An organization supporting amateur baseball in America. Based in Marshall, Michigan, it spon-

sors six major national tournaments for different age groups. All of its divisions are named for players ranging from Pee Wee Reese (12 and under) to Stan Musial (unlimited age).

American   Association 1. Professional league that existed between 1882 and 1891.
2. Current name of the *AAA* minor league with franchises in Buffalo, Denver, Indianapolis, Iowa, Louisville, Nashville, Oklahoma City and Omaha.

American Baseball Coaches Association
Name of a group with more than 5,000 members who coach at various levels of the game. Among other things, it originated the NCAA College World Series and holds national clinics. It is based in Hinsdale, Illinois.

American League   One of the two leagues in the major leagues. It was formed in 1901 by former sportswriter Byron Bancroft "Ban" Johnson with eight teams, their franchises in Boston, Baltimore, Chicago, Cleveland, Detroit, Milwaukee, Philadelphia and Washington, D.C. Since it came into being after the National League, it has always been called the "junior circuit." One of the immediate differences between the older league and the new was that Johnson gave the umpires stronger authority over the game.

American League President.   See LEAGUE PRESIDENT.

American League style   The real and imagined differences between the two major leagues, which has been accentuated since the American League adopted the designated hitter. Among other things, the strike zone is supposedly higher in the American, where there is supposedly less emphasis on the running game.
SEE   *National League style.*

American Legion Baseball   A national program for 15- to 18-year-olds that culminates in an annual eight-team World Series tournament.

America's pastime   *n.* The game of baseball, which is more commonly termed the National Pastime.

America's Team   A name that *Atlanta Braves* owner Ted Turner tried to give his team, presumably because Braves games, televised on Turner's national television station, are accessible to most of the United States. The precedent for the name was the Dallas Cowboys, who, at one time, had similarly sold themselves as America's Team in football.

Anaheim Stadium   Home of the American League California Angels since 1966. Located in Anaheim, California it has been called the "Big A" since it opened.

anchor   *v.* To be at the base or heart of; for instance, several pitchers are often said to "anchor a rotation" on a particular team.

anchorage   *n.* BASE.
1ST   1915. "Having reached the middle anchorage in this manner, the local base runner was amazed on getting a sign from the manager to steal third." (Gilbert Patten, *Covering the Look-in Corner;* DS)

anchor man   *n.* Batter who hits first in the lineup. (MHW)

angel   *n.* **1.** A cloud that comes to the aid of a fielder by blocking out the blinding glare of the sun and therefore making it easier to catch a high fly ball.
1ST   1909. An early example of the term in use appeared in the August 1909 issue of *Baseball* magazine: "Pitilessly, the sun beats down from a sky, broken only by the fleecy-white clouds that the players call 'angels' because they afford so benevolent a background for the batted ball." (DS)
2. *n.* One who invests money in a team with scant hope of financial reward. "Starry-eyed owner who thinks baseball is a sport," as defined by Bert Dunne in his irreverent *Folger's Dictionary of Baseball*, published in 1958 by Folger's Coffee and given away to San Francisco Giants fans.

angler   *n.* Player or his agent who "casts" about looking for testimonials, product endorsements, speaking engagements and other off-field sources of income.

Annie   *n.* BASEBALL ANNIE.

Annie Oakley   **1.** *n.* A free pass to a baseball game.
2. *n.* By extension, a base on balls (often described as a free pass or free ticket to first base). "Lemon's No-Hitter Lift to Tribe, Only Three Tigers Get On—All Via Annie Oaklies." (Headlines announcing Bob Lemon no-hitter, *San Francisco News-Call Bulletin,* July 1, 1948; PT)
ETY   Obviously, named for the legendary star of Buffalo Bill's Wild West Show. As part of her act, Oakley used to show off her sharpshooting skills by putting bullets through the suit symbols of playing cards. Since free passes to baseball games have traditionally had holes punches in them, the jump to baseball was a natural one. (For this same reason, in the 1930s especially, complimentary tickets were sometimes called machine-gun tickets.)
    While the inspiration for the term is easily traced to the famed sharpshooter, its transfer to the game of baseball has been a matter for much conjecture. The earliest and most widely accepted usage of Annie Oakley as a baseball term appeared in the 1927 biography *Annie Oakley, Woman at Arms,* by Courtney Ryley Cooper. The full Cooper account:
    "And by one of her tricks, Annie Oakley

Annie Oakley. The imposing figure of a woman whose name became part of baseball and theatrical slang. *Prints and Photographs Division, the Library of Congress*

achieved a form of notoriety which she did not expect. The feat was to place a playing card, the ace of hearts, as a target at a distance of twenty-five yards. Then, firing twenty-five shots in twenty-seven seconds, she would obliterate that ace of hearts in the center, leaving only bullet holes in its place. A card thus shot by Annie Oakley formed quite a souvenir in the Eighties.

"There came into being a baseball magnate who looked with some disfavor upon passes—as all baseball managers look upon these avenues of free admission. It is the custom, that the doortender may know the ticket to be free, to punch a hole or two in the card, thus saving a miscount when the proceeds of the day were checked. One day a card came through to the gate which had been thoroughly perforated. The magnate remarked laconically:

" 'Huh! Looks like Annie Oakley'd shot at it!'

"The remark was repeated—and re-re-peated. Soon along Broadway, a new name came into being for a free ticket of admission. It was an Annie Oakley, and passes remain

Annie Oakleys to this date. The surprising thing being that Annie Oakley herself denied ever having had one of the things.

" 'I always pay my way,' she averred."

Oakley herself established that the baseball magnate was none other than Ban Johnson, long-time American League president. In an interview in the *New York World* for June 28, 1922, (reproduced in the February 1933 *American Speech* along with the letters mentioned below) she told of Johnson looking at a pass "and suggested that the man has been letting me use it as a target. Now the term is in use in Australia and England, as well as America."

Several readers of the *World* were not happy with this explanation and in the following days the newspaper published their letters. One man insisted that it came from Oakley's first appearance with the Barnum and Bailey Circus at Madison Square Garden, when ". . . a number of her pictures, ticket size, were scattered throughout the streets of the city. Finders were entitled to free admission to 'the greatest show on earth.' You can imagine the resultant eagerness of small boys and their equally boyish fathers, to find an 'Annie Oakley.' "

A second writer insists that virtually all slang comes from the underworld and its fringes. He insists that the term in question ". . . originated among the hangers-on of circuses and street fairs and was, like so many bits of argot, an opprobrious word, usually accompanied with profanities and obscenities. If you have ever experienced the mood of circus people on a rainy day, when the paid admissions were few and passes many, you will understand how the expression in question came to be used."

The final letter insisted that the term originated from an incident at Madison Square Garden when a man walked through the gates and was asked to produce a ticket. "Don't need one," he said, "I'm Annie Oakley's brother." He was let in free and the next evening 37 of Miss Oakley's brothers showed up to see her act.

Despite these alternative theories, it is the Ban Johnson version that seems to have the greatest credibility (probably because this is Oakley's own version). When Johnson died on March 28, 1931, the obituary carried in many newspapers noted that he had coined the term when he "likened a well-punched baseball pass to a discarded Annie Oakley target." (*San Francisco News*, March 30, 1931; PT)

ant *n./arch.* FAN.
ETY According to Patrick Ercolano in his 1987 book, *Fungoes, Floaters and Fork Balls,* "The word dates from the early 1900s and stems from the observation that fans in the stands often appear as small as ants to the players (and to some players, as insignificant as ants)."

ant-killer *n./arch.* A hard-hit ground ball; one that appears to be hit so hard that it will kill insects in its path.
1ST 1874. (*Chicago Inter-Ocean,* July 7; EJN)

Aparicio double *n.* A walk and a stolen base.
1ST/ETY 1959. "When larcenous Luis Aparicio, a .260 hitter, stole fifty bases in his first sixty-one tries, an 'Aparicio double' became renowned throughout the league as a walk and a stolen base." (*New York Times Magazine,* September 27; DS)

APBA *n.* A tabletop baseball game that takes its name from the original American Professional Baseball Association. It has been said that more than 500,000 Americans play the game, including David Eisenhower, President George Bush and New York Mayor Ed Koch. It was created in 1932 by Richard Seitz and has recently been issued in a computerized version.
USE Seldom stated in letters, but pronounced "app'-bah."

appeal *n.* An official notice that a rule has been broken or a request that a call be reexamined. Specifically, when:
a. The fielding team claims that a member of the batting team has violated a rule or that an umpire has made a decision that is in conflict with the rules.
b. The fielding team asks the home plate umpire to seek the help of the first or third base umpire in determining if the batter took a full swing at the ball for a strike, or only took a half swing (not a strike) for a ball. Such an appeal is made after a pitch that was called a ball.

appeal play *n.* If a base runner neglects to touch a base when running, it is the responsibility of the fielding team, not the umpire, to point this out. To make an appeal play, the pitcher must first put the ball back in play by stepping on the pitching rubber. He then steps off the rubber and throws the ball to a teammate who tags the base in question. At this point the umpire decides if the runner is safe

or out. The appeal play and the appeal must be made before the next pitch is delivered.

appearance game *n.* An exhibition game played to show the talents of certain stars or to pair two teams that do not play normally. "The All-Stars met little resistance from the Elite Giants. It was the Giants' second game of the day, an 'appearance' game as they called it, a game set up for the fans instead of the players." (William Brashler in *The Bingo Long Traveling All Stars and Motor Kings;* CDP)

apple *n.* One of the commonest slang terms for the baseball.
1ST 1922. (*Saturday Evening Post,* October 28; EJN)

apple comes up, the *v.* Fails to accomplish a desired result in a key situation. A reference to one's Adam's apple; to choke.

apple-knocker *n.* BATTER.
1ST 1937 (*The Sporting News Record Book;* EJN)

apple tree *n.* A verbal symbol for choking and an allusion to the Adam's apple. When Dick Young once wrote, "The tree that grows in Brooklyn is an apple tree," he was using what George Vecsey said later was "the ultimate sports phrase for choking in the clutch." (*New York Times,* September 2, 1987)

apply the whitewash *v.* To shut out. To keep the opposite team from scoring.
1ST 1888. (*The Chicago Inter Ocean,* July 3; EJN)

April Cobb *n./arch.* Spring whirlwind; a rookie who looks like the next Ty Cobb for a short period of time.

aqueous toss *n.* SPITBALL.
1ST 1920. (*New York Times,* October 7; EJN)

arbiter/arbitrator **1.** *n.* An umpire. Famous umpire Bill Klem was known as the "Old Arbitrator."
1ST 1908. (arbitor, *Baseball Magazine,* July; EJN)
2. *n.* A labor negotiator.

arbitration *n.* The method employed since 1974 to settle salary disputes between players and the team owners. In the case of such a dispute, an independent labor arbitrator holds a hearing to decide whether or not the player is being fairly paid. If not, a raise can be granted by the arbitrator. The judgment made is bind-

Arby's RBI Award. The American League version of the trophy that goes with the award. *Courtesy of Arby's*

aren't your hands bleeding yet? Traditional taunt for player hogging or spending too much time at the plate during batting practice.

Arlie Latham   1. *n./arch.* Used to describe an infielder making a futile attempt to catch a ground ball. The term, used rarely today, was once a major eponym among baseball players and writers.
2. *n./arch.* Player or coach who makes a lot of noise.
3. *v./arch.* To yell and gesticulate in the coach's box in order to distract the opposing pitcher.
ETY/1ST 1907. Named for Walter Arlington "Arlie" Latham who played for seven teams over a period from 1880 to 1909. Toward the end of his career, Latham's arm had become so weak that his name became synonymous with making a weak or half-hearted attempt at fielding a grounder. His arm had been injured in a

ing and not subject to further appeal. The results of the off-season hearings are often tallied like a game. After reporting a player win and an owner win, *USA Today* for February 12, 1986, added, "The split gave the players four victories and the owners six in the ten arbitration decisions this year."

As of this writing, players have to have at least three years of service to be eligible. Prior to the end of the 1986 season, the pre-arbitration period was only two years.

Arby's RBI Award   An award first given in 1986 for the hitter in each league who drives in the most runs. The prize is a coproduction of major league baseball and the Arby's fast-food chain. For each run batted in by the winners, $1,000 is donated to the Big Brothers/Big Sisters of America. The first winners of the award were Mike Schmidt (Philadelphia Phillies) of the National League and Joe Carter (Cleveland Indians) of the American League, with a collective total of 240 RBIs. The actual prize given to the players is known as the Hank Aaron Trophy. Aaron, baseball's all-time RBI leader, served as the first national spokesman for the award.

Arlie Latham. Walter Arlington Latham poses for a tobacco card (1888). *National Baseball Library, Cooperstown, N.Y.*

contest with Doc Bushong, a St. Louis Browns teammate, to see who could throw a ball the farthest. Latham won the contest—and the $100 put up by their manager, Charles Comiskey—but had neglected to warm up, thus causing the injury. The second definition of the eponym—to distract the pitcher from the coacher's box ("doing an Arlie Latham")—dates from his coaching days with John McGraw's New York Giants when, according to Fred Lieb in *Comedians of Baseball Down the Years*, "he amused New York fans by dancing jigs in the coaching box and performing other acrobatic gyrations." (*New York Evening Journal*, April 24, 1907; EJN)

Arlie Latham hit   *n./arch.* A grounder that evades the infielder (as in meaning 1 of *Arlie Latham*, above).

Arlington Stadium   Home of the American League Texas Rangers, located in Arlington, Texas. Built in 1965, it was originally a minor league park known as Turnpike Stadium, until the Rangers arrived in 1972.

arm   **1.** *n.* Player's throwing or pitching arm. **1ST** 1863. (*New York Sunday Mercury*, n.d. clipping; EJN)
2. *n.* Throwing ability, usually applied to a fielder who makes fast, accurate throws.
3. *n.* A player with throwing ability is known as having an arm.

arm fake   *n.* A deceptive, defensive move in which the player with the ball simulates throwing the ball to one base in the hope of drawing a runner off another base.

arms   *n.* A team's PITCHING STAFF. "Young arms have Rangers riding high in the AL West." (*USA Today* headline, May 30, 1986)

arm thrower   *n.* Said of a fielder who fails to coordinate his stride or body momentum with arm motion in the act of throwing. An arm thrower is often said to have poor mechanics.

around the horn   **1.** *adj.* Describing a force double play in which a ground ball is fielded by the third baseman who throws to the second baseman who then throws on to the first baseman. "The ball is thrown to second . . . to first . . . and the Seals pull a twin killing around the horn." (San Francisco Seals telecast, July 19, 1956; PT) Many modern writers, however, drop the a in the word around. Here is Tom

Boswell in the April 7, 1987, *Washington Post:* "Knight started two 'round-the-horn double plays both of which required hard-nosed, low-bridge pivots by Burleson with spikes aimed at his knees."
USE   This would appear to be the older and more traditional of two current meanings, the newer being:
2. *adv.* Throwing the ball around the infield for practice and/or show. This can take place during practice or during a game, when it is common for the infield to throw the ball "around the horn" after the first or second out has been made and nobody is on base.
3. *n./arch.* A specific pitch; "Side-arm curve to batter when count is 3 and 2," according to the *Sporting News Record Book* of 1937.
ETY   The term is an old nautical one referring to the long voyage between the Atlantic and the Pacific Ocean, which, before the opening of the Panama Canal, required a vessel to go around the tip of South America at Cape Horn. In *Salty Words*, Robert Hendrickson notes, "Cape Horn, incidentally, isn't so named because it is shaped like a horn. Captain Schouten, the Dutch navigator who rounded it in 1616, named it after Hoorn, his birthplace in northern Holland."

The custom of throwing the ball around the infield is an old one. In 1970 Lenny Anderson of the *Seattle Post-Intelligencer* asked Casey Stengel about this: "They were doing it in the fall of 1912 when I went to the big leagues. They did it in '13 and '14. Then later on they started to say it took too long. I'll tell you why they changed. One reason was they doctored the ball. The second reason though was the games were too long when they started at 3:30 and when they went too long it got very dark."

artificial grass, artificial turf   *n.* Synthetic field surface textured and colored to resemble grass. The first such surface was installed in the Houston Astrodome in 1965.
USE   Although the term is a perfectly good one, the concept is not without its strong critics who will let you know what they think of it when they hear it. Leonard Koppett, in the *New York Times* ". . . artificial turf spoils all the formulas and ruins the rhythms of the game, especially in the outfield." (March 30, 1986)

Even its supporters will grant the point that it changes the nature of the game. It is generally agreed that balls hit along artificial turf move faster and that the turf produces more injuries than its natural and more forgiving counterpart.

SEE *Astroturf, Tartan Turf.*

artillery   *n.* A team's most powerful batters.
1ST 1912. (*New York Tribune,* September 6; EJN)
ETY Perhaps inspired by *battery,* a much older term for the pitcher and catcher as a unit.

artists   *n.* A term that was often used in the last century and the early part of this one to honor certain players. Henry Chadwick defined it this way in *The Game of Baseball:* "The most experienced players of a nine come under this head, viz, such as are not only physically active and expert but mentally quick, and shrewd in judgement of the 'points' in the game."

art of misdirection   *n.* A pitcher's ability to throw strikes effectively by confusing batters with breaking balls of all types.

Red Barber has said that this was the quality that had enabled Mike Scott to win the 1986 National League Cy Young Award. (National Public Radio, "Morning Edition," November 14, 1986)

A's   *n.* A nickname used periodically for the Philadelphia, Kansas City and Oakland Athletics.

ascend   *v./arch.* To become nervous or rattled.
1ST 1901. (Burt L. Standish, *Frank Merriwell's Marvel;* EJN)

ash   *n.* The bat. From the fact that most bats are made out of white ash.
1ST 1874. (Chadwick Scrapbooks; EJN)

ash-handle   *n.* The smaller end of the bat. "You ain't never goan hit that bawl if you don't choke up on the ash-handle, Horsefoot." (Stephen King, in *It;* CDP)

ash heap   *n./arch.* Derogatory term for a hard and rocky infield.
ETY The reference is to the hard, flinty residue of burned coal that is piled in ash heaps. Before World War II bad infields and ash heaps were much more common sights.
SEE *Contractor's backyard, Hogan's brickyard.*

aspirin/aspirin tablet   *n.* A ball thrown so fast that it gives the illusion of being pill-sized. It is explained by pitcher Dizzy Dean in his personal lexicon, *Dizzy's Definitions,* as, "A fast ball that shrank up to the size of an aspirin when it reached the plate." Former player and writer Jim Brosnan called it, "The best way for a pitcher to cure his manager's headache."

assigned to the bench   Said of a player kept out of the game by the manager.

assist   **1.** *n.* Any throw or deflection of the ball by one fielder to another contributing to a putout.

On a strikeout the assist is credited to the catcher, with this one exception: the rare occasion when the pitcher fields an uncaught third strike and makes a throw that results in a putout.
1ST 1865. (Chadwick Scrapbooks, EJN)
2. *n.* A credit that is given by the official scorer to a fielder who contributes to a put-out. Credit for an assist may be granted to a player even if the player attempting to make the put-out is charged with an error.
3. *v.* To make a play in which an assist is registered.

Assisto glove   *n.* Special training glove that uses a strap to force the batter to keep his hand on the bat when swinging.

assortment   *n.* The combination of different types of pitches that a pitcher may throw during a given outing.
1ST 1898. (*New York Tribune,* June 7; EJN)

asterisk   **1.** *n.* In the context of baseball, this term is used in conjunction with entering an event or achievement in the official baseball record. Because the record book merely portrays things in a numerical or statistical fashion, the historical context in which an event takes place or an achievement is accomplished can be lost. The inclusion of an asterisk, along with a verbal explanation to which it refers, is felt to be a way to retain the historical context of an item entered into the record book. "An asterisk should be placed on Gooden's start that game, since his removal was due to a rain delay." (New York *Daily News,* July 6, 1987)
2. *n.* Specifically, the term invokes the long-held and sometimes bitterly disputed asterisk that was thought to have been attached in the record book to an accomplishment by Roger Maris when he was with the New York Yankees. The asterisk was allegedly affixed by Commissioner of Baseball Ford Frick when, in 1961, Maris topped Babe Ruth's single-season home

run record. Because Maris broke the record during a 162-game schedule—giving him eight more games than the 154-game schedule in which Ruth set the record—some fans and sportswriters felt that Maris' achievement should only be entered in the record book with an asterisk, calling attention to these extra games. In fact, no asterisk was ever affixed to Maris' achievement. It was suggested at one point, but it never appeared in the official record. For eight years there were separate records kept for 154- and 162-game seasons.

But in 1969 the Special Baseball Rules Committee ruled that baseball would have one set of records and that "no asterisk or official sign shall be used to indicate the number of games scheduled." Despite this, the myth of Maris' asterisk persists. In the July 2, 1986, *USA Today*, Tony Kubek is quoted supporting the idea of putting asterisks next to the names of teams setting batting records with designated hitters: "If Commissioner Ford Frick put an asterisk by Roger Maris' name, which was ridiculous, then you should do the same here."

In his autobiography, *Games, Asterisks and People*, Ford Frick points out that the asterisk was discussed at a press conference: "Oh yes, during the conference the word 'asterisk' was mentioned; not by the commissioner but by Dick Young, one of the outstanding baseball writers of his time. Dick remarked kiddingly, 'Maybe you should use an asterisk on the new record. Everybody does that when there's a difference of opinion.'"

SEE *Year of the Asterisk.*

Astroturf The brand name for one of the earliest and most popular forms of artificial grass; it got its name from the Houston Astrodome, where it was first installed. Originally, transparent panels on the Astrodome's roof allowed in adequate sunlight to grow real grass, but this made conditions too bright for the players, and two of the eight panels had to be painted to control the sun's glare. This killed the real grass and by June of the 1965 inaugural season, the artificial turf had been laid.

at bat 1. *v.* To be at home plate for the purpose of batting; to be "up."
2. *n.* A turn at the plate, as in, "He walked in his last at bat."
3. *n.* An official plate appearance for statistical and record-keeping purposes. In any given game, it is the number of times a batter comes

At bat, on deck, in the hole. The legendary Harry Wright, who both managed and played in the game in Belfast where the terms "at bat, on deck and in the hole" were first used. Hall of Famer Wright has been credited with introducing the knicker-style baseball pants that he is wearing in this photograph. *National Baseball Library, Cooperstown, N.Y.*

to the batting box; however, an official "at bat" is not charged if the batter walks, sacrifices, is hit by a pitched ball or is interfered with by the catcher.
1ST 1861. (*New York Sunday Mercury*, August 10; EJN)
EXT Referring to a person "in the spotlight." For example, a jazz reviewer commenting on the soloist in a big band concert, "I can't tell which one is at bat." (*San Francisco Call-Bulletin*, September 24, 1960; PT)

at bat, on deck, in the hold *adjs.* Sequence of terms traditionally used in reference to the current batter and the player scheduled to bat next, followed by the subsequent player in the lineup. In the modern era it is usually given as "at bat, on deck, in the hole," but this is a corruption of "in the hold," a reference to the interior of a ship, below decks.
ETY Few borrowings are as evident as these words, except for at bat, which came directly to the ball field from a ship, where to be on

deck is to be on the main deck (or floor) and the hold is the area of the ship below the main deck. That these terms have obvious roots in nautical language is made clear in Joanna Carver Colcord's *Sea Language Comes Ashore:* ". . . the newspaperman's dogwatch, the baseball player's on deck and in the hole (hold), the contractor's wrecking crew, the bus-driver's and the soda-fountain clerk's double-deckers, are also sea-borrowings."

According to one important source, it can be traced to an official scorer of a game played in Belfast, Maine, a town with both a rich baseball and nautical history.

The source is a short, unsigned story that appeared in *The Sporting News* for March 24, 1938, and was based on a report sent to its offices by Robert P. Chase, a nonagenarian from Belfast. According to *The Sporting News'* report the Boston team was making a tour of Maine in 1872 and played, among others, The Pastimes of Belfast on August 7th of that year. At that time there were no scorecards, so the scorer for each team was called upon to announce the batters. The Boston scorer simply announced, "G. Wright at bat; Leonard and Barnes next." To quote from the original story, "But when the Belfast team had its turn, the Belfast scorer would say, 'Moody at bat, Boardman on deck, Dinsmore in the hold,' using nautical terms which made such a hit with the Boston scorer that he carried them back to Boston, after which they became general."

The Sporting News added that the final outcome of the game was Boston 35, Belfast 1. "So all the Maine town got out of that contest was the distinction of being a contributor to the lexicon of the game."

Further investigation of this claim was made by the author of this book on a visit to Belfast, Maine, in August 1987. The investigation revealed the following:

- The game in question did occur, on the 6th (not the 7th) of August, 1872, according to the *Republican Journal*, which came out on the 8th. It said in part, "The visit of the famous Boston Red Stocking Baseball Club to our city on Tuesday the 6th was an unusual treat to the lovers of the national game."
- According to the *Republican Journal* the pitcher for the Pastimes was named Chase. No other name or initial is given, but it suggests that the man who gave the report to the *Sporting News* may have been more than an observer,

perhaps a participant. He would have been 25 at the time of the game and was the only Chase in the local city directory who seemed to have been of playing age in 1872. Chase was a well-known and respected resident of Belfast who died when he was nearly 100.

Ironically, the story was known locally in Belfast, but had been largely forgotten until after a local Belfast reporter picked up the story on vacation when he read it in the scorecard at the Houston Astrodome. Jay Davis, editor of the local Waldo (County) *Independent*, published in Belfast, says that his paper then reinvestigated the story and while it could not prove it conclusively, it could not find anything to cause him to doubt its authenticity.

The terms at bat, on deck and in the hold do not show up in print until after the Belfast game. Edward J. Nichols traced "on deck" back to the year 1881.

"A" team *n.* A group composed of a club's top players by position. The term is used figuratively to refer to a team's best players (as in "He's potential 'A' team material.") as well as literally, such as during spring training, when the assembled players are divided into an 'A' and a '*B' team* for the purpose of practice play. **EXT** Any elite grouping.

at 'em ball *n.* A ball hit right at a defensive player—at him—resulting in a double play because of the extra time it gives to make a second out. Also, ATOM BALL.

athletic hose *n.* Long, white socks worn under player's colored stockings. **SEE** *sanitary.*

athletic supporter *n.* An elastic undergarment worn to protect the genitals and to hold in place the protective cup.

An old Philadelphia gag (which lost its punch when the city's American League Athletics moved to Kansas City):

Q. Are you an Phillie fan?

A. No, I'm an Athletic supporter.

Atlanta Braves The name of the National League's western division team in Atlanta, Georgia. The name Braves has followed the team since its inception in Boston in 1912, stayed with the franchise when it moved to Milwaukee in 1953 and then on to Atlanta where the team has been located since 1966.

Atlantic luck. The Brooklyn Atlantics (bottom row) pose with the original Philadelphia Athletics. The image is a wood engraving made from a photograph. It appeared in *Harper's Weekly* on November 3, 1866.   *National Baseball Library, Cooperstown, N.Y.*

Atlanta-Fulton County Stadium   Home of the Atlanta Braves since their arrival in the city in 1966.

It was the site of Hank Aaron's record-breaking 715th home run, hit on April 4, 1974.

Atlantic luck   *n./obs.* Good fortune.
ETY/1ST   1870. Edward J. Nichols has written that luck was characteristic of the early Atlantic League clubs. He first found the term in the June 1, 1870, *New York Tribune*.

atom ball   *n.* A punning variation of AT 'EM BALL; a ball hit right at the defensive player.
SEE   *nuclear fission ball.*

attendance clause   *n.* A provision of some modern contracts that promise a bonus to a player if the home attendance for a season goes above a certain number. The assumption here is that the player in question is a draw who will help the gate. Associated Press sportswriter Howard Smith on Harry Caray, who then announced for the White Sox: "Caray supposedly even has an attendance clause in his contract." (*Cleveland Plain Dealer,* August 27, 1978) In his book *Baseball Lite,* Canadian sportscaster Jerry Howarth defines the word attendance, "Formerly a noun of interest to major league owners, it is now an adjective for 'clause' when players negotiate salary bonuses."

at the plate   *adj.* AT BAT.

audible signal base   *n.* A base that emits sound when it is touched and an idea that has been kicked around for decades, but which never attracts much interest. Consider this description by Lester L. Sargent in the March 1914 issue of *Baseball* magazine: "A step toward the dawn of universal peace has been taken in the audible Signal-Base for Baseball Fields, which is the invention of Stephen H. Wills. Those terrible things that are said about the umpire will be said no more. Everybody will know for sure whether or not the runner reached the bag safe, for when he does touch base an electric bell will be rung by the base itself."

Autographed ball. Luis Tiant participates in the traditional rite of adding a signature to a kid's souvenir baseball. *Courtesy of the Cleveland Indians*

authority *adj.* A hitter who swings the bat with power and purpose is said to have this.

autographed ball A long-standing baseball tradition has been the autographing of baseballs by players. Autographs themselves have become a baseball commodity, with stars getting up to $10 to sign their names at baseball card collector conventions. A 1987 UPI story reported that Mickey Mantle gets a flat $10,000 for four hours of autographing.

automatic strike *n.* Often said of a pitch delivered when the count on the batter is three balls and no strikes. It is so called because, in the hope of receiving a *walk*, the batter will not swing at the next pitch. (Sometimes in this situation the manager of the batting team will order a batter to *take* a pitch.) Knowing this tendency of batters and managers, pitchers are more likely to put the ball in the strike zone.
1ST 1937. (Red Barber, World Series broadcast, Oct. 6)

automatic take *n.* The batter's situation in a 3-0 automatic strike situation. The batter is ordered to take the next ball—that is, not swing at it—hoping for a fourth ball and a free trip to first base.

Autumn Classic, The THE WORLD SERIES.
USE It is a cliche of such magnitude that the term is commonly capitalized. "But if the Autumn Classic is baseball's prime-time ode, opening day is when baseball's fans are born and reborn, when hope springs eternal for all teams." (*USA Today*, April 7, 1987)

average *n.* There are several key averages in baseball. See individual entries for *batting average, earned run average* and *fielding average.*

away **1.** *adj.* The number of outs in an inning.
1ST 1981. (*New York Herald,* July 15; EJN)
2. *adj.* A pitch outside the strike zone.
3. *adj.* Playing a game in another team's ball park.

away game *n.* Game played on the other team's field, as opposed to a home game. The 162-game major league schedule comprises 81 away games and 81 home games.

AWOL See *furlough.*

B

B **1.** Class of minor league baseball that is at the fourth level following AAA, AA and A: sometimes referred to as "B-ball."
2. Standard abbreviation for BUNT.

BA Common abbreviation for BATTING AVERAGE.

Babe **1.** *n.* The most famous nickname in baseball, the one given to George Herman Ruth. The 1933 edition of *Who's Who in Baseball* gives this explanation, "The nickname 'Babe' was originally applied to him when he joined the Baltimore Orioles in 1914. Coach Steinam, who was owner Dunn's right hand man, greeted the big fellow when he came into the ball yard, shouting to the other Baltimoreans: 'Boys, here's Jack's New Babe!' " (Jack Dunn was owner and

Babe. Life-sized wooden carving of Babe Ruth on display at the National Baseball Hall of Fame and Museum in Cooperstown, New York. It depicts Ruth at age 34. The museum has found this to be one of its most popular attractions. *National Baseball Library, Cooperstown, N.Y.*

manager of the Baltimore Orioles.) In his autobiography, *The Babe Ruth Story*, Ruth pointed out that the "clincher" came a few days later when he was playing with the controls of a hotel elevator. After almost decapitating himself, Ruth was chewed out by Dunn. One of the older players, taking pity on him, called him a babe in the woods. "After that," said Ruth, "they all called me Babe."

Ruth was not the only player to be called Babe. Probably the most famous was Floyd C. "Babe" Herman who was also known as "the other Babe."

The importance of the names Babe and Babe Ruth is underscored in Eleanor Gehrig's book *My Luke and I*. At various points she mentions that her late husband, Lou Gehrig, is deemed "the Babe Ruth of the high schools" and the "college Babe Ruth."

Ruth may have been able to claim a record for the most aliases in the history of baseball. Though some of the names only existed in the vocabulary of sportswriters, he was called, at various times: Bam, Bambino (Italian for little baby), Behemoth of Biff, Big Bambino, Caliph of Clout, Colossus of Club, Colossus of Sport, Goliath of Grand Slam, Home Run King, King of Clout, King of Swat, Jidge, King of Clout, Monk, Monkey, Prince of Pounders, Slambino, Sultan of Swat and Wizard of Whack.
2. *n.* Term used for any big, fat player but only after Babe Ruth began showing the effects of excessive drinking and eating.
3. Element of infield chatter, as in *Hum babe.*

Babe Ruth *n.* HOME RUN.
ETY As a player Babe Ruth hit so many home runs that his name actually became synonymous with a home run. In the 1930s, when Ruth did his greatest slugging, his name was a common sports page eponym.

Babe Ruth Baseball A nonprofit organization founded in 1951 that supports summer leagues for groups ranging in age from nine through 18.

Babe Ruth curse *n.* Some believe that this is the cloud under which the Boston Red Sox have toiled since owner Harry Frazee sold the great slugger in 1920. There are many aspects to the curse but one of them is that the Sox have a penchant for losing the seventh and deciding game of the World Series (which they did in 1946, 1967, 1975 and 1986). "The Red Sox Have Babe Ruth Curse" read the headline for a George Vecsey column, *New York Times*, October 28, 1986, after the Sox were beaten by the Mets in game 7 of that year's World Series.

Babe Ruther One who plays Babe Ruth Baseball. "Knox Babe Ruthers Place Third in State." (Headline, the Camden (Maine) *Herald*, July 31, 1986)

baby act *n./obs.* Term used by Adrian "Cap" Anson and other late 19th-century ballplayers to describe the bunt. They felt that the strategy of the bunt could potentially ruin the game.
ETY The clear point made by Anson and others who used the term is that the bunt was a weak and pitiful thing that might be fine for infants and youngsters but not for grown men.

baby boomers *n.* Nickname that has been attached to a group of strong, young power hitters, most of whom came up in 1986.
ETY The term baby boomer refers to the children of the period after World War II when the birthrate skyrocketed. In the 1980s the baby boomers were seen as coming into a time of great influence. The baseball baby boomers were born much later but the term fit because they were young (babies) and could hit the long ball (boomers).

Baby Ruth The name of a candy bar that many have long assumed was named after the baseball player. The manufacturer has long insisted that its product was so named in 1917, when the candy bar came out, for the daughter of President Grover Cleveland. Regardless, the closeness of Baby Ruth to Babe Ruth had the effect of tying the candy bar to the slugger. Writer Robert Hendrickson has been able to shed additional light on the situation by adding this comment: "In fact, when another company got Babe Ruth to endorse Babe Ruth's Home Run Candy in 1926, Baby Ruth's manufacturer appealed to the Patent Office on the grounds of infringement and won, the Babe's candy bar never appearing."

back-door slide *n.* Slide in which the runner touches the base with his hand as he slides beyond the bag with his body. Something of a rarity, this slide is performed when an advancing base runner sees that he is about to be tagged out. He fakes a conventional slide, throws himself beyond the base, and reaches back to the bag with his hand. It is a desperation play that only works when it confuses the fielder.

backhand *v.* To field a batted or thrown ball by extending the gloved hand across the body.

backlots *n.* Sandlots; amateur and semi-pro baseball fields.
1ST 1908. (*Baseball* magazine, December; EJN)

back of squeedunk *adj.* Said of a team that is very low in the standings; that is out of contention.

backstop **1.** *n.* Screen behind and extending over the home plate area to keep the ball in the playing area and protect spectators from foul balls. In the majors the backstop must be at least 60 feet from home plate.
2. *n.* CATCHER.

backstopper *n.* CATCHER.

back through the box *adv.* Said of a ball that is hit sharply through the pitcher's box. Such hits often end up as centerfield hits.

back-to-back *adj.* Two consecutive hits of the same type, such as back to back doubles.
1ST/EXT ca. 1900. In *Good Words to You*, John Ciardi reports that this term started in baseball about the turn of the century and long ago generalized to the language at large. He also points out that the term can become absurd in a sentence like, "Remember when Reggie Jackson hit three back-to-back homers in one World Series Game?" His answer: "I do as a matter of fact, but after the third, what was his position relative to the other two, and after the second, what was his position relative to the first and third?"

back up/backup **1.** *v.* To move into a supporting position to help the player who is fielding the ball or being thrown to in case it is missed, dropped or overthrown. For instance, if the ball is coming in from the outfield for a play at third base, the pitcher's job is to get behind the third baseman. So, too, the pitcher often goes behind the plate to back up the catcher.
2. *n.* Player in a support position.
1ST 1869. (DeWitt Official Base Ball Guide; EJN)

backward runner   *n.* Describing a base runner who, having advanced one or more bases, is forced to return to a previous base. If such a runner has tagged a new base while advancing, he must retouch that base before returning to the original one. For example, a runner leaves first base as a ball is hit to the outfield. Thinking the ball will hit the ground, the runner crosses second base and advances toward third. If the ball is caught, however, he must return to first, making sure to retag second base on the way.

bad ball   *n.* Pitched ball thrown outside the strike zone in hopes of enticing the batter to swing.

bad-ball hitter   *n.* Batter who willingly swings at pitches outside the strike zone. Usually a deficiency because such hitters tend to produce strikes and fly balls, but some players have turned it into an asset. Roberto Clemente, Joe Medwick, Yogi Berra and Hank Aaron were all considered excellent bad-ball hitters.

bad call   *n.* Term used when it is felt that the umpire has made an incorrect ruling on a play. The term is commonly used by the real or imagined victim and applied to a ball crossing the plate (was it a ball or a strike?) or a runner arriving at a base (safe or out?).
EXT   Any perceived misjudgment.

bad hands/bad paws   *n.* Player with poor fielding ability, especially when it comes to holding on to the ball; one who has trouble with short hops. Or, as Jim Brosnan put it in *The Long Season,* "A physical affliction common to ball players with poor fielding averages. There is no known cure."

bad head   *n.* An ugly player.

bad hop   *n.* A batted or thrown ball that suddenly changes direction because it hits an object or irregularity on the field.
    In her *New York Times* article, "Terms for Parents of Little Leaguers," Marian Edelman Borden defined a bad hop as ". . . any ball that comes toward your son and doesn't roll into his glove."
SEE   *base on stones.*

bad hose   *n.* Said of a player with a bad arm.

bad lamps *n.*   **1.** Said of a player with poor eyesight.
2. A poorly lit field.

Bad News Bears   *n.* The name of an unruly, motley Little League team in a 1976 movie; they went on to star in *The Bad News Bears Break Training* (1977) and *The Bad News Bears Go to Japan* (1978). It was also the name of a television series. The name has been used to characterize a club in decline or in the midst of a losing streak.

bad wood   *n.* Poor contact between the bat and ball.

bag   *n.* BASE (except for home plate, which is a rubber slab). Canvas bags have been used for first, second and third base since the earliest days of baseball.
1ST   1857. "The first, second, and third bases shall be canvas bags, painted white, and filled with sand or sawdust." (an issue of the newspaper *Spirit of Times,* quoted by DS)

bagger   **1.** *n./arch.* A one-base hit; a single bagger.
1ST   1880. (*Chicago Inter Ocean,* June 3; EJN)
2. *n.* Word used in describing the extent of a hit; as in two-bagger for double and three-bagger for triple.
3. *n.* Word used in describing a first, second or third baseman who can be a first-, second- or third-bagger.

bagman   *n./arch.* BASEMAN.
1ST   1880. (*Chicago Inter Ocean,* June 3; EJN)

bag of bones   *n.* An extremely thin player.

bag of peanuts   *n.* Broken and misshapen hands, like those of a veteran catcher.
1ST   1963. "His hand looked like a bag of peanuts." (Leonard Shecter, *Baseball Digest,* June 1963)

bag puncher   *n./arch.* A player who talks too much. An article titled "Baseball Terminology," in the April 1930 issue of *American Speech,* claimed this was a term used in the National League. Its American League equivalent was *barber.*

bags clogged   BASES LOADED.
1ST   1913. (*Harper's Weekly,* September 6; EJN)

bail out   *v.* When batting, to step back or fall away from a pitch. The act is seldom voluntary and usually takes place when the ball is coming at the batter or when it appears that the ball is coming at the batter. A common situation in which the batter bails out is when he is expecting a fastball and the pitcher serves him a breaking pitch.

bait the hitter *v.* To throw the ball just outside the strike zone in an attempt to get the batter to swing at a bad pitch.

Baker *n./obs.* HOME RUN. Before *Babe Ruth*, Frank "Home Run" Baker was the most dominant home run hitter in baseball. As with Ruth, Baker's name was synonymous with home run. **1ST** 1912. (*New York Tribune*, October 15; EJN)

balk **1.** *n.* Any motion by the pitcher that the umpire deems to be an attempt to deceive a base runner into making a move that may get him picked off base. Specifically, failure by a pitcher to complete the delivery of the ball to home plate once his foot has made contact with the rubber. Most balks are called as the pitcher shows a move that seems to be to deliver the ball to the plate. It is a departure from the pitcher's regular delivery that is, ostensibly, designed to deceive the base runner. A common balk occurs when the pitcher does not come to a stop after his stretch. All runners advance one base on a balk, which can be especially costly if a runner scores on a balk. The official rules spells out 13 specific balk situations.

Even without a change in the rule, the degree to which balks are called changes, depending on the strictness with which the rule is being interpreted. Scores of balks were called at the beginning of the 1988 season, which probably would have been ignored the previous year.

Sportswriter Bob Considine once termed the balk, "a misdemeanor which permits runners to advance a base under the protection of a temporary armistice." (*The Saturday Evening Post*, April 9, 1938; PT) **USE** In 1978, a year in which the balk rule was being strongly enforced, Ira Miller wrote in the *San Francisco Chronicle*, "It is one of baseball's least understood rules. It even sounds funny. Say 'balk' and people hear 'ball.' It's pronounced 'bawk' as in the first syllable of awkward, which is how umpires are making pitchers feel about it." (May 16, 1978; PT) **2.** *v.* To commit the balk. **3.** *n.* An act of interference in which a runner on third is trying to score on a steal or squeeze and the catcher or other player covering home blocks the plate from the runner without possession of the ball, or touches the batter or his bat. In such a case a balk is charged and the batter awarded first. The ball is dead.

1ST 1845. The original Knickerbocker Rules; number 19.
ETY From *balca,* the Anglo-Saxon word for beam. Balcas were put across the doors of huts in the days before locks and keys to thwart or stop intruders. Tracing the term through "baulk" for a false shot or mistake, Peter Tamony wrote this note: "The sense of this word seems in general to be to stop short, to frustrate, to disappoint. In billiards, the balk-line is a line drawn a certain distance from the cushion, and used in connection with certain methods of playing billiards. In baseball, a feint or false motion made by the pitcher in the delivery of the ball to the batter, which is penalized."
EXT To recoil; to fail to deliver, such as a politician balking on tax reform.
SEE *catcher's balk.*

balkamania *n.* Term created to describe the early weeks of the 1988 baseball season when the balk rule was reinterpreted along stricter lines. During the first 11 days of the season, 88 balks had been called in the American League and 36 in the National League, a situation which caused the *Sporting News* to headline its article on the subject "Balkamania Unchecked." (April 25, 1988)

balk move *n.* A pitcher's move that suggests a balk.
USE This is a highly subjective notion as a "balk move" is something alleged by the team at bat. A pitcher charged with making a balk move to first will insist that it is nothing more than his regular move.

ball **1.** *n.* A pitch that is not swung at by the batter and that is judged outside the strike zone by the umpire.
2. *n.* The baseball itself.
3. *n.* A synonym for the game of baseball, as in, "He plays good ball." In some childhood circles this term actually overwhelms the proper one. "We did not know our game as baseball but merely as 'ball,' and in other respects we failed to conform to the orthodox formula," wrote journalist Mark Sullivan about his childhood in his autobiography, *The Education of An American.*

The ball is also known as the apple, horsehide, marble, nugget, onion, pill, rock.
1ST 1845. (Original Knickerbocker Rules)

ball-and-strike umpire *n.* Umpire who, situated behind home plate, is responsible for judging whether a pitch was in or out of the strike zone; the plate umpire.

Ballantine blast   *n.* HOME RUN. One of a number of product-inspired names for the home run used over the years by radio and television announcers to please their sponsors. Including the White Owl Wallop, a Case of Wheaties and a Case of Lucky Strikes, which respectively turned long balls into ads for cigars, breakfast cereal and cigarettes. A 1988 example is shown in this spiel given by New York Yankee announcer Phil Rizzuto linking the homer to one of his broadcast's sponsors, Budweiser beer: "Hey, Yankee fans, you know what happens everytime a Yankee hits a homerun: Dave Winfield, this Bud's for you."

ball boy or ball girl   *n.* Person whose job it is to keep foul balls off the playing field.

ball club   **1.** *n./arch.* The BAT.
2. *n.* A team.
1ST   1845. (Chadwick Scrapbooks, October 13; EJN)

balldom   *n.* The realm of baseball.
1ST   1905. (*Sporting Life,* September 2; EJN)

ball field   *n.* Baseball playing area.
1ST   1864. (*Brooklyn Daily Eagle,* September 20; EJN)

ballgame   **1.** *n.* A baseball game.
2. *n.* The moment or event that determines the outcome of a game. For instance, Earl Weaver is quoted on a key out in Tom Boswell's *How Life Imitates the World Series,* "That one at-bat was the ball game."
3. *n.* A player with strong identification.
EXT   A coherent event, such as the movement of a bill through Congress. "Duncan's only comment on the close vote yesterday was 'The ball game isn't over yet.' " (AP dispatch, May 30, 1986; PT)
   "A whole new ballgame" means a new start. It alludes to the situation inside baseball when a sudden turn of events in a game in progress brings on the comment that it is now a "new ballgame."
SEE   *new ballgame.*

ball game is at first, the   Way of saying the fact that if the runner on first base scores, it will win the game. Similarly, "the ball game is at second" and "the ballgame is at third" allude to the game-winning potential of runners at second and third base, respectively.

ball girl   *n.* BALL BOY/BALL GIRL.

ball hawk   **1.** *n.* An especially fast and adept outfielder; one who covers a lot of ground.
1ST   1920 (*New York Times,* October 10; EJN)
2. *n.* Person who collects as souvenirs balls that are hit outside a ballpark. They are very common at the smaller major and minor league parks and at those that are used for exhibition games during spring training, for the simple reason that more balls land out of the park at such sites.

ball hound   *n.* One who will chase and return stray baseballs.
1ST   1935. "A couple of 'ball hounds', youngsters not quite old enough for the team yet loyally interested in it, should be relied upon to rescue balls going out of the grounds." (Ralph H. Barbour, *How to Play Better Baseball;* DS)

ballites, ball-ites   *n./arch.* Fans.

balloon   **1.** *n.* A ball that looks big to the batter because it is moving slowly and gives the illusion of being oversized. The opposite illusion comes into play with an especially fast fastball which is likely, for example, to be termed an aspirin. Of course, both the balloon and the aspirin are regulation-size balls.
2. *n.* Fly ball.
1ST   1920. (*New York Times,* October 6; EJN)
3. *n.* Type of umpire's chest protector (see chest pad) worn outside the uniform. "Although 'the balloon' was difficult to master, it did provide more protection . . ." (Ron Luciano in *Strike Two;* CDP)
ETY   The name is an allusion to the puffy, bloated look of the outside protector.

balloon ascension   *n./arch.* A BLOW UP; when a pitcher loses his effectiveness. The term was commonly framed in terms of spectators witnessing a balloon ascension.
1ST   1907. (Burt L. Standish, *Dick Merriwell's Magnetism;* EJN)

balloon ball   *n.* A slowly thrown pitch that is thrown upwards. It arches high in the air and drops precipitously as it passes through the strike zone. It is a rarely thrown pitch that can be effective when the odd trajectory is enough to throw the batter's timing off.
1ST   1913. "My team had their batting eyes along, but that balloon ball fooled us every time." (Alan Douglas, *Fast Nine;* DS) Another early reference: 1919. "Unfortunately Frazer

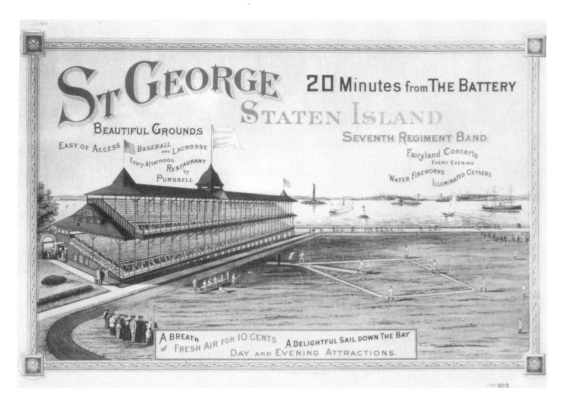

Ballpark. An 1886 lithograph of the St. George Grounds on Staten Island. Both the American Association Metropolitans and the National League Giants played there in the 1880s.   *Prints and Photographs Division, the Library of Congress*

could not vary his speed and drops and curves with an occasional deceptive Mathewson 'balloon ball.' " (Donald Ferguson, *Out for the Pennant;* DS)
SEE   *eephus ball.*

balloon flier   *n./arch.* High fly ball.
1ST   1919. "Horatio Juggins was an elongated chap whose specialty, besides capturing balloon fliers out in right field consisted in great throwing." (Donald Ferguson, *Out for the Pennant;* DS)

ballpark/ball park   *n.* An enclosed baseball field, including its seating areas; a stadium. It is a short form of *baseball park.*
1ST   1908. (*Baseball* magazine, June; EJN)
ETY   The first such enclosed playing area was Union Grounds in Brooklyn, New York, which opened on May 15, 1862. The enclosure was invented and designed by William Cammeyer.
EXT   A given realm; a field of activity. "Senators Knock FmHA [Farmers Home Administration] All Over the Ballpark." (headline,

Washington Post, September 10, 1986) By extension, in the ball park refers to something (a cost estimate, plan etc.) that is within the realm of consideration, while out of the ballpark is something that is, as John Ciardi defined it, "beyond negotiable limits."

ballpark figure   *n.*
EXT   A rough estimate. This has an decidely odd connection to baseball given that most figures having to do with the game (batting averages, earned run averages and other statistics) are relentlessly precise. Lexicographer Stuart Flexner is quoted by William Safire on its evolution in the book *I Stand Corrected:* "Our Random House dictionary citation files show the term first started out as *in the ballpark* (1962), as when talking about figures, estimates, etc., with 'I hope that's in the ballpark.' Then, in 1968, we first recorded *ballpark figure* from The Seattle Times."

ballpark frank   *n.* A hot dog. Possibly the most beloved food sold by vendors at baseball games, it is often felt that they taste better there than elsewhere. At some parks they are given local nicknames such as the Fenway Frank (Boston) and the Dodger Dog (Los Angeles).

On the other hand, not everyone is convinced that these franks are superior. "I ask you, is there anything in the world tastier than a ballpark frank?" writer Rick Horowitz asked himself in a *Washington Post* article on ballpark food. "Are you kidding?!" he answers. "Hot dogs steamed since the 1958 World Series? Buns carved out of broken bat handles?" (April 8, 1987)

ball player/ballplayer   *n.* One who plays the game.
USE   This term carries its own honor. In *Baseball America* by Donald Honig, "Smoky" Joe Wood is quoted on his phenomenal 1912 season when he had a 34–5 pitching record and a batting average of .290. "I wasn't just a pitcher, I was a ballplayer."
1ST   1862. (Correspondence of the Knickerbocker Base Ball Club, EJN)

balls and strikes   *n.* The COUNT on a batter.

ball-shoe   *n.* Baseball footwear.
1ST   1909. ". . . and most of all I'll want my glove and ball-shoes." (Zane Grey, *The Short Stop*)

ball team   TEAM.
1ST   1902. (*Sporting Life,* April 26; EJN)

ball town/ball-town   *n.* City that supports baseball, such as one that keeps a team in the black. "Time was when the name of Toledo as a ball town was one to conjure with," according to the 1905 *Official Guide* of the National Association of Professional Base Ball Leagues, "but that time has passed." (DS)
1ST   1883. "Detroit is one of the best paying ball-towns in the country . . ." (*Sporting Life* for July 22)

ball with eyes on it   *n.* A batted ball, usually a grounder, that barely gets past the outstretched gloves of two fielders. So described because it would seem to need "vision" to chart such an elusive course.
SEE   *seeing eye single.*

ballyard   *n.* BALLPARK.
USE   Used by some sportswriters, but far from universal. In fact, it would seem to be something of a taboo or red flag to traditionalists. After Dave Kindred of the *Washington Post* called Baltimore's Memorial Stadium a ballyard, the paper printed a letter from a reader named Caroll Beaulac, which said in part: "Since the birth of baseball, the area where the game is played has been called the ball*park*. Will Kindred grow tired of calling that area the ball*yard* by next year and start calling it the ball*patio* or the ball*lot* or perhaps the ball*arena*?" (*Washington Post*, October 16, 1982)

Nonetheless, there are those who seem able to get away with it, especially if they are affecting a gushy style. Writing about Candlestick Park at the beginning of the 1987 National League playoff series Tom Boswell of the *Washington Post:* "Oh, thou loveliest of ball yards, how have you been maligned." (October 11, 1987)

Baltimore bounce   *n./arch.* Baltimore chop.

Baltimore chop   *n.* A batted ball that hits the ground close to home plate and then bounces high in the air, allowing the batter time to reach first base safely. It is occasionally described as a ball that hits the plate.
ETY/1ST   1910. Despite the fact that it did not begin to show up in print for several decades (*Baseball* magazine, April 1910; EJN), it got its name, by all accounts, in the 1890s when the tactic was perfected by Wee Willie Keeler of the old Baltimore Orioles. Two other Baltimore batsmen, John McGraw and Wilbert Robinson, also used it as a method to get on base. Evidence suggests that at the Orioles' field, the dirt near home plate was purposely hardened to make the ball bounce higher. A description of the tactic from an 1896 edition of the *Baltimore News* appears in Dan Schlossberg's *Baseball Catalog:* "A middle-height ball is picked out and is attacked with a terrific swing on the upper side. The ball is made to strike the ground from five to ten feet away from the batsman and, striking the ground with force, bounds high over the head of the third or first baseman."

"Today's Baltimore chops, however, are almost always accidental," says Mike Whiteford in his book, *How to Talk Baseball.* However, the term is very much alive, as this kind of hit comes more easily on artificial turf.
SEE   *butcher boy.*

Baltimore farewell   *n.* By fans at a game, the collective act of waving handkerchiefs in a

Baltimore chop. The innovative Wilbert Robinson, shown here as the manager of the Brooklyn Dodgers, who were also known as the Robins in his honor. As a Baltimore Oriole on June 10, 1892, he had seven hits in seven at bats in a nine-inning ballgame. *National Baseball Library, Cooperstown, N.Y.*

derogatory fashion upon the departure of an opposing pitcher who has been removed from the game.

ETY   An article in *The Baltimore Evening Sun* of April 12, 1955, by Murray Wieman reveals that the custom was spawned in Baltimore, back when the Orioles were an AAA International League team. Wieman wrote, "In spite of critics who called it 'small town' the farewell blossomed again last season [1954] as the Orioles went big league."

Baltimore Orioles   Traditional name for several baseball teams that have played in Baltimore, Maryland. The original Baltimore Orioles played during the 19th century and the first two years of the 20th century in the American Association and National and American Leagues. That team was followed by the AAA

International League team. The current Orioles of the American League's Eastern division moved to Baltimore in 1954 from St. Louis where they had been the Browns.

ETY   The black and yellow Baltimore Oriole is the Maryland state bird and has always been linked to the city because of its name. According to legend, the bird was named by Cecilius Calvert, the second Lord Baltimore.

The Orioles of the present era are also known as the "Birds" and the "O's."

Bambi   *n.* A meek or extremely mild-mannered player, manager or coach, from the name of the fictional deer. "Though he never kicked dirt on an umpire or turned his cap around to argue nose-to-nose as Weaver is famous for, Ripken says he will be no Bambi with the umpires." (*USA Today* profile of manager Cal Ripken, January 28, 1987)

banana   *n.* A good player; a prospect that makes the team. "There isn't a scout in the business who hasn't touted more lemons than bananas." (Dick Friendlich, *Relief Pitcher;* CDP)

banana boat   *n.* Player who has played winter ball in Latin America. Reported by writer Joseph C. Goulden, who recalls: "A derisive name for minor leaguers who played Central American and Mexican baseball during the off-seasons in the late 1940s, employed chiefly by bench jockeys of opposing teams. This was the period when a three-year man in Class C baseball might earn upwards of $225 monthly during the regular season, so he went south for both the money and the experience. The next summer, however, he would hear the growl, 'banana boat, banana boat, TOOT TOOT TOOT!' from the other team's dugout."

banana stalk/banana stick   *n.* A bat of inferior wood or low quality. "This banana stalk won't crack an aspirin." (Ad in *Time* with a theme of baseball slang, November 22, 1948; PT)
1ST   1937. (*Sporting News Record Book;* EJN)

bandbox/band box/bandbox field   *n.* A ballpark whose small dimensions make it easier to hit home runs. In the 1950s the label was often applied to Ebbets Field, while today it is most likely to attach itself to Fenway Park (which John Updike termed a "lyric little green bandbox") and Wrigley Field. The term is sometimes used to suggest that a batter's numbers are less impressive because of the dimensions of his home field. At the end of the 1988 season, Jose Canseco of the Oakland A's said that the record posted by Mike Greenwell of the Boston Red Sox was diminished "because he plays in a bandbox." (The *Sporting News*, October 10, 1988)

"The best moments of my life were spent in the old [San Francisco] Seals Stadium at 16th and Potrero, a beautiful little bandbox of a ball park." (*Anderson Valley Advertiser*, Boonville, California; "Sports Notes" column for May 21, 1986)

1ST 1906. (*Sporting Life*, February 10; EJN)

ETY A reference to the bandstands and band boxes that were common in small towns at the turn of the century.

bang *n.* A base hit.
1ST 1888. (*New York Press;* EJN)

bang-bang/bang-bang play *n.* An attempted tag or force play at a base when the runner and the ball arrive simultaneously. The action happens in quick succession, making it difficult for the umpire (and spectators) to determine whether the runner is safe or out. "I blew a play at first base. I admit it. I was wrong. But I wasn't *that* wrong. It was a bang-bang play and I anticipated the throw arriving before it did and I called the runner out." (Ron Luciano, *The Umpire Strikes Back;* CDP)

bangup game *n./arch.* A well played, exciting contest.
1ST 1914. (*New York Tribune*, September 27; EJN)

banish *v.* For an umpire to eject from a game a player, coach or manager.
1ST 1912. (*New York Tribune*, April 21; EJN)

banjo eyes *n.* The wide-eyed look of a batter attempting to steal a sign from the catcher while at the plate. In *Comedians of Baseball* J. G. Taylor Spink attributes this term to Cub & Dodgers second baseman (1931–1941) Billy Herman.

banjo hit *n.* A weak hit as the result of a poor swing or accidental contact with the ball, such as one made on a checked swing.
ETY/1ST 1937. According to Tim Considine in his *Language of Sport*, it was "named in 1924 by Jersey City second baseman, Ray 'Snooks' Dowd, for the way the ball 'plunks' off the bat." Edward J. Nichols first found it in print in the January 11, 1937, *Pittsburgh Press*.)

banjo hitter *n.* Term denoting a batter who cannot hit the long ball.
USE Although it underscores the inability to hit for distance, the term is not necessarily derogatory as it can be applied to an effective place hitter. "Campy happy as banjo hitter," read a headline for an October 17, 1973, Associated Press dispatch (PT) which is followed by this first sentence: "NEW YORK—As a baseball player, little Bert Campaneris dreams of powering the ball over distant fences such as Hank Aaron or Willie Mays, but he is happy at being a banjo hitter with a pair of speedy legs."

banjo hitting *adj.* Applied to an individual or team that does not hit the ball long distances. "The banjo-hitting Los Angeles Dodgers have added new muscle to their attack for their 1971 run at the National League pennant." (*San Francisco Examiner*, December 12, 1970; PT)

Banks' Dictum Name given to Ernie Banks' famous line, "It's a great day for a ball game. Let's play two!"

The line is quoted often and widely and tends to be uttered when the weather is mild and the players are primed. To many, the line captures the spirit and joy of the game of baseball. It could never, for instance, be applied to football where a second game would amount to cruel and unusual punishment.

banner **1.** *n.* PENNANT.
1ST 1880. (*New York Herald*, August 30; EJN)
2. *n.* Paper or cloth sheet emblazoned with a message from a fan or fans. A product of the television age because tv cameras often focus on them, banners took on great importance during the early seasons of the New York Mets. Possibly the most famous banner of all time was displayed by Michael Sergio who parachuted into Shea Stadium with a "Go Mets!" banner at the beginning of the sixth game of the 1986 World Series.

banner day/night *n.* A game. Time when fans are encouraged to display posters and banners. The idea evolved from the practice of fans bringing to ballparks placards and bedsheets emblazoned with slogans proclaiming feelings toward the teams and players on the field.

baptism *n.* The act of removing the smooth, slippery surface of a new baseball before bringing it into play. This is usually performed prior

Banner Day. August 8, 1965, at Shea Stadium, when 2,500 fans carried banners during a parade staged between the games of a doubleheader. The parade took an hour and 10 minutes. The winning entry was a bedsheet emblazoned with the line, "To error is human, to forgive is a Mets' fan." *National Baseball Library, Cooperstown, N.Y.*

to the start of a game by the home plate umpire, who uses a special rubbing mud.

barber 1. *n./arch.* A garrulous player; one who engages in chatting and joking during a game, in the manner of an extroverted barber; a willing and eager conversationalist. Compare with bag puncher.

1ST 1927. (*New York Sun*, July 18; EJN)

ETY Baseball writer Hy Turkin maintained that Waite Hoyt coined the term when he was a pitcher with the New York Yankees. One of the earliest appearances the term makes in print is in the glossary to Yankee teammate Babe Ruth's 1928 book, *Babe Ruth's Own Book of Baseball*.

This meaning of the term was the only one that obtained in baseball until about 1950 when the next two began to be heard.

2. A pitcher who throws close to the batter's head; one who gives "close shaves."

The late sportswriter Dick Young on Sal Maglie: "He was the barber because he shaved hitters. That's what they call a good knockdown, a close shave." (New York *Daily News*, October 20, 1980)

Barber. Sal Maglie, the man who apparently carried the "Barber" nickname for two reasons: his persistent stubble and his ability to throw "close shaves." *National Baseball Library, Cooperstown, N.Y.*

3. A pitcher with enough precision and control to "shave" the corners of the strike zone.

barbering   *n.* Chatting, as one is likely to do in the barber chair. Listed by Hall of Famer Dizzy Dean in his booklet *Dizzy Daisies*, in which he presented some of his "favorite broadcastin' expressions" and defined it as, "Conversing, chinning, or chewing the fat."

bare-handed   *adj.* Describes the act of fielding a batted or thrown ball without the use of a glove. Such plays are usually made on slowly hit balls and often result in quick, off-balance throws. A bunt for instance will often take a third baseman by surprise and his only hope of making the play at first in time is to bare-hand the ball and whip it across the infield in the same motion.

bargain bill/bargain day   *n.* DOUBLE HEADER, so called because you get to see two games for the price of one.

barker   *n.* FIRST-BASE COACH.
1ST   1937 (*Sporting News Record Book;* EJN)

barn ball   *n.* Forerunner of baseball that survived after baseball was created. It was a game of two players, a ball, a bat (usually an ax handle or stick) and the side of a barn or other building. One player threw the ball against the barn for the other to hit with the bat. If the batter missed and the pitcher caught it, the batter was out and the pitcher was up. However, if the batter hit the ball he had a chance to score a run if he could touch the barn and return to his batting position before the pitcher could retrieve the ball and hit the batter with it. As John Allen Krout points out in *The Annals of American Sport,* "Here were the fundamentals of the game of baseball; the pitcher, the batter, the base hit and the run."

barn door   *n./arch.* Easy pitch to hit; one that is slow and seems to be the size of a barn door.
1ST   1912. "If I was pitchin' barn doors and you was battin', you'd swear every door I threw would be the size of a French pea." (*Sporting Life,* May 18)

barnstorm   *v.* To play exhibition games in small towns and cities without a baseball team of their own.
1ST   1902. (Edward J. Nichols finds both barnstormer and barnstorming in *Sporting Life*—July 5, September 27—but does not find barnstorm until 1922.)
ETY   The term was borrowed from both the world theater and the political arena whence it

Barnstorm. Undated photograph sent to the Hall of fame in 1972 by Fred C. Snodgrass, one of the players depicted. Snodgrass described them as a National League troop that barnstormed from Chicago to Honolulu in the off-season. *National Baseball Library, Cooperstown, N.Y.*

originally meant to appear where and when one could—even if it was in a barn. The spirit of the term was noted by Peter Tamony in a quote, which appeared in P. T. Barnum's *Struggles and Triumphs*, about the great singer Jenny Lind's arrival in Madison, Kentucky: "We were not a little surprised to learn upon arriving, that the concert must be given in a 'pork house'— a capacious shed which had been fitted up and decorated for the occasion."

A. G. Spalding wrote that baseball's first barnstorm tour took place in 1860 when the Excelsiors of Brooklyn played in several cities of central and western New York State.

Long after these other applications it was applied to aviation. In his 1936 *Phrase Origins*, Alfred H. Holt wrote: "Since the War, 'barnstormer' has also been applied to an aviator who parks his 'crate' (usually an old OX-5 with a Liberty motor) in a barn at some conveniently large and level pasture, and takes people joyriding at a dollar or two a shot."

barnstorming loop/barnstorming tour *n.* A series of exhibition games played in various cities and towns, sometimes on the way from spring training to the Opening Day game or after the regular season had ended.

Earlier in the 20th century it was common for major league teams to barnstorm from their spring training sites back to their home cities in time for opening day. Groups of individuals also engaged in off-season barnstorming, a practice which was generally frowned on by big league owners who did not want to see their best players hurt playing for pick-up "All-Star" teams. "The players participated in a major vs. minor all-star game in Los Angeles on February 15, thus breaking the barnstorming rule which prohibits big leaguers playing for money later than thirty days after the World Series ends." (*San Francisco Examiner*, March 8, 1948, PT)

For the players, barnstorming was an important source of income. Yogi Berra recalled the ways he used to make money in the 1950s in an article in the *New York Times* (January 11, 1988) and said, "And we'd go barnstorming. We did it to make money."

barrage *n.* A number of hits in close succession.

barrel *n.* The top or heavy part of the bat; often referred to as good wood.

barrelhoop curve *n.* A sweeping curveball.
1ST 1910. (*American* magazine, June; EJN)

base *n.* Each of the four corners or points of the baseball diamond. Only one runner is allowed on any base at one time. Each base is 90 feet from the next and, with the exception of the rubberized home plate, is made of canvas and measures 15×15 inches. Each base is an incremental unit used in reaching the fourth unit and scoring a run.
SEE *bag, cushion, hassock, pillow, sack, station.*
1ST 1845. (Rules of the Knickerbocker Club)
EXT To "touch base" is to make contact, to "touch all the bases" is to be thorough, to be "off base" is to be wrong and to be "off one's base" is to be out of one's mind.

base ball **1.** *n./arch.* Earlier way of writing baseball that is seldom used today but was dominant in the 19th century. It has been suggested elsewhere that it became one word between 1925 and 1940, but there are many examples that show up earlier. Here is one from 1903: "The first game of baseball is said to have been played at Hoboken, N.J. on the Elysian Fields . . ." (*Springfield Republican*, July 27)
1ST 1845. (Knickerbocker Rules; however, see *base-ball* below)

base-ball **1.** *n./arch.* Earlier way of writing baseball. The term was commonly hyphenated around the turn of the century. For instance, the 1896 rules and specifications of the Government Printing Office call for it to be written in this manner.
2. *n.* The traditional British game of ROUNDERS.
1ST 1744. By all accounts one of the first uses of the term appears in *The Little Pretty Pocket Book* published in London. It also shows up in this form in Jane Austen's *Northanger Abbey*, which was written in 1798 but not published until 20 years later.

baseball **1.** *n.* The game itself, comprising a body of rules, records and traditions and played at a number of levels from that of young children to seasoned professionals. It is defined in the first rule (1.01) in the *Official Baseball Rules* this way: "Baseball is a game between two teams of nine players each, under the direction of a manager, played on an enclosed field in accordance with these rules, under jurisdiction of one or more umpires." It has also been defined many ways in many quarters, including this

Baseball. Woodcut showing a precursor of baseball. It first appeared in the book *Children's Amusements,* published in New York in 1820.   *Courtesy of the New York Public Library*

Freudian interpretation: "The pitcher-father tries to complete a throw into the mitt of his mate crouched over home plate. A series of sons step up and each in turn tries to intercept the throw. If any of them is successful, he can win 'home' and defeat the pitcher—if he is able first to complete a hazardous journey out of the adult world of the father's allies." (Thomas Gould, *The Ancient Quarrel Between Poetry and Philosophy;* quoted in the *New York Times Magazine,* September 11, 1983)

2. *n.* The leather-covered ball used to play the game, which is not less than nine nor more than 9¼ inches in circumference and not more than 5¼ ounces in weight. "Save that old Spalding major league baseball. It'll soon be a collector's item." (*The Washington Star,* June 21, 1975)

3. *n.* The organized game in its entirety; the "industry." "Baseball has never answered any charges directed against it by anyone regarding the war records of its players." (*Springfield* [Mass.] *Union,* May 5, 1954)

4. *adj.* Having to do with the game. ". . . that phase of his baseball life." (*Boy's Life,* March 1952)

EXT   1. *n.* A general metaphor for other organized activities relying on teamwork. "R. Sargent Shriver, Jr., director of the Peace Corps, said today the Corps will be operated like a baseball team, with the manager empowered to yank out a player before he ruins the game." (AP dispatch, May 18, 1961; PT)

2. *n.* In gambling, a method of wagering. Here it is applied to dog racing. "And the most popular method of selecting quinellas is called, by golly, a 'baseball.' Since there generally are eight greyhounds in each race, students of the sport have noticed there can be a problem in forecasting the two which will run best. So, in a 'baseball' you select three lean pooches which means you're betting on three combinations. With this baseball though, there are more wild pitches than two-baggers." (Harry Jupiter, *San Francisco Examiner,* March 20, 1967; PT)

3. *n.* Any of a number of games that ape the scoring of baseball but that do not involve other elements of the game. For instance, there is a mumblety-peg-like jackknife game mentioned under the heading for *baseball* in the *Dictionary of American Regional English* in which one gets hits by throwing the knife in the ground but is out if the knife falls flat.

baseball Annie *n.* Generic name for unattached woman who favors the company of baseball players. The phrase was given prominence after the Phillies' Eddie Waitkus was shot without provocation on June 15, 1949. "He sat up in bed and tolerantly described Ruth [Steinhagen, a 19-year-old] as a 'Baseball Annie,' one of an army of hero-worshipping teen-age girls who follow the players around." (*Time,* June 17, 1949; PT) The Waitkus incident is portrayed fictionally in the film, *The Natural.*

Although the term is not as commonly used as it once was, it is still used in special situations, such as this one written about by Ira Berkow in the *New York Times* of August 12, 1988: "Margo Adams, who has filed a $6 million palimony suit against [Wade] Boggs, has been categorized by some as a Baseball Annie, a woman attracted to ballplayers."

baseball arm *n.* Painful throwing arm that can take a pitcher out of the rotation and hamper a fielder. It is a lay (i.e., non-medical) term and can describe any sore arm produced from playing baseball.
EXT It can be applied to players in other sports as well. "Baseball arm will be the long range football problem at Stanford during the interim until plans start for the next big game." (*San Francisco Call Bulletin,* November 24, 1952; PT)

baseball bet
EXT *n.* Horse-racing bet involving a parlay on three or more horses.

baseball bride
EXT *n.* One's ninth wife, after the fact that there are nine on a baseball team. "Bandleader Charlie Barnett breezed into town last night with his 'baseball bride.' " (*San Francisco News,* August 18, 1955; PT)

baseball cage *n.* BATTING CAGE.

baseball cap *n.* The billed hat worn by baseball players. It was once rigid custom for players to doff or touch the peak of their cap when crossing home plate after hitting a home run.
EXT The term is just as likely to show up in a news story as on the sports pages: "Two gunmen wearing black baseball caps escaped with an estimated $2,500 from the Gary Federal Savings and Loan at 36th and Grant this morning." (*The Gary Post Tribune,* August 12, 1967)

baseball card *n.* A piece of cardboard depicting a baseball player, a group of players or a team. Besides tobacco and gum, they have been included as a premium with such widely diverse products as soft drinks, bread, potato chips, candy and breakfast cereals. They have been produced in many shapes and sizes.

There are no rules as to what can or cannot appear on a baseball card, but the established format is to feature a portrait or action photograph of the player on one side of the card and statistics and biographical information on the flip side. The growing variety of baseball cards is suggested in these lines from a Topps Chewing Gum Inc. press release, "The 1988 card series will consist of 792 cards. This will consist of 700 regular player cards, 26 team cards, 26 manager cards, 22 All-Star cards, 7 record-breaker cards, 6 checklists and 5 Turn-Back-The-Clock cards. Included among the 700 regular player cards will be five cards designated as 'Future Stars' and ten cards designated as 'Topps All-Star Rookie.' "

Baseball Chapel Organization of religious major and minor league baeball players dedicated to spreading Christian Gospel to players throughout North America. It is based in Bloomingdale, New Jersey.

baseball diamond *n.* DIAMOND.

baseballdom *n.* The domain of baseball, especially professional baseball. "Current Gossip From Baseballdom" was once a typical name for a column on the sport.
SEE Balldom.

baseballeer *n./arch.* Rarely used name for a player in the earlier days of the 20th century. The most recent example of its use was found in Frank G. Menke's *New Encyclopedia of Sports,* published by A. S. Barnes in 1944: ". . . the report was like some heaven-sent gift which arrived for the harassed baseballeer."

baseballer *n./arch.* A PLAYER. "And Mr. Clarke sadly advises all golfers, cricketeers and baseballers that the moon, with its reduced gravitational pull, is no place to swat a ball." (*New York Times* Book Review, April 25, 1955)

baseballese **1.** *n.* The overall language of baseball, comprising official terminology, slang and jargon.

CHAMPIONS OF AMERICA.

Entered according to Act of Congress, in the year 1865, by CHAS. H. WILLIAMSON, in the Clerk's Office of the District Cour' of the United States, of the Eastern District of New York.

Baseball card. This small photographic depiction of the Brooklyn Atlantics, with an 1865 copyright, is exactly the size of a modern baseball card (3½x2½). It was discovered in the Library of Congress' vast photographic holdings by George S. Hobart, curator of documentary photographs.   *Prints and Photographs Division, the Library of Congress*

"They liked his language—some of it authentic American baseballese, but most of it just plain Dizzy Dean." (Norman Cousins, *Saturday Review*, August 2, 1946)
1ST 1912. "Some writers call it 'baseballese'; you call it either one you please." (Edmund Vance Cooke, *Baseballology*)
2. *n.* The language of the players themselves as distinguished from that of those who write about the game. This distinction is made forcefully by William G. Brandt in his October 1932 *Baseball* magazine article, "That Unrecognized Language—Baseballese." After giving some authentic examples, Brandt writes: "That's baseballese. [*You Know Me Al* author] Ring Lardner's half-wit bushers don't talk that way. Nor any of the sluggers in the baseball yarns you read in 'Flimsy Stories.' In fact you won't read baseballese anywhere."

baseball farm *n.* A minor league team. "The San Jose Bees, a very minor league team, almost won a championship in 1973, providing a semi-

dramatic framework for a determinedly undramatic overview of life on the modern, mechanized baseball farm." (Robert Lipsyte in the *New York Times*, April 6, 1975)

baseballfield/baseball field *n.* The surface on which the game is played, usually located in a park, or stadium. "A baseballfield is found on the edge of the settlement and baseball seems to be the favorite sport." (*Harper's* magazine, June 1902)

baseball finger *n.* A "disruption of the tendon to the tip of a finger caused by the ball striking the finger," as defined in a 1952 issue of the *Annals of Western Medicine and Surgery*.
1ST 1889. "Then, can you tell me what a baseball finger is?" "A WHAT?" "A base-ball finger! I heard an American lady use that term." (A. C. Gunter, *That Frenchman;* DS)

baseball fingers *n.* "Thickened, distorted fingers caused by injuries received in excessive playing of baseball," according to *The New Social*

THE FIRST BASE.   6

"WAKE UP, WAKE UP, MY DUCK LEGGED MAN,
AND STIR YOUR SOLID PEGS."

From *Base ball as viewed by a Muffin. Illustrated by S. Van Campen*
New Bedford, Mass.: Taber Bros., 1867

Baseballese. This captioned illustration from an 1867 baseball book, *Base ball as Viewed by a Muffin*, underscores the point that some attempts at creating a baseball jargon have been shortlived. One must wonder if anyone other than the author of the book ever uttered the line, "Wake up, wake up, my duck legged man, and stir your solid pegs." *Courtesy of the New York Public Library*

Worker's Dictionary by Erle Fiske Young, published in 1941.

EXT The term also shows up as a generic name for distorted fingers. "Fingers distorted at the joints by accident are called 'baseball fingers' and are frequently marks of identification." (*New York Daily Tribune*, December 20, 1903)

baseball grenade
EXT *n.* Nickname for a hand-held explosive device which is baseball-shaped and meant to be thrown in the manner of a baseball. "Pieces of a 'baseball grenade' that sent half a dozen policemen scurrying from Taraval station will be turned over to Army ordnance experts." (*San Francisco News*, March 25, 1954; PT)

baseball grip *n.* The general manner in which the bat is held by a batter—firmly, with one's two fists touching but not linked.

EXT *n.* Method for holding a golf club that was made popular by professional golfers Bob Rosberg and Art Wall in the late 1950s. It bears some resemblance to the grip used by a baseball player in holding a bat, although the left thumb is not tucked in but extends along the shaft.

baseball gum *n.* The thin piece of aromatic, pink bubble gum included in certain packages of baseball cards. The practice of pairing gum and baseball cards began in 1933 when the Goudey Gum Co. of Boston issued a set of cards depicting 239 famous players. Though paper and latex shortages during World War II brought production to a halt, a number of companies began issuing gum and cards as soon as the war ended. When the Topps Co. of Brooklyn, New York, began manufacturing its own cards in 1951, the collecting and trading of baseball cards became a fad.

"Just chew it like baseball gum." (Hunter S. Thompson, *Fear and Loathing in Las Vegas*)

Baseball Hall of Fame   HALL OF FAME.

baseballia   *n.* Materials concerning or characteristic of baseball and the culture of baseball; collectible baseball Americana.

baseballically   *adv.* Relating to the game; name of the sport fashioned into an adverb. "The Babe was one of my children, you know, baseballically speaking. First Lou [Gehrig] and now the Babe"—Edward G. Barrow, retired Yankee president and the man who converted Babe Ruth from a pitcher to an outfielder, quoted at the time of Ruth's death. (*The Washington Star*, August 17, 1948)

baseball immortal   *n.* One of the greatest and most influential players to play the game, an individual who presumably will never be forgotten. The title is totally subjective and seems to be bestowed on those who have had an effect on the very nature of the game. It is bestowed by common and repeated usage—in other words, if almost all of the nation's sportswriters call Ty Cobb a baseball immortal, he is one. Caption for a *New Yorker* cartoon in which two angels eye a uniformed New York Yankee with a halo and wings: "I don't care if he *is* a baseball immortal, he should wear a robe and carry a harp like the rest of us." (August 16, 1982)
SEE   *Hall of Famer.*

baseballism   *n.* An expression or custom peculiar to the game of baseball. Calling a team's locker room a clubhouse, as is the practice, is a baseballism. Another is that the manager of a baseball team customarily dresses in the team uniform (unlike the coach in other sports who wears street clothes.)

baseballist/base-ballist   *n./arch.* One who plays or is in some other way closely associated with the game of baseball. It was a term of honor, as can be heard in a speech by Rep. J.M. Glover of Missouri and reported in *The Congressional Record* for April 2, 1886: "[He is well known] as a baseballist among constitutional lawyers, and a constitutional lawyer among *baseballists.*"
USE   This was a fairly common 19th-century term for a person who would be termed a ball player today. A headline in the September 20,

1890, *National Police Gazette:* "Young Lady Baseballists."
1ST   1866. ". . . that illustrious base-ballist, Mr. Blindman, was appointed umpire . . ." (*The Galaxy;* DS)

baseballite   *n./arch.* FAN. A person with an enthusiasm for the sport. The term seems to have been in vogue in the 1930s and may have been a poke at the word socialite.

baseballitis   *n.* Mock-disease name for infatuation with the game. "Since early childhood I've been afflicted with a near-fatal illness known as diamond fever or, to call it by its medical term, baseballitis." (Frank Barnicle in the *Clearwater* (Fla.) *Times,* April 4, 1986)

baseball jacket   *n.* The short coat designed to keep the upper body and arms warm. Players often wear this when they are warming up or practicing before a game or in the dugout during a game, but never when actually playing the game.
EXT   An outergarment of the same style. "He wears a baseball jacket piped in red . . ." (*New Times* describing a rock star, November 1973)

baseball jackknife
EXT   *n.* A children's game on the order of mumblety-peg, which is played by tossing a pocketknife with two open blades. It is played by two or more children using flexible rules. Depending on how the knife sticks in the ground and how the game is set up, the thrower is credited with a single, double, triple or home run. If the knife lands flat, the thrower is out. According to *The Dictionary of American Regional English*, the game is commonly known as baseball.

baseball leather   *n.* According to *The Dictionary of Leather Terminology*, 4th ed., published by the Tanner Council of America (1946), it is "Usually made from fronts of horsehides and used for covering baseballs. Sheepskin is used for inexpensive baseballs."

baseball man   *n.* Professional who knows, loves and understands the game whether he be an owner, manager, coach, player or trainer.
USE   To be called one is a major compliment, and to be told that you are not one is to be marked an outsider to the game. "Kobritz is a good businessman, but no matter how much research he did and how many books he read he could not turn himself into a baseball man."

Baseball man. Manager Sparky Anderson exemplifies the concept of baseball man.   *Courtesy of the Detroit Tigers*

(Profile of Jordan Kobritz, owner of the Maine Guides, *Maine Sunday Telegram,* August 31, 1986)

baseball mother   *n.* Dedicated woman who, in the process of ferrying her children to baseball practice and games, becomes a dedicated supporter. "In her case she is a baseball mother," explained an article on the phenomenon in the *New York Times* for July 3, 1976. "So even though she was due at a class reunion one recent evening and perhaps should have been at home washing her hair or on her way to the Detroit airport to pick up her husband, Lou, there she was in the bleachers, watching her 14-year old son Ken play in a Babe Ruth League game."

baseball mud   *n.* A special composition of earth used to rub up a baseball to give it a uniform gripping surface.

baseball parachute
EXT   *n.* From the January 7, 1946, issue of *Life* magazine, ". . . the 'baseball' parachute used by the Navy during the war for mine-laying and precision deliveries of delicate cargoes. Unlike conventional chutes, which swing their loads in pendulum fashion, the baseball chute has a hemispheric canopy cut like a base-

ball cover and deposits its burden gently and vertically on the ground."

baseball park   *n./arch.* Ball park.

baseball pass
EXT   *n.* A basketball term for a one-handed, overhead pass that requires making a motion similar to that when throwing a baseball.

baseball pitcher's arm   *n.* A malady often caused by throwing a baseball. According to the *Century Dictionary* (1909 ed.): ". . . a condition of sprain, with pain and soreness over the points of insertion of the muscles, occurring sometimes as a result of overuse by base-ball players."
SEE   *baseball arm.*

baseball pitcher's elbow   *n.* Defined in a 1930 issue of the *Journal of the American Medical Association* as a "fracture of bone or cartilage from the head of the radius at the elbow due to strenuous baseball pitching."

baseball player   *n.* BALL PLAYER.

baseball poker
EXT   *n.* Form of seven-card stud. According to *The Complete Card Player* by Albert A. Ostrow it varies from the conventional game of seven-card stud through these exceptions.

a. A three of any suit dealt face up makes a player's hand dead, and he must drop out of play. b. A three of any suit dealt face down is wild. c. A four of any suit dealt face up entitles the player to have an extra card dealt face up. d. All nines are wild. The fact that it is called baseball poker probably derives from the fact that a face card with a three on it puts one out in the manner of three strikes being an out in baseball.

baseball pool
EXT   *n.* An illegal lottery in which one wagers on the appearance of a certain set of winning numbers taken from the box scores of different baseball games. It is a form of gambling that has been popular since about 1900 and is a variation on the numbers game or numbers pool, which gets its winning number from horse racing or stock market totals. It has existed in many variations, including, it seems, crooked ones: "It's anybody's guess as to how much money fans have tossed into a bottomless well playing phoney baseball pools." (*Easy Money* magazine, July 1936)

baseball-rounders *n./obs.* A largely forgotten hybrid game of American baseball and British rounders, according to J. M. Walker in his book *Rounders and Quoits* (London, 1892)

Baseball Sadie *n.* Woman whose weakness is ballplayers, aka *Baseball Annie.*

baseball's attic *n.* Nickname for the NATIONAL BASEBALL LIBRARY in Cooperstown, New York. "A Library Known as 'Baseball's Attic.' " (*New York Times* article, heading, July 31, 1984) This was probably inspired by the old nickname for the Smithsonian, which is "the nation's attic."

baseball sense *n.* Instinct for making the correct move whether it be in a play on the field or an advantageous trade.

baseball shoe *n.* Special shoe designed for and worn by baseball players which features *cleats* for traction and a full set of laces for support. Or, "A shoe built of leather for the sport indicated with sole having cleats or plugs to prevent slipping. Usually laced to the toe," according to *The Shoe Dictionary,* by Harold R. Quimby, published by the National Shoe Manufacturers Association in 1955.

baseball shot
EXT *n.* A basketball term for an attempt to score by throwing the ball with a motion similar to that of throwing a baseball. In December 23, 1959, *Sporting News,* then Boston Celtic head coach Red Auerbach forecast that this technique would have a major impact on the future of basketball. "It can't miss. Some kid with unusually big hands will come along and wind up like a baseball pitcher, or a football passer, and throw the ball in."

baseball shoulder *n.* Painful and debilitating shoulder of a player, usually a pitcher, which expresses itself medically with calcific deposits and fraying of the tendons. Discussed in detail in the November 21, 1959, *Journal of the American Medical Association.*

baseball sleeve *n.* Cuffless, shorter—usually ¾ length—sleeve common to the shirts worn under the short-sleeved uniform shirt. According to the June 4, 1952, *Woman's Wear Daily* it is "the important detail of jersey blouses worn under dresses, jackets and jumpers which have short sleeves of their own and a cutaway neckline which reveals turtle neck, cowl-drape or two-inch band of the jersey neckline."

"Baseball's Sad Lexicon" See *Tinker to Evers to Chance.*

baseball stitch *n.* A sewing technique for making two edges meet exactly rather than overlap as is done when seaming a baseball.
EXT This technique is often used when mending sails. It is also likely to show up in other areas, such as tent repair: "Better way still is to sew large tears with a baseball stitch using greased thread." (*The Great Outdoors,* by Joe Godfrey, Jr. and Frank Dufresne; McGraw-Hill, 1949)

baseball toss *n.* A context to determine ability to throw a baseball for distance and accuracy.

baseballwise *adj.* In a manner pertaining to baseball.
1ST An early use was recorded on the radio broadcast of the October 6, 1946, first game of the World Series when it was observed ". . . baseballwise the day is perfect . . ."

baseball with cards
EXT *n.* A game in which the various situations and events from the game of baseball are evoked by turning over playing cards from a shuffled deck.

baseball with dice
EXT *n.* According to *Foster's Complete Hoyle* published by F. A. Stokes in 1928, the complete rules of this game are contained in these three sentences: "Each side has 3 dice, to represent 3 strikes. Only aces count as runs, and as long as a side scores it continues to throw. Nine turns in a game."

base-ballyhoo *n./arch.* Hyperbole and boosterism sometimes associated with the game; bunkum baseball-style.

base clogger *n.* Slow runner. Mickey Mantle on New York Yankee teammate Elston Howard in his autobiography, *The Mick:* "We called him 'base clogger' because if you hit a double you had to stop at first and wait up for him." (CDP)

base coaches *n.* The two coaches positioned in the coach's box (first or third base). They are positioned to direct base runners and relay signals.
SEE *coacher's box.*

base-getter *n./arch.* One who gets on base and advances with regularity.
1ST 1911. "But Arthur has made him into a

great field captain and a base-getter of remarkable skill." (Zane Grey, *The Young Pitcher;* DS)

base hit *n.* A batted ball on which the batter advances safely to, but no farther than, first base.
1ST 1874. (Henry Chadwick's *Baseball Manual;* EJN)

base knock *n.* Base hit.

base line(s) *n.* The path along which the base runner travels. Specifically, the chalk marking between home plate and first base and home plate and third base. Also, the imaginary lines between first and second and first and third.
1ST 1869. (*New York Herald,* August 5; EJN)

baseman *n.* Defensive player assigned to cover first, second or third base.
1ST 1891. (*New York Evening Post,* July 9; EJN)

basement *n.* Lowest position in the *standings.*
1ST 1911. (*Baseball* magazine, October; EJN)
SEE *cellar, last place.*

basement troop *n.* Team at the bottom of the standings.

base on balls *n.* An advance to first base awarded to a batter who, while at bat, accepts four pitches outside the strike zone without swinging.
   In 1889, it was ruled that, in the course of one at bat, four balls would result in a walk. In the years preceding 1889, the rule changed with confusing regularity:
   Before 1880: 9 balls for a walk
   1880–1882: 8 balls
   1882–1884: 7 balls
   1884–1886: 6 balls
   1886:   7 balls
   1887–1889: 5 balls
   1889–   4 balls
   Abbreviated as BB.
1ST 1858. Chadwick Scrapbooks; EJN)
EXT To "wait for a base on balls" is to forgo action in the hope that something will happen; to assume a passive posture in an attempt to force one's opponent to make a false move. "U.S. Should Stop Waiting for Bases on Balls." (Headline in the *San Francisco News,* February 22, 1950. The article concerned diplomatic relations with Bulgaria. PT)

base on stones *n.* Ground ball that hits a pebble or other impediment causing it to bounce

away from a fielder for a base hit. The use of this term has declined in direct proportion to steady advances in groundskeeping and use of artificial turf.
1ST 1937. (clipping, National League Service Bureau files; EJN)

base open *n.* Said when second and third base are occupied but first is not.

base path/basepath *n.* Six-foot-wide runway that connects the four bases and serves as a path along which base runners run. The base runner cannot leave the base paths to avoid a tag.
1ST 1910. (*Baseball* magazine, December; EJN)

baser *n.* SINGLE.
1ST 1880. (*Chicago Inter Ocean,* May 19; EJN)

baserunner *n.* What the batter becomes on the way to first base. The goal of the base runner is to score by crossing the home plate.
1ST 1875. (*DeWitt's Base Ball Umpire's Guide;* EJN)

base-running **1.** *n.* The integral facet of the game by which one travels from one base to the next; including such skills as leading and sliding.
2. *adj.* Pertaining to one's ability as a base runner.

bases *n.* Stations along the path to scoring a run; first, second and third collectively.
EXT Incremental levels of achievement. In the language of teenage sexuality, knowing your way around the bases was (is?) to know that first base was kissing, second base was petting above the waist, third base was petting below the waist and a home run was sexual intercourse.

bases choked *n./adj.* BASES LOADED.

bases crowded *n./adj.* BASES LOADED.
1ST 1912. (*New York Tribune,* September 5; EJN)

bases drunk *n./adj.* BASES LOADED.

bases empty When there are no runners on base.

bases-empty home run *n.* A home run which scores no additional runs. It contrasts with the bases-loaded home run which scores four runs.

bases full *n./adj.* BASES LOADED.
1ST 1894. (*Spalding's Official Base Ball Guide;* EJN)

bases loaded *n./adj.* When there are runners on first, second and third base.

bases-loaded home run *n.* A home run hit with players on each base resulting in four runs. Many regard it to be the game's most spectacular offensive play.

base stealer *n.* Player who advances from one base to the next by taking the base without the aid of a hit, balk, passed ball, wild pitch or base on balls. Generally, base stealers are fast runners with an ability to judge the pitcher's attention and reflexes.
1ST 1892. (*New York Press,* August 7; EJN)

bases tenanted *n./adj.* BASES LOADED.
1ST 1908. (*Baseball* magazine, 1908; EJN)

base-sticker *n.* Base-runner who takes either a short lead or no lead at all off a base.

bases waterlogged *n./adj.* BASES LOADED.
1ST 1910. (*New York Tribune,* July 10; EJN)

base umpire *n.* Umpire stationed at first, second or third base.

bash *v.* To hit the ball with great power.

basket catch *n.* Style of fielding in which a defensive player cups his glove and bare hand together—close to his body and belt-high—to trap the ball. Although several prominent players—starting with Hall of Famer Rabbit Maranville—used the technique, Morris A. Shirt advises, "It is not a very good way for you to catch the ball," in his book *Warm Up for Little League Baseball.*
ETY A likely shortening of breadbasket catch.

bass ball **1.** *n.* A variant form of rounders.
2. *n.* Synonym for rounders.
1ST 1852. "He also plays at cricket and bass ball, of which the laws are quite too complicated for me to describe." (*Little Charlie's Games and Sports;* DS)

bastard play *n.* According to former Houston pitcher Don Wilson, who is quoted in Jim Bouton's book *Ball Four,* a play that is so-called because ". . . if the play works, it's a real bastard for the other team."

The actual play as described by Wilson takes place in a bunt situation. The first and third basemen charge in for the ball. The shortstop

Basket catch. Rabbit Maranville demonstrates the catch that he made famous. Elected to the Hall of Fame in 1954, his career spanned 23 years, during which time he played in 2,670 games. *National Baseball Library, Cooperstown, N.Y.*

sneaks to third and the second baseman sneaks over to cover first. "Then," says Wilson, "whoever fields the ball, fires it to third base. The guy on third fires to first and maybe we get the double play. If we don't, we at least get the lead runner."

baste *v./arch.* To hit a ball hard.
1ST 1891. (*Chicago Herald,* May 12; EJN)

baste ball *n.* An early form of baseball played on the campus of Princeton University in 1786. The name comes up in discussions of other precursors to baseball along with such terms as *bass ball, poisoned ball, stool ball.*

bat **1.** *n.* The wooden implement that is used to hit a pitched ball. There are different regulations for bats at various levels of organized baseball and softball, but the Major Leagues require that it be made of a single piece of wood, which cannot be longer than 42 inches or thicker than 2¾ inches at its thickest point.
1ST 1845. (Original Knickerbocker Rules)
2. *v.* To take a turn as batter.

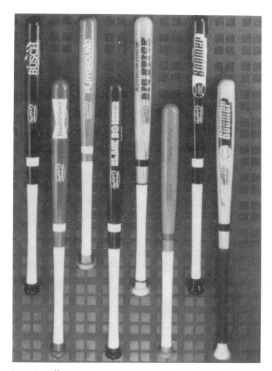

Bat. A collection of softball bats with names like the Bomber, the Boomer and the Shady Lady. The trade-names, graphics and colors used on softball bats have become increasingly less inhibited. *Courtesy of Rawlings*

1ST 1875. (*DeWitt's Base Ball Umpire's Guide;* EJN)
3. *n.* One's hitting ability. "Cards' Ozzie Smith bulks up in hopes of improving his bat." (*St. Petersburg Times,* April 2, 1987)
4. *n.* A player seen in his role as a hitter. Brewers manager Tom Trebelhorn is quoted in the *St. Petersburg Times* of February 29, 1988, "We're looking for a left-handed bat."
EXT This baseball term has long been borrowed by the greater language:
- Right off the bat: from the start, or immediately. "The producers got the verdict right off the bat, and they are wise enough to fold up and depart when the decision is thumbs down." (*The National Police Gazette,* January 14, 1928)
- To go to bat for: to take up someone else's cause or argument. "When Morgenthau went strongly to bat for [the new tax bill], Roosevelt turned on him sharply." (Drew Pearson's "Washington Merry-Go-Round," *San Francisco Chronicle,* May 23, 1939; PT)

- To not get the bat off one's shoulder: not given a chance. On an attorney not being able to make his case: "Being well-known as a Wall Street attorney he didn't even get his bat off his shoulder." (*San Francisco News,* June 8, 1933; PT)
- To bat two for three, to bat three for four, etc.: to be successful but not altogether successful. "Mayor Bats Two for Three on the Washington Circuit." (*San Francisco Call-Bulletin* headline, June 17, 1960; PT)

bat around *v.* When all nine batters in a team's lineup come to bat during an inning.
1ST 1880. (*Chicago Inter Ocean,* May 19; EJN)

bat a thousand *v.* See *bat 1.000.*

bat bag *n.* A canvas or leather duffle bag in which bats are carried.
1ST 1892. (*Brooklyn Daily Eagle,* August 22; EJN)

bat boy/batboy *n.* A young man employed by a team to take care of its players' personal equipment before, during and after games. Traditionally the most important responsibility of the job has been to retrieve each player's bat from home plate where it has been dropped or tossed and put it back in its proper place in the bat rack. The bat boy is also responsible for keeping the home plate umpire supplied with baseballs. "The New York Yankees . . . forgot to vote World Series money to their batboys, but rectified the problem the other day by tapping the fine fund and sending each the grand sum of $100." (Melvin Durslag, *San Francisco Examiner,* February 28, 1977)
1ST 1909. (*Baseball* magazine, July; EJN)

batboy shot *n.* A home run of such clear and immediate magnitude that the batter is simply able to hand his bat to the bat boy because he has the time for such a ritual.
ETY According to Joe Goddard in *The Sporting News* for March 6, 1982, "This is the brainchild of Yankee Oscar Gamble, who says he knows when he hits one well and it's out of the park. 'I don't even look at it,' Gamble says. 'I know it's gone. I just turn around and hand my bat to the batboy.' "

bat breaker *n.* A hitter who swings the bat with tremendous force; one whose powerful swings often result in a broken bat.

bat day/night *n.* Games at which, as a promotion, patrons are given a souvenir bat.

Batboy. Batboy John McBride is shown between Lou Gehrig and Babe Ruth in this photograph from the 1933 All-Star Game. *National Baseball Library, Cooperstown, N.Y.*

bat dodger   *n.* One of Satchel Paige's nicknames for a deceptive pitch. Bob Uecker, in his book *Catcher in the Wry,* lists some of Paige's colorful pitch names: "He described his repertoire of pitches as the blooper, looper and drooper, the jump ball, hurry ball and nothing ball, and the ever-dangerous bat dodger." (CDP)

Bates   *n./arch.* A worn-out or declining player.

Batesy   *n./arch.* Veteran player who has seen his best days.

batfest/bat fest   *n.* BATTING FEST.
1ST   David Shulman, in his article on baseball language in the February 1951 issue of *American Speech,* noted that the earliest use of the term was in *Frank Merriwell Jr.'s Athletic Team* by Burt L. Standish: "For some reason his teammates were beginning to hit Merriwell and Needham wanted his share in the batfest." The book was published in 1929 but had a 1913 copyright as it had appeared earlier as a magazine serial.

bat grip   *n.* A sleeve or coating that is placed over the bat handle to give the batter a firmer grip when swinging. It also protects the handle, the thinnest part of the bat, from chipping.

bat-handle blooper   *n.* A ball hit on the slender end of the bat, which lacks power but nevertheless falls in for a hit. "But a bat-handle blooper into right drove both men home, the runner going to second on the throw to the plate." (*Relief Pitcher* by Dick Friendlich; CDP)

bat 1.000/bat one thousand   *v.* Perfection at the plate. Because an average of 1.000 is a virtual impossibility after a dozen or so at bats, the term finds greater application in baseball fiction—e.g., a 1951 children's book, *The Kid Who Batted 1.000*—than in real life.

Bat Day. June 4, 1967, at Cleveland, as the young fans show their new bats to the camera.   *Courtesy of the Cleveland Indians*

EXT   To be absolutely correct; to perform flawlessly.

baton swinger   *n./arch.* BATTER.
1ST   1915. "Only when I use baseball terms—about swiping sacks . . . fanning the baton swinger . . . you say you don't like to hear me talking slang." (Gilbert Patten, *Covering the Look-In Corner;* DS)

bat rack   *n.* In the dugout, an open, slotted box that holds a team's supply of bats during a game.
SEE   *lumber yard.*

bat ring   *n.* In softball, a standard measuring device umpires use to monitor the size of all bats to be used in a game. If the head of the bat will not fit through the ring, the bat is deemed to be illegal and is disallowed for play.

batsman   *n./arch.* BATTER. This term was commonly used in the old days; defined by

Henry Chadwick as "The striker at the bat."
1ST   1863. (Chadwick Scrapbooks; EJN)

batsmanship   *n.* A player's ability as a batter.

bat speed   *n.* In a hitter's swing, the velocity of the bat as it approaches the ball. It is generally regarded that, to be successful, a hitter must generate good bat speed.

batter   *n.* Offensive player with a bat who is positioned in the batter's box in order to hit or get on base through a base on balls. The main focal point of the game of baseball is the contest between the batter and the pitcher.
1ST   1869. (*DeWitt Official Base Ball Guide;* EJN)

batter's box   *n.* Rectangular 6 × 4 foot area in which the person at bat must stand. There are actually two boxes—each is positioned six inches on either side of the plate for right- and left-handed batters. Though the boundary for each box is lined with white lime before the

Batter's box. The batter's box is evident in this scene from the 1944 World Series in which Don Gutteridge of the St. Louis Browns is shown striking out. The St. Louis Cardinals won the game in question and went on to take the Series, four games to two.   *Prints and Photographs Division, the Library of Congress*

game, batters have been known to scrape away the back line with their feet to distort the umpire's ability to determine if they have stepped out of the batter's box.

batter's circle   *n.* See ON-DECK CIRCLE.

batter's glove   *n.* BATTING GLOVE.

batter's wheelhouse   *n.* That part of the strike zone in which a hitter swings the bat with the most power. Pitches thrown in a batter's wheelhouse are often hit for home runs.
ETY   In nautical terms, a wheelhouse is the pilothouse or the place from which a vessel is controlled.

"Batter Up!"   *v.* Umpire's call to the batter that it is time to step into the batter's box and for play to start.
   Traditionally the call is made at the beginning of the game, at the start of each half inning and after a long time out, such as that taken for a change of pitchers.

battery   **1.** *n.* The pitcher and catcher collectively. In the novel *Changing Pitches* by Steve Kluger a successful battery is described as one in which the pitcher and catcher could switch brains and nobody would know the difference.
ETY   The explanation offered in the glossary in R. G. Knowles and Richard Morton's 1896 book *Baseball*: "The term has its origin in telegraphy, the pitcher being the transmitter, and the catcher the receiver." In 1897, however, in a slim volume in the Spalding's Athletic Library entitled *Technical Terms of Baseball*, Henry Chadwick clearly implies a military borrowing when he gives this definition: "This is the term applied to the pitcher and catcher of a team. It is the main attacking force of the little army of nine players in the field in a contest." Most later attempts to pin a history on the term have

alluded to this comparison to a military artillery unit. Metaphorically, it fits nicely with *firing line,* a now dated, but once popular term for the pitcher's mound, and *powder* and *smoke,* two synonyms for fastball.

Perhaps the most contrived attempt to explain the exact origin of the term appeared in a letter published in *The Sporting News* on January 18, 1940. In response to an appeal for clues to the origin of the term, Frank J. Reiter of Kenmore, New York, wrote, "It may possibly have arisen as follows: General Abner Doubleday, the founder of baseball, being a military man, may have originated the phrase, or someone in the army so named it in honor of General Doubleday. As the word 'fire' is a military command, and as the pitcher literally 'fires' the ball to the plate much in the same manner as a field artillery battery fires a cannon, this may have prompted the name of a military unit to be applied to the pitcher and the catcher."
2. *n.* Before the 1880s the term was commonly used for the pitcher alone.
1ST 1868. (Chadwick Scrapbooks; EJN)

battery mate *n.* The catcher is the pitcher's battery mate and vice versa.

batting **1.** *n.* Attempting to hit the ball; the act of coming to home plate with a bat in an attempt to become a base runner.
2. *n.* A team's offense from the plate.
1ST 1861. (*Sunday Mercury,* August 10; EJN)

batting around *v.* Said of a team when a batter comes to bat for the second time in the same inning.

batting average *n.* The standard numerical measure of a player's ability at the plate. The number of hits a player gets in relation to his number of official at bats. It is expressed in thousandths (three decimal places) and is quickly calculated by adding three zeros to the total number of hits and dividing by the total number of at bats. They can be carried beyond three places. In 1983 Robin Yount ended the season with a .3307 average, which was .0009 short of Willie Wilson, who won the batting titles.

The standard of excellence is an average of .300 (three hundred) or better, while .400 has only been achieved by eight batters since 1900, the last of whom was Ted Williams (.406 in 1941).

1ST 1880. (*Brooklyn Daily Eagle,* August 16; EJN)
EXT Success or failure in other realms is often measured in terms of "batting a thousand" or "batting zero." An ad from an investment corporation in the October 6, 1986, *Forbes* opens, "If the S&P is hitting .333, then our top two hitters are batting over .630."

batting bee *n.* A succession of hits.
1ST 1905. (*Sporting Life,* October 7; EJN)

batting cage *n.* A metal framework that is wheeled behind home plate during batting practice to prevent foul balls from being hit into the stands. A time-honored prank is to ask a rookie or batboy to go back to the clubhouse and pick up the "keys" to the batting cage.
2. *n.* An enclosed indoor framework used for batting practice and instruction. They can be used in bad weather, in the off season and when a batting coach wants to work with a batter in private.

batting championship **1.** *n.* The imaginary crown and real title that is given to the player in a league to complete a season with the highest batting average over the course of that season.
2. *n.* The race for the title of batting champion.

batting clothes/togs *n.* A player who is hitting well is said to be wearing these. It is a figurative term for a period of good hitting and does not refer to a special uniform (although batters have been known to wear the uniform during a batting streak).
1ST 1890. (*New York Press,* July 28; EJN)

batting crown *n.* BATTING TITLE.

batting eye *n.* A batter's ability to hit safely.
1ST 1913. "My team had their batting eyes along . . ." (Alan Douglas, *Fast Nine;* DS)

batting fest/bat fest/batfest *n.* A hitting spree, often celebrated at the expense of a single pitcher.
1ST 1916. ". . . after turning the enemy down in one, two, three order, High School proceeded to indulge in another batting-fest." (Christy Mathewson, *First Base Faulkner;* DS)

batting glove *n.* A thin leather or vinyl glove used by batters to gain a better grip of the bat and lessen the pain associated with batting the ball. Introduced by Ken "Hawk" Harrelson in 1964 when he was with the Kansas City A's.

Batting glove. Milwaukee Brewers' centerfielder Gorman Thomas shows off his batting glove while in the on-deck circle.   *Courtesy of the Cleveland Indians*

(Bobby Thomson of the New York Giants wore golf gloves in spring training as early as 1949, but he never wore them during the regular season.)

batting helmet   *n.* Protective headgear made of hard plastic, to be worn while at bat and on the bases. Designed to fit over a player's cloth baseball cap, the latest version of the helmet includes a flap to cover the ear and the temple. They are mandatory at all levels of organized baseball, including the Major Leagues. A light plastic liner was first adopted experimentally for a whole team by the 1941 Brooklyn Dodgers; however, they had been used by individual batters before then. Research conducted by the National Baseball Library at Cooperstown and reported in 1969 by Librarian John Redding, concluded: "[On] January 24, 1905 the A. J. Reach Co., patented and later manufactured the Reach Pneumatic Head Protector, which served the same purpose as today's helmet. The head protector was not widely accepted, but some players, amongst them Roger Bresnahan, did wear it."

In more recent times, the 1953 Pittsburgh Pirates was the first team to adopt them permanently.

batting-list   *n./arch.* LINEUP CARD.
1ST   1907. "The head of the batting-list came up again, and now by using his combination ball Merriwell succeeded in fanning Strothers." (Burt L. Standish, *Dick Merriwell's Salvation;* DS)

batting order   *n.* Official listing of the sequence in which batters will come to the plate. The batting order must be submitted to the home plate umpire before the game begins and cannot be changed. Substitutes must be inserted in the batting order in the position of the player being replaced.
1ST   1901. (*Frank Merriwell's Marvel;* EJN)

batting out of turn/order   A player who appears at the plate out of the proper place in the batting order is "out of turn" and the proper batter will be declared out by the umpire because of this infraction of the rules, but only on appeal from the other team.

batting practice   *n.* A period of about an hour before each game during which players from both teams are given an opportunity to rehearse their hitting. The batting practice period has its own rituals and traditions. For instance, it is customary for each batter to take the same number of practice pitches and some teams have established cycles of batting, such as starting each practice plate appearance with a bunt. It is also a time for a batter to work on timing and adjust for the wind, lights and other environmental factors.
BP, for short.
1ST   1908. (*Baseball* magazine; June, EJN)

batting-practice pitch   *n.* Derogatory term for pitch thrown during a game that is slow and easy to hit. Such a pitch is said to have "nothing on it."

batting-practice pitcher   *n.* Person who regularly pitches to the team during batting practice. There are no rules on who performs this chore but it is commonly a member of the club staff who is not on the roster.

batting practice screen   *n.* Protective screen put in front of the batting practice pitcher.
A 1973 letter from public relations man Barry Landers, on file at Cooperstown, reads as follows:
"It may be of interest as to the reason behind the use of the screen in front of the batting practice pitcher. It is obvious as to why it is there; however, back in 1927, there was no screen. An incident involving my father, who

pitched batting practice for the New York Yankees in Spring training of that year, sparked the use of the screen. He was pitching to the immortal Babe Ruth, when 'the Babe' slapped a hard line drive back at him, striking him in the face and knocking out all his teeth in front. From that day to this, a screen is used to protect the batting practice pitcher."

batting stance *n.* The position one takes at the plate as the ball is about to be delivered by the pitcher. Not only do different batters have different stances, but the same batter may change stances during the course of a game.

batting streak *n.* A string of consecutive games in which a particular player is officially in a game and has gotten at least one hit.

batting tee *n.* A large adjustable pole on which the ball rests, allowing a player to practice without the services of a batting practice pitcher. Also used for playing tee-ball.

batting title *n.* The honor earned by the batter in each league with the highest batting average at the end of the regular season. In the major leagues a player must have at least 502 official at bats to be eligible.

bat weight *n.* A metal or plastic, doughnut-shaped ring that is slipped onto the barrel of a bat to make it feel twice as heavy as normal. The purpose of the weight is to strengthen the batter's arms and wrists and to make the bat feel lighter in the batter's box. It is used by the on-deck batter while limbering up and replaces the old method of swinging two bats simultaneously.
SEE *doughnut.*

Bauer and Black player *n.* One who is always playing with a lot of bandage tape, from the name of a company that makes such tape. The term appears in J. G. T. Spink's (et al.) *Comedians of Baseball* along with the traditional comment for such a player, "As long as the tape and baling wire hold up, you ought to have a hell of a year."

bazooka **1.** *n.* Strong throwing arm. Term is used for a pitcher, catcher or fielder. "He's got a bazooka."
2. *n.* Mechanical device used to shoot fly balls, line drives, for fielding practice.

BB **1.** *n.* Abbr. for a base on balls; a walk.
2. *n.* A ball thrown with such speed that it

Bazooka. Los Angeles Angels coach Jack Paepke (assisted by Bob Lemon) gets ready to fire the club's bazooka during spring training. The picture was taken in the early 1960s before the team became known as the California Angels. *Los Angeles Angels publicity photo in the author's collection.*

seems as small as a ball bearing pellet when it crosses the plate.

beachhead *n.* A batter who reaches first base to start an inning. See furlough.

bean **1.** *n./arch.* A player's head.
2. *v.* To hit a batter in the head with a ball.
1ST 1910. "A 'bean' you ask? Why, bean is baseball language for head." (Frank Leroy Chance's *The Bride and the Pennant*) Peter Tamony noted that TAD used the term in a June 19, 1910, cartoon in the *San Francisco Examiner*. In the cartoon, a man is hit in the head with a ball, which causes another character to remark, "Right on the bean."
ETY An explanation that appeared in 1920 when the term was still novel: "The slang expression 'bean' was derived from descriptions of pitchers throwing the ball at the heads of batsmen. This was originally described as a 'bean ball' and from that the word 'bean' became synonymous with 'head.' " (Sid Mercer in the article, "Baseball's New Catch Phrases," *San Francisco Call & Post,* July 2, 1920; PT)

EXT   The head—as in, use your bean—and to hit someone in the head.

beanball/bean ball/beaner   *n./adj.* A pitch thrown intentionally at a batter's head for the purpose of either moving the batter away from home plate or to punish him, his team or another player for something he has done. Pitchers who throw beanballs are supposed to be ejected from the game, but it is usually difficult for the umpire to determine that the act was premeditated. "Another Epidemic of Beanballs" read a New York *Daily News* headline, June 20, 1964.

The only player ever to be killed in a major league game was Ray Chapman of the Cleveland Indians who was hit by a pitch thrown by Carl Mays of the New York Yankees on August 17, 1920. But there have been deaths at other levels of the game. A chilling headline from the *San Francisco Call-Bulletin* of September 23, 1947: " 'Bean Ball' Is Fatal To S. F. Sandlotter." (PT)

1ST   A very early use appears in *The Athletics of 1905* by Charles Dryden: "While pitching, Mr. Bender places much reliance on the bean ball." (DS)

EXT   A direct shot meant to do damage, often verbal. "Wallace Winds Up to Pitch Bean Ball at Truman Doctrine." (Headline in the *San Francisco News*, April 16, 1947)

beanball war   *n.* Series between two teams characterized by potentially lethal retaliatory pitches thrown at batters' heads and bodies, often spread over a number of days. "Baseball must act to defuse beanball war." (Headline in the *Christian Science Monitor*, August 3, 1987)

Bean Eaters   *arch.* Nickname for various professional teams from Boston.
1ST   1880. (*Chicago Inter Ocean*, June 29; EJN)

beaner   *n.* BEANBALL.
1ST   1912. "Bing! Up comes another 'beaner.' " (Christy Mathewson's *Pitching in a Pinch;* DS)

beanie   *n.* BATTING HELMET.

beany   *adj.* A bit off mentally, a condition attributed to being hit in the head by a ball. Hugh Fullerton added, in his 1912 definition: "Condition similar to 'The Dance,' a disease among prizefighters struck on the head often."

Bearded Wonders   Generic name for renegade teams, explained by Franklin P. Huddle

in his 1943 article in *American Speech* on "Baseball Jargon":

"One occasionally sees references to barnstormers or non-league traveling teams. These are, quite often, pretty disreputable outfits, since they are likely to be made up of men who have been thrown out of organized baseball. Many of these gentry grow beards and call themselves (in imitation of the real thing) *House of David* teams or *Bearded Wonders.* The beards serve the twin purpose of advertising and disguise."

bear down   **1.** *v.* In pitching, to give one's all; to use the last ounce of energy.
2. *v.* To exert total concentration and maximum effort in any aspect of the game.
1ST   1931. (*New York World*, February 26; EJN)

bear's nest   *n.* A shabby hotel.
ETY   This may have been a bit of slang common to the Los Angeles Dodgers. In Fresco Thompson's *Every Diamond Doesn't Sparkle* (1964) it is part of the baseball language that Dodger rookies would learn on arriving at the team's spring training camp at Vero Beach, Florida.

beast of the East   During the season, a reference often used to describe the best teams in the eastern divisions of the American and National Leagues. The equivalent term for the western divisions is "Best of the West."

beat a tag   *v.* For a runner to reach a base before being touched by the ball in the hand—gloved or bare—of the infielder covering that base.

beat a throw   *v.* To reach base ahead of the ball.
1ST   1892. (*Brooklyn Daily Eagle*, February 26; EJN)

beat out   *v.* To reach first base on an infield ground ball. Implied is that the batter was fast enough to beat the infielder's throw to first.
1ST   1896. (*Frank Merriwell's Schooldays;* EJN)

beauty   *n.* A called strike that should have been hit out of the park.

Becket   In baseball card collecting, the leading and most reliable price guide is the *The Baseball Card Price Guide* by Dr. James Becket and Dennis W. Eckes. The name Becket has become an important point of reference in pricing cards; for instance, one card that has gotten particularly hot may sell for "50% over

Beat a tag. Softballer throws himself hard and headfirst into second base to beat the tag.   *Courtesy of the Amateur Softball Association of America*

Becket" while run of the mill cards sell "under the Becket price."

beef   1. *n.* A loud and prolonged protest.
ETY   According to Hy Turkin in the *Baseball Almanac,* it sounds "as if noises come from lowing [mooing] cattle or beef."
2. *v.* To make such a protest; to have a dispute (beef) with.

1ST 1908. (*New York Evening Journal*, May 27; EJN)

bee liner *n.* A batted ball that travels fast and straight, not far from the ground; a low line drive.

Beep Ball/Beep Softball A variant form of baseball adapted to people who are blind. The game features a ball that emits a beeping noise and buzzing bases.

Beer Night Promotional event where beer is sold at a game for a greatly reduced price. On June 4, 1974, the Cleveland Indians let their fans drink all the beer they could hold for ten cents a cup. Predictably the fans became intoxicated and unruly, forcing umpire Nestor Chylak to forfeit the game.

bees in the bat Expression for the stinging sensation a batter's hands feel when a pitch strikes the handle or end of the bat. In a 1972 article by Wayne Minshew in the *Atlanta Constitution*, Braves' pitcher Jim Nash explained that it, "usually happens on a cold day against a pitcher throwing heat."

behind in the count *adj.* Said of a pitcher when there are more balls than strikes on the batter. Said of a batter when there are more strikes than balls. The opposite of *ahead of the count*.

behind the hitter *adj.* Said of a pitcher who is behind in the count. A pitcher in trouble is often one who keeps getting behind in the count.

beisbol *n.* Spanish for baseball; the term often used when Latin baseball is discussed. "People of Cuba have serious case of 'beisbol' fever." (Headline in *USA Today*, April 29, 1987)

belabor a pitcher *v.* For a group of batters to get a number of hits off of a pitcher.

belly slide *n.* HEADFIRST SLIDE.

belly whopper *n.* HEADFIRST SLIDE, characterized by a long, airborne dive into the base.

Dizzy Dean's definition: "Hittin' the dirt head first on your stummick. Pepper Martin was the last great belly-whopper" (*Dizzy's Definitions*)

belt **1.** *v.* To hit a ball hard.
1ST 1891. (*Chicago Herald*, August 25; EJN)
2. *n.* A ball that has been hit hard.
1ST 1907. (*Harper's Weekly*, December 14; EJN)

belt buckle ball *n.* A pitched ball that has been scratched or cut on the pitcher's belt buckle. The defacing of the ball makes it curve unnaturally, putting the batter at an unfair disadvantage. The umpire, detecting such a pitch, can eject the pitcher from the game.

bench **1.** *n.* Seating area in the dugout for a team's players, substitutes and coaching staff.
1ST 1891. (*Chicago Inter Ocean*, May 5; EJN)
2. *n.* Collectively, the players a team holds in reserve. Even though they don't sit on the bench, pinch hitters are part of the bench in this metaphorical sense.
3. *v.* For a manager to remove a player from the line-up for one or more games. To demote a starting player to the role of substitute player.
1ST 1902. (*Sporting Life*, July 12; EJN)
EXT Figurative location of those who are not participating or have been taken out of participation. "Blonde Miss North Gets Off Bench for First of Monroe Roles." (*Life* magazine subheadline on Sheree North getting a Marilyn Monroe role, March 21, 1955)

bench blanket *n.* BENCH WARMER.

bench clearing *n.* A quick emptying of the dugout, leaving an empty bench in its wake. It can be prompted by an altercation on the field or by the umpire who can clear the bench in order to retain control over the game.

bench-clearing/benches-clearing *adj.* Describing players coming out of the dugout, it usually modifies a word like brawl or incident. "George Foster hit his 13th career grand slam, triggering a benches-clearing melee . . ." (*USA Today*, May 28, 1986)

bench jockey **1.** *n.* A player who verbally abuses or "rides" players from the opposing team while in the dugout. In an essay on baseball, Bruce Catton called him, ". . . the man who will say anything at all if he thinks it will upset an enemy's poise. . ."
2. *n.* A substitute who rides the bench; BENCH WARMER.
1ST 1939. "The doctor's orders were soon grapevined around the league, and all the bench jockeys on the circuit were quickly counting ten [i.e., keeping quiet] on every pitch Lefty made." (G. S. Corchrane's *Baseball, the Fans' Game*; DS)

bench polisher *n.* A substitute player whose constant presence on the bench is said to polish it.

Belly whopper. Photograph from the 1930s of a belly whopper in progress. The picture belies the notion that women's softball has become tough only in recent years. *Prints and Photographs Division, the Library of Congress*

bench warmer *n.* A substitute player whose constant presence on the bench is said to warm it.
1ST 1892. On January 9 the *Sporting Times* declared that, "The days for 'bench warmers' with salaries are also past." (DS) A 1912 report on baseball in *The Saturday Evening Post* told of, "A certain rich man [who] offered a manager $10,000 if the manager would carry his son as a combination of mascot and bench-warmer."
EXT A judge (who also sits on a bench) is sometimes called a benchwarmer. A book on judges by Joseph C. Goulden was entitled *The Benchwarmers.*

bench-warming *n./adj.* Sitting in the dugout. "The most unplayed, but not unpaid, athlete of his time, Charlie [Silvera], as Yogi Berra's stand-in with the Yankees, collected over $50,000 in bonus pelf for six World Series,

during which he did nothing but practice the gentle art of bench warming." (Jack McDonald column, *San Francisco Call-Bulletin*, September 23, 1960)
1ST 1916. "Bench-warming for a week or so, and then a trial." (*Redbook*, April; DS)

bender *n./arch.* CURVEBALL. Seldom used, it was described as "A term not often used in modern times" in Parke Cummings' 1950 *Dictionary of Baseball.*
1ST 1901. (*Frank Merriwell's Marvel;* EJN)

Bengals Nickname for the Detroit Tigers. Rarely used today, this moniker was commonly used before about 1950.

bent-leg slide *n.* Technique in which a runner bends both legs when sliding into a base. Sliding with straightened legs, a runner's spikes can catch in the dirt, causing serious injury.

Berraism *n.* Aphorism from the lips of Yogi Berra, also called a YOGIISM or YOGISM.

berth **1.** *n.* A player's position on a team. **2.** *n.* A team's position in the standings. **1ST** 1908. (*Baseball* magazine, September; EJN)

best *v.* To defeat—and one of many, many terms for one team winning a game from another. To note some such terms collected in the space of a week's newspaper reading in the summer of 1987: down/trim/trounce/blast/fend off/thump/spank/outlast/stun/shock/tame/foil/ defeat/beat/nip/upset/clobber/spill/pound/wallop/ edge/outlast/roll past/whip/rout/unplug/shade/ stop/ upend/ tip/ trip/ drill/ drop/ top/ stifle/ dump/ take/hold off/shake down/halt/haunt/quell/power over/and sweep Team B. **1ST** 1912. (*New York Tribune*, September 6; EJN)

best interest clause *n.* Legal empowerment that gives the Commissioner of baseball jurisdiction to determine that which is and that which is not "in the best interests of the game."

best-of-seven *adj.* Describing the means of determining the modern League Championship and World Series play-off format in which the first team to win four games is the champion.

between the lines/between the white lines On the field of play; the location of the action of the game itself, as opposed to off the field activity. The "lines" are the foul lines, which both physically and symbolically mark the realm of the actual game itself. Players have been known to say that what another player does off the field is his own business and that all that matters is what goes on "between the lines." *Houston Post* TV critic Ken Hoffman, criticizing Vin Scully: "If it's not between the white lines, Scully pretends it doesn't exist." (June 27, 1987; CDP)

Probably the most famous line using the phrase was uttered by Early Wynn who once said, "That space between the white lines— that's my office. That's where I conduct my business."

between the seams The location, on the surface of a pitched ball, of the spot most advantageous for the batter to hit. **1ST** 1910. (*American* magazine, July; EJN)

biff *v.* To bat a ball hard.

1ST 1888. (Gerald Cohen has found several examples of this term in the *New York World* for that year, with the earliest being on June 7. One example, "It was biff! bang! from the start, and Cleveland was not in it.") **ETY** H. L. Mencken stated in *The American Language:* "Said to have been coined by William T. Hall, a Chicago sports reporter."

biffer *n./arch.* A hard-hitting batter. **1ST** 1908. (*New York Evening Journal*, February 24; EJN)

biff stick *n.* BAT. **1ST** 1908. (*New York Evening Journal*, March 16; EJN)

Big A, the See ANAHEIM STADIUM.

big as a balloon *adj.* A pitched ball that is very easy to hit. **1ST** 1910. (*American* magazine, June; EJN)

big bang theory *n.* One of several names for Earl Weaver's hypothesis that pitching, defense and three-run homers—"one swing, then trot"—win baseball games. The name was given to the theory by Tom Boswell of the *Washington Post*.

big Bertha **1.** *n.* CLEANUP HITTER; the fourth player in the batting order. **2.** *n.* A vastly oversized catcher's mitt that was designed by Paul Richards, when he was managing the Baltimore Orioles, to make it easier for Gus Triandos to handle Hoyt Wilhelm's most unpredictable knuckleball. The mitt, the Wilson model #1050 CL, was 45 inches around and would be illegal today because of a 1964 rule stipulating that no glove can have a circumference of more than 38 inches. **3.** *n.* A favorite bat. **4.** *n.* Said of a colossal hit. When, on July 13, 1921, Babe Ruth became the first and only player ever to hit a home run into the old, wooden center field bleachers at the *Polo Grounds,* the *New York Times* said, "The Babe had had it upon his mind to perpetrate this Big Bertha shot for some time, but never seemed to get around to it." **ETY** Big Bertha was the nickname for the German Army's mammoth 420-millimeter gun of World War I. It was named for Bertha Krupp, the sole heir to the Krupp armament empire.

big bill *n.* Long easy bounce, particularly the last bounce of a batted ball before it reaches the fielder. It is an easy bounce to catch and tends to make the fielder catching it look good.

1ST 1932 (*Baseball* magazine, October; EJN)

ETY It has been suggested that this name comes from the fact that on such a bounce, the ball often reaches the fielder at head level and is named for the bill of the baseball cap. (*How to Talk Baseball* by Mike Whiteford, 1983) On the other hand, Edward J. Nichols cites a letter, which appears in the April 15, 1937, *Sporting News*, in which it is asserted that the term is named for Bill Bradley (who played for several teams between 1899 and 1915), who hit many such bounders.

big classic/big series *n.* Nicknames for the WORLD SERIES.

1ST 1915 (*Baseball* magazine, December; EJN)

big fly *n.* HOME RUN.

In *Bats*, the diary of the 1985 New York Mets season by Davey Johnson and Peter Golenbock, Keith Hernandez is quoted on his thoughts on going to the plate with the idea of hitting a home run: "I'm looking in. I'm looking in. If I get it, I'm going big fly."

The term is clearly a player's term of the mid-1980s. A 1986 article, which uses R. J. Reynolds to explain the latest terms reports: "It all begins with a relatively new term, the 1986 version of what once was called a dinger or tater. The home run. Down on the pine (bench), no one calls it any of those outdated things. That would be like saying something was cool or groovy. Today, the long ball is the big fly."

biggies, the *n.* The MAJOR LEAGUES.

big guns *n.* A team's best batters.

1ST 1902. (*Sporting Life,* September 27; EJN)

big hit *n.* A key hit; one in the clutch.

big hit, the *n.* HOME RUN.

1ST 1922. (*Spalding Official Guide Book;* EJN)

big inning *n.* An inning in which three runs— or more, usually—are scored by one team. Often it occurs as the result of home runs being hit with runners on base. As a bonafide statistic, the big inning has started to show up with some rgularity in newspapers. Prior to the 1986 World Series, *USA Today* was looking for a number or statistic that tipped off a winner: "Big innings are excellent indicators. Teams that have had 'big innings' are 40–7 (.851)."

ETY A July 12, 1950, article on Babe Ruth in the *Sporting News,* by Frederick G. Lieb, was entitled "Ruth Originator of the Big Inning." In the article Lieb asserts that Ruth's ability to hit the home run "revolutionized" baseball— creating what seemed to be an entirely new game. He compares the second place 1908 White Sox (who were eliminated by the Tigers on the last day of season) to the fourth place 1947 Giants. The White Sox had had only three home runs all year, but the Giants hit 221 of them. "That's what the Ruthian influence did to baseball," concluded Lieb.

The term comes into play in a well-worn baseball riddle:

Q: Where is baseball mentioned in the Bible?

A: Genesis: In the big inning.

big league **1.** *n.* Major league baseball, comprising the American and National Leagues together. The highest level of organized baseball.

2. *n.* All six professional major leagues in the history of baseball, comprising the American Association (1882–1891), the *Union Association* (1884), the *Players League* (1890), the *Federal League* (1914–1915) and the current *National League* (1876–) and *American League* (1901–). In 1968, the Special Baseball Records Committee decided that these six leagues would be considered "Major League" for purposes of the official record. Some baseball historians consider the National Association (1871–1875) to be the first professional league in the big league category, but the Records Committee cited the Association's "erratic schedule and procedures" as reason enough for exclusion.

3. *adj.* Of big league proportions or scale: "big league ball," "big league aspirations" etc.

1ST 1901. (*Frank Merriwell's Marvel;* EJN)

ETY Under the heading "Baseball Language in the 1890s," the *Bill James Historical Abstract* says: "The term 'big league' apparently referred originally to the size of the one major league, which had twelve teams in it. But the 'big league' came to stand for the 'major league,' and 'big leagues' became a synonym for 'majors.'"

EXT The highest level in any given field; major; large; important—for instance, "a big league appetite." The opposite of bush league.

SEE Major Leagues.

big leaguer *n.* Player in the majors. One who plays baseball at the highest professional level; major leaguer.
1ST 1911 (*Baseball* magazine, October; EJN)

big mit/big mitt *n.* The large padded glove worn by the catcher.
1ST 1905 (*Sporting Life*, October 5; EJN)

big one 1. *n.* The third strike, especially in a key situation.
1ST 1907 (*New York Evening Journal*, n.d.; EJN)
2. *n.* Put out at first base.
3. *n.* The last out of an inning.

Big Red Machine Nickname for the CINCINNATI REDS. This moniker is more commonly used when the team is playing well, such as when the Reds won back-to-back World Series in 1975–76.

bigs, the *n.* Shortened form of the BIG LEAGUES. "Winterport's Bordick headed for the Bigs?" (headline in the *Waldo* [Maine] *Independent* for December 3, 1987)

big show *n.* The MAJOR LEAGUES.

big stick *n.* A heavy hitter; one given to hitting home runs and extra-base hits.
ETY The term probably entered baseball in the wake of Theodore Roosevelt's line delivered on September 2, 1901 at the Minnesota State Fair, "Speak softly and carry a big stick."

big swat *n.* HOME RUN.

big team *n.* The parent major league club to a minor leaguer.

big tent *n.* The MAJOR LEAGUES, an obvious reference to the circus.

big time *n.* The MAJOR LEAGUES.

big Van Heusen VAN HEUSEN.

big W *n.* A victory based on the abbr. w for win. It can be achieved by a team and/or a pitcher. "I ended up with my first big W, as we baseball players call it. It was my first major-league win earned with a knuckleball." (Jim Bouton in *Ball Four*; CDP)

bill 1. *n.* A game in the schedule, such as tomorrow's twin-bill.
1ST 1912 (*New York Tribune*, September 8; EJN)
2. *v./arch.* To schedule a game.
1ST 1902 (*Sporting Life*, July 12; EJN)
3. *n.* The visor of a baseball cap.

Bill Hassemer Bounce *n./arch.* A batted grounder that jumps neatly into a fielder's glove, named presumably for a man known for hitting such ground balls.
1ST 1937. (*Pittsburgh Press*, August 4; EJN)
ETY Although this term was current baseball slang when Edward J. Nichols wrote his thesis on baseball terms in 1939, it does not seem to be named for a player of that era. The only major league player with a name close to Hassemer was William Louis "Roaring Bill" Hassamaer who played from 1894 through 1896.

billiard *n.* A ball that, when batted, hits the ground in front of the plate and rolls back toward the batter. Named, according to EJN, "from a reverse spin similar to that produced with a billiard ball."
1ST 1937 (*Pittsburgh Press*, January 4; EJN)

Bill Klem *n.* Any person in baseball who is never wrong.
ETY An eponym for infallibility inspired by Hall of Fame umpire Bill Klem who is credited with a number of statements in which he never admits a bad call, e.g., "It ain't nothin' till I call 'em."

Bill Klem. Klem, who earned the nickname "The Old Arbitrator," worked in 18 separate World Series. *National Baseball Library, Cooperstown, N.Y.*

Billy Ball   Term created to describe the style of aggressive, alert, fan-pleasing baseball management practiced by Alfred Manuel "Billy" Martin in his various terms as manager with the Athletics, Twins, Tigers, Rangers and Yankees.

"In Billy Ball," wrote Red Smith in 1981, "the players run. Rickey Henderson stole 100 bases last year, breaking Ty Cobb's American League record. They work the double steal, they squeeze and they steal home. They sacrifice and they hit behind the runner. They worry runs out of the opposition, while their pitchers hold the varmints off at the pass." (*New York Times*, April 22, 1981) For all of its successes, Billy Ball has also been characterized by controversy and dissension. "Feuding rips away facade of Billy Ball" screams a sports section headline in the *San Francisco Examiner* for March 7, 1983.

Martin himself simply defines it as "old-fashioned baseball." (*Houston Post*, May 10, 1987; CDP)

bing   *v.* To hit a ball hard. Edward J. Nichols calls it an "onomatopoetic term."
1ST   1909. "Bing one, Cap!" says a character in Zane Grey's *The Shortstop.*

bingle   1. *n.* Base hit, usually a "clean one."
2. *v.* To hit safely.
ETY/1ST   1902. One of the first to tackle this was lexicographer David Shulman in the February 1937 *American Speech*, who conjectured: "If it is not an erroneous reading of *single,* perhaps it may be a blend of *bang* or *bing* with *single.*" Responding to Shulman's suggestion, Peter Tamony posed a counter-theory in the October 1937 *American Speech*. Tamony did not doubt that the term was based "on the onomatopoetic *bing,* the sound of the bat solidly meeting the pitched ball. . . ," but he also asked, ". . . was such a hit first called 'bingo,' from the exclamation in use, and later blended with *single?*" Tamony cites an example of bingo in use: " 'Truck' Egan is showing his form of other seasons, playing a swell short and getting his timely bingoes as of yore." (*Sporting News,* Nov. 15, 1902) But Tamony is quick to point out that a year before that *bingle* was in use: "You must give him credit for being good on ground balls, but he is not a good ground coverer, loses bingle after bingle near second base and is a light hitter." (*Sporting Life,* September 6, 1902)

bird cage   *n./arch.* Slang nickname for the CATCHER'S MASK, so-called because of its resemblance to a small, wire cage. "So in 1875 Fred W. Thayer hit upon the nose-saver we call a mask, but which people then called a 'bird cage.' " (*The Mutual Baseball Almanac,* CDP)
1ST   1906 (*Sporting Life,* March 3; EJN)

Bird cage. A young man in a catcher's mask, when they really looked like bird cages.   *Author's collection*

bird dog   *n.* Friend or associate of a scout who tips him off to high-schoolers and other young players with major league potential; an assistant scout. They are not paid, but occasionally one is given a small bonus for having spotted a boy who eventually becomes a major leaguer.

They are the first people you meet in Pat Jordan's *A False Spring,* published in 1973:

"The bird dogs came first. They just appeared one spring day in your sophomore year of high school as if drawn by the odor of freshly cut outfield grass . . . They were called bird dogs because they sniffed out talent, although the name does not do justice to the men. The bird dogs were kindly old men in plaid shirts and string ties. They owned taverns and hardware stores, and had even played ball with Kiki Cuyler and Georgie Cutshaw. Now in their last years, they measured out the weekday afternoons at an endless succession of high school baseball games."

After the bird dogs, wrote Jordan, "came the full-time scouts."

1ST   1950. The term appears in the glossary to Sam Nisenson's *Handy Illustrated Guide To Baseball.* (DS)

ETY   An obvious reference to the dog used by a hunter to hunt and retrieve birds. To bird-dog is also general slang for watching closely.

Birds   Nickname for the present-day BALTIMORE ORIOLES. For some reason the so-briquet has not worked for the other avian teams, the Toronto Blue Jays and the St. Louis Cardinals.

However, the term is used from time to time in print for other teams, such as an article on the Toronto Blue Jays in *Sports Illustrated,* entitled "Birds on the Wing."

bite   *v.* To swing at a bad or unexpected ball, as a fish bites at a baited hook. The term has usually been applied to the hapless batters who cannot resist swinging at and missing the elusive slow curve. In 1912 Hugh Fullerton wrote of the term, "The message 'he will bite' passed through the league among the players generally means the end of the usefullness of that player."

1ST   1905. (*Sporting Life,* September 2; ENJ)

2. *v.* To hit a batter with a pitch; to take a "bite" out of him.

bite the dust   *v.* To SLIDE.

1ST   1910. (*New York Tribune* July 9; EJN)

ETY   Since approximately 1870 this has been slang for dying or being killed violently. It is also used as an expression of defeat (as in "my idea bit the dust"). Baseball uses the term literally, as a player sliding is likely to send up a cloud of dusty soil.

BK   Standard abbreviation for BALK.

black   *n.* The perceived inside and outside edges of the strike zone. It refers to the area above the borders of the plate.

ETY   There is no black border to the regulation rubberized home plate but its edges show up in sharp contrast to the surrounding dirt and give the illusion of darkness or being black. The impression of a black or dark edge is strengthened by drawings and illustrations, that show a black outline and non-regulation plates (such as plastic toy store renditions) that have black edges.

Black and Decker   *n.* A player used for odd jobs such as warming up bullpen pitchers; one used like a tool from the Black and Decker tool manufacturer.

ETY   Explained in TSN for March 6, 1982: "This one originated in Kansas City, where the Royals' bullpen applied this tag to catcher John Watham. 'A weak tool, less than human,' said [Dan] Quisenberry. It is often used to describe a bullpen catcher."

black betsy   *n.* Name for the large black bat first popularized by the great hitter "Shoeless" Joe Jackson, but any black bat thereafter. According to Edward J. Nichols the name was originally given to the bat by its manufacturer, A. G. Spalding and Co.

1ST   1922. (*The Spalding Official Base Ball Guide;* EJN)

blackout   **1.** *v.* To keep a game off of television or radio for any of a number of reasons, usually economic. For instance, a team may have an agreement with a local television station or cable system that a game cannot be shown unless a certain number of tickets are sold in advance of the game.

2. *n.* The act of blocking the television broadcast of a game. When a Red Sox game versus the Yankees was kept off a New England cable TV system, the Boston *Globe* ran an explanation

Bite the dust. Paul Richards of the Tigers raises a cloud as he slides safely into home in a game against the Philadelphia Athletics on July 1, 1945. *Prints and Photographs Division, the Library of Congress*

under the headline, "Light shed on blackout." (June 27, 1986)

Black Sox Derogatory name for the 1919 Chicago White Sox team on which eight players illegally conspired with a gambler to lose the World Series to Cincinnati. Black Sox was a nickname coined to bring shame to the team. The whole incident became known as the Black Sox scandal and the trial of the players, whose presiding judge was Kenesaw Mountain Landis, was known widely as the Black Sox trial. To bring respectability back to the sport, the powerful office of Commissioner of Baseball was created, and Judge Landis became the first commissioner. In the 1982 novel *Shoeless Joe* by W. P. Kinsella, the narrator muses, "Instead of nursery rhymes, I was raised on the story of the Black Sox Scandal, and instead of Tom Thumb or Rumpelstiltskin, I grew up hearing

of the eight disgraced ballplayers: Weaver, Cicotte, Risberg, Felsch, Gandil, Williams, McMullin, and, always, Shoeless Joe Jackson." **SEE** *"Say it ain't so."*

Blade Commonly used nickname for thin, wiry player, for example, Mark Belanger during his days with the Baltimore Orioles.

blank(s) **1.** *v.* To shut out. A term beloved of headline writers.
1ST 1862 (*New York Sunday Mercury* June 29; EJN)
2. *n.* A scoreless inning. "Relaxed Gooden throws three blanks." (headline in the New York *Daily News*, March 14, 1987)

blast out of the box *v.* To remove from the pitcher's mound for giving up too many hits.

blaze *v.* To bat a hard ball, to "blaze one."
1ST 1912. (*New York Tribune*, October 13; EJN)

Black Sox. The 1919 White Sox. (Front row: Lynn, Risberg, Leibold, Kerr, McClellan, Williams, Cicotte. Middle row: Schalk, Jenkins, Felsh, Gleason, E. Collins, J. Collins, Faber, Weaver. Back row: Jackson, Gandil, McMillin, Lowdermilk, James, Mayer, Murphy, Sullivan, Wilkinson.) *National Baseball Library, Coopers-town, N.Y.*

blazer   *n.* FASTBALL.

bleacher(s)   **1.** *n.* Originally, the uncovered, unreserved, backless benches for spectators at a ball park. Now they simply refer to the most distant and inexpensive seats, which are beyond the outfield wall and may be covered, in the case of domed stadiums.

They carry with them a certain rowdy, ro-mantic image: "The democracy of the game is at its best on the bleachers and in the grand-stand. There the wealthy banker, straight from downtown by the 'Wall Street subway special,' hobnobs with the office-boy for once, on terms of perfect equality." (*New York Evening Post*, September 14, 1911)

One appeal of the bleachers has always been their relative cheapness. *The Sporting News* of July 14, 1954, reported "Ebbets Field prices will continue to be $3 for lower boxes, $2.50

upper boxes, $1.75 grandstand, and 50 cents, bleachers." Another draw has been the party atmosphere that exists in some parks. A recent report from Fenway Park: "Beachballs are only the newest, and most visible, of the bleacher game-time activities. But while beer-spilling, Frisbee-throwing and marijuana-smoking are time honored traditions in the cheap seats, this season seems to have brought, if anything, an improved situation." (*The Boston Globe*, June 25, 1986)

2. *n.* The spectators in the bleachers. "The bleachers nursed their wrath until the game was over when they swarmed into the field and started to mob the offending official." (*Sporting Life*, May 13, 1905; PT)

ETY/1ST   1888. Derived from "bleaching boards," a jocular reference to people bleaching in the sun. In his humorous 1888 book of baseball definitions, Thomas W. Lawson gives

Bleachers. Fans crowding into the bleachers at the Brooklyn Ball Grounds (c. 1920), when a "field seat" cost a mere two bits.   *Prints and Photographs Division, the Library of Congress*

this definition of "bleaching boards": "the resting place for the *kranks* who are not acquainted with the doorkeeper of the grandstand . . ." A very early reference appeared in the Cincinnati *Inquirer* in 1877 under the byline of O. P. Caylor (and which was reprinted in *The Sporting News* for May 16, 1956): "The bleaching boards just north of the north pavillion now holds the cheap crowd which comes in at the end of the first inning at a discount." (PT)

Hugh S. Fullerton in his "Primer" of 1912 added this racial twist to the etymology of the term when he announced that the "Term originated in the south where the colored spectators were forced to sit in the sun, and were 'bleached.'"

EXT   The term that originated in baseball is now applied to the cheaper backless seats in football stadiums, gymnasiums and even nightclubs. Bleacher seats are offered for rock concerts and religious revival meetings. Every four years they become Inaugural fixtures in Washington: "A mile of tiered board bleachers flanked Pennsylvania Avenue from the Treasury to Capitol Hill." (*New York Times*, January 19, 1969)

bleacher bums   *n.* Hoard of boisterous, often shirtless fans who inhabit the bleachers of such places as Wrigley Field in Chicago (where the term originated). The term appears to have been in use since the late 1960s.

bleacher critic   *n.* A critic who, to use another sport's terminology, sits on the sideline. "But Secretary of State Cordell Hull, speaking directly over the Columbia network, was performing primarily for the home folks answering bleacher critics of his foreign policy pitching." (*Newsweek*, April 17, 1944)

bleacher entrance   *n.* At a ball park, an admission gate reserved exclusively for the bleachers. "The tickets will be sold at the bleacher entrances, not at the main box office . . ." (The *St. Petersburg Times* on tickets for a Red Sox vs. Mets exhibition game, March 14, 1987)

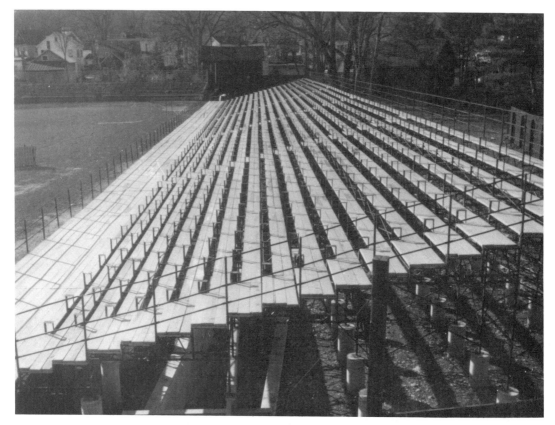

Bleachers. The bleaching boards at Doubleday Field in Cooperstown, New York.   *National Baseball Library, Cooperstown, N.Y.*

bleacherite   *n.* Person who sits in the bleachers. "Another Brooklyn first baseman earned the jeers of the bleacherites by being picked off base, after singling, on a version of the hoary hidden-ball trick." (Bennett Cerf, *Shake Well Before Using*, 1948) Certain popular players of the past, Zack Wheat for one, have been referred to as an "idol of the bleacherites." A later example of the term in use appeared in the "Jocks" column of *People*, June 24, 1974: "In Cincinnati, bleacherites poured beer on Houston outfielder Bob Watson as he lay stunned after running into the left field fence."

When Hugh Fullerton set out to define the term for his "Primer" of 1912 he gave them a certain nobility with lines like this: "The bleacherites usually are much better posted on the game than those patrons who occupy the grand stand boxes and seats and are much more dreaded by the players because of their caustic criticism."
1ST   1890 (*New York Press,* July 10; EJN)

bleacheritis   *n.* Mock disease name for the deteriorated physical conditioning of those who have given up active participation in athletics and become mere spectators: "The active athlete of the teens succumbs to bleacheritis by 30 and is interested only because he has money on the Giants." (*The Next Hundred Years* by C. C. Furnas, 1936)

bleachers diplomacy   *n.* Foreign affairs conducted in an aloof manner. "In that part of the world [Southeast Asia] Washington seems to practice 'bleachers' diplomacy, as a non-participating spectator of events." (Blair Bolles, *Headline Series—78*, Foreign Policy Association, Nov.–Dec. 1949)

bleaching boards   *n./obs.* This term evolved into BLEACHERS but also coexisted with it. From an article on opening day: ". . . the horney handed sons of toil made a brave show upon the bleaching boards, where they were jammed and crowded without a seat to spare, so that they overflowed the grounds and crowded in upon the players." (*The Illustrated American,* May 10, 1890)

bleeder 1. *n.* A batted ball that, as the result of an erratic roll, pop, bad bounce or overall slowness, becomes a base hit. Dizzy Dean once described it as, "A weak scratch hit that is just slow enuff so the runner can beat it out to first base." A typical bleeder is a ground ball that slows to a stop about halfway down the baseline (with a possible assist from the infield grass), but some are underpowered fly balls that drop unexpectedly for hits. "Marquez beat out a bleeder over the pitcher's head, advanced to second on a sacrifice, stole third and came home when Surkont hoisted a fly to left." (*San Francisco Examiner,* April 21, 1951; PT)
ETY/1ST 1937. In his book *How to Talk Baseball,* Mike Whiteford says: "The term is a sarcastic one, suggesting the ball was hit so hard that it's bleeding. Following such a hit, players often say, 'Wipe the blood off it.' "

A tad more logical, perhaps, is Bert Dunne's explanation in his *Folger's Dictionary of Baseball* (1958) in which he states that the term grew out of the phrase "That hit had blood on it!" Dunne goes on to indicate that, "while the ball was hit on the handle, the batter's fists were figuratively responsible, bled in the process, and left blood on the ball."

Yet one of the earliest uses of the term in print strongly suggests that it is based on a pun. In his March 11, 1937, *San Francisco Examiner* article, "Baseball Slang, Growing Fast," Curley Grieve wrote: "A bleeder aptly describes a scratchy single . . ." (PT)
2. *n./obs.* A sharply hit ball, according to William G. Brandt in his 1932 article on baseballese, "threatening to split the first finger that's laid upon it." This meaning appears to have been totally cancelled out by the first.

blind *n./obs.* A club's scoreless inning. In Henry Chadwick's 1987 *Technical Terms of Base Ball* this word is already considered of historic interest only, when it is defined as, "An old-time term used to indicate the retirement of a side in a game without their being able to score a single run."

blinder *n.* Archaic term defined by Henry Chadwick in his *The Game of Base Ball* as "the provincial term in the Middle States for a blank score in a game."

blind mice *n.* Derogatory term for a group of UMPIRES at a game.

blind staggers *n.* Awkward maneuvering of a fielder positioning to catch a high, wind-blown fly ball.

blind tom *n.* UMPIRE. Part of a litany of references (*blind mice, three blind mice* etc.) that link umpiring with blindness. Writer Robert Hendrickson found and forwarded this bit of typical and traditional doggerel:
> Breathes there a fan with soul so dead,
> Who never to the ump hath said:
> Yer blind, you bum!

USE An affront that can, nevertheless, be used affectionately. ". . . Palo Alto's Bill Engein [is] about to start his fourth season as a National League umpire and his twentieth as a blind tom." (Jack McDonald, *San Francisco Call-Bulletin,* January 25, 1955; PT)
1ST 1912. "I get me a newspaper, so I can keep me lamps off that high-ball sign, and right there at the top o' the page is a spiel printed in letters that Blind Tom could read." (*Bonehead* by "The Wise Guy"; PT)
ETY Quite likely that the term originated with and was appropriated from Old Blind Tom, a popular black musical prodigy of the period just after the Civil War.

block/block off a base *v.* Action taken by a defensive player to prevent a runner from tagging a base; accomplished with the aid of the defensive player's body and commonly performed by the catcher. It is illegal and can be ruled an obstruction if the block occurs without the blocker having the ball or being in the process of fielding it.
1ST 1902. (*Sporting Life,* July 12; EJN)

blocked ball *n.* A ball in play that is touched, stopped or handled by a person not engaged in the game. Such an occurrence causes a dead ball.
1ST 1891. (*Chicago Herald,* June 25; EJN)

blocker 1. *n.* Catcher or other defensive player who blocks either a base or home plate.
1ST 1905. (*Sporting Life,* September 2; EJN)
2. *n.* Base runner who "takes out"—throws himself into—the second baseman to prevent a double play.

block the plate *v.* For a catcher (or a pitcher, if he is covering the plate) to stand in the way of the runner and use his body to prevent a base runner from scoring while attempting to tag him out. It is only legal when the catcher has the ball or is in the process of fielding it.

blood bounty   *n.* Money paid for retaliatory action on the field. Term that shows up in Burt Dunne's *Folger's Dictionary of Baseball*, where it is defined in these words: "Money irate manager offers to player who will drag ball down first, cause pitcher (who has been throwing at hitters) to cover, offering opportunity to 'run up his back' and spike pitcher."

bloomer   *n.* Player who looks good in spring training, but is a failure when the regular season starts. Most probably this is a corruption of "early bloomer." Also, a player who blows hot and cold.

bloop   1. *n.* (TEXAS LEAGUER.) A badly-hit ball that drops between the infielders and the outfielders for a hit. Onomatopoetically named for the "bloop" sound that is suggested when the bat hits the ball, which writer and former player Jim Brosnan wrote has the sound "of a soft tomato struck by a broomstick."
2. *v.* To hit such a ball. "I made a pretty good pitch, but that's how you hit .350. You hit one hard, then bloop one in." (Mike Flanagan, quoted in the *Washington Post*, September 25, 1986)

blooper   1. *n.* A bloop hit.
1ST   1937. (*New York Times*, October 8; EJN)
2. *n.* A pitch that is lobbed into a high arc, which, when thrown correctly, drops precipitously through the strike zone, tantalizing the batter in the process. It has also been termed a "glorified" slow ball thrown with a high arc.

bloop single   *n.* A blooper that allows the batter to reach first base safely. ". . . Gutierrez moved him to third with a bloop single to center." (*Boston Globe*, August 11, 1984)

blow   1. *v.* To fail in any of a number of ways; for examples, to lose a game, misplay the ball or, in the case of an umpire, to make a bad call.
2. *n./arch.* A base hit. Probably what Babe Ruth and his Yankee teammates called a single as this is the only alternative to single offered in *Babe Ruth's Own Book of Baseball*.
3. *n.* A big or clutch hit, as in: the big blow in extra innings that won the game.
1ST   1907. (*New York Evening Journal*, April 27; EJN)

blow by   *v.* BLOW 'EM PAST/BLOW IT BY.

blow-down pitch   *n.* Rarely used synonym for BRUSHBACK PITCH. Defined in Ralph H. Barbour's 1935 *How to Play Better Baseball* as, "A pitched ball high and close to the batsman designed to drive him away from the plate." (DS)

blow 'em past/blow it by   *v.* To deliver a pitch with great speed.

blown call   *n.* A bad judgment by an umpire. "He had another homer in the game but it was ruled a double on a blown call by umpire Dan Morrison." *Tampa Tribune*, March 30, 1986)

blowout   1. *n.* A leg or foot injury, a play on "bad wheel."
2. *n.* A one-sided game, such as one in which a team outscores its opponent by a wide margin.
3. *v.* To defeat overwhelmingly.

blow smoke   *v.* To throw a fastball or fastballs. Blow the lid off.

blow up   *v.* In pitching, to lose one's ability to throw strikes; to come unglued. Writing about the semantics of sports writing, Calvin T. Ryan addressed this term: "It is one of those rare examples of slang which just about hits the nail on the head." (*Word Study*, February 1952)
1ST   1908. (*Brooklyn Daily Eagle*, May 27; EJN)

bludgeon   1. *n.* Bat.
1ST   1908. (*New York Evening Journal*, March 18; EJN)
2. *v.* To hit the ball.

bludgeon wielder   BATTER.
1ST   1913. (*Harper's Weekly*, September 6; EJN)

blue   *n.* Derogatory term for an UMPIRE.
USE   This term has decidedly provocative overtones, as if the term were a reference not to the color of the empire's uniform but to someone who "blew it." Overheard at an industrial league game: "Get a flashlight up there, blue."

bluecoat   *n.* An UMPIRE. ". . . the ball game went on—fortunately, without any especially difficult calls to challenge the bush-league bluecoats." (Roger Angell describing a game during an umpires' strike in *The Summer Game*; CDP)

blue dart/blue darter   *n.* A hard, low LINE-DRIVE. Blue darts are difficult to field. "And how about Billy Hunter? I never saw a shortstop make the play he did on Joe Astroth's blue dart. If that wasn't a hit, I never saw one."

(Alva "Bobo" Holloman in a May 7, 1953, UPI article on his no-hitter. (*San Francisco News;* PT) Holloman won only three games in his career, of which one was a no-hitter.

ETY It is described by Mike Whitford in *How to Talk Baseball* (1983) "as though it were propelled by a blue gas flame."

board *n.* Flat and/or stiff glove or mitt from which balls are likely to bounce, as if it were a board or plank. This term is used less often today than it once was because modern gloves come with deep, pre-formed pockets and break in quickly.

bob-and-weave *n.* The KNUCKLEBALL, so-called because of its erratic nature. "But the bob-and-weave became Nipper's bread-and-butter pitch yesterday, as the veteran right-hander survived a rocky first inning and went on to a 9-4 victory over the Yankees at Fenway Park." (*Boston Globe,* June 21, 1987)

bobble **1.** *v.* To mishandle a batted or thrown ball—often resulting in an error.
2. *n.* A ball that has been mishandled.
ETY It appears that this term was first used in the early American West as slang for a mistake or blunder. "But, Sal," says a character in William C. Campbell's 1901 *Colorado Colonel,* "I'm mighty afeerd you'll make a bobble of it." (DS)
1ST 1893. Listed in a "Texas Vocabulary" by F. K. Wister, which appears in the 1968 collection, *Owen Wister Out West.* (DS)

boiler *n.* A player's, manager's or coach's stomach, especially when upset. A gastro ailment such as an ulcer or an upset stomach is known as a "bad boiler."

boiling out place *n./arch.* A spring training camp, usually situated in a hot climate.
1ST 1908 (*New York Evening Journal,* February 11; EJN)

Bolshevik League Name given by the press to the National League of Base Ball Clubs, a league created in the late 19th century by the Brotherhood of Professional Base Ball Players, a union.
ETY The term was applied after the fact because the Bolshevik party did not emerge until 1903 in Russia. They seized power in that country in November of 1917. In the United States the term Bolshevik and its variations (including the slangy bolshie or bolshy) were applied to

that which was wild-eyed, radical and anti-capitalistic. The application to a group of baseball players was clearly meant to be derogatory. As Leonard Shecter points out in his book, *The Jocks,* "The league was called the Players' National League of Base Ball Clubs but, sportswriters being a conservative lot, it came to be called the Bolshevik League." (CDP)

bolt *n.* A LINE DRIVE.

bomb/bombard/bombard a pitcher **1.** *v.* To get a number of hits off one or more pitchers during a finite period (an inning, a game etc.). "Bombed," Jim Brosnan wrote in *The Long Season,* is said of "pitchers whose pitches return from the plate traveling faster than they were going when they arrived."
1ST 1905. (*Sporting Life,* September 2; EJN)
2. *v.* To defeat decisively and with a large number of hits.

bombardment *n.* Rash of hits; a bombing.

Bombers *n.* Nickname for the NEW YORK YANKEES, short for BRONX BOMBERS.

bone **1.** *v.* To rub the maximum hitting point or "sweet spot" of one's bat with a soupbone to harden the bat. Perfectly legal; such noted hitters as Frank Howard and Joe DiMaggio have boned their bats. Even Roy Hobbs, the tragic main character of Bernard Malamud's novel *The Natural,* took care of his bat in such a fashion. Says Hobbs speaking of his beloved bat Wonderboy, "Hadn't used it much until I played semipro ball, but I always kept it oiled with sweet oil and boned it so it wouldn't chip."
2. See bone play.

bone play *n.* A heedless or foolish play, also, a boner. Often stated as "pulling a bone."
ETY See boner.
1ST 1915. "Among the spectators not a few expressed the belief that Ganton had 'pulled a bone' by his failure to try for Runyan instead of Schmidt." (Gilbert Patten, *Covering the Look-In Corner;* DS)

bonehead/bone-head **1.** *n.* Dumb player.
2. *adj.* Stupid.
ETY This "sweet word" we are told by lexicographer Gretchen Lee in *American Speech* (April 1926) began in baseball as a term of ridicule for particularly unintelligent players or actions.
Many sources agree that the origin and certain initial popularity of both bonehead and boner stem from a single incident. Describing

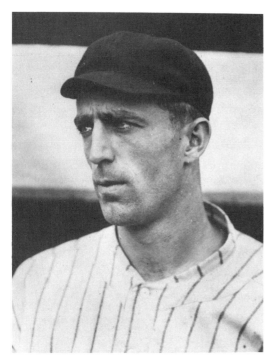

Bonehead. Fred Merkle. *National Baseball Library, Cooperstown, N.Y.*

an event that took place on September 23, 1908, Mark Sullivan stated, "At the Polo Grounds, New York, a dispute historic in baseball, which enriched the language with two exceedingly forceful words, 'bonehead' and 'boner,' arose over whether Frederick Charles Merkle did or did not touch second base." (*Pre-War America* [Vol. III of *Our Times*] 1930)

The incident in question took place under the most dramatic circumstances. It was the last half of the ninth inning in a 1-1 tie game between the New York Giants and the Chicago Cubs. Tied for first place, the winner of the game would take the lead in the National League. New York had two out and two men on base; one on third and Merkle on first. The man at bat singled into center field and the runner at third ambled across the plate with what appeared to be the winning run. The play, however, would not be complete until Merkle touched second base ahead of the ball. If Merkle did not touch second he could still be retired by a force at the base. With two outs, no runs can score until a possible force play has been completed.

Although there were claims to the contrary

on the part of Merkle and others (including 8,000 fans who signed a petition that said they had seen him touch the bag), he apparently turned right toward the club house before touching second. He was presumed to have thought the game was over when his teammate crossed the plate, causing him to stop short of the bag. At this point, Chicago second baseman Johnny Evers signaled for the center fielder to throw him the ball so he could tag second. Jubilant with their apparent victory, fans and Giant players rushed out onto the field creating mass confusion. Before Evers could retrieve the ball and record the out at second base, a spectator grabbed ahold of it and threw it into the stands. The Giants pushed Merkle back to the base, as the ball, recovered by a Chicago fan, was tossed back to Evers. But all this took place after the umpires had left the field. Despite the fact that the New York papers credited the Giants with the win, it was decided by the National League President Harry C. Pulliam that the game would be recorded as a tie. The drawn game was replayed a day after the season ended and Chicago won both the game and the pennant.

As to the origin of bonehead and boner in their modern sense, Sullivan reported, "In their wrath at Merkle, an excellent player, the New York fans fixed upon a previously anaemic and almost meaningless word, and gave to it a significance with which every reader is familiar. For more than twenty years, there has been rarely a game when from some part of the stands there did not arise from time to time, in shrill falsetto or hoarse bellow, the cry 'bonehead' directed at any player disapproved, not always justly, by a 'fan.' "

The sad part of the story is that Merkle is remembered for this one play, but he had an otherwise respectable career playing for the Giants, Dodgers, Cubs and Yankees from 1907 to 1926.

As Sullivan suggests there is evidence to hint that bonehead (but not boner) predates the Merkle play. Alfred H. Holt in *Phrase Origins* reports that the term has been spotted in print as early as 1903 for a person who acts stupidly (presumably with bones where there should be brains) and that it was popularized by the 1908 incident; however, the earliest Edward J. Nichols can date it is March 9, 1908, five and a half months before the Merkle affair (in the *New York Evening Journal*). A specific point of origin was suggested by Hy Turkin when he wrote, "First used by manager George Stallings to describe the brainless play of his 1898 Phillies." In the *Hot Stove League,* Lee Allen agrees but insists that it was applied mainly to John I. Rodgers, who Stallings released in 1898.

As is often the case with American slang, researchers are faced with conflicting claims that are long past the point of being sorted out; however, what is clear and conclusive in this case is that the term was a slang rarity until the 1908 error.

EXT   Stupid or foolish. "I don't like ta knock ya, but when ya pull a bonehead stunt like ya did yesterday, y're in love, or else y're getting balmy in the bean." (*Railroad Man's Magazine,* August 1916; PT)

bonehead play   *n.* A blunder; an error.
1ST   1912. "I don't know as I'd call it a vice so much as a bonehead play." (Alfred H. Lewis, *The Apaches of New York;* DS)

boner   **1.** *n.* A dumb play, usually as the result of an error of judgment or lack of concentration as opposed to a mere physical mistake. A boner, for example, might be a base runner taking off on a catchable fly thinking that there are two outs when, in fact, there is only one.
2. *n.* Any stupid move on or off the field. "Bill Sullivan the old White Sox catcher talked to me and told me not to pull no boner by refusing to go where they sent me." (Ring W. Lardner, *You Know Me Al;* 1916)
USE   Historically, this term has not been used lightly in baseball and tends to be reserved for only the most serious gaffes. In its most extreme case—the infamous Merkle Boner—it hung on Fred Merkle for the rest of his life. An AP obituary for March 2, 1956, was headlined: "Fred Merkle, Of 'Boner' Fame, Dies." (PT)
ETY   Quoting Gretchen Lee, from her article "In Sporting Parlance" in the April 1926 issue of *American Speech:* "The sweet word 'Bonehead' began with ball players, and from it has sprung the useful term 'boner,' meaning an error in judgement." The full etymology from the Fred Merkle play of 1908 is discussed under BONEHEAD.
EXT   An error, but without the sting it carries in the context of baseball. It has also specifically come to mean a hilarious classroom gaffe or howler.
SEE   *bonehead, Merkle's boner.*

boneyard   *n.* The imaginary dying grounds for washed-up pitchers.

boneyard aggregation   *n.* Team made up of old or worn-out players.

bonus   **1.** *n.* A cash incentive and reward given to a player for signing with a team.
2. *n.* A special incentive payment built into a player's contract, based on a particular aspect of that player's performance—such as, Roger Clemens being promised $150,000 for making the All-Star team in 1987 (a position he did not make).
SEE   *signing bonus.*

bonus baby/bonus kid   *n.* A bonus player. Pat Jordan, who signed with the Milwaukee Braves in 1959, defined the term in his book *False Spring:* "The term 'bonus baby' is usually applied to any player receiving more than $10,000 upon signing a contract. Naturally, whenever a team invests such money in a player they treat him more tenderly than they would a player in whom they invested little money. A bonus baby had only to hint at improvement in order to advance in the minors. But a non-bonus baby had to fashion a record of unquestionable success before he advanced."

bonus player   *n.* A prospective player who is given a cash bonus as an extra incentive for signing with a particular baseball team. "A ball player who is paid a fortune to watch ballgames," according to the iconoclastic sportswriter Jimmy Cannon who watched a number of such bonus players fail to live up to expectations.

The first such player appears to have been Tommy Henrich who was signed by the Cleveland Indians in 1936. The contract was deemed to be illegal and then-Commissioner of Baseball, Kenesaw Mountain Landis declared Henrich a free agent. Henrich was then offered—and he accepted—a contract along with a $25,000 bonus just for signing with the Yankees. But the first bonus player to capture wide popular attention was Dick Wakefield who, in 1940, was given a $52,000 bonus to sign with the Detroit Tigers upon his graduation from the University of Michigan.

The practice of offering signing bonuses was common up to 1965 and the first amateur player draft. The draft was created to end bidding wars that, among other problems, created large bonuses. Young players are still paid bonuses for signing and they are not insignificant. On June 11th, 1988 the Baltimore Orioles gave Gregg Olson, their number one draft choice, a $200,000 signing bonus.

The old bonus system had its share of successes but is still recalled for such players as Paul Pettit, signed in 1955 by the Pittsburgh Pirates. He was given a $100,000 bonus and only won one game for the team.

Despite this history, the term "bonus player" did not attract attention as a new word until after World War II. For instance, it is listed as new in 1947 in Kenneth Versand's *Polyglot's Lexicon*.

boob *n.* A fool; a dolt.
ETY In an article in *American Speech* (February 1951) David Shulman terms this a word that is not baseballese, but seems to have originated with baseball players. The earliest use that Shulman could find was in Christy Mathewson's *Pitching in a Pinch:* "There's a poor 'boob' in the hospital now that stopped one with his head." It may have been inspired by the much older term booby, for a fool.

boo bird *n.* A fan given to jeers, boos and catcalls when the home team falters. "The boo birds in the Cleveland stands were in full voice. Even Earl Averill, a star for eight years and one of the great hitters of all time, came in for his share of sour notes from the fans." (Bob Feller in *Strikeout Story;* CDP)

book 1. *n.* The official rules of the game.
2. *n.* Conventional strategic approach to the game; the unwritten but widely observed rules and assumptions followed by the game's managers, players and fans. Perhaps, the most often-cited example of a tenet of the book is that left-handed batters face right-handed pitchers and vice versa. Not universal, however, as longtime manager Dick Williams pointed out in 1980: "I never play by the book because I never met the guy that wrote it." A manager who makes an unconventional move is said to be going against the book.
3. *n.* The knowledge that a team has of an opposing pitcher, batter or manager, especially when it comes to specific strengths and weaknesses. Also, clubhouse food, out of town restaurants, umpires and practically any other variable may have a book. Ken Singleton, quoted in the *Sporting News:* "You keep a book on umpires the way you do with pitchers." (June 13, 1981)

4. *v.* To move very fast; with maximum speed, as in, "Brock was really booking around the bases for a stand-up triple."

bookends *n.* Used to describe the two pairs of defensive players who are positioned on opposite sides of the playing field, the left and right fielders collectively, and the first and third basemen collectively. The term has been used, for example, to describe Don Mattingly and Mike Pagliarulo of the New York Yankees (ca. 1986).

boom *v.* To hit the ball hard.
1ST 1909. (*Baseball* magazine, July; EJN)

boomerang ball *n.* Batted ball that comes back to the pitcher.

boost *v./arch.* When batting, to contact the bottom half of the ball causing it to pop up in the air.
1ST 1908 (*New York Evening Journal,* August 26; EJN)

boot 1. *n.* An error, such as one made while handling a ground ball. Typically, the ball bounces off the fielder's glove, as if it were kicked or booted. Originally, a booted ball was (and still is on occasion) one that had actually been kicked—booted—in error, but the term has long since generalized to any fielding error. "Why does he waste his efforts booting baseballs, when Yale is mourning the lack of a punter?" is a line quoted by Hugh Fullerton who used it to illustrate the term in his 1912 "Primer."
2. *v.* To commit such an error.
1ST 1907. (*New York Evening Journal,* May 2; EJN)
EXT To err; to mishandle.

booth *n.* In a ballpark, where radio and television announcers work, usually from an elevated position behind home plate. This is a traditional baseball term that is often used when the work area bears no resemblance to a booth. "This spring, after dreaming of it for years, I finally entered 'the booth.' Actually, it's not a booth at all; it's more like a pen, open to the elements except for some light wire mesh designed to protect the announcers from irate fans." (J. Anthony Lucas, *New York Times,* September 12, 1971)

Borough Hall *n.* A sidearm pitch in Brooklyn when that borough was Dodger territory.

Bosox Nickname of BOSTON RED SOX.

Boston Bees   Temporary name for the NL Boston Braves. In 1936 a contest was held among fans of the Boston Braves to rename the team (this came after a disastrous 1935 season). From some 1,327 entries the name Bees was selected as the new official team name. It only lasted for five seasons, when the name reverted to Braves. If nothing else the Bees were a headline writer's dream. Not only could the team's name be abbreviated as "B's," but stories would be introduced with lines like "Bees Swarm South" and "Bees Sting Again." The old name was brought back in the 1941 season as a new group of owners took over the team. The new owners concluded that the fans much preferred the old name and, in fact, many people had persisted in calling them the Braves during the Bees' years.

Boston Braves   Early National League teams in Boston were given a number of nicknames, including Red Caps, Beaneaters, Beanies, Rustlers and Doves. In 1912 they became the Braves after James E. Gaffney bought the team. Gaffney was a contractor and Tammany Hall chieftain. The name, suggested by John M. Ward, one of Gaffney's partners, came from the fact that members of the Tammany machine were often referred to as braves. The Tammany Society, which had been formed in New York City in 1789, was named for a Delaware Indian chief, Tammany, known for his sagacity. Tammany Hall was the most famous of the big-city political machines and had a major influence in New York politics for about 100 years (roughly from the middle of the 19th to the middle of the 20th century). In his *Political Dictionary* William Safire characterizes the Tammany influence as, "often corrupt, sometimes effective . . ."

The name has remained with the team through two moves: to Milwaukee in 1953 and then to Atlanta in 1966.

Boston Game   MASSACHUSETTS GAME.

Boston Massacre   Widely used nickname for the 1978 fade by the Boston Red Sox. "Red Sox rooters have known heartbreak. They haven't forgotten the Boston Massacre in 1978 and the 14½-game lead that vanished like an apparition." (Tom Pedulla, *The Gannett Westchester Newspapers,* June 25, 1986)
ETY   The name comes from the event that took place on March 5, 1770, when British soldiers fired on a crowd of Colonists in Boston.

Three people died and the word of the Boston Massacre spread rapidly and served to strengthen the spirit of revolution.

Boston Red Sox   The name of the American League's Eastern Division franchise in Boston, Massachusetts. Long associated with Boston, the name actually originated in Ohio with the Cincinnati Red Stockings, baseball's first professional team. When the Red Stockings broke up in 1871, many team members headed to Boston to form a new National League team and they carried with them both the name and the red stockings for which they were famous. The name was gradually dropped in the 1880s but revived and reapplied in 1904 for a new American League team that had come to town in 1901. The Boston Americans had been called the Somersets (in honor of owner and AL vice president Charles W. Somers), the Puritans, Pilgrims, Plymouth Rocks and Speed Boys, and became the Red Sox under the ownership of the Taylor family, which also owned the *Boston Globe*. The team is sometimes called the Bosox or the Rouge Hose.

"both feet on the rubber"   *n.* In softball, a point often made by the coach or other players to the pitcher to reiterate the fact that both feet much touch the pitcher's rubber before the ball can be delivered.

bottle   *v.* To contain an opponent; to bottle a game is to win it or make certain of winning it.

bottle bat   *n.* A bat with an especially large barrel, a short taper and very small handle, which gives it a bottle-like appearance. The bat was made famous by Heinie Groh who used it with great effectiveness from 1912 to 1921 when he played for the Cincinnati Reds and the New York Giants. (A bottle-shaped bat would be legal today as long as it was not more than 2¾ inches at its thickest and not more than 42 inches in length.)

bottom   **1.** *n.* The latter half of an inning, when the home team bats. The home team's scoring always appears on the bottom line of the scoreboard.
2. The last few players in a team's batting order—usually comprising the weaker hitters and in the National League, the pitcher.

bottom of the order   *n.* Generally, the last three batters in the batting order, almost always a club's least effective hitters.

Bottle bat. A tobacco label from 1867 shows a bottle-style bat. *Prints and Photographs Division, the Library of Congress*

Boudreau shift *n.* WILLIAMS SHIFT.

bounce a beauty *v.* To make a safe hit with a well-directed ground ball.

bouncer *n.* A ground ball that takes a series of moderate bounces.

bounce target *n./arch.* CUT OFF MAN.
1ST 1935. "Bounce target—Provided by a player placing himself in line between the home base and an outfielder making a throw-in to indicate the length and direction of the throw and to intercept it if advisable." (Ralph H. Barbour, *How to Play Better Baseball;* DS)

bounder *n.* A high-bouncing, easy to field ball.
1ST 1880. (*Brooklyn Eagle*, August 20; EJN)

bounds *n.* Synonymous with BASE in some early forms of baseball.
SEE the *Massachusetts game.*

Bowery, the *n.* Row of lockers reserved for players who are passed their prime.

ETY The term dates from the middle 1930s and is a direct reference to the Bowery, a street running diagonally across the east side of lower Manhattan. The street and the area around it have long been associated with grim poverty and human dereliction. Metaphorically, it stands for the end of the road. The name comes from the Dutch word, *bouwerji,* for farm.

box *n.* On the playing field, a designated area within which a player or coach is obliged to stand. The boxes of the ballpark include the batter's box, catcher's box, pitcher's box (or mound) and coach's (or coacher's) box. However, in the 19th century it was all but exclusively a reference to the pitcher's position or, as one reference put it, "the little square in the middle of the diamond."
1ST 1883. (*Sporting Life,* May 20; EJN)

box artist *n.* A PITCHER.
1ST 1908. (*Brooklyn Eagle,* May 20; EJN)

boxcar town *n./arch.* Small town.
EXT In the derogatory talk of players the term suggested a sleepy town whose main feature was a siding where the railroad stored boxcars.

boxman *n./arch.* Pitcher.

box score *n.* A condensed statistical summary of a baseball game; traditionally a feature of newspaper sports sections. Although the first one to be published was in the *New York Clipper* on July 16, 1853, (recording the Knickerbockers' 21-12 defeat of the Gothams), they did not appear with regularity until 1876 and the founding of the National League. Henry Chadwick is given credit for the creation of the shorthand ("phonographic") box score, although some have insisted that *New York Herald* writer Michael J. Kelly deserves the credit.
1ST 1908. (*Baseball* magazine, June; EJN)
ETY According to Edward J. Nichols, "Named from the old newspaper custom of placing the data in a boxed-off section on the page."
EXT The term has long been used for statistical summaries in other sports and as a metaphor for results in other areas. For example, Edward J. Nichols found a headline in the *New York Herald Tribune* for October 4, 1936, that proclaimed "Republicans See Errors in 'Box Score' of New Deal." The story under the headline read in part: "Arthur M. Curtis, assistant to the chairman of the Republican National

Box score. Henry Chadwick's Hall of fame plaque, which credits him with baseball's first box score. *National Baseball Library, Cooperstown, N.Y.*

Committee, Friday issued a statement calling attention to 'five errors' and one 'deliberate misplay' which belong in the 'box score' brought to the nation by President Roosevelt's Pittsburgh address." Roosevelt had talked of "the box score of the government of the United States" in his speech.

This political use of the term continued. When Harry Truman became President he issued periodic "box scores" scoring congerssional action on his legislative program. "Truman 'Box Score' Hits Congress Again." (*San Francisco Call-Bulletin,* August 12, 1948; PT)

box seats *n.* The choicest and most expensive seats at the ballpark, located near home plate, first base and third base.

box-work *n./arch.* PITCHING.
1ST 1888. (*New York Press,* April 2; EJN)

boy blue *n.* UMPIRE.
ETY Almost certainly inspired by the horn-blowing "Little Boy Blue" of nursery rhyme fame and a tie-in to the traditional blue umpire's uniform.

boys in blue *n.* UMPIRES.
1ST 1937. (New York *Daily News,* May 6; EJN)
ETY An obvious borrowing from the nickname of both the Union soldiers of the Civil War and police forces of modern times, who have both been recognized by their blue uniforms.

Boys of Summer **1.** A retrospective name for the Brooklyn Dodgers of the 1950s, created by Roger Kahn in his 1972 book on the Brooklyn Dodgers, *The Boys of Summer.* The book, according to Kahn, was "not on sports but on time and what it does to all of us."
2. In recent years the term has been used by broadcasters and writers to connote all baseball players. An opening day story from *USA Today* begins, "The Boys of Summer are back—at last." (April 7, 1987)

There has been some play on the term; for instance, players in spring training are called the Boys of Spring and popular Baltimore Orioles' broadcaster John Miller is called the Voice of Summer in the *Washington Post* (July 31, 1988).
ETY The term itself comes from a Dylan Thomas poem entitled "I See the Boys of Summer," which Kahn quotes at the beginning of his book.

BP Abbreviation for batting practice.

Brabender's Law *n.* Facetious "natural law" of postseason play that states: "The most inactive player during the World Series will be the most active during the clubhouse follies." Discovered by George Vecsey of the *New York Times,* the law is named for Gene Brabender of the Baltimore Orioles who drenched the clubhouse after spending all of his time in the bullpen as his team swept the Los Angeles Dodgers in the 1966 World Series.

brace of homers Two home runs, such as when a player scores a brace of homers during a game.

braille-man *n./arch.* Coach skilled at sending signs and hand signals to base runners. Most signs involve use of the hands.

brains *n.* The MANAGER.

brain surgeon *n.* A ballplayer. "What it's easier to become than a successful ball player," according to Leonard Shecter in his June 1963 *Baseball Digest* article on baseball slang. Shecter quotes a disgusted pitcher, "I think I'll take up something simple, like brain surgery."

brander   *n./arch.* A ball that is hit hard by the batter; one that dents or brands the ground. **1ST**   1869. (*New York Herald,* September 16; EJN)

brass   *n.* A team's management, including the owner, general manager and field manager. "Evans takes [verbal] shot at Red Sox brass." (AP dispatch, July 4, 1987) **1ST**   1946. "Manager Frankie Frisch is the 'CO,' the 'Old Man' or 'The Brass,' and he and his coaches have come to be known as 'GHQ.' " (Chester L. Smith, "Diamond Slang Goes G.I." from the May 1946 *Baseball Digest.* Smith discusses a number of terms brought to baseball from the military. Others are mentioned under the entry for *furlough.*) **ETY**   The term originated during World War II and was a reference to the decorative metal insignias (usually made of brass) worn by officers. It established itself as service-wide military slang for officers as a class. It was brought back and reapplied by baseball players returning from the war.

bravery suit   *n.* The protective gear worn by the umpire. "On occasion an umpire will forget to wear part of his 'bravery suit.' " (Ron Luciano, *Strike Two; CDP*)

Braves Field   Home grounds of the Boston Braves from 1915 through 1952.

bread and butter pitch   *n.* The specific pitch by which the pitcher earns a living; the pitch that gives him the edge over the batter. Burt Dunne pointed out, in his definition of this term: "When pitcher is denied right to dust off batter, he cries, 'You're taking away my bread and butter.' "

breadkbasket catch   *n.* Method of fielding a high fly ball with the glove held just above the waist as opposed to one's arms over one's head. Breadbasket has been a slang word for stomach since the 16th century. **SEE**   *basket catch.*

break   **1.** *n.* Deviation in the trajectory of a pitched ball; generic name for any pitch that does not go straight. **1ST**   1905. "The deceptive feature of this delivery (spit ball) is the fact that it is nothing but

a straight ball until just as the batter swings at it, then it 'breaks' sharply." (*Sporting Life,* May 13, 1905; PT)
2. *n.* A runner's start toward the next base, taken when the opportunity arises.
3. *n.* A lucky or unlucky event; such as a good or bad break. To make your own breaks is to create your own luck.
4. *n.* The turning point in a game; one crucial play—often a mistake—that a team capitalizes on. "Time and again these two have kept the score board clean as far as the sixth or 'lucky seventh' and then would come the break for which each team was working." (*The Book of Baseball,* published by P. F. Collier, 1911; PT)
5. *v.* To end something, such as breaking a batting streak or breaking (another person's) record.
SEE   *breaks, the.*

break his dishes   *v.* To break a batter's bat handle, as in "He [the pitcher] got in his kitchen [inside] and broke his dishes." In *The Encyclopedia of Sports Talk,* Phil Pepe reports, "The term has been refined as in, 'He got in his refrigerator and broke his eggs.' "

break in   **1.** *v.* To make good with a club; to make the team.
2. *v.* To make one's professional debut at a particular level of the game—for example, to break into the minors or break into the majors. **1ST**   1906. (*Sporting Life,* March 10; EJN)
3. *v.* To condition a glove or mitt for game use.

breaking   *adj.* Deviating. *Curve balls* are variously described by the manner of their deviation—high-breaking, low-breaking, fast-breaking, slow-breaking.

breaking ball   *n.* Any pitched ball—slider, sinker, knuckleball, screwball, and curveball—that deviates from a relatively straight and natural trajectory. The generic nature of the term was underscored when Brooks Robinson admitted during his August 18, 1987, telecast of a Baltimore Orioles game that this was the term broadcasters used when they were not sure what kind of pitch had just been thrown. Robinson is not alone in this perception. In his 1986 book, *Baseball Lite,* Jerry Howarth defines it this way: "A term used by radio and television sportscasters who have difficulty detecting the difference between a slider and curve." **1ST**   1905. (*Sporting Life,* October 7; EJN)

breaking stuff   *n.* An assortment of breaking balls.

break one off   *v.* To throw a breaking ball.

breaks, the   *n.* Luck and good fortune; often created by another's mistake or miscue.
EXT/1ST   1908. From a game that "breaks" right or contains a lucky "break." As early as 1908 (the *American* magazine for June), this was identified as a baseball term by Edward J. Nichols and it appears in V. Samuels' 1927 listing of "Baseball Slang" in *American Speech:* "The player of the side favored by luck 'gets the breaks' or the 'lucky breaks.'" The term appears to have still been regarded as exclusive to baseball as late as January 1943 when an article entitled "The Breaks" appeared in *Baseball* magazine. In it, the author, Franklin Faskee, reports, "Some call it fate. The old-time player called it the jinx. And players and fans now call it 'the breaks.'"
EXT   The breaks and the breaks of the game are common ways of connoting luck in many realms of modern life.

breaks off the table/breaks one off the table   *v.* Describing the motion of a curve ball that drops suddenly. "He has a variety of serves, but is primarily a curve baller. In the jargon of the trade, his downer is described as one that 'breaks off the table.' In other words, it drops all of a sudden—just like a round object rolling off the edge of a flat surface." (Syd Russell on 16-year-old prospect Frank Bertaina in the *San Francisco Examiner,* February 26, 1961)

break the wrists   *v.* For the batter to take a full swing at the ball, which involves turning one's wrists, that is, bringing the top hand over the bottom wrist through the action of one's wrists. The term and concept come into play when a batter starts to swing at a pitch and then attempts to stop. If, in the view of the umpire, the wrists have broken, the pitch will be called a strike. If not, the pitch will be judged—as a ball or called strike—as if the bat had not moved at all.

break-up   *v.* To score the game-winning run(s) with a flurry of hits.
1ST   1905 (*Sporting Life,* October 7; EJN)

break-up slide   *n.* A slide that is made to halt—"break up"—a double or triple play. The base runner who is about to be forced out attempts to slide into the infielder making the

play so that he will not be able to relay the ball.
SEE   *Neighborhood play.*

break up the double play   *v.* To prevent a second out with the *break-up slide.*

breeze   **1.** *v.* To work with ease whether it is to run the bases without interference or to win easily against easy competition. Sometimes stated as breeze through.
2. *adj.* Easily. "He won it in a breeze."
1ST   1910. (*Baseball* magazine, September; EJN)
3. *v.* To throw the fastball.
4. *n.* An easy victory
EXT   Baseball's popular term of ease has been long applied to other easy conquests, such as breezing through an examination. "It was a breeze."

breeze through   *v.* BREEZE.

Brew Crew   Nickname for the MILWAUKEE BREWERS.

brick   **1.** *n.* An inexpensive ball; a rock-like ball.
SEE   *nicklebrick.*
2. *n.* In baseball card collecting, a lot of 50 or more cards sold as a unit and packed like a solid brick. Bricks usually contain cards of one type (a "Mariners brick" for example) and do not normally contain star players or rarities.

bridge   *v.* To hit a home run. "When a pitcher is 'bridged' he has allowed a home run." (*Sports Illustrated,* September 13, 1982)

Briggs Stadium   Name for the home grounds of the Detroit Tigers from 1938 to 1960 when it became known as Tiger Stadium.

bring in   *v.* To score a runner, such as a single that brings in the runner on second base.
1ST   1865. (Chadwick Scrapbooks; EJN)

bring it   *v.* To throw a pitch with great velocity.

Broadway   **1.** *n.* The middle of the plate. A ball may be thrown right down/on Broadway.
2. *n./arch.* "A flashy dresser, loud talker," according to the 1937 *Sporting News Record Book.* Once a popular baseball catchall nickname, it may have last been widely used to describe Charlie Wagner of the Red Sox (1938–1946). It may have made a permanent transfer to football with the dubbing of "Broadway" Joe Namath of the New York Jets.
Lyn Lary, whose major league career ex-

tended from 1929 through 1940, served as the epitome of the player who attracted the name. Today it is hard to find his name in print without an adjective like dapper or snappy. When Lary and Leo Durocher, another snappy dresser, were both on the Yankees in 1929, Durocher got nicknamed "Fifth Avenue" presumably because he was a bit less flashy than Lary.

broken-bat hit/broken-bat single   *n.* A hit achieved in spite or because of a bat that breaks when it comes in contact with the ball.

broken in   *adj.* State or readiness commonly used to describe a glove that has been softened and conditioned to fit a player's hand.

broken wrist   *n.* The rolling of the batter's wrist when he swings. Not breaking one's wrists is the key to a check swing.

Bronx Bombers   Nickname for the New York Yankees that first became popular when heavyweight champion Joe Louis was known as the Brown Bomber. The term is still in common use.

Bronx bunnies   A nickname for the New York Yankees used, for example, in Roger Angell's classic *The Summer Game.*

Bronx cheer   *n.* A contemptuous razzing sound made by sticking the tongue between the closed lips and expelling air; the bird. Long associated with New York baseball fans who have never been shy about directing them at players in disfavor: "Bronx Cheers Hit DiMaggio At Failure to Clout Ball." (headline on a UPI story, May 13, 1946, *San Francisco News;* PT)
  Although there is no direct evidence to support the connection, the term may have been created in reference to the Bronx-based New York Yankees.
1ST 1931. "The Bronx cheer has even invaded Forest Hills. During tight tennis matches there this last summer the gallery with increasing frequency undertook to line the matches." (*San Francisco News,* December 31; PT)
SEE *Razzberry.*

Bronx Zoo   Derogatory nickname for the New York Yankees during the ownership of George Steinbrenner, taken from the name of the famous zoo of the same borough. The clear implication is that of a motley assortment of wild animals. "Not for nothing are the New York Yankees of George Steinbrenner known as the Bronx Zoo." (William Gildea, *The Washington Post,* April 27, 1986)
1ST 1979. In that year Sparky Lyle and Peter Golenbock published an account of the Yankees' 1979 season called *The Bronx Zoo.* According to Golenbock's preface the title was the "masterstroke" of the book's editor, Larry Freundlich of Crown Books.

Brooklyn Dodgers   Name of the National League franchise that played in Brooklyn, New York; founded in 1890 and played in Ebbets Field from 1913 through 1957.
  The nickname Dodgers was originally used by baseball writers in the late 1890s when the team was known as The Bridegrooms and it was customary to refer to the residents of Brooklyn as trolley-dodgers. Trolley-dodging was a term for jaywalking in Brooklyn, where pedestrians had to avoid being hit by the numerous street cars that crisscrossed the borough. The team went through several nickname changes. They were the Superbas for a while (from the name of a popular Broadway play) and the Robins when Wilbert Robinson took over as manager (1914–1931), but always seemed to revert to the name Dodgers.
  The name went with the team when it moved to Los Angeles in 1958.

Brooksian   *adj.* Adroit fielding, in the manner of Brooks Robinson, especially in defense play at third base. "[Wade] Boggs has been semi-Brooksian at third base . . ." (Tony Kornheiser in the *Washington Post,* October 25, 1986)
ETY   Named for Brooks Robinson who won virtually every possible award and accolade for defensive play during his career with the Baltimore Orioles (1955–1973). In 9,165 chances he made only 263 fielding errors. Along with *Ruthian* and *Koufaxian,* this is one of those rare cases where a player has been honored with an eponymous adjective.

Brotherhood, The   Union of players that emerged in 1889 to protect and promote the rights of players and that eventually created its own league, the Players League, in 1890. The story broke in the *Sporting News* under a succession of three headlines:

THE BROTHERHOOD.
Every Man But Anson Pledged to Jump the League.

The Greatest Move in the History of the National Game.

The Players League did not have the organization or money to compete with the established leagues and had gone out of existence by the beginning of the 1891 season.

brown *adj./arch.* Inept.
1ST 1889. "Some of the brownest work ever seen on a baseball field characterized the home team's play in the second. It was enough to drive a baseball man to drink . . . It was one complete jumble of uncanny mistakes, high-salaried muffs and skyscraping throws . . . People who can't play any better than they did here shouldn't be allowed to eat." (*New York World,* August 18. The quote is reprinted in Gerald Cohen's article on baseball slang in the February 1987 *Comments on Etymology.*)

Brownies Nickname for the old St. Louis Browns, which tended to be used in order to underscore the chronic ineptitude of the team; a play on brown as a term for imperfection.

brown spitter *n.* Spitball moistened with chewing tobacco juice. In his book *Me and the Spitter,* Gaylord Perry admits it is one of the few variations on the spitball that he did not throw. "I couldn't take to the tobacco." (CDP)

Bruins *n.* Nickname for the Chicago Cubs.
ETY Bruin is a synonym for a bear; it originated in the character of Sir Bruin, a bear in the medieval German epic, *Reynard the Fox.*

brush *n.* Whisky broom used by the umpire to keep home plate dusted off and easy to see.

brush back 1. *v.* To move a batter away from the plate with the aid of a *brushback pitch.*
2. *adj.* Relating to the pitch. "Torre remembered when there were some brush-back wars with other teams . . ." (*New York Times,* August 1, 1987; JCG)

brushback pitch/brush-ball/brush-off pitch *n.* When a batter crowds the plate, taking away some of the pitcher's target area, a pitcher may decide to throw a pitch close to the batter's body to encourage him to move back. Or, as Jim Brosnan put it, "to let the batter know the pitcher may, occasionally, lose control and to keep him from digging in at the plate with confidence."

It is not to be confused with a beanball, which is intentially thrown *at* the batter. Red Smith once wrote that the brushback pitch, coming after two strikes, was, "in the classical pattern, as rigidly formalized as the minuet." Others are less understanding. "That is what they call a ball thrown 90 miles an hour in the general direction of someone's nose—a 'brushback pitch,' " says columnist Mike Royko. (*Houston Chronicle,* August 6, 1987; CDP)

brushback pitcher *n.* Pitcher who uses the ball to keep the batter away from the plate. When Red Sox manager Billy Herman was asked who was the best brushback pitcher in baseball, he replied, "Freddie Fitzsimmons is my man. He once hit me in the on-deck circle."

However, the distinction is sometimes blurred. Referring to Manager Don Zimmer in *The Wrong Stuff,* Bill Lee writes, "He constantly encouraged his pitchers to loosen batters up with a brushback. One pitcher turned to me and asked, 'How bright can this guy be? Here he is walking about with a plate in his head, the souvenir of a serious beaning, and he's talking about knocking guys down.' "

Brush Rules The basic set of rules for staging the World Series. Established in 1905 by John T. Brush, owner of the New York Giants. Many important features of these rules are still followed today, including the best-of-seven game

Brush Rules. Giants' owner John T. Brush. *National Baseball Library, Cooperstown, N.Y.*

format. The Brush Rules also established the principle of a date after which no new players could be added to a team in anticipation of postseason play.

"B" Team   *n.* A second team created from a team's roster for the purpose of playing an *"A" Team,* composed of the best players at each position. In the major leagues such teams are created to play each other in practice games and are a fixture of spring training, especially during the first week or two. "Outfielder John Morris homered off John Tudor to start the game and later tripled, pacing the St. Louis Cardinals' 'B' team to an 8-1 intrasquad victory Thursday over the squad's veterans." (*The St. Petersburg Times,* March 7, 1986)

bubble-gum ball   *n.* Spitball pitch pioneered by Orlando Peña. He is quoted in Gaylord Perry's *Me and the Spitter,* "I mix tobacco with a piece of gum and chew it good . . . Tastes like sweet tobacco. When you blow a bubble with that mixture, anybody who sees it wants to throw up. I knew guys playing winter ball in Cuba who would put a spot of gum right on the ball. Every time the umpire found it, he would throw out the ball. But you could win a ball game in a tight spot with it."

bubble-gum card   *n.* Genre of premiums to which the baseball card belongs and are sometimes called. For many years, however, the cards have become far more important than the gum, and in reality the gum is now the premium and the cards are the prime product being sold. From *Sports Collectors Digest:* "When someone asked Doug Rader what advice he would give a kid, he suggested that they eat bubble-gum cards. 'Not the gum,' he said, 'but the cards. They have a lot of good information on them.' " (November 26, 1982)

Buccos   BUCS.

bucket hitter   *n.* Batter who often steps back from the pitch; one who "steps in the bucket."

buck-fifty   *n./adj.* Batting average of around .150—as in, "He's batting about a buck-fifty."

Bucs   Nickname for the Pittsburgh Pirates. It is short for Buccaneers which has tended to be used interchangeably with Pirates. In 1986 the club came up with a new slogan: "The New Bucs: We Play Hardball."

budder   *n.* ROOKIE.

buffalo   **1.** *v.* To bluff.
2. *v.* To intimidate.
1ST   1905. (*Sporting Life,* September 2; EJN)

bug   *n./arch.* Baseball enthusiast; fan.
1ST   1907. (*New York Evening Journal,* May 10; EJN)

bugaboo   *n./arch.* A sore arm.
1ST   1935. " 'Bugaboo,' or sore arm necessitates the applications of dry heat." (Ralph H. Barbour, *How to Play Better Baseball;* DS)

bug bruiser   *n./arch.* A hard-hit ground ball.
1ST   1874. (*Chicago Inter Ocean,* July 7; EJN)

bug crawler   *n.* Defined by Carol R. Gast in *Skill on the Diamond* (1953) as, "a ball that when hit has a lot of over-spin, eliminating the usual hop."

bug on the rug   *n.* Originally, a ground ball that eludes one or more fielders and gets into the outfield, usually into one of the corners. The term has been around for decades, but became more popular with the advent of rug-like artificial playing surfaces, after which announcers tended to use the term to describe a ball bouncing on plastic grass. It has been attributed to Bob Prince, the Pittsburgh Pirates announcer, who supposedly introduced it about 1970, but it appears in much earlier listings of baseball slang.

bulb   *n./arch.* The BALL.
1ST   1908. (*New York Evening Journal,* March 5; EJN)

bulge   *n./arch.* A slow curveball.
1ST   1907. (*New York Evening Journal,* April 25; EJN)

bull   *n./arch.* BONER.
1ST   1902. (*Sporting Life,* July 5; EJN)

Bull Durham   See bullpen.

bullet   *n.* A hard-hit line drive.

bullpen/bull-pen/bull pen   **1.** *n.* Where the relief pitchers and warmup catcher are during the game. There are two bullpens, one for each team, which are located outside of fair territory usually either at opposite ends of the outfield or along each foul line. Then appointments differ, but all major league bullpens contain mounds and home plates. The primary purpose of the bullpen is as a place where relief pitchers can prepare and warm up for entry into the game.

Bullpen. Spectators draped over a mammoth Bull Durham sign. The picture was taken on August 9, 1911, at the Old Huntington Avenue Baseball Grounds in Boston when a record crowd of 33,904 came to see Boston play Detroit. *National Baseball Library, Cooperstown, N.Y.*

Joe Garagiola was quoted in the May 16, 1956, *Sporting News* on the subject: "A bull pen is supposed to be a place for warming up pitchers. That's what it is a little bit of the time. Mostly it's a place for eating peanuts, trading insults with the fans, second-guessing the manager and picking all kinds of silly all-star teams, like the all-screwball team or the all-ugly team or the all-stackblowing team."

2. *n.* The relief pitching staff as a group.

3. *n.* Pitchers appearing in relief in a given game. "Bullpen collapses after Ron's seven no-hit innings." (*New York Post* headline after a stunning Mets loss, June 29, 1987)

USE Currently, the bullpen is the realm of high-priced specialists rather than a place for pitchers who simply couldn't pitch for a full game or were out of favor. The degree to which the situation has changed is underscored by the fact that as recently as 1966, Jack McDonald of the *San Francisco Chronicle* was able to define the bullpen as "a group of ex-starting pitchers in the manager's doghouse."

The term is variously written as bullpen, bull pen and bull-pen; however, it is mostly written as one word. (*USA Today, Sports Illustrated,* the *Sporting News,* and the *New York Post* treat it is as one, but the *New York Times* uses two.)

ETY/1ST 1915. The earliest use of bull pen for a place where pitchers warm up was discovered by Edward J. Nichols in the December 1915 *Baseball* magazine. Another early example shows up in the Tamony collection, which includes a line from T. A. Dorgan's "Indoor Sports" in the *San Francisco Call and Post* for June 7, 1917: "I been out here in the bull pen all season warming up—I ain't been in one game yet."

The origin of this term has long been debated in baseball. In 1967, an article by Joseph Durso of the *New York Times* provided two interesting theories. Written during spring training (March 10), the piece first quoted long-time baseball man Casey Stengel, then the manager of the New York Mets: "You could look it up and get 80 different answers, but we use to have pitchers who could pitch 50 or 60 games a year and the extra pitchers would just sit around shooting the bull, and no manager wanted all that gabbing on the bench. So he put them in this kind of pen in the outfield to warm up, it looked like a place to keep cows or bulls." Stengel's quote was followed by this contrasting opinion from Johnny Murphy, who had spent more than a dozen years in the bullpen for the Yankees. "It came from Bull Durham tobacco, I was always told. All the ball parks had advertising signs on the outfield fences and Bull Durham was always near the spot where the relief pitchers warmed up."

Murphy's explanation has been given various twists. Michael Gartner in his nationally syndicated column on language (*Newsday,* April 27, 1986) asserts that the bullpen/Bull Durham connection originated in the days when all games were day games and when ". . . pitchers warming up for relief duty often chose to limber up in the shade of those big signs."

In the early days of the 20th century the Bull Durham name was, indeed, closely associated with the ballpark. In fact, by 1910, the big bull-shaped signs were on the outfield fence of almost every park in the country. As part of its advertising campaign, Bull Durham drew minor and major league attention to the 40-foot-long, 25-foot-high signs by offering a reward to any batter who could hit a ball off one. Quoting from the 1911 edition of *The 'Bull' Durham Base Ball Guide:* "Any player who hits the bull with a fairly-batted fly ball, during a regular scheduled league game on any of the grounds where these 'Bull' Durham signs are located on the field will receive $50.00 in cash." In addition, any player hitting home run in a park with a bull on the fence got a carton containing 72 packs of the tobacco.

In 1909, the first year of the hit-the-bull contest, there were 50 signs in place and 14 players won. The next year, with nearly 150 Bull Durham signs being hit 85 times, Blackwell's Durham Tobacco Company gave out $4,250 in cash and more than 10,000 pounds of tobacco. According to the *'Bull' Durham Base Ball Guide,* the sign promotion scheme was expanded because "interest in the National Game was then waning in various parts of the country" and this was seen as a way to stimulate interest, which it apparently did.

While there is significant merit to the Bull Durham theory—particularly because the term hadn't been used in baseball until after the signs were in place—the term *bull pen* had long been used in the United States to denote either a log enclosure for holding cattle or a holding area for prisoners. This concept of the bull pen as an enclosure may have strongly influenced and

helped corroborate the notion of the bull pen as an enclosure for pitchers, perhaps giving an assist to the influence of Bull Durham. In fact, it was in use in baseball as early as 1877 for an area in foul territory beyond first and third bases where spectators could stand penned in like bulls. O.P. Caylor wrote in the *Cincinnati Enquirer* on May 7, 1877, "The bull pen at the Cincinnati grounds with its 'three-for-a-quarter' crowd has lost its usefulness." (Quoted by Lee Allen in the *Sporting News* for May 16, 1956; PT) Peter Tamony theorized that this use of the term came from the Civil War when soldiers on both sides used the term "bull pen" for roped-off corrals where prisoners of war were herded like cattle. Tamony was also of the opinion that the Bull Durham signs reinforced and redefined the term bull pen in baseball.

Early bull pens for pitchers were almost always placed along the outfield foul lines (as some still are), which would suggest how this term developed.

One other theory which is published from time to time likens the relief pitchers to the reserve bulls in bullfighting who are penned near the arena should the starting bull be found to be lacking. There is a certain neatness to this idea, but it would appear to be pure conjecture.

Incidentally, the first area set aside for major league relief pitchers was probably at the Polo Grounds in 1905.

EXT   The term has a number of specialized meanings for defined spaces and enclosures outside of baseball, which may or may not have been inspired by the baseball bullpen. These include the barracks in a lumber camp, a used car lot, cashier's cages in banks, the box in some courtrooms where defendants sit during trials, room for railroad crewmen, work areas in large companies, the sale ring at a horse auction, a smoking area for oil refinery workers, the penalty box in ice hockey, the area in a jazz club where a youngster can pay to sit without being bothered by a waiter, an area where prisoners are kept during a riot, an enclosure for prostitutes, and a flop house for men only.

bullpen ace   *n.* Team's best relief pitcher; one who can "close" games.

bullpen boss   *n.* BULLPEN COACH. "Birds' bullpen boss Elrod Hendricks claims his boys are into each pitch. But every so often he jolts them with his favorite pastime, a pop quiz on the count." (*The Washington Weekly*, "Bullpen Buddies," June 21, 1985)

bullpen coach *n.* Pitching coach who spends all or most of his time in the team's bullpen advising and preparing the relief pitchers. Most major league teams have such a coach.

bump *v.* To hit a ball squarely; as in, "He really bumped the ball." Not nearly as common today as it was when reported in *American Speech* in 1927.
1ST 1908. (*Brooklyn Daily Eagle*, May 23; EJN)

bumps *n./arch.* As defined when the term was in vogue by Hugh S. Fullerton in his 1912 "Baseball Primer": "Overwhelming defeats. A pitcher gets his 'bumps' when his delivery is hit hard, a team 'gets its bumps' when it is badly beaten. Synonymous with 'Gets his,' 'Gets his trimmings,' 'takes his beatings.' "
1ST 1910 (*Baseball* magazine, September; EJN)

Bums A nickname for the old Brooklyn Dodgers, more commonly *Dem Bums*.

bunched hits *n.* A cluster of safe hits that come in one inning.
1ST 1880. (*New York Herald*, July 23; EJN)

bungle **1.** *n.* An error or misplay.
2. *v.* To make an error.
1ST 1898. (*New York Tribune*, May 29; EJN)

bunt **1.** *n.* A batted ball that is tapped softly into the infield. The purpose of a bunt is to advance a base runner (sacrifice bunt) or get the batter to first base on the element of surprise. Its success depends to a large degree on the placement of the ball on the infield. An ideal bunt is one that proves difficult for infielders to get hold of. The bunt is performed as the batter loosens his grip, flexes his knees, and squares around to face the pitcher. The hands are separated along the handle of the bat and it is presented as if the batter wants the pitcher to read the bat label. The bat is not swung at the ball, rather the ball is tapped with the bat.
ETY Credit for introducing the bunt goes to Dickey Pearce of the original Brooklyn Atlantics in 1866, but the practice did not become common until after 1876 when Tim Murnane of the Boston National League Team started "butting" the ball with a special flat-sided bat. In *A Baseball Album* Gerald Secor Couzens adds, "The bunt was referred to as a freak play in

Bunt. Richard D. Pearce, father of the bunt. *National Baseball Library, Cooperstown, N.Y.*

accounts of 1888 and did not take on its importance in game strategy until much later." This is confirmed in a profile of Pearce written in 1911, three years after his death. "It was not known as a bunt at that time and Dickey himself had no idea that he was making baseball history." (Article by Sam Crane, *New York Journal*, December 20, 1911)
2. *v.* To execute a bunt or bunt play.
1ST 1891. (Glossary to *Baseball*, by Knowles and Morton; EJN)
ETY The word itself is a nasalized variation or corruption of the term butt which comes from the batter butting at the ball with his bat in the manner of a goat butting. Columnist Michael Gartner has suggested the original butt ". . . quickly became known as a *bunt*, probably because somebody misheard the word in Brooklyn." (*Newsday*, April 27, 1986) But *Webster's Ninth New Collegiate Dictionary* says that bunt as an alternative term for butt can be dated back to 1582.

The term itself may have come into baseball by rail. In railroading to bunt was used to describe the shoving of a car onto a side track or—and this may be even more to the point—the nudging of an uncoupled freight car to get it moving.
USE Knowing what a bunt is has long been a test of whether one knows anything about baseball. A character in a 1952 *Boy's Life* story is ridiculed for not knowing "a bunt from a Buffalo" and a story by Jerome Beatty in the March

1917 *McClure's* magazine contains the following incident:

> An' another thing I asks him. I used to be the greatest sacrifice hitter in baseball. So I asks him. "Young man, can you bunt?" "Mister Ryan," says he,—Jake fairly yelled his protest against such disgusting incompetence—"Mister Ryan, I don't like to brag about myself, but I can bunt farther than any other man on the team!" Them's his very words! Can you beat it?

bunt and run   **1.** *n./arch.* SQUEEZE BUNT. **2.** *v.* To effect a SQUEEZE BUNT.

bunting   *n./arch.* The pennant itself. **1ST**   1902. (*Sporting Life*, September 20; EJN)

burglar   **1.** *n.* Quick-thinking player who takes advantage of the *breaks;* one who is said to "steal" opportunities. **2.** *n.* A *base stealer.*

burn a hole/burn a hole in the mitt   *v.* To pitch or throw a ball with great velocity. **1ST**   1907. (*Dick Merriwell's Magnetism;* EJN)

burn ball   *n.* Variant of baseball in which a base runner can be put out—or burned—by being hit with a ball. **1ST**   1888. "The boys used to play 'burn ball,' if you were hit by the ball before reaching the base, you were out." (M. J. Kelly, *Play Ball;* DS) **ETY**   The burn in burn ball is an overt reference to the fact that an object of the game was to inflict pain and leave bruises.

burn off   *v.* To run close behind another base runner thereby forcing—or burning—your teammate to advance or be put out.

burn up the circuit   *v.* To win routinely and decisively on the road.

The term is applied to teams, pitching staffs, individual pitchers and, on rare occasions, to dominant batters (such as one with a string of game winning RBI).

Busch Memorial Stadium   In St. Louis, Missouri, the home grounds of the National League St. Louis Cardinals since 1966. Before moving to its present downtown location, the Cardinals had played at Sportsman's Park since 1920. In the period 1953 to 1966, Sportsman's Park was known as Busch Stadium. Named by and for the Busch family and the owners of the team of Anheuser-Busch, the large, St. Louis-based brewery.

bush   **1.** *adj.* Unprofessional, unsportsman-like, amateurish. From bush league, it is used to refer to both crude play on the field and poor behavior off the field. It can be applied at any level of the game; for instance, it is bush to talk too much on the field, wear your uniform incorrectly, show too much enthusiasm or steal a base when your team is way ahead. **USE**   Scornful to the point that this is one of the labels that a player at any level of play strives to avoid. **2.** *n.* Exile; a low rung of the minor leagues at the end of a baseball career. "The 'bush' with its sadness of cheap hotels, rancid food, and fetid dressing-rooms; of inferior craftsmanship and memories of gone glories." (*The Book of Baseball,* published by P. F. Collier and Son, 1911; PT) **1ST**   1905. (*Sporting Life*, September 2; EJN)

bushie   **1.** *n.* Busher. **2.** *adj.* Bush/Bush League. **EXT**   Amateurish or inferior, such as an actor who is accused of a bush performance.

bushel basket   *n.* A large glove.

busher   *n.* A ROOKIE, just up from the bush leagues. "Jerome Dean reported to Joe Schultz who managed Houston that season. 'What's your name, busher?' asked Schultz. 'Just call me Dizzy,' replied Dean." (Undated player bio for Dizzy Dean put out by the St. Louis Cardinals.)

The term was given a boost with the publication of Ring Lardner's novel *You Know Me Al* (1916), which is the tale of Jack Keefe. The word busher is key to the book (Keefe has a fight with one of his girlfriends because he thinks she called him one), and each of the six chapters has the word in its title ("A Busher's Letter Home," "The Busher Comes Back," "The Busher's Honeymoon," etc.). **1ST**   1909. "In the major leagues there are three classes of players designated in the picturesque language of the game as 'bushers,' 'bone-heads' and 'topnotchers.' The 'busher' is the freshman, inexperienced but promising and derives its name from the fact that he recently graduated from the 'bush' or minor league." (Hugh S. Fullerton, "Winning Baseball Pennants," *Collier's*, September 11, 1909) **2.** *n.* A player in the bush leagues.

bushes   *n.* Place outside the majors; wherever the grass grows tall.

The opposite of bush league is big league both inside and outside baseball.

bush league   1. *n.* Lesser minor league teams in small cities or towns, such as when a player has slipped from "the big leagues to the bush" or one who has "just come up from the bush league."
ETY   From the nickname for the lower levels of the minor leagues, which were traditionally typified as out where the bushes grow, where the land has not been cleared.
2. *adj.* BUSH
1ST   1908. (*Baseball* magazine, July; EJN)
EXT   Having to do with a group or class of things that is at best mediocre, but more likely inferior.

bush leaguer   BUSHER.
1ST   1906. (*Sporting Life*, February 10; EJN)

bushness   *adj.* Inexperience. " 'Dobie, I hate to bug your ointment,' said Tommy, 'but there is a distinct chance your bushness is showing.' " (*Changing Pitches* by Steve Kluger; CDP)

businessman's special   *n.* A weekday game played in the mid to late afternoon; it caters to a salaried white-collar clientele that, presumably, can get out of work for a few hours. As day games have become less common there are fewer and fewer of these games every year. St. Louis Cardinal manager Whitey Herzog was quoted in the *Village Voice* for September 2, 1986, saying that Club reliever Lee Smith had the biggest advantage in baseball because he gets to pitch "those damn three o'clock businessman specials" at Wrigley Field. He added, "It's hard enough to hit that guy in the daylight, much less the twilight."

bussie/bussy   *n.* Player's nickname for the team bus driver. This term was popular among major leaguers before teams started traveling by plane. Today the term is still used by players during spring training and in the minor leagues where bus travel is still common. According to an item in *Comedians of Baseball,* the ritualistic joke is to ask the bussie if the regular driver is off. In *Ball Four*, Jim Bouton says that the way you tell a driver that he is going too slowly is to call out, "Hey, bussy, there's a dog pissing on your rear wheel."

The term has stayed alive through new incarnations. In 1963 Leonard Shecter reported in an article on baseball slang: "Once this meant simply bus driver. But times change and now it's applied to those in charge of vehicles of any sort, from bus driver to pilots of jet aircraft." Tim Horgan added in a 1964 *Baseball Digest* article that the term also applied to "the park employee who drives the relief pitcher in from the bullpen."

In one odd case the bussie label has been used as a nickname. Devon White picked it up in the minors when he tried to turn on the air conditioning in a hot bus while waiting for the driver to show up. White accidentally got the bus rolling and it ran through a fence. The label stuck with him when he came up to the majors as a California Angel in 1987.

bust the batter inside   *v.* To throw a pitch close to the batter's body in an effort to move the batter away from home plate.

butcher   *n.* A bad defensive player; one who has a hard time holding onto the ball.

butcher boy stroke   *n.* Descriptive term coined by Casey Stengel for a batter's downward chopping swing to ensure a high-bounding groundball. In situations calling for a ground ball, he told his players to use the butcher boy and likened the motion to that which a boy in butcher shop would use when chopping meat.
1ST   1959. " 'I know what Casey's telling him,' Mr. Rizzuto said. 'He's telling him, "Don't swing hard now. Just butcher-boy the ball. Just butcher-boy it." ' " (John Lardner, *The New Yorker*, July 18; PT)
SEE   *Baltimore chop.*

buttercup/buttercup hitter   *n./arch.* Batter without power; a weak hitter.
1ST   1937. (*The Sporting News Record Book;* EJN)

butterfinger   *adj.* Clumsy, inept, error-prone. "The ancient 'butterfinger' plague is making itself a factor in the major league pennant races." (Howard Sigmand in the *San Francisco Call & Bulletin,* August 25, 1952)

butterfingers/butter fingers   *n.* Derogatory term for a player who drops the ball.
1ST   1888.
> The buttercups I gather
> While the batsman waits and lingers,
> And now you know the reason
> Why they call em 'butter-fingers.'

(Thomas W. Lawson, *The Krank: His Language and What It Means*) As late as 1927 *American Speech* (April) it was reported as a term peculiar to baseball rather than to the language at large.

ETY   Butter-fingered is cited as early as 1615 in *Slang and Its Analogues* for a person who is likely to let things drop. It is clearly old English slang that appears to have entered both cricket and baseball.

EXT   This term, which saw its early American popular use in baseball, has since been used for anyone who is clumsy and drops things.

butterfly   *n./arch.*   Term for KNUCKLE-BALL because of its similarly erratic flight.

1ST   1937. More common in the earlier days of this century; for example, it first shows up in a list of players' terms in the 1937 edition of *The Sporting News Record Book,* but is rare after about 1950.

buzzer   *n.* Fastball that asserts itself by the noise it makes as it passes a batter's ear. A hummer, but presumably louder.

"bye-bye baby"   Trademark home run call of New York/San Francisco Giants broadcaster Russ Hodges.

C

C The fifth level of minor league baseball, following B.

Cactus League *n.* Nickname for the American and National League teams that conduct spring training in the Southwest, as opposed to the *grapefruit league,* which comprises teams training in Florida.

Cactus clubs are the Angels, Cubs, Indians, Brewers, A's, Padres, Giants and Mariners. At present all the teams that train in the Cactus League work out of Arizona, with the exception of the California Angels who prepare for the season in Palm Springs, California.
ETY The term comes from the cacti that are common to this area of the United States.

caddie *n.* A reserve player who generally is used as a substitute in the late innings of a game. "As a rule," wrote Jim Brosnan in *The Long Season,* "the 'caddie' is younger, quicker, but has less experience and makes less money than the player for whom he is substituted."

Cactus League. First spring meeting of the 1966 Indians with Manager Joe Adcock, at Corbett Field in Tucson. *Courtesy of the Cleveland Indians*

Cadillac trot *n.* Easy jog around the bases made by high-salaried sluggers, often staged to show up high-priced pitchers and opponents. During the 1986 National League Playoff Games on CBS radio, Johnny Bench said that it should now be called "the Mercedes trot."

An interesting variation on this was collected by Peter Tamony who noted that, during a June 1966 interview of John Roseboro by broadcaster Vin Scully, Roseboro, who thought he had hit a home run during the game, said, "I was just Cadillac-ing along . . ." The ball did not go out of the park and Roseboro should not have been trotting around the bases.
ETY This certainly can be traced to a famous line uttered by Hall of Famer Ralph Kiner in the 1950s: "Hitters of homeruns drive Cadillacs, singles hitters jalopies." On another occasion he told a reporter that he never choked up on the bat because the Cadillacs were down at the end of the bat.

cage **1.** *n.* Short for the movable BATTING CAGE used in batting practice.
1ST 1910 (*Baseball* magazine, September; EJN)
2. *n.* Catcher's mask.
SEE *bird cage.*
1ST 1908 (*Baseball* magazine, July; EJN)

cake and coffee *n.* See coffee and cake.

cakewalk *n.* An easy, lopsided victory.
ETY From the dances and promenades (or walks) that were once staged as contests. Popular among 19th-century black Americans, the couple who won the contest often got a cake as their prize, hence the name. The idea of being able to win with a set of fancy steps no doubt conveyed the idea of an easy win to baseball.

California Angels Name of the American League's Eastern Division franchise in Anaheim, California. Joining the American League as an expansion team in 1961, the team, then based in Los Angeles, took its name from the Pacific Coast League's Los Angeles Angels. The name is derived from Los Angeles, Spanish for "the angels." When the team moved to Anaheim in 1966, the name of the city was replaced by that of the state. After the Minnesota Twins, the Angels were the second team to take a state name. The name allows some nice word play—calling the GM the "Archangel" for instance.

call **1.** *n.* An umpire's stated or signaled ruling on a pitch (ball, strike, balk, foul ball or hit batsman) or a play (safe or out).
2. *v.* To make an umpiring decision.
3. *n.* The catcher's signal for a specific pitch.
4. *n.* The manager's decision on a starting pitcher or his signal to the bullpen for a relief pitcher or for a relief pitcher to begin warming up.

called ball *n./arch.* A term for a pitched ball delivered outside the strike zone, which is not swung at and is deemed to be a ball by the umpire; but *not* a called strike.

called game *n.* A game that has been terminated by the home plate umpire. Games are most commonly called for rain, but they have also been called for fog, wind, sleet, snow and darkness. In the American League, games can be called for going past the curfew time. The rulebook states: "All night games must be called at 1 a.m. local time. But if an inning is started prior to 1 a.m. city [local] time, it can be completed."

If a game is called before the trailing team has batted in five innings, the game is replayed from the beginning. If the losing team has had its five innings and the game is called, it is recorded as a "shortened game."
1ST 1866. (Henry Chadwick, *Base Ball Player's Book of Reference;* EJN)

called shot *n.* A hit whose destination is predicted in advance; however, it is usually used to describe *the* called shot, which was allegedly made by Babe Ruth in 1932. When Ruth died in 1948 the story of the "called shot" appeared in almost every newspaper in America and some even made it the central anecdote of his life. *The Evening Star* of Washington, D.C., for August 17, 1948, headlined a huge 98-paragraph article on the Babe, "Ruth Climaxed Fabulous Career by Calling Shot on Homer in '32." The article opened:

As long as baseball is played, the memory will live of a bulbous man on matchstick legs pointing in eloquent gesture to Wrigley Field's faraway centerfield barrier, the jibes of 50,000 Chicago fans searing his ears.

There were two strikes on George Her-

man "Babe" Ruth that World Series day of October 1, 1932, like there had been two strikes on him many times during his career. The score was 4 to 4 in the fifth inning and Ruth's Yankees were gunning for their third straight win.

Two called strikes and there stood baseball's greatest hitter in the sunset of his career, majestically drawing a bead on a spot 400 feet away. Contemptuously, the Babe held up two fingers, then pointed to the centerfield flagpole.

Charlie Root pitched. He shouldn't have done it. Like a projectile the ball left the Ruthian bat to scream on a line over the right centerfield wall.

Depending on the source the story is likely to be embellished with any of a number of extra details, such as these two:
—That one of those who witnessed the called shot was Franklin Delano Roosevelt, who would be elected President a month later.
—That Ruth pointed to the sky with one finger after the first strike, and with two fingers after the second; as if to show the assembled multitude that a singular event was taking place.

The issue of whether Ruth actually called his shot is still being argued. When old-timer Bill Wambsganss, who played between 1914 and 1926, was interviewed by *Sports Collectors Digest*

No. 4---Ruth Calls His Shot

Called shot. Cartoon in the old *Washington Star,* shortly after the Babe's death, depicting Ruth's called shot. *Courtesy of the Martin Luther King Library, Washington, D.C.*

in 1983, he was asked about Joe Sewell (who played between 1920 and 1932 and was in a Yankee uniform when the incident occurred). His answer, "Sewell is fine. He and Riggs Stephenson are still in Alabama fighting over whether Babe Ruth called his shot in 1932." (June 24)

When the debate was sparked again in the letters columns of the Washington *Post* during the summer of 1988, an Alexandria, Virginia man wrote to point out that he seemed to be one of the few survivors of the year 1932 who was not present at Wrigley Field that day. He then put his tongue firmly in cheek and concluded, "I find it most interesting, however, that while the capacity of Wrigley Field is 39,008, to this date (by my count) 55,603 living witnesses from the Washington area alone who have written to The Post to verify that the Babe did in fact predict his blast." (September 9, 1988.)

called strike *n.* A pitch that a batter does not swing at, but which is judged to have passed through the strike zone by the home plate umpire.

call for the ball *v.* To yell claim to a ball to prevent a misplay or collision. When two players are headed for the same hit ball, one or the other, usually the one in the best position, takes command and claims it.

call time *v.* To create a temporary cessation of play at the command of the umpire; to take time out.

call up *v.* To bring a player up from a minor league club during the season to the majors because the parent team needs his services.

camp *n.* Spring training home for a given team. News from the grapefruit and cactus leagues is often reported in the newspapers under the heading "Around the camps" or "News from the camps."

camp under it *v.* To set up and wait for a pop fly or high bouncing ball to come down.

can **1.** *v.* To be removed; to be taken out of service by an umpire, manager etc.
2. *v.* To be released or discharged from the team.
1ST 1908. (*New York Evening Journal*, May 30; EJN)

Candlestick Park Home of the National League San Francisco Giants since 1960. Candlestick Point, which overlooks the park, is named for the rocks and trees that poke up from the surrounding area like giant candles. Known for its inhospitable winds and chilliness. "Somebody once told me that putting a dome on Candlestick would be like putting lipstick on a pig," was Mets broadcaster Fran Healy's reaction to the question of whether a dome would improve things.

cannon *n.* A strong throwing arm. "You talk about a cannon; you could've had a 30:30 and you wouldn't have gotten him," Padre announcer Jerry Coleman quoted on the speed of a runner in the December 1983 *Baseball Digest*.

cannon ball *n.* Ball pitched or thrown with great velocity.
1ST 1891. (*Chicago Herald*, May 7; EJN)

cannon's mouth *n.* Said of an infielder's location when positioned close up to the batter during a probable bunt situation. Implied is the danger that batter may unexpectedly take a full swing and imperil the fielder with a hard-hit ball.

can of corn/can o'corn *n.* An easily caught fly ball; a high fly ball that allows a defensive player time to stand under the ball and catch it easily.
ETY The phrase has long been assumed to have come from the old time grocery store where the grocer used a pole or a mechanical grabber to tip an item, such as a can of corn, off a high shelf and let it tumble into his hands or his apron, which was held out in front like a fire net.

An alternate theory is suggested in Mike Whiteford's *How to Talk Baseball*, in which he quotes Pittsburgh Pirates announcer Bob Prince who said, "It's as easy as taking corn out of a can." Still another, suggested by Burt Dunne in the *Folger's Dictionary of Baseball*, is that the "can of corn" ball is hit with a "kerplunk" sound—presumably that of a can being hit with a stick.

Peter Tamony developed a separate theory, which was published in the form of a letter appearing in Bucky Walter's "Mail Bag" of August 24, 1977, in the *San Francisco Examiner*. " 'Can of corn' no doubt developed out of the complex of usage surrounding 'cornball,' a confection made of pop corn and molasses, munched by the young for over a century.

Popped corn flies wildly, of course, making a handy word association with a light popup to the outfield."

Tamony, incidentally, determined that the term was in use in the early to mid-1920s, based on a series of interviews in 1953 with semi-professional players.

USE From time to time, this is deemed to be an archaic bit of slang (see Introduction, p. xiv) but it is still used by sportscasters with regularity. "That's a can of corn for Shelby." (ABC Monday Night Baseball, June 8, 1986, New York Yankees vs. Baltimore Orioles) Players may see it as more of a verbal antique. The term was brought up in an article on baseball slang in the *St. Petersburgh Times* for March 5, 1987. "That's ancient history," laughed New York Mets catcher Gary Carter, "Now we say 'can of rice and beans,' he added with a wink."

EXT 1. *n.* An easy accomplishment.

2. *n. can of corn decision.* A phrase that underscores the degree to which a bit of baseball slang can work its way into other realms. It refers to a court decision in San Francisco that made the sponsor of a semi-professional baseball team responsible for an injury to a bystander. In the case, a player for a team sponsored by the Double Play Tavern dropped an easily catchable fly ball (i.e., a can of corn) with two out and the bases loaded in the bottom of the ninth inning during a scoreless tie. The player who had dropped the ball was so angry that he threw it across the street, accidentally hitting a woman at a gas station. The woman won the case. (Reported in full under the headline, "Can of Corn Decision," in the May 12, 1959, *San Francisco News;* PT)

cantaloupe *n.* A pitched ball that looks big to the batter; e.g., "How can you miss that cantaloupe that he throws?"

"can't anyone here play this game?" Lament and backhanded rallying cry first uttered by Casey Stengel after taking over as manager of the inept 1962 New York Mets.

can't catch cold *arch.* Said of a poor defensive player, who is unable to catch anything from a baseball to a common cold.
1ST 1915. (*Baseball* magazine, December; EJN)

can't hit a balloon *arch.* Said of a poor batter.
1ST 1908. (*Baseball* magazine, September; EJN)

can't-miss *adj.* A term describing young players who appear headed for baseball success whether it be to the majors or for stardom.

"In 1983, that heaviest of burdens—'can't miss' status—was conferred upon a dozen or so major-league rookies." (Bruce Lowitt in the *St. Petersburgh Times*, March 30, 1988)

canto *n./arch.* INNING. Like *stanza*, it is a borrowing of the term for a division in poetry to connote the divisions of a baseball game.
1ST 1920. (*New York Times*, October 4; EJN)

can't pitch hay *v./arch.* Said of an ineffective pitcher.
1ST 1915. (*Baseball* magazine, December; EJN)

cap *n.* The visored hat that is a standard element of players' uniforms at all levels of baseball. It is usually decorated with the team's initials or insignia.

captain *n.* An honorary title bestowed on a player acknowledging leadership. In both the Major and Minor Leagues, such appointments are rare: "First baseman Eddie Murray, clearly the most respected man on the Orioles, was named the first captain in the history of the franchise by manager Earl Weaver yesterday during a team meeting." (*The Baltimore Sun*, February 28, 1986)

Sometimes, but not always, the team captain will wear a small letter "c" on his uniform sleeve.

cap-tipper *n./arch.* Term for a show-off in the 1930s; a showboat.

cardboards *n./arch.* Admission tickets to a baseball game.
1ST 1912. (*New York Tribune*, September 26; EJN)

Cards Long-established nickname for the St. Louis Cardinals.

career year *n.* Term for what is, or seems like it will be, the best season of a player's career.

caress the ball/caress the horsehide *v./ arch.* To hit the ball.
1ST 1912 (*New York Tribune*, Sept. 7; EJN)

carnage *n.* A clobbering in which many runs are given up.

carom/carom shot *n.* A batted ball that bounces or ricochets off a wall or fence in the manner of a carom shot in billiards.

1ST   1908. (*Spalding's Official Base Ball Guide;* EJN)

carpet   *n.* The infield playing surface, whether it be real or artificial grass. It has been recently reported (in Mike Whitford's book, for example)—that this term applies only to synthetic surfaces, but it shows up in print for the natural surface as early as:
1ST   1908. (*New York Evening Journal,* August 21; EJN)

carry   *v.* The way a batted ball travels away from home plate. It is often used in the context of atmospheric factors like humidity, fog or wind. For instance, the question of whether the presence of fog affected the ability of the ball to carry was raised by sportscasters during the final game of the 1986 World Series. (Back to back hits by the Red Sox had Vin Scully conclude that the fog was not a factor.)

carry a club/carry a team/carry the club   *v.* To be able to singlehandedly hit and score enough to keep a team in contention. " 'When Jack Clark is hot,' the word was then, 'he can carry a club for three or four weeks at a time.' " (Kevin Horrigan in the *St. Louis Post-Dispatch,* May 29, 1987)

carry a safe   *v./arch.* To run slowly; to run as if weighed down by a heavy object.

carry the mail   *v./arch.* To run swiftly. The phrase appears in Herbert Simons' 1943 *Baseball* magazine article ("Here's Some More Slang"): "He is a fellow who can 'carry the mail,' or get from here to there in a hurry, and frequently it is said he 'can high tail it' or is a 'deer.' "
1ST   1937. (New York *Daily News,* February 14; EJN)

carve nicks in the weather   *v./arch.* As a batter, to swing at pitches without making contact.
1ST   1912. (*American* magazine, June; EJN)

Casey   *n.* A player who strikes out at the crucial moment in a game; one who fails in the manner of Casey, the figure in Ernest L. Thayer's *Casey at the Bat.* Usually stated as "doing a Casey" or "pulling a Casey," it recalls the last stanza of the poem:

> Oh! Somewhere in this favored land the sun is shining bright;
> The band is playing somewhere, and somewhere hearts are light.

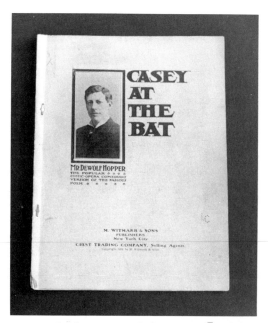

Casey at the bat. Copy of the original pamphlet version of "Casey at the Bat." Such was the popularity of the man who recited the poem that his name and picture appeared on the cover, but the man who wrote it is not even mentioned. *Public Information Office, the Library of Congress*

> And somewhere men are laughing, and somewhere children shout;
> But there is no joy in Mudville—mighty Casey had struck out.

Casey act   *n.* STRIKE OUT; one occurring at an especially crucial moment in a game and in the manner of "Casey at the Bat."
1ST   1912. (*New York Tribune,* October 15; EJN)

"Casey at the Bat"   Poem by Ernest L. Thayer that gives epic quality to a single strikeout. More than 100 years old, the work has established itself as baseball's most popular and enduring literary adjunct. It was termed "the nation's best known piece of comic verse" in Martin Gardner's *Annotated Casey at the Bat* (a book that contains, among other things, 27 variations and updates in the style of the original). Though the poem first appeared in the June 3, 1888 issue of the *San Francisco Examiner,* it attracted little attention until it was recited by a Shakespearian actor named DeWolf Hopper later the same year. Hopper went on to recite the poem more than 10,000 times during his lifetime.

Casey at the bat. Bust made in 1939 of DeWolf Hopper, the man who made Casey famous; in the possession of the Baseball Hall of Fame. *National Baseball Library, Cooperstown, N.Y.*

cashew *n.* An undisciplined, zany non-conformist; a "nutty" guy. "I felt at home with the Phillies, when I reported to camp at Clearwater in March. The roster included such cashews as Richie Allen, who liked everything about a ball park except getting there . . ." (Bob Uecker, *Catcher in the Wry;* CDP)

castoff *n.* A player who has been let go or dismissed by a team. Occasionally, a castoff from one team goes on to become successful with another.
1ST 1900. (*New York Tribune,* July 4; EJN)

casualty pass *n./arch.* Base on balls.
1ST 1922 (*Baseball Cyclopedia;* EJN)
ETY This is almost certainly a reference to the pass given to a wounded soldier to allow him to retreat from the front lines to seek medical attention.

cat *n.* A great fielding pitcher; one with feline agility.

cat/catball *n.* A simple game of ball, called, according to the number of batters available, *one old cat, two old cat* etc.
SEE *old-cat.*

catbird seat *n.* A position of control and mastery; to be sitting pretty and in control of the situation, often stated as sitting in the catbird seat. Popularized by Brooklyn Dodger announcer Red Barber, who would use it, for example, to describe a batter with a count of three balls and no strikes. The term is often used to describe a team's first place position in the standings. A *Sporting News* headline from October 5, 1987 announced, "Twins, Giants in Catbird Seat" as those two teams were on the verge of clinching playoff berths.
ETY The term has long been attributed to Red Barber. Though he denies having created the term, he does explain how he once "bought" it. In his 1968 biography *Rhubarb in the Catbird Seat,* Barber tells the story of how, while playing penny ante poker in Cincinnati with friends, he sat for hours unable to win a hand. Then he relates, "Finally, during a round of seven-card stud, I decided I was going to force the issue. I raised on the first bet, and I raised again on every card. At the end, when the showdown came, it was between a fellow named Frank Cope and me. Frank turned over his hold cards, showed a pair of aces, and won the pot. He said, 'Thank you, Red. I had those aces from the start. I was sitting in the catbird seat.' I didn't have to be told the meaning. And I had paid for it. It was mine."

One question that has never been satisfactorily answered is why the catbird? "The catbird commands a good view from its lofty perch, but then, so do many birds," says James Rogers in *The Dictionary of Cliches.* "Why the catbird's vantage point was signaled out is beyond explaining."
EXT The term is used to describe anyone finding themselves in an advantageous situation. "Peres in the Catbird Seat," is a headline in the September 29, 1986, *Newsweek,* which refers to Israeli Foreign Minister Shimon Peres.

The phrase eventually became so popular that James Thurber wrote a short story for *The New Yorker* (which also appears in a collection of stories called *The Thurber Carnival*) entitled "The Catbird Seat." In the story a mild-mannered chap is driven to distraction by a woman in his office who asks questions in the colorful, metaphoric Barber manner: "Are you tearing up the pea patch?" "Are you hollering down the rain barrel?" "Are you sitting in the catbird seat?" "Are you lifting the oxcart out of the ditch?" Another employee must explain that the woman, named Ulgine Barrows, is a Dodger fan who has picked up these Barberisms from the radio.

catch   **1.** *v.* To retrieve and control a thrown or batted ball, usually with the aid of a glove or mitt. Most commonly applied to a ball that has not hit the ground.
1ST   1883. (*Sporting Life,* April 22; EJN)
2. *v.* To play the position of catcher.
3. *n.* A batted ball judged to have been fielded and controlled by a player before it hits the ground.
1ST   1862. (*New York Sunday Mercury,* June 29; EJN)
4. *n.* Name for the practice of two or more people throwing a ball back and forth.

Catch, The   The over-the-shoulder catch in deep center field at the Polo Grounds made by Willie Mays of the New York Giants. The play occurred in the 8th inning of the first game of the 1954 World Series off a hit by Cleveland Indians' first baseman Vic Wertz. A special insert on the 1981 World Series, which appeared in *Time,* carried this line, "When baseball heads into the 22nd century, they'll still be talking about The Catch . . ."

catcher   *n.* The player behind home plate to whose mitt the pitcher aims the ball.

The role of the catcher is relatively complex and extends far beyond being a target for and receiver of pitched balls. Among other things, the catcher orders (calls) the pitches to be thrown through the use of signals, backs up throws to first base, attempt to field pop fouls, sets defensive alignments and attempts to throw out would-be base stealers.
1ST   1854. (Knickerbocker Rules; EJN)

catcher's balk   *n.* Correct but rarely used term for interference with the batter by the catcher. See *catcher's interference.*

catcher's box   *n.* A four-by-six-foot rectangular area found at the rear edge of the batter's box in which the catcher must remain until the pitch is delivered.

catcher's equipment   *n.* Protective gear worn by the catcher consisting of a catcher's mask, mitt, chest protector and shin guards. The equipment is designed to protect the catcher from being injured by the baseball (and to a much lesser extent, the bat).

In the early days of the game there were catchers who chose to work without this equipment. In the display case with the early equipment at the Baseball Hall of Fame, there is a poem by one George Ellard, a nonprofessional catcher, which contains these lines:

We used no mattress on our hands,
No cage upon our face;
We stood right up and caught the ball,
With courage and with grace.

catcher's interference   *n.* An action in which the catcher hinders the batter or base runner. Examples: pushing the batter, touching the batter's bat, running in front of the batter to catch a pitched ball or blocking home plate without holding the ball. In cases involving the batter, the batter is awarded first base and the catcher is charged with an error. In such cases the batter is not charged with an official at bat. Should this be called when a base runner is attempting to steal base, he is awarded that base.

catcher's mask   *n.* A padded metal grate that protects the catcher's face from the baseball. Invented by Fred Winthrop Thayer, a Harvard coach and player of the 1870s, the mask was first worn by a Harvard catcher named James Alexander Tyng. Tyng first used it in a game on April 12, 1877, against the Live Oaks, a semi-professional team from Massachusetts.

Not only did the new invention protect the catcher's face from the ball and bat; it allowed him to move closer to the plate and pay greater attention to the runners on base.

It attracted quick criticism. An article on Thayer by John Hanlon, which appeared in the Portland, Maine, *Sunday Telegram* on June 1, 1896, recounted a number of critics including a sportswriter who commented, "There is a great deal of beastly humbug in contrivances to protect men from things which do not happen. There is about as much sense in putting a lightning rod on a catcher as there is a mask."

But, as the demand for masks grew steadily, Thayer realized that he had come up with a good idea. On January 15, 1878, he applied for a patent, which was granted less than a month later as patent 200,358. One of the three "original" models used in conjunction with the patent application has been silvered and is on display at the Harvard Varsity Club in Cambridge, Massachusetts.
1ST   1877. It was first mentioned in print on April 20, 1877, eight days after its debut, by

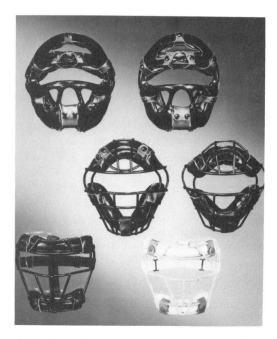

Catcher's mask. An array of modern masks from Rawlings.   *Courtesy of Rawlings*

the *Harvard Crimson*, which deemed it "a complete success, since it entirely protected the face and head and adds greatly to the confidence of the catcher, who need not feel that he is every moment in danger of a life-long injury."

catcher's mitt   *n.* Large padded glove worn by catchers since the 1890s.

catch leaning   *v.* To pickoff a base runner who has moved or is moving too far from the base occupied toward the next base. One is said to have been caught leaning when picked off by the pitcher or catcher after leading and trying to get a jump on the next base.

catch looking   *v.* To fool or deceive a batter with a pitch that crosses the plate for a called third strike.

catch napping   **1.** *v.* To surprise a less than alert runner with the result that he is picked off or suddenly caught between bases, also known as being asleep at the switch or caught asleep. An 1889 definition of baseball napping in Mrs. John A. Logan's *Home Manual* is both quaint and accurate, "When a player through carelessness or sleepy-headedness is caught off his base."

1ST   1862. (Chadwick Scrapbooks; EJN)
2. *v.* Outwitted on any point of play.

catch stealing   CAUGHT STEALING.

catch-up game   *n.* Game in which one team comes from behind to lead or win.

caught leaning   *v.* CATCH LEANING.

caught looking   *v.* CATCH LOOKING.

caught stealing   *adj.* Tagged out while attempting to steal a base or home plate. Tabulated as an official statistic—along with the S for successful steals—it is commonly abbreviated CS in scorecards and boxscores. In 1982 when Rickey Henderson set the all-time single-season steal record of 130, he was also caught stealing a record 42 times.

cellar   *n.* Position in league or divisional standings held by the team with the won-lost record.

cellar championships   *n.* Facetious way of describing two or more teams determining which will end up in last place in the final standings. **1ST**   1905. "With a team which never had a look-in for anything better than cellar championship . . . the club made money." (*Official Guide, National Association of Professional Base Ball Leagues—1905;* DS)

cellar dweller/cellar tenant   *n.* Said of a team with the worst won-lost record in the standings at any given moment during the season.

cello pack   *n.* Common term for a set of baseball cards packaged in transparent cellophane. The term is used by collectors to distinguish cellophane-packed cards—which collectors tend to prefer because the top and bottom cards in each pack are exposed—from those in a *wax pack*, cards wrapped entirely in opaque wax paper.

center field   **1.** *n.* The area beyond second base, which is not regularly covered by either the right or left fielder; the center of the outfield.
2. *n.* The position of the player who defends center field.
1ST   1854. (Knickerbocker Rules; EJN)

center fielder   *n.* The defensive player who is positioned in center field. Because of the size of the area the center fielder must patrol, the player in this position is usually quite fast and a strong, accurate thrower.

CG Common abbreviation for COMPLETE GAME. "They have only nine CGs for the season in 82 games." (New York *Daily News*, July 6, 1987)

chaffing *v./arch.* To complain about an umpire's decision.
1ST 1863 (Chadwick Scrapbooks; EJN)

chain baseball/chain-store baseball *n./arch.* Names for the system by which a team gets first option on the players on certain minor league teams; the name for the farm system before it was called the farm system.

chair position *n.* Defined by Morris Shirts in his 1971 book, *Warm Up for Little League Baseball,* as, "The right position for a catcher to catch the ball as the pitcher throws it; he looks almost as if he is sitting on the edge of a chair."

chalk *n.* The white powder that is spread on the playing field to mark the foul lines, base lines, on deck circles, and the coaches', catcher's and batter's box. Lime is often used as a substitute for chalk.

chalk line *n.* Any line drawn on the field, although it usually refers to one of the foul lines.

chalk raiser *n.* A batted ball that is ruled fair because in hitting the chalked foul line, it raises a corroborating puff of white lime dust.

chalk up **1.** *v.* To produce hits or victories, as they would be on a blackboard.
1ST 1912. (*New York Tribune*, September 12; EJN)
2. *v.* Words once commonly hollered by players after a batter hits a ball off the end of the bat. The allusion, of course, was to billiards where the end of the cue is chalked up.

challenge the hitter *v.* To pitch to that area of the strike zone where the batter displays his greatest strength, as opposed to avoiding it. This is most likely to occur when the pitcher's strength seems to match that of the batter.

Chalmer's Award Early name for the Most Valuable Player Award. Between 1911 and 1914, the players picked as the top men in the American National leagues were given a Chalmer's automobile.

champagne celebration *n.* A post-game, clubhouse ritual in which a victorious team celebrates by spraying and drinking champagne. It usually occurs when a team clinches its division, the pennant or wins the World Series, but not exclusively. In 1950 the St. Louis Browns held a champagne celebration upon winning their 55th game, which (under the old 154-game schedule) meant that it was impossible for them to lose 100 games.

championship season **1.** *n.* The regular season, during the course of which the divisional championships are established. Before there were divisions, the term referred to the period between Opening Day and the winning of the pennant.
2. *n.* A specific season in which a particular team wins the championship.

Championship Series *n.* Name for the series of playoff games played between the division-winning teams in each league to determine the winners of the American and National League pennants.

champions of the world *n.* Resplendent title claimed annually by the winner of the World Series. Many have commented on this all-embracing title, including linguist Peter Tamony who in 1939 wrote: "That baseball . . . is played only in the United States, and that the game is not international is of little moment in the excitement attending the outcome of the series. Whichever team wins holds the Championship of the World, and is thus, in our scheme of things entitled to a place just to the right of that of the gods." (*News Letter and Wasp,* October 13, 1939)

chance **1.** *n.* A reasonable opportunity for a defensive player to field a batted ball with the opportunity of making or assisting a put-out. Generally the first baseman accepts the most chances in a game since he ends most infield outs. A fielder's total chances are determined by adding putouts, assists and errors.
1ST 1867. (Chadwick Scrapbooks; EJN)
2. *n.* An opportunity to perform well. Baltimore Oriole manager Earl Weaver once said, "I gave Mike Cuellar more chances than my first wife."

change *adj./arch.* Description for relief or substitute player or players, such as a change pitcher or a change battery.

Champions of the world. Cap Anson (front row, to the right of the man with the bat) and a mid-1880s version of the Chicago White Stockings, in front of a banner declaring them the "Champions of the United States." It is a title that was uncommon to begin with and has long been abandoned in favor of "Champions of the World." *Prints and Photographs Division, the Library of Congress*

1ST 1883. "The Athletics pitted their change battery against the amateur Hartville Club . . ." (*Sporting Life,* April 15; DS)

change livery *v./obs.* To change teams.

change of pace *n.* A once commonly used term for changeup; a slowly pitched ball, thrown in an effort to deceive the batter into thinking it is a fastball thereby throwing off the batter's timing. "A slow ball throwed with a fast ball motion," according to Dizzy Dean.

Formerly, it was known simply as a *slow ball.* The term change of pace has gone out of style because of the tendency to use the term changeup to describe the same pitch.
1ST 1868. (Chadwick Scrapbooks; EJN) The term also appears in an 1889 baseball glossary where it defines the strategy of a pitcher who "alternates in his delivery between a slow and

swiftly pitched ball." In other words, this would indicate that when it was first used it was applied to both fast and slow balls.

changeup/change-up *n.* Modern incarnation of the change of pace; specifically, a slow ball thrown after one or more fastballs; a let-up pitch thrown to look like a fastball to upset the batter's timing.
1ST 1952. "A change up is a good pitch, if you don't pull it too consistently. A change up means to take a little off your curve ball or your fast ball, with the same motion." (Dizzy Dean in *Dizzy Baseball*) A more formal use and definition shows up in 1953: "The slow pitch that follows the fast breaking curve is the change-up off the curve ball." (Arthur Mann, *How to Play Winning Baseball*)
USE Still pretentious way of saying slow ball

to older ears. In his essay "The Grand Old Game" Jim Murray quotes veteran writer Jack Olsen: " 'Know what they call a "slow ball" nowadays?' he demanded, 'A "change-up"! Now, I ask you!' " (From *The Best of Jim Murray*)

charge *n.* Player on a team.

CHARGE! *v.* To prepare to attack; i.e., rally. It is a rallying cry bellowed in unison by many a modern fan after a bugle (which is usually on a tape recording) sounds the cavalry charge. Such charges are often prompted by instructions appearing on electronic scoreboards. Despite the fact that it seems more appropriate to football or a sport where players charge down the field, it has become a very popular form of baseball fan participation.

charge the ball *v.* As a defensive player, to rush forward to field a batted ball in an effort to reduce the time it takes to reach the ball and make a play. An important action because the time that is saved charging a ball (often fractions of a second) may be crucial.

charity hop *n.* A batted ball that bounces waist-high, making it easy to field; a gift to an infielder; *big bill.*

charley horse *n.* Name for a muscular cramp, especially one in the legs, usually produced as a result of physical exertion.
ETY/1ST 1887. One of those wonderful terms that have fascinated a number of people, all of whom seem to have come up with a different theory of its origin. This may be one of those cases in which a number of stories, seemingly contradictory, contributed to give a term the momentum it needed to become popular.

In *The American Language: Supplement II* H. L. Mencken cites Bill Clarke, an original Baltimore Oriole of the 1890s, who argued that the term had come "from the name of Charley Esper, a left-handed pitcher, who walked like a lame horse." This theory was discredited when it was learned that the term was already in use by the time Esper joined the Orioles in 1894.

Another version involving members of the same Orioles team appears in Forrest C. Allen's *My Basket-ball Bible* (1930) and was repeated in the April 1947 *American Notes and Queries*. One day at a local race track, several players put money on a horse called Charlie who, winning throughout the race, pulled up lame in the

final stretch. The following day a player pulled a tendon in his leg and was likened by one of the coaches to "our old Charlie horse."

In the *Baseball Almanac* (1955), Hy Turkin relates a similar story with the Chicago Cubs, asserting the term was, "Coined by either Billy Sunday or Joe Quest in the 1880's after a horse backed by the Chicago players had pulled up lame in the stretch." A note written by Peter Tamony in the Tamony collection, attributed to "Baseball Slang and Origins" (but not further identified), agrees but taps Sunday as the one who coined the term. It reads, "When George Gore hit what should have been an inside-the-park homer and strained a thigh muscle rounding second, so that he had to limp into third, Billy cried, 'Here comes the Charley horse.' "

Lee Allen, on the other hand, used his column in the May 2, 1962, *Sporting News* to insist that it was Quest who coined the term in 1882. Allen reported, "Son of a blacksmith from New Castle, Pa., Quest noticed that players hobbling around with a peculiar muscle injury of the legs reminded him of an old white horse, Charlie, employed at his father's shop." (PT)

A letter of June 1, 1957, on file at the National Baseball Library in Cooperstown from Henry R. Viets, M.D., curator of the Boston Medical Library, begins, "I have been trying to trace for some months the derivation of the term 'Charley horse,' and have gotten back to the year 1889 where we have found a reference in the *Cincinnati Commercial Gazette* for March 17 of that year stating that one of the players 'was affected with a "Charley horse" ' and that ended his ball-playing for 1888." (Since then etymologist Gerald Cohen traced the term to the June 19, 1887, *New York World.*)

In his *Language of Sport,* (1982) Tim Considine came up with this unreferenced explanation: "Often in the 1800s, old workhorses kept on the grounds of ballparks were called Charley. The movements of the injured, stiff-legged ballplayers were likened to the labored plodding of these old horses, and the injury itself eventually became known as a 'charley' or 'charley horse.' " In his book *A Baseball Album* (1980), Gerald Secor Couzens traces the term back to the Sioux City, Iowa, team of 1889 and an old white horse named Charley. Couzens attributes this version to a minor league coach named Walter McCredie. This same story appears in an unsigned article printed in the *San Francisco Chronicle* of July 2, 1934, but the old white horse in this version inspired the coinage in 1890, not 1889.

EXT   The leap from the slang of ballplayers to standard English is described in Tristram Potter Coffin's *The Old Ball Game* (1971) as being so complete "that most people would have trouble describing the ailment if the phrase were taken [away] from them." He adds, "In fact, the *Journal of the Medical Association* printed an article as long ago as November 30, 1946, entitled 'Treatment of the Charley Horse' rather than 'Treatment of Injury to Quadriceps Famoris.' Such a usage indicates the phrase to have been a part of even the most formal American English for a quarter of a century."
SEE   *"Here comes Charley."*

chart   *v.* To keep a detailed record of the exact type of pitching in a game. To record pitches on a *pitching chart.* It is an old and widely-observed custom in baseball that on a given day the next day's pitcher charts the game.

chase   **1.** *v.* For the offense to force the removal of a pitcher by getting hits.
2. *v.* To be ejected from the game by the umpire.
3. *v.* To persue first place in the standings and ultimately the pennant and world championship.

chase flies   *v.* To play the outfield.
1ST   1905. (*Sporting Life,* February 10; EJN)

chatter   *n.* Lively, often meaningless, talk spoken for team morale. Infield chatter is intended to keep everyone alert and on their toes and encourage the pitcher, while chatter from the bench or dugout is meant to inspire the batter. Writer Courtland Milloy tried to capture some chatter from the Continental League of the District of Columbia. It came out in an article in the *Washington Post* like this: " 'Dada boy. Dadda boy, baby,' the catcher yelled out to the pitcher's mound during a recent game. 'Make him think. Pick 'em up. Lay it on 'em, baby. [ball one, above the strike zone] Too high, but no damage done.[the next pitch strike one] Dada boy, baby. That's the one. Do it for me two mo' times.' " (*The Washington Post,* May 26, 1987)
1ST   1891. (*New York Post,* June 8; EJN)

Chavez Ravine   The location of Dodger Stadium in Los Angeles, California. The ravine

Chaw. Nellie Fox displaying a cheekful.   *Courtesy of the Cleveland Indians*

itself is on a hill overlooking downtown. When the Angels played here from 1962 to 1965, it was only referred to as Dodger Stadium when the National League club was in residence. When the Angels were at home, it was referred to as Chavez Ravine so as not to refer to the Dodgers.

chaw   *n.* Chewing tobacco; a smokeless form of the weed that has long been common in baseball circles. "A cud of tabaccer," according to Dizzy Dean. "Some pitchers can't even start warmin' up without at least one good chew."

An article on a campaign to battle smokeless tobacco among Little Leaguers contained this line on anti-chaw pitcher Nolan Ryan: "After his two sons began playing Little League baseball, Ryan said he saw youngsters as young as 10 years of age using dip [snuff] and chaw." (*The Houston Post,* September 29, 1987; CDP)

cheap hit   *n.* Subjective term applied to a ball that is batted into fair territory for a hit, but that lacks power and relies on an odd bounce, fortunate placement or some other "lucky" factor.

cheap seats   *n.* The bleachers and other areas distant from home plate. The term is not used to comment on the spectators or their chosen seats, but on the distance of a home run or deep foul ball, as in, "He just put one in the

cheap seats." The seats are cheap because they are far from most of the action.
1ST   1912 (*American magazine*, August; EJN)

cheating   *n*. Term used to describe infielders who, with runners on base, position themselves closer to the bases than normal in the hopes of preventing a stolen base or taking part in a double play.

check/check swing   1. *n*. A half or partial swing of the bat; one stopped midpoint before the batter's wrists turn (or are *broken*). If a ball is thrown outside of the strike zone and the batter check swings (or checks the swing), it will be called a "ball" by the umpire. But if the batter swung the bat across home plate, or, in the opinion of the umpire, intended to hit the ball, it would be called a strike. Often when the umpire rules "no swing" the catcher or pitcher will appeal the decision, at which time the first or third base umpire will verify or overrule the plate umpire's call.
2. *v*. To hold a swing after it has begun.

checker   *n*. Batter who is able to keep the wrists from breaking and his bat from crossing the plate when a pitch is not to his liking.

checking the runner   *v*. Gesture made by the pitcher who glances at the base runner to dissuade him from taking too long a lead.

checklist card   *n*. A particular type of baseball card that does not feature a player but rather lists the numbers and names of other cards in the set. For instance, all the Red Sox in a set may appear on a Red Sox checklist card.

cheddar   *n*. CHEESE. "Doc blew some big-league cheddar past D," Met Lenny Dykstra was quoted in *Newsday* (March 1, 1988) on Dwight (Doc) Gooden throwing fastballs past Darryl Strawberry in a spring training intrasquad game. (D)

cheer leader   *n*. Term for the loudest bench jockey on a team.

cheese   *n*. Contemporary player's term for the fastball. In *The Wrong Stuff*, Bill Lee translates Dennis Eckersley's "cheese for your kitchen" as meaning "a fastball up and in." Lee added that Eckersley also called himself the "Cheese Master."

chemistry   *n*. A distinct sense of teamwork, cooperation and friendship created by a mix of individuals on a team; often stated as "good chemistry." In the Chicago Cubs' magazine *Vineline* (August 1987), Keith Moreland offered this formula: "The makeup of an organization—the players, coaches and the fans. And the talent. The total ingredients that go into a team's makeup."

cherry pie   *n*. An unflattering term for a poor hitter, an easy out. This is one of a handful of terms that were created and used almost exclusively by the late Casey Stengel.
ETY   It is probably a play on "easy as pie" applied to an easy out.

chestiness   *adj./arch*. Conceit.
1ST   1909 (*New York Evening Journal*, July 14; EJN)

chest pad/chest protector   *n*. A pad used by catchers and home plate umpires to protect the body from the shoulders to the waist from pitched and fouled off balls. Most are worn but some umpires' models are held like a warrior's shield. They are especially important as protection from foul tips.
1ST   1889. "[When] he sprained the bosom of his pants . . . it was worth a gold medal to see Jim shift his chest protector around to his rear." (*Cincinnati Commercial Gazette*, March 17; cited in Mitford M. Mathews, *Americanisms*)
ETY   A small item from the popular *Leslie's Weekly* of October 15, 1914, gives this account of the origin of the protective device:
A Woman's Gift to Baseball
   Charles Bennett, famous as a catcher for the noted Detroit team of 1886–1887, delights in telling the story of how his wife made the first catcher's breast protector. It was a constant source of worry to Mrs. Bennett to watch her husband acting as a target for the speedy twirlers of 30 years ago, and she determined to invent some sort of an armor to prevent the hot shots from the pitchers playing a tattoo on the ribs of her better half. After much planning, assisted by practical suggestions from her husband, she shaped a pad which answered the purpose and which bore some resemblance to the "protector" of the present day. In a private tryout it worked well and Charles, after permitting the ball to strike him repeatedly without feeling a jar decided to use it in public. The innovation created

Chest protector. Charles W. Bennett. *National Baseball Library, Cooperstown, N.Y.*

almost as great a sensation as Bresnahan's shin guards, but it made a hit with the catchers and they were quite ready to follow Bennett's lead.

Chicago   *v./arch.* To shut out the opposing team. To have been Chicagoed (or Chicago'd) was to be shut out. Most recent use that could be found was in the slang section of the 1958 *Comedians of Baseball* where it is listed as an "old term." Arthur "Bugs" Baer wrote a column on the term in 1953, which he opened with the line, "Baseball word you never hear any more is 'Chicagoed.' " (*San Francisco Examiner*, January 19; PT)
ETY/1ST   1874. In the 1914 *Balldom, The Britannica of Baseball*, George L. Moreland concluded, "The word was coined by some wag when on July 23, 1870, the Mutuals of New York shut out the Chicago team by a score of 9 to 0. Shutouts prior to that date had been few and far between, for previous to this game but five shutout games had ever been played."

A contrary theory suggests a later coinage and says that it is based on the effectiveness of the Chicago White Stockings of the 1880s. In his book *Fungoes, Floaters and Fork Balls*, Patrick Ercolano argues that a more likely theory is that it came from the 1876 Chicago National

League team featuring their ace Al Spalding who threw eight shutouts.

Clearly, theories about the 1880s and the Spalding season of 1876 must give way to the fact that Edward J. Nichols was able to find the verb in use in 1874 (*New York Herald*, July 19), meaning to shut out.
EXT   The term was applied to a shutout in card-playing.

Chicago Cubs   The name of the National League's Eastern Division franchise in Chicago, Illinois. The team was originally called the White Stockings, then the Colts, the Cowboys, Broncos and Rainmakers. Two sportswriters, Fred Hayner and George Rice, came up with the name Cubs and a logo featuring a bear cub to go with it in 1901. The name was created to reflect the number of young players on the team.

With an eye on the team's generally lackluster standing, former Manager Herman Franks once commented, "The Chicago Cubs fans are the greatest fans in baseball. They've got to be."

Chicago Shirley   *n.* Synonym for BASEBALL ANNIE that appears in Bill Lee's *The Wrong Stuff.*

Chicago slide   *n.* The original HOOK SLIDE, which was invented and first employed by Mike "King" Kelly when he played for the Chicago White Stockings from 1880 through 1886.
1ST   1911. (*American* magazine, May; EJN)

Chicago White Sox   The name of the American League's Western Division franchise in Chicago, Illinois. Originally the Invaders, the club took the name White Stockings and turned it into White Socks after it had been discarded by their National League neighbors. The name was used when the club entered the American League in 1901. Sportswriters Carl Green and I. E. Sanborn shortened the name to Sox. Sometimes known as "Chisox" for short.

chief of staff   *n.* Umpire-in-chief of any umpiring crew.

chill a bat   *v.* For a hitter in a slump to discard his regular bat and borrow a bat from a player who is in the midst of a batting streak; to take the "heat" out of a bat. A batter in a slump is said to have a cold bat while one on a streak is said to have a hot bat.

Chinese blow   *n.* A lucky hit; a fluke.

Chinese home run. The Honolulu-based Chinese Baseball Team left this poster as a memento of their 1913 tour of the mainland United States. It suggests the additional possibility that the Chinese home run may somehow have been linked to one of these tours. *Prints and Photographs Division, the Library of Congress*

Chinese homer/Chinese home run 1. *n.* A derogatory term for home run hit over the portion of the outfield fence closest to home plate, often one that lands just inside (or hits) the foul plate in a ballpark with small dimensions. The most famous locale for Chinese homers was the Polo Grounds, which had 280- and 258-foot foul lines. Pinch-hitter Dusty Rhodes' three-run homer that won the opening game of the 1954 World Series for the New York Giants was described as a "270-foot pop fly."

The term is not to be used lightly, as a letter printed in the August 21, 1971, *Sports Illustrated* attests: "Shame on you for calling Bobby Thomson's historic sudden-death home run against the Dodgers in the 1951 National League playoff a 'Chinese home run' (*Baseball's Week*, Aug. 9). It is the first time I ever heard it characterized in such a demeaning way, and I can only conclude that the writer, Larry Keith, is an anguished Dodger fan who still doesn't believe it happened." (letter from Phil Harmon, New York City)

Common in the 1950s, the term has been used sparingly since the demolition of the Polo Grounds. It did come into play, however, when the Dodgers relocated to the Los Angeles Coliseum in 1958 and home-run balls began landing in the left field seats, which were only 251 feet from the plate. A *Sporting News* headline in the May 7, 1958, issued read, "16 of first 29 HR's in L.A. Labeled 'Pekinese Pokes.' " (PT) For the same reason, cartoonist Willard Mullin labeled the Coliseum "Flung Wong O'Malley's Little Joss House in Los Angeles."

2. *n.* A long foul ball, perhaps used mostly in sandlot baseball. In Stephen King's *Skeleton Crew* there is a story called "The Monkey," which contains this line, "Hal was too small to play, but he sat far out in foul territory, sucking his blueberry Popsicle and chasing what the big kids called 'Chinese home runs.' " (CDP)

This use may very well be limited to New England. A query to Stephen King about his use of the term brought this reply: "I first heard the term 'Chinese Home Run' in Stratford, Connecticut learning to play the game. When I moved back to Maine in 1958, the term was also used—in both cases, a Chinese home run was a foul ball, usually over the backstop . . ."

USE A note in Herb Caen's *San Francisco Chronicle* column for May 18, 1981, underscores why the use of the term is now an invitation to controversy and charges of racial insensitivity: "Bill King, the Oakland A's announcer, got off a racist line Thurs. night, but he'll learn. After describing Bobby Murcer's homer as 'not a Chinese home run'—meaning it was well hit— I'm sure he has heard from militant Oriental groups, all of which hit hard." (PT)

This point was made obliquely by Jimmy Cannon in 1956 when he gave Chinese home run this definition in a *Baseball Digest* article: "A cheap homer which would be called something else if the Chinese had enough influence."

ETY When Dusty Rhodes hit his aforementioned 1954 Chinese homer, Joseph H. Sheehan of the *New York Times* attempted to trace the term. He reported, "According to Garry Schumacher of the Giants' front office, who in his baseball writing days was a noted phrase-coiner, 'Chinese homer' was one of the numerous Thomas Aloysius (Tad) Dorgan contributions to the lexicon of American slang." (NYT, October 1, 1954)

Dorgan, known far and wide as Tad, used his cartoon "Indoor Sports" to introduce—or popularize—slang. Such terms as "dumb-bell," "skimmer" (for hat) and "hot dog" have been traced to Tad's cartoons.

The *Times'* Sheehan concluded that the connotation of a cheap homer came from the association in Dorgan's era of the name Chinese with coolies and cheap labor. "The term carried the added connotation of a homer of little account," he adds, "in line with the cynical observation of a colorful political leader who reportedly once stated, 'Why should we care about the Chinese. There ain't a vote in a million in them.'"

Dorgan's coinage fit in with a larger group of Chinese terms, such as a "Chinese Rolls-Royce," which is a Ford according to Abraham Roback in his *Dictionary of International Slurs,* and probably was not intended to be especially disparaging. Sheehan pointed out that Tad was a "benign and gentle" satirist with two adopted sons of Chinese ancestry.

In the May 7, 1958, issue of the *Sporting News,* J. G. Taylor Spink does an exhaustive search for the origins of the term and comes to the same conclusion that Sheehan did. However, the Spink article was reprinted in the *Los Angeles Times* and inspired a number of letters to the newspaper, including one from a retired San Francisco sports writer named Travis McGregor. His thoughts appeared in the May 28 *Sporting News* and are repeated here in part:

The use of the term Chinese homer goes far beyond the answers given in Mr. Spink's article, and I think you will find it originated in San Francisco prior to World War I. There was a young China boy there at about 1912 or 1913, of my memory is correct, who had an unpronounceable name, keen sense of humor, a degree from Stanford and a great yen to be a newspaperman . . . The typewriter jockeys gave up on spelling his name and renamed him Mike Murphy, and he was a one-man show at the ball games . . . While Mike was educated beyond any trace of an accent his quips were all in Chinese dialect, and made with a perfectly straight face. "Ow," he would wail, "look the way he bat. Wave at ball like Mandarin with fan." The old Oakland park's short fence caught the most of it from Mike and his "Mandarin fan" waving balls out of the park were knocked back to "Chinese homers."

Later in the letter McGregor gets to Dorgan. "For two or three seasons Mike was a riot—an Oriental Fred Allen, and Tad Dorgan drew a number of cartoons featuring Mike's comments." He adds that a number of writers picked up and used the term, including Ring Lardner and Damon Runyon and he thought that the first writer to put it into print was either Ed Hughes or Harry Smith of the *San Francisco Chronicle.*

While not disputing the Dorgan story, Dan Schlossberg points out in *The Baseball Catalog* that the term was used in the 1920s by *New York Tribune* sports editor Bill McGeehan to describe the right field wall, which looked "thick, low, and not very formidable—like the Great Wall of China."

But this seems to be one of those terms that has attracted a fascinating collection of explanations. Russ Hodges, longtime Giants announcer, gave this explanation to the *San Francisco Call-Bulletin:* "Years ago in the Polo Grounds, Chinese gamblers were wont to gather in the leftfield stands at the foul line, a little over 250 feet. Any hit that went out at that point was followed by cries of: 'There goes one for the Chinese.'" (April 21, 1958; PT)

Other explanations, such as those that appeared in Joe Falls' *Sporting News* column, which solicited etymologies from readers, seem to be purely conjectural: that a short homer is so named because the Chinese are a shorter people, that the outfield seats in the Polo Grounds used to stick out like a pagoda and that it was inspired by the "short jump" of Chinese checkers.

Without question, the wildest of all the theories was one suggested to Falls by a St. Louis man, Tom Becket. As far-fetched as it sounds, however, it does offer an explanation—even as an elaborate pun—for the fact that, in New England, Chinese homer may refer to a long, foul ball.

In this version the term harks back to the turn of the century and a game in Salem, Massachusetts, between teams of Irish and Polish immigrants. The game lasted into the 17th inning at which point there was only one ball left to use because the others had been lost. At this point, Becket explains, "A shortstop named Chaney fouled a fast ball into the high grass deep beyond the backstop. After 20 minutes of searching for the ball, the umpires declared the victory for the Irish. They ruled that the Polish team, which was the home team, had failed to furnish the necessary amount of baseballs to complete the game."

The term? "So the cheer went up," wrote Becket, " 'Chaney's home run won the game.' From then on, any foul ball clearing the backstop was heralded as another Chaney's home run. Various misunderstandings as to dialects eventually brought it to the now-familiar 'Chinese home run.' "

Chinese liner *n./arch.* Pop fly.
1ST 1935. "Pop, pop-up—a fly ball . . . a Chinese liner." (Ralph H. Barbour, *How to Play Better Baseball*)
USE This term carries the same derogatory implications as *Chinese homer* and was probably inspired by it.

chin music 1. *n.* A beanball or knockdown pitch that passes close to the batter's jaw. "He served Dykstra a little chin music down in the dome. It almost set his hat spinning,"—said of Nolan Ryan by Brent Musberger during the National League Playoff Game on October 14, 1986.
2. *n./arch.* "Back-talk, especially impudent backtalk from a player or umpire, or from the grandstand or bleachers is 'chin-music' or 'chin-chinning,' " as defined by V. Samuels in his 1927 article on "Baseball Slang." (AS, February 1927)
3. *n./arch.* Shouting.
1ST 1888. "Nearly 10,000 people witnessed the game, each one of whom wasted an inordinate amount of chin-music in the general effort to brace the Giants up to victory or death." *(New York World,* September 4; cited by Gerald Cohen in *Comments on Etymology)*

chipmunk *n.* Punning, self-deprecating name for a sportswriter who, in the words of Milton Gross, is so called, "Because in the long run all we do is nibble around the edges." Gross is quoted calling himself the first chipmunk of sportswriters in Pat Jordan's *Suitors of Spring,* in this interchange on the subject:

"But what about the heart of a story?" says the novice. "Don't you ever try to get to the heart of the matter?"

Milton smiles and shakes his head. "Kid, when you've been in the game as long as I have you'll learn there is no heart." (CDP)

chips *n.* Calcium deposits, such as those that sometimes develop in a pitcher's elbow and that can be debilitating.

Chisox Nickname for the Chicago White Sox, akin to calling the Boston Red Sox the Bosox.

choke/choke in the clutch 1. *v.* To play badly in a crucial situation or lose one's resolve. Players, managers, coaches and umpires have all been accused of choking.
2. *n.* A bad showing, especially in a pinch.
USE According to baseball tradition, this is not a term to be used lightly, especially when emotions are running high. "In fact," Tristram Potter Coffin wrote in *The Old Ball Game,* "so strong is the feeling concerning the word 'choke' that a player needs only to hold his hand to his throat after an umpire's decision to get thrown out of the game."
1ST 1937. (clipping, National League Service Bureau; EJN)
EXT The choke is a factor and a term in most every sport and in situations outside baseball from business to military conflict.

choke grip *n.* Method of holding the bat several inches from the narrow end.
ETY See choke up.

choke hitter *n.* Batter who does badly under pressure, a choker.

As used in *Babe Ruth's Own Book of Baseball* (1928), "The other division is the 'choke hitters' . . . [where they] stand flatfooted and take half a swing."

choker *n.* CHOKE HITTER.

choke up/choke up on the bat *v.* To grip the bat above the customary lower end; to move one's hands up the handle of the bat to achieve greater control (but also cutting down on the power of the swing).
1ST 1909. (Zane Grey's *The Shortstop;* EJN)
ETY From the impression that the bat is being grabbed by the neck and choked.

choose up *v.* To form sides for an informal game of baseball, softball or their variations. Usually two captains are decided on and alternate in picking players for their teams.

choose-up game *n.* Contest between two teams formed by choosing up.

chop *v.* To swing down on the ball, a move that often results in a grounder.
1ST 1902. (*Sporting Life,* July 12; EJN)

chop one off the high limb *v.* To swing at a ball that is pitched above the strike zone.

chopper *n.* A batted ball that hits the ground sharply and bounces high.

chopstick *n.* The BAT.
1ST 1908. (*New York Evening Journal,* April 25; EJN)

chuck *v.* To throw or pitch.
1ST 1907. (*New York Evening Journal,* May 7; EJN)

chucker *n.* Pitcher, usually a fastballer. Once this referred to a pitcher who threw *only* fastballs and no breaking balls.
1ST 1937. (New York *Daily News,* January 31; EJN)

chucker/chukker *n.* An inning.
ETY A borrowing from polo in which a chukker is a discrete period of play usually lasting 7½ minutes.
1ST 1934. "Chucker, n. (baseball)—inning." (definition in *Journalism Quarterly*)

chump *n.* Dupe or stupid person.
One of the terms that David Schuman noted were not strictly baseball terms but which, because of their original context, "seem to have been originated by ballplayers . . ." His earliest example is from the *Sporting Life* of May 27, 1883: "Maybe Manager Bancroft isn't regarded as a chump by baseball people."

chute *n.* The area over the plate where it is easiest for the batter to hit the ball; the middle of the strike zone. "The next afternoon, he threw Rick nothing but fastballs down the chute, and Manning got two base hits." (Bill Lee in *The Wrong Stuff;* CDP)

cigar box *n.* A small field or stadium.
1ST 1937. (New York *Daily News,* January 17; EJN)

cigarette card *n.* Name for the baseball cards that came in cigarette packs. In *My Luke and I,* Eleanor Gehrig says that her late husband, Yankee great Lou Gehrig, saved and traded "the cigarette cards that carried pictures of Ty Cobb, Zach Wheat and Christy Mathewson" when he was a boy of 12. (CDP)

cinch *n.* Easy victory.

Cincinnati Redlegs Name of the Cincinnati Reds, 1953–1959.

Cincinnati Reds The name of the National League's Western Division franchise in Cincinnati, Ohio. It is a direct descendant of the Cincinnati Red Stockings, who became known as the Red Legs or, simply, the Reds in 1876. During the early days of the Cold War, there were some who were disturbed by the name Reds. In the early 1960s, a justice of the Pennsylvania Supreme Court admonished the team for its unpatriotic name. "Let the Russians change," was the altogether proper response of *Cincinnati Enquirer* sports editor Lou Smith. "We had it first."

Cincinnati Red Stockings The name of the first professional baseball team, which was formed in 1869. Named for the color of their hose, the original team won 130 games over two seasons before suffering its first loss.

Cinderella *n.* Applied to teams that emerge from the lower levels and become contenders in the manner of the fairy tale of Cinderella.
"The game pitted two Cinderella teams making their state tourney debuts." (*Bangor Daily News* account of a state American Legion tournament, August 11, 1986)

Cinderella Softball Leagues A Corning, New York-based association that seeks to promote girls' and women's softball nationally and internationally.

circle **1.** *v.* To run around the bases.
2. *n.* Short for the on-deck circle.

circuit **1.** *n.* The four bases; that which is covered by a home run.
2. *n.* A league—the National League has been called "the Senior Circuit" and the American "the Junior Circuit."
1ST 1880. (*Brooklyn Daily Eagle,* July 22; EJN)
ETY Although the first meaning follows the standard definition of a circuit as a circular journey, the second meaning may stem from the theatrical use of the term for a group of theaters visited on a regular basis.

circuit belt/circuit blow/circuit clout/circuit drive/circuit smash/circuit tripper/circuit wallop *n.* A HOME RUN.
USE Today these are terms of exaggeration and intended archaism used sparingly and for emphasis. An article in the October 1932 issue

Cincinnati Red Stockings. A trophy—in the form of a giant bat—given to the 1869 Red Stockings in honor of their winning 65 games.   *Courtesy of the New York Public Library*

of *Baseball* magazine contained this: "It is really remarkable that so few of the actual terms used in baseballese ever see the light of a printed page. Now and then they make the newspaper sporting pages, but the commendable modern journalistic trend away from the silly jabber of twenty years ago, when every strikeout was a 'breeze' and every home a 'circuit clout,' has also militated against the popularization of dozens of words that have become full-standing baseballese by the prime standard of word-legitimization . . ."
1ST (circuit clout) 1908. (*New York Evening Journal,* May 14; EJN)

circus catch   *n.* A spectacular catch, suggesting the moves of a circus acrobat. Such a catch may involve a jump, dive, flip, roll or combination thereof. "Circus Solly" Hofman, an outfielder with the Chicago Cubs between 1904 and 1912, was given his nickname because he was known for making acrobatic catches of fly balls.
   "But, replays showed, the Rangers outfielder came up a glove-length shy of a circus catch." (Tom Boswell in the *Washington Post,* August 8, 1986)
1ST 1888. As it appears in Thomas W. Lawson's *The Krank: His Language and What It Means:*

"Circus Catch. Catching the ball between the upper and under eyelid."
EXT   The term has been applied to spectacular football catches for some time and is used metaphorically for any melodramatic feat.

circus play   *n.* A spectacular play.
1ST 1885. (*Chicago Inter-Ocean,* July 15; EJN)
   By extension, there is also the circus stop and the circus throw. They even appear in combination. "He made circus catches, circus stops, circus throws . . ." (Zane Grey, *The Redheaded Outfield,* 1915; DS)

clamshell catch   *n.* Style of catching in which a player with wrists flat together, traps the ball between his glove and bare hand. This two-handed method is surer than trying to catch the ball in one hand.

clang/clank   *n.* A bad fielder, presumably from the metaphoric noise made by his IRON GLOVE and skillet-hard hands.

class   *n.* The level at which the game of professional baseball is played, with the major leagues at the top followed by the ranking of the minor leagues (AAA, AA, A, B, etc.). The class ranking system was originally set up on the basis of the population of the city or town in which the team played and was used to fix the salaries and prices of players.

class F   *n./arch.* "A term of contempt used among players toward weak players, insinuating that they rank below all organized clubs," according to Hugh S. Fullerton in his "Baseball Primer." At that time the minor leagues ranged from class AA down to class E.
1ST   1912. (*American Magazine,* June)

classic   *n.* The WORLD SERIES, more commonly, the FALL CLASSIC.

Class of '25   *n.* Name given to the remarkable group of nine rookies who came into the major leagues in 1925: Jimmy Foxx, Mickey Cochrane, Charlie Gehringer, Freddie Fitzsimmons, Charley "Red" Ruffing, Moses "Lefty" Grove, Chick Hafey, Mel Ott and Lou Gehrig.
SEE   Year of the Rookie.

clean hit   *n.* A safely batted ball that at no point looked as if it would be fielded for an out; a solid hit.
1ST   1880. (*Chicago Inter Ocean,* June 29; EJN)

clean the bases   *v.* To get a hit, usually a home run, on which all base runners score; one that rids—or cleans—the bases of all base runners.
1ST   1910. (*New York Tribune,* July 3; EJN)

clean their clocks   *v.* To beat a team decisively.

cleanup/clean-up/cleanup hitter/clean-up hitter/cleanup position/clean-up position   *n.* The fourth position in the batting order, which is reserved for a player with a high batting average and the ability to drive in runs with extra-base hits. The assumption is that he is most likely to get a hit that will score any or all of the preceding batters who have reached base, thus cleaning or clearing the bases of base runners.
1ST   1907. (*New York Evening Journal,* April 15; EJN)
EXT   **1.** The most dependable or most skillful person in any group, such as a team of lawyers.
2. A political candidate who can help effect reform or a sweeping change in policy. In supporting congressional candidate William S. Mailliard in 1952, an editorial in the San Francisco *Examiner* termed him a "clean-up hitter" who would help get rid of ". . . the New Deal, the Square Deal, the Fair Deal and all the rotten deals we've had for the 20 long years." (PT)

Cleanup Hitter. Mike Schmidt belts another long home run.   *Courtesy of the Philadelphia Phillies*

clear the bases   CLEAN THE BASES.
1ST   1870. (*New York Herald,* May 8; EJN)

clear the bench   **1.** *v.* A provision of the Official Rules by which an umpire can order all the substitute players from the dugout for objectionable conduct—notably the "violent disapproval" of a call—when the offender or offenders cannot be singled out. A warning must first be given, but if the bench is cleared all substitutes must go to the club house. Players can be recalled by the manager but only as needed for substitution in the game. "The base ump threatened 'to clear the bench' if Anderson Valley had the temerity to question calls following a chorus of groans at one of his calls." (*Anderson Valley Advertiser,* April 10, 1985)
1ST   1914. (*New York Tribune,* October 2; EJN)
2. *v.* To send in all the substitute players, as when a team is leading or losing by a seemingly insurmountable margin.

cleats   **1.** *n.* The projections on the bottoms of shoes, used to achieve greater traction on the field. They are made of rubber, plastic or metal.
2. *n.* BASEBALL SHOES.
1ST   1935. "Cleats—Metal attachments . . . commonly called spikes." (Ralph H. Barbour, *How to Play Better Baseball;* DS)

Cleveland Indians. Louis Francis Sockalexis, the first American Indian to play in the Major Leagues. *Courtesy of the Cleveland Indians*

Cleveland Indians   The name of the American League's Eastern Division franchise in Cleveland, Ohio. The team mascot is a cartoon Indian named "Chief Wahoo."

The team went through a series of name changes before becoming the Indians. They began in 1869 as the Forest Citys (Forest City being a nickname for Cleveland). Due to a number of tall and skinny players, the management changed the name to the Spiders in 1889. They became the Blues the following year to celebrate their bright blue uniforms. In 1902 the players themselves voted for a more powerful nickname and settled on Broncos. In 1903 they got rid of the blue uniforms and a local newspaper asked its readers to rename the team. As a result of the contest, they became the Naps in honor of Napoleon Lajoie, their star second baseman. In 1915, after Lajoie left the team, there was another newspaper contest in which the winning entry came from a fan who suggested *Indians* in honor of Luis Francis Sockalexis, a Cleveland Spider who was the first American Indian to play in the majors. Sockalexis, a Penobscot from Old Town, Maine,

played at Holy Cross and then at Notre Dame where he was spotted and signed by a Cleveland scout. In 1897, his rookie year, he batted .338 and captured the imagination of the fans who saluted him with loud war-whoops when he took to the field. But two seasons later it all came to a quick halt. In an article on Sockalexis in the *Maine Sunday Telegram,* Herbert Adams reports: "A man of pride and intelligence, Sockalexis' Catholic education and trusting nature left him unprepared for the pressure and exploitation of a big-business game. Alcohol and high living took their toll, and in 1899 he played only seven error-riddled games 'before being booted from the big leagues forever,' says one blunt account, 'due to drunkeness.' " (August 10, 1986)

Cleveland Stadium   Immense home grounds of the Cleveland Indians, situated on the edge of Lake Erie, Cleveland, Ohio. It has a seating capacity of 74,208, the largest in professional baseball.

Nobody has ever hit a ball into the center field bleachers of this monstrous stadium. It is also the site of one of the few forfeited games in modern times, when unruly fans took over the field on the night of June 4, 1974, during a special promotional event called Beer Night.

click on all nine   *v.* To possess good teamwork.

cliff-hanger   *n.* A close, hotly-contended game whose outcome is decided late in the game.

clinch   **1.** *v.* To be assured a particular position in the final standings based on an exact number of wins and losses, such as clinching first place.
2. *v.* For a player to establish a spot on a team's roster or in its starting lineup.

clincher   *n.* Game in which a championship is, or is likely to be, won. "Ojeda Gets Call for Clincher." (*New York Times* headline, September 4, 1986)

Clincher   *n.* Brand name for the widely used softball, manufactured by J. de Beers and Sons, Inc.

clinic   **1.** *n.* Instructional session where players and/or coaches instruct others—usually children—on the finer points of the game. Clearly implied by the term is that problems are brought to the clinic where a solution will be sought.

Cleveland Stadium. Massive stadium described by Philip J. Lowrey in the book *Green Cathedrals* as an example of "major league classic" style.   *Courtesy of the Cleveland Indians*

2. *n.* By extension, players or teams who perform magnificently in a game are said to be "holding a clinic." "Espinoza sparks Twins with clinic on fundamentals." (*Orlando Sentinel* headline, March 22, 1987)
ETY This term, originally indicating a medical facility, appears to have made the leap to other realms in the 1930s and 1940s when, as H. L. Mencken noted in his *American Language: Supplement II* (1948), clinic was being used for a beauty parlor. A letter by Atcheson L. Hench of the University of Virginia, which appears in the October 1949 issue of *American Speech*, notes 13 other non-medical clinics dating as far back as a 1933 "Clothing Clinic." Hench notes several baseball clinics starting with a 1944 announcement in the *Baltimore Sun:* "The second meeting of the baseball clinic sponsored jointly . . . is scheduled for tonight." (January 21, 1944) Another early baseball clinic noted by Hench appeared in a dispatch from Mobile,

Alabama, which also appeared in the *Sun:* "Little Eddie Stankey . . . announced he would open his second annual free baseball clinic for youngsters and oldsters here." (January 7, 1946)

clinker *n.* An ERROR.
1ST 1937. (*The Sporting News Record Book;* EJN)

clip (one) *v.* To hit a ball sharply.
1ST 1905. (*Sporting Life*, October 7; EJN)

clip a pitcher *v.* To get hits from a pitcher.

clip the corner *v.* To pitch a ball that just passes inside one of the four corners of the strike zone.

clobber **1.** *v.* To hit a ball hard.
2. *v.* To hit very well against a pitcher; to "pin his ears back."

clock/clock one *v.* To hit a ball hard; term used in reference to the precise timing required to be a successful hitter.
1ST 1932. (*Baseball* magazine, October; EJN)

Clinic. Cleveland pitcher Sonny Siebert at a 1969 clinic.   *Courtesy of the Cleveland Indians*

close call   *n.* Umpire's ruling on a split-second play. Because the distances between the bases seem so perfectly set, such calls are common.

closed stance   *n.* A batting position taken in which the front foot is closer to home plate than the rear foot. Compare to open stance.

closer   1. *n.* A starting pitcher who often pitches complete games.
2. *n.* A team's most reliable relief pitcher, one who is commonly used to get the final outs of a ball game.

close shave   1. *n.* Any ball that is pitched close to a batter's head, as if it were close enough to shave the whiskers on his face; a knockdown pitch.
2. *n.* Any play that is close.

closing reliever   *n.* CLOSER. "Pitching for the first time since shoulder surgery in September, the Atlanta Braves' closing reliever appeared to be his old dominating self in one perfect inning against the Kansas City Royals." (profile of Bruce Sutter, *USA Today,* March 12, 1986)

clothesline/clothesliner   *n.* A low line drive that heads to the outfield as straight as a taut clothesline. Rarely, a clothesline is stopped by an infielder but this is difficult since they are normally too far (10–15 feet) off the ground.
1ST   1937. (*Philadelphia Record,* October 11; EJN)

cloud-hunter/cloud-scraper/cloud-searcher   *n./arch.* A ball batted high in the air.
1ST   (All three terms traced to the late 19th century by EJN, with the earliest going back to 1874.)

clout   1. *v.* To hit the ball with power.
1ST   1908. (*New York Evening Journal,* February 24; EJN)
2. *n.* A hard-hit ball.
1ST   1908. (*New York Evening Journal,* May 14; EJN)

clouter   *n.* A power hitter, one who is known for hitting long home runs.
1ST   1908. (*Spalding's Official Base Ball Guide;* EJN)

clouting spree   *n.* An impressive display of hitting by a team.

clout king   *n.* A powerful and outstanding hitter regarded as tops in his league.

clown   *n.* An individual who performs comically on the field—but outside the game itself. They range from professionals who have clowned for a fee to the antics of catcher Rick Dempsey who occasionally put on his own one-man show during rain delays at Memorial Stadium in Baltimore.

clowning   *n.* An old baseball tradition in which an entertainer, often a former player, put on a sideshow to go with the game. The clowning took place before the game, between innings and during the break between two games of a doubleheader.

Clown Prince of Baseball   A title first taken by Al Schacht after his playing days were over and he became baseball's most famous clown. He was a pitcher with the Washington Senators during the 1920s. The next man to adopt the title was Max Patkin.

Clown Prince. Baseball's first Clown Prince, shown here in a Liberator Bomber during World War II while on his way to the South Pacific to entertain the troops. Schacht spent three years in the majors with the Washington Senators (1919–1921). *National Baseball Library, Cooperstown, N.Y.*

club   **1.** *n.* A team. From the beginning of baseball. The original baseball rules from 1854 were for the Knickerbocker Club. Today, however, a club is not just the team but also its supporting staff.
2. *n.* The bat.
3. *v.* To hit the ball.

clubhouse/club-house   *n.* The area at a ball park comprising a team's locker room, showers, lounge and the manager's office. Every park has two clubhouses, one for the home team and one for the visiting team. "Many ballplayers seem caught in adolescence, their development perhaps arrested by long enclosure, early wealth, and their teammates' high spirits and scrutiny. They call their locker rooms 'the clubhouse.' " (*New York Times*, September 11, 1983)
1ST 1869. "Gould's light foul was taken by Foran, up by the club-house . . ." (Chadwick Scrapbooks, DS)

clubhouse lawyer   *n.* A player given to complaining and talk of reform and "rights." In the 1937 edition of *The Sporting News Record Book* this term is defined as, "A player who airs bolshevik views in the clubhouse." With the unionization of players through the Major League Player's Association, clubhouse lawyers are less common than they once were. "Bob Farley, a top prospect as an outfielder-first baseman with the Giants a year ago, denied today that he is hard to manage or a clubhouse lawyer, as tagged by Chicago White Sox pilot Al Lopez when traded to Detroit the other day for veteran outfielder Charley Maxwell." (*San Francisco News Call Bulletin,* June 28, 1962; PT)
1ST 1937. *The Sporting News Record Book,* as above.

cluster   *v.* To get, as a team, a series of hits or runs in quick succession.

clutch   *n.* A difficult or critical situation, often one in which the outcome of a game hinges on the success or failure of a team or individual player. Also known as the *pinch*.
1ST 1937. "But Gabby has always had the knack of inserting base hits in what the ballplayers call 'the clutch.' When the score is tied and there's a man on, those Chicago players love to see Gab walk up there with his heavy stick." (Quentin Reynolds on Gabby Hartnett in *Collier's* for August 21, 1937; PT)
ETY This etymology is suggested in the 1954

Gillette World Series Record Book (edited by Hy Turkin): "When a clutch is engaged in any machinery, parts are made to move, and any defect in the clutch will cause faulty operation or danger." (PT)
EXT A key situation in any endeavor.

clutch hitter *n.* Player known for his ability to get a hit in key situations and/or with runners in scoring position. Players with reputations as clutch hitters included Tommy "Old Reliable" Henrich, Hank Aaron and Pete Rose. At least one player, Dutch "the Clutch" Vollmer, had his role acknowledged in a nickname.
EXT Anyone who can come through when it counts most.

coach **1.** *n.* An assistant to the manager. Major league clubs today usually have four or five of them: pitching coach, bullpen coach, first base coach, third base coach, and a batting instructor. The rulebook states that the coach shall be a "team member in uniform."
Coaches perform a number of jobs during and between games. The most visible is that of the first and third base coaches who give orders to base runners and relay hand signals from the manager to the players on the field.
2. *v.* To serve as a coach or coacher.
1ST 1890. (*New York Evening Post,* May 3; EJN)

coacher *n.* Early term for the first and third base coaches which is still used officially in the Rules of Baseball. "In the early days of the game," says part of the definition that appears in the 1912 "Baseball Primer" in the *American Magazine,* "the duties of the coaches were to play clown, make noise and strive to excite or anger opposing players. The coacher in the modern game usually is quiet, studying the movements of the opposing pitcher and catcher and assisting base runners."
1ST 1891. (*Chicago Herald,* May 4; EJN)

coaches' boxes/coacher's boxes *n.* Designated areas where the first and third base coaches must remain while the ball is in play. In baseball the boxes are 5 x 20 foot rectangular areas marked off with chalk and are situated along the base lines eight feet in foul territory. In softball, the rectangle is six feet from the baseline and is only 15 feet long.
1ST 1896. (glossary to Knowles and Morton *Base Ball;* EJN)

coaching lines *n.* The outlines of the coaches' boxes.
1ST 1897. (*New York Tribune,* April 26; EJN)

coach's interference *n.* Called by an umpire when a coach touches, grabs or gets in the way of a base runner in an attempt to stop the runner. In such cases the runner is called out.

coax a pass *v.* To be given a base on balls.
1ST 1910. (*New York Tribune,* July 18; EJN)

Cobb's Lake During Ty Cobb's time, this was the area of dirt in front of home plate at Tiger Stadium, which the groundskeepers kept wet in order to slow down Cobb's bunts and cause infielders to slip as they tried to field them.

cob-fence route *n./arch.* Term for the circuit of small, rural towns visited by teams in the low minor leagues. "The regulars followed the cob-fence route, playing exhibition games each afternoon with minor-league clubs . . ." (Gilbert Patten's *Courtney of the Center Garden,* 1915; DS)

cocked arm *n.* Describes the position of a player's arm pulled back in preparation to throw the ball.

cockeye *n./arch.* Left-handed, particularly a pitcher.
1ST 1937. (*Sporting News Record Book;* EJN)

cocking the bat *v.* Describes the position of a hitter's bat and arms, slightly tensed and pulled back in preparation to swing at a pitch.

cock of the arm *n.* Preparatory action of the arm and wrist prior to the forward movement of a throw.

cock of the bat *n.* The slant or cant of a hitter's bat. During the 1986 World Series, NBC announcer Vin Scully noted, "Strawberry cocks his bat towards the pitcher."

coffee and cake *n.* Long-established player slang for low pay, usually said in reference to the salaries of minor league players.
1ST 1934. "How would you feel if you'd been playing the cakes and coffee route for years and somebody suddenly dropped you in soft on the champagne and caviar circuit." (Pat Robinson, *Fort Worth Star-Telegram,* February 5)
ETY Presumably, a reference to the fact that the player got something to eat and drink and little else. Often, mere cake and coffee.

EXT   Peter Tamony found the term used in jazz circles as early as 1936 for a very poor-paying job; one that might only pay carfare. Also, boxing, he found, had coffee-and-cakes fighters willing to enter the ring for little pay.

coked up   *v.* Term used by Casey Stengel to describe a player on fire, ready for anything.
ETY   The allusion here points to heat and fire, which strongly suggests that Stengel was thinking of the carbon fuel as opposed to cocaine or Coca-Cola.

collar   *n.* Figurative term for the cause or result of a player going hitless during a game. "He's got a collar," Oriole announcer Brooks Robinson describing Juan Bonilla at the end of a July 29, 1986, telecast. Also stated as, "He wears the collar" or "He took the collar." Also, horse collar.
1ST   1932. (*Baseball* magazine, October; EJN)
ETY   A literal "zero" from the round shape of a collar, according to Harwell West's 1933 *Baseball Scrapbook*.

college try   *n.* OLD COLLEGE TRY.

collision   *n.* Player fresh from college. Perhaps a Dizzy Dean-like interpretation of "collegian."
1ST   1937. (*Sporting News Record Book;* EJN)

collusion   *n.* A secret agreement or arrangement. In the context of baseball, it usually is applied to the real or imagined agreements between team owners to forego the purchase of high-priced free agent players.

color/color man   *n.* Radio or television broadcaster brought in to deliver background information and sidelights to supplement the talk of the play-by-play announcer. Pittsburgh sportscaster Bill Currie once described a color man as, "A guy paid to talk while everybody goes to the bathroom."

color bar/color line   *n.* The unwritten rule that prohibited black players from playing in the major leagues. It was broken on April 15, 1947, when Jackie Robinson donned a Brooklyn Dodger uniform. On the occasion of a commemorative postage stamp honoring Robinson, *Sports Illustrated* contained the line, "People remember that he was the man who broke big league baseball's color bar . . ."
USE   For reasons hard to fathom, these terms were particular to baseball. Other sports and endeavors had to deal with segregation or discrimination, but only baseball had to deal with the color bar.

colors   *n.* Two or more colors by which a team is identified and known. When Charles O. Finley owned the Oakland A's, he insisted that his team's colors were Kelly Green, Fort Knox Gold and Wedding Gown White.

comb   *v.* To hit the ball straight up the middle of the field, usually coming close to hitting the pitcher; such a hit is said to comb the pitcher's hair.
1ST   1912. (*New York Tribune,* September 7; EJN)

combination ball   *n./arch.* Pitch that combines elements of two or more pitches, such as a sinking fastball.
1ST   1907. "The head of the batting-list came up again, and now by using his combination ball Merriwell succeeded in fanning Strothers." (Burt L. Standish, *Dick Merriwell's Salvation;* DS)

combination card   *n.* A baseball card containing the images of two or more players.

combine   *v.* To join with one or more other pitchers in establishing a win or loss, such as four pitchers combining on a three-hitter.

comeback   *n.* A rally by a team behind in the score or the standings. It can be applied to an individual game or a number of games over the course of a season.
2. *n.* A ball that is hit to the pitcher; COMEBACKER.
3. *n.* A good season following a poor or mediocre one. It can be applied to a team, manager or player.

comb the curves   *v.* To bat.

comebacker   **1.** *n.* Ball that is hit right back to the pitcher, as in a batter who is "out on a comebacker to the mound."
2. *n.* Game in which a team, losing at one point, comes back to tie or take the lead.

"Come back, little Sheba"   Trademark phrase used by sportscaster Red Barber as he announced a ball that was hit and bounced back to the mound.
ETY   The name of a William Inge play that was made into a motion picture, a popular 1952 film that won an Oscar for actress Shirley Booth. It is an apparent play on the term comebacker.

Color bar. The *USS Maine* baseball team. All of the members of the team, except for the man marked J. H. Bloomer, were killed when the ship was blown up in Havana harbor (February 15, 1898). This is also a fascinating photo because it shows a black player on an otherwise white team, a rarity then and for the next half century. *Prints and Photographs Division, the Library of Congress*

comeback player of the year *n.* Title conferred on one player in each league after each season by a United Press International poll of sportswriters. The award honors those players who make a dramatic reversal from a season or more of decline and poor play.

come home *v.* To score.

come home dry *v.* To fail to take advantage of a scoring opportunity.

come in *v.* To pitch the ball so it crosses over home plate toward the batter.

come off *v.* To have played a particular kind of game or series or finished a particular kind of season. For instance, it is sometimes said that a player is coming off a good (or bad) spring training season.

comer *n.* Promising player.
1ST 1902. (*Sporting Life*, July 12; EJN)

come through *v.* To win.

come to eat *v.* Said of a fastball that moves in on the batter; one that is likely to take a "bite" out of the batter.

"coming down" *v.* Traditional call made by the catcher to alert the second baseman to the fact that he is about to throw the ball his way. The call and the throw are made to clearly signal the end of the pitcher's warm-up between innings.

Comiskey Park Located in Chicago, Illinois, the home of the Chicago White Sox since 1910 and named for the long-time team owner, Charles A. Comiskey. Site of the first All-Star

Comiskey Park. Opening Day, July 10, 1910 (top); the first All-Star Game, July 6, 1933 (middle); aerial view of "White Sox Park," early 1970s (bottom).   *Courtesy of the Chicago White Sox*

Game (1933) and the first exploding score-board.

command   *n.* Control by a pitcher.

Commission   Prior to the appointment of the first Commissioner of Baseball in 1921, organized baseball was run by a national commission composed of the presidents of the two major leagues and a chairman hand-picked by them. When Hugh Fullerton wrote about the Commission in 1912 he was able to describe the scope of the Commission's vast major and minor league domain as "about 42 leagues, composed of about 338 clubs, and over 10,000 players."

commissioner of baseball   The chief official of major league baseball who is appointed and employed for an undetermined period by the National and American League club owners.

The office was established in 1921 in the wake of the Black Sox scandal in an effort to restore public confidence in the game. Judge Kenesaw Mountain Landis was baseball's first commissioner, and he served in that capacity until his death in 1944.

The duties of the commissioner are varied:
- Run the World Series.
- Settle grievances of players, teams or leagues that cannot be settled at lower levels. (The commissioner's jurisdiction covers the minor leagues.)
- To be the final judicial authority on all matters of appeal.
- Investigate and resolve acts that may be detrimental to the game.

Commissioner's Games   The World Series, so-called because the commissioner has supreme authority over these games. Critics say that the Commissioner has relinquished some of that authority to the television networks who have a lot to say about the hour at which the games begin.

commit oneself   *v.* To make a half swing in which the wrists break. If the umpire determines that the batter has committed himself, a strike is called.

common card/common   *n.* In the realm of baseball card collecting, this refers to the vast majority of cards, which, depicting average players who are not stars or particularly notable for any reason, are not rare. Having no pre-mium value, all common cards from a given year may bring a standard price.

comp   *n.* A free ticket to the game; short for complimentary ticket.
1ST   1902. (*Sporting Life,* October 4; EJN)
EXT   A free ticket to any event for which there is a paid admission charge.

complete game   *n.* An official statistic credited to a pitcher who pitches an entire game without relief. Complete game is usually abbreviated as CG in box scores and scorecards. The all-time single season record for complete games belongs to New York Giants pitcher Amos Richie, who completed 50 games in 1893. A fascinating complete game record belongs to Walter Johnson who pitched 38 complete game 1–0 victories during his career with the Washington Senators (1907–1927).

concentration   *n.* The edge or advantage a pitcher must possess in order to succeed; what was once known as rhythm.
1ST   1974. "When a veteran pitcher recently explained an early KO by saying, 'I lost my concentration,' my first thought was, 'What the hell does he have to concentrate on for 2½ hours?' Then it occurred to me that this was just another change in the jargon of ballplayers." (*Sporting News,* July 7)
USE   This is a tricky term because it does not relate to concentration in the traditional sense as much as to the concept of effectiveness on the mound. In fact, a seemingly distracted pitcher throwing a no-hitter might be described as having concentration.

confederate soldier   *n.* Term for a visiting player in his gray uniform, as opposed to the white uniform traditionally worn by the home team.

conference   **1.** *n.* A discussion on the pitcher's mound between the manager and his players. The purpose of the meeting may be to set defensive strategy or to call for a relief pitcher.
2. *v.* To meet on the pitcher's mound. "The Orioles conference on the mound." (Radio announcer Jon Miller on an Orioles vs. White Sox game, May 10, 1987)

connect   **1.** *v.* To hit the ball successfully—squarely and solidly.
1ST   1905. (*Sporting Life,* September 2; EJN)
2. *v.* To hit a home run.

Connie Mack Stadium   The name for Shibe Park in Philadelphia between 1953 and 1970.

contact hitter   *n.* A batter known for his ability to get hits by squarely meeting the ball with the bat, as opposed to the power hitter who meets the ball and drives it powerfully with the bat. Contact hitters are more likely to hit singles than extra-base hits. "When you talk about contact hitters the discussion must begin and end with Joe Sewell." (*Sports Collectors Digest*, April 15, 1983).
USE   The term is not universally loved. In a column on overworked sports terminology, sportswriter Jim Murray put contact hitter at the top of his list with this comment, "If a guy isn't a good 'contact' hitter, what kind of 'hitter' is he? There's no such thing as a 'non-contact' hitter. Every hit is 'contact,' isn't it?"

contend.   *v.* To be in the race for the championship. "Weaver confident that O's will contend." (*Baltimore Sun* headline, April 2, 1982)

contract   *n.* A written agreement between a player and his club in which the terms of employment are set forth.

contract-jumper   *n.* Player who breaks his contract with one team to play with another team. The term got much play when members of the union known as the Brotherhood formed their own Players' League and a number of players quit their old teams and joined new ones. When the new league folded the contract-jumpers were allowed to rejoin their old teams without penalty.
   There have been other cases of contract jumping in the 20th century, including the handful of players who joined the "outlaw" Mexican League in 1946.
1ST   "Barnie and Mike McDonald raised their holy hands in horror at the thought of employing any so-called contract-jumper . . ." (*Sporting Times*, October 31, 1891; DS)

contractor's back yard   *n.* Term describing the bumpy or uneven surface of a poorly kept infield, used before the advent of modern groundskeeping techniques.

control   *n.* A pitcher's ability to vary the speed, trajectory and placement of the ball *within* the strike zone; the pitcher's accuracy. Having good control is, as it was when stated by Hugh Fullerton in a 1912 definition, "the pitcher's principal stock in trade . . ."
1ST   1887. (*Base Ball Tribune*, June 9; EJN)

control pitcher   *n.* One known for his ability to pitch the ball to a precise desired location both inside and outside the strike zone.

controman   *n.* Modern name for an individual in baseball who always seems to get in trouble when talking to the press. A player who, according to the *Sporting News* for March 6, 1982, "creates controversy with his quotes."

Coogan's Bluff   The name of the hill behind the Polo Grounds; once synonymous with the name of the ball park, it was sometimes also known as Coogan's Hollow.

cookie   *n.* A pitch that is easy to hit; one that is easy to "get your teeth into."

coop   *n.* DUGOUT.
1ST   1909. (*American* magazine, May; EJN)

co-op club   *n.* Minor league club that agrees to develop players from a number of different major league organizations rather than serve as a farm for a single club. "As a co-op club, they're dependent on last-minute deals with major league teams who don't have room for all their signees on their Class A squads." (*USA Today*, June 17, 1986)

Cooperstown   New York State home of the Baseball Hall of Fame. The name of the town is used as a synonym for the Hall itself: "If he stays healthy, Dwight's on his way to Cooperstown." (Gary Carter on Dwight Gooden in *Newsweek*, September 2, 1985)

cop   *v.* To win.
1ST   1907. (*Lajoie's Official Baseball Guide;* EJN)

cork   **1.** *n.* A team's most effective relief pitcher.
   According to Zander Hollander in his *Baseball Lingo*, "The expression became popular with Ted Wilks, who choked off many rallies as a relief pitcher for the St. Louis Cardinals in the 1940's." It also fits nicely as a synonym for STOPPER.
2. *v.* To doctor a bat. See corked bat.

corkball   *n.* Baseball variation that has been played in the St. Louis, Missouri, area since the early 1900s. A brochure on the subject published by the Markwort Sporting Goods Company of St. Louis describes it as "a game that has many of the features of baseball yet can be played in a very small area. It is a good summertime game because no exhausting action is required—the action is centered around the pitcher, the catcher and the batter; there is no baserunning. Corkball is also played in winter in netted areas in gymnasiums."

The ball is cork-centered and weights 1¼ ounces and is 6¼ inches in circumference. The bat cannot be any longer than 38 inches and cannot be thicker in diameter than the diameter of the ball. It is normally played inside a cage that is about 75 feet long and about 20 feet wide. Teams usually have five players, but can have as few as two—a pitcher and a catcher.

Two strikes constitute an out, five balls a walk and a hit is any ball landing in fair territory. Four walks, four hits or a combination thereof, constitute a run. Each additional walk or hit in the same inning adds a run. There are five innings in a game and three outs to an inning. A batter is out if he hits a foul ball, or hits a fair ball that is caught before hitting the ground or the cage.

There are a number of corkball leagues in and around St. Louis and Memphis. Longtime catcher and now announcer, Tim McCarver, points out in his *Oh, Baby, I Love It!* that when he was a youngster in Memphis, "I got an early start on my announcing career while playing corkball, imitating Harry Caray on the play-by-play."

cork center *n.* The distinguishing feature of the new baseball introduced in 1910 to replace the rubber-centered ball. The credit for inventing the cork-centered ball was given to George A. Reach of the sporting goods company that carried his name. "Reach Dies at 86, Pioneered Cork Center in BB," was the headline carried above his obituary in the *New York Mirror* on December 8, 1954. (PT)

corked bat *n.* A bat that has been partially hollowed out at the barrel end and filled with cork, rubber or any of several other substances for the purpose of giving the batter an added advantage over the pitcher. There are two theories as to the benefits of corking a bat. One proposes that the nature of the cork acts as a springboard, allowing the batter to hit the ball farther. The other theory suggests that the reduction in weight in the barrel of the bat allows the batter the advantage of a faster swing. As with ball doctoring, any such bat tampering is expressly illegal, but not uncommon. Norm Cash, who won the 1961 American League batting title (.361 average), later admitted he used such a bat.

corker *n./arch.* A good player.
1ST 1867. (*New York Herald*, August 27; EJN)

cork one *v.* To bat a ball hard.
1ST 1876. (*Chicago Inter Ocean*, May 1; EJN)

cork popper *n.* OPENING DAY. ". . . yesterday's cork popper witnessed nine full innings of errorless ball." (Undated clipping from a Jack McDonald column, *San Francisco Call-Bulletin;* PT)

corkscrew-er *n./arch.* Tricky curveball.
1ST 1909. "And how did you like that *corkscrew-er? (Redney McGaw* by Arthur E. McFarlane; PT)

corkscrew twist *n.* Characteristic of a curveball that takes more than one change in direction.
1ST 1891. (*Chicago Herald*, May 8; EJN)

corner clippers/corner cutters *n.* Pitches that cross over the edges of the plate.
1ST 1913. (*Harpers Weekly*, September 6; EJN)

corners **1.** *n.* The two parallel sides of home plate which provide the empire with a visual basis for determining the inside and outside edges of the strike zone. To be successful, a pitcher must keep his pitches "on the corners" where they are harder for the batter to hit.
1ST 1896. (*Frank Merriwell's Schooldays;* EJN)
2. *n.* The points where the foul lines meet the outfield fence or wall.
3. *n.* The bases, especially first and third base.
1ST 1891. (*Chicago Herald*, May 5; EJN)

corps *n.* A team's pitchers as a collective group, as in "the Mets pitching corps."
1ST 1902. (*Sporting Life*, April 26; EJN)

corral **1.** *v.* To catch or field a ball.
1ST 1902. (*Spalding's Official Base Ball Guide;* EJN)
2. *v.* To collect accomplishments, as in "he corralled four assists."

"couldn't hit a bull in the ass with a shovel"/"couldn't hit the inside of a barn"/ etc. *v.* Any of a number of highly-exaggerated phrases used to typify a player who does not do well at the plate. "He couldn't hit water if he fell out of a boat," is what Tommy Lasorda said about a former shortstop named Willie Miranda during the NLCS on October 9, 1982.

Similar taunts and insults are used in other realms, from marksmanship ("couldn't hit the inside of barn") to prizefighting ("couldn't punch his way out of a paper bag") to selling ("couldn't sell ice water in hell") and are not a baseball exclusive.

count   1. *n.* At any given moment, the tally of balls and strikes charged to a batter; always given with the number of balls followed by the number of strikes. The count is determined and kept track of by the home plate umpire. **1ST** 1915. (Ring Lardner short story, "Horseshoes"; EJN)
2. The paid attendance.
3. *n./obs.* A run in the earliest days of baseball. **SEE** *Ace.*

counter   1. *n./arch.* A run.
2. *n.* One of several names for the small handheld device that umpires use to keep track of balls, strikes and outs, more commonly called INDICATORS.

counting house   *n.* Home plate.
1ST 1910. (*Baseball* magazine, April; EJN)

"counting your money?"   Once a common put-down hollered to a runner picked-off base.

country   *adj.* Solid, powerful, as when *Time* described Hank Greenberg as "a good country hitter." (November 20, 1950; PT)

country-fair hitter   *n.* A good hitter, a reference to the big, tough farmers who showed up to play baseball at country fairs.

country fair player/country fair   *n.* a grandstander; a showoff; a busher.
1ST 1937. (*Sporting News Record Book;* EJN)

country mile   *n.* Describing the distance traveled by the long ball. "He is the answer to a scout's prayer. He can throw a baseball into a barrel at 100 yards, is a ten-second sprint man and can hit a ball a country mile." (*The Saturday Evening Post,* March 9, 1935; PT)
EXT A good distance for anything from a golf ball to a thrown football.

country sinker   *n.* A spitball. In Arnold Hano's *Roberto Clemente: Batting King* it is named in a list of pitches as, ". . . that new-old pitch, the 'country sinker,' which you and I know as the spitball."

count the stitches   1. *v.* To look at a slowly pitched ball as it drifts to the plate.
2. *v.* To pitch slowly.
1ST 1937. (clipping, National League Service Bureau; EJN)
ETY This is, of course, based on an exaggerated notion because it would be impossible to see the individual stitches on any pitched ball,

no matter how slow. As a matter of fact, there are 216 stitches in a regulation baseball.

County Stadium   Milwaukee, Wisconsin, stadium that was the home of the Milwaukee Braves of the National League from the beginning of the 1953 season to the end of the 1965 season, when the team moved to Atlanta. Since the beginning of the 1970 season it has housed the American League Brewers.

courtesy runner   *n.* In amateur play, there are times when a substitute is allowed to run for a player without driving that player out of the game.

cousin   1. *n.* A particular pitcher who a batter consistently finds easy to hit; a batter's favorite pitcher. "To [Fred] Lynn, [Angels pitcher Jim] Slaton is like a favorite cousin who just doesn't get to town often enough"—Tom Mahr, WFBR, on May 22, 1986, following a Lynn home run off Slaton.
2. *n.* On a rare occasion, a batter who a pitcher finds easy to strike out.
3. *n.* Occasionally, a whole team is regarded this way, such as the Royals who were cousins to the Orioles in a period between May 1969 and August 1970 when they were beaten 23 times in a row. "A's Take 'Tiger' Cousins Into Camp for 6th Time"—headline in the May 27, 1957, *San Francisco Examiner* (PT)
1ST 1928. "Yeah—they was all callin' him 'Cousin Dick.' "—said of a pitcher who has just been yanked in T. A. Dorgan's column "Outdoor Sports" in the *San Francisco Call & Post,* August 23. (PT) It also appears in *Babe Ruth's Own Book of Baseball* published in 1928. Babe writes of Paul Zahniser who "was a 'cousin' of mine." He added, "Every time he pitched against us I knew I would get two or three hits—and so did he."
ETY The term has been widely attributed to New York Yankees pitcher Waite Hoyt who likened certain batters who faced him to cooperative family members. It was apparently a term more commonly used by players than writers in its early days. In his article, "That Unrecognized Language—Baseballese," which appears in the October 1932 *Baseball* magazine, William G. Brandt lists it as one of the terms "unfamiliar to the public." In making it "public" Brandt said, "Every batter has a list of 'cousins,' pitchers whose deliveries he finds comparatively easy to slap upon the nostrils."

Cousin. Yankee Hall of Fame pitcher Waite Hoyt. *National Baseball Library, Cooperstown, N.Y.*

EXT An easy opponent in other sports. An article on how basketball player Bob Lanier commonly scored many points when he played against the Portland Trailblazers was headlined, "Piston Center Finds Cousins." (*San Francisco Examiner*, November 29, 1972; PT)
SEE *Coz.*

cover **1.** *v.* To protect a base from an advancing runner by positioning oneself on or near it.
1ST 1861. (*New York Sunday Mercury*, August 10; EJN)
2. *v.* For the pitcher to hide a ball that is about to be pitched so that the grip cannot be spotted and interpreted by the opposition. Some gloves have tightly-woven basket-style webbing to help hide the ball.
3. *v.* To efficiently protect a section of the playing area. Great fielders are known for their ability to cover and the ultimate compliment of this nature may have been issued by Ralph Kiner who once said, "The earth is two-thirds covered by water, and the other one-third is covered by Garry Maddox."

cover a base *v.* COVER.

cover ground *v.* To run across a large amount of the field
1ST 1905. (*Sporting Life*, September 2; EJN)

cow pasture *n.* Derogatory term for a field that is in poor playing condition.

cowtail/cowtail a bit *v.* To take a long swing of the bat, with the bat held at the very end of the handle.
1ST 1937. (World Series Broadcast, October 6, Red Barber announcing; EJN)
USE Edward J. Nichols likened the long swing to the motion of a cow's tail swishing.

coz *n.* COUSIN, for short. "Hello, Coz," is an occasional (and provocative) greeting for pitcher who is easily hit by a batter.

cozy roller *n./arch.* Slowly batted ground ball.
1ST 1907. (*New York Evening Journal*, June 5; EJN)

cp/nc Scouting report shorthand for "can't play" and "no chance." " 'Bad even in wartime baseball . . . cp and nc,' Frank Cashen said of his mid-'40s run as the pepperpot second baseman for Loyola College in his native Baltimore." (*The Washington Post*, October 7, 1986, from an article about the Mets general manager)

crab **1.** *n.* Player who finds fault with others; a grouch.
2. *v.* To complain; to show a quarrelsome nature.
    Although this slang meaning of crab predates baseball, it was so commonly used in baseball circles early in this century that it was considered to be a baseball term. "Many of the worst 'crabs' in baseball are the pleasantest and most genial when off the field, their crabbedness evidently being the result of the nervous strain of playing," said Hugh Fullerton in 1912.
1ST 1909. (*New York Evening Journal*, July 8; EJN)

crackerjack *n.* Term used to describe a first-rate or spectacular player or team.
USE Sometimes spelled *crack-a-jack* in early applications.
ETY/1ST 1908. The term was in use for many years as slang for: a sailor's biscuit using salted meat; and anything first-rate or excellent. "Tom Stevens brings two cracker-jack two-year-olds from Mobile, so the touts say, in Wary and Poteen." (*The Spirit of the Times*, May 1, 1886; PT)
    The term did not come into its own until 1896 when the firm of F. W. Rueckheim and Brother of Chicago started selling a confection

of popcorn, peanuts and molasses under the name and trademark "Cracker Jack." (It had been sold as early as the Columbian Exposition in 1893 but without the name.) Before long, it was a baseball stadium staple (along with peanuts and popcorn) and even shows up in the words to the song "Take Me Out to the Ballgame." In *Mr. Dooley's Opinions* (1910), we read: "A good seat on th' bleachers, a bottle hand f'r a neefaryous decision at first base an' a bag iv' crackerjack was as far as iver I got tow're bein' a sportin' character an' look at me now!"

Evidence points to the conclusion that the specific use of the term crackerjack for baseball players follows its use for the popcorn confection popular at ballparks. This can be said because it does not show up in a baseball context until after the candy is a well-established product. Edward J. Nichols traces it back to 1908 and the short story "Dick Merriwell's Magnetism," while Peter Tamony was unable to find anything before 1910, when he finds three citations. An early example: "Good players of all kinds are wanted by every manager, but a 'cracker-jack' third baseman has a strangle hold on his job as long as he bats .200 or better." (*Letters of a Baseball Fan to His Son*, S. DeWitt Clough, 1910; PT)

Cracker Jack Old Timers Classic Since 1982, an annual all-star game between old timers of the National League vs. old timers of the American League. The game is played at Robert F. Kennedy Stadium in Washington, D.C.

cradle *n.* A training device built of long wooden slats used to sharpen the reflexes of infielders. Shaped like a large cradle, balls are thrown into it so they will carom off it at odd and unpredictable angles.

cradle-snatcher *n.* Said of a scout or bird dog who trails extremely young prospects.

crank **1.** *v.* To pitch. "Beefy Max Surkont cranked his sixteenth victory of the PCL [Pacific Coast League] season tonight as his Sacramento Solons trimmed Los Angeles, 8 to 5." (*The San Francisco News*, August 5, 1950; PT)
2. *n./obs.* A baseball fan.

In his work on baseball slang used in the *New York World* in the 1880s and reported on in the April 1986 issue of *Comments on Etymology*, Gerald Cohen reports, "At least from 1888 through 1890 the standard term for a baseball fan was a *crank*, short for *baseball crank*. I don't recall

seeing the term *fan* used at all in this time span."
1ST 1882. Cohen reports others finding the term in use from 1882 to 1910 and gives 13 examples of it in use including this from the *World*, "The arrival of Father Adrian Clapdoodle Anson and his lavender conspirators in the metropolis is always a signal for a general uprising of the cranks . . ." (May 23, 1889)
SEE *crankess, crankism, krank.*

crankess *n./obs.* Term for a female fan, a "humorous and artificial creation" according to Gerald Cohen in his report on crank. He gives this example from the *New York World:* "It was 'ladies' day' at the grounds, and . . . about five hundred crankesses took advantage of the Giants' invitation to see the game." (May 24, 1890)

crankism *n./obs.* Term for what Gerald Cohen in his work on crank defines as "oddball pessimism." One of his examples from the *World:* "The surprisingly good work by the New York team has finally put to rest all adverse criticism, and even those persons who are soaked and sodden with crankism are at last losing sight of their *ignis fatuus* in the broad glow of hope which the Giants are shedding . . ." (Aug. 5, 1888)

crank up **1.** *v.* To wind up to deliver the pitch.
2. *v.* To hit the ball. "If knuckle ball is not moving . . . if it just floats up to the batter, big and fat, batters crank up on pitcher." (San Francisco Giants pitcher Billy Muffet, pre-game radio interview, June 17, 1959; PT)

crash **1.** *v./arch.* Defined by Hugh S. Fullerton in his 1912 *Baseball Primer:* "Verb used in baseball, not to signify a single sound, but a series of hard hits. A team 'starts crashing,' when three or four batters in succession make hits." Today the term would suggest a team that was falling apart.
2. *n./arch.* A hard batted ball.
1ST 1912. (*Outing* magazine, June; EJN)

cream *v.* To hit a ball hard.

cream puff *n.* An easy ball to hit, such as one thrown by a batting practice pitcher. "He showed . . . his stuff Monday, serving up big, fat, medium fast cream puffs for the All-Star hitters to feast on." (*Houston Post* article by Mickey Herskowitz on the 1986 All-Star game

batting practice pitcher, Joseph 'Stretch' Suba, July 15, 1986; CDP)
SEE *Cuban sandwich, lollipop.*

crew **1.** *n.* The group of umpires working a particular game.
2. *n.* The workers tending the grounds at a particular ballpark. Also referred to as GROUNDCREW.

crew chief *n.* Umpire in charge.

cripple **1.** *v.* For the pitcher to get into a position where he must throw a strike because he is behind in the count. He is crippled in that he is obliged to throw the ball over the plate and cannot use his trickier deliveries. Generally reserved for situations where the count is 3–0, 2–0 or 3–1.
2. *n.* Pitch thrown when the count is against the pitcher (3–0, 2–0, 3–1) and he must sacrifice power for accuracy to make sure the ball is in the strike zone.
1ST 1914. (*New York Tribune*, October 13; EJN)

cripple shooter **1.** *n.* Batter who takes advantage of a crippled pitcher.
2. *n.* Batter who becomes especially dangerous when ahead in the count 3–0, 2–0 or 3–1.

crocus sack *n.* Impending victory. One of the terms that became part of the stunning verbal delivery of broadcaster Red Barber. He would say that a game was "all tied up in a crocus sack" if it were almost won.

crook *n./arch.* CURVEBALL.
1ST 1908. (*New York Evening Journal*, May 7; EJN)

crooked arm *n.* Uncomplimentary reference to a left-handed pitcher or any pitcher with an unorthodox delivery.
1ST 1932. (*Baseball* magazine, October; EJN)

crooked pitch *n.* The CURVEBALL.
   The term was used by Martin Quigley to title his magnificent history of the curveball, *The Crooked Pitch.*

Crosley Field The home of the Cincinnati Reds from 1912 to 1970, which was known as Redland Field until 1933 when it was renamed for team owner Powell Crosley, who built the Crosley automobile.

cross bats *v./obs.* To compete in a game.

crossfire/crossfire delivery *n.* A sidearm pitch that appears to cross the strike zone on the diagonal. It is accomplished when the pitcher begins his delivery by stepping toward the baseline rather than taking the usual step toward home plate—that is, a right-handed pitcher stepping toward third base. Lefty Eddie Plank who pitched for the Philadelphia A's in the early days of this century was known for this pitch and helped make it famous.
1ST 1902. (*Sporting Life*, September 13; EJN)

cross-firing *v.* To throw a sequence of pitches as explained in Lester Chadwick's *Baseball Joe of the Silver Stars* (1912): "Cross-firing is merely sending the ball first over one side of the plate then the other and then right over centre." (DS)

cross-handed grip *n.* An incorrect hold on the bat in which the batter's hands are crossed. "[Hank] Aaron started as a cross-handed hitting softball player . . ." (UPI dispatch on the occasion of Hank Aaron's admission to the Hall of Fame, August 1, 1982)

cross-over pivot *n.* Footwork often required of a second baseman when turning a double play. After receiving the ball from the shortstop, the second baseman touches second with his left foot and relays the ball to first base as he swings his right foot over the bag and plants it.

cross the plate/cross the platter/cross the rubber *v.* To score.

cross up *v.* To fool or mislead a player on your own team. It is commonly used to describe a pitcher throwing the catcher off balance by pitching something unexpected; for example, a breaking ball when a fast ball is anticipated.

crouch **1.** *n.* The catcher's playing position: balanced on the balls of his feet with his weight on his haunches.
2. *v.* To take a low batting stance.

crowd **1.** *n.* The spectators as a collective body.
2. *v.* To take a batting stance close to the plate, to CROWD THE PLATE.

crowd the corners *v.* To fill the bases with runners.

crowd the plate *v.* To hover close to the strike zone; to crouch on the inner edge of the batter's box as close to the plate as possible.
1ST 1901. (*Frank Merriwell's Marvel;* EJN)

crow hop   *n.* An extra little step at the end of a pitcher's motion.
USE   Is this term an antique? In *The Old Ball Game*, Tristram Potter Coffin reports, "In the spring of 1969, pitcher Jerry Johnson was interviewed on the radio. He told how he had rid his pitching motion of a little 'crow hop' . . . during winter ball. Two weeks later members of the Houston Astros . . . denied the phrase was still in use."

crow hopping   *n.* A softball term for jumping off the mound *before* the ball has been released. It is an illegal pitch that is often associated with the *windmill pitch*.

crown   *n.* An honor figuratively worn by a player or team that comes in first place, either in the standings or in the statistical accounting of some aspect of performance. For instance, the batting crown goes to the player who has the highest batting average in his league.

crush   *v.* To hit a pitched ball with great power.

crush zone   *n.* Pitch thrown to the point where the batter is most likely to hit the ball; the batter's wheelhouse. "A pitch thrown right in the crush zone, I mean, when it leaves the pitcher's hand the ball is right in a place where the batter was swinging—and he got all of it." (Keith Moreland on "wheelhouse" in the August 1987 *Vineline*)

CS   Standard box score and scorecard abbreviation for CAUGHT STEALING.

cub   *n./arch.* Recruit or rookie, a term popular around the turn of the century, which probably influenced the naming of the youthful Chicago Cubs.
1ST   1906. (*Sporting Life*, March 10; EJN)

Cuban   *adj.* In the days before a number of Latin Americans were in the majors and well before the color line was broken, this was a name for black American ballplayers. In his 1943 article on "Baseball Jargon," Franklin P. Huddle wrote, "Since Negroes have, by devious means, been kept out of major league baseball, their evasion is to sometimes call themselves Cubans. Thus, Cuban All-Stars is a frequent name of a Negro team."

Cuban forkball   *n.* SPITBALL. The term got a boost through an often repeated comment by relief pitcher John Wyatt who played during the 1960s. "I use a Cuban fork ball. I learned to use it while I was swimming in the Mediterranean Sea." The pitch was also used by Orlando Peña when he staged a comeback in 1973. As Gaylord Perry recalled it in *Me and the Spitter*, "He returned to the major leagues at the age of thirty-eight—thanks mostly to a pitch he calls a 'Cuban fork ball.' It is not a dry pitch." (CDP)

Cuban palmball   *n.* Spitball. "A prime suspect in those days was Pedro Ramos, who resembled [Gaylord] Perry by touching his cap and shirt frequently before pitching his 'Cuban palmball.' The ball did so many tricks en route to the plate that the umpire once made Ramos go into the clubhouse and change his shirt three times a game." (Joseph Durso in the *New York Times*, August 31, 1982)

Cuban sandwich   *n.* An especially tantalizing batting practice pitch, such as those thrown by Minnesota Twins' hitting instructor Tony Oliva. " 'The Cuban sandwich is a confidence builder,' Oliva said, 'If you cannot hit a long ball off a Cuban sandwich, you are in trouble.' " (*Sporting News* report from the Twins' 1986 spring training camp, by Patrick Reusse)

Cubs factor   *n.* Theory, annually brought out during post-season play, which proposes that the team with the most ex-Chicago Cubs will lose the World Series. The theory was given new life in the 1986 World Series when the Mets, with no former Cubs on their roster, beat the Red Sox, whose first baseman, ex-Cub Bill Buckner committed a critical error in game six. On October 30, 1986, *USA Today* concluded that there was something to the theory: "Since 1970, a dozen ex-Cubs have played for world championship teams and 23 have played for losing teams."
USE   The basis for the "Cubs factor" is the fact that this is the team that has gone the longest without winning a World Series. As of this writing the last year the Cubs won the World Championship was 1908.

cudgel   *n.* A baseball bat.
1ST   1908. (*Baseball* magazine, June; EJN)

cue ball shot   *n.* Fluke hit hit off the top of the bat suggesting a cue stick striking a billiard ball. Such a hit is sometimes said to have been cued up.

cunning thumb/cunning thumber/cunny thumb/cunny-thumb/cunnythumb/cunny-thumber 1. *adj.* Describing a pitcher, or pitchers, who throws slow balls. "And it's a crime to get beat by the cunny-thumb pitching they have. Brother, I'd like to be playing them during the regular season." (Marty Marion, a manager of the St. Louis Browns, quoted in the *San Francisco Examiner,* April 4, 1953; PT) **1ST** 1937. (New York *Daily News,* January 17; EJN)
2. *n.* A player who cannot throw, or throws, as is often characterized, "like a woman."
ETY This is an old term used in marbles playing by children on both sides of the Atlantic. In marbles it refers to shooting in the "female manner," that is, from a closed fist with the thumb tucked under the first three fingers. According to Eric Partridge in his *Dictionary of Slang,* cunny is a reference to female genitalia dating back to the 17th century. Despite this clearly sexual reference, there seems to have been no taboo about its use in baseball (or in marbles for that matter) as it shows up in such places as the New York *Daily News* (January 17, 1937) and Dizzy Dean's various glossaries. Its decline in use as a baseball term has paralleled the decline in marbles as a childhood pastime.

cup *n.* A small, hard metal or plastic device commonly worn by players to protect their genitals. Jim Bouton in *Ball Four:* "What baseball players do to each other is punch each other in the groin and say 'cup check.' " (CDP)

cup of coffee *n.* A brief trial with the parent club by a minor league player. "Billy Williams' cup of major league coffee cooled in just 10 days." (UPI story, *San Francisco Chronicle,* August 29, 1969; PT)
These trials often take place during the month of September, when teams are allowed to expand their rosters to 40 players. It allows the brass of the major league team to get a glimpse at its new talent.
1ST 1908. (*Baseball* magazine, August; EJN)
ETY The phrase seems to have derived from the observation that a young player's first taste of the major leagues is usually quite short, figuratively just long enough to drink a cup of coffee.
EXT The term has been applied to quick trial periods in other sports. An example from pro football: "Schichtle had a cup of coffee last season with the New York Giants and was picked up by the new Atlanta Falcons and put on waivers there before the 49ers took a look at him." (*San Francisco Chronicle,* August 2, 1966; PT)

cupped bat *n.* TEACUP END.

curfew 1. *n.* Time players must be in quarters, according to rule set down by the manager.
2. *n.* Time that a game must end in accordance with league *curfew rule* or local regulations. "Suspension of Saturday's game after eight innings because of the league's 1 a.m. curfew was the first at Memorial Stadium since July 31, 1978." (*USA Today,* June 22, 1987)

curfew rule *n.* Hour set by the municipality or the league at which a game must be terminated or suspended. For instance: American League: "All night games must be called at 1 a.m. local time. But if an inning is started prior to 1 a.m. city time, it can be completed."

curtain call *n.* The practice of a player coming out of the dugout to acknowledge the call of the fans. The call usually starts in the form of a chant of the player's name ("Rusty-Rusty-Rusty" or "Ed-die-Ed-die-Ed-die") to honor the player for a home run, personal milestone, crucial hit or, in the case of a pitcher, a number of strikeouts.
No clear idea exists as to when the practice began, but it certainly dates back no further than the late 1970s. "Can you imagine what Early Wynn would have done to the next batter after somebody took a bow for hitting a home run?" asked George Vecsey in the *New York Times* on August 15, 1982. "There is reason to believe the current practice of curtain calls did not begin until Bob Gibson was safely retired after 1975."
During his last at bat in Fenway Park, Ted Williams hit a home run that John Updike recalled in *The New Yorker:* "Though we thumped, wept, and chanted 'We want Ted' for minutes after he hid in the dugout, he did not come back." Updike later learned from the papers that both the players and the umpires had begged Williams to come out and acknowledge the crowd.
Compare this to Carl Yastrzemski's final at bat in Fenway in 1983. He popped out to the first baseman, and then, as described by Stephen Williams in the January 1984 *Inside Sports,* "The fans clamored for Yaz and he came out

Curtain-raiser. Opening Day 1886 at the Polo Grounds: New York vs. Boston. *Prints and Photographs Division, the Library of Congress*

and lifted his hat, and then he came out again, and later that night, when he was supposed to be attending a cocktail party in his honor, he stood on a street in the Back Bay and signed autographs for an hour."

curtain-raiser   *n.* The first game of the season, a series or a doubleheader.
1ST   1912. (*New York Tribune*, September 9; EJN)

curve/curve ball/curveball/curved ball   *n.* A pitch that is thrown with a forceful, downward spin and snap of the wrist, causing it to drop or break and veer to the side as it nears home plate. A right-handed pitcher's curveball tends to veer to the left while that thrown by a left-handed pitcher heads to the right.

Although few now doubt the fact that the ball actually curves, there have been those who maintained that it was an illusion. Several experiments determined that it was real. For instance, in a well-publicized 1959 experiment, physicist Dr. Lyman J. Briggs (with the aid of former Brooklyn Dodger infielder Cookie Lavagetto) determined that a curveball does in fact curve. Briggs determined that the absolute maximum curve—or break from the line of trajectory—that could be created was 17.5 inches over the distance of 60.5 feet from the mound to the plate.
1ST   1874. (*New York Herald*, July 7; EJN)
ETY   The pitch has been credited to Hall of Famer Candy Cummings of Brooklyn who first began working on it in 1864 at boarding school. He later said he came on the idea in 1863 while throwing clam shells, which naturally curved. In 1867 he first applied it in a game while playing for the Brooklyn Excelsiors.

But there are many other claims. In 1973 the National Baseball Library collected the various claims made by or on behalf of five other men.
EXT   1. *n.* A surprise, as in "Russians Throw Curve Into Suez Parley." (*San Francisco News*, August 10, 1956; PT)

Curveball. The Hall of Fame plaque for the father of the curveball, William Arthur "Candy" Cummings. *National Baseball Library, Cooperstown, N.Y.*

2. *n.* Specifically, a tough, tricky question, such as one that shows up in an examination. A character in a Steve Canyon comic-strip says, "That's an unfair curve to throw at a newspaperman." (*San Francisco Examiner,* July 17, 1956; PT)

3. *adj.* By extension, *curvy* has come to mean dishonest or full of surprises. "Some of these make-money-at-home outfits are curvy." (Ann Landers column for June 13, 1964; PT)

4. *n.* Also, a *curveballer* is a person with questionable ethics. "In a business [prizefighting] full of curve ballers, Fran threw right down the middle." (*San Francisco Chronicle,* March 2, 1968; PT)

cushion   **1.** *n.* A BASE.
1ST   1891. (*Chicago Herald,* May 5; EJN)
2. A comfortable lead in a game, a series of games or the overall standings.

cushion night   *n.* Game at which, as a promotional attraction, seat cushions are given away to fans. More often than not, it seems, many fans forego sitting on the cushions for throwing

them on the field. "For the second straight year, the Chicago White Sox 'Cushion Night' resulted in a delay of play Friday night." (*Des Moines Register,* May 31, 1987)

cuspidor curve   *n./arch.* Spitball pitcher.

cut   *n.* The batter's swing. "Lord, he has a wicked cut." (Dennis "Oil Can" Boyd on first pitching to Jose Canseco, *USA Today,* May 16, 1986)
1ST   1932. (*Baseball* magazine; EJN)

cut ball/cut fast ball   *n.* A ball that is cut, slit or deeply scratched so that when thrown it will create an irregular airflow, which will cause it to break unnaturally. "Mike Scott throws the best one. It's scraped on one side of the ball. If you hold it in the middle to throw it the ball will break in the opposite direction of where you cut it." (Keith Moreland, *Vinelane,* August 1987)

cut base   *v.* To fail to touch a base while advancing.

cut down   *v.* Throw out a runner, especially when an extra base or stolen base is being attempted.
1ST   1912. (*New York Tribune,* September 5; EJN)

cutdown date/cutdown time   *n.* The day on which a major league team must cut its roster to the maximum number of players allowed (currently 25). The surplus players must be traded, sold or sent to minor league teams by the deadline.

cutey   *n.* Pitcher who specializes in curves and slow stuff on the corners.

cut off   **1.** *v.* To intercept a throw coming in from the outfield on its way to home plate. The intercepting infielder then decides whether to relay the ball to the plate or another base.
2. *n.* The interception itself.
1ST   1863. (Chadwick Scrapbooks; EJN)

cutoff man   *n.* Player who intercepts or intends to intercept a throw from the outfield. "With a runner on second and a hit to center field, it is vital to hit the cutoff man. That can be one of the toughest plays in baseball." (Toronto Blue Jay outfielder Lloyd Moseby, *USA Today,* April 6, 1987)

cutoff play   *n.* On a ball hit to the outfield with one or more runners on base, the ball is thrown in from the outfield and intercepted by an infielder who then must make the play. Ideally, the infielder should try to get out the lead runner who may be attempting to score. But if it is too late to stop the lead runner, the infielder will throw it to a lesser base in an effort to prevent other runners from advancing.

The unpredictable outcome of the cutoff play based on the fielder's split-second decision makes it an exciting play for the spectator.

cutoff position   *n.* A point where a throw from the outfield can be intercepted.

cutouts   *n.* The heel and toe areas of a player's outer or team socks which have been left out of the socks to create a stirrup and allow some of the white understockings or SANI-TARIES to show. "Frank Robinson, the celebrated Baltimore outfielder, wears the highest cutouts in the American League." (*The Summer Game* by Roger Angell; CDP)

cutter   *n.* Batter who swings at a lot of pitches outside of the strike zone.

cut the corner/cut corners   *v.* To pitch a ball across the inside or outside edge of the plate, making it hard to hit and a called strike if passed up.
1ST   1908. (*Spalding's Official Base Ball Guide;* EJN)

cut the plate   *v.* To pitch the ball right over the center of home plate, as if to cut it in half.

cut way to bases   *v./arch.* To slide into a base feet first with one's spikes up.
1ST   1911. (*American* magazine, May; EJN)

cycle   *n.* When a batter gets a single, double, triple and home run in the same game. It is usually stated in the phrase hit for the cycle.

cyclone pitcher   *n.* Pitcher who delivers with great speed. It is for this that Denton True Young became known as Cy. The name Cy-clone has been used to describe some young pitchers of the modern era because of their resemblance to previous winners of the Cy Young Award. A story on the resemblance of pitcher Storm Davis to his Oriole teammate Jim Palmer received this headline: "Storm Davis: A 'Cy Clone' Composite." (*Washington Post,* June 12, 1983)
1ST   1891. (*Chicago Herald,* July 1; EJN)

Cybex   *n.* A machine for exercise and reha-bilitation favored by a number of players. "The Royals . . . have become so attached to their Cybex machine, which allows isolation of spe-cific muscles for rehabilitation and condition-ing, [that] they take it on road trips." (*USA Today,* February 13, 1986)

cyclops   *n./arch.* A player who wears glasses.

Cy Young Award   Annual award given to the pitcher in each league who is deemed by the Baseball Writers Association of America to have been the outstanding performer. It is named for Cy Young who won 511 games between 1890 and 1911. The award was first handed out in 1956 and went to the single best pitcher in the Major Leagues. Don Newcombe of the Brooklyn Dodgers was the award's first recipient. Since 1967, there has been a winner named for both the American and National Leagues. In 1981 Fernando Valenzuela became the first rookie to win the award.

Some think that a jinx exists, which sabotages a pitcher's season the year following winning the award. In *Baseball Lite,* Jerry Howarth de-fines the award as, "The kiss of death, often followed by an arm injury, surgery or simply an off year."

Cy Young Award. Denton True "Cy" Young.   *National Baseball Library, Cooperstown, N.Y.*

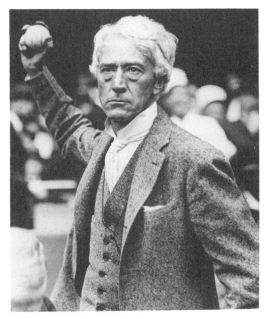

Czar. Kenesaw Mountain Landis throwing out the first ball to start the second game of the 1922 World Series. *National Baseball Library, Cooperstown, N.Y.*

Czar   *n.* Name associated with the Commissioner of Baseball because of his great personal power when dealing with issues having to do with the good of the game.

Before there was a commissioner the term was applied to the presidents of the two major leagues. It is hardly a misnomer, as the commissioner has absolute power in a few critical areas. When, in the wake of the 1919 "Black Sox" scandal, Judge Kenesaw Mountain Landis was appointed the Commissioner of Baseball, he was often referred to as "Czar" Landis in the newspapers.

Besides the other commissioners following Landis, the title has been bestowed on other powerful baseball figures. A UPI story on Walter O'Malley of the Dodgers, which appeared in the *San Francisco Chronicle* in 1969, is titled "Baseball Czar." (January 29; PT)

1ST   1912. (*Hampton* magazine, May; EJN)

ETY   Originally the title of the powerful Russian emperors, the term was applied to railroad magnates and political bosses, among others, before it came to baseball. "Czar is what they call me in the papers when they do not call me 'rogue.'" (*The Boss, and How He Came to New York* By Alfred Henry Lewis, 1902) It was also used as a nickname for T. B. Reid (1839–1902) during the years he was speaker of the House of Representatives and ran that body with rigid, rigorous adherence to the parliamentary rules. Since the title was pinned on Landis it has been used liberally for people given extraordinary powers.

D The lowest level of minor league play after the E level was eliminated. Traditionally, D-level teams were situated in cities with a population of less than 100,000 people.

daffiness boys **1.** *n.* Nickname for a team with a madcap or clownishly inept reputation. "No manager ever had more woes than Stengel in the days when he piloted the 'daffiness boys' of the Brooklyn Dodgers and later the equally inept Boston Braves." (*San Francisco News*, June 21, 1956; PT)

The daffiness label seems to have a special place in baseball, where it can stick with a team or player for years. This is the opening line of a November 30, 1987, *Washington Post* obituary: "Floyd Caves (Babe) Herman, 84, one of baseball's top batters who was probably best known for his part in bringing the Brooklyn Dodgers and Brooklyn itself a national reputation for irrepressible daffiness, died yesterday in a hospital in Glendale, Calif."

Daffiness boys. Jay Hanna "Dizzy" Dean on the left and Paul Dee "Daffy" Dean on the right. *Prints and Photographs Division, the Library of Congress*

2. *n.* Collective nickname for Dizzy and Daffy Dean, brothers from Arkansas whose real names were Jay Hanna and Paul Dee Dean. Both were first-rate pitchers for the St. Louis Cardinals, a team that captured the public fancy as cut-ups and pranksters. "Me and Paul can do it all," was Dizzy's famous line on the combo.

daily win *n.* Club meeting held before the game.

daisy clipper/daisy cutter/daisy dipper/ daisy scorcher *n.* Long-established terms for a hard-hit ground ball that skims the grass without rebounding, presumably removing any daisies in its path. Henry Chadwick wrote of the daisy cutter: "It is a hit ball very difficult to field, and, consequently, shows good batting."
1ST 1866. Daisy cutter may be the oldest of the three as Edward J. Nichols traces it back to an 1866 article in the *New York Herald*. Daisy clipper shows up in Thomas W. Lawson's *Krank* of 1888 where it is defined in terms of a ball bouncing through a meadow as "The sphere in the act of parting a Kranklet from her bonnet."
EXT The term shows up in the 1881 glossary in the turf section of the *New York Clipper Almanac* as "A horse that keeps his feet near the ground in trotting or running." (PT) Much later the term became a name for small World-War II rockets. "Marines promptly nicknamed the skipping, hell-raising rocket shells 'Daisy Cutters.'" (*Time*, February 7, 1944) It was also the official nickname for a bomb of the Vietnam War.

D&M model glove With D&M standing for "dropping and moaning," this is the type of glove presumably worn by a fielder who has committed an error. Such players were once taunted by their teammates: "What are you using, the D&M model?" D&M was a legitimate brand name of yore.

Daniel Webster *n.* Name for a player who is good at taunting umpires and other verbal skills. A player who looks or acts wise. It refers to the oratorical skills of the 19th-century statesman, Daniel Webster.

Day. Cy Young (left) and catcher Lou Criger on Cy Young Day, August 13, 1908. The caption written on the back of the original photograph says, in part, "Crowd of 28,000 attended. Young received $8,500." *National Baseball Library, Cooperstown, N.Y.*

darter *n.* A line drive.

dash off with the pennant *v.* To win the league championship.

Day **1.** *n.* A game used to commemorate a player, manager or coach. There is usually a ceremony attached to such a day and gifts are given to the player being honored. Days can be set for players about to retire, retiring or after retirement. "Guidry was a classy member of the Yankees for 11 years. His exit should have been marked by a 'day' at Yankee Stadium at the end of his career, not by a meaningless midnight telephone call to Lafayette, La." (Murray Chass, *New York Times*, at a moment when it looked like Ron Guidry would retire, January 11, 1987)
2. *n.* A promotional event that is given this name except when it is held after sundown, when it is called a night. Charles Poe jotted down some of the special days and nights that

he encountered while reading baseball books. They include Cap Day, Bat Day, Poster Day, Hot Pants Day, Senior Citizen's Day and Fan Appreciation Day.

day at the beach *n.* Derogatory term for a poor hitter, one considered an "easy out." Usually stated in the negative—"he's no day at the beach"—to designate a wily hitter, this is a recent addition to baseballese.

day ball *n.* Baseball played during the day, as opposed to night ball. " 'Everybody wants to say we [the Cubs] lost in '69 because of day ball,' says catcher Randy Hundley." (*Sport*, October 1984)

day game *n.* A game played in natural light. It is a distinction that came about with the advent of artificial lights and night games.

daylight play *n.* Defensive maneuver performed by an infielder and the pitcher in an effort to pick off a base runner. While the runner takes his lead, the infielder quietly slips back to the base. Simultaneously the pitcher steps off the rubber and spins around toward that base. If the pitcher feels there is a chance to pick off the runner—if he sees "daylight" between the runner and the base—he throws the ball to the infielder for the attempted pick-off. If the pitcher doesn't see daylight, he simply holds the ball, having at least moved the runner back to the base.

dead ball   **1.** *n.* A ball that is not in play for any one of a number of reasons, including temporarily suspended play. It may be deemed dead if it has hit a batter, been handled by a spectator, come in contact with an umpire or hit foul. If an area of the field is ruled dangerous for play, a ball hit to that area is ruled dead. The ball becomes live again when the umpire allows the pitcher to take the ball and step on the pitching rubber.
1ST   1869. (*New York Herald* August 1; EJN)
2. *n.* A baseball that, due to certain properties of its component materials, deadens the impact when hit with a bat.

dead ball era/dead ball times   *n.* Period before 1920 when men like Ty Cobb and Honus Wagner played the game with a much less lively baseball. Ruth and Gehrig on the other hand are considered to have played in the early live ball days.

The dead ball was phased out of the game by organized baseball to give Babe Ruth better opportunity to show off his home run hitting ability. It also served to take some of the attention away from baseball's moment of shame: the 1919 Black Sox scandal.

dead batter   *n.* Batter who approaches the plate without a bat. In his dictionary, Burt Dunne adds: "Dugout legalists claim there is no rule in book that forces batter to use a bat at the plate, and that umpire must proceed in normal fashion, calling balls and strikes."

dead body   *n.* Bench jockey's description of a nonchalant or low-key player.

dead fish   **1.** *n.* A pitch. Usually, a slowly pitched ball; a nothin' ball, but sometimes used for an unorthodox pitch of any kind. "Ron Guidry calls his new pitch the 'dead fish.' It's a little like a screwball, and it has him off to a 2–0 start for the New York Yankees in 1986." (*Washington Post*, April 14, 1986)

2. *n.* A bunted ball that scurries a short distance and then stops—dies in the grass. Such hits rarely occur on artificial turf.

dead hands   *n.* Said of a batter who keeps his hands locked in a rigid position while swinging, rather than rolling his wrists.

deadhead   **1.** *v./arch.* To get a base on balls; to get a free ride.
1ST   1912. (*New York Tribune*, October 6; EJN)
2. *n.* Front-office slang for a spectator admitted on a complimentary ticket.
ETY   Appears to have been in use as a theatrical term (for a patron admitted free) and railroad term (person who takes a free ride) before its baseball application.

dead mackerel   *n.* Slow ball. "He kept feeding me the dead mackerel and what could I do?" ("Jargon of the Field," *Baseball Digest*, August 1945)

dead red   *n.* A FASTBALL.

Dead Sox   *n.* Derogatory nickname for the Boston Red Sox. In Stephen King's *Different Seasons* a character's mood is elevated when the 1967 Red Sox win the pennant: "There was a goofy sort of feeling that if the Dead Sox could come to life, then maybe *anybody* could . . ." (CDP)

dead spot   *n.* A period of ineffective pitching.

"Pitchers go through a dead spot in the spring where they try to throw something good and nothing comes out," Jimy Williams told the *St. Petersburg Times* in a March 26, 1986, article: "Your arm feels good and your delivery is good but it's just not there. I think some of our guys are going through that now."

deal   **1.** *v.* To trade a player or players. To say that a team will not "deal" a certain player is to say he will not be traded.
2. *n.* A trade.

deal from the bottom/deal from the bottom of the deck/deal off the bottom   *v.* To pitch underhand.
1ST   1937. (*The Sporting News Record Book;* EJN)
ETY   Edward J. Nichols wrote, "Named from the poker term indicating an unfair or 'underhand' passing out of cards."

Deanism   *n.* Term for any one of scores of words, phrases and statements coined by the late Dizzy Dean. Though many were grammat-

Deanism. A 1948 NBC publicity photograph shows Dean a few days before he made his network radio debut. *National Baseball Library, Cooperstown, N.Y.*

ically incorrect, they often were quite inventive and descriptive. In his own vernacular, for instance, players always "slud" into base. In his book of baseball terms, Jerry Howarth insists that Dizzy helped establish the popularity of the live television "Game of the Week" when, on the air, he referred to an act of courage as "testicle fortitude."

death valley *n.* Term for a particularly deep outfield area in a given ballpark. Because of the deep dimensions, it is harder to hit home runs and fly balls are an almost certain out. A well-known "death valley" is left-center field in Yankee Stadium.

decision **1.** *n.* The scoring outcome of a game, such as 3–2 decision.
2. *n.* Ruling by an umpire.

deck **1.** *n.* Location of the player next in line to hit after the present batter; the on deck position.
2. *n.* A layer or tier or seats in a baseball stadium.
3. *v.* To knock a batter down with a pitch (either by intimidation or a direct hit).

decking *n.* The act of being knocked down by a pitch.

decoy **1.** *v.* To run in such a manner as to deceive a defensive player. For instance, a batter hits the ball and acts as if he will stop at first to trick the fielder into thinking the play is ending. At this point he breaks for second.

2. *v.* For the offense to lure a player out of position or off base. For example, employing the hidden ball trick. A rarer example would be a second baseman who acts in such a way as to get the runner on first to try and steal; he is said to be decoying the runner.
3. *v.* To lead a batter to guess incorrectly the type or location of the next pitch.
4. *n.* The deceptive act itself; decoying.

deep **1.** *adv.* Far from the plate, as opposed to shallow, which is close to the plate. Both infielders and outfielders may play deep, while the batter may hope to hit the ball deep or "go deep." A batter planning to touch up a pitcher will say, "I'm going to take him deep."
2. *adj.* Rich in talent; such as a deep bench or deep bullpen. Earl Weaver's term for a team with much talent in reserve was "deep depth."

deep count *n.* A tally against the batter of either two balls and two strikes or three balls and two strikes (2-and-2 or 3-and-2).

deep in the hole *adj.* Said of a ball fielded toward the outfield in the area between the shortstop and third base.

deer *n.* A fast runner; a player who can "high tail it."

deface *v.* To mar the surface of the ball so that it moves erratically when pitched.

defense **1.** *n.* The team, or any player on that team, in the field.
2. *n.* The total strategy of the team in the field, involving such variables as the positioning of fielders, pick-off plays and pitchouts. The purpose of the defense is to get three outs per inning without allowing the offense to score a run.

defo *n.* In softball, the DESIGNATED PLAYER who is only playing defense.

deke *n.* Short for decoy.

delay *n.* An official suspension of play before or during a game.
   "The [Pittsfield, Mass.] Cubs drew an estimated 3,600 fans for their Fireworks Night game with the Albany-Colonie Yankees. But after a 36-minute pre-game sun delay, an 86-minute delay due to power failure, and 10 innings of baseball, the Cubs and Yankees finished in a 4–4 tie in a game suspended by an Eastern League curfew rule." (*The Berkshire Eagle,* July 5, 1985)

delayed double steal   *n.* A deceptive base running maneuver attempted when runners are at first and third base. The play begins as, on the pitch, the runner at first moves toward second on an apparent steal attempt. Before the catcher—who has the ball—makes the throw to second, the runner stops as if to return to first. If the catcher relaxes, the runner then starts again for second at top speed to induce the catcher's throw. As the ball is thrown, the runner on third breaks for home.

delayed steal   *n.* A play in which the runner steals after the ball has been returned to the pitcher or after the defensive team has started another play. The success of the play hinges on the extent to which the element of surprise has caught a fielder unaware or out of proper defensive position.
1ST   1908. (*American* magazine, May; EJN)

deliver   1. *v.* To pitch; to complete one's delivery.
1ST   1866. (Constitution and By-Laws of the Olympic Baseball Club of Philadelphia; EJN)
2. *v.* To come through in a pinch.

delivery   *n.* The complete combination of pitcher movements in executing a pitch, from windup to the release of the ball.
2. The manner and quality by which a pitch is executed.
1ST   1876. (*New York Tribune*, July 26; EJN)

Dem Bums   Traditional nickname for the Brooklyn Dodgers established and characterized by a cartoon tramp drawn by Willard Mullin.
ETY/1ST   1937. In 1958 Mullin revealed the origin of the bum in a television interview, which was then retold in the *Sporting News* (December 3, 1958). He said that the idea came from a cab driver in 1937. It seems that Mullin was on his way home from a doubleheader in Brooklyn in which the Dodgers had won one game, putting them in fourth place and then lost the second, knocking them back into the second division.

The character was inspired when the taxi driver turned to Mullin and asked, "How did our Bums come out?"

dent it/dent the ball   *v.* To hit the ball hard.

dent the garden wall   *v.* To hit a ball off the outfield fence.

Dem Bums. Willard Mullin's Bum in 1955, after the Brooklyn Dodgers defeated the Yankess in the World Series four games to three. *National Baseball Library, Cooperstown, N.Y.*

department   *n.* A position on a club, for instance, the catching department.

deposit the pill   *v.* To hit a ball a long distance. Hitting a home run is often stated, "to deposit the pill in the seats."

derrick   *v.* To remove or yank a pitcher; to "lift" from the game.

designated hitter   *n.* In the American League, the pitcher does not bat but rather a 10th player known as the designated hitter or DH is inserted into the batting order. This rule has been in effect since the beginning of the 1973 season.

There is no DH in the National League except during the World Series when teams from both leagues can use a DH in games played in the American League park. Neither team can use a DH in a World Series game played in a National League park. Between 1976 and 1986, before this World Series plan went into effect, the rule had been to use the DH in alternating years.
1ST   1973. "In the baseball box scores this summer, he will be listed as the 'dh,' the des-

Designated hitter. Yankee slugger Ron Blomberg visits his own display at the Baseball Hall of Fame in 1975. His historic appearance as the first DH was on April 6, 1973.   *National Baseball Library, Cooperstown, N.Y.*

ignated hitter for the pitcher . . ." (Joe Durso, *New York Times*, February 4)
ETY   The idea was not a new one when it was adopted by the American League. It was actually first suggested by National League President John H. Heydler in 1928.
EXT   Designated hitter and DH are beginning to show up as terms for an announcer who steps in and helps out. "Nice DH job turned in by Brent Musburger for the ailing Harry Caray . . . Tuesday, during the Cubs' opening 9–3 loss to the St. Louis Cardinals." (*USA Today*, April 8, 1987)

designated pinch-hitter   *n.* Early term for the designated hitter, which has seldom been used since its adoption by the American League.

designated player (DP)   *n.* Used in fast pitch softball since 1987—a player who may be substituted for any player in a game but who must

remain in the same position in the batting order while remaining in the game. The DP is designated before the game and may reenter once as long as reentry is into the same position in the batting order. The DP can play defense, or the player whose bat has been taken over by the DP can stay in the game defensively. The defense-only player is known as the "defo."

designated runner   *n.* Player whose only role is to pinch run; to enter the game as a substitute base runner. Term was created to cover Herb Washington, a track star hired by Charlie Finley in the mid 1970s to run for the Oakland As. Washington scored 33 runs without ever once appearing at the plate.

designated sitter   *n.* Informal reference to the American League DH during World Series games played without one. Applied to the Red

Sox's key hitter Don Baylor (frequently) throughout the 1986 World Series.

Detroit Tigers   The name of the American League's Eastern Division franchise in Detroit, Michigan. Originally known as the Wolverines because Michigan is the Wolverine State, this American League team was nicknamed the Tigers in 1901 by a writer for the *Detroit Free Press* named Phil J. Reid. Noting that the blue and orange stockings of the team reminded him of the Princeton colors, he suggested the team use the same mascot as the Ivy Leaguers.

They have also been referred to as the Bengals and, during Ty Cobb's reign (1905–1928), the Tygers.

deuce   1. *n.* The CURVEBALL.
ETY   A borrowing from the most basic level of sandlot baseball where the catcher has two signals: one finger for the fastball and two for the curve. (DS)
2. *n.* A double play. "They're going to turn the deuce—Murray to Ripkin and back to Murray." (John Mahr, June 30, 1986, Orioles vs. Brewers)

deuces wild   *n.* Situation in which there are two outs; the count is two balls/two strikes on the batter and, perhaps, two runners are on base. Popularized by broadcasters Vin Scully and Joe Garagiola on NBC-TV's "Game of the Week," this term is occasionally used to describe such situations by radio and television announcers.

development contract   *n.* Name of the legal arrangement made by a major league team and a minor league club under which the latter will work to develop the skills of a specific player. A recent estimate is that a third of the cost of running a minor league club can be offset with the money from such contracts.

DH   Standard abbreviation for both designated hitter and doubleheader.

DH-ing   *v.* Acting as the designated hitter; batting but not fielding.
" 'I'd rather be DH-ing, and that's God's truth,' said [Reggie] Jackson, whose two forays into right field this season were, to be kind, an adventure." (Doug Cress, *The Washington Post*, May 18, 1986)

dial 8   *v.* To hit a home run; to hit the long ball, from the practice of dialing the number 8 on a hotel phone to get long distance.

Diamond. Alexander Joy Cartwright, Jr. In this undated photo he is shown in his role as chief of the Honolulu Fire Department. *National Baseball Library, Cooperstown, N.Y. (original in the Hawaii State Archives)*

diamond   1. *n.* The surface on which the game of baseball is played. ". . . you looked down, and there was the diamond. It glistened. The grass was green. I've been to Ireland, and they have the greenest grass I've ever seen since, and still it wasn't as green as the grass at Ebbets Field." (Bill Reddy in Peter Gollenback's *Bums*)
2. *n.* The infield square formed by home, first, second and third bases.
3. *adj.* A synonym for the game of baseball, as in diamond artists. "The diamond sport's flaw." (title of a *Christian Science Monitor* editorial, April 3, 1987)
1ST   1858. (Chadwick Scrapbooks, EJN)
ETY   Immediately after Alexander Cartwright laid out the first regulation playing field in 1845, the term came into play. Dan Schlossberg points out in *The Baseball Catalog* that it is actually not a diamond at all: "A true diamond has two acute and two obtuse angles, but the

infield has four 90-degree angles. Since the diamond is best viewed from the catcher's perspective, however, the diamond reference is apparent."

Originally, the term referred only to the infield but it has long since become a term for the total playing area as well. However, it is clear that the distinction was blurred before the beginning of the 20th century. In their 1896 book *Baseball,* R. G. Knowles and Richard Morton explain, "The ground is called a diamond by reason of its appearance when viewed from the grand stand."

diamond artists *n./arch.* Term used during the 1930s for ballplayers.

Diamond Ball *n.* A forerunner of modern softball. The term came into use as a replacement for Kitten Ball in 1922 by the Minneapolis Park Board. The first group that tried to organize softball on a national scale was the National Diamond Ball Association, which was founded in 1925 and continued until the formation of the Amateur Softball Association in 1933.

diamond bugs *n./arch.* Term used during the 1930s for fans.

diamondeers *n./arch.* Term used during the 1930s for ballplayers.

Dick Smith *n.* A loner; a player who won't be one of the boys, who travels and eats alone and, according to Dizzy Dean, "seldom ever treats." A sponger or freeloader.

In a *Collier's* article on Joe and Dom DiMaggio by Tom Laird, Joe is asked about his younger brother, "Will he be a Dick Smith?"

Joe answers: "Not if I can help it. That was one of my big mistakes—being a lone wolf. I was afraid to talk about anything, not only to the newspapermen but to my teammates as well, and I got to be known as a Dick Smith." (March 22, 1940; PT)

Peter Tamony, who did much work on this term, pointed out that it was virtually unknown to fans, but common among players. "He is the man who has never been known to say 'Here's how,' to anyone," Tamony wrote of the generalized "Dick Smith." "If he is treated he does not return the favor, and if in company he is the chap who never picks up the check."

ETY/1ST 1876. This clearly does *not* appear to be the name of an old ballplayer as has often been asserted. In one of several manuscripts

which he prepared on the subject, Tamony points out that he "must have been a well known character before baseball became the national pastime. He is mentioned in the *Congressional Record* for June 29, 1876, and his name is there used as a synonym for sponging."

It came up in the context of the custom of the House of Representatives to provide lemonade and iced tea for its members in the warm months. The drinks were paid for out of the House contingency fund until the practice was halted by Rep. "Blue-Jean" Smith of Indiana. Members then had the choice of running to the Senate for drinks or drinking "iced Potomac" (river water, which apparently caused its share of illness and intestinal distress).

In supporting a bill to rectify this, Rep. Conger of Michigan proposed that the House enable itself "to supply the necessary wants of its member, without either playing 'Dick Smith' on the Senate or leaving so many of its members confined to their rooms by sickness resulting from drinking iced Potomac."

Tamony asked himself who this man could have been and by examining the *Dictionary of American Biography* showed that there was, in fact, a well-known person whose reputation was such that it could have become an eponym for sponging.

Richard Penn Smith (1799–1854) fit the bill. Tamony wrote:

> In 1821 he published a series of moral and literary essays under the title of 'The Plagiary.' Between 1825 and 1833 he wrote twenty plays, of which fifteen were performed. Some of these plays were of extreme and lasting popularity, and Smith is given much space in the histories of the drama in America. But Smith was a practical playwright. His essays were titled, 'The Plagiary.' For his dramas he depended mainly on foreign writers for his inspiration. Did this plagiarism, this dependence on others for ideas and inspiration, make Smith's name a synonym for sponging? It is very likely that it did.

EXT H. L. Mencken notes in *The American Language: Supplement II* that the term is also used on the racetrack. Tamony finds it as a logger's term for a drink of liquor consumed privately and a bar term for a lone drinker. Columnists from Damon Runyon to Charles McCabe have used the term in the context of bar culture. "One proprietor I know has a great fancy for Irish bartenders, and for a peculiar reason. He knows they are addicted to Dick Smithing and other weaknesses." (Charles McCabe, *San Francisco Chronicle*, December 17, 1974; PT)

die   **1.** *v.* To be left on base at the end of an inning.
2. *v.* To be put out; to be "retired."
1ST   1880. (*Chicago Inter Ocean*, June 29; EJN)
3. *v.* To have failed; to have had a bad day at the ballpark.

differentials   *n.* What Dizzy Dean called "credentials" when he was in broadcasting.

dig in   **1.** *v.* To twist one's spikes into the dirt, especially with the back foot, to gain better traction for swinging the bat; to anchor one's self in the batter's box.
2. *v.* To focus one's concentration on a key play or situation.

dig out/dig out of the dirt   *v.* To field successfully a poorly thrown ball, one that bounces in the dirt.
1ST   1909. (*Frank Merriwell's Schooldays;* EJN)

dilly   *n./arch.* A spectacular hit.

dime hit   *n.* SCRATCH HIT.
1ST   1907. (*New York Evening Journal*, May 8; EJN)

dimensions   *n.* The specific word used to describe the particular measurements of a given ballpark both in terms of overall size and of the playing field itself. By extension, the term also serves to underscore the differences among ballparks whose dimensions may vary considerably.
SEE   *band box.*

dime player   *n.* Infielder who lacks hustle and spirit; one who cannot or will not "get off the dime."

dime 'ya   *v.* For a pitcher to display exceptional control. When speaking of a particularly capable pitcher, Casey Stengel was known to say, "He can dime 'ya."

dinger   *n.* Home run. "Bang, there goes another one. It seems every day in baseball is dinger day, every park a homer dome." (*USA Today*, June 30, 1987)

dink/dink up   *v.* To pitch a slow ball.
1ST   1916. (*American* magazine, August; EJN)

dinky-doo   *n.* DIPSY-DOO.

dinky fly   *n.* A batted ball that goes neither high nor far and is easily caught.

dinner tongs   *n./arch.* Hands, also known as "lunch hooks" in the parlance of the sports writer in the early 20th century (both show up in the September 1909 *Baseball* magazine in an article on sports writing).

dipso-do / dipsy-doo / dipsy-dew / dipsey-doodle / dipsey-dow / etc.   **1.** *n.* A slow, tantalizing curveball.
2. *n.* Term for any odd-breaking pitch, including a suspected spitter. " 'Say, that's a regular dipsy doodle you got there!' he said with admiration. 'How do you do it, Professor?' " (Valentine Davies, *It Happens Every Spring;* CDP)
1ST   1932. (*Baseball* magazine, October; EJN)
3. *n.* A swinging strikeout in the trademark talk of pioneer sportscaster Rosey Roswell in Pittsburgh, who called such an out "the old dipsey doodle."
USE   "This uncertainty as to spelling," wrote Edward J. Nichols, "is typical of terms invented by the players rather than the sports reporters."

dirt   *n.* The ground around homeplate and the base paths.

dirter   *n.* Casey Stengel's term for a ground ball.

dirty ball   *n.* Dishonest or unsportsmanlike play.
1ST   1902. (*Sporting Life*, July 12; EJN)

disabled list   *n.* A player is said to be on the disabled list when he has been removed from the team for a period of 15 or 21 days because of illness or injury. This allows the player to remain on the roster, but also allows the team to add a replacement player during the time the disabled player is out of action.

Disco Demolition Night   Promotional night held on July 12, 1979, by Bill Veeck at Comiskey Park; it resulted in the White Sox forfeiting the second game of a doubleheader to the Tigers as fans poured onto the field. The idea was to have a gigantic bonfire between games, during which thousands of disco records would be burned. The anti-disco ritual was enough to attract about 6,000 fans onto the field.

dish   *n.* Home plate, an obvious play on the word plate.

Diving catch. A softball player in the initial phase of a dive. *Courtesy of the Amateur Softball Association of America*

1ST 1907. (*New York Evening Journal*, April 17; EJN)

disputed *adj.* Applied to a umpire's call or to an entire game whose outcome is being questioned by one of the teams.

dive *v.* To slide into base head first.

divide a twin bill *v.* To split a doubleheader.

diving catch *n.* Acrobatic move in which a fielder throws himself to the ground in order to reach the ball. It is one of the more dramatic ways a player shows off his fielding skills. Dan Sperling says in his *Spectator's Guide to Baseball:* "Diving catches made at the 'hot corner' are perhaps the most remarkable of all, because third basemen usually have only a split-second in which to react."

division **1.** *n.* In the majors, the American and National Leagues are divided into two divisions, East and West. At the end of the regular season, the two Eastern teams with the best records meet the two Western teams with the best records in a playoff series to determine which teams will represent their leagues in the World Series.
2. *n.* Before Eastern and Western Divisions were created, the informal classification determined by standings, with a team in the top half

in the first division and one in the bottom half in the second division.

DL Standard abbreviation for disabled list.

do a Casey *v.* To strike out.
SEE *Casey Act, Casey at the Bat.*

do a Sammy Vick *v.* SAMMY VICK.

doctor **1.** *v.* To gain an edge, by secretly tampering with the bat, ball or grounds. Most doctoring is both hard to detect and illegal. Real or imagined doctoring has lead to some of the most heated and prolonged debates in baseball. "I'm not accusing the Yankees of doctoring the infield but it's very thick-sodded and that's certainly a great help to their infield." (Tiger Manager Jack Tighe, quoted in an AP dispatch, May 1, 1958; PT)
2. *n.* Temporary nickname for someone caught or suspected of the act of doctoring. "Doctor Sutton not the only one." (reference to pitcher Don Sutton in a *San Francisco Examiner* headline, July 19, 1978; PT)
ETY The term was applied to baseball high jinks long after establishing itself elsewhere as a term for secret product adulteration. "There is very little beer that is not 'doctored' and made even worse than in its original state by deleterious drugs." (*Sunlight and Shadow, At Home and Abroad,* John B. Gough, 1881; PT)

Dodgertown. Calisthenics at Vero Beach.   *Courtesy of the Florida Division of Tourism*

doctor the ball   *v.* To do something illegal to the ball to make it move erratically after it has been pitched. This may involve the use of a substance or damage to the ball. Any list of agents that have been used to doctor balls would have to include: BB shot, bottle caps, dirt, emery paper, nutmeg graters, oil, paraffin, phonograph needles, pine tar, resin, slippery elm, spikes, spit, talcum powder, K-Y jelly and vaseline.

doctor the bat   *v.* To modify a bat for the advantage of the batter. This is usually done to make the bat lighter and livelier while maintaining the mass of a heavier bat. This feat is accomplished by drilling out a hole in the heavy end of the bat and leaving a hollow spot or filling it with a light material such as cork. The hole is hidden with a plug of wood shavings and glue.

doctor the grounds   *v.* To modify the grounds or its boundaries to give the home team the advantage.

A number of ways exist by which the grounds can be doctored; here are two:
• A spot near first base can be kept wet or soft to deter an especially good base stealer.

• The pitching mound in the visitors' bullpen can be raised, lowered or tilted to confuse pitchers who warm up on an unconventional mound and must perform on a conventional one.
SEE *Cobb's Lake.*

do damage   *v.* To score a run or runs.

Dodger Stadium   Home of the Los Angeles Dodgers from 1962 to the present. It is located in Chavez Ravine on a hill overlooking downtown Los Angeles, California. The Dodgers moved there from the Los Angeles Memorial Coliseum where they had been since 1958. Between 1962 and 1965, it was also the home field of the American League Angels, who chose to call the park Chavez Ravine instead of Dodger Stadium. The Angels moved to their own stadium in Anaheim to begin the 1966 season.

Dodgertown   A 450-acre complex in Vero Beach, Florida, where the Dodgers hold spring training. Dreamed up in 1949 by Branch Rickey when he was president of the Brooklyn Dodgers, it soon got the reputation as the most progressive and well-equipped of the spring camps. In 1956 Arthur Daley described it this way in the *New York Times:* "It is a factory that rolls ball players off an assembly line with the steady surge of Fords popping out of the River Rouge plant." (March 18)

Today it features two golf courses, a conference center, and villas for the players. Streets are named for Dodger greats.

dodge the bullet *v.* To get out of a threatening situation, especially appropriate to pitchers.

doghouse *n.* Figurative place of exile for players who have displeased the manager.

(Red Sox Manager John "McNamara is also a manager without a doghouse." (*New York Times,* October 23, 1986)

dog it 1. *v.* To malinger; to slow down for a minor ache or pain. "Richards had been complaining of injuries all season, and his teammates had thought he was 'dogging' it . . . When the true seriousness of Richards' injuries became known, the team pulled together and became a winning unit." (Edwin Silberstang, *Playboy's Guide to Baseball Batting,* 1982; CDP)
2. *v.* To not play one's best; to play lazily. Often applied to a runner who does not try to beat the ball to first base or to a fielder who backs away from a sharply hit ball.
ETY In his 1958 dictionary, Burt Dunne suggests that the term is a literal and graphic reference to the infielder who "lifts his leg" to get out of the way of a hard-hit ground ball.

dome *n.* Enclosed stadium used for baseball and other sports, all of which (to date) have "dome" in their name—the Metrodome (Minneapolis), Superdome (New Orleans), King Dome (Seattle), Silverdome (Detroit) and the original enclosed stadium, the Astrodome (Houston).

domeball *n.* Baseball played under a dome—term used to emphasize differences between indoor and outdoor baseball. "Inside Information: The Mysteries of Domeball." (heading, *Sport* magazine, April 1984)

dome dong *n.* DOMERUN.

dome head *n.* Houston Astros fan in the Astrodome.

"The Astrodome which Larry McMurtry first likened to [the] 'working end of a gigantic roll-on deodorant,' rocks with standing-room-only crowds of Dome Heads as the Astros challenge

the Mets in a best-of-seven series for the National League pennant." (David Maraniss, *The Washington Post,* October 9, 1986)

domerun *n.* A home run hit in a domed stadium, such as the "cheap" homers that can be hit in the Seattle Kingdome whose configuration and controlled atmosphere can be kind to powerful hitters who find it easier to hit homers under a dome. Clearly implied is that the domerun would not have been a home run if hit in a traditional open air stadium.

donkey *n.* Term for rookie or a minor league player up for a tryout with a major league team.

donkey ball/donkey baseball *n.* A game played for laughs by players mounted on donkeys. Although still staged, such intentional fiascos are not as popular as they once were.

don the spikes *v.* To take part in a baseball game.

don't lose the glove Traditional barb yelled by the opposition to a player who is a good fielder but not much of a hitter.

donut 1. *n.* Heavy circular weight that fits around the head of one's bat and used when warming up to bat.
SEE DOUGHNUT.
2. *n.* A rubber circle that some batters wear on their thumbs while batting to cut down on the painful reverberation of the bat.

do one's chores *v.* To perform well in a game.

doozy maroony *n.* Term for an extra base hit coined by pioneer Pirates broadcaster Rosey Roswell. Often stated as "The Ol' Doozie Marooney."

dope 1. Inside information or opinion. "The dope will prove that a care-free player will do better than one who carries his troubles on the diamond." (*Letters from a Baseball Fan to his Son,* S. DeWitt Clough, 1910)
1ST 1902. (*Sporting Life,* September 20; EJN)
2. *n./arch.* The curve and speed of the ball; STUFF.
3. *n.* Term applied to a substance other than rosin that a pitcher puts on his hands. Used commonly in softball.
ETY In his 1936 *Phrase Origins,* Alfred H. Holt wrote, "Though cursed with a multiplicity of uses in American slang, the little word seems to be traceable in almost every sense to the

Doubleday Myth. A 1919 view of the pasture where, 70 years earlier, Abner Doubleday supposedly invented baseball.   *National Baseball Library, Cooperstown, N.Y.*

Dutch *doop* (pronounced 'dope'), a thick liquid or sauce." Holt points out that one form of dope is any drug used to stimulate a horse in a race. To have knowledge of this may have lead to the idea of inside or secret information as "dope."

dope book   *n.* Book containing baseball records and statistics.
ETY   Peter Tamony noted that dope-book in the earlier context of horse racing is a book containing a chart of previous performances of race horses.

dopesters   *n.* Those who compile statistics and other information.
1ST   1915. (*Baseball* magazine, December; EJN)

"do they show movies on a flight like that?"   Colorful quip about a long, high home run. Similar aviational reference to a home run is the line "That ball traveled so far that it should have a stewardess on it."

double   *n.* A hit on which the batter reaches second base safely.
    There are many archaic amplifications of the word (double bag, double bagger, double baser), but they all mean the same thing: double
1ST   1880. (*Brooklyn Daily Eagle*, August 27; EJN)

double clutch   *n.* A motion made by a fielder in which he pumps his arm once before throwing the ball.

Doubleday myth   *n.* Term that has arisen out of the controversy surrounding the claim that General Abner Doubleday invented baseball in 1839, in Cooperstown, New York. Though Doubleday never claimed to have invented the game, credit was given to him after his death by A. G. Spalding and a commission formed to prove that baseball was a purely American creation. Since then, its debunkers have become legion. "The Doubleday myth, however, is as much a part of our culture as George Washington's chopped-down cherry tree." (Bill Tammeus, *The Kansas City Star*, August 21, 1986)
    The debunkers have had a field day creating lines on the subject. "Abner Doubleday didn't invent baseball," wrote Harold Peterson in *The Man Who Invented Baseball*. "Baseball invented Abner Doubleday." Sportswriter Bob Allison once said, "Columbus didn't discover America either, but he was the one who made it pay."

double duty pitcher   *n.* A pitcher who, within a single season or over the course of a career, is used both as a starting pitcher and as a relief pitcher. Few pitchers have matched the combined effort in this regard of Woodie Fryman who had 322 starts and 302 relief appearances over the course of his career (1966–1983).

double elimination   *n.* Form of tournament play in which teams participating or all finalists can lose once and still stay in the tournament. This was used in the College World Series for its eight finalists until the NCAA decided to switch to a final four format for the 1988 season.

doubleheader/double-header   *n.* A set of two games played in succession on the same day between the same two teams and to which spectators are admitted for the price of a single game. Traditionally, there is a 20 minute break between games. The second game of the set has long been known as the *nightcap*.

Historically, there have been two reasons for doubleheaders: They were necessitated by postponements of previously scheduled games or they have been scheduled in advance as a means of attracting fans. The first major league twinbill took place on September 25, 1882, between Worcester and Providence, both of the National League.

They are becoming rarer and rarer in the Major Leagues. "Like the movie double features, the baseball doubleheader is on the verge of extinction," was the conclusion of an article in the March 9, 1987, issue of *Forbes.*
ETY/1ST   1897. Dating back to the 1870s this term was used in railroad circles to describe a railway train having two engines or two trains traveling so close together that they move as one. "The two extras were bowling along merrily when they struck this grade; and although there is a time card rule that says that trains will be kept ten minutes apart, they were right together, helping each other over the grade. In fact, it was one train with two engines, something of a double header with the second engine in the middle." (*Tales of the Telegraph, The Story of a Telegrapher's Life and Adventures in Railroad, Commercial and Military Work,* by Jasper Ewing Brady, 1900) The earliest use of the term applied to baseball was found by Edward J. Nichols in the July 4, 1897, *New York Tribune.*
EXT   Two paired or consecutive events. For instance, in a report from San Quentin in the San Francisco Examiner, "A doubleheader at the big prison is the simultaneous execution of two inmates in the state's pale green gas chamber." (July 4, 1967; PT)

double hit   *n.* Rare situation in which the batter's bat actually hits the ball twice. This usually occurs on a lightly hit ball when a batter accidently lets go of the bat. Moving faster than the rolling ball, the bat catches up to it and hits it again. The batter who accomplishes this feat is summarily called out by the home plate umpire.

double-name job   *n.* Uncommonly heard term defined by Leonard Shecter in his June 1963 article on baseball slang in *Baseball Digest:* "This is rookie talk. When spring training camps are crowded with players from all over the system there aren't enough individual lockers to go around. The rookies are asked to double up. That means there are two names hung over the locker, both with astronomically high uniform numbers, like 73 and 94. That's the kind of number you get when you're in one of those double-name jobs."

double off   *v.* To be caught off base and put out before tagging up after the batter has flied out, resulting in a double play (hence, to be doubled off).

double play   *n.* When two outs are recorded by the fielding team in continuous action, providing that no error is committed. Both outs must occur between the time the ball leaves the pitcher's hand and is returned to him in the pitcher's box.

Speaking for many fans, reporter Alistair Cooke once said, "Next to a triple play, baseball's double play is the most exciting and graceful thing in sports."
1ST   1858. (Chadwick Scrapbooks; EJN)
ETY   Hall of Fame shortstop George Wright has been credited with having made the first such play while playing for the Cincinnati Red Stockings. Wright supposedly used the hidden ball trick. However, Edward J. Nichols revealed a published reference to the double play before the Red Stockings came in to being in 1866.
EXT   Two accomplishments made at the same time.

double-play ball   *n.* A ground ball hit to a fielder at a speed and location ideal for turning an easy double play.

double-play combination   *n.* The shortstop and the second baseman collectively, because the most common double play involves a precisely timed maneuver between these two play-

Double play combination. Giant infielders Frankie Frisch and Travis Jackson practice their double play toss in spring training, 1924.   *National Baseball Library, Cooperstown, N.Y.*

ers. The shortstop fields the ball and tosses it to the second baseman. He steps on second base to force the runner coming from first and then throws on to that base to retire the batter. "But the day when he forms a double-play combination with his brother Cal may not be that far away." (*Washington Times* profile of the Orioles' then-minor league second baseman Billy Ripken, February 26, 1987)

double-play depth   *n.* Position taken by the shortstop and second baseman to enhance the possibility of turning a double play. This position is taken when there are fewer than two outs and first base is occupied.

double-play pivot   CROSS OVER PIVOT.

double pump   *n.* Applied to that part of a pitcher's windup when he throws his arms back over his head twice before delivering the ball.

double steal   *n.* Strategic baserunning maneuver in which two base runners advance to the next base without the aid of a hit, error, balk, base on balls or hit batter. Usually employed when first and second are occupied.

This is a risky play that is not easy to execute, so it is something of a rarity.
1ST   1897. (*New York Tribune,* July 6; EJN)
SEE   *delayed double steal.*

double switch   *n.* Line up shuffle used to get a good batter into the pitcher's place in the batting order while bringing in a relief pitcher. It usually comes in the late innings of a close game in the NL or at any other level of the game where there is no designated hitter. It occurs on defense as the manager needs to remove the pitcher on the mound for a reliever. Knowing that the pitcher's turn in the batting order is coming up in the next offensive inning, the manager then brings in the reliever as well as a second new defensive player. The new player who is not the pitcher (and presumably a good batter) is inserted into the pitcher's spot and the new pitcher is put in the spot from which the original player has been taken.

double up   *n.* To be retired by a double play, usually applied to the second player to be put out, as in, "Jones is out, Smith is doubled up."
1ST   1880. (*Chicago Inter Ocean,* August 2; EJN)

doughnut   *n.* Common name for the bat weight used by batters warming up in the on deck circle. It is a modern alternative to the earlier practice of warming up by swinging two bats at once. It was introduced by New York Yankees catcher Elston Howard in the early 1960s and, according to the *Sporting News*, was in use in most spring training camps by 1968.

Marketed originally as "Elston Howard's On-Deck Bat-Weight," it was immediately dubbed the doughnut or iron doughnut by those who used it. "The purpose of the weight is to help a batter in such areas as speeding up his swing and developing stronger wrists and forearms," said Howard (*The Sporting News*, April 27, 1968), who added that it also loosened shoulders, would fit over the bat one actually used during a game and could be removed by simply tapping the bat handle against the ground.

down   1. *adj.* Out; "two down" is two out.
1ST   1888. (*Chicago Inter Ocean*, July 12; EJN)
2. *adj.* Defeated or trailing the opposing team.
EXT   In his *Language of Sports,* Tim Considine states that when one says, "Two down, one to go;" this is a borrowing from baseball.
3. *adj.* Toward second base from home plate. An item in the December 1956 *American Speech* on the confusing terminology of directional words uses this example, ". . . the pitcher who stands on a mound to deliver the ball, throws his pitches up to the plate, whereas the catcher . . . pegs the ball down to second. Oddly enough, the same pitcher while in the process of warming up is described as throwing down to his receiver, and none of the fielders is said to throw up to the plate."
4. *adj.* Toward home plate from the mound.

down and up   *n./arch.* POP-UP SLIDE.
1ST   1935. "There are several variations on the feet-first slide, as the hook, fall-away, down-and-up, etc." (Ralph H. Barbour, *How to Play Better Baseball;* DS)

downer   *n.* An overhanded curve that drops close to the batter's ankles. Also known as a dropball or sinker.

down shoot   *n./arch.* A pitched ball that drops precipitously as it nears home plate.

down the alley/down the cock/down the middle/down the pike/down the pipe
adv./adj. Said of a pitch, usually a fastball, that is delivered straight through the center of the strike zone. Such a pitch, if taken by the batter, is said to be an "automatic" strike.

down the middle   *adj.* Reference to the four defensive players positioned on the center line of the field from home plate to center field. These players, catcher, second baseman, shortstop and center fielder, are said to anchor the defense. "But we've got to be solid down the middle or none of us will look good to anyone." (Brooks Robinson, *Third Base is My Home;* CDP)
USE   In what seems contradictory, in baseball parlance a synonym for down the middle is UP THE MIDDLE.
2. *adv./adj.* Describing a ball that is pitched across the center or middle of the plate. "But all Jones wanted was an out and the first ball was down the middle for a strike." (*Relief Pitcher* by Dick Friendlich; CDP)

down the river   *adv./adj.* Said of a trade or sale that sends a player to the minors or a team that is lower in the standings.

down the slot   *adv.* Across the plate. "However, a third fast ball down the slot seemed to find him unprepared for again he was late swinging and got underneath the pitch, raising a pop fly that climbed in front of the plate." (*Relief Pitcher* by Dick Friendlich; CDP)

down to the wire   *v.* GO TO THE WIRE.

downtown   1. *n.* The figurative landing site of a deep home run ball. To hit a home run is often referred to as "going downtown."
2. *v.* To hit a long home run. "Come on, Lefty, downtown one and gag those bench jockeys." (Edward R. Walsh in the USAir inflight magazine, September 1982)
ETY   Peter Tamony suggested that this had an early association with Ollie Lee Brown. It started in 1964 when he played for the minor league team in Fresno that played on the outskirts of town. According to Tamony's notes, the fans came up with the cheer, "Hit it downtown, Ollie."

downtowner   *n.* HOME RUN. "His startling production of downtowners (forty to date) may bring him within range of Roger Maris's record by mid-September." (Roger Angell on Reggie Jackson in *The Summer Game;* CDP)

DP   1. Common box score and scorecard abbreviation for double play.
2. Abbreviation in softball for the designated player.

draft **1.** *n.* Established procedures by which team representatives meet to acquire players. There are now four of them:

1. The free-agent draft, in which eligible high school and college players are picked. Teams choose in reverse order of their position in the final standings of the previous season.
2. The minor league draft, in which major league teams can select players from other teams' farm clubs *when* they have spent more than a specified period in the minors.
3. The free-agent reentry draft, in which veteran players who have played out their options and chosen to be free agents are selected.
4. A special draft is held when expansion teams are created. Existing teams are required to make available a group of (non-starting) players from which the new teams draft their rosters.

1ST 1905. (*Sporting Life,* September 2; EJN)
2. *v.* To acquire a player in the draft.

drag *v.* To execute a drag bunt.
1ST 1927. (*New York Sun,* July 18; EJN)

drag bunt *n.* A bunt purposely hit away from the pitcher down the first base line. A properly executed drag bunt is nearly impossible to defense. Seeing the batter setting to bunt, the infielders charge to the spot directly in front of home plate, the most common location of a bunted ball. Meanwhile, the ball trickles along so slowly down the line that the batter is able to beat it to first base. It gets its name because the ball appears as if it is being dragged by the batter on his way to first. With the drag bunt, the batter is bunting for a base hit as opposed to a *sacrifice bunt* where the batter's primary goal is to advance a runner already on base.

A few of the most proficient drag bunters were Mickey Mantle, Rod Carew and Maury Wills.
1ST 1934. "He put everything he had into every pitch after Goslin had opened with a double and Rogell had beaten out a drag bunt to Collins." (*New York American,* October 8; DS)

draw **1.** *v.* To make a fielder throw to a base, such as taking a lead at first to "draw" the ball to first base. Forcing a draw can benefit the offensive team if it causes a wild throw or helps another runner steal. The gist of this strategy is to give the fielder the impression that he can get the runner out.

1ST 1896. (*Frank Merriwell's Schooldays;* EJN)
2. The number of people in attendance at a game.

draw a base on balls/ draw a free base/ draw a pass/draw a walk/etc. *v.* To be walked; issued a base on balls.

draw a blank *v.* To fail to score.
1ST 1865. (*New York Herald,* July 25; EJN)

draw a throw *v.* DRAW.

drawing card *n.* Player who attracts paying customers.
1ST 1895. (*Spalding's Official Base Ball Guide;* EJN)

drawn game *n./obs.* A game that ends with each team having the same number of runs after each has batted in the same number of innings.
1ST 1867. (*New York Herald,* July 4; EJN)

dreamer *n.* A player who is not paying attention to the game.

GEORGE HERMAN (BABE) RUTH
BOSTON—NEW YORK, A.L.; BOSTON, N.L.
1915–1935
GREATEST DRAWING CARD IN HISTORY OF
BASEBALL. HOLDER OF MANY HOME RUN
AND OTHER BATTING RECORDS. GATHERED
714 HOME RUNS IN ADDITION TO FIFTEEN
IN WORLD SERIES.

Drawing card. Babe Ruth's Hall of fame plaque points to his role as a drawing card. *National Baseball Library, Cooperstown, N.Y.*

dreamer's month   *n.* The month of March, because the regular season does not get underway until early April and the only games being played are spring training exhibition games. At this point in the baseball year, anything seems possible for any team. To quote Bob Uecker from *Catcher in the Wry:* "They call it Dreamer's Month. In March, on paper, every team looks stronger than it did a year ago, and they are counting heavily on a player they got in a trade with a team that no longer wanted him." (CDP)

dream game   *n.* Term used by the press to describe the All-Star game when it was first being planned as an event for the Century of Progress Exposition in Chicago in 1933. Although the first game was successful and exciting (Babe Ruth won the game with a two-run homer), it was not until the second All-Star game in 1934 that the "dream game" description seemed to fit. An article in the September 1934 *Baseball* magazine by Kenneth B. Byrd, entitled "Carl Hubbell and the Dream Game," ends: "But we will wager that twenty or thirty years from now the score will be forgotten. All that will be remembered of the classic is the phenomenal pitching performance of Carl Hubbell. He has assured the permanency of the 'dream game' by making it—for Ruth, Gehrig, Foxx, Simmons, and Cronin—a nightmare."

Dream Week   *n.* Name for one session of a commercial fantasy baseball camp in which adults pay to train and work out and play baseball with ex-players.

dream weeker   *n.* Attendee of dream week.

dribbler   *n.* A slow-rolling ground ball.

drill   1. *v.* To hit a ball hard, deep and well-placed.
2. *n.* A physical conditioning exercise or routine.
3. *v.* To be hit hard or hurt. The term is applied when a player is hit by a thrown, pitched or batted ball, by a bat, or collides with another player. "One of the worst feelings in baseball is seeing someone get drilled like that." (Alan Ashby on Dickie Thon's severe beaning, *Washington Post*, October 14, 1986)

drive   1. *n.* A hard-hit ball.
1ST   1881. (*New York Herald,* July 23; EJN)
2. *v.* To hit the ball hard.
1ST   1861. (Chadwick Scrapbooks; EJN)

3. *n.* A campaign, such as a playoff or pennant drive.

drive from the hill   *v.* To remove a pitcher by getting hits from him.

drive in   *v.* To score a base runner by way of a hit or sacrifice.

drive to the showers   *v.* To get so many hits from a pitcher that his manager removes him from the game.

drizzler   *n.* A weakly hit ground ball.
1ST   ". . . only pounded out a little drizzler that Sam quickly gathered in and threw to first." (Lester Chadwick's *Baseball Joe of the Silver Stars,* 1912; DS)

Dr. Longball   *n.* Home run.
ETY   Creation of Oriole manager Earl Weaver, who often described hitting a home run as a "call to Dr. Longball."

drooler   *n.* A spitball.

drooper   *n.* TEXAS LEAGUER.
1ST   1932. (*Baseball* magazine, October; EJN)

drop/dropball   *n.* A pitch that suddenly sinks as it nears the plate. Although the term is still in use, it is now more likely to be called a sinker.
1ST   1890. (*New York Press,* July 16; EJN)

drop down   *v.* To pitch sidearm.
"Rusty Staub's the last left-handed batter I ever dropped down on . . . It was in 1980 when Rusty was with the Texas Rangers and he ripped a pea to Dewey [Dwight Evans]. I've never dropped down since and won't." (Bob Ojeda to Hal Bodley, *USA Today,* June 6, 1986)

drop off the table   *v.* OFF THE TABLE.

drop one   *v.* To bunt.

dropped ball   *n.* A batted ball that is handled by a fielder but not held long enough to constitute a catch.

dropped third strike   *n.* An error on the part of the catcher that allows the batter to advance safely to first base. This mistake only results in an opportunity to take first base when the bases are empty. The pitcher is still credited with a strikeout even if the batter reaches first base on a dropped third strike.

dropper   *n.* Fly ball that falls in for a hit.
1ST   "White's contribution was a dropper into left field, on which he reached second, while

McVey scored." (*The Spalding Scrapbooks*, vol. III, 1876; DS)

drop pitch   *n.* A breaking ball that drops sharply as it nears the plate.

drop-the-bat   *n./obs.* A now-illegal ploy in which the batter would drop his bat during the pitcher's windup to cause a halt in the delivery and a balk. It was once practiced on unexperienced pitchers with runners on second or third.

drought   *n.* A slump—at the plate or on the mound or for a whole team. "Overdue Bill: Drought Ends for Dawley." (headline, *St. Louis Post-Dispatch*, May 29, 1987) Baseball's longest drought is, as of this writing, being experienced by the Chicago Cubs who last won the World Series in 1908.

drub   *v.* To defeat.
1ST   1883. (*Chicago Inter Ocean*, May 24; EJN)

drunk   *adj.* Said of the bases when they are loaded.
Commenting on the slang in Keith Hernandez's 1987 book, *If at First*, *Newsweek* pointed out (May 15, 1987) that "the sacks are drunk" was how he explained that the bases were loaded.

dry spitter   1. *n.* Slider that behaves like a spitball and that batter insists is a spitball (but which, of course, when examined by the umpire is dry).
2. *n./arch.* Term that Eddie Cicotte used to describe his emery ball.

dub   *n./arch.* A poor player.

ducks on the pond   Runners on base.
EXT   Coined, or at least brought to baseball, by broadcaster Arch McDonald, the former Yankee and Senators announcer who was called "the Barnum of the bushes."
1ST   1939. "DiMaggio's runs batted in record would indicate he doesn't hit when there's 'ducks on the pond.' " (*San Francisco News*, August 5, 1939; PT)

dues collector   *n.* A BAT.
ETY   Scott Ostler of the *Los Angeles Times* wrote in 1986 that this is a Reggie Jackson creation, adding, "In '74, Reggie actually took a felt-tip pen and wrote 'Dues Collector' on the sweet spot of his lumber."

Duffy's cliff   One of the fabled phenomena of Fenway Park (along with "The Green Monster"). It was a 10-foot-high mound that formed a steep incline in front of the left field wall. It

was there from the opening of the stadium in 1912 until 1933 when it was greatly reduced, but not eliminated. It got its name from Red Sox left fielder Duffy Lewis who excelled at playing on and around the cliff.

dugout   *n.* An enclosure for the players' bench. Major league rules state that it must be roofed and closed at the back and at either end. It gets its name because dugouts are traditionally dug into the ground, with the bench below the playing field. Despite the name, many dugouts are built on top of the ground, especially in parks where amateurs play.
1ST   1912. (*New York Tribune*, October 17; EJN)
EXT   Realm of non-participation. "State Stayed in the Dugout"—*San Francisco Examiner* headline on California passing on the first ballot at the Democratic Convention in which John F. Kennedy was nominated, July 14, 1960; PT.

dummy signals   *n.* Signs or signals from the catcher, dugout or coacher's box that are meaningless and meant only to mislead and confuse those trying to steal the signals.

dumper   *n.* Player who works to throw or lose a game; a traitor.
"One of these cities was Louisville and it collapsed because in its second season, it collected the dumbest group of dumpers the baseball world has ever known." (Leonard Schecter in *The Jocks*, discussing the barring of Louisville players in 1877.)

dump one   *v.* To bunt the ball.
1ST   1922. (*New York Times*, June 4; EJN)

dungeon   *n.* The last place in the standings.

dunk   *v.* To hit a ball that drops quickly.

dunker   *n.* A batted ball that pops up over the infield; a TEXAS LEAGUER.
1ST   1937. (*The Sporting News Record Book*; EJN)

Dunlap   *n./arch.* A spectacular catch.
1ST   1893. "A volley of cheers followed the drive and doubled in volume when Long was seen to make what the players called a "Dunlap" or grand-stand catch." (*Donahoe's Magazine*, August 27; DS)

duro seam   *n.* A type of softball that has concealed stitches.

dust bowl   *n.* A particularly dusty field; one that has not been watered down before play begins.

Dugout. The Yankee dugout, replete with lumberyard, April 1923.   *Prints and Photographs Division, the Library of Congress*

duster   *n.* A dust off pitch. *Sporting News* headline for June 20, 1970: "Danger in Dusters."
1ST   1932. (*Baseball* magazine, October; EJN)

dust off/dust   *v.* To pitch a ball so far inside that the batter has to drop to the ground (in the dust) to keep from being hit. Although the distinction is often lost on the batter when one comes his way, a dust off pitch is not a beanball because it is not aimed at his head.
1ST   1928. In *Babe Ruth's Own Book of Baseball,* a dusting off is defined as "Making the hitter drop to the ground by pitching at him."(DS)

dust sprayer   *n.* Player who slides a lot.

dyed-in-the-wool-fan   *n.* An extremely enthusiastic and loyal fan.
1ST   1902. (*Sporting Life,* September 27; EJN)

dying quail   *n.* A batted ball that drops suddenly and unexpectedly, like a bird that has been shot on the wing. A wind blowing in from the outfield may be an important factor here.
   "That was a dying quail single that will look like a line drive in the paper tomorrow." (Brooks Robinson, WMAR-TV, May 29, 1986)

dying seagull   *n.* DYING QUAIL, when close to either coast; or as Peter Tamony notes in his

MILLER JAMES HUGGINS
1904–1929
MANAGER OF ST. LOUIS CARDINALS
AND NEW YORK YANKEES.
LED YANKEES TO 6 PENNANTS
IN 1921, 1922, 1923, 1926, 1927 AND 1928 AND
3 WORLD SERIES VICTORIES 1923, 1927 AND 1928.
SECOND BASEMAN IN PLAYNG DAYS
WITH REDS AND CARDINALS, 1904–1916.

Dynasty. Miller Huggins' role in the Yankee dynasty of the 1920s is spelled out in bronze at the Hall of Fame. *National Baseball Library, Cooperstown, N.Y.*

file on the term, "This figure of speech would probably not be familiar to inlanders."

dying swan *n.* DYING QUAIL. "Then Gil McDougald pumped a dying swan over second base that no one could reach. I scooted home for my first World Series run, knowing my father was in the stands." (Mickey Mantle in *The Mick;* CDP)

dynamite bat *n.* Bat wielded by a strong, powerful hitter.

dynasty *n.* Subjective term used in baseball to describe a team able to come up with a cluster of championship seasons. The team generally acknowledged to have established the most dynasties is the New York Yankees, who have lorded it over eight of them, starting with the 1921–1923 dynasty.

ETY From the dynasty established by a string of rulers from the same family or group; for instance, the Ming Dynasty.

USE For reasons unclear, baseball never has empires, periods or eras but only dynasties.

dypsydo *n.* A slow, tantalizing curveball. Same as dipsy-doo.

E

E Common box score and scorecard abbreviation for error. ". . . he still stencils 'E-5' (the scorekeeper's shorthand for 'error-third baseman') on his glove to remind him 'to be humble.'" (description of Craig Nettles, *New York Times*, August 29, 1982)

In the ballpark the E takes on special meaning as it is flashed on the scoreboard when the official scorer decides that a particular player has committed an error. (If the batter reaches base safely on a tough chase for a fielder, the official scorer may in fact call the play a hit rather than an error. In such cases, the letter H is flashed to indicate a "hit.") One of the more ingenious, if commercial, systems for showing E's and H's appeared in Ebbets Field after World War II. It was a huge sign, for Schaefer Beer, whose H or one of whose E's lit up when the scorer made his ruling.

eagle claw *n./arch.* A common term for glove in the 1930s.

eagle eye *n.* Sharp eye for judging pitched balls.

ear bender *n.* Hotel stranger who talks with players.

ear flap *n.* An enlargement of the standard batting helmet, which covers the batter's ear on the side facing the pitcher. It began as a Little League safety precaution and, according to Frederic Kelly in the *Baltimore Sun*, ". . . worked its way into the big leagues when Baltimore's Brooks Robinson adopted it." (April 5, 1981)

early bloomer *n.* A rookie who looks particularly good in spring training or the early days of the regular season, but who fades quickly and must be dropped from the team.

early man *n.* A player who takes his batting practice before the players who are in the starting lineup that day. "The 'early men' were those not in the day's lineup, or who needed extra batting practice. The starters monopolized the batting cage once the formal practice began." (Dick Friendlich, *Relief Pitcher;* CDP)

early shower *n.* Destination of a player ejected from the game by the umpire.

early swing *n.* A swing at the ball, which is far out in front of the plate. The ball is usually missed altogether or, at best, hit into foul territory.

earned run *n.* A run scored without the aid of an error, passed ball, obstruction or interference. A run that is charged to the pitcher. **1ST** 1871. (*New York Herald*, September 5; EJN)

earned run average *n.* (ERA) A pitcher's statistic representing the average number of runs legitimately scored from his deliveries per full nine-inning game (27 outs). The figure is usually carried to two decimal points. It is calculated by dividing the number of earned runs by the number of innings pitched, then multiplying by nine. For instance, if a pitcher has worked 20 innings in three games and has given up seven earned runs, his earned run average is $20 \div 8 = .250 \times 9 = 2.25$.

Along with the won-lost record, this statistic is the mark of a pitcher's efficiency over the course of a season. Generally, an ERA of under 3.00 is considered good.

earned runs prevented *n.* Statistic that accounts for the number of earned runs below the league average collected by a given pitcher.

Eastern Division Those portions of the American and National Leagues that are grouped around eastern cities and that have their own standings throughout the course of the season. The Eastern Division winners in each league are entered in playoff series against their Western counterparts to determine who wins the pennant and plays in the World Series. The divisions were created in 1969 to replace a system in which there were no such separations within the Major Leagues.

Eastern Shuttle series Nickname that attached itself to the 1986 World Series between the New York Mets and the Boston Red Sox. Despite the best efforts of Pan American, which

Ebbets Field. Players hauling the flag for Opening Day, April 14, 1914, the first game played in Ebbets Field. *Prints and Photographs Division, the Library of Congress*

had just initiated a shuttle service between the two cities, the name of the long-established Eastern Air Lines air bus between the two cities is the one that stuck.

easy *adj.* Vulnerable, quickly dispatched. Neither a batter nor a pitcher would like to be known as easy.
1ST 1897. (*New York Tribune*, July 14; EJN)

easy money *n./arch.* Opponent who is weak.
1ST 1907. (*New York Evening Journal*, April 17; EJN)

easy out **1.** *n.* A player who poses no substantial threat at the plate; often applied to pitchers when they come to bat.
2. Common cliche chanted at the amateur level of the game. It is used to rattle the batter who may, in fact, be a good hitter.
EXT Applied to anyone or anything that can be dealt with easily.

eat up *v.* To field a ground ball quickly and skillfully.
1ST 1907. (*New York Evening Journal*, April 18; EJN)

Ebbets Field Home grounds of the Brooklyn Dodgers in Brooklyn, New York, from 1913 to 1957. Named for Charlie Ebbets, the man who had it built, the park was demolished in 1960, and a housing development is now located on its former site.

E-card In baseball card collecting, this is a reference to a candy or gum card (as opposed to one given out with tobacco) issued before 1930.

ecology pitch *n.* The 55-mile per hour fastball.
ETY Attributed to Allen Ripley of the Chicago Cubs by Joe Goddard in the March 6, 1982, *Sporting News*. It was inspired by the 55-mph speed limit imposed after the OPEC Oil Embargo.

Edison *n./arch.* A pitcher who is always experimenting with new pitches. From Thomas Edison.

Edna *n./arch.* Generic name for the wife of a baseball player (ca. 1958) who, according to

Burt Dunne in his *Folger's Dictionary*, is "married to a genius," namely the player in question.

eephus *n.* Pronounced "eee-fuss." A high-arcing pitch likely to reach an apex of 25-feet above the ground between the mound and the plate. The ball is thrown overhand and aimed upwards in the hope that it will, at its most effective, drop from the top to the bottom of the strike zone as it crosses the plate. The pitch will always be associated with pitcher Truett (Rip) Sewell. In the 1946 All-Star Game in Fenway Park, Sewell threw three straight eephus pitches to Ted Williams. Anticipating the third one after taking the first and fouling off the second, Williams ran up a few feet toward the mound and drove the ball over the right-field fence.

Eephus is one of a number of names for this unorthodox pitch, which is also known as the blooper, gondola, parachute, balloon pitch and La Lob. However, eephus seems to be reserved for the bloopers of the most outlandish trajectory.

ETY/1ST 1942. The pitch was first thrown by Sewell in an exhibition game the Pirates played against the Tigers in 1942 in Muncie, Indiana. Catcher Al Lopez called for a changeup with a count of 3 and 2 on Tiger Dick Wakefield, and Sewell threw the blooper.

In an interview published on July 12, 1981, Sewell told Ray Fitzgerald of the *Boston Globe* what happened next:

"Wakefield started to swing, then he stopped, and then he swung again and almost fell down when he missed. After the game, when everybody stopped laughing, Frisch wanted to know what I called the pitch, and Maurice Von Robays, an outfielder, said 'that's an eephus ball.'

" 'What's an eephus?' I asked him.

"Eephus ain't nuthin'. So it was always eephus after that."

Sewell also told Fitzgerald that he had developed the pitch as a result of a hunting accident that left 14 pieces of buckshot in his foot. After the accident, he was unable to pivot as before and adopted a straight, overhand motion, "something like an Australian crawl." The eephus came out of this and was thrown "by holding the ball in the palm of his hand with the fingers on top and delivered much in the manner of a shotputter."

Before the term was used by Sewell, ephus, e-phus or ephus ophus was used as slang for dependable information; the low down or the right "dope." Peter Tamony notes its use in both underworld and political contexts before and after Sewell's time in the majors, e.g., "The ephus is that by delaying things this long, Governor Olson has quietly knocked the election into a cocked-ballot." (*San Francisco News*, June 19, 1939)

USE Since Sewell's retirement the term has held on, but seems to be used humorously. For instance, in a March 6, 1988, Grapefruit League contest between the Toronto Blue Jays and the Philadelphia Phillies, Blue Jay pitcher Jose Nunez, unaccustomed to hitting because of the DH Rule, came to the plate and stood on the first base side of the batter's box even though he is right-handed and was wearing a right-handed hitter's helmet. After getting a laugh from the crowd he went to the other side of the plate. According to the account of the game in the *St. Petersburg Times*, the Phillies thought Nunez was making a joke out of appearing at the plate and Mike Schmitt was heard yelling to Phillies pitcher Kevin Gross, "Throw him the eephus, eephus." Gross threw one and Nunez got enough of it to ground out to second.

ee-yah Call/shout made famous by coach Hugh Jennings before World War I.

egg *n.* A baseball.

egg feast *n.* Low-scoring game; one with a lot of goose eggs on the scoreboard.
1ST 1891. (*Chicago Herald*, June 8; EJN)

800 Club Name for a select group of pitchers who have worked in 800 or more major league games. Members include Hoyt Wilhelm (1,070) and Cy Young (906).

eject *v.* To remove a person from the playing area.

ejection *n.* The banishment from a game of a player, coach, manager or spectator who, in an umpire's judgment, has violated a given rule or behaved in an unsportsmanlike manner.

Several managers have been so contentious that they normally get ejected more than once during a season. The most notable ejectee of the modern era was Earl Weaver of the Baltimore Orioles whose personal record for ejections in a season, according to the *Baltimore Sun*, was 10 in 1975.

elbow bender *n.* Pitcher.
1ST 1937. (*Philadelphia Record*, August 22; EJN)

800 Club. Club member Hoyt Wilhelm.   *Courtesy of the Cleveland Indians*

elbowing   *n.* Pitching.

electronic pitcher   *n.* Term used for a pitcher outfitted with a transistorized radio device, which is used to receive instructions from the dugout.

This idea has been experimented with in the Minor Leagues; the Atlanta International League team used them during the 1964 season. However, the bench-to-mound radio has never gathered much long-term interest.

elevator shaft   *n.* Figurative destination of a pop-up hit high and straight up from the batter's box.

USE   A play on the notion that the ball is shot up into an elevator shaft.

eleven immortals   *n.* Name for the select group of living inductees who were present at the Hall of Fame when it was dedicated in 1939. Their names: Ruth, Cobb, Johnson, Sisler, Lajoie, Mack, Young, Wagner, Alexander, Collins and Speaker.

Election to the Hall of Fame has since invoked the notion of baseball immortality. A modicum of reality was imposed at the moment when Dizzy Dean was told that he had been elected and he responded, "Well, I guess now I'm 'mongst them mortals."

Eleven Immortals. Ty Cobb missed the picture session so only 10 of the 11 immortals are in this photo taken at the dedication of the Hall of Fame in 1939. Left to right, in the front row: Eddie Collins, Babe Ruth, Connie Mack and Cy Young; back row: Honus Wagner, Grover Alexander, Tris Speaker, Nap Lajoie, George Sisler and Walter Johnson.   *National Baseball Library, Cooperstown, N.Y.*

Elias scale *n.* A set of statistics compiled by the Elias Sports Bureau to rank, by playing position, all major league players who are eligible to be free agents. Under the terms of baseball's collective bargaining agreement, this ranking determines if a team will be compensated if a player signs with a new team.

First compiled in 1981, the first player to be given a perfect ranking score of 1.000 was New York Yankees first baseman Don Mattingly in 1987.

emergency swing *n.* Defensive action taken when a ball is coming at the batter.

emery ball *n.* A pitched ball that has been roughed up with emery cloth, sandpaper or other abrasive agent. When such a ball is pitched, the scuffed side is more resistant to the force of air, causing it to move erratically as it nears the plate.
EXT/1ST 1914. An article by Lenny Anderson, published in the September 29, 1971, *Seattle-Post Intelligencer*, asserts that the emery ball was discovered "by accident" before the First World War by right-handed pitcher Russell Ford. The source of this information was an octogenarian, William L. (Doc) Green of Mercer Island, Washington, who knew Ford. In addition, Ford's account appeared in an Asso-

Emery ball. A dapper Russell Ford at spring training camp in Gray, Georgia, c. 1909. *National Baseball Library, Cooperstown, N.Y.*

ciated Press interview with a dateline of November 15, 1968, two months before his death.

According to Ford, he came on the trick pitch in the spring of 1908 while with Atlanta of the Southern Association. On a rainy day, while working under a grandstand, he accidentally threw a ball into a wooden upright, marring the ball's surface. He used the ball again and was surprised by the "amazing curve" that it made. He noted the scuff and went back to his customary technique (a then-legal spitball using tobacco and slippery elm). He applied what he had learned the next season, winning 26 games for the New York Yankees.

As for the emery ball, Green recalled, "He worked out a very careful way of scuffing up the ball with emery cloth. He had the emery cloth on his middle finger and when he got the ball, he slid his finger out through a hole in the pocket of the glove—a lot of players used to cut out the middle of the glove—and scuff up the ball."

Ford gave up the emery ball after that first season with the Yankees, choosing instead to rough up the ball with his fingernails. The emery secret got out in 1914 and everybody wanted to use it. This is also the year that the term began to appear in print (*New York Tribune*, September 20; EJN)

As Ford later recalled, "Some pitchers even used files to rough the ball. Others used potato graters." The emery ball was declared illegal in the winter of 1914–1915 at the meeting of the baseball rules committee.

emigre *n.* Player who moves from one team to another.

endorsement *n.* A practice pioneered by baseball players as they found they could earn a few extra dollars by lending their name and face to a product or service. Some have been more successful than others. Modern players sometimes make hundreds of thousands of dollars through endorsements.

English **1.** *adj.* Characteristic rotation of a ball—batted or pitched—with just enough spin to cause it to veer from its natural course.
1ST 1910. (*American* magazine, June; EJN)
2. *v.* To bunt or bat a ball that acts oddly thanks to spin. Referring to certain Negro League players in a 1940 *Saturday Evening Post* article, Ted Shanehan wrote, "Some are positive magicians at bunting, being able to English it so

Endorsement. Babe Ruth (center) used other Yankees, including Lou Gehrig (unfolding undergarment, to Ruth's right), to help him model his own Babe Ruth All-American Underwear. Unlike pitcher Jim Palmer, Ruth had limited success as an endorser of such garments.   *National Baseball Library, Cooperstown, N.Y.*

that it either stops dead as a fielder reaches for it, or corkscrews back around a catcher as he tries to pounce on it."(July 27, 1940; PT)
ETY   From the spin of a billiard or pool ball, which is accomplished by hitting the cue ball off center.

entrepreneur/entrepreneurial player   *n.* Player who takes the assets he has and puts them to especially good use. The *Boston Globe* once called Carl Yastrzemski the "best and last great entrepreneurial player." (June 1, 1986) It is a compliment of the first order.

Epworth League   *n./arch.* Figurative repository for players outside the game. In his April 1943 article on "Baseball Jargon," Franklin P. Huddle writes that to be sent to the Epworth League is "to be dropped outside of organized baseball."

equalizer, the   **1.** *n.* The curveball.
2. *n.* A run that ties a game—especially late in the game.

equipment   **1.** *n.* A team's game paraphernalia, including such items as bats, gloves and the catcher's protective gear.
2. *n.* A pitcher's stuff.

equipment manager   *n.* Club official responsible for obtaining, maintaining and transporting his team's equipment.

ER   Standard scorecard and box score abbreviation for earned run.

ERA   Standard abbreviation for earned run average, which is always stated as an initialism rather than as a word.

erase   *v.* To put out a base runner or to retire a batter.

eraser rate *n.* A statistic marking a team's success at catching opposing base stealers. Listed as a percentage, it is computed by dividing the number of opponents caught stealing by the number of their attempted steals. For a period in the early 1980s Eraser Rate Awards were awarded to the team with the best record in each league. It was sponsored by major league baseball and Eraser Mate, a pen produced by Paper Mate. In 1982, the award went to the Pittsburgh Pirates who threw out 71 of 179 runners attempting to steal (.396) and the California Angels who took care of 77 of 143 would-be thieves (.538).

Ernie Banks' dictum See Banks' Dictum.

error *n.* A misplay on the part of the defensive team that helps the offensive team. Errors occur when a batted ball is missed or dropped, when a wild throw is made or when a putout is missed because the ball is mishandled. Errors are determined by the subjective judgment of the official scorer and are given to a specific player and his team. They are recorded in the most basic accounting of a game, which calls for giving each team's tally in terms of "hits, runs and errors."
1ST 1858. (Chadwick Scrapbooks; EJN)

error-alls *n.* The Baltimore franchise on a bad defensive day. It is a punning play on the name Orioles. "Meet the Baltimore Error-alls" is the lead to an article in the *St. Petersburg Times,* for March 24, 1986. "The Orioles committed six errors, including two by all-star shortstop Cal Ripken, against the Philadelphia Phillies Sunday."

errorless *adj.* Having completed a game, a series of games or a string of consecutive innings without committing an error. Applied to individuals, parts of a team (an infield collective, for example) and teams as a whole.

ethyl chloride *n.* A chemical spray that is used as a local anesthetic to "freeze" a painful area so that a player may stay in the game. Often used after a batter has been hit by a pitch.

even the count *v.* When a batter or pitcher is able to make the count even—that is, the same number of balls and strikes.

everyday eight *n.* Lineup that seldom changes; applied to teams that see strategic value in using the same men (minus the pitcher) day after day, as opposed to platooning players at one or more positions. *USA Today* headline: "Yankee strategy for pennant drive: Every-day eight." (August 14, 1986)

ex- *n.* Former player, and one of the stages in the life cycle of a player. The full list of stages appeared in an article on Tom Seaver in the July 27, 1987, *Sports Illustrated:*
  I. Prospect.
  II. Phenom
  III. Regular
  IV. Star
  V. Established Star
  VI. Hero
  VII. Superstar *cum* Celebrity
  VIII. Disappointment (?)
  IX. Comeback Kid (!)
  X. Leader
  XI. Controversial Leader
  XII. Trade Bait
  XIII. Appreciated Elsewhere
  XIV. Disabled
  XV. Restored (El Comebacko Segundo)
  XVI. Veteran
  XVII. Hanger-On
  XVIII. Ex-

excuse-me hit/excuse-me swing *n.* A checked swing in which the batter, unintentionally making contact with the pitch, gets a hit. The hit, most commonly a single, is such a fluke that the batter is expected to excuse himself.

execute *v.* To make a play or carry out a specific action dictated by a situation in the game.
1ST 1912. (*New York Tribune,* September 5; EJN)

exhibit card *n.* A form of baseball card, which is also known as an arcade card because they were often sold from vending machines in amusement park arcades. According to Beckett's *Baseball Card Price Guide,* the name comes from the Exhibit Supply Co. of Chicago, which was the principle manufacturer of these cards.

exhibition game *n.* One of many unofficial games that do not count in the standings; they are often staged to pit against each other teams that do not meet during the regular season. Most are played before the season to get the teams prepared; however, occasional exhibition

Exhibition game. Al Lange Field in St. Petersburg, Florida, spring home of the St. Louis Cardinals (and the New York Mets until 1988).   *Courtesy of the Florida Division of Tourism*

games are played during the regular season. Teams sometimes make exhibition tours of Japan after the World Series has been played. The annual All-Star Game is a special example of an exhibition game as is the one staged every year at Doubleday Field in Cooperstown, New York, at the time when new members are inducted into the Baseball Hall of Fame.
1ST   1874. (*Chicago Inter Ocean*, July 25; EJN)

Exhibition Stadium   Located in Toronto, Ontario, Canada, the home of the Toronto Blue Jays since 1977.

expansion   *n.* The addition of a new franchise or franchises to the Major Leagues. A special draft is held at such times to enable the new teams to select nonstarters from a pool of players from existing teams. Between 1901 and 1960 there was no expansion in the Major Leagues, but new teams have since been added in 1961, 1962, 1969 and 1977.

expansion team   *n.* Tag that goes with a team that has been created through expansion. Such teams are often referred to as such for

many years after their entry into the league. The Mets, Padres and Angels are examples.

expectoration exhibitor   *n./arch.* One of the more flamboyant synonyms for spitball pitcher. **1ST**   1907. (*New York Evening Journal*, June 7; EJN)

ex-pilot   *n.* An ex-manager.

explode   **1.** *v.* To get maximum energy behind a hit or throw.
2. *v.* To unleash a barrage of hits, usually applied to a team.

exploding scoreboard   *n.* A scoreboard configured to make a flashy, noisy display when the home team scores a home run or accomplishes some other feat.
ETY   The term and the concept came from the fertile mind of Bill Veeck who introduced the first one in Comiskey Park in Chicago.
   Replete with mortars for Roman candles, smoke and strobe lights, Veeck later reported in his autobiography *Veeck as in Wreck* that it was inspired by a pinball machine that hits the

Exploding scoreboard. The original version in Comiskey Park.   *Courtesy of the Chicago White Sox*

jackpot at the finale of William Saroyan's play, *The Time of Your Life.*

extra-base hit   *n.* A double, triple or home run. A hit on which the batter advances safely past first base.

extra inning   *n.* Any additional inning of play beyond a game's regulation nine-inning length.

extra-innings game   *n.* Any game that goes beyond the regular nine innings. In the event of a tie after nine innings of play, play continues until one team has scored more runs than the other at the end of a complete inning or when the home team scores the tie-breaking run.
1ST   1885. (*Spalding's Official Baseball Guide;* EJN)

extra pitch   *n.* A pitch that pitchers are encouraged to develop when they are not successful with their particular repertoire of pitches.

eye   *n.* A batter's ability to determine from the sight of an oncoming pitch its location vis-a-vis the strike zone
1ST   1901. (*Frank Merriwell's Marvel;* EJN)

eye in the sky   *n.* A strategic observer in the person of a coach in the press box or other elevated position who communicates with the dugout. ". . . Astro General Manager Dick Wagner does not permit opposing teams to use an eye-in-the-sky . . ." (*San Francisco Chronicle,* June 6, 1987)
USE   This may amount to a term for coaching in Siberia. Reporting on Billy Martin's fifth return as Yankees manager, *The Sporting News* described the prospects for coach Jeff Torborg on the 1988 Yankees: "Torborg, never a Martin favorite has one year remaining on his contract and is expected to be the club's 'eye-in-the-sky' coach." (November 9, 1987)

eyes on it   *n.* Said of a batted ball that seems to find its way past fielders.

F

face a pitch *v.* Come to bat.
1ST 1874. (*New York Sun,* July 31; EJN)

face ball *n.* Brushback or knockdown pitch.

face mask *n.* Protective head device, worn by the catcher and home plate umpire which covers the face with a wire cage.

factory set *n.* A complete set of baseball cards assembled and collated at the printing company rather than one assembled and collated by a dealer or collector.

fadeaway *n./arch.* A term for the screwball that is seldom used today outside of historic context.
1ST 1908. (*New York Evening Journal,* March 5; EJN)
ETY First attributed to Christy Mathewson (active 1901–1916), who is credited with its invention and naming ca. 1908. The term apparently derives either from the fact that the

Fadeaway pitch. Christy Mathewson as he looked in 1916 in the final year of his career. *National Baseball Library, Cooperstown, N.Y.*

pitcher seems to fall off the mound after he has delivered the ball or, as Hugh Fullerton put it, that the ball, "loses speed suddenly as it approaches the batter and falls, or 'fades' away at an unnatural angle."

fader *n.* FADEAWAY.

fagot *n./arch.* The bat, a nickname of the last century.
ETY From the word for a bundle of sticks.
1ST 1891. (*Chicago Herald,* May 21; EJN)

fair *adj.* In fair territory, playable.

fair ball *n.* A ball in play; a batted ball that lands in fair territory (between the foul lines), or remains in fair territory until it passes first or third base, or remains between the foul lines until it clears the outfield fence or wall.
1ST 1854. (Knickerbocker Rules; EJN)

fair ground *n.* FAIR TERRITORY.

fair side *n.* The infield edge of the first and third bases.

fair territory *n.* The playing area within the foul lines.

faithful, the *n.* Fans.
1ST 1902. (*Sporting Life,* September 13; EJN)

fake bunt *n.* Bluff in which the batter squares the bat as if to bunt, but then pulls the bat back or takes a full swing.

fall away *n./arch.* A curveball that drops slowly toward the ground as it nears the plate.

fallaway slide/fall-away slide *n.* A slide into a base featuring a sudden, evasive drop to the ground just before reaching it.
1ST 1910. (*Baseball* magazine, May; EJN)

fall classic *n.* The World Series. This is one of baseball's oldest cliches, fully expressed in the large cliche of "titans clashing in the fall classic."

fall on a pitcher *v.* To get many hits off a pitcher during an inning or over the course of a game.

falsies *n.* Extra-thick sliding pads.

Fall Classic. Fans line up outside the Polo Grounds for World Series tickets (c. 1912).   *Prints and Photographs Division, the Library of Congress*

family day/family night   *n.* Promotional afternoon or evening in which either: (a) families get a special rate on tickets, or (b) the players are brought onto the field before the game with their families.

fan   **1.** *n.* An enthusiastic follower of the game; a devotee.
2. *n.* By extension, it has been diluted to mean any spectator at the game.
1ST   1889. "Their work on the diamond is a revelation to local 'fans,' . . ." (*Breeder and Sportsman,* December 7; PT) Also, "Kansas City baseball fans are glad they're through with Dave Rowe as a ball club manager." (*Kansas Times & Star,* March 26; PT)
ETY   While it is commonly assumed and quite often stated that this is a back formation or clipping of *fanatic,* other evidence has been presented. In his article "The Sports Section," which appeared in the March 1929 *American Mercury,* William Henry Nugent shows how many common sports terms used in North America are not Americanisms but rather much older

transplants from the British Isles. Nugent traces a number of terms back to the writings of Pierce Egan who he calls "the father of newspaper sports slang." Egan, who published a number of books and articles on sports in the 1820s, used much of the "flash and cant" of the boxing ring and race track in his account of events while others writing on the same subjects left them out. This was not just the slang of the sportsman but, as Nugent points out, "words that he had picked up from the speech of vagabonds, jail birds, bartenders, soldiers and actors."

Among others, Nugent traced these terms to Egan's era and his writings: *palooka* (for a fifth-rate boxer, from a pure Gaelic word), *ham* (for a poor performer, from a cockney abbreviation of amateur to am which was pronounced h'am), and *Chinaman's chance* (which has nothing to do with Asiatics, but came from a light-hitting boxer of the 1820s named Tom Spring who was likely to break during a long fight—a china man meaning a fragile individual, one made out of porcelain).

Family Day. Cleveland Indians John Romano (left) and Jerrry Walker (right) pose with two of a dozen pedigreed pups that were given away at one of the Tribe's early-1960s Family Days. *Courtesy of the Cleveland Indians*

Nugent's evidence on *fan* comes in part from a lexicon that Egan compiled in 1823 and that was published in the third edition of a book first issued in 1785 by Francis Grose, titled *Francis Grose's Dictionary of the Vulgar Tongue as Revised and Corrected by Pierce Egan.* The book contains the following entry:

The Fancy: one of the fancy is a sporting character that is either attached to pigeons, dog-fighting, boxing, etc. Also, any particular article universally admired for its beauty; or which the owners set particular store by, is termed a fancy article, as a fancy clout, a favorite handkerchief, etc; also, a woman, who is the particular favourite of any man, is termed his fancy woman and *vice versa.*

Nugent concludes, "The *fancy* was long a class name in England and America for followers of boxing. Baseball borrowed it and shortened it to *the fance, fans* and *fan.*"

(Other terms with a familiar ring that Nugent found in Egan's dictionary: to kid, to fake, to crab, to sting, to pony up, sucker, lame duck, faker, lucky break, pink of condition, racket and scab.)

An even earlier use of fancy can, in fact, be found in Egan's *Boxiana* published in 1818 in which he talks of, "The various gradations of the fancy hither resort to discuss matters incidental to pugilism." The term was firmly established and, for example, shows up in J. S. Farmer and W. E. Henley's monumental *Slang and its Analogues* (published in several volumes between 1890 and 1904) where it is defined as, "The fraternity of pugilists: prize-fighting being once regarded as THE FANCY *par excellence.* Hence by implication people who cultivate a

Fans. Jolly crew at the Polo Grounds, April 12, 1911.   *Prints and Photographs Division, the Library of Congress*

special hobby or taste." Farmer and Henley also point to *fancy-bloke*, a sporting man, as a variation.

Despite all of this evidence, the word fan is still regularly asserted to be a clipped form of fanatic. According to Gerald Secor Couzens in his *Baseball Album*, the supposed clipper of the word was T. P. Sullivan, manager and scout of the early 1880s. Others claim it was clipped by Chris Von der Ahe, owner of the St. Louis Browns in the 1880s, who supposedly had trouble pronouncing the word fanatic with his thick German accent.

Peter Tamony did much research on the term and sided with the Sullivan theory, which he spelled out in a letter to Jim Brosnan of December 9, 1963. The crucial paragraph: "A much better claim to origination is made by T. P. (Ted) Sullivan, one of the real founders of the modern game, in his book, *Humorous Stories of the Ball Field, A Complete History of the Game and Its Exponents* (Chicago, 1903, p. 253). Sullivan writes that Charles Comiskey called an enthusiast who visited the clubhouse in St. Louis

a 'fanatic' and that he [Sullivan] clipped the word to 'fan.' He sets the date as 1883: he was then building the St. Louis team which was later to be taken over by Comiskey to win the league championship four times, and the World Championship in 1885–1886; Von der Ahe was owner of the Club."

While these two are the major theories there are several lesser ones as well. Occasionally, one runs into a restatement of the claim made by Connie Mack that fan was first created to describe spectators who fanned themselves to keep cool.

3. *v.* To strike out a batter; to be put out on strikes; to whiff.

4. *v.* To swing and miss.

Edward J. Nichols collected a number of constructions based on this meaning, including *fan the air/fan the climate/fan ether* and *fan ozone*.

fancy Dan   *n./arch.* Player who works to make every play seem spectacular; a poser.
1ST   1927. (*The Sporting News Record Book; EJN*)

fandom   *n./arch.* Fans collectively; the realm of the fan. "Fandom also means agony, and one agony in being an Orioles fan is that the only seats they'll sell you for games with the Red Sox, Yankees, Indians, Blue Jays, Tigers and Brewers are so high above the field that acrophobia can make you hysterical . . ." (Russell Baker in 1980 *New York Times* magazine)

fanning bee   *n.* An artful display of pitching in which swinging strikes are plentiful.

fantasy baseball camp   *n.* A mock training camp in which ordinary fans can, for a hefty fee, practice and play baseball with retired Major Leaguers. An August 1986 ad in the *Wall Street Journal* for "The Mickey Mantle Whitey Ford Fantasy Baseball Camp" carried the line: "Play ball with your Yankee Heroes."
ETY/1ST   1983. The first of these camps took place in 1983 featuring ex-Cubs and ex-Dodgers. The word fantasy was quickly attached to them. "Baseball fantasy to Be fulfilled." (AP story on the Dodger camp in the *Oneonta Star*, February 3, 1983) An earlier story in the *Washington Post* (January 23) on the Cubs camp referred to it as "Fantasy Island in the desert."

fantasy-camper   *n.* One who pays to come to a fantasy baseball camp. "Luis Tiant hurls a pitch to a fantasy-camper Sunday afternoon in Winter Haven"—photo caption in the *St. Petersburg Times*, February 8, 1988.

fantasy game   *n.* Game in which two teams clash on paper, in a computer or by some other artificial means. These were popular during the baseball strike of 1981 when some radio stations took to broadcasting them.

fantasy league   *n.* Simulated baseball game, such as Rotisserie League Baseball, in which the statistical performance of real major league players determines the outcome.

far corner   *n./arch.* Third base.
1ST   1913. (*Harper's Weekly,* September 13; EJN)

farm   **1.** *n.* A minor league club where players are cultivated for a parent club (or clubs) in the Major Leagues, which has first option on the players. "Phils Plan Harvest of Farm Products." (headline in the *Philadelphia Daily News,* June 25, 1987)
SEE   *baseball farm.*
2. *v.* To send a player to a lower-level team for development.

ETY/1ST   1898. The term and concept date back into the 19th century. Edward J. Nichols found reference to a farm team in the *New York Herald Tribune* for June 17, 1898. However, the farm system as it exists today was the brainchild of Branch Rickey who created it while in the employ of the St. Louis Cardinals. He came up with the idea "by necessity" after the 1918 season when the Cards finished in last place. As he later told a congressional subcommittee on monopoly power, which was looking into "Organized Baseball" in 1952, he needed a way to compete with the richer clubs by ensuring himself a steady supply of replacement players. He started by buying half-interest in a Class D team in Arkansas for "a pittance." Using borrowed money, he bought half interests in the Houston and Syracuse teams in the Texas and International Leagues.

farm hand/farmhand   *n.* A minor league player. One who labors in the farm system. "Pirate Farm Hand Fans 27 in Hurling No-Hit Victory"—headline in the *San Francisco News,* May 14, 1952, describing Ron Necciai's Class D-league baseball feat: the throwing of the maximum number of strikeouts in a nine inning game.

farm out   *v.* To relegate a player to a minor league club; to send him back to the farm. "The Denver team sold him to Pittsburg for $5000. In 1908, Pittsburg 'farmed him out' to Louisville." (*The Book of Baseball,* P. F. Collier and Son, 1911; PT)
    Before there was a farm system as such, teams would place players on minor league teams to let them gain experience. It was regarded by some as an abuse by which the richer teams were able to reserve younger players and recall them at will.
1ST   1902. (*Sporting Life,* July 12; EJN)
EXT   To reassign: "I'd like to farm out some of this work."

farmhand   *n.* Minor league player who belongs to a major league club, from the name for a hired man in agriculture (farmhand, hired hand, ranch hand).

farm system   *n.* A major league club's network of affiliated minor league clubs. A team in the farm system may be owned by the parent club or may be independently owned and operated. In the case of independent ownership, the minor league club contracts with the major

Farm System. Branch Rickey's Fall of Fame plaque gives top billing to his role as father of the farm system. *National Baseball Library, Cooperstown, N.Y.*

league team on an exclusive basis to manage and develop players.

ETY The first modern farm system was created by Branch Rickey when he ran the St. Louis Cardinals in the 1920s and announced that the team would cultivate its own talent. Before that players had been optioned to minor league teams on an individual basis.

far turn *n./arch.* Third base.
1ST 1912. (*New York Tribune*, September 8; EJN)

fashion a hit *v.* To hit safely.
1ST 1928. (*New York Times*, October 7; EJN)

fastball/fast ball *n.* Overhead pitch thrown at top speed and with great power. It has a relatively even trajectory but usually has a backward spin, which can cause it to hop when it reaches the plate. It is the most common pitch in baseball.
ETY Because overhand pitching was not allowed until 1884, the fastball as we know it did

not come along until then. Before then fastballs existed, but came from the waist or below.
1ST 1905. (*Sporting Life*, September 2; EJN)

fast company *n./arch.* The Major Leagues.
1ST 1902. (*Sporting Life*, April 26; EJN)

Fast Food Fall Classic 1984 World Series, which pitted the Tigers against the Padres. The former club was owned by Tom Monaghan of Domino's Pizza and the latter by the heirs to McDonald's.

fast hook *n.* A manager's tendency to remove a pitcher at the first sign of trouble.

fast pellet *n.* One of many nicknames for the livelier ball, which was introduced after the Black Sox scandal of 1919.

fast pitch softball *n.* That branch of softball in which the pitcher is allowed to use full power in delivering an underhanded pitch that does not arc.

fat **1.** *adj.* Said of a pitch that is slow and easy to hit, of a pitch that is so hitable, it appears larger to the batter.
2. *n.* The thickest part of the bat, where the ball is best hit; the best wood; as in, he hit it right on the fat of the bat.

Fast pitch softball. Jimmy Moore, one of the top fast-pitch pitchers, is photographed in 1986, when his record in National Championship play was 22-4. *Courtesy of the Amateur Softball Association of America*

Fatal Fenway   What some pitchers call the home grounds of the Boston Red Sox. Bob Feller uses the nickname in his book, *Strikeout Story*.

fat cat syndrome   *n.* Term used to describe a team that falls apart the season after winning a championship. It implies a certain level of collective self-satisfaction seasoned with a dash of winter dissipation.

Father of Baseball   Patronym assigned to Henry Chadwick.

"A cloud was cast upon the opening of the season by the death on April 20 of Henry Chadwick, 'the Father of Baseball.' 'Father Chadwick,' who was eighty-three years old at the time of his death, had been a baseball enthusiast for more than half a century." (*Collier's*, May 2, 1908)

Chadwick, who was born in England, had advanced the theory that baseball had evolved from the British game of rounders. This led to the appointment of a National Commission of "fans," which was to determine the origin of the game. A short time before Chadwick's death

Father of Baseball. Henry Chadwick, a writer who had tremendous influence on the development of the game. (The title, Father of Baseball, has sometimes also been applied to Alexander Cartwright.) *National Baseball Library, Cooperstown, N.Y.*

the Commission concluded that baseball was a purely American invention.

fat one   *n.* A home run pitch; one that is delivered down the middle of the strike zone and easy to hit. "Mariners Go Far, 5–1, On Dixon's Fat Ones." (*The Washington Post*, June 5, 1986)

fat part of the bat   *n.* The barrel end of the bat.

fat pitch   *n.* Ball that is easy to hit; FAT ONE.

fatted calf   *n./arch.* A player out of physical condition.
1ST 1937. (New York *Daily News*, September 5; EJN)

fatten the average   *v.* To hit safely, thereby increasing one's—or a team's—batting average.
1ST 1897. (*New York Tribune*, June 2; EJN)

favorite cousin   Same as COUSIN (1. and 2.)

FC   Standard scorecard abbreviation for fielder's choice.

Federal League   Short-lived major league (1914—1915) created when a minor league elevated itself.

feeder   **1.** *n.* One of a number of games that were forerunners of baseball. In his book, *Baseball (1845–1881) from the Newspaper Accounts*, Preston D. Orem reveals that feeder was discussed in the *Boy's Own Book* published in London in 1829 as a variation on the game of rounders in which the bases were arranged in the form of a diamond.
2. *n.* During batting practice, a player or coach who stands behind the mound and supplies the pitcher with balls.

fence   **1.** *n.* Any boundary surrounding the field of play. " 'When you go into the fence, you use the fence to come back throwing,' Willie Mays said. 'Don't let the fence use you.' " (*New York Times*, March 3, 1986)
2. *n.* That portion of the field's boundary over which home runs are hit.

fence-buster   *n.* A heavy hitter. "Fence-busters Marshall, Mize, Cooper"—photo caption, in *Time*, August 25, 1947, accompanying a picture of New York Giant sluggers Willard Marshal, Johnny Mize and Walter Cooper.
1ST 1907. (*New York Evening Journal*, April 8; EJN)

Fenway Park   Home grounds of the Boston Red Sox since 1911. Located in Boston, Massachusetts, it is one of the last old-time stadiums and is much admired for its cozy atmosphere and odd dimensions (LF-315′, CF-390′, RF-302′), which were dictated by the path of railroad tracks rather than the ingenuity of architects. It is the smallest stadium in the Major Leagues and is dominated by a gigantic left-field wall known as the Green Monster. The park was named by former owner John I. Taylor for the fact that it was in the Fenway section of Boston. "I love this park. I think Fenway is the essence of baseball." (Tom Seaver in the *Boston Globe,* July 1, 1986)
ETY   A fen is an area of low marshland, which described the Back Bay section of Boston until it was filled in during the late 1800s. However, part of the area was maintained in its original state as a park and the road between downtown Boston and this Back Bay fen was named the Fenway. The name attached itself to the neighborhood surrounding the site of the ballpark. Owner John I. Taylor officially gave the name to the stadium.

fernalia   *n.* Catcher's equipment.
ETY   "Obviously, a corruption of the word paraphernalia. Some catcher couldn't pronounce it and gave up," reports Frank Gibbons in his 1959 *Baseball Digest* article on "fieldese."

fiddle hitcher   *n.* A Deanism that Dizzy explained was ". . . usually a pitcher who's been up there a long time and has lost his stuff, so he takes to fiddle hitchin' to get them batters out. He's a guy what fiddles around—hitchin' his trousers, fixin' his cap, kicken' around in the dirt—so's the opposin' batter will get riled up and blew up."

field   **1.** *n.* The playing area; the baseball field itself.
1ST   1845. (Knickerbocker Rules)
2. *v.* To catch or control a batted or thrown ball.
1ST   1870. (*New York Herald,* May 15; EJN)
3. *n.* The defensive team; that which is in the field.
4. *v.* To deploy defensively, such as fielding a top infield.

fielder   *n.* A player in any defensive position, although it is seldom applied to the pitcher or catcher.

fielder's choice   **1.** *n.* Act by which a defensive player fields a batted ball and decides to put out a base runner rather than throw out the batter. In other words, the fielder has chosen to let the batter take first in order to put out a runner farther along the base path.
   Whether or not there has been a fielder's choice is determined by the official scorekeeper. When one is ruled, the batter is charged with a turn at bat, but he is not credited with a base hit, even though he reached base.
1ST   1898. (*New York Tribune,* May 1; EJN)
2. *n.* Term used by the official scorer to account for either a batter who reaches base safely when the defense attempts to put out a runner farther along the basepath, a base runner who advances a base while the attempt is made to put out another runner, or a base runner who makes an undefended steal of a base. (This last case is called a fielder's choice at the discretion of the official scorer.)

field general/field manager   *n.* A team's manager as opposed to the general manager.

fielding   *n.* The defensive act of catching and controlling batted balls and turning as many of them as possible into outs.

fielding average   *n.* A statistic that is used to evaluate a player's fielding ability. It is computed by dividing a player's total number of putouts and assists by the sum of his chances (putouts, assists and errors). A player with 670 putouts and assists in 687 chances has a fielding average of .990.
1ST   1902. (*Sporting Life,* September 20; EJN)

fielding glove   *n.* GLOVE.

fielding practice   *n.* Pregame warm-up, which usually involves a coach hitting balls with a fungo bat.
1ST   1908. (*Baseball* magazine, June; EJN)

field umpire   *n.* An umpire stationed anywhere but behind home plate.

fifth infielder   *n.* A role that belongs to—but is not always assumed by—the pitcher. It is a term used by coaches and managers to emphasize the importance of a pitcher being ready to field a ball after it has been delivered. Pitcher Vic Raschi once put it this way: "Most balls hit through the box go for base hits, which is why the pitcher should be the fifth infielder." (*San Francisco News,* July 6, 1949; PT)

55-foot breaking ball/55-footer/56-foot fastball/etc.   *n.* Facetious reference to a bad pitch that bounces in the dirt before reaching home plate. The actual distance from mound to plate is 60 feet 6 inches.

fight the ball   *v.* For a defensive player to have a difficult time fielding a batted ball.
1ST   1910. (*New York Evening Journal*, March 10; EJN)

fill the bases   *v.* To put runners at first, second and third bases.
1ST   1884. (*DeWitt's Official Base Ball Guide;* EJN)

find/find a pitcher   *v.* To get hits off a pitcher, as if one has found his secret weakness.
1ST   1888. (*Chicago Inter Ocean*, July 7; EJN)

find the handle   **1.** *v.* The ability of a defensive player to control successfully a batted or thrown ball.
2. *v.* The phrase can also be stated as a command to a fielder who has just made a glaring error.

fine   **1.** *n.* A monetary penalty imposed on a player, coach or manager for behavior deemed detrimental to the club, the league or all of baseball. Fines can be imposed by the manager, the owner, the league president or the commissioner.
2. *adj.* Precise, such as when pitcher Eric Bell used the term in telling a *Washington Post* reporter, "That's when I stopped trying to be so fine with every pitch and just threw the ball." (July 24, 1987)

finesse pitcher/finesser   *n.* One who relies on such things as placement, deception, change of speed and guile over velocity and power. "I know that there will come a day when I'll have to make a transition from a power pitcher to a finesse pitcher, but by that time I'll have 11 years in the game." (Ron Guidry, quoted in the *Baltimore Sun*, June 13, 1982)

fingering   *n.* What has been described as the "mysterious science" used by pitchers to obtain the proper grip on the ball, depending on the desired pitch. It is accomplished by employing a combination of finger position and pressure on the ball. An important element of fingering is how the pitcher's fingers are positioned in regard to the seams of the ball.

fingernail ball/fingertip ball   *n.* A form of the KNUCKLEBALL thrown by gripping the ball with one's fingertips. It appears to have been first delivered by Eddie Summers in 1908.

finger system   *n.* System of communication by which the catcher signals a suggested pitch to the pitcher by flashing the fingers on his bare hand. From the crouched position, the catcher gives the finger signals between his legs to keep the batter from seeing them. Traditionally, one finger is given for a fastball and two for a curveball. Many catchers put white adhesive tape on their fingers so they can be seen from the mound.

Finleyites   Nickname for the Oakland A's when the team was owned by Charles O. Finley.

fire and fall back   *v.* To swing the bat with such force that one falls backwards. It is a play on the recoil that results from firing a powerful firearm.

fireball/fire-ball   *n.* FASTBALL.
1ST   1931. (*New York World*, February 26; EJN)

fireballer   *n.* A pitcher whose primary pitch is the fastball.

fireman   **1.** *n.* A relief pitcher; a reference to one who comes in to put out a "fire" (a rally by the opposition).
2. *n./arch.* Player who showers and dresses quickly after a game, in the manner of a fireman preparing to go out and fight a fire. (As recently as 1937, in a glossary printed in the *Sporting News Record Book*, this was the only baseball meaning of this term; its common application to relievers began in the 1940s when the role of the relief pitcher became more prominent.)
USE   An interesting distinction was made when both meanings coexisted in Herbert Simons' January 1943 article on baseball language: "A 'fireman' in baseball writers' parlance, usually is a relief pitcher who rushes in to quench the conflagration, but to the player, he's the teammate who showers and dresses the fastest after a game."
ETY/1ST   1940 (for a reliever). In a letter to Jack McDonald of the *San Francisco News-Call Bulletin*, Peter Tamony pointed out that the term had been in use colloquially in the 1920s (based on his interviews with players of the period), that it was showing up in print by 1940 and, by the end of the 1950s, was "the name

. . . of a new era in baseball." (June 12, 1960; PT) The first player whose name was broadly associated with the term was Johnny Murphy, Yankee relief pitcher. As Tamony put it in another letter on the term (to the *San Francisco Chronicle,* February 26, 1979): "As he doused rallies, Johnny Murphy's fourteen 1934 wins for the Yankees evoked the term 'fireman.' " In fact the earliest use of the term that Tamony could find in print was this line from a 1940 article on the decline of the Yankees: "Johnny Murphy is no longer the fireman of old." (*San Francisco News,* May 23, 1940)

In the late 1940s, the great Yankee relief pitcher Joe Page was nicknamed The Fireman and, in fact, posed for publicity photographs in a fire chief's hat.

fireman of the year   *n.* Informal title given to the best relief pitcher in each league at the end of the season.
SEE   *Rolaid's Relief Man Award.*

fireplug   *n.* A short, stocky player.

fireworks   *n.* An impressive offensive display, usually involving a rapid succession of extra-base hits.

firing line   *n.* The pitcher's box and mound. The term jibes nicely with battery.
1ST   1902. (*Sporting Life,* April 26; EJN)

first   *n.* See *first base.*

first, a   *n.* That which is new to the game. Baseball is usually fascinated by firsts. An exception was pointed out in a *Life* editorial on the 1971 All-Star Game: "They [the announcers] didn't allude to an All-Star 'first'—for the first time both starting pitchers were black." (August 13)

To underscore the game's infatuation with firsts, here are a few examples from the file marked "firsts" in the National Baseball Library in Cooperstown.

- The first woman to receive a World Series share. (Edna Jameson, who worked for the Cleveland Indians, was given a slice of the Series proceeds in 1920.)
- The first player in baseball history to be still active while eligible for a pension. (Hoyt Wilhelm, according to the May 3, 1969, *Sporting News*)
- The first professional player to hit a home run from opposite sides of the plate in the

same inning. (Gary Pellant of the Carolina League Alexandria Mariners on April 30, 1979)
- The first wedding at home plate. (September 18, 1893, at League Park in Cincinnati)
- First team to wear shorts. (The Hollywood Stars on April 1, 1950)
- The first major league club to travel by airplane. (The Boston Red Sox flew from St. Louis to Chicago on July 30, 1936.)
- The first written reference to the existence of a ball. (The Bible, Isaiah 22:18)

first and fifteenth player   *n.* One who thinks only of payday, as in the first and fifteenth of the month.

first ball   **1.** *n.* A ceremonial ball-tossing, which is most commonly associated with the opening day of the season but which has increasingly been used at other games, such as the All-Star Game, World Series, etc.

At its most spectacular, the President of the United States throws out the first ball on Opening Day to signal the beginning of another season. Sometimes the symbolism is even greater than the actual event. When President Harry Truman threw out the first ball in 1946 at Griffith Stadium, he was showing the nation that the war years were indeed over and that the President once again had time for such trivial pursuits as throwing out the first ball.

At a lower level, various people are asked to throw out balls as an honor, for reasons as simple as being the president of the company sponsoring Seat Cushion Night.
2. *n.* The first offering made by a pitcher to a batter

first ball hitter   *n.* Batter who routinely swings at the first pitch.

first ball itch   *n.* Compulsion to swing at the first pitch.

first base   *n.* "The first in order of the fair stations comprising the diamond," as Edward J. Nichols described it.
1ST   1845. (Knickerbocker Rules)
EXT   **1.** Initial success, often phrased in the negative: "I never got to first base."
2. In teenage slang, at various times since the 1930s, it has meant kissing. In this context each base represents a further level of sexual involvement up to the ultimate home run.

First baseman. Steve Garvey. *Courtesy of the San Diego Padres*

first base coach   *n.* Member of the managerial staff whose primary job is to instruct the runner on first on whether or not it is safe to advance. He may also relay signals from the manager to the batter or to a runner on second.

first baseman   *n.* Defensive player stationed at first base.

first division   *n./obs.* The top half of a league's standings before 1969 when each of the two major leagues was broken into two divisions.
1ST   1892. (*Chicago Herald,* June 30; EJN)

first sacker   *n.* First baseman.

first string   *n./adj.* The collection of players on a team who are best at their position.
1ST   1912. (*New York Tribune,* April 15; EJN)
ETY   See second string.

first stringer   *n.* Starter.
1ST   1920. "Cady was a young pitcher . . . even though he had not been accepted as a first stringer." (Burt L. Standish, *The Man on First;* DS)

first ups   *n.* The team to come to the plate at the very beginning of the game. In organized baseball, the visiting team always has first ups. "We used to choose up sides by palming our hands on a bat and the guy whose fist last closed around it got 'first ups.'" (Jim Murray in *The Best of Jim Murray*)

fish   *v.* To swing at a bad pitch.

fish cakes   *n./arch.* Low pay, particularly that which is paid in the Minor Leagues. The term appears to have been popular in the 1930s.

fisherman   *n.* Batter who chases—or "bites for"—pitches out of the strike zone.

fish hook   *n.* CURVEBALL, also hook.

fishing trip   *n.* A swing at a bad pitch.
1ST   1937. (*Pittsburgh Press,* May 2; EJN)

fist/fist him   *v.* To jam the batter; to throw the ball in at his fists.

fitness of the ground   *n.* Field conditions as they are affected by the weather, groundskeeping, other uses of the playing surface (e.g., football) etc.

$5 ride in a Yellow Cab   *n.* A long home run.

5 o'clock lightning   *n./arch.* To score late in the game. This term was used back when baseball was played exclusively during the day, with most games beginning around 3 o'clock. Phil Rizzuto has said the ability to strike 5 o'clock lightning was characteristic of some of the Yankee teams he played on.

flag   **1.** *n.* The PENNANT.
1ST   1883. (*Sporting Life,* August 13; EJN)
2. *v.* To signal a runner as he approaches a base.
3. *n./arch.* To catch or stop a batted ball, probably named from the railroad term for stopping a train with a red flag.
1ST   1920. (*New York Times,* October 10; EJN)

flag chase   *n.* PENNANT RACE.

flake   *n.* An odd or eccentric player. "Reporters, for reasons no one can really understand, want to be kind to them. A flake can literally go berserk in the clubhouse and the news never gets out." (Wells Twombly in a column on the flake, *San Francisco Examiner*, December 1, 1970; PT)

USE The term carries a certain element of endearment and tends to be applied to likable, but not always reliable, kooks.

ETY In a 1982 article in the *New York Times Magazine*, Tim Considine reports that the term "was first applied in the 1950s by baseball Giants teammates . . . to the offbeat San Francisco outfielder Jackie Brandt, from whose mind, it was said, things seemed to flake off and disappear." Other famous baseball flakes: Phil Linz, Denny McLain, Bill Lee, Doug Radar, Ross Grimsley and Jay Johnstone.

The term, however, had earlier slang meanings. For one, it has referred to a small packet of cocaine since the 1920s. In another earlier incarnation, Walter Winchell noted in an article on Harlem slang that it was one of several nicknames (along with ofay, pink and keltch) for a white person. (*San Francisco Call-Bulletin*, February 8, 1935; PT)

flaky/flakey *adj.* Strange; eccentric; a bit off; applied to any player who behaves oddly. "I found it's much easier to have a flaky front and do as you wish underneath, rather than present a straight intellectual front. Then when you do something flaky, they say, 'Oh, my gosh, look at this one.' Now they come to expect it and you do something weird and they say, 'Yeah, that's him.' " (Texas Rangers bullpen ace Jim Kern on the subject of "floating with life," *San Francisco Examiner*, November 30, 1979; PT)

ETY See *flake*.

Eric Partridge noted in his 1949 *Dictionary of the Underworld* that it has been a term for cocaine addiction since the 1920s.

EXT It is used widely in other realms, such as when President Reagan said that Col. Muammar el-Qadaffi was flakey. Ann Landers said in a 1962 column, "This man is as flakey as mother's apple-pie crust."

flamethrower *n.* Fastball pitcher.

flame-throwing *adj.* Possessing a superior fastball.

flare *n.* A looping fly ball likely to fall in between the infield and outfield; since the 1970s this has been still another synonym for Texas Leaguer or blooper.

" 'Against a righthander like Boddicker the lefthanders have to get on [base],' Schmidt said, 'You can't expect a righthander to hit defensively against him and get a flare to right.' " (*New York Post*, October 13, 1983)

USE Vin Scully said during the Oct. 21, 1986, World Series broadcast that the modern player preferred this term to Texas Leaguer.

flash **1.** *v.* To give signals quickly in the hope that one's opponents cannot steal them.
2. *n.* A signal given only once and given quickly, such as a tug of the belt.

flat *adj.* A pitch that has a straight trajectory, one that has no deceptive movements and is usually easy to hit. The opposite of *live*.

flat-footed **1.** *adj.* Unprepared; asleep; not on one's toes. To be caught flat-footed is to be caught napping.
2. *adj.* Describing runners who do not run on the balls of their feet; who run on their heels.

flat-footed position *n.* Batting stance with both feet flat on the ground as opposed to a stance in which the batter rests on the balls of his feet. The position is considered to be the optimum one for hitting a sacrifice fly.

flea-box *n.* A very small ballpark.

flinger *n.* Pitcher.
USE Term is often used in a context with a clear derogatory edge. Long paired with "alleged," which makes it an outright insult.
1ST 1909 (*New York Evening Journal*, July 8; EJN)

flip **1.** *v.* To throw a pitch in the direction of the batter's body, causing him to hit the dirt. "A good flip," wrote Jim Brosnan in *The Long Season*, "may require that the pitcher throw the ball at a spot where the batter would be if he knew the pitch was meant just for him, and duck."
2. *n./arch.* A player's throwing arm, FLIPPER.
3. *v.* To toss the ball underhanded without much velocity.
4. *n.* A light, underhanded toss that only goes a short distance.

flipper **1.** *n.* Pitcher.
2. *n.* Player's throwing arm.

flip-ups PULL-DOWN SUNGLASSES.

flivver *n./arch.* Player who fails to use or show his ability.
1ST 1915. (*Baseball* magazine, December; EJN)

floater *n.* Slowly pitched ball with very little spin or twist, intended to catch the batter off balance; pitch that seems as if it floats its way toward home plate. According to research conducted by the National Baseball Library in the 1970s, the pitch was first made popular by Bill Phillips at Indianapolis around 1906.
1ST 1906. (*Sporting Life,* March 3; EJN)

flocked hits *n.* BUNCHED HITS.

floop *v.* To hit weakly, but safely; to bat poorly but successfully. Perhaps a blend word of flub + bloop.
1ST 1937. (*New York Tribune,* October 10; EJN)

fluffy duff *n.* A player easily hurt, a term used by Dizzy Dean and which may have been coined by him.

flutterball/ flutter ball *n.* Pitched ball that wobbles and travels slowly; a knuckleball variation delivered with a snap of the wrist.

fluttering cuff *n.* Term that refers to the loose, ragged sleeve of pitcher Dazzy Vance, which so distracted batters that a rule was established that prohibited pitching with ragged or slit sleeves.

fly **1.** *n.* A batted ball that rises high into the air before it drops. (A traditional rule of thumb is that, to be called a fly ball, the ball should reach a height of around 15 feet before dropping.)
   A fly ball that is caught before touching the ground is an out. This fly was not part of the original *Knickerbocker Rules,* but one member of the club, J. W. Davis, waged a long campaign to have it adopted. The Knickerbockers adopted it in 1865.
1ST 1860. (EJN found two references for this year: the minutes of the Knickerbocker Base Ball Club and *Beadle's Dime Base Ball Player.*)
2. *v.* To bat a ball into the air that is caught by a fielder before touching the ground.
1ST 1908. (*Brooklyn Daily Eagle,* May 28; EJN)
3. *n.* A pest; a persistent fan who will not leave a player alone.
SEE *green fly.*

fly ball *n.* Ball that is batted into the air, as opposed to one batted on the ground.
SEE *fly.*
1ST 1865. (*New York Herald,* August 25; EJN)
EXT Someone who is wifty, semi-nutty, an oddball.

fly catch *n./arch.* The fielding of a fly ball before it touches the ground. Used, presumably, to distinguish the first two meanings of fly from one another.
1ST 1862. (Chadwick Scrapbooks; EJN)

fly chaser *n.* An OUTFIELDER.

flyer *n.* Fast runner.

fly out **1.** *v.* To hit a fly ball that is caught for an out before it hits the ground.
1ST 1870. (*New York Herald,* May 8; EJN)
2. *n.* With the exception of the *foul tip,* a ball batted in either fair or foul territory that is caught before it touches the ground. It counts as an out.
USE Although the past tense of this verb is sometimes stated as *flew out,* as in, "Last time up at bat, he flew out," it is proper and traditional to say or write flied out. As William Safire points out in his book, *On Language,* "When a batter has hit a fly ball which is then caught, the past tense of his action is 'flied out.' The only time 'flew out' would be correct is if the batter dropped his bat, flapped his arms, and soared out of the stadium, thereby earning himself the frothiest head in the *Guinness Book of World Records.*"

fly the flag *v.* To win the league championship, to win the pennant.

FOB's **1.** *n./arch.* Initialism from the days of the Brooklyn Dodgers; it stood for bases that were "full of Brooklyns" or "full of bums." At about the same time it was used in Pittsburgh for "full of Bucs."
2. *n.* One modern adaptation: Baltimore Orioles' announcers using it for "full of birds."

fog *n.* Fastball, derived from fog it through.
1ST 1937. (New York *Daily News,* September 5; EJN)

fogger *n.* Fastball pitcher.
1ST 1937. (New York *Daily News,* January 31; EJN)

fog it through *v.* To fire a fastball past a batter. Phrase created and associated with Dizzy Dean's delivery, but applied to others; a Deanism.
ETY Dean explained that when he reached back for that something extra for his fastball, it appeared so quickly that it seemed to be coming out of a fog.

fold 1. *v.* To fall from a strong position in a game or in the standings.

"I don't look at 1978 as a fold." (Dwight Evans, quoted in the July 28, 1986, *USA Today* on his Red Sox team that blew a 14-game lead.) **2.** *n.* The point at which a team fails, which is often referred to as "the fold." A *Washington Post* headline of October 10, 1988, after the Oakland Athletics won the American League Championship, simply read, "Red Sox 'Outplayed' in '88 Version of Fold."

follow-through 1. *n.* The continuation of the arm and body in the direction of a pitch or throw; the final stage of a pitcher's motion. **1ST** 1909. (*American Magazine*, May; EJN) **2.** *n.* The continuation of the swing by the batter after the ball has been hit or missed; bringing the bat all the way around for maximum power.

folly floater *n.* Blooper ball by New York Yankee pitcher Steve Hamilton. Though Hamilton described it as a "gag" or novelty pitch, he actually did use it in games.

foot in the bucket 1. *n.* Descriptive of a batter who pulls away from the plate as he swings at the ball. It may come as a result of fear of being hit by the ball. It is an awkward move that suggests that the batter's back foot is stuck in an imaginary bucket. More commonly, however, it seems to result from the batter being fooled by the speed or delivery of a pitch, causing a premature swing and shift of weight. This causes the front foot to come forward. **2.** *n.* Descriptive of an unorthodox stance in which the batter's front foot is pulled back toward the foul line rather than pointed out toward the pitcher. Once described by Dizzy Dean: "Sort of a sprattle-legged stance at the plate. The batter looks like he has got a pain in the hip and he sticks his left foot out toward third base." Though such a stance might be interpreted as a sign of timidity in a batter, it is actually an effective, respected stance, used by such successful hitters as Arky Vaughn, Roy Campanella and Al Simmons. So closely was Simmons associated with this stance that when he died on May 26, 1956, the first line of his AP obituary read, "Al Simmons, whose batting feats with an odd 'foot in the bucket' stance earned him a niche in baseball's Hall of Fame, died here early today four days after his 54th birthday."

Foot in the bucket. Al Simmons displays his foot-in-the-bucket stance. Simmons posted a magnificent record at the plate, hitting over .300 for eleven seasons in a row. Simmons entered the Hall of Fame on the strength of a career batting average of .334. *National Baseball Library, Cooperstown, N.Y.*

ETY/1ST 1913. In his section on baseball terms in *The Encyclopedia of Sports Talk*, Phil Pepe says that the stance took its name from the front foot, which is withdrawn toward the foul line, "toward the old water bucket in the dugout." This conforms with the earliest use of the phrase found by David Shulman: "Take your foot out of the water-bucket, Mister Conley, says Buzz . . ." (C. E. Van Loan, *Score by Innings*, published 1919, copyrighted 1913) **EXT** To have one's "foot in the bucket" is to act timidly. "Secretary-General Thant of the United Nations shows signs of having his foot in the bucket in getting ready to duck a formal request by the South Vietnamese Government for U.N. observers at the September elections." (*San Francisco Examiner*, June 7, 1966; PT)

foot in the dugout *n.* FOOT IN THE BUCKET.

foozle *n.* A bungled play. "Goldblatt . . . scor[ed] on Shaneman's foozle of Sullivan's fly." (*The Dartmouth Alumni Magazine*, February 1922; DS) **1ST** 1905. (*Sporting Life*, September 9; EJN)

Forbes Field   Located in Pittsburgh, Pennsylvania, the home of the Pittsburgh Pirates between 1909 and 1970. When the Pirates moved into their current park, Three Rivers Stadium, (1971) Forbes Field was closed and demolished. The original site is now part of the University of Pittsburgh. According to Philip J. Lowry in his *Green Cathedrals:* "Home plate remains in its exact original location, only now it is encased in glass on the first floor walkway of a University of Pittsburgh library."

It was named for British General John Forbes who captured Fort Duquesne and renamed it Fort Pitt during the French and Indian War.

The fact that there was never a no-hitter thrown here is just one of a number of odd facts about the park.

SEE   Greenberg Gardens and Kiner's Korner.

force   *n.* A play in which a runner loses his right to a base for the simple reason that two runners cannot occupy the same base at the same time. In such plays a hit or stolen base forces the runner or runners to advance to the next base.

1ST   1869. (*DeWitt's Official Base Ball Guide;* EJN)

force double-play   *n.* A fielding play in which two putouts are made on a force play. Typically, a man is on first base and the batter hits a ground ball, which is thrown to the fielder covering second, who touches the bag for a force out and then throws the ball to first base to get the batter out. The fielder at second base is the key to this play because he must touch the bag and fire the ball to first base while avoiding the sliding runner. In his *Spectator's Guide to Baseball,* Dan Sperling writes: "Although it's a fairly common baseball occurrence, a force double-play involving the batter, a base runner and three fielders is a thing of beauty to behold because of the clockwork precision with which it is executed."

force in   *v.* When the bases are loaded and the pitcher walks the next batter, the man occupying third base must come home; thus, forcing him in to score.

force out/force-out/forceout   *n.* The putout of an advancing base runner who is forced to move to the next base. Example: A runner is on first and the batter hits the ball to the third baseman, who throws to second. The second baseman touches the bag and the base runner, forced to move up by the advancing batter, is automatically out.

1ST   1870. (*New York Herald,* May 8; EJN)

force play   *n.* The defensive action that results in the retiring of a base runner by touching the base to which he is headed and must—is forced to—occupy because there is an advancing runner behind him. In a force play, the runner does not have to be tagged.

foreign substance   *n.* Generic term used in the rules of baseball to outlaw pine tar, petroleum jelly, hair dressing and other illegal materials applied to the ball to give the pitcher an advantage. The one substance that is officially allowed is rosin.

forfeit/forfeited game   *n.* A game in which a victory is awarded to a team by the umpire because the opposition acts in an illegal manner. A team can be forced to forfeit a game if it refuses to play, delays the game, or fails to remove an ejected player. A game may also be forfeited to the visiting team in the case of unruly behavior on the part of the hometown fans. The official score of a forfeited game is 9-0. Only the umpire-in-chief can declare a forfeiture.

SEE   *beer night, disco demolition night.*

"forget it!"   *v.* Exclamation used by some sportscasters to describe a long, powerful hit that is obviously a home run. It is said when the outcome of such a hit is never in doubt. Also stated as, "you can forget about that one."

forkball/forkball/forked-ball pitch.   **1.** *n.* A pitch that breaks on a downward path as it approaches home plate. It is gripped between the thumb and the first and middle finger, which are spread apart, suggesting a two-pronged fork. This grip limits the spin of the ball and causes it to drop or sink sharply as it reaches the plate.

It is a pitch associated with certain players, including Ernie Boham of the Yankees and Elroy Face, who helped popularize it during his years with the Pittsburgh Pirates. The first pitcher to become known for his forkball was Joe Bush.

1ST   1923. (Edward J. Nichols traced it back to *Spalding's Official Baseball Guide* of this year.) **2.** *n.* Euphemistic name for a spitball. "He also acquired another pitch for his repertoire, a pitch he sometimes calls a 'spitter' but most

Force-out. Softball force during the 1986 Slow Pitch National Championship in Burlington, North Carolina.   *Courtesy of the Amateur Softball Association of America*

frequently refers to as a 'forkball.' " (profile of Gaylord Perry, *American Way*, September 1962)

for the first time in history   A phrase that, when written or spoken, indicates the occurrence of an event in baseball that has never happened before. Because such events are rare, the words have taken on a special significance. "For the first time in history, three grand slams were hit in a major league game—a phenomenally bizarre 13-11 Texas Rangers victory over the Baltimore Orioles tonight in Memorial Stadium." (Thomas Boswell, *The Washington Post*, August 6, 1986)

45-foot lane/45-foot line   *n.* A designated area that the batter must stay in when running to first base. Three feet wide, the lane begins halfway down the base line from home plate and extends the 45 feet to first base. The lane is designed to keep the runner from going inside the diamond and interfering with the throw to first. Any runner, ruled to have left the lane in a deliberate attempt to interfere

with the defensive play, is called out by the umpire.

40-40 Club   *n.* Figurative place for players who have hit 40 or more home runs while stealing 40 or more bases in a single season. It came into prominence at the end of the 1988 season as these lines from Eric Brady in *USA Today* (October 4, 1988) explain: "[Jose] Canseco hit 42 home runs and stole 40 bases. Baseball records go back 112 years, but you can count the 40-40 club members on one finger. Canseco. Period. End of list."

foshball.   *n.* Pitch attributed to Mike Boddicker that combines the properties of a change-up and a forkball or other breaking pitch. *USA Today* said that, "It breaks away from left-handers and is the pitch [Rod] Carew, George Brett and other lefties have found so frustrating." (September 8, 1983) See FUSH BALL.

foul   **1.** *n.* A FOUL BALL.
1ST   1845. (Knickerbocker Rules)

2. *v.* To hit a ball into foul territory.

3. *n.* Foul Territory.

foul back/foul one back *v.* To hit a ball backward into foul territory.

foul ball *n.* A legally batted ball that is hit and lands in foul territory before reaching first or third base, or first touches the ground in foul territory beyond first or third base, or, to quote the game's official rules, "while on or over foul territory, touches the person of an umpire or player, or any object foreign to the natural ground."

A foul ball counts against the batter as a strike, unless it is caught on the fly, which then counts as an out. A batter cannot strike out on a foul ball, however, unless he bunts the ball foul with two strikes.
1ST 1860. (*Beadle's Dime Base Ball Player:* EJN)
EXT A bad egg; an ignorant person.
"Where do I find the bartender?"
"He's in the can. He was a foul ball. He tried to work a swindle on some rich dame and called cops. They stepped in and put him away for five years." (Michael Brett, *The Flight of the Stiff*)
There is much evidence to suggest that cartoonist/writer T. A. Dorgan was the first to apply the term to an individual. Peter Tamony collected a number of examples from Dorgan's work, including a piece from July 1, 1925, in which one of his characters says in reference to a boasting athlete, "Oh, he's just a foul ball." (*San Francisco Call & Post*)

foul ball indicator *n.* Device that determines if a long ball has passed the foul pole in fair or foul territory. Several such devices have been developed over the years, but none has yet to establish itself in the game. One system that got a lot of press attention in 1949 was based on a foul pole with free-swinging rods attached. If the ball touched one of the rods on the foul side a red light went on while a green light was lit if it passed on the fair side. It was granted U.S. patient 2,461,936.

foul bound *n./obs.* Foul ball caught after taking one bounce. Under early rules of the game this was an out.
1ST 1874. (*New York Sun,* June 24; EJN)

foul bunt *n.* A bunt that lands in foul territory. If a player bunts foul after two strikes, it is counted as a third strike.

foul fly *n.* A foul ball that goes high in the air.

foul ground *n.* FOUL TERRITORY.

foul lines *n.* The white boundary markings that extend from home plate to the left-field foul pole and from home plate through the right-field foul pole, forming a 90° angle.
1ST 1875. (*DeWitt's Base Ball Umpire's Guide;* EJN)

foul off *v.* To hit a pitched ball foul.
EXT *adj.* Screwed up. "I have seen a buffoon platoon become the pride in eight weeks, and I have seen a foul-off gun crew develop into a crack outfit in three weeks . . ." (Robert C. Ruark on the new draft, in the *San Francisco News,* August 6, 1948; PT)

foul out *v.* To hit a fly ball that is caught for an out in foul territory.
1ST 1880. (*Chicago Inter Ocean,* June 29; EJN)

foul pole *n.* A set of vertical posts or polls erected at the intersection of the outfield fence and each foul line. They are there to help the umpires determine if a ball that is hit over the fence is fair or foul. A batted ball that hits the foul pole is a home run. The rules dictate that the foul poles in major league parks must be at least 10 feet tall.

foul screecher *n.* Untutored spectator who cheers foul balls not knowing that they are not hits. Dizzy Dean's definition was: "A ladies' day fan who screams on every pop foul."

foul strike *n.* Proper term for a foul ball—batted with fewer than two strikes—that is not caught on the fly. Originally, a ball batted foul was counted as a strike, but the rule was changed in 1901, allowing the batter as unlimited number of foul balls.
1ST 1954. (*Knickerbocker Rules;* EJN)

foul territory *n.* All area outside the lines of the 90° angle formed by the two foul lines. A fly ball is playable within foul territory unless it is in an area that has been deemed to be *dead.* Charles F. Dery, who collects baseball broadcast slang and phraseology, prizes this brilliant but probably unintentional pun: "The ball landed in foul territory, in the midst of a flock of seagulls."
1ST 1908. (*Brooklyn Daily Eagle,* May 21; EJN)

foul tip *n.* A ball that glances off the bat directly into the catcher's hands. It counts as a

regular swinging strike rather than as a foul ball, thus the batter is out if he foul tips a ball with two strikes against him. A tipped ball is not counted as a foul tip if it hits any part of the catcher's body before landing in his hands. Although touched by the batter a foul tip is considered in play.
1ST 1861. (*Beadle's Dime Base Ball Player;* EJN)

four-bagger   *n.* A HOME RUN.
1ST 1883. (*Chicago Inter Ocean,* June 25; EJN)

.400 hitter   *n.* A benchmark season's batting average. This feat was last accomplished by Ted Williams in 1941 when he batted .406. Ever since Williams' achievement, a perennial question is asked: Will there ever be another .400 hitter? Rod Carew, George Brett and Wade Boggs have flirted with the number for parts of seasons but all have come up short. Should another one come along, his manager would do well to listen to manager Joe McCarthy's decades-old comment on the subject: "Any manager who can't get along with a .400 hitter is crazy."
EXT A heavy hitter in any realm. A column in the July 18, 1987, *Bangor Daily News* on the performance of Maine's senators in the Iran-Contra hearings was headlined: ".400 hitters on a mediocre team."

four-master   *n./arch.* A HOME RUN.

four-ply blow/four-ply wallop   *n.* HOME RUN.

four-seamer   *n.* Variety of HOME RUN described in an article on player jargon in the March 6, 1982, *Sporting News:* "The ball doesn't move at all. It goes straight down the middle, about thigh-high, and the hitter gets all four seams. The result makes the fans go 'ooh-ah.' "

Fourth of July   Roughly halfway through the regular season, this date is a standard landmark for measuring a team's success. It's often said that the teams in first place on the Fourth of July will win their divisions, but this actually happens less than half the time.

four wide ones   A BASE ON BALLS.

FP   Standard abbreviation for fielding percentage.

frame   *n.* An INNING.
1ST 1910. (*New York Tribune,* July 13; EJN)
ETY Edward J. Nichols concluded that this was taken from the bowling term as, "both 'inning' and 'frame' constituting divisions of play in their respective games."

frame the pitch   *v.* For a catcher to keep his glove in the strike zone, or as close to it as possible, when receiving the pitch. This is done in order to give the home plate umpire the impression that a pitch is in the strike zone, even if it is not.

franchise   *n.* The formal agreement or grant that establishes the existence and ownership of a club. It amounts to a license, which can only be legally granted by Major League Baseball and either the American or National League. When a club moves from one city to another, the franchise or license remains in force but has been relocated.
1ST 1913. "Besides the legitimate expenditure charges . . . or the 'franchise,' as it is usually called, the depreciation charges, the interest on money invested in players, and the 'charge off' for the depreciation in the value of human flesh and blood must be considered before profits can be reckoned." (*Technical World,* January)

franchise player   *n.* A superior player around whom a successful team can be built; one who gives significant added value to the franchise.
   "In short, he is what baseball men covet beyond all else, a franchise player. The pilings on which pennant-winners rest, a neophyte Mike Schmidt or Johnny Bench." (Phil Musick on Cal Ripken, Jr., *USA Today,* March 16, 1983) Franchise players: Lou Brock with the St. Louis Cardinals, Tom Seaver with the New York Mets, Mickey Mantle with the Yankees and Willie Mays with the Giants. *Time* headlined its article on Tom Seaver's 1977 trade from the Mets to the Reds, "How the Franchise Went West." (June 27; PT)
1ST The term was not used in this sense until after World War II according to research conducted by Peter Tamony, and it may not have come into its own until it began to be attached to Willie Mays. Curley Grieve, sports editor of the *San Francisco Examiner,* once pointed out that Mays was "the franchise" just as Carl Hubbell was "the meal ticket." Grieve added that the Mays partisans pointed out, "Hubbell showed once every four days. Willie you can see every day. That's why he's the franchise and not merely a meal ticket." (September 29, 1957; PT)

Franchise player. Photo taken June 4, 1912, of Nap Lajoie after he was presented with a horseshoe embedded with 1,009 silver dollars. The cash was given to him by fans in honor of his 10th anniversary in a Cleveland uniform. *Prints and Photographs Division, the Library of Congress*

frank *v./arch.* To be given a base on balls.
1ST 1922. (*Base Ball Cyclopedia;* EJN)

Frank Merriwell finish *n.* A game that ends dramatically in the manner of Burt Standish's novels starring Frank Merriwell.

fraternization *n.* Conversation between players of opposing teams on the field of play. Significant because it is actually prohibited by the rules—"Players of opposing teams shall not fraternize at any time while in uniform"—but the prohibition is seldom enforced. The term was used frequently during the 1950s when it was argued that the practice would somehow reduce the intensity of performance. In his book *How to Watch Baseball,* Steve Fiffer points out that different managers have different policies on fraternization. For instance, Mets Manager Davey Johnson is quoted, "I don't believe in fraternization. I frown on my players talking to guys on the other team, but I don't have a rule." In *The Rules and Lore of Baseball,* Rich Marazzi points out that first baseman Willie Stargell of the Pirates was so given to chatting with runners who stopped at his station that some players and writers ironically referred to the rule as "the Stargell Rule."

freak delivery *n.* Unconventional method of pitching, usually designed to throw off or fool the batter. It is sometimes applied to illegal pitches, such as emery balls and mud balls, but also to a pitch that is legal but ideosyncratic.

"Most of the 'freak' deliveries have been developed because of some hunch on the part of the pitcher," writes Babe Ruth in *Babe Ruth's Own Book of Baseball.* "For instance, in my pitching days, the balls we used had printed on them the trade mark and the name of the league president. It was my hunch that this ink on the side of the ball gave just an added atom of weight to the printed side. Consequently in pitching a curve ball I was careful to hold the inked side of the ball on the side that I wanted the curve to break. A foolish notion, perhaps, but one that I always followed."

freaky floater *n.* BLOOPER. A Phil Niekro pitch was described by Wayne Minshew as: "The pitch is off-speed but slower than the normal change-up. It floats to a height of about 10 to 15 feet, but not as high as the blooper Rip Sewell threw a few years ago." (*Sporting News,* August 28, 1971)

free agency **1.** *n.* The state of being a free agent.
2. *n.* The system under which free agents operate.

"In moves that may signal the rebirth of free agency in major league baseball, two significant players switched teams yesterday." (Richard Justice in the *Washington Post,* December 2, 1987)

free agent **1.** *n.* A professional player who has no contractual obligation to play for one team and is free to negotiate directly with any team, including the one he was playing for when the contract expired. One can also become a free agent when released by a club.

Modern free agency was born in 1975 with the decision of an arbitrator, Peter Seitz, who ruled in favor of two players. Ten years later Murray Chass wrote in the *New York Times,* "After Seitz created free agency, free agency created millionaires, agents and unhappiness among owners, but it also produced unprecedented popularity for baseball." (December 22, 1985)

1ST 1908. (*Brooklyn Daily Eagle,* May 23; EJN)
2. *n.* A player who has been discharged or is unemployed. This euphemistic application of the term is significantly different from its true meaning.

free check *n./arch.* BASE ON BALLS.
1ST 1902. (*Sporting Life,* July 12; EJN)

free pass/free passage/free passes *n.* A BASE ON BALLS.
1ST 1917 (free passage only). (*New York Times,* October 8; EJN)

free ride *n.* BASE ON BALLS.

free spirit *n.* A player who lacks inhibition; a nonconformist. "Reliever Randy Niemann is the New York Mets' comic relief specialist who is gaining recognition as one of baseball's funniest free spirits." (Gannett Westchester Newspapers, June 28, 1986)

free swinger *n.* Batter who tends to swing for pitches out of the strike zone.
1ST 1909. (*Baseball* magazine, November; EJN)

free ticket/free transit *n.* BASE ON BALLS.
USE These are seldom simply thrown or delivered but issued: "Boggs was issued a free ticket in the second inning Friday night." (*Boston Globe,* August 10, 1986)
1ST 1917. (*New York Times,* October 7; EJN)

free transportation/free trip **1.** *n.* BASE ON BALLS.
2. *n.* An awarded base given to a batter who has been hit by a pitched ball.

freeze a ball **1.** *v.* To catch a fly or field a grounder gracefully.
1ST 1868. (*New York Herald,* August 14; EJN)
2. *v.* To dampen a ball's life by keeping it in a freezer or refrigerator in an attempt to help a pitcher. The practice and the belief that a warm ball goes farther than a cold one goes back many years. Talking of Connie Mack, Frederick Lieb wrote in *The Pittsburgh Pirates:* "There used to be an icebox in the Pittsburgh Club's offices, and Connie conceived the idea of stuffing boxes of baseballs into the icebox, and freezing them overnight. The practice supposedly froze the life out of baseballs." (CDP) Writing about Josh Gibson, the Hall of Fame slugger from the old Negro Leagues, in *It's Good to be Alive,* Roy Campanella said, "Freezing the balls was supposed to deaden them and help to keep those heavy-hitting Homestead Grays down to size. It never stopped Josh." (CDP)

freeze the runner *v.* To cause the base runner to hold his lead.

freight delivery *n./arch.* Slow pitching.
1ST 1892. (*Chicago Herald,* May 4; EJN)

friendly confines *n.* Descriptive of many home ballparks, but often used to describe the particularly cozy quarters of Wrigley Field.

front, the *n./arch.* PITCHER'S BOX.
1ST 1915. (*Baseball* magazine, December; EJN)
ETY Edward J. Nichols noted in his 1939 thesis, "The influence of the World War added this synonym to one already in use . . . firing line."

front-and backer *n./arch.* "[A] perfect strike through the plate, which was one of Kid Gleason's favorite expressions," according to Herbert Simons in his 1943 article on baseball slang in *Baseball Magazine.*

front office *n.* The business and financial side of the club and the realm of a club's general manager and his staff. This part of a baseball organization is responsible for obtaining, contracting for, and trading players.
ETY/1ST 1948. The term has a long history as an underworld term for police headquarters, an interrogation room, or the warden's office in a prison. Peter Tamony first found it applied to baseball in two 1948 newspaper articles, including this from the *San Francisco Call-Bulletin:* "More than 250 baseball executives gathered here today for a unique five day 'school' on front office matters." (January 19)

front runner **1.** *n.* An individual who only favors a successful team.
   "He's no front runner, he was here when they were struggling."—John Lowenstein on Boston Red Sox fan Tip O'Neill, Home Team Sports telecast, September 10, 1986.
2. *n.* A player who only performs well when his team is winning.

frozen rope *n.* A hard-hit line drive, so-called because of the rigid path it takes. "You can almost see the icicles dripping off it," said Leonard Shecter in defining the term. Because it is so much hyperbole, the image is often embellished with something on the order of broadcaster Red Rush's, ". . . a frozen rope . . . you could hang a week's wash on it and not have to worry."

fudge *n.* Informal pick-up game played by a few players who periodically switch positions.

"Sometimes enough boys were present to permit of a game what they called 'fudge,' each taking his turn at fielding, playing first base, pitching, catching and batting." (Christy Mathewson in his 1914 *Pitcher Pollock;* DS)

full count   *n.* Three balls and two strikes on a batter.
1ST   1937. (NBC-radio World Series broadcast, Tom Manning announcing, October 6; EJN)

full house   *n.* Bases loaded.
ETY   A clear borrowing from the game of poker.
1ST   1922. (*Base Ball Cyclopedia;* EJN)

full route   *n.* All of the game; nine innings or more in the case of an extra-inning game. A pitcher who has gone the full route has pitched a complete game.

full swing   *n.* A strike at the ball with the full reach of the arms.

full wind-up   *n.* A legal method of delivery begins with the pitcher swinging his arms above his head as he steps back with one foot. It is the full and complete pitching delivery. Usually taken when the bases are empty, rather than the abbreviated *stretch* delivery, which is usually taken with a man or men on base. A full windup takes more time and allows runners to take a longer lead.

fumble/fumble the pill   *v.* To make an error.
1ST   1879. (*Spirit of the Times,* August 23; EJN)

fungo   1. *n.* A fly ball hit to a player during practice. "Then him and Carey was together in left field, catchin' fungoes, and it was after we was through for the day that Carey told me about him." (Ring Lardner, *Round Up,* 1929)
2. *v.* The act of hitting a fly ball to a player during practice. It is usually thrown up in the air by the batter or fungoer and hit as it descends through the strike zone. The primary purpose of this is to give fielders practice catching fly balls. The batter is often a coach. Sometimes stated as "to fungo bat," as below:
1ST   1915. "He used to come out sometimes on Saturdays and fungo bat for the players." (Gilbert Patten, *Covering the Look-In Corner;* DS)
3. *n.* A very long, light bat used in practice to hit flies to the outfield. Its design gives the batter the ability to place his hits with greater accuracy.

4. *n.* A scratch hit.
1ST   1867. According to *Joe Reichler's Great Book of Baseball Records,* a newsstand publication of 1957, it first appeared in *Haney's Book of Reference,* which was published by Henry Chadwick. In it fungo is defined as: "A preliminary practice game in which one player takes the bat and, tossing the ball up, hits it as it falls, and if the ball is caught in the field on the fly, the player catching it takes the bat. It is useless as practice in batting, but good for taking fly balls."

David Shulman was able to date the use of fungo back to a March 3, 1886, issue of *Sporting Life:* "While watching some of our freshmen practicing 'fungo' batting the other afternoon it occurred to me that it was about the worst kind of practice a batsman could imagine in training his eye in batting." Edward J. Nichols was able to find fungo used as a verb as early as 1892 (*Brooklyn Daily Eagle,* July 17).
ETY   The etymology of this word is uncertain, which allows for plenty of good theories and a certain amount of linguistic frustration. In *Good Words to You,* John Ciardi wrote: "Fungo in baseball has never been explained. I have seen efforts to derive it from L.[atin] *fungo,* I do, undertake to discharge an obligation." He then adds with clear disdain, "Having noted the suggestion, I understand to believe the form remains unexplained."

1. The 'Fun/Go' Theory. Writing in the February 1937 *American Speech,* David Shulman said: "My guess is that the word fungo, which is baseball slang, may be explained through the elements of a compound word, fun and go." An item in the *Sporting News* (May 23, 1981) reports on research by Bill Bryson of the *Des Moines Register,* who says that the chant "One goes, two goes" etc., comes from a street game in which a player catching a certain number of fly balls was qualified to replace the batter.

A variation on this appears in Patrick Ercolano's *Fungoes, Floaters and Fork Balls* when he said, "Still others believe that the word has its derivation in rhyme recited during early versions of fungo, a rhyme consisting of the words 'run and go.'" Hy Turkin, in his *1956 Baseball Almanac,* suggests, "an old game in which the man using this style of hitting would yell, 'One go, two goes, fun goes.'"

Still another variation on this theory appears in William Safire's *What's the Good Word;* Safire publishes no less than 13 theories—genuine and tongue-in-cheek—that were originally sent to him in response to a query in his *New York Times* language column. A letter from Frederick L. Smith of Short Hills, N.J., says: "In a substantial amount of this century's earlier English literature, especially some humorous things by P. G. Wodehouse, there is reference to the warm-up for cricket matches involving 'fun goes,' i.e. practice strokes before the game began in earnest. I have always taken it as a fact of life that 'fungo' represents a shortening of this English usage."

2. The Fungible Theory. As stated in Zander Hollander's *Baseball Lingo:* "The word 'fungible' means something that can be substituted for another and it is thought that in baseball the thin fungo stick got its name because it replaces the conventional bat."

3. The Fungus Theory. According to a note made by Peter Tamony, the matter was discussed on KLX radio in San Francisco on April 10, 1956. Burt Dunne, radio-TV director of the San Francisco Seals and a student of baseballese, attributed it to an unnamed Princeton professor who claimed the bat hitting the ball sounded like fungus wood. Dunne added that the early fungo bats were regular bats that had been split in two and then bound with tape. Tamony himself had written in the October 1937 *American Speech* that the word "refers to the lightness of the instrument."

A number of others think it came from the feel rather than the sound of fungus. For instance, Joseph McBride explains in his *High and Inside:* "the bats, with very narrow handles and extra thick heads, were so soft that they seemed to be made of fungus."

Another fungus variation appears in the Safire collection of letters. It is from Stephen V. Fulkerson of Santa Paula, California, who says he first heard it 50 years ago as a synonym for nongenuine or not bone fide, such as a fungo that is not a real fly ball. He relates this to fungus in the sense that rural people regard a fungus as lacking the character of a real plant, which puts its roots in the ground.

4. The Fangen Theory. In the February 1, 1987, *Comments on Etymology* Professor Gerald Cohen of the University of Missouri-Rolla writes, "Perhaps its origin is to be sought in German *fangen* 'to catch'; we now think of fungoing a ball as hitting it, but the early quotes . . . show clearly that the emphasis of a fungo game was on the ball's being caught."

One of Cohen's citations is this explanation of a fungo game from *American Folk-Lore IV,* 1891:

"The game is played on a vacant lot, or in the middle of a wide street. One boy is chosen for batsman, and the others stand around at some distance from him. A base ball is used, and the batsman throws it in the air, and then bats it out to the fielders, who endeavor to catch the ball 'on the fly.' The one who first catches the ball a certain number of times that has been agreed upon, takes the batsman's place for another game."

Cohen also provides some instances of fungo as it was used in the *New York World* in the 1889–1890 period, including this one from the October 26, 1889, edition, "Ward's fungo was simply pousee-café for Corkhill, and he swallowed it smoothly."

5. The Fung Theory. One of the letters on fungo that appear in William Safire's *What's the Good Word* is from Joan H. Hall, associate editor for the *Dictionary of American Regional English* (DARE), in Madison, Wisconsin. She asserts that it is from a Scottish verb, fung. Her letter reads in part: "According to *The Scottish National Dictionary,* the verb 'fung,' meaning 'to pitch, toss, fling,' was in use in Aberdeen as early as 1804: 'Ye witches, warlocks, fairies, fien's! Daft fungin' fiery pears an' stanes.' " She says that the connection with ball playing is that the ball is flung into the air before it is hit and that the "-o" ending is common in other games (bingo, beano, bunco and keno).

EXT To club with a bat or stick. "I'm sure that if most Americans should walk through the crowded wards [of wounded] they would grab baseball bats and hit a few fungoes the next time the Communists assemble in Union Square." (Jimmy Cannon on a Communist rally in New York, quoted in *Time,* August 28, 1950; PT)

fungo bat/fungo stick   *n.* Bat for pregame hitting practice. It is usually longer and thinner than a regular bat.

fungo bazooka   *n.* A mechanical device that uses air pressure to fire balls into the air for fielding practice.

fungo circles   *n.* Two circular patches of dirt located on either side of home plate in foul territory. They are used by fungo batters and average about seven feet in diameter.

fungo hit   *n./arch.* A high fly ball; a ball that appears to have been hit with a fungo bat.
1ST   1897. "Fungo Hits—The weakest batting is shown when the batsman indulges in fungo hitting . . ." (Henry Chadwick, *Technical Terms of Baseball;* DS)

fungo hitter   *n./arch.* A batter with a reputation for fungo hits.

furlough   *n./arch.* BASE ON BALLS.
ETY   This apparently was one of the terms brought back from World War II by players who had been in the Armed Forces. It appears in an article in the May 1946 *Baseball Digest* entitled, "Diamond Slang Goes G.I.," by Chester L. Smith (condensed from the *Pittsburgh Press*). The term stuck as a lesser synonym for a walk, but most of the other terms cited by Smith, who had obviously been listening to the Pittsburgh Pirates, did not. Notable exceptions were *brass* for the management and *old man* for the manager.

Those that did not make it past the immediate postwar period included: *AWOL,* for a fielder who does not make it under a pitch; *KP duty,* for assignment to the bullpen; a *beachhead,* for getting the first man on base in an inning; *man overboard,* for a player who has overslid or overrun a base; and *policing the parade grounds,* for the work of a groundskeeper and his crew.

fush ball   *n.* A change-up forkball that the pitcher delivers by pushing the ball from between his spread-out index and middle fingers; a blend of fork + push. Named by Baltimore pitching coach Ray Miller in 1983 and practiced by Mike Boddicker. Appears to be a term that quickly turned into FOSHBALL.
1ST   1983. "Boddicker calls it a fork ball, but since he pushes it from between his fingers with a sidespin that produces a screwball, his

Future Hall of Famer. The all-time strikeout king and author of a record five no-hitters, Nolan Ryan is certain to be inducted into the Hall of Fame. *Courtesy of the Houston Astros*

pitching coach, Ray Miller, has named it the 'fush ball.' " (Tom Boswell, *Washington Post,* July 17, 1983)

future Hall of Famer   *n.* Term applied to an active player whose career of statistics and accomplishments in the game all but assures his being voted into the Hall of Fame.

"Future Hall of Famer Nolan Ryan is hardly on future Hall of Famer Mike Schmidt's 'loves to face' list." (*USA Today,* May 2, 1986)

G

G Standard abbreviation for game.

gab-circuit *n.* The off-season baseball talk (chatter, conjecture, speechifying etc.) beloved of fans, which is more commonly called the *hot stove league.*

gaijin *n.* The Japanese word for outsiders. It has a specific meaning and application in the context of baseball as it is used to describe American players who are contracted to play for teams in Japan. "Even if none of this year's gaijin measure up, the 'cash-flapping rush' for new [Bob] Horners, as one magazine called it, will continue." (*The Washington Post,* February 4, 1988) The *gaijun waku,* or outsider quota, for each team is two.

game **1.** *n.* A contest between two teams that is the basic unit of baseball competition. A game usually consists of either nine or eight and a half innings (when the home team is ahead after eight and a half innings have been played, the last half-inning is not played). Games are also deemed complete if play is suspended for rain or other reason after the team that is losing has been at bat at least five times. A game is won by the team with the most runs, which means that extra innings must be played if the two teams are tied at the end of the ninth inning.
USE In recent years, it has become customary in both the electronic and print media to refer to games in the League Championship Series and World Series as Game 1, Game 2 etc. When used in this context, the word game is always capitalized.
2. *n.* Unit of measurement used to determine a team's exact place in its league standings. This unit is expressed in terms of full and half games out of first place or "games behind." To compute the number of games a team is ahead or behind, you add the difference in the number of wins and the difference in the number of losses and divide by 2.
SEE *games back/games behind.*
3. *n.* The call made by the umpire to signify the end of a contest.

game ball *n.* A ball that has actually been in play as opposed to a souvenir ball.

game face *n.* A look of determination affected for play.

game of inches *n.* Baseball. This time-honored phrase encompasses a number of givens about the game. For instance, a runner is often safe or out at first base by a matter of inches, a ball is batted for either a hit or a foul by a matter of inches, and a player stealing a base is usually safe or out by a matter of inches. "Baseball is, after all, a game of inches and even fractions." (Shirley Povich, *Washington Post,* October 21, 1986)

gamer **1.** *n.* A player who approaches the game with a tenacious, spirited attack and continues to play even when hurt. A compliment, most especially when it comes from another player.
    "On the difference between the two, he said, 'Cerone is a gamer and a fighter, Butch is more the quiet type.' " (New York *Times* article comparing catchers Rick Cerone and Butch Wynegar, February 22, 1983) "His ever protective teammates counter that Murray is a 'gamer,' that he is playing in pain." (*Washington Times* article on Orioles first baseman Eddie Murray, August 28, 1986)
ETY From the idea of a player who is "game."
EXT Anyone who is willing to carry on in the face of adversity.
2. *n./arch.* Any player in a game.
3. *n.* The winning run.
USE A rare modern application of this word, but one which shows up occasionally.
1ST 1980. "Reggie Jackson singled home the gamer." (*New York Post,* October 21; DS)

games back/games behind *n.* The number of games by which a team in a division or league is out of first place. It is expressed as a combination of whole and half numbers, with each victory or loss counting as a half of a game.

game-winning RBI *n.* The run batted that gives the winning team the lead it never relinquishes. The game-winning RBI appears in the box score of a game and is an officially kept statistic.

gap *n.* The space between outfielders. Because only three players cover the entire expanse of outfield territory, wide stretches of uncovered field exist. The size of the gaps, one each between the center and left fielders and between the center and right fielders, is determined by the defensive position of the outfielders.
SEE *hole.*

gapper/gap shot *n.* A batted ball that goes into the gap. If such a ball falls safely, it usually goes for an extra-base hit.

garden *n./arch.* The outfield, short for "outer garden" (as opposed to the infield, which is always the "inner garden").
1ST 1869. (*New York Herald*, September 14; EJN)

gardener *n./arch.* An OUTFIELDER.
1ST 1902. (*Sporting Life*, July 12; EJN)

garner/garner hits *v.* To hit safely.
1ST 1892. (*Chicago Herald*, June 13; EJN)

Garrison finish *n.* A game in which a team, which initially seems hopelessly behind, comes through to win the game. It has been said that a true Garrison finish requires the winning team to have been down by five runs with two outs in its last at bat.
ETY From the legendary ability of 19th-century jockey Snapper Garrison to win horse races at the wire.

gas **1.** *n.* The FASTBALL. "He just came in throwing gas." (Marty Barrett on Roger Clemens, *Boston Globe*, August 4, 1986)
2. *n.* fastball pitching.

Gashouse Gang Nickname given to the St. Louis Cardinals of the mid-1930s, but most strongly associated with the 1934 team. They were a rowdy, passionate crew that included Dizzy Dean, Pepper Martin, Ducky Medwick, Leo Durocher and manager Frank Frisch.
ETY Originally, the Gashouse District was an area on the lower East Side of Manhattan that once housed a number of large gas tanks. It was a rough neighborhood described in part in *The American Metropolis* (1897) by Frank Moss; ". . . but perhaps the most unique of all vicious drinking places is a 'dead house' on 18th Street in what is called the 'gas-house district,' a 'Mecca'

for vagrants and 'bums' of New York, Brooklyn and New Jersey . . ." The neighborhood, however, was best known for a vicious band of thugs known as the Gashouse Gang.

There are several versions of how the cognomen was applied to the Cardinals. One version has the St. Louis team coming into New York from Boston where they had just played in the rain. Their uniforms were particularly dirty because they were a "sliding" team, and the equipment man did not have time to have them cleaned. When they appeared on the field at the Polo Grounds, one shocked reporter commented that they looked like "the gang from around the gas house." This version was given by Frisch in a May 11, 1963, radio interview in which he acknowledged that his was not the only version of the story. Frisch added that he thought the reporter was Frank Lamb of the *New York Evening Journal*. (PT)

More commonly heard is the story of a conversation between Frank Graham of the old *New York Sun* and Leo Durocher. Graham said that the Cards were so good that they could play in the American League, then regarded as superior to the National. Durocher replied, "They wouldn't let us play in the American League. They'd say we were just a lot of gashouse players." From then on Graham called the team the Gashouse Gang. The very same story has been told and published with Pepper Martin in Durocher's place.

Finally, one must consider what Durocher himself put in his autobiography, *Nice Guys Finish Last*. He tells of the team arriving dirty and unkempt for the confrontation with the Giants. Says Durocher, ". . . the next day I saw a cartoon in the *World-Telegram* by Willard Mullin. It showed two big gas tanks on the wrong side of the railroad track, and some ballplayers crossing over to the good part of town carrying clubs over their shoulders instead of bats. And the title read: 'The Gas House Gang.' "

gate **1.** *n.* Total paid attendance.
2. *n.* The gate receipts.
1ST 1888. "There is a 'big gate' awaiting the championship should they decide on making the trip." (*Sporting Life*, November 21, 1888; DS)

gatecrasher *n.* Person who gains admission to an important sports event, such as the World Series, without paying admission. The practice became something of a fad in the 1920s when

Gate. A panoramic picture of a game played in September 1914 in Cleveland, which proves that the big gates have not all been in the majors. The attendance claim on this photo of an Amateur Championship Game is 100,000. *Prints and Photographs Division, the Library of Congress*

the newspapers covered several daring gate-crashers who seemed able to get in everywhere.

gate money *n.* The money that is collected at the turnstiles. Research conducted at the National Baseball Library concluded that the first game of baseball where gate money was charged was one between the Knickerbockers and Brooklyn on July 20, 1858.
1ST 1869. (*DeWitt's Official Base Ball Guide;* EJN)

gateway *n.* First base; the threshhold to the other bases and the opportunity of scoring. It is an element of the most flamboyant base-ballese under which the ball is a pellet and second base is the keystone sack.

gather in *v.* To field a batted ball.
1ST 1874. (*Chicago Inter Ocean,* July 30; EJN)

gazoonies *n./arch.* ROOKIES.
1ST 1943. " 'Gazoonies' is probably the most modern nickname for recruits, who through the years have come to be known as 'rookies,' 'bushers,' and 'yannigans,' as well as many others." (Herbert Simons, "Do You Speak the Language?" *Baseball,* January)

Gehrig's Disease *n.* LOU GEHRIG'S DISEASE.

general admission *n.* Catchall term that refers to areas of the ballpark where sets are not reserved and are filled on a first-come, first-served basis. The term commonly applies to seating in bleachers in portions of the upper deck. General admission tickets carry a common price although there are sometimes special prices for children and/or senior citizens.

general manager *n.* A team's director of business and personnel, who, among other things, is in charge of signing and trading players. GM, for short. According to Lou Piniella, in his autobiography *Sweet Lou* (written in 1986 with Maury Allen), "The definition of a good general manager is a guy who can call up another GM at three o'clock in the morning and have the guy help him out with a player, instead of screaming at him for the early wake-up call."
ETY According to the *Bill James Historical Baseball Abstract,* "The term 'General Manager' was first applied to William Evans, a former American League umpire who became General Manager of the Cleveland Indians in 1927."

George Brett numbers *n.* 1980s shorthand for a player posting batting statistics in the vicinity of those collected by slugger George Brett, an excellent hitter whose numbers have constituted a standard of excellence.

George Stallings pitcher *n.* As defined in G. S. Cochrane's *Baseball, the Fans' Game,* published in 1939, "A 3-and-2 pitcher; one who gets behind every batter; a 'wild hurler.' " (DS)

get **1.** *v.* To put out.
2. *v.* To deceive another player; to trick an opponent. In an article entitled "The American National Game," in the April 1910 issue of the *Century,* Walter Camp gives a number of examples, including one in which catcher Lou Criger of Boston *got* Cleveland great Nap Lajoie. "There were two strikes and three balls on Lajoie. Criger had returned the ball to the pitcher, but had his mask off and was pretending to fasten a buckle on it, saying to Lajoie, 'We'll get you this time.' Lajoie turned slightly, and, seeing Criger with his mask off said, 'You will, will you?' when the pitcher shot the ball over the plate, catching Lajoie entirely unpre-

George Brett Numbers. George Brett adds another hit to his impressive record.   *Courtesy of the Kansas City Royals*

pared as he heard the umpire say, 'Strike three, and out!' "

get across   *v.* To score a run.

get a jump   **1.** *v.* As a base runner, to make a quick break toward the next base as the pitcher begins his motion toward the plate.

George Stallings Pitcher. Stallings as Yankee manager (1909-1910) at spring training in Gray, Georgia.   *National Baseball Library, Cooperstown, N.Y.*

2. *v.* As a fielder, to begin to move before, or just as, the ball is hit toward the point on the field where the ball can be caught.

get all of it/get all of the ball   *v.* To hit the ball solidly and with power.

get a piece of it/get a piece of the ball   *v.* As a batter, to make contact with the ball. Batting with two strikes, a player will try to "at least get a piece of it" to keep from striking out.

get around/get around on a fastball   *v.* To swing the bat fast enough to pull a fastball.

get a ticket   *v.* To receive a base on balls.

getaway bag   *n./arch.* FIRST BASE.
1ST   1907. (*Lajoie's Official Base Ball Guide;* EJN)

getaway day   **1.** *n.* The last day of a long homestand for a team; the day the club gets away for a road trip.
2. *n.* The last day of a series between two teams, on which one or both of the teams leaves for another city. Both teams have a getaway day when the visitors leave and the home team ends its homestand.

get healthy   *v.* To hit successfully, individually or as a team, against a pitcher or group of pitchers, especially for an individual or team that has not been hitting well. "A lot of Red Sox got healthy tonight." (Jack Wiers, WTOP-radio, in a game in which the Red Sox beat the Orioles 15 to 4, June 10, 1987)

get him over   *v.* To advance a base runner with a bunt or sacrifice.

get hold of it/get hold of one/get hold of the ball   *v.* To connect solidly with the ball.
1ST   1914. (*New York Tribune*, October 12; EJN)

get in one's kitchen   See *kitchen.*

get it started   *v.* As a batter, to begin the swing. " 'It's the lightest bat I've ever used,' Clark said. 'When I was with the Giants I swung at least 35 ounces and used a bat with a thicker barrel. This bat feels like a toothpick in comparison, but I can get it started quicker.' " (Jack Clark quoted in the *Philadelphia Daily News,* June 25, 1987)

get naked   *v.* To bear down, a pun in the same class as bases drunk for bases loaded. Put into context by Leonard Shecter in his article "Baseball Spoken Here": ". . . a coach might yell to a pitcher who seems to be losing his concentration: 'Hey, get naked out there.' "

get on   *v.* To advance to first, second or third base.
1ST   1909. (*Baseball* magazine, July; EJN)

get one's innings   *v.* HAVE ONE'S INNINGS.

get-small-quick ball   *n.* HOME RUN.

get the call   *v.* To be chosen to play, often applied to relief pitchers as they get the signal to come into the game.
1ST   1920. (*The New York Times*, October 4; EJN)

get the gate   *v.* To be thrown out of the game by the umpire.

get the leading lady   *v.* See *leading lady.*

"get the spring out"   *v.* Said to a fielder who looks in his glove after committing an error.

get the thumb   *v.* To be ejected from the game.

gettin' in their kitchen   See *kitchen.*

get to   *v.* To hit successfully, individually or as a team, against a particular pitcher.
1ST   1905. (*Sporting Life*, September 2; EJN)

get to first base   *v.* To make an offensive start by getting a player to first whether it be by means of a hit, base on balls or hit batsman.
EXT   To reach the first step in a procedure or activity. See bases.

get two   **1.** *v.* To turn a double play
2. *n.* A cry of encouragement to the infielders when there is a runner at first with fewer than two outs.

get under it/get under one   **1.** *v.* To swing a bat and hit the bottom portion of the ball, causing it to pop-up or go for a long fly ball.
2. *v.* To position oneself in preparation to catch a ball hit high in the air.
1ST   1905. (*Sporting Life*, October 7; EJN)

get-up off the bench hitter   *n.* Pinch batter who comes in cold and is often successful.

GIDPs   Pronounced gidap, a rarely used acronym for "grounded into double plays; akin to calling RBIs ribbies. It is used in referring to the statistic that accounts for "times grounded into double plays."

gift   **1.** *n.* A base on balls.
1ST   1895. (*New York Press*, July 3; EJN)
2. *n.* An error or misplay that has put a man on base or allowed a runner or runners to advance.
1ST   1879. (*Spirit of the Times*, August 28; EJN)

Gillette   *n.* A ball thrown in the direction of a batter's head; a brushback pitch that is likely to come close to—in the manner of a Gillette razor—but not hit the batter. The term is an obvious play on the idea of a "close shave."
1ST   1937. (*The Sporting News Record Book;* EJN)

gilt-edged ball   *n./obs.* Good playing. In his dissertation on baseball language, Edward J. Nichols noted, "This phrase was in constant use throughout the 1880s and 90s, but appears to have dropped out of baseball writing shortly after 1900."

ginger   *n.* The zest and vigor of a player.
1ST   1890. (*New York Press*, July 10; EJN)

give him the player/give up the line   *v.* Direction given to fielders instructing them to play away from the foul lines.

give oneself up   *v.* To hit the ball behind a teammate on base in an effort to bring him home or advance him to scoring position.

giver   *n./obs.* The PITCHER.

give the nod 1. *v.* For a manager to indicate that a player, usually a starting or relief pitcher, has been selected to play. It is commonly used to indicate which pitcher has been given the nod to come in from the bullpen.
2. *v.* To get a favorable decision from the umpire.
ETY From the nod of approval. In *The Dictionary of American Slang* Harold Wentworth and Stuart Berg Flexner say that it has been a common sports expression since about 1920 and was first used to describe a boxer who won a prizefight—who got the nod—because of the referee's or judge's decision rather than a knockout.

give up *v.* To allow the opposition an advantage whether it be a walk, hit or run.

glass arm 1. *n.* A sore throwing or pitching arm.
2. *n./adj.* By extension a player with a chronically weak or sore arm. "The Glass Arm Pitcher Is No Worse Off Than The Slugger With a Hole in His Bat." (headline in the *San Francisco Call,* September 27, 1913; PT)
1ST 1891. "For a back number with a 'glass' arm, George Hanley seems to be holding up his own end in [keeping] the San Jose team in great shape." (*Sporting Times,* June 13, 1891) David Shulman, who found this first reference, also reported a comment from the following issue of the same sports weekly reporting that the term "glass arms" was becoming obsolete and was being replaced with "crockery limbs." Peter Tamony noted that the glass metaphor is not limited to baseball as it was a reference to fragility in other sports, such as the boxer's "glass jaw."
ETY In *The American Language: Supplement II,* H. L. Mencken thanks the late Admiral C. S. Butler for this explanation, which appeared in a letter of November 30, 1943. He said that it was usually *myositis* (inflammation) of the long tendon of the biceps muscle. "Its action is three- or four-fold and its relations to synovial sheaths, bursas and joints complicated. Damage of these structures often produces a stiffness and rigidity accompanied by loss of the power to supinate the forearm . . . The arm feels rigid, and as if likely to break like glass."
EXT It has been applied to stiff or weak arms in other realms. In "Ham Lingo," an article on shortwave radio in the October 1929 *American Speech,* its use is reported as a synonym for "telegrapher's cramp."

globe *n./arch.* The ball.
1ST 1891. (*Chicago Herald,* May 7; EJN)

glory circle *n./arch.* Baseball's elite; its unofficial hall of fame before there was a Hall of Fame.
1ST 1908. (*Spalding's Official Base Ball Guide;* EJN)

glory time *n.* Period late in a game during which a relief pitcher earns a save.

glove 1. *n.* Padded leather hand covering used to protect the hand and help catch a batted or thrown ball. They were originally solely intended as a means of protecting a player's hand but soon began to evolve as a means to better fielding.
  Traditionally, the gloves used by the catcher and the first baseman have been called mitts.
2. *n.* Fielding ability. An exceptional defensive player is said to have a good glove.
USE The term glove alone means the same as good glove. In an article on baseballese in the June 1964 *Baseball Digest,* Tim Horgan wrote, "If you chance to overhear Player A say to

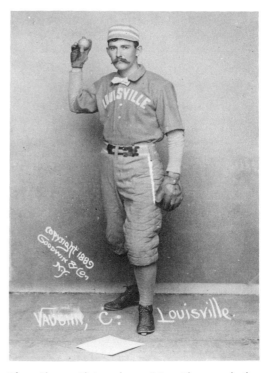

Glove. Player with two gloves. It is not known whether he actually played with both, or simply used them when posing for baseball cards. *Prints and Photographs Division, the Library of Congress*

Player B, 'Don't lose your glove,' it doesn't mean there's a sneak thief in the house. It means Player B can't hit his weight and the only thing that keeps him in the lineup is his fielding prowess."
3. *v.* To catch and control a ball.
1ST 1887. (*Harpers Weekly*, September 10; EJN)

glove and a prayer   What a poor pitcher is said to have. See prayer ball.
1ST 1912. "All he has when he goes to the box is a glove and a prayer." (*Sporting Life*, May 18, 1912)

glove hand   *n.* The catching hand on which the glove or mitt is worn. A fielder who throws with his right hand wears his glove on the left.

glove man   **1.** *n.* Good defensive player. Applied sparingly, this term is used to identify top-notch fielders like Marty Marion, Brooks Robinson and Ozzie Smith.
2. *n.* A weak hitter. Joseph McBride points out in his *High and Inside* that the term is used as a "back-handed insult."

glue to the bag   *v.* To keep a runner close to his base.
1ST 1910. (*New York Tribune*, July 12; EJN)

GM   *n.* Standard abbreviation for general manager.

go   **1.** *v.* To pitch.
2. *v.* To try to advance to the next base.

go against the book   *v.* To violate the conventional wisdom of baseball strategy.

go-ahead run   *n.* The run that puts a team ahead; often used to describe a man on base, as in, "The tie run is at second, the go-ahead run is on first."

goal tender   *n.* Batter who patiently waits for good pitches to swing at.
1ST 1937. (New York *Daily News*, September 5; EJN)

goat   *n.* Derisive name for a player who is singled out for a serious lapse in performance; one who loses (or appears to lose) a game for his team. Because of the severity of the term, it is more likely to come into play after the loss of an important regular season game or during the playoffs or World Series. It is correctly known as a "postgame sobriquet." "Mickey 'Goat' As Sox Win"—headline for an article on a game in which Mickey Mantle allowed a run to score because he had collided with another player

(*San Francisco Call-Bulletin*, May 22, 1957; PT).
The term and the concept are regarded with some seriousness. As Doug DeCinces put it when talking about playing in the World Series, "In the back of every player's mind is the hope not to be the goat."

On occasion it is applied to a manager or an umpire. "Often the player seeks to cover up his own blunder by making the umpire the 'goat.' " ("The Ethics of an Umpire" by Billy Evans in *Pearson's Magazine*, September 1912)
1ST 1910. Peter Tamony first found it in T. A. Dorgan's comic strip when a character says, "No more for me, I've quit being the goat." (*San Francisco Examiner*, January 5)
ETY Most references to this term say that it is a derivative or "clipped" form of scapegoat and applied to a player whose error is being blamed for a team's defeat. In a short article in *Comments on Etymology* (December 1, 1985), Gerald Cohen insists that there is a major "discrepancy" in this theory. He writes, ". . . a scapegoat is innocent, whereas the goat is not; he has blundered, usually at a crucial moment. And the standard etymology of *goat* as a shortening of *scapegoat* is therefore almost certainly in error."
Cohen then posed his theory:
"Through serendipity I have found a likely answer in the 1889 sports pages of *The* [New York] *World;* the scene is the Polo Grounds, then in Staten Island, where the Giants played:
'. . . even the meek and lowly goat, whose job it is to haul the peanut wagon up and down the board walk . . .'
"So the original 'goats' were players severely humbled by their errant play."

goatland   *n.* The mythic resting place for baseball's famous goats.
1ST 1920. (*Spalding's Official Base Ball Guide;* EJN)

goat's beard   *n.* Dangling flap hanging down from a catcher's or umpire's mask as a means of protecting the throat.

gobble   *v.* To field a throw or batted ball, often stated as "gobble the ball" or "gobble up."
1ST 1873. (*New York Herald*, August 10; EJN)

go deep   **1.** *v.* To hit a home run.
2. *v.* To hit a ball for a long distance.

go down looking   *v.* To strike out on a called third strike.

go down swinging   *v.* To strike out on a swinging third strike.

go downtown   *v.* To hit a homerun.

go for the downs   *v.* To try to hit a home run.

go for the fences   *v.* To consciously swing for a home run.

"going, going, gone"   *v.* Popular and dramatic description of a home run ball in flight.
ETY   Made popular by Yankee announcer Mel Allen who used it to describe balls heading into the outer reaches of Yankee Stadium. Sometimes the "gone" has to be left out of the phrase, if the ball is caught at the wall. This serves to heighten the drama for those moments when the announcer pauses after "Going, going . . ."
Allen did not invent the phrase and probably was not the first to apply it to baseball. In his book on baseball terminology, *Floaters, Fungoes and Fastballs,* Patrick Ercolano claims it was "coined" by Reds announcer Harry Hartman in 1929. It is, after all, an echo from the auction house where the same words are used to signal a sale. It was also an advertising slogan used for a bottled hair-remover known as Newbro's Herpicide.

gold coast   *n./arch.* Term for the group of clubhouse lockers reserved for "bonus babies."

golden age/golden era   *n.* Period when baseball seems to have been played to near perfection. The term was given a special baseball context and perspective in Lawrence Ritter's *Glory of Their Times.* "From an emotional standpoint, I think each individual fan has his own 'Golden Age.' It's the period when that fan was between 8 and 16 years old. That's when baseball first captured the imagination; when players had appeal beyond human bounds."

Golden Glove Award   An annual award given to a player at each position in each league who has been voted the best fielder.

golf ball   *n.* Said of a very low pitch, which is batted in an upwards fashion in the manner of a golf swing. Golf balls are usually fly balls.

golf hitter   *n.* A batter given to swinging at low pitches.

golf one   *v.* To bat a low pitched ball, lifting it up as if it were a golf shot. "He golfed the ball into right field for a home run when the Mets were an out away from trailing the series, 2-1." (*USA Today,* October 16, 1986)
1ST   1917. (*New York Times,* October 9; EJN)

GOM   Initialism applied to Connie Mack, which was short for "grand old man." In *I Managed Good, But Boy Did They Play Bad,* Jim Bouton insisted that Mack was the GOM of the GOG (great old game). In his *Political Dictionary,* William Safire says that British statesman William Gladstone was also known as the GOM.

gone   **1.** *adj.* Out, as in "Two gone in the bottom of the 5th."
1ST   1899. (*Frank Merriwell's Double Shot;* EJN)
2. *v.* Ejected from the game.
3. *adj.* Said of a ball hit for a home run.
SEE   *"Going, Going, Gone."*

gonfalon   Pennant; actually the Italian word for flag.
1ST   1910. (*Baseball* magazine, September; EJN)

gonfalonia interruptus   *n.* Facetious pseudo-medical term for a team that bogs down in its quest for the pennant (gonfalon).
"Seaver, however, is a pitcher, with stronger stats than two previous pennant-year additions, Gary Bell and Rick Wise. The type of pitcher he is and the type of person he is may cure that ancient regional affliction of *gonfalonia interruptus.*" (*The Boston Globe,* July 1, 1986)

good   *adj.* Excellent in the context of baseball. This understatement is present in the next group of entries, from good arm through good wood.

good arm   **1.** *n.* Fielder with the ability to throw the ball accurately and for distance.
2. *n.* Pitcher with a strong delivery and a good fastball.

good ball   *n.* A pitch in the strike zone.

good camp   *n.* Successful spring training. "Despite a 'good camp' in St. Petersburg, the Mets finished 40-120." (article on the 1962 Mets, *St. Petersburg Times,* March 1987)

good cheese/good express   *n.* Modern player slang for a blurring fastball.
ETY   Even though this is relatively new to baseball it may have a much older basis.
As early as 1818, when it is defined in *London Guide,* cheese has stood for "the best thing of its kind." It appears in most 19th-century slang dictionaries as meaning anything first rate in quality—as in "That's the cheese"—and is usu-

ally traced to the word *chiz*, which means "thing" in Hindustani and Anglo-Indian, rather than the food. In the *Dictionary of Cliches,* James Rogers traces the term *chiz* to an origin in Persian and Urdu and points out that it is also the source of "the big cheese."

"good cut!" *n.* Said when a batter takes a mighty swing at the ball and misses. In a *New York Times* article entitled "Terms for Parents of Little Leaguers", Marian Edelman Borden points out that this is "yelled to the batter who has swung with a great deal of force at the ball over the umpire's head."

"good eye!" *n.* Exclamation made when a batter does not swing at a pitch out of the strike zone.

good field, no hit *adj.* Classic description of the exceptional defensive player is who is not a good hitter. "Fittingly, it was good-field-no-hit Marty Castillo who got one of the night's few fat pitches—a high fastball that he returned to the upper deck for a two-run second-inning homer." (*Newsweek,* October 22, 1984)
  ETY All accounts trace this back to Cuban-born Miguel "Mike" Gonzalez whose command of English was less than perfect. Writing in *P.M.* on the retirement of Moe Berg a week after the Japanese attack on Pearl Harbor (he was retiring to become a spy for the U.S. government), Tom Meany said, "It is ironic that the suave and polished Berg should have been the subject of baseball's most illiterate message: 'Good field, no hit.' But it was so. Moe was with Brooklyn at Clearwater in the spring of 1924 and so was Miguel Gonzales, a coach for the Cardinals. Mike Kelley of Minneapolis wanted to buy Berg and wired Gonzales for his opinion, which resulted in Miguel's famous four-word telegraphic message of the young shortstop."

good pair of hands *n.* Said to be the asset of a good defensive player.

good stuff *n.* Said of a pitcher who has command of his pitches and is using them effectively.
  USE To be told that you have good stuff is to be paid a major compliment. It can be applied to a particular pitching performance or to a pitcher's overall ability.

good town *n.* Player's term for an enjoyable city to visit on a road trip. " 'Good town' is as much a part of the baseball vernacular as line drive. Montreal is perhaps the best, but San Diego and Chicago are not far behind in the opinion of the Braves, who were asked to rate National League cities." (TSN, July 1, 1978)

good wood *n.* The thickest part of the bat, where the ball is hit with the greatest power. To hit with good wood on the ball is to hit the ball solidly.

go on the pitch *v.* To try to steal a base at the moment the pitcher goes into his motion.

goose egg *n.* A zero on the scoreboard, which somehow come to suggest a goose egg. "Goose-Egg Diet Plunges Seals Into Basement"—headline in the *San Francisco News,* June 27, 1952. In the story that followed it was claimed, "The Seals recently have accumulated enough goose-eggs to open a market." (PT)
  1ST 1867. "The Buckeyes in this inning were treated to a goose egg . . ." (Chadwick Scrapbooks, October; DS)
  In his book *A Hog on Ice and Other Curious Expressions* Charles Earle Funk points out that the egg in the expression, "to lay an egg," is derived from the goose egg of the scoreboard

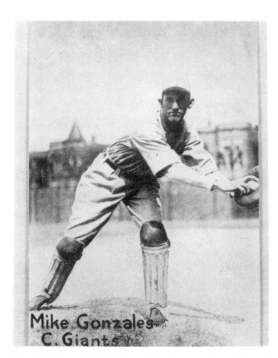

Good field no hit. Author of the famous line, Miguel "Mike" Gonzales was a catcher for the New York Giants between 1919 and 1921. *National Baseball Library, Cooperstown, N.Y.*

and "has no bearing whatsoever on the output of a hen."

EXT   The egg stands for the zero cipher in other sports. To crack or break an egg is to begin to score in cricket (just as not scoring is to lay an egg), and the zero-term in tennis, love, derives from *l'oeuf*, which is French for egg. Both goose egg and "lay an egg" have generalized to any realm in which one fails to score.

go out   *v.* To get credited with an out.
1ST   1863. (Chadwick Scrapbooks; EJN)

gopher/gopher ball   *n.* Pitch that is destined to be hit for a home run; one that will "go for" a run; the long ball. Jim Brosnan wrote in *The Long Season:* "Similar to the ordinary, legal-size baseball, but dangerous for pitchers to handle . . . should be avoided."

In some earlier explanations of the term it is said that it is a contraction of "go far."
USE   Term now used without a hint of its punnish origin: "Any informed student of the game knows that no pitcher wants to go down in the record books as having been the pitcher who served up a record-breaking gopher ball; thus careful pitching is the order of the day." (letter to the *International Herald Tribune*, Sept. 22, 1986, from Tom Mitchel)
1ST   1932. (*Baseball* magazine, October; EJN)
ETY   In his 1955 *Baseball Almanac* Hy Turkin reports that it was coined by Lefty Gomez when he pitched for the Yankees (1930–1942); he used it in lines like, "When they hit that pitch, it will go fer (gopher) a homer."

Although there have been many published explanations of this term being a play on "go fer," opinion is not unanimous. In *The Dictionary of Baseball*, Parke Cummings reports, "Like the gopher, which vanishes into its hole, the ball quickly vanishes into the stands or out of the park." Along those same lines, Ray Corio adds, "But there's also the line of thought that the expression reflects how a pitcher feels as he watches his pitch soar over a fence: like digging a hole and crawling into it, gopher style." (*New York Times*, February 8, 1988)

gophergate   *n.* Term created by Tom Boswell to describe the scandal surrounding the huge increase in the number of home runs hit in 1987.
ETY   It is one of a number of words that were created after the Watergate scandal to indicate irregularity by using the suffix "gate." See also scuffgate.

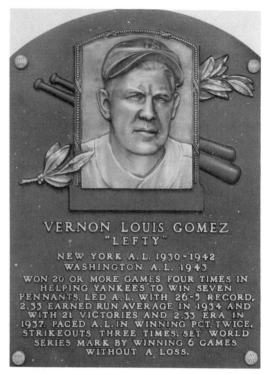

Gopher. The Hall of Fame plaque for the man who may have given the baseball world the gopher ball. *National Baseball Library, Cooperstown, N.Y.*

gopher hunter   *n./arch.* A sharply batted ground ball.

gorker   *n.* Term for a cheap hit; used by long-term Baltimore Orioles manager Earl Weaver. "The Yankees did not give up on this one easily. In the ninth, Tippy Martinez (2-4) gave up two cheap singles. 'You hate to take a guy out after two gorkers,' Manger Earl Weaver said." (*Washington Post*, June 12, 1983)

go sign/go signal   *n.* Coach's signal telling a base runner to steal or to advance to the next base.

go south   **1.** *v.* To head off to spring training.
1ST   1906. (*Sporting Life*, February 10; EJN)
2. *v.* To lose a game.
1ST   1915. (*Baseball* magazine, December; EJN)

got a big one left   Said of a batter with two strikes against him.

go the distance/go the route   *v.* To pitch a complete game.

go the other way   *v.* To hit to the opposite field.

"got him!"   Broadcaster's terse way of saying that a batter has been struck out—"a simple salute to the strikeout" said one critic after hearing Vin Scully use it.

got too much   Said when a pitcher has an excess of deceitful motion (curve, slide etc.) on the ball and therefore cannot control his delivery.

go to school   *v.* To learn from another player through experience.

go to the hat   *v.* For a pitcher to touch, tug and otherwise fuss with his cap while on the mound. It is an affectation that can come in handy if one has hidden an illegal substance on the cap and is "loading up" for an illegal pitch, or, as Gaylord Perry has been known to do, touch a clean cap to encourage the batter to think you are fueling up for an illegal pitch.

go to the mouth   *v.* To touch the lips or mouth. This action is illegal if it is made by a pitcher while on the mound and can cause him to be ejected from the game. The move is illegal because it suggests that the pitcher may be preparing to throw a spitball. If a pitcher needs to touch his mouth, he must step down from the mound. On particularly cold days, pitchers can ask for and receive from the home plate umpire permission to blow on their hands without stepping off the mound.

go to the wire   *v.* To be decided at the end of a game; used, for instance, to characterize a game whose outcome is not known until the 9th inning.
ETY This term originated in horse racing for a close race. Wire is long-established track slang for the finish line.

go up   **1.** *v.* To break into the Major Leagues. **2.** *v.* To move to a higher level of minor league play.
1ST 1909. (*Baseball* magazine, October; EJN)

go with the pitch   *v.* To hit the ball to the side of the plate where it is pitched rather than trying to pull or "overpower" it. A right-handed batter would therefore hit an outside pitch to right field while a left-handed batter would hit an outside pitch to left field.

grandmother   *n.* Woman whose fictional funeral traditionally figures into excuses for people to get out of work for an afternoon at the ballpark. The death rate among grandmothers has decreased in direct proportion to the decrease in day games played during the workweek.

Here is how grandmother was defined by R. E. Sherwood in the September 1913 issue of *Baseball*: "An elderly female in high favor with office boys in general. Her death often forms an excuse among them for leave of absence. If the home team is on the road, the excuse goes; if at home the office boy GOES—to look for another job."

An earlier and more disarming reference appears in the August 1908 *Atlantic* in the form of this immortal stanza:

> Lives there a man with soul so dead
> But he unto himself has said,
> "My grandmother shall die to-day
> And I'll go see the Giants play?"

In the next paragraph, an expert fixed "the average daily baseball mortality among grandmothers at seven thousand."

"Grand Ol' Game"   The game of baseball.

grand salami   *n.* A punning play on GRAND SLAM.

grand slam/grandslam/grand slammer   *n.* A home run hit with the bases loaded.
1ST 1940. "Jim Tabor smashed out a 'grand slamer' against Johnny Humphries in the fourth inning after Jimmy Foxx had belted his thirty-third circuit drive of the year." (*San Francisco News*, August 20, 1940; PT) Evidence that this term did not come into use until 1940 can be found in the fact that it was *not* mentioned in Edward J. Nichols' 1939 thesis on baseball language.
ETY This term, which is now used in a number of sports, was first used in the game of contract bridge where it applies to the taking of all 13 tricks. It would appear that it first moved to golf in 1930 when it was widely applied to Bobby Jones' feat of winning all of golf's four major championships—the British and U.S. Opens and the British and U.S. Amateurs. It has since been applied to the four major tennis tournaments (Wimbledon and the French, Australian and U.S. Opens).
EXT Anything extraordinary and/or powerful. The term has been applied to a diversity of things and events outside sports. Peter Tamony collected a number, including these two headlines: "A Grand Slam for Culture" (when two new theaters opened in Los Angeles) and "Grand Slam Driver Held" (he ran into four other cars). It was also the name of a powerful

British bomb during World War II. In fact, when the first atomic bomb was dropped on Japan in 1945 it was said to have 2,000 times the power of the British "grand slam" bomb, the largest previously used. It is also the name of a cocktail (made by mixing ½ jigger of blended whiskey, ¼ jigger of vermouth, ⅛ jigger of Curacao and ⅛ jigger of lime juice).

grandstand   1. *n.* The location of the main seating area at a ball park, traditionally behind the box seats. The grandstand is usually covered and contains reserved seats, which are priced between the cheap (bleachers) and the expensive (box) seats.
2. *v.* To play for the admiration and applause of the crowd. To show off. An earlier definition: "The custom prevalent among players of taking a drink of water in front of the grandstand after making a home run." (R. E. Sherwood, *Baseball* magazine, September 1913)
1ST   1888. See play to the grandstand.
EXT   To show off in other realms.

grandstander/grand   stander   1.   *n.* GRANDSTAND PLAYER.
2. *n.* Person sitting in the grandstand.
1ST   1891. "During the four New York games there were never less than 2,200 people at a game, and 50 per cent of the patrons here were 'grand-standers' . . ." (*Sporting Times*, May 23, 1891; DS)

grandstand manager   *n.* A spectator who second-guesses the manager and tends to be quite vocal about it. "Grandstand managers, some of them with horns, have sprouted up all over since Lefty O'Doul sent outfielder Joe Brovia to Portland." (*San Francisco Call-Bulletin*, March 4, 1949; PT)

grandstand play   1. Any play that is staged to elicit applause. The play may be a simple one but it is embellished and made to look difficult and even heroic.
2. *adj.* Descriptive of a flashy style of playing. "When necessary, bench a man for each at-

Grandstand. Entry to the grandstand at Briggs Stadium, Detroit, in August 1942, when the turnstiles were called stiles.   *Prints and Photographs Division, the Library of Congress*

tempt at grandstand play. Most coaches need a little courage in this respect." (Coleman R. Griffith, *The Psychology of Coaching*, 1926)

1ST 1902. (*McGraw's Official Base Ball Guide;* EJN)

EXT **1.** *n./adj.* A showy move or style that is usually both spectacular and ineffective. "They spent so much time in arguin' and makin' grandstand play, that the interests of the city were forgotten." (William L. Riordan, *Plunkitt of Tammany Hall*, 1905; PT)

2. *n.* In legal jargon, a grandstand play has come to mean an unexpected and dramatic move in the courtroom. "Defense attorneys in the Nick De John murder trial demanded perjury charges yesterday against Mrs. Anita Rocchia Venza, and were met by snorts from the prosecution of 'grandstand play.' " (*San Francisco Examiner*, February 26, 1949; PT)

grandstand player *n.* One who plays for the adulation of the crowd and routinely makes easy plays look hard.

USE Although a grandstand play here and there is tolerated and even appreciated, a player does not want to become known as a grandstand player. Alfred H. Spink once wrote of Charles Comiskey, "He had no use for the grandstand player who could hit the ball over the fence when the bases were clear and his side a mile ahead, but he loved the man who could hit the ball right on the nose when a run was needed and a good clout meant the game." (*The National Game*, 1910)

1ST 1888. "It's little things of this sort which makes the 'grand stand player.' They make impossible catches, and when they get the ball they roll all over the field." (M. J. Kelly, *Play Ball;* DS)

grand tour *n.* See *home run trot.*
1ST 1912. (*New York Tribune*, October 7; EJN)

grapefruit circuit *n.* GRAPEFRUIT LEAGUE.

grapefruit game *n.* Spring exhibition game played in Florida.
1ST 1961. "Last year 306,000 attended 143 grapefruit games in Florida." (*New York Times*, February 19; DS)

Grapefruit League Commonly used name for the major league teams that conduct spring training and play exhibition games against each other in Florida, as contrasted with those that train in Arizona's Cactus League.

Grapefruit League. Philadelphia Phillies loosen up at their Grapefruit League camp at Jack Russell Stadium in Clearwater, Florida. *Courtesy of the Florida Division of Tourism*

Although the first team to make a southern spring training trip was the Chicago White Stockings, who went to New Orleans in 1870, the first to train in Florida was the 1888 Washington Nationals who went to Jacksonville.

ETY/1ST 1937. The term is of course based on the fact that Florida is a prime growing area for citrus fruit. It was in common use by the 1950s. Edward J. Nichols traced the term grapefruit loop back as far as the March 31, 1937, edition of the *Philadelphia Record*. Grapefruit circuit seemed to come into play in the 1940s (*Time* headline for March 25, 1946: "News From the Grapefruit Circuit"). The first use of grapefruit league in Peter Tamony's collection was this quote from Neill Sheridan of the Red Sox, who struck out in the only at bat of his major league career: "I wound up hitting over .300 in the Grapefruit League. But once the season started I only rode the bench." (*San Francisco Call-Bulletin*, May 10, 1948)

grapefruit loop *n.* GRAPEFRUIT LEAGUE.

graphite bat   *n.* Baseball bat made from a lightweight, virtually unbreakable combination of graphite, fiberglass and polyester resin. Although they are in use in softball and at various levels of baseball, their only plate appearance in major league baseball has been in spring training experiments. Unlike aluminum bats, which give off a 'ping' sound, graphite sounds more like wood when the ball is hit.

grass   **1.** *n.* Traditional vegetation that is grown as the surface for a baseball field and that covers everything except the pitcher's mound, basepaths and other specific areas, which are covered with dirt. In some parks the field is covered with green synthetic turf which is laid like carpet.
2. *n.* Term that is applied to the grass of the infield and is used in phrases like "Jones is in the grass" to indicate an infielder who, for defensive reasons, has come in close to the plate and out of the base path.

grass burner/grass clipper/glass cutter   *n.* Sharply hit grounder that skims along the grass.
1ST   1868. "Wright goes to first on his short grass clipper to center field." (Chadwick Scrapbooks; DS)

grasser   *n.* A GROUND BALL.

grass puller   *n.* COACH, so-called because some signals literally involve pulling grass.
1ST   1908. (*Baseball* magazine, July; EJN)

gravy hop   *n.* Term for when a ground ball takes a high, easy-to-field bounce.
   "Hit sharply towards third, takes a gravy hop." (Tom Marr, WFBR radio, June 11, 1983; Orioles vs. Red Sox)

grays   *n.* Road uniforms which contrast with *home whites.* They are traditionally gray or darker than the home uniform.

grazer   *n.* An outfielder.

grease ball   *n.* Name for a type of illegal pitch, this being a reference to one that has been doctored with a secret dollop of hair dressing, petroleum jelly, lard or similar sticky substance to give the ball an unpredictable trajectory. "Today, people still talk about the spitter, but the spitter is dead. Nowadays, it's a grease ball the pitchers are throwing." (Gaylord Perry in *Me and the Spitter;* CDP)

Greatest Week in the History of Baseball   Description that was used widely during the 1986 National and American League playoff series in which the Mets and Red Sox emerged with their respective pennants after particularly exciting and suspenseful wins over the Angels and Astros. "The greatest week in baseball history is over. The World Series begins tomorrow night at Shea Stadium," wrote Bill Livingston in the *Cleveland Plain Dealer* on October 17th. Livingston was one of many to deem it the greatest week yet beheld.

Greenberg Gardens   When Hank Greenberg joined the Pittsburgh Pirates in 1947 the team erected a shorter fence in left field to encourage more home runs from the slugger. The fence was moved in 30 feet from 365 to 335 feet and the area between the old and new fences was dubbed Greenberg Gardens in his honor. Years later when Ralph Kiner became the team's great slugger, the same happy hunting ground became known as *Kiner's Korner.*
1ST   1947. "The 'Greenberg Gardens' plot in the Forbes Field home of the Pittsburgh Pirates has sprouted a flourishing crop of home runs—nine in four games." (lead to AP dispatch of April 20, which appeared in the *San Francisco Examiner* on April 21; PT)

green fly   *n.* Derisive name for female who is constantly working to be in the company of professional players; baseball equivalent of the rock groupie. "When a green fly comes around," wrote Mike Gonring in his article on baseball lingo, "you may hear someone yell, 'Get the swatter.' " A quote from the *Boston Globe,* which was reprinted in the *Atlantic,* said, ". . . [Players] speak disparingly of this pesky breed as *'greenflies'* referring to the species that is softbodied, pear-shaped and gathers in colonies." (July 1987)
ETY   Named for the most persistent and obnoxious kind of fly.

green light   *n.* A coach's "go" sign flashed to a batter telling him to swing. It is most commonly given when there is a 3-0 count on the batter. It also refers to the sign telling a runner to take an extra base on a hit or to attempt to steal. An obvious borrowing from the green light of traffic control.

Green Monster, The   The imposing left-field wall in Fenway Park, 310-feet from home plate and a.k.a. The Wall. "Myth-killer Hurst doesn't fear the 'Green Monster.' " (*USA Today* headline, October 23, 1986) Before it was painted green in 1947, it was covered with advertisements. It has been blamed and credited for things ranging from turning line drive home runs into sliding doubles as they bounce off the wall to converting high fly balls into home runs as such balls are lofted over it.

green pea *n.* ROOKIE, especially one with little experience; a real novice.
1ST 1912. This was Casey Stengel's favorite term for a young and inexperienced player and one that was eventually regarded as an element of Stengelese. It was probably a term that Stengel picked up during his playing days, as it shows up in the 1912 *Sporting Life* article on player slang, in the line, "You're the green pea of the American League." By the 1920s it appears to have been common slang.
EXT A novice in other areas. "The delegation which arrived here last Saturday for the most part 'green peas' in national convention work, are now veterans." (article on the 1952 Democratic National Convention, *San Francisco News,* July 26, 1952)

green weenie **1.** *n.* A gag store plastic hot dog painted green, which was first brought into play by the Pittsburgh Pirates in 1960 when a trainer noted that when it was pointed at an opposing pitcher—when he was given "the green weenie"—the Pirates started hitting. They went into mass production and sold as souvenirs in 1966, and one was wielded by sportscaster Bob Prince in the booth to put hexes and jinxes on opponents of the Pittsburgh Pirates on their way to the 1971 pennant.
2. *n.* A pitch that a batter does not like, according to Jim Brosnan in *The Long Season,* who uses it in the context of "slipping the green weenie past" Ernie Banks.

Greyhound squad *n.* A name for the daily list of players cut from a major league club's spring training roster (who then presumably headed out to their minor league assignments on Greyhound buses), according to Bub Uecker in *Catcher in the Wry.* (CDP)

Griffith Stadium In Washington, D.C., the home grounds of the Washington Senators from 1911 to the end of the 1960 season. It was a quirky, classic stadium whose center field wall detoured around five houses and a large tree.

It was named for Senators owner Clark Griffith.

Griffmen *n./arch.* The WASHINGTON SENATORS under the stewardship of owner Clark Griffith. It was used in the same sense that McGrawmen was used for the New York Giants under John McGraw, and the Philadelphia Athletics were the Mackmen under Connie Mack. Charles Poe notes that on the day that Babe Ruth hit his 60th home run in 1927 the Associated Press noted that the Yankees would play the Griffmen next.

grinder *n.* Reliable workhorse pitcher; one who grinds out victories. "Grinder Sutton Polishes off No. 300." (headline in *Sporting News* on Don Sutton's 300th win, June 30, 1986)

grip **1.** *n.* The exact manner in which a batter holds the bat at the plate. It will vary considerably depending on whether a batter is, say, batting away or bunting. Batters use batting gloves and pine tar to keep their grips from slipping.
2. *n.* The exact manner in which a pitcher holds the ball as he prepares his delivery. The grip taken for a given pitch pretty much determines the type of pitch to be thrown.

grooming *n.* The preparation and maintenance of the playing field by the grounds crew.

groove **1.** *n.* The path a pitch takes down the middle of the strike zone, the location where a batter would most easily hit it.
1ST 1912. (*New York Tribune,* October 6; EJN)
2. *v.* To throw a pitch down the middle of the strike zone—in the groove—where it is most hittable for the batter.
1ST 1911. (*Spalding's Official Base Ball Guide;* EJN)
3. *v.* To experience a period when one performs at one's absolute best; to be in consistently high form.

groover *n.* A pitch delivered to the heart of the strike zone; one that is an AUTOMATIC STRIKE.
1ST 1914. (Ring Lardner's *You Know Me Al;* EJN)

ground ball *n.* Batted ball that hits the ground as it comes off the bat and then rolls or bounces along the ground.
1ST 1860. (*Beadle's Dime Base Ball Player;* EJN)

ground ball-to-shortstop-for-a-double-play pitch   *n.* Self-explanatory term for a pitch thrown with the intention of inducing the batter to ground the ball to the shortstop who, with a runner on first, would convert a double play. (from a quote by Scott McGregor in article by Richard Justice, *Washington Post,* March 17, 1986)

ground coverer   *n.* A defensive player who is able to field successfully balls hit to a wide range of the field.
1ST   1902. (*Sporting Life,* July 12; EJN)

ground crew   *n.* A group of workers who, under directions of the groundskeeper, prepare and maintain the condition of the playing field. The crew's duties include protecting the field from rain, sweeping the basepath and chalking the various lines and boxes on the field.

grounder   *n.* GROUND BALL.
1ST   1861. (*New York Sunday Mercury,* August 10; EJN)

ground hog   **1.** *n./arch.* Member of the grounds crew
2. *n./arch.* GROUNDSKEEPER.

ground out   **1.** *v.* To be thrown out as the result of hitting a grounder. The word "out" is sometimes omitted when it is said that a player who has grounded out to the third baseman has "grounded to third."
2. *n.* An out resulting from a ball being hit on the ground.

ground rule double   *n.* Two-base hit that results from hitting into a special situation outlined in the ground rules. The term almost always refers to the situation in which a batted ball bounces in fair territory and goes over the fence or into the stands and the umpire awards the batter a double.
ETY   Researching baseball slang of the 19th century, Gerald Cohen came upon an article in the *New York World* that contained, "what seems to be an account of the first ground rule double in baseball history, although the term was yet to be coined."
   The article, which appeared on August 26, 1889, under the headline "Stopped by the Police," tells of a game in Hamilton, Ohio, between teams from Brooklyn and Cincinnati, which drew such an immense crowd that the game had to be halted. At one point in the account of the shortened game, we hear, "The entire outfield was lined with people, and the fences were black with humanity. The crowd within so completely filled the grounds that hundreds refused to go in when they found that there were no accommodations . . . The crowd encroached so on the fielders that a ground rule allowing but two bases on a ball batted into the crowd was made." (Cohen's article appears in the April 1, 1986, *Comments on Etymology.*)

ground rules   *n.* A set of special rules unique to the specific conditions and dimensions of each ballpark; made by the home team and must be understood by both teams before play begins. Many have to do with whether or not a ball is in play if it hits an obstacle such as a rolled tarp.
   Though most ground rules are peculiar to each stadium, there are some that generally apply to all, including:
·   The runner gets two bases if the ball is thrown into the dugout, into the stands or over a fence.
·   The runner gets two bases for a ball that bounces in fair territory and then into the stands.
·   A home run is granted when a ball bounces from a fielder's hand or glove and into a stand in fair territory without hitting the ground first.
   One of the odder ground rules ever established was during the first game of the 1965 World Series, which was attended by then Vice President Hubert Humphrey. It was decided that even if a ball hit the Secret Service man sitting on the field in front of Humphrey, *it would remain in play.*
EXT   A basic set of rules and procedures that is set out in advance whether it be for an election debate or pie-eating contest.

grounds   *n.* Area in which the game is played, including both the field and the stands.
1ST   1845. (*Brooklyn Daily Star,* October 23; EJN)

groundskeeper   *n.* The chief of the grounds crew. Because the way in which grounds are kept can give the home team small advantages the position can have a certain strategic importance. Or, as Bill Veeck once put it, "A good groundskeeper can be as valuable as a .300 hitter." For instance, such factors as the length of the infield grass, the moistness of the base-paths, and the subtle slope of the ground around the foul lines are variables in the hands of the groundskeeper.

In his "Rookie Diction-err-y" of 1947, Milt Richman identified the groundskeeper as, "The guys who smoothen every position except your own."

GS *n.* Abbreviation for a grand slam home run. It tends to be used in headlines, such as this one from the *Bangor Daily News* of August 3, 1988: "Greenwell GS powers Red Sox past Rangers."

guardian angel *n.* ANGEL.

guarding the line *v.* A defensive strategy, usually taken in the late innings of a close game, in which the first and third baseman play close to the base line. Because balls hit down the line usually go for extra-base hits, a manager will position his player closer to the line to guard against that possibility.

guard the bag *v.* To play close to a base.

guard the lines *v.* Describing the strategic, defensive move by which the first and third basemen stay very close to their respective foul lines to prevent an extra-base hit, which goes down the line. It is a strategy that often comes into play in the late innings of a close game.

guard the plate *v.* Advice given to a batter with two strikes to swing for any pitch close to the strike zone.

guesser *n./arch.* An umpire.
1ST 1937. (*The Sporting News Record Book;* EJN)

guess hitter **1.** *n.* Batter who tries to anticipate or out-guess the pitcher based on the situation at hand (bases loaded, 3-2 count etc.). "As with all big sluggers, there were frequent strikeouts and [Hank] Greenberg was sometimes labeled 'guess hitter.' He resented it. 'Guess hitter, bull,' he said. 'We're all guess hitters, if everybody would only tell the truth.' " (Shirley Povich, *The Washington Post*, September 9, 1986)
2. *n.* Batter who is indecisive and often swings at any pitch.

gun **1.** *n.* A strong throwing arm.
2. *n.* A pitcher's arm; his wing.

gun, the *n.* Electronic device used to determine, in miles per hour, the speed of a pitched ball.

gun down *v.* To throw out a base runner with a strong throw.

gun-shy *adj.* Applied to a player who is afraid of the ball—often after having been hit by a pitched or batted ball.

guy *v./obs.* To jeer at, to rib. In his research into baseball slang of the 19th century, Gerald Cohen has concluded, "It is now clear from *The* [New York] *World* that the term was entrenched in baseball speech of the late 19th century, and the only question is why it later died out." An example from the August 4, 1888, *World* in which "black" refers to the New York Giants: "They guyed the red stockings and cheered black."

GWRBI *n.* Standard scorecard and box score abbreviation for game-winning run batted in.

H

H Standard scorecard and box score abbreviation for hit or hits.

hack **1.** *v.* To swing without form or grace. **2.** *n.* A poor swing; a clumsy swing at a pitch out of the strike zone.

hacker *n.* A batter with poor form at the plate, one who regularly takes reckless swings at pitches outside the strike zone.

hair *n.* Velocity as applied to a pitch. San Diego Padres announcer Jerry Coleman was quoted in the December 1983 *Baseball Digest* for this description of fastball: "that one had a little hair on it."

Hairs vs. Squares Nickname for the 1972 World Series, which pitted the hirsute Oakland A's—"The Mustache Gang"—and the clean-shaven Cincinnati Reds.

half *n.* HALF INNING.

half gainer/half gaynor *n.* Name for a headfirst dive for either a catch or a slide. **ETY** From the name of a common dive in aquatic sports.

half inning *n.* One of two equal portions of a full inning, when one team is at bat and the other is in the field. During the top half, the visiting team bats and during the bottom half the home team bats. When the fielding team records three outs, the teams switch positions and begin a new half inning.

half-rubber *n.* A schoolyard baseball variation played with a sponge rubber ball that has been cut in half and a thin bat, which is likely to have been fashioned from a broomstick. Its appeal comes from the fact that it allows for a number of odd sidearm breaking pitches and difficult to get hits. There are two players on each team and there is no base running but rather bases are reached by imaginary men and earned when the ball is hit beyond a designated line.

The game is discussed in detail in a letter entitled "A Depression-Days Schoolyard Ball Game," which appears in the January 1975 issue of *Western Folklore.* In it, the writer, Hugh M. Thomason, goes into a detailed description of the game as he played it in rural southeastern Georgia in the middle 1930s. Another article, "Half-Rubber," in the August 1927 *American Speech* and written by Lowry Axley, claims that the game and its name were invented in Savannah, Georgia, where, according to one player, "[It] was originated . . . some eight or ten years ago by two boys who got the idea when they were hitting pop-bottle caps with broom handles."

half swing *n.* CHECKED SWING.

halfway **1.** *adj.* The position taken by a base runner between bases when a fly ball is hit so that he will have time to get back to base if the ball is caught. **2.** *adj.* Defensive position often taken by infield when there is a slow runner on third base with fewer than two outs. The position puts the fielder in a spot midway between regular depth and the "in" position. It sets up an opportunity for a play at home plate without fully compromising the defensive positioning.

Hall of Fame **1.** *n.* The pantheon of the game's greatest players in the form of a list of those players. **2.** *n.* The name of baseball's museum and the place within that museum reserved for bronze plaques depicting and honoring the great players who have been elected and inducted into the Hall of Fame. Both the museum and the Hall itself were established in a building—baseball's "shrine"—in Cooperstown, New York, in 1939; however, the first players were elected to the Hall of Fame in 1936. The first group of inductees, selected by a special committee, were Ty Cobb, Walter Johnson, Christy Mathewson, Babe Ruth and Honus Wagner. In addition to the great players, there are separate honor rolls for writers, managers, umpires and owners who have contributed to the game.

The rules governing election to the Hall of Fame require that players be retired for five years and that the election is conducted by

Hall of Fame. The Hall of Fame as it looks today, much expanded from the original configuration of 1939 when it was dedicated.   *National Baseball Library, Cooperstown, N.Y.*

polling baseball writers by secret ballot. (Jimmy Cannon's candid definition of the Hall of Fame was, "Where baseball writers send their friends.") A candidate must receive a vote from 75 percent of those voting in order to be elected.

1ST   The term predated the establishment of the Cooperstown shrine by many years. In his dissertation, submitted in 1939 when the Hall of Fame was created, Edward J. Nichols says that it originally meant, "An honor roll of pitchers who have pitched full games without allowing opposing teams to hit safely." He first found the term in the November 1908 *Baseball* magazine.

ETY   The idea for the Hall of Fame was proposed by Ford Frick in 1935 soon after becoming National League president. Many other Halls of Fame have followed the one in Cooperstown, which, though the most famous, was not the first American example. The prototype American institution is the Hall of Fame at New York University, which honors the names of important Americans. In sports alone, there are now dozens of Halls of Fame, including the National Jockeys Hall of Fame, the Lacrosse Hall of

Fame and Museum, and the U.S. Croquet Hall of Fame.

Hall of Fame Game   Special exhibition game played in Cooperstown, New York, between two major league teams and in conjunction with the annual induction ceremonies. The game is played on a Monday, usually the first Monday in August.

hall of famer   *n.* An individual inducted to the Hall of Fame.

hall of shame   *n.* Name used for lists, books, articles and other places where poor performances, error rates and other negatives are collected. It is, of course, a play on Hall of Fame.

Authors Bruce Nash and Allan Zullo have turned the idea into a series of books, but they seem to be running out of material. Does Mike Schmidt really belong in *The Baseball Hall of Shame* because he once forgot to buckle his pants and walked onto the playing field?

ham-and-egg reliever   *n.* Relief pitcher who is usually brought in after the game has been decided. "He is reliable but nondescript," says Patric Ercolano in his *Fungoes, Floaters and Fork Balls,* "like a meal of ham and eggs."

ham hitter   *n./arch.* An inferior batter.

hammer   **1.** *v.* To hit the ball with great power.
  "I don't use the strike zone much," said Dick Allen on more than one occasion, "I'm looking for something to hammer."
1ST   1895. (*New York Press,* August 7; EJN)
2. *v.* To hit well against a pitcher in a particular game.
1ST   1869. (*New York Herald,* August 7; EJN)

hand   *n./obs.* A turn at bat during the earliest days of baseball. In his book *Baseball* Robert Smith talks about the early game as a gambling vehicle and makes this point: "The very language of early baseball, as evolved by the Knickerbockers, was that of the gaming table: a turn at bat was a 'hand' and a run was an 'ace.' "

handcuff   **1.** *v.* To defy easy handling when a ball is batted into the field, such as "A bullet that handcuffed the third baseman." (Keith Jackson, ABC-TV broadcast of Mets vs. Astros playoff game, October 14, 1986)
2. *n.* The situation that takes place when a fielder simply cannot get his glove hand on a batted ball, as if he were wearing handcuffs. Handcuffs are likely to come with hard-hit balls.
1ST   1935. "An infielder is said to be 'hand-cuffed' when unsuccessfully attempting to catch a hard drive." (Ralph H. Barbour, *How to Play Better Baseball;* DS)
3. *v.* For a pitcher to hold the opposition to a very few hits, with the batters being hand-cuffed.
1ST   1939. "Morris Handcuffs Seals." (*San Francisco News,* April 10; PT)
ETY   This term may have had its first sports application in boxing where it referred to a fighter who was not using his hands to full advantage. A 1933 report by Stuart Bell of the *Cleveland Press,* on a fight discovered to be a fake, contained these lines: "Bell had every reason to believe that one of the fighters was wearing handcuffs. Not only did the referee toss the middleweights from the ring, but the fans did some rioting." (*San Francisco News,* May 4; PT)

hand grenader   *n./arch.* PITCHER.

handle   **1.** *n.* The narrow end of the baseball bat.

2. *v.* To field successfully a batted or thrown ball.
1ST   1862. (Chadwick Scrapbooks; EJN)
3. *n.* The fieldable nature of batted or thrown ball. Players attribute this to a non-existent piece of the ball which must be grasped in order to field it successfully, as if the ball had a "handle."
4. *n.* Ground ball that takes a high, easy hop for the fielder.

handle a pitcher   *v.* To effectively play the role of catcher for a particular pitcher. As stated by Edward J. Nichols, "usually refers to the ability of the catcher to obtain effective cooperation from a pitcher." The handling of a pitcher also involves giving the pitcher good direction in the form of signals and being able to keep the pitcher calm when he is having difficulties.
1ST   1894. (*Spalding's Official Baseball Guide;* EJN)

handle hit   *n.* A hit made off the handle of the bat.

handle the stick   *v.* To bat well. "You'd be surprised. A guy who handles the stick the way you did isn't forgotten so easily." (from *Squeeze Play,* by Paul Benjamin)

handout   *n.* BASE ON BALLS.

hands   **1.** *n.* Fielding ability. A capable defensive player is said to have "good" hands.
2. *n.* Hitting ability. A capable hitter is said to have "good" hands.
  "A player who hits singles has baby hands. A player in a slump, well, his hands went on vacation. Dave Kingman has feet for hands." (*Rotisserie League Baseball,* edited by Glen Waggoner)

hands lost   *n./obs.* Henry Chadwick defined this as "the old way of recording the outs in a match. Whenever a player is put out, a 'hand is lost,' and an 'out' is recorded in the score books."

hands out   *n./obs.* Players declared out. Edward J. Nichols noted, "This term was carried over from cricket but dropped before the Civil War."
1ST   1845. (Knickerbocker Rules)

handyman   *n.* Player who can play a number of positions as well as bat; a handy man to have around. An article on Rick Cerone in the May 22, 1988, *Boston Globe* is headlined "Designated Handyman," in this case alluding to the fact that he had been used for short periods at a number of positions, including an inning each in two different games as a pitcher for the 1987 Yankees. Brought in as a last resort, Cerone gave up no hits and walked only one batter.

hang   *v.* To throw a pitch that does not break or breaks slowly and slightly; one that hangs over the plate.
1ST   1937. Edward J. Nichols traces it to an interview he conducted with William Weir, pitcher.

hang a clothesline   *v.* To hit a line drive.
1ST   1932. (*Baseball* magazine, October; EJN)

hanger   *n.* Same as hanging curve.

hanging curve   *n.* A high curveball that only breaks slightly, thereby giving the batter an easy target. It is the bane of pitchers and the delight of batters. "For a pitcher, a mortal sin," wrote Jim Brosnan in *The Long Season.* "He who hangs too many curves, soon hangs up his glove forever."

hang out the clothes   *v.* HANG A CLOTHESLINE.

hang out hemp   *v.* To hit a line drive.
ETY   It is a play off other terms with the same meaning: clothesline, frozen rope etc.

hang out to dry   *v.* To pick off a base runner.

hang-up   *v.* To catch a runner between bases; to catch in a rundown.

hang up one's spikes   *v.* To retire from playing professional baseball.

Hank Aaron Trophy   Proper name for the Arby's RBI Award given at the end of the season to the players with the most *RBI*s in the American and National Leagues.

hard   *adj.* With velocity and power, as in, a hard liner or a hard sinker.

hardball   *n.* A term that seemingly refers to baseball—the game itself, as well as the ball itself. When the term is used in the context of baseball it refers to a tough style of play. " 'Billy' campaign adds major hard sell to A's hard-ball style"—headline in the *San Francisco Examiner,* March 25, 1981, on Oakland manager Billy Martin and the efforts of the A's front office to promote his style of management at the gate. (PT)
USE   The term does not sit well with baseball

purists who see it as misnomer. As the late Red Smith commented in his *New York Times* column of July 1, 1981, it is a "misbegotten term" that has been given "an unappetizing usage, signifying nothing." Smith was quick to point out, "There is a game called softball; in fact, there are two—slow-pitch and fast-pitch softball. There is no game called hardball. Nobody plays hardball."
1ST   1944. In a discussion of the highly-competitive newspaper business in Chicago, it was stated in the October 30 issue of *Times:* "Last week a man with a winning streak stepped into what he called this 'hard-ball league.' " (PT)
ETY   It is commonly assumed that hardball came into being as a way to distinguish baseball from softball, e.g., "What will we play Sunday? Softball or hardball?"

However, Peter Tamony discovered an item in a club newsletter (the Olympic Club's *Olympian,* March/April 1945) that discusses the club's changeover from a "soft ball" (a tennis ball) to a "hard ball" (black-rubber Irish handball).
EXT   Currently, it seems to be used most commonly to refer to a tough, relentless adversary or adversarial situation. Presumably, no soft balls are thrown when hardball is being played. "More Hardball Over Big Government" reads a *Washington Post* headline for January 6, 1987. *USA Today* headlined an article on Jim Bunning, a new congressman and a former big league pitcher, "Bunning ready to play some hardball in D.C." (October 6, 1986) In addition to the meaning just discussed, it has a specific use among drug addicts: "Mixing cocaine with heroin is called speedballing or hardballing." (*San Francisco Examiner* on the death of John Belushi, March 12, 1982; PT)

hard cheese   *n.* Fastball. "He threw some good hard cheese up there," Wally Backman said of Nolan Ryan. (*St. Petersburg Times,* March 5, 1987)

hard one   *n.* See fastball.

hard out   *n.* A player who is hard to retire; a good hitter with a good eye for balls out of the strike zone.

harness   *n./arch.* Uniform and equipment of a player, especially a catcher.
1ST   1902. (*Sporting Life,* July 5; EJN)

Harvey's Wallbangers   Nickname given to the hard-hitting 1982 Milwaukee Brewers after Harvey Kuenn became manager in June of that year. According to *Newsweek,* Kuenn told his players, "Look, you guys can flat-out hit. So just go out there and have some fun." The name was a play on the name of a mixed drink called a Harvey Wallbanger.

hassock *n./arch.* BASE.
1ST 1907. (*Dick Merriwell's Magnetism;* EJN)

hat trick *n.* Said when a batter has *hit for the cycle.* The term is only occasionally used in baseball but is much more commonly used in hockey or soccer for a player who has scored three goals, or in horse racing for a jockey who wins three races in a row.
ETY The term comes from cricket where it was created in the 19th century for the practice of presenting a bowler a new hat when he took—or knocked down—three wickets on three consecutive balls. The Oxford English Dictionary lists the term in use as early as 1882 in this context. "He thus accomplished the feat known as the 'hat trick,' and was warmly applauded." (*Daily Telegraph,* May 19)

It has also been stated that the term is Canadian and that it was created to describe spectators collecting money in a hat for a player who had just scored three goals. This practice may well have been common, but the application of the term to hockey clearly postdates its appearance in cricket by many years.

haul it in *v.* To catch a batted or thrown ball.

have bells on *adj.* Said of a ball that has been hit hard.
1ST 1908. (*New York Evening Journal,* June 19; EJN)

have one's innings *v.* To have one's proper turns at bat.
EXT To have had a chance.

hawk *n.* An outfielder who covers his territory with speed and skill; a ball hawk.

hazzards *n.* BASES, in the parlance of Dizzy Dean, who was giving his own twist to hassocks.

HB/HBP/HP Standard scorecard and box score abbreviations for hit by pitch(er) and hit batsman, or batter.

head *n.* One's physical appearance, usually used in a negative context. "Men who are considered to have 'the bad head' include Rocky Bridges, Don Mossi and Yogi Berra," wrote Leonard Shecter in his 1963 article on baseball slang.

head fake *n.* A deceptive tactic by which the player with the ball looks at a base runner in the hope that the glance will be enough to get the runner to stop or return to a base, allowing the man with the ball to throw to another base.
SEE *arm fake.*

headfirst slide *n.* A dive with arms outstretched to reach or return to base. It is a risky move, hence it is used as a measure of a player's mettle.

head hunter/headhunter *n.* A beanball pitcher; one who aims for the head. "There are certain pitchers who are known as headhunters, there are other pitchers who won't throw at anybody, like Catfish, and then there are pitchers who can't throw at anybody, like Wilbur Wood." (Ron Luciano, *The Umpire Strikes Back;* CDP)

head in the locker *n.* Figurative condition of a player with little or nothing to say to anyone, including his teammates.

head of the bat *n.* The thick end of a baseball bat.

heads up **1.** *adj.* Alert and quick-thinking, such as a heads-up play or, generally, heads-up ball.
2. *v.* Command to stay alert.

head work/head-work *n./arch.* Term applied to the thinking of a player using good judgment in his work.

This term was common in the late 19th century. Here is what Henry Chadwick had to say about head work in *The American Game of Base Ball:* "This is a term specially applied to the pitcher who is noted for his tact and judgement in bothering his batting opponents by his pitching. A pitcher who simply trusts to pace, in his delivery, for effect will never succeed with skillful batsmen opposed to him. A pitcher, however, who uses head-work in pitching tries to discover his adversary's weak points, and to tempt him to hit at balls, either out of his reach or pitched purposely for him to hit to a particular part of the field. Pitchers, in general, have greatly improved in this respect within the past few years."
1ST 1876. (*Chicago Inter Ocean,* April 28; EJN)

Head-first slide. An aggressive softballer dives for the plate.   *Courtesy of the Amateur Softball Association of America*

healthy   *n./arch.* A batter's swing at the ball. Edward J. Nichols gives this example: "He walked to the plate and took his healthy."
1ST   1915. (Ring Lardner, "My Roommate"; EJN)

healthy average   *n.* A good percentage, usually applied to batting average.

hear the bell ring   *v.* To open the season. "Maybe the Cincinnati Reds hear the bell ringing. That's old baseball talk meaning the start of the season." (*Tampa Tribune*, April 4, 1986)

heart of the game   *n.* Pitching, so called by those who see it as the key to the sport.

heart of the order   *n.* That part of the batting order with the best hitters, commonly positions three, four and five.

heat   *n./arch* An inning, borrowed from horse racing.

heat/heater   *n.* A fastball of high quality. To lose one's heat is to lose the ability to throw the fastball: "Baseball can bring you to your knees

. . . I never thought this could happen when I was on top and I had my heat, but now I know . . . baseball can knock you right down to your knees." (Dennis Eckersley, quoted in Michael Madden's column in the *Boston Globe*, July 10, 1983)

heave   *v.* To pitch or throw.
1ST   1907. (*Harpers Weekly*, December 14; EJN)

heave-ho   *n.* Ejection of a player from the game. Commonly stated as "the old heave-ho."

heaver   *n.* A PITCHER.
1ST   1914. (*Harpers Weekly*, May 2; EJN)

heavy ball   **1.** *n.* A ball that feels heavy to the catcher because of the way it was thrown. An odd or eccentric spin on the ball is often the cause. It brings an extra sting to the hands of the catcher or, if it is hit, to the batter's hands.
2. *n.* A sinking pitch that a batter has a hard time hitting in the air.
3. *n.* One saturated with water.

heavy batter/heavy hitter   *n.* Player who hits the ball hard.
1ST 1883 (heavy hitter only). (*Sporting Life,* April 15; EJN)
EXT Person to be reckoned with; someone important. "Stephen King's apparent desire to be a literary heavy hitter weighs down his already elephantine new novel." (*Newsweek,* September 1, 1986)

heavy pitch   *n.* Ball that drops sharply as it nears the plate.

"he can't spit"   *v.* "[S]cout's comment on a pitcher who is inclined to go into a panic in a tight situation," says Herbert Simons in his January 1943 *Baseball* magazine article, "Do You Speak the Language?" "It derives from the fact that fear or excitement usually stops the flow of saliva."

"he could throw a lamb chop past a wolf"   Line created by Arthur "Bugs" Baer to describe the speed of Walter Johnson's fastball. Baer pointed out in a 1956 column that he came up with the line after Johnson had hung up his spikes. (*San Francisco Examiner,* March 27; PT)

heifer step   *n.* A unit of measurement used by Dizzy Dean in his broadcasting incarnation to describe such things as the distance a runner was short of a base. It lacked a certain precision, however, because he defined it as 2½ feet in *Dizzy Daisies* and "about 36 inches" in *Dizzy's Definitions.*

helicopter   *n.* A high, breaking pitch.
1ST 1987. "Look out for that helicopter (translation: Be ready for the high breaking pitch)." (*The St. Petersburg Times,* March 5, 1987)

"Hello, Coz"   See coz.

helmet   *n.* A protective hat used by batters. See batting helmet.

help out   *v.* For a batter to try to obstruct or hinder the throw of the catcher who is trying to stop an advancing runner.
1ST 1911. (*American* magazine, May, EJN)

hemp   *n.* A hard-hit line drive and a variation on rope. "Hisle was laying out some hemp." (*Baseball Digest,* June 1979)

hen fruit   GOOSE EGG.
1ST 1891. (*Chicago Herald,* June 24; EJN)

hen is on, a   *arch.* Phrase meaning something important is in preparation; from the image of a hen sitting on her eggs, which will soon hatch. Gerald Cohen found examples in his research on baseball slang, including this from the July 1, 1890, *New York World:* "From what Ewing says there is no longer any doubt that there is a very large National League hen on."

"Here comes Charley"   *arch.* Greeting for a limping player presumed to be suffering from a charley horse.

herky jerky   *adv.* Describing the motion of a pitcher with an especially awkward delivery.

hesitation pitch   *n.* A pitch that is delivered with a pause, or hitch, between the windup and the throw. Such an abnormality can cause the batter problems in timing his swing. The pitch was developed by Satchel Paige before he came to the Major Leagues from the Negro Leagues in 1948.

he took a drink   *v.* To have struck out, an obvious play on the fact that many batters head back to the dugout for a sip of water after failing at the plate.

Hickok Belt   A jewel-studded belt given to the professional athlete of the year. Named for Stephen Rae Hickok, of the Hickok Belt Com-

Hesitation pitch. LeRoy "Satchel" Paige in the uniform of the Kansas City Monarchs.   *National Baseball Library, Cooperstown, N.Y.*

pany. Its official name is the S. Rae Hickok Professional Athlete of the Year Award and it was first presented in 1950. Baseball players who have won the award include Willie Mays and Phil Rizzuto.

hickory *n./arch.* The BAT, despite the fact that most bats are made of ash.
1ST 1892. (*Chicago Herald,* May 31; EJN)

hidden ball trick **1.** *n.* A time-honored legal ruse in which a baseman conceals the ball and hopes that the runner believes it has been returned to the pitcher. When the runner steps off the base, he is summarily tagged out with the hidden ball.

One of the oddest versions of the hidden ball trick came in 1958 when Nellie Fox asked Billy Gardner to step off the bag for a moment while he cleaned it off. Gardner obliged and got tagged out by Fox.
1ST 1908. (*Spalding's Official Base Ball Guide;* EJN)
2. *n.* An illegal play in which a hidden second ball is brought into play. If the trick is still occasionally performed, it is rarely detected. However, cases come to light from time to time. Here, for example, is the beginning of an Associated Press story with a June 26, 1964, dateline from Binghamton, New York.

"As a high fly hit by Dan Napoleon soared toward the fence last night, evidently bound for home run territory, it was suddenly snared from the air in a spectacular catch—or so it appeared.

"But later, Outfielder John May of the Binghamton Triplets in the Class A New York-Pennsylvania League admitted he didn't catch the ball after all. He said he went through the gestures, but actually substituted a ball from his pocket for the one that was hit out of the park."

The story goes on to say that Napoleon was credited with the homer and the Binghamton team lost the game.
3. *n.* On rare occasion it is applied to a pitcher's ability to keep the ball hidden from the batter's view until it is delivered. Because the pitcher's grip on the ball determines the type of delivery, a pitcher will try to hide the ball until the last moment. " 'Hidden Ball Trick' Gave Carwell $2000 'Bonus' "—on how Cubs pitcher Don Cardwell credited his no-hitter to his ability to hide the ball; UPI dispatch of May 17, 1960. (PT)
ETY There is also a hidden ball trick in foot-

ball, which dates back to the last century and was first employed by Vanderbilt in a game with Auburn in 1895. (PT)
EXT Used for deceptive move in other areas, but particularly politics. In a comment on the House of Representatives' "quick fixes" for problems, *San Francisco News* columnist Thomas L. Stokes wrote, "Those are 'hidden ball' plays—now you see it, now you don't." (August 9, 1948; PT)

hide *n./arch.* HORSEHIDE.

high *adj.* A pitched ball that comes in over the top of the strike zone. Unless swung at, a high pitch should be called a ball by the umpire.

high and hard *n.* HIGH, HARD ONE.

high and inside *adj.* A tough ball to hit; it is pitched high in the strike zone, close to the batter.
EXT Describing something hard to handle; thorny. "Mayor Elmer Robinson wound up and pitched a fast one high and inside today to Supervisor Edward T. Mancuso. (*San Francisco Call-Bulletin,* September 8, 1953; PT)

high-arc ball *n.* A variation of softball.

high-ball hitter *n.* A batter with a reputation for swinging at balls that come in above his belt.

high cheese *n.* A fastball delivered high in the strike zone.
"High cheese for strike two." (description of a Dwight Gooden pitch on WOR-TV, April 8, 1986)

high five *n.* Celebratory hand-slapping that takes place with one's arms extended high over one's head. It began to show up in baseball in 1980 as a way of welcoming a man at the plate after hitting a home run. It is one of a number of slaps, clasps and other congratulatory gestures that have been popular.
ETY The origin of the gesture and the term were claimed by Derek Smith of the University of Louisville basketball team, which won the NCAA championship for the 1979–80 season. Smith was quoted in the *Sporting News, New York Times* and elsewhere to the effect that he and two fellow Georgians on the Louisville squad, Wiley Brown and Daryl Cleveland, decided to come up with something "a little odd." The high five was created during preseason practice and introduced to the nation in 1979 as the team made numerous tv appearances.

High five. The high five is an extension of the traditional home plate handshake. Here Larry Doby (left) of the 1954 Cleveland Indians greets teammate Al Rosen after one of his 24 homers that year. The pair reversed the ritual greeting 32 times for Doby home runs.   *Courtesy of the Cleveland Indians*

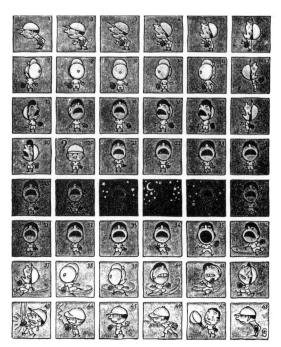

High fly. An interpretation of the term from the September 17, 1914, *Life. Courtesy of the New York Public Library*

high-flier   *n./arch.* See high fly.
1ST   1867. "Smith sent a high-flier toward the right field, but King took it in nicely." (Chadwick Scrapbooks, DS)

high fly   *n.* Ball that is hit high in the air.
1ST   1881. "Another part of a shortfielder's work is his attending to the class of high fly-balls hit over the heads of the third or second baseman . . ." (Chadwick Scrapbooks; DS)

high, hard one   *n.* A powerful FASTBALL that comes in high in the strike zone.
1ST   1928. (*New York Times,* October 7; EJN)

high-low   *n.* A warm-up drill for fielders in which the ball is deliberately thrown high and low for added difficulty.
1ST   1910. (*American* magazine, April; EJN)

high mass   *n./arch.* Sunday doubleheader.

high pockets   *n.* Name for a skinny player with long legs.

high school   *adj.* Amateur, BUSH LEAGUE.

high school hop   *n.* A batted ball that takes a big bounce that is easy to field.

high sky   *n.* Cloudless, bright blue sky under which it is difficult to judge fly balls.

hightail it   *v.* To move quickly.
1ST   1939. "On throws from right or center field, with no play at the plate suggested, the pitcher should hightail it over behind the third base man." (G. S. Cochrane, *Baseball, the Fan's Game;* DS)

hill/hillock   *n.* The pitcher's mound. " 'I was interested to see you out there on the hill in the ninth,' he remarked with a quizzical look." (*Relief Pitcher* by Dick Friendlich; CDP)
1ST   1908. (*New York Evening Journal,* March 11; EJN)

hilltop   *n.* The pitcher's mound.
1ST   1920. "They continued to play well, but not well enough to beat a team like the Hawks—not with Powder Hurley on the hilltop . . ." (Gilbert Patten, *Man on First; DS*)

hind snatcher   *n./arch.* CATCHER.

hipper-dipper   *n./arch.* Curveball with a sharp break in the trajectory.

hippodroming   *n./arch.* Practice of promoting baseball with stunts, like using prizefighters

ROBERT CAL HUBBARD
UMPIRE
AMERICAN LEAGUE 1936-1951
ONE OF MOST RESPECTED, EFFICIENT AND
AUTHORITATIVE UMPIRES IN HISTORY OF
MAJORS. GENTLE GIANT BOASTED SPECIAL
KNACK FOR DEALING WITH SITUATIONS ON
FIELD. WORKED FOUR WORLD SERIES AND
THREE ALL-STAR GAMES. SERVED AS LEAGUE'S
ASSISTANT UMPIRE SUPERVISOR IN 1952 AND AS
UMPIRE SUPERVISOR FROM 1953 TO 1969.

His Umps. One of the umpires who earned the title. *National Baseball Library, Cooperstown, N.Y.*

John L. Sullivan and Jim Jefferies as umpires. "When he got to the big leagues, Barrow eschewed all such hippodroming for he felt baseball by itself was all the entertainment a man needed." (Robert Smith in *Baseball's Hall of Fame;* CDP)
ETY   From the name of ancient structures and arenas used for equestrian shows and other spectacles. Among other things, chariot races were held in ancient Greek and Roman hippodromes.

his ump/his umps   *n./arch.* An umpire's title, a play on "his honor," "his highness" etc.
1ST   1908. (*Baseball* magazine, July; EJN)

hit   **1.** *n.* A batted ball that moves in fair territory and allows the batter to reach a base safely before the ball and without the help of an error and without the ball being caught on the fly. Although most are obvious and automatic, the official scorer may have to decide whether a given batted ball is to be credited as a hit or an error.
   The ability to get 200 hits in a season is

regarded as an exceptional feat. Ty Cobb had nine such seasons, a record.
   There are many, many terms for specific hits. To give an inkling of how many and how diverse they are, here a few that Charles Poe found while reading Roger Angell's *The Summer Game:* hopper, roller, bouncer, tap, bloop, dying single and hit and run ball.
1ST   1892. (New York Sunday *Mercury,* July 13; EJN)
2. *n.* Any batted ball.
3. *v.* To bat a ball.
   There are many verbs for hitting, including some found, as above, during a reading of *The Summer Game:* dribble, bomb, bang, sail, line, tap, stroke and waft.
1ST   1866. (*New York Sunday Mercury,* September 16; EJN)
4. *v.* To take a turn at the plate.

hit a buck-eighty/hit about a buck   *v.* References to a low batting average, with a buck equaling .100. They are clearly used to disparage as was the case when Vin Scully said that Met Mookie Wilson was "hitting about a buck" during the 1986 World Series.

hit air   *v.* To swing and miss.
1ST   1908. (*Baseball* magazine, July; EJN)

hit an air pocket   *v.* Said of a fly ball that has been dropped by a fielder.

hit-and-run play   *n.* Offensive play put on by the manager, in which a runner on first base starts to run as soon as the pitcher releases the ball. With the base runner heading to second, either the shortstop or second baseman moves to cover the bag, giving the batter a gap in the infield defense through which to hit the ball. If the batter gets a hit, the base runner usually is able to advance to third base. If the ball is hit to an infielder, the base runner's head start reduces the defense's chance of turning a double play. However, if the batter swings and misses, the runner may be thrown out, and if the ball is hit for a pop fly the runner is likely to become part of a double play.
1ST   1902. (*Sporting Life,* October 4; EJN)
ETY   The play was, by all accounts, created by the Baltimore Orioles of the mid-1890s, specifically, John McGraw and Willie Keeler. According to Frank Graham, in his book, *McGraw of the Giants,* "They trained in New Orleans in that spring of 1894. With the enthusiastic encouragement of Hanlon, McGraw began to de-

Hit-and-run play. The two men standing—Willie Keeler (left) and John McGraw (right)—are given credit for inventing the hit-and-run play. Along with Joe Kelley (left, sitting) and Hughey Jennings, these four Baltimore Orioles were known as baseball's "Big Four" in the mid-1890s. *National Baseball Library, Cooperstown, N.Y.*

vise plays calculated to upset the enemy. He and Keeler originated the hit-and-run play. They all polished their bunting game. They invented so many tricks, that, in order to curb them, the owners of the other clubs had to draft new rules or change some of the old ones."

EXT 1. This term began showing up as a description for automobile accidents in which injury is done and the driver of the car leaves the scene. Edward J. Nichols gives a number of examples, including this *New York Herald-Tribune* headline of December 6, 1936: "Mother Jailed in Hit-and-Run Injury of Boys." Peter Tamony found examples dating as far back as 1929.
2. Generally, anything that strikes quickly. A letter to "Dear Abby" opens: "There is a cheap little flirt who is a freshman at school and she is the hit and run type. She likes to go after a boy who is going with another girl just to see if she can get him. After she breaks them up, she drops the boy and finds somebody else to break up." (*San Francisco Chronicle*, October 18, 1968; PT) *Time* of November 20, 1950, de-

scribes certain strike techniques used against American Telephone and Telegraph as " 'hit and run' picketing." To create maximum impact, the pickets would show at one locale, where follow workers would refuse to cross picket lines, and then abruptly move to another site.

hit a ton *v.* To be on a hitting streak, reserved for batters in the .300 range.

hit away *v.* To take a full swing at the pitch.
USE This term tends to be used to describe the batter in situations where one might assume that the batter would not take a full cut at the ball—for instance, when the count on the batter is 3-0 or at a point when a bunt seems appropriate.

hit back to the box *v.* To bat the ball back to the pitcher.

hit batsman/hit batter *n.* A batter hit by a pitched ball. If he makes a reasonable effort to get out of the way and does not swing at the ball, he is awarded first base.
ETY The rule first came into play in 1884 in response to a minor league pitcher named Will White who made a practice of hitting batters to keep them away from the plate.

hit-batter pitch *n.* A pitch intended to hit a batter's body but not to hit him in the head. Explaining his hit-batter pitch in the *New York Times*, Bob Gibson writes: "Note that I didn't say 'beanball' pitch. Nobody in his right mind throws a rock 90-plus miles an hour at a guy's head." (July 13, 1986)

hit behind the runner *v.* To bat the ball down the first base side of the field to help the runner move to second or third base. This is a common element in successful hit-and-run plays in which the ball is hit into right field. One of the earliest and strongest advocates of hitting behind the runner was John J. McGraw, who once said: "You see, the fact that a baseball diamond is so laid out that the runners advance by turning to the left and away from right field puts a premium on hits in that direction when the bases are occupied."
USE It would be hard to underemphasize the degree to which this phrase—and the advice behind it—has become an element of the game. Arthur Mann once wrote down the conventional wisdom on this matter: "But the biggest problem found among young players is pre-

sented by the chronic left-field hitter. No matter how good a young batter may be, he must be taught to 'hit behind the runner,' or into right field when a man is on base, for this placement facilitates the runner's trip around the base paths." ("Rehearsing for Baseball," *American Mercury,* March 1933; PT)

hit by pitch/hit by pitcher   *v.* To be struck by a pitched ball while at the plate. Unless the batter leans in or is clearly at fault in not getting out of the way, the batter is awarded first base.

If the umpire deems that a pitcher has intentionally hit a batter, the pitcher will be ejected from the game.

1ST   1905. (*Sporting Life,* September 2; EJN)

hitch   **1.** *n.* A hesitation or other abnormality in a batter's swing that usually affects his timing and prevents a "smooth swing."

A common hitch occurs when the batter drops his hands just before the pitch is delivered. Another type of hitch occurs when the batter draws the bat backwards just before starting his swing. Depending on the context in which it appears, the term can be used to refer to a flaw or a strength, but it tends to be used more often in pointing to a defect.

Here it is used in a positive way: "One of the things the Orioles liked about Traber this spring is that he has enough of a hitch in his swing to spray the ball to all parts of the field." (*The Washington Post,* July 23, 1986, on rookie Jim Traber) Walker Cooper, with the St. Louis Cardinals and New York Giants, Jimmy Foxx and Rudy York were all players noted for the flaw. And as Joe Garagiola put it during a telecast, "Nobody complained about Hank Aaron's hitch." **2.** *n.* A pause in a pitcher's windup intended to throw off the batter's timing; the key element in a hesitation pitch.

EXT   This may be nautical in origin, coming from a hitch in a rope, a jam that prevents it from running smoothly through a block.

hitchy-koo   *n./arch.* Fidgeting at the plate.

"hit 'em where they ain't"   Rallying cry for batters through the decades since 1897, when William "Wee Willie" Keeler hit .432. He was asked by a reporter how a man of his size could put together such an average. "Simple," was Keeler's reply. "I keep my eyes clear and I hit 'em where they ain't."

Though the line was undisputedly Keeler's,

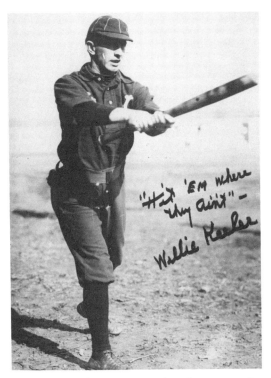

"Hit em where they ain't." Lest there be any question as to Keeler being aware of his famous line, note how he signed this photograph.   *National Baseball Library, Cooperstown, N.Y.*

the idea behind it was hardly new. "For the Mutuals, Hunt sent a very safe one to center, where 'nobody was,' and Bearman sent him home." (*New York Clipper,* September 7, 1867; PT)

It is one of baseball's hoariest axioms and shows up in various contexts. "Willie Keeler hits them where they ain't," wrote Arthur "Bugs" Baer in the 1920s. "Babe Ruth hits 'em where they're never going to be." Some even tried to turn it into a nickname for Keeler. In J. G. Taylor Spink's *Judge Landis and Twenty-Five Years of Baseball,* we read of: " 'Hit 'em Where They Ain't Willie Keeler,' laughing over his cups at the stupidity of club owners. 'The saps pay me for playin ball,' said Willie. 'Why, I would pay my way into the ball park if that was the only way I had to get in a game.' "

hit famine   *n.* A batting slump for a team or individual.

hit for the circuit   *v.* Relatively uncommon variation of HIT FOR THE CYCLE.

hit for the cycle   *v.* For a player to hit a single, double, triple and home run (not necessarily in that order) within the course of a single game. It is a rarity.

"He becomes the first Oakland player ever to hit for the cycle and only the fourth ever to do it against the Orioles (Larry Hisle, George Brett, and Bob Watson are the others)." (Tony Phillips hitting for the cycle, as reported by *The Washington Post,* May 17, 1986)

It is a rare feat that many top hitters never accomplish in a career. There have been only two players who have done it three times: Babe Herman and Bob Meusel. Willie Keeler, Ty Cobb, Babe Ruth and Willie Mays never batted for the cycle.

USE   The emphasis on this feat has increased in recent years and, as Brooks Robinson has pointed out, many "old timers" may never have heard of it during their playing years. Dave Kingman drove this home when he hit for the cycle as a rookie on April 16, 1972: "When Chris Speier mentioned it to me in the dugout, I didn't know what it meant. I had never done it, and I had never even heard of it." (*San Francisco Examiner,* April 17, 1972; PT)

An odd variation appears in Ron Luciano's *The Umpire Strikes Back.* After asserting that Lou Piniella was the worst base runner of all times, he points out that he did something unequaled in baseball history ". . . he ran for the cycle. In a single game he managed to get himself thrown out at every base." (CDP)

Odder still is the variation that appears in Robert Whiting's *Chrysanthemum and the Bat* when he discusses the impact of American Daryl Spencer on Japanese baseball. In the course of the 1967 season, Spencer takes out a man at first, decommissions a second baseman "with a vicious slide," slides into a third baseman who needs stitches and removes a catcher from "both the play and the game." (CDP)

hit in a pinch   *v.* PINCHHIT.

hit in the slats   *v.* To be hit by a pitched ball.

hitless   *adj.* Describing a team or player without a base hit.

USE   This is usually given in terms of a number of at bats or games.

Hitless Wonders   Nickname given to the early 20th century Chicago White Sox for their ability to win games with light batting. The name got special play in 1906 when the team won the pennant with a team batting average of .228—the weakest of all teams in either league. They went on to win the World Series with an average of only .198. The key was the team's pitching staff, which, among other accomplishments, recorded 32 shutouts during the season.

In *Commy, the Life of Charles A. Comisky,* G. W. Axelson wrote: "In hitting the [White Sox] had, year after year, gradually dropped from .275 in 1901 to .237 in 1905. They had already acquired the title of 'hitless wonders,' but they were rapidly becoming more hitless without being wonders."

1ST   1905. (*Sporting Life,* October 7; EJN)

hit metal   *v.* Said of a batted ball that is misplayed by a fielder; one who is, presumably, playing with an iron glove.

hit off the fists   *v.* Pitch that the batter hits off the handle portion of the bat.

hit one's weight   *v.* To bat poorly; to have a low batting average. Usually phrased negatively, as in, "He's not even hitting his weight."

The phrase links a player's three-digit weight with three-digit batting average and, because most players weigh less than 225 pounds, a player not hitting his weight would not have a very good average.

hit over one's head   *v.* To bat better than expected; to hit over one's average for an earlier period, such as the previous season.

hit safely   *v.* To bat the ball so that it cannot be fielded for an out. A ball that in the opinion of the official scorer should have been fielded for an out, but is not, is considered an error.

"Hit Sign, Win Suit"   Long-famous words on a sign in Ebbets Field; they were put there in 1931 by clothier, politician and Dodger fan Abe Stark. The sign advertised Stark's family clothing store and was a pledge that any player hitting the right-center field sign on the fly would be given a free suit from the store. The sign stayed in place until 1958 when the Dodgers moved to Los Angeles. The first two balls to hit the sign were hit by Mel Ott of the rival Giants.

hitsman   *n./arch.* Batter.

hitsmith   *n.* Term for a good hitter used around the turn of the century.

CHICAGO WHITE SOX

1. ALTROCK
2. DAVIS
3. DOUGHERTY
4. DONAHUE
5. DUNDON
6. JONES
7. ISBELL
8. HAHN
9. McFARLAND

WORLDS CHAMPIONS —1906—

10. O'NEIL
11. OWEN
12. PATTERSON
13. ROHE
14. SULLIVAN
15. TANNEHILL
16. TOWNE
17. WALSH
18. WHITE

Hitless Wonders. The 1906 Chicago White Sox hit only seven home runs and batted a mere .230 as a team. *National Baseball Library, Cooperstown, N.Y.*

1ST   1907. (*New York Evening Journal*, April 5; EJN)

hit straightaway   *v.* To hit the pitch up the middle or to the opposite field rather than pulling it.

hittable   *adj.* Describing a pitcher who is relatively easy to hit against.

hitter   **1.** *n.* Batter.
1ST   1883. (*Sporting Life*, April 15; EJN)
2. *adj.* A means of describing a pitching performance or game in terms of the number of hits allowed; . . . no hitter, 1-hitter, 2-hitter, etc.

hitterish   *adj.* Player or team in the midst of a hitting streak, a term brought into play by Dizzy Dean.

"Hit the Bull"   Motto associated with a scheme, hatched by the makers of Bull Durham tobacco prior to World War I, that awarded a player $50 for hitting their sign. The signs were cutout in the shape of a bull and placed on the outfield fences of as many as 150 major and minor league parks.
1ST   1909. (*Baseball* magazine, June; EJN)
SEE   *bullpen*

hit the corners   *v.* To throw pitches that pass just inside the edges of the strike zone.

hit the dirt   **1.** *v.* For a batter to drop to the ground to avoid getting hit by a pitched ball. Reaction to a duster.
2. *v.* For a base runner to begin his slide into base.
1ST   1908. (*New York Evening Journal*, April 18; EJN)
3. *v.* For a base runner to dive back toward the base he occupies to avoid being picked off.

hitting streak   *n.* A series of games in which a player has gotten at least one hit.

"**Hiya kid.**" Babe Ruth poses with the kids in the bleachers and the local sheriff at Brooks' Field, Scranton, Pa., in 1926. The picture was taken after the World Series, when the Babe was probably barnstorming. *National Baseball Library, Cooperstown, N.Y.*

"**Hiya kid**" Babe Ruth's traditional greeting, used often because of his legendary inability to recall names. There were a few variations. Older men were "Doc" and he sometimes called teammates "Stud."

"**hoe her down**" *n./arch.* An encouragement yelled to a base runner to run fast.
ETY A clear derivation from hoedown, Gerald Cohen found this example in the August 13, 1889, *New York World:* "Ewing stood on the coaching lines with his hat in his hand and his hair standing straight on end. 'Go it, John,' he yelled. 'Hoe her down.' John was 'hoeing her down' for all he was worth."

HOF Common abbreviation for Hall of Fame.

Hogan's brickyard *n./arch.* A rough or stony ballfield. The term may have derived from an early (ca. 1905) comic strip called "Hogan's Alley."

hog tie *v.* To keep the opposition from scoring.

hold **1.** *v.* HOLD A RUNNER.
2. *v.* For a runner to remain at a base when a ball is pitched or hit.
3. *n.* A statistical credit given by some teams to

a relief pitcher who enters a game with his team ahead and doesn't relinquish the lead. The opposite of a hold is a squander.
SEE *Miller-Brown System.*

hold a runner/hold up a runner **1.** *v.* To keep a man on base from taking a large lead. Infielders do their part by staying close to the bag, awaiting a possible pickoff throw from the pitcher. The pitcher keeps his eye on the runner and occasionally throws to the base in question.
1ST 1912. (*American Magazine,* June; EJN)
2. *v.* To prevent a base runner, who is not forced to run, from advancing to the next base during a play. This is usually accomplished by the fielder with the ball either faking a throw toward the runner being held or just looking in his direction.
3. *v.* Signal—usually a coach with his hands held up—for runner telling him not to advance to the next base.

holdout/hold-out *v.* A player who has not come to terms with his team and misses part or all of spring training and, in a few cases, some of the regular season. The player is said to be "holding out" for more money or better terms in his contract. "Clemens Ends 29-Day Holdout." (*Washington Post* headline, April 5, 1987).

In an extreme case, Edd Roush of the New York Giants sat out the entire 1930 season because his team wanted him to take a pay cut after coming off of a .324 season. Traditionally, a player becomes a holdout when he returns his unsigned contract to the team's front office. Babe Ruth had been a holdout on several occasions.
ETY/1ST 1888. In *The Baseball Catalog* Dan Schlossberg reveals this about the term: "First used by the *New York Press* (1888), to describe a player who delayed in accepting salary terms, it caught on when Brooklyn pitcher Tommy Lovett held himself out of the game for the entire 1893 season in a salary dispute." The practice may have predated the term. In *A Baseball Album* Gerald Secor Couzens suggests that the first holdout was Charles Sweeney, second baseman of the Cincinnati Reds. "In the 1869 season he was paid $800 which he thought was insufficient. The following year he held out for $1,000 and didn't report until he was paid that sum."

hole *n.* See *in the hole.*

hole, the   *n.* The space between any two in-fielders but commonly applied to the space to the right of the standard shortstop position. "But with two men out and runners on second and third, he'd go into the hole, backhand the ball, and throw the runner out by a step and a half." (Bill Lee in *The Wrong Stuff;* CDP) Compare to the gap, which is the space between outfielders. Tradition dictates this distinction, although hole is occasionally applied to the space between outfielders.

hole in the bat   *n.* Humorous excuse for a missed swing, as if the ball went right through the bat.
1ST   1908. (*New York Evening Journal,* May 20; EJN)

hole in the glove   *n.* Humorous excuse for a ball that is totally missed by fielder, as if it went through a hole in the glove.

holiday   *n./arch.* A doubleheader.

holler guy   *n.* A coach or player known for his constant chatter and shouts of encouragement.

hollow bat   *n.* A doctored bat; one that has been made lighter by drilling a hole in the thick end, which is then filled with a light material such as cork or sawdust and capped to avoid detection.

Hollywood hop   *n.* A batted ball that takes an easy bounce into a fielder's glove, which presumably makes him look good enough for the movies (Hollywood).

"holy cow!"   Signature phrase of Harry Caray, which was also adopted by New York Yankees broadcaster Phil Rizzuto.
   It achieved a certain notoriety when Rizzuto repeated it several times after Yankee Bucky Dent hit the game-winning home run in the 1978 division playoff against the Boston Red Sox. (At Phil Rizzuto Day at Yankee Stadium, the veverable Yankee shortstop and announcer was presented with a live cow furnished with a gleaming halo!)

home   1. *n.* Short for HOME PLATE.
1ST   1845. (Knickerbocker Rules)
2. *n.* Short for home grounds.
3. *n.* Another way of saying that a player has scored: a hit may bring one home and move another to third.
4. *n.* Short for home team.
5. *n.* A game played on one's home grounds.

home field/home grounds   *n.* Place where the home team plays.

home bagger   *n.* HOME RUN.

home-brew field   *n.* A rough pebble-strewn playing surface; one on which a ground ball takes many unexpected hops. This is a play on "hops" as an ingredient of beer.
1ST   1937. (*Sporting News Record Book;* EJN)

homefield advantage/homefield edge   *n.* The combination of factors that give a team extra help at home ranging from knowledge of the grounds to the enthusiasm of the fans.
   "I don't know why we can't turn playing in Candlestick into the biggest homefield edge in baseball." (San Francisco Giants Manager Roger Craig, quoted in *USA Today,* March 4, 1986)

home game   *n.* A contest a team plays at its own park.

home orchard/home pasture   *n./arch.* HOME FIELD.

home plate   *n.* The base from which one bats and that one must touch in scoring a run. It is the focal point of the game. Physically, it is a five-sided slab of white rubber that is securely set in the ground. It is 17 inches wide at the end facing the pitcher and 17 inches deep. Its width determines the vertical width of the strike zone. The rear end of the plate forms a right angle, which determines the direction of the foul lines.

homer   1. *n.* HOME RUN.
1ST   1891. (*Chicago Herald,* May 5; EJN)
2. *v.* To hit a home run.
3. *n.* A broadcaster or sportwriter or one who shows obvious bias for the home team.
4. *n.* An umpire whose decisions seem to consistently favor the home team.
1ST   1888. (*New York Press,* June 3; EJN)
EXT   The term is used for officials in all major sports and is just as likely to show up in football where it may have come into use earlier. For instance, Peter Tamony found this quote from a football coach in the November 13, 1932, *San Francisco News:* "Referee Arthur Badenock is an out and out 'homer.' He cost Stanford a game and did his best to take the UCLA game away from the Gaels."

homer ball   *n.* HOME RUN BALL.

homer hankie   *n.* An imprinted souvenir handkerchief that achieved visual prominence

Home plate. The sculpture *Play at Home* greets visitors to the Softball Hall of Fame and Museum in Oklahoma City. Its inscription reads, "To all softball players and umpires, worldwide." *Courtesy of the Amateur Softball Association of America*

during the 1987 American League Championship Series and World Series. They were held and waved with vigor by great numbers of Minnesota Twins fans to encourage home runs, hits and rallies. They were dreamed up and sold as a promotional stunt by the local newspaper, the *Star Tribune,* whose name was on each piece of cloth.

homer ratio   *n.* See home run percentage.

home run/homerun   *n.* A four-base hit on which the batter scores. It is usually accomplished by driving the ball out of the playing area but into fair territory. The batter and his team are awarded a run when he has touched all four bases. A ball that does not leave the park but allows the batter to score without the help of an error is an *inside-the-park* home run. A home run causes all the runners on base to score.

The home run provides baseball with much of its excitement and drama. Home runs routinely change the course of a game and are instrumental in putting fans in the seats. The ability to hit the home run has been at the core of the star quality of many greats, including Babe Ruth, Mickey Mantle and Hank Aaron.

There are many slang synonyms for the home run, including homer, circuit clout, four-ply swat, moon shot, rainbow drop, round tripper, and seat-boomer.

ETY   The term also predates baseball in cricket, where it refers to a ball outside the boundaries of the game scoring multiple runs.

EXT   1.   *n.* Applied to big scoring plays in other sports. A spectacular touchdown or a three-point play in basketball may be called a home run. It may even apply to a boxing punch: "He earned it the way a real champ should by blasting home runs with a lethal right that

Home run. Cover to a piece of 1861 sheet music that uses the term to describe a dance.   *Prints and Photographs Division, the Library of Congress*

caused many to compare it with the blockbusters Rocky Marciano used to fell challengers before he retired undefeated." (report of Ingemar Johansson's defeat of Floyd Patterson, *San Francisco Examiner,* June 30, 1959)
2. *n.* The home run has become a common metaphor for an action that has been a clear success. An article that questions the ability of a major corporation to come up with a dramatically new product is headlined: "Does Kodak Have Any Home-Run Hitters?" (WP, Sept. 11, 1986) When Dan Rather defended in court an investigative report on insurance fraud, which had appeared on "60 Minutes," he declared the segment "a home run." (AP, May 31, 1983)
3. *n.* Intermittent teenage slang for sexual intercourse, on a scale of physical involvement that starts at first base. A letter to "Dear Abby" from a teenage girl, which was published in her column on December 31, 1967, ended this way: "So far I've gone only to 'second and third base.' I'm afraid I can't stop myself. Is something wrong?" Abby's answer in part: "If, at age 14, you've gone to 'second and third base' you had better get out of that league or you'll

be known as the 'Home-Run Queen' by the time you're 16."

home run ball   *n.* Pitch that is hit for a home run.
1ST   1937. (*Philadelphia Record,* September 28; EJN)

home run cut   *n.* A very powerful swing in which the batter is obviously swinging for the fences. It is often cautioned against by managers and batting instructors who see it as an ineffective way to get a home run and an effective way to increase strikeouts. For instance, it was reported during the 1986 World Series that New York Mets Manager Davey Johnson had told Len Dykstra to lay off this swing for the duration. (Despite this, Dykstra scored big home runs in both the playoffs and the World Series.)

home run derby   **1.** *n.* Any game in which a large number of home runs are hit by one or both teams.
2. *n.* An exhibition game in which a few sluggers compete to see how many home runs they can hit. In such contests, anything short of a home run is considered an out.

home run in an elevator shaft   Facetious comment reserved for balls hit straight up and especially high. They are usually caught on the fly a few yards from home plate.

home run king   **1.** *n.* Unofficial title for the player in each league with the greatest number of home runs at the end of the season.
2. *n.* The player with the most home runs in the history of the game.

home run percentage   *n.* A statistic that accounts for the number of homers hit per 100 times at bat. The homer ratio is computed by dividing the number of home runs by at bats and multiplying by 100. Babe Ruth's homer ratio was 8.5 while Hank Aaron and Willie Mays both had career ratios of 6.1.

home run pitch   *n.* HOME RUN BALL.

home run trot   *n.* The jog of a batter touching the bases after hitting a home run.

homestand/home stand   *n.* A series of two or more consecutive games played at home. "They entered play Saturday with a nine-game losing streak and had recently finished the franchise's worst homestand in history (0-7)."

(Richard Justice, *The Washington Post,* May 16, 1987)

homestretch/home stretch **1.** *n.* Roughly, the last month of the regular season when teams jockey for their place in the final standings. It is an obvious borrowing from horse racing.
2. *n.* The ninth inning of a given game.
1ST 1881. (*New York Herald,* August 10; EJN)
3. *n.* The path between third base and home plate.

home sweet home team *n./arch.* A team that plays well at home but badly on the road.

home team *n.* The team that hosts a visiting team on its own grounds. By tradition, the home team always bats in the bottom, or second half, of each inning, which gives it the final chance to score.
1ST 1880. (*Brooklyn Daily Eagle,* July 7; EJN)

home turkey *n.* HOME PLATE.

home umpire *n./arch.* Term for what is a HOMER today. "They [the players] at once seek to discover if he is a home umpire. Woe unto him if the players see he has a penchant for favoring the home team." (Billy Evans, "The Ethics of an Umpire," *Pearson's Magazine,* September 1912; PT)

home whites *n.* Traditional uniform worn on a team's home grounds.

hoodoo *n.* An unlucky object, sign, player or anything else about which a player, coach or manager is superstitious. "Cuellar Authority on Whammies and Hoodoos." (headline, *The Sporting News,* August 5, 1972)
ETY Although direct links are hard to find, it seems quite likely that hoodoo is a play on the word voodoo. One link of sorts appears in a *Sporting News* article on superstition (December 26, 1929), which talks of the players and their "versions of voodoo medicine."
USE Although synonymous with jinx, hoodoo seems to have a closer association with the game of baseball, and one is much less likely to hear it applied in other areas. Under the heading "Jinxes and Hoodoos," *The SABR Bulletin* for October 1986 gave a sampling that included spilling coffee, cutting oneself while shaving, picking up the wrong bat, stepping on a base line, seeing a dog on the diamond, having the entire team on the bench at once and chewing gum in the outfield.
1ST 1883. (*Chicago Inter Ocean,* June 26; EJN)

hook **1.** *n.* CURVEBALL, because of its hook-like trajectory.
1ST 1910. (*American* magazine, June; EJN)
2. *n.* The tendency of a manager to remove a pitcher from the game. Some managers with a hook will remove a pitcher at the first sign of trouble while others simply make a lot of pitching changes during the course of the season. Depending on how he removes pitchers, a manager may therefore be said to have a "quick hook" or, if he does it enough, maybe called "Captain Hook" or "Dr. Hook."
3. *n.* The removal of a pitcher who is getting into trouble, usually used in the phrase "to get the hook."
"In case the Mets get hot, they'll go for the hook."—Vin Scully on the situation during the October 19, 1986, World Series game between the Mets and Red Sox.
ETY From the theatrical image of an actor or performer who is so bad that he or she is pulled off the stage by a theater manager with a long pole with a hook on its end. This was reportedly a custom practiced on amateur nights during the age of vaudeville and became a staple sight gag in movie cartoons.

hook arm *n.* LEFT-HANDER.

hooks *n.* Hands, as in a "good pair of hooks" on an adept fielder.

hook slide *n.* A feet first slide during which the runner tucks one leg under his body and uses the other to catch, or hook, the side or one corner of the bag as he passes it. The reason for this is to try to avoid being tagged by giving the defensive player a smaller target.
Also known as the Chicago slide and fallaway slide.
1ST 1906. (*The Independent;* EJN)
ETY It is generally agreed that the hook slide was first perfected by Mike Kelly of the Chicago White Stockings who taught it to other members of his team. Thus it became known as the Chicago slide.
SEE *"Slide, Kelly, Slide"*

hook-worm league *n./obs.* Derisive nickname for spring training played in the southeastern United States, a region with a prevalence for the hook-worm parasite.
1ST 1917. (*American* magazine, July; EJN)

hooter *n.* A particularly noisy fan. "Winning baseball isn't all that's missing at Comiskey Park this season. Each night, Chicago broadcaster

Don Drysdale has his camera scan the stadium looking for 'The Hooter,' the rumpled old man whose howl could be heard all over Comiskey when the White Sox were hitting." (*USA Today*, May 13, 1986)

hoover 1. *n.* A highly adept infielder who sucks up batted balls in the manner of a vacuum cleaner.
2. *n.* A batter adept at hitting successfully with men on base; a base cleaner. Pittsburgh sportscaster Bob Prince would often use the expression "We need a Hoover" when the opposition got men on the bases. In other words, he was calling for a vacuum to clean the bases. Writing about this in *TV Guide* (May 17, 1975), Mel Durslag reported: "The station Prince works for was unhappy. They figured this was a commercial reference Hoover wasn't paying for. Prince started observing, instead, 'We need a J. Edgar.' "

hop 1. *n.* A bounce of a thrown or batted ball. A ball that bounces erratically takes what is commonly called a bad hop, while a bounce that makes it easy for a fielder is called a good hop.
1ST 1908. (*New York Evening Journal*, March 19; EJN)
2. *n.* The jumping motion of an extremely fast pitch.

hop ball *n.* Fictional pitch in the movie and book *It Happens Every Spring*. It was a ball that hopped like "Barnum's flea."

hopper 1. *n.* A batted ball that bounces, often modified as a high hopper, lazy hopper, two-hopper etc.
2. *n.* A fastball that has a hop on it.
1ST 1915. "Courtney missed a hopper, though he·almost fancied his bat lightly touched the whistling ball as it sped past." (From Gilbert Patten's *Courtney of the Center Garden;* DS)

horse-and-buggy league *n.* A minor league in which the teams travel by bus rather than by air or, when the phrase first came into use, by rail.
1ST 1937. (New York *Daily News,* September 5; EJN)

horse collar 1. *n.* See collar. "The Yankees won yesterday, but Joe DiMaggio didn't get a hit. It was his first 'horse collar' in six games." (*San Francisco News,* June 6, 1940)
2. *v.* For a pitcher to hold an opposing team or batter hitless.

1ST 1907. (*New York Evening Journal,* April 25; EJN)
ETY The term derives from the shape of the box-score cipher (0), which resembles the horse collar of a work horse.

horsehide *n.* The BALL itself. Baseballs are covered with horsehide or cowhide.
Horsehide had been the traditional cover for baseballs since the 19th century, but a shortage of quality horsehide in the early 1970s prompted the Baseball Rules Committee to allow cowhide covers along with horsehide. Cowhide balls began showing up in the Major Leagues in 1974.
1ST 1895. (*New York Press,* July 20; EJN)

horseshoes 1. *n./arch.* A lucky catch or stop.
2. A lucky player.
1ST 1915. (Ring Lardner short story called "Horseshoes"; EJN)
ETY Both of these relate to the long-established superstition that horseshoes bring good luck.

hose 1. *n.* A player's throwing arm.
2. *n.* A play on the word socks, which comes into play when, for example, the White Sox become the Pale Hose. In Roger Angell's *The Summer Game,* for instance, hose is used as a synonym for the Red Sox.

hostilities *n.* Play; competition, a term likely to be used during a particularly hard-fought series of games.

hot 1. *adj.* Hard-hit; hard-smashed, as in a "hot grounder," "hot shot" or the archaic "hot balls," which were defined in the baseball glossary in Mrs. John A. Logan's *Home Manual* of 1889 as, "The lightning-like shots thrown or hit to the infielders."
1ST 1869. (*DeWitt's Official Base Ball Guide;* EJN)
2. *adj.* Performing at one's best in the field, on the mound or at the plate.
"He's so hot he could fire a gun up into the air and kill a fish."—Giant outfielder Candy Maldonado on teammate Will Clark, first base, after the pair hit back to back home runs in the bottom of the 9th to beat Houston 6-5 on August 10, 1987, in a critical National League West game. (from researcher Tom Gill)
1ST 1899. (*Frank Merriwell's Double Shot;* EJN)

hot box 1. *n.* Location of a runner caught between two bases and two infielders who are trying to tag him out.
2. *n.* Game in which a runner travels back and

forth between two bases trying to beat the tag. It can be used as a drill for infielding and baserunning.

hot-bread belt   *n./obs.* Term for the Southern spring training area, which was so named, according to E. J. Nichols, from the "association of southern training regions with hot bread."
1ST   1910. (*American* magazine, April; EJN)

hot corner   *n.* THIRD BASE. "The game was nice, too. I liked the whiplash grace of a third baseman's throw from the 'hot corner,' the sharp crack of a line drive rifled into the outfield." (Ted Berkman on "Growing up with the Dodgers," *Christian Science Monitor*, March 10, 1983)
ETY/1ST   1889. It is commonly assumed that the term came about because of the hot shots aimed at the third baseman, but the explanation is not universally accepted. An article on "Baseball Lingo" in the October 1935 issue of *Fan and Family* says: "Third base was so named about 40 years ago when most of the star sluggers were right-handed. Nowadays, however, with so many hard-hitting left-handers, first

base is equally 'hot.' " In his *Baseball Almanac* Hy Turkin traces the term to Cincinnati writer Ren Mulford, who created it during a certain game in 1889 during which third baseman Hick Carpenter, "fielded seven sharp drives that almost tore him apart." Mulford wrote, "The Brooklyns had Old Hick on the hot corner all afternoon and it's a miracle he wasn't murdered."
EXT   Any particularly tough or tight spot.

hot dog   **1.** *n.* Player who calls attention to himself with theatrics; one who plays to the crowd and/or the TV camera; a "showboat" player who grandstands. "A ballplayer who exaggerates his place in the mortal scheme of things," according to Jim Brosnan in *The Long Season.* Defenders of hot dog players have puckishly suggested the term came from the fact that these guys play the game "with relish." **2.** *n.* A traditional food of ballpark denizens.
ETY/1ST   1906. Reportedly, hot dogs were introduced to baseball in 1901 at the Polo Grounds, home of the New York Giants. It seems that concessionaire Harry Stevens was having a hard

Hot dog. Fans load up on hot dogs while waiting for the gates to open at Ebbets Field for the second game of the World Series, October 6, 1920. *Prints and Photographs Division, the Library of Congress*

time selling ice cream and soda in April and so he decided to offer small wursts, which were commonly known as "dachshund" sausages. He had them loaded into tanks and sent his vendors out into the stands chanting, "They're red hot! Get your red hots here!" Research conducted by Peter Tamony suggests that they were first called hot dogs in print and in a humorous context, by sports cartoonist T. A. "Tad" Dorgan in 1915. According to Tamony, the earliest appearance in print was in an article in the *New York Sun* for August 12, 1906, about Coney Island, where they were called "hot dog sandwiches."

hot dogging/hotdogging   *adj.* Playing the game in manner of a hot dog. When asked about his antics on the mound by Richard Justice of the *Washington Post,* Dennis "Oil Can" Boyd replied, "That ain't hot doggin'. That's the way we pitch back home." (July 23, 1986) **ETY**   The term is used in other sports and activities and may first have been applied to acrobatic skiing. In his *Second Browser's Dictionary,* John Ciardi defined it as, "A recently popular form of suicide on skis," and added that it was "perhaps so called by association with festive exuberance; perhaps because the skier is likely enough to end up as dog meat."

hot grounder   *n.* Ball hit along the ground with great speed.

Hot Shot   A commercially-produced protective device that attaches to a baseball glove or catcher's mitt to protect the inside part of a player's wrist. It was invented by Russ Gould of the Portland State University baseball team. When it was introduced in March 1973, Gould told the *Portland Oregonian* that he came up with it after getting hit on the wrist.

hot stove league   *n.* Term for the gab, gossip and debate that takes place during the winter months when baseball is not being played.

It was given added popularity with the publication of Lee Allen's book, *The Hot Stove League.* **ETY**   Quoting from Allen's book: "No one knows when baseball followers first began to gather in winter around the hot stove of a barber shop or country store. Obviously, there has been talk about baseball as long as the game has existed. The phrase, *hot stove league,* is of uncertain origin. Ernest J. Lanigan, historian at the game's Hall of Fame . . . thinks it was almost certainly coined by a sports writer around

the turn of the century, perhaps by Ren Mulford, who covered baseball in Cincinnati and wrote long winter columns about the sport. A glossary of baseball terms published in 1897 does not include it."

However, Peter Tamony assembled information showing that the term predates the turn of the century when it was used to describe the off-season in horse racing. A dispatch from Knoxboro, New York, which appeared in the March 20, 1886, *Spirit of the Times,* contained this line, "The sleighing has gone, and most of the trotting is done around the hot stove at present." And even earlier report in the *Spirit* (March 17, 1877) contained a reference to "stove speed" ascribed to a trotter. It would seem to be a clear reference to a speed imagined during a gathering of the hot stove league.

The general idea is even older. Tamony discovered this quotation from P. T. Barnum's *Struggles and Triumphs,* under "hot stove league": "In nearly every New England village, at the time of which I write [in the 1820s], there could be found from six to twenty social, jolly, story-telling, joke-playing wags and wits, regular originals, who would get together at the tavern or store, and spend their evenings and stormy afternoons in relating anecdotes, describing their various adventures, playing of practical jokes upon each other, and engaging in every project out of which a little fun could be extracted by village wits whose ideas were usually sharpened at brief intervals by a 'treat,' otherwise known as a glass of Santa Cruz rum, old Holland gin or Jamaica spirits." **1ST.**   1912. ". . . O'Day decided to try some of his new material which will win the pennant sometime in February in the Hot Stove League . . ." (*New York Tribune,* September 13; DS)

hot-stover   *n.* Follower of the game who is given to off-season talk of baseball. "Metropolitan hot-stovers believe that Sergeant Joe DiMaggio was on the verge of getting a medical discharge from the Army Air Force because of threatened stomach ulcers, just when the European war situation became grave." (*San Francisco News,* December 25, 1944; PT)

hot stoving   *n.* Rehashing plays, decisions, calls, trades etc. Analogous to Monday morning quarterbacking.

Houdini   *n.* Pitcher with a repertoire of trick pitches and deceptive deliveries.

house dick *n./arch.* A player who spends most of his spare time in the hotel lobby while on the road.

ETY This is a clear allusion to the hotel detective, who has long been known as a house dick in American slang and who also hangs around the hotel. The presumption at work here is that the hotel-bound player might be mistaken for the hotel's detective.

house man *n.* Sportscaster who is unequivocally and relentlessly loyal to the home team. "I called it the way I saw it and that's the reason I'm losing my job. I wouldn't be able to get up and shave my face in the morning without cutting my throat if I became a house man."—Jimmy Piersall, after losing his job as a pregame/postgame show host on a Chicago White Sox cable television program. (*Washington Post,* April 7, 1983)

House of David Nickname given to a number of barnstorming teams whose distinguishing characteristic was that all the players wore long beards. In his article on "Baseball Jargon" (*American Speech,* April 1943) Franklin P. Huddle pointed out that because such teams were likely to have members who had been thrown out of organized baseball, "The beards serve the twin purpose of advertising and disguise." According to Huddle, they were also known as *The Bearded Wonders.* "You got to watch out for the other barnstormers like Max Helverton's Hooley Speedballers and them white teams from Michigan, them House of David boys with the beards," says a character in William Brashler's *The Bingo Long Traveling All-Stars and Motor Kings.*

house pet *n.* Management favorite; "player who sits in manager's lap," according to Burt Dunne (*Folger's Dictionary of Baseball*).

House that Ruth built, The YANKEE STADIUM, so called because of the fame Babe Ruth brought to the Yankees and their ballpark.

Houston Astrodome Home of the National League Houston Astros since their arrival in the city in 1965. The first domed sports arena, it was originally called the Harris County Domed Stadium, and was termed "The Eighth Wonder of the World" by its promoters.

Houston Astrodome. The Texas-sized dome where Astroturf was first introduced. *Courtesy of the Houston Astros*

Houston Astros The name of the National League's Western Division franchise in Houston, Texas. At its inception in 1962, the team was named the Colt 45s, but the Colt Arms Company complained. When the team moved into the brand-new Astrodome in 1964, it sported a new name, the Astronauts, but this was quickly shortened to the Astros.

Houston Colt 45s The first name of the Houston, Texas, National League franchise from the time of their first season in 1962 to 1964, when they became the Astros. Despite their firearms name, almost everybody referred to the team as the Colts.

"How about that!" Comment that followed a home run when Mel Allen was in the broadcast booth.

Hubert H. Humphrey Metrodome Located in Minneapolis, Minnesota, the domed home of the Minnesota Twins since 1982. The name honors the late senator and vice president from Minnesota.

hug 1. *v.* To position oneself very close to a base or a foul line.
1ST 1869. (*DeWitt's Official Base Ball Guide;* EJN)
2. *v.* To stand close to the plate when batting.

human rain delay *n.* Batter who takes a great deal of time preparing to receive each pitch.

humidity dispenser *n./arch.* A particularly waggish synonym for a spit ball.
1ST 1912. (*New York Tribune,* September 22; EJN)

humm-babe A unit of chatter that permeates every level of the game from the schoolyard to the Major Leagues. Roger Craig of the San Francisco Giants used it so much that in the 1987 season *Sports Illustrated* termed it "a cult phrase in San Francisco."
ETY It probably evolved from more articulate chatter along the lines of encouraging the pitcher to "Hum that ball," "Throw the hummer."

hummer 1. *n.* The FASTBALL, named for the whizzing sound it seems to make as it comes across the plate. "At age 59, if that's what he was, Satch had lost the hummer." (Jack Mann, *The Washington Times,* June 10, 1982)
2. *n./obs.* A hard-batted ball.

hump-back liner/humpbacked liner *n.* A batted ball that soars like a line drive then sinks precipitously.
1ST 1938. According to Harwell West's *The Baseball Scrap Book* of 1933 this term got its start in the Southern Association.

humpty-dumpty 1. *n.* A player, often unskilled, who is unpopular or unproven with his teammates.
2. *n.* A substitute. Leo Durocher uses the term in *Nice Guys Finish Last:* "The way it has always been in baseball, the humpty-dumpties, the substitutes, come out early to take their batting and fielding practice, and then the bell rings and the hitting cage belongs to the regulars."

hung him out to dry. *v.* Picked a runner off base.

hunt leather *v./arch.* To try to hit the ball.
1ST 1885. (*Chicago Inter Ocean,* May 3; EJN)

hurl 1. *v.* See *pitch.*
2. *v.* To throw the ball.

hurler *n.* A pitcher.
1ST 1908. (*Baseball* magazine, November; EJN)

hurry the throw *v.* To get rid of the ball as quickly as possible, especially when trying to turn a slow roller, bunt or bobbled ball into an out.

hurt *v.* What an opposing player can do to your chances of winning if he is effective at the plate or on the mound.

hustle *v.* To play aggressively, quickly and alertly. A noted modern player who performs in this manner is Pete Rose who attracted the nickname "Charlie Hustle." New York *Times* sportswriter Ira Berkow has written that it was a derisive nickname at first, but Rose wore it as a "badge of distinction."
ETY Although this has often been described as an Americanism, Peter Tamony showed that it was, in fact, ". . . a term that was employed by English pickpockets from about 1750 on." In a paper he delivered to the International Society for General Semantics on October 19, 1962, he summarized his findings: "Hustle, the English word, has cognates in Dutch and Low and High German, and the import in these languages is 'to shake together, to toss.' In the early 19th century, these older terms came to mean 'to push forward, to impel, to urge, to

move hastily, to hurry, to bustle' . . . 'to work busily,' As hustle and bustle characterized American life and seemed so characteristic of Americans, hustle was up-graded or ameliorated, and became an admired American trait . . . The meaning has persisted in criminal slang, and indicates almost anyone who seems to be getting by without visible means of support—someone with a racket. It has been closely connected with prostitution and pimps and, of course, all kinds of gambling and games of chance."

hustle blister   *n.* STRAWBERRY.

hustle bumps   *n.* "Marks and bruises on a player's body," according to Fresco Thompson in his book *Every Diamond Doesn't Sparkle.*

hustlersville   *n./arch.* Figurative breeding ground of hustlers.
1ST   1891. "Murnane is a hustler from Hustlersville and when there is anything on writing a baseball war, his sensational and newsy stories are looked for and read by all." (*Sporting Times,* November 14; DS)

I

ice cream cone *n.* A ball that is caught in the top of the webbing of a fielder's glove. It is so called because the ball sticks up out of the glove like a scoop of ice cream.

ice down *v.* To use ice or some other cooling agent to soothe and reduce swelling or inflammation, such as icing down a pitcher's throwing arm after coming out of a game. When asked if he did this during his years as a major league pitcher, Warren Spahn answered, "Ice is for mixed drinks." (*Boston Globe,* May 21, 1988)

ice it *v.* To all but assure the final outcome of a game through a hit or defensive play.

ice man *n.* RELIEF PITCHER; one who is able to freeze an opposing team's rally. Interestingly, this is a synonym of fireman.

ice wagon *n./arch.* A slow player, one with the labored movement of an ice wagon.
1ST 1908. (*New York Evening Journal,* May 4; EJN)

IF Standard abbreviation for infield.

"If you're waving at me, howdy." Said to a player who has struck out swinging, according to a September 13, 1982, item in *Sports Illustrated* on the latest in player talk.

"I'll be there" play *n.* A play in which an infielder throws the ball to a place where a teammate *will* be when the ball arrives, such as a catcher throwing to second base with the knowledge that the second baseman or shortstop is on his way to cover the bag.
   "Gedman pulls off an I'll be there play."—Joe Garagiola during the October 27, 1986, World Series game between the Red Sox and Mets.

illegal *adj.* Contrary to the rules of the game.

illegal defense *n.* Concept that primarily exists in a hypothetical sense: "The Twins tried everything short of an illegal defense, but the left-handed Boggs raised his average from .378 to .399 as the Red Sox beat the Twins two-of-three games." (*USA Today,* June 2, 1986, article by Mel Altonen on Wade Boggs)

illegal pitch *n.* A pitch that violates the rules. Specifically, one delivered to the batter by a pitcher who is not in the proper position, namely, his pivot foot is not in contact with the rubber or pitcher's plate; also, when he throws a quick return pitch, a doctored ball or commits a balk, which is an illegal pitch when runners are on base.
   When ruled, it is a balk with anyone on base and a ball if there is nobody on base, provided that the batter does not swing at it. If a batter reaches first base on an illegal pitch, the play counts.

illegally batted ball *n.* A ball hit with either of the batter's feet outside the batter's box. In such cases, the ball is dead and the batter is out. The same is true for a ball that is hit twice, such as one that is popped up in front of the batter and hit again as it comes down. A ball hit with a bat that has been doctored is also deemed to be illegally batted.

illegally caught ball *n.* A ball stopped or caught with a cap, glove or any other part of the player's uniform or equipment that is detached from its proper place. For example, it is illegal for a fielder to throw his glove to stop the progress of a batted ball. Such action results in an automatic triple being awarded the batter.

immortal *n.* See Eleven immortals.

import *n.* A player's wife or girlfriend brought on a road trip.

in **1.** *adv.* Toward the plate, such as an infield that is playing close in anticipation of a bunt or play at home plate.
2. *adv.* Toward the batter, such as a ball that is pitched inside or close to the batter.
3. *adv.* Short for "in the strike zone."
4. *adj.* Across home plate as in "a run is in to tie the score."
5. *n.* The side at bat.
6. *adj.* Participating; he is "in."

in a breeze BREEZE.

in a hole **1.** To be at a distinct disadvantage in a game, such as trailing by five runs in the third inning.
2. To be behind in the count.

in and out play *n.* Game or innings characterized by a quick succession of outs.

incentive/incentive clause *n.* A bonus promised in the contract of a professional baseball player for achieving certain goals and/or honors during the season. A common incentive stipulates that a player will be given a cash bonus if he makes the All-Star team.
"Once upon a time, general managers tossed incentive clauses into contracts because (a) they wanted to get an obnoxious agent out of their office, (b) they thought giving incentives instead of higher base salaries would keep payrolls lower or (c) they figured the incentives wouldn't be met." (Richard Justice, in *The Washington Post*, August 24, 1986)
These incentives can be many and varied. In his 1987 contract with the Oakland A's, Reggie Jackson was given a number, including these:
· $1,000 per plate appearance from his 476th through the 600th.
· .15¢ for each home admission from 1.6 to 1.7 million; .20¢ for each home admission from 1.7 to 1.8 million and .30¢ for each admission over 1.8 million.
· $250,000 if he is named the league's most valuable player, $125,000 for second through fifth in voting, $50,000 for sixth through tenth.

in curve/incurve *n./arch.* A screwball pitch thrown by a right-handed pitcher that curves toward a right-handed batter or a similar left-handed curve to a left-handed batter.
1ST 1901. (*Frank Merriwell's Marvel*; EJN)

Indian sign *n.* A jinx or hoodoo
1ST 1908. (*Baseball* magazine, June; EJN)

indicator *n.* A card or a small mechanical device used by an umpire to keep track of balls, strikes and outs. Some modern indicators have the capacity to display runs scored as well.
"Tom Gorman, the supervisor of National League umpires, says, 'Steve Zabriskie and Ralph Kiner are second-guessing umpires so much, I am going to give them indicators.' " (*Newsday*, June 30, 1986, from a Steve Isaacs piece on announcers and umpires)
1ST 1905. (*Sporting Life*, October 7; EJN)

individual offensive bunt *n.* A bunt batted to get the batter on base rather than one whose purpose is to advance a runner(s) already on base.

Indoor Baseball *n.* The original name for the game from which modern softball derived. Its rules were written by Chicagoan George W. Hancock who was one of the group of young men who created the game, using a boxing glove for a ball and a broomstick for a bat while waiting for the telegraphed results of the Army-Navy football game on Thanksgiving Day, 1887, at the Farragut Boat Club.

Indoor-Outdoor *n.* Second name for the game from which modern softball derived. Less than a year after *Indoor Baseball* was invented, it had caught on to such an extent that by the summer of 1888 it was being played outdoors and some preferred to call it by this name.

indoor team *n.* Any team that plays its home games in a domed or enclosed stadium.

industrial leagues/industrial teams *n.* Generic name for baseball and softball leagues and teams that are sponsored by and named after industrial and commercial enterprises.

infield **1.** *n.* The area on the playing field bounded by the four base lines; the diamond. Since there is no official definition of where the infield actually ends and the outfield begins, we have this second definition:
2. *n.* The same area as above but bounded by the "outside edge" of the base paths.
1ST 1858. (Chadwick Scrapbooks; EJN)
3. *n.* The defensive players assigned to first base, second base, third base and shortstop collectively. Technically, the pitcher and catcher are infielders but generally are not being referred to when a team's infield is being discussed. Collectively, the pitcher and catcher are called the battery.
1ST 1883. (*Sporting Life*, May 27; EJN)

infield chatter *n.* The rhythmic talk of infielders intended to bolster spirit and encourage the pitcher.

infielder *n.* A player defensively positioned on the infield positions of first, second and third base and shortstop.
1ST 1865. (*New York Herald*, July 1; EJN)

infield fly/infield fly rule *n.* A batted ball popped up over the infield, which, deemed

Indoor baseball. From 1897, this may be the earliest known photo of an indoor baseball team.   *Prints and Photographs Division, the Library of Congress*

easily controllable by the umpire, is automatically called for an out even if it is ultimately dropped or missed by the fielder. The rule comes into effect when all of these conditions are met: (1) the fielder must be in a reasonable fielding position, normally, facing the infield; (2) first and second bases or all three bases are occupied; (3) there are fewer than two outs.

The umpire declares the rule is in effect by saying "infield fly" and signals it by raising a clenched fist straight overhead. If the ball is near the base lines, the umpire should yell, "Infield fly, if fair."

The rationale for the infield fly rule is to prevent the defensive player from intentionally dropping the ball, picking it up quickly and forcing the offensive team into a double play. In other words, it removes the force situation, which would cause two runners to be doubled up after an intentional drop.

All base runners advance at their own risk on an infield fly. If a runner is off base and hit by the ball, both the runner and the batter are out. However, if the runner is on the base and

is hit by the ball, only the batter is out. In either case the ball is dead.

1ST   1909. (*American* magazine, May; EJN)

infield hit   *n.* Any hit that does not escape the infield but allows the batter time to reach first base safely. Such hits must be either hit slow enough or placed well enough to allow the batter to outrun the eventual throw to first base.

infielding   *n.* Infield defensive play.

infield out   *n.* An out made on a ball hit within the infield.

infield roller   *n.* A ball that is batted onto the infield grass (or turf). It tends to roll slowly and can therefore present a challenge to the defense.

infield up   *adj.* Describing the situation in which the infield positions itself closer to home in anticipation of a play at the plate. The infield usually plays up when a man on third base is advancing to home.

Industrial Leagues. Great numbers of baseball and softball teams are sponsored by industrial or commercial firms. These 1986 softball champs represent Tire Centers of Richmond, Virginia.   *Courtesy of the United States Slo-Pitch Softball Association*

in flight   *adj.* A batted, thrown or pitched ball that has not yet hit the ground or been touched by a fielder.

in his kitchen   See kitchen.

I-95 Series   Nickname for the 1983 World Series that pitted the Philadelphia Phillies against the Baltimore Orioles, their two cities linked by Interstate 95.

initial bag/initial corner/initial cushion/ initial sack   *n.* First base. These terms were popular from the late 1880s until about 1910.

in jeopardy   *n.* State of an offensive player who, while the ball is in play, is in a position to be put out.

injured reserve   *n.* Status of a player who, not playing because of an injury or illness, can return to the team at any point because he has not been permanently replaced on the roster. During his time on the injured reserve list, he can be temporarily replaced.

ink   *v.* To put one's signature to, as in a contract or other legal document. "One might be tempted to wonder, given this mythic rise, if Ripken hasn't also inked a contract with the devil: Shoeless Joe Hardy in a Baltimore reprise of 'Damn Yankees.' " (*The Washington Post*, April 1, 1984, article by Paul Hendrickson on Cal Ripken, Jr.)
USE   This term of self-conscious sports talk is beloved of sportswriters, just as "hoop tilt" is for a basketball game.

inner game   *n.* The strategy and tactics of the game as they relate to such things as batting order, defensive positioning and the use of pinch hitters.

inner garden.   *n./arch.* The infield, as opposed to the outfield, which is the outer garden.
1ST   1907. (*New York Evening Journal*, May 24; EJN)

inner works   **1.** *n./arch.* The area in which the infielders play.
2. *n./arch.* The infielders as a working unit.
1ST   1908. In his glossary John B. Foster used it in context: ". . . the inner works held together well."

inning   1. *n.* That portion of a game within which the two teams alternate defense and offense and during which there are three outs for each team.
2. *n.* In referring to the work of a pitcher, inning (sometimes stated as half inning) refers to the opposition's time at bat. This can be expressed in fractions with each out counting as one third of an inning. Statistically, a starting pitcher removed with one out in the seventh inning is credited with working 6⅓ innings.
ETY   The term was used in its modern sense in the rules of the original Knickerbocker Club in 1854, but not in the first 1845 set of rules. Inning was borrowed directly from cricket, a sport in which the team at bat is "in" and the one on the field is "out." A time at bat—an at bat—in an inning. British writers taking a crack at writing about baseball will initially refer to an inning as innings.
EXT   1. *n.* A opportunity or chances; to have had one's inning or innings. It is hard to tell whether or not the American use of the word inning outside of baseball is a product of baseball or cricket. It may well be cricket. In *Words and Idioms*, Logan Pearsall Smith listed "to have one's innings" as a borrowing from cricket. Other cricketisms on Smith's list :

to be bowled over	to catch up
to be bowled out	to stop the rot
to keep one's end up	to score heavily
to back up	it isn't cricket

2. *n.* A period of play in other sports and games; for instance, a bowling frame (one bowler's turn) is also called an inning.

in order   *adv.* The retirement of the first three batters in an inning, as in, "The team goes down in order."

in play   *adj.* Describing a ball that is still live, when runners can advance or be put out and runs can score; of that time when the game is being played as opposed to periods when plays cannot begin or continue. The ball is in play until it is ruled dead by the umpire, time out is called or a third out is made. A ball is put back in play only after it is in the hands of the pitcher in position and the home plate umpire has called "Play!"

inshoot/in-shoot   *n.* A curveball that curves toward the batter. The fictional Frank Merriwell, hero of such books as *Frank Merriwell's Double Shot* and *Frank Merriwell's Schooldays*, had a super inshoot which he called his "double shoot." See screwball.
Although the term is now seldom used in baseball, it is still a very common term in softball where it refers to an underhanded curve that heads in toward the batter.
1ST   1881. (*New York Herald*, July 13; EJN)

inside   *adj.* A pitched ball that comes between the batter and the strike zone; one that may intimidate. Jimmy Cannon once facetiously defined it as, "A bean ball thrown by your own team's pitcher."
During a 1986 World Series broadcast Vin Scully said that the best story to come out of that year's spring training involved a pitching coach telling a rookie pitcher that he would have to learn to pitch inside. The pitcher's response: "Have I been traded to Houston?"

inside baseball/the inside game/inside work   *n.* Smart strategic baseball involving the use of good teamwork and such techniques as stealing and sacrificing. John B. Foster said of it in his 1908 glossary: ". . . a much abused expression to denote clever team work much of which is the result of a vivid imagination."
1ST   1902 (inside ball). (*Sporting Life*, April 26; EJN)
EXT   In his *New York Times* column of June 19, 1988, William Safire explores the term's new "political or professional denotation," which he defines as "minutiae savored by the cognoscenti, delicious details, nuances discussed and dissected by aficionados." Safire gives a number of examples of the term in use outside baseball, including this line from Richard Weiner, chairman of the Michigan Democratic Party: "The people in my state are interested in jobs, the economy and education. The rest is inside baseball." The earliest example mentioned by Safire was in 1978 by Senator Edward M. Kennedy in a letter quoted by Myra MacPherson of the *Washington Post;* Kennedy speaks of a legislator who "chairs endlessly boring hearings . . . then cuts through testimony with inside baseball jokes that no visitors understand but laugh at anyway."

inside corner   *n.* The corner of the strike zone that is on the batter's side of the plate.
1ST   1896. (*Frank Merriwell's Schooldays;* EJN)

inside hitter   *n.* A batter who is good at hitting balls thrown close (inside) to him.
1ST   1932. (*Baseball* magazine, October; EJN)

inside-out swing *n.* A swing in which the batter's hands move ahead of the barrel of the bat so that when contact is made the ball tends to head toward the opposite field.

inside pivot *n.* A defensive maneuver in which—to turn a double play—the shortstop or second baseman receives the ball and then tags second base as he relays the ball to first base.

inside-the-park home run *n.* A hit on which the batter scores a home run with the ball not leaving the field of play.

Boog Powell of the Baltimore Orioles holds the distinction of being the heaviest batter to hit an inside-the-park home run. The homer in question was hit on August 16, 1969 in the 9th inning of a game against Seattle, according to writer and baseball historian L. Robert Davids of Washington, D.C., at a point when Powell weighed about 250 pounds. Powell was also the first player to play in both the Little League World Series (for Lakeland, Florida) and the Major League World Series (for the Baltimore Orioles.)

inspect the ball *v.* For an umpire to examine the ball to see if it is fit for continued play. This is commonly done after a batted ball is returned to the pitcher or if a ball is thrown in the dirt. If the ball is nicked, badly scuffed or has pulled stitches it is taken out of play. A ball may also be inspected if there is suspicion that it has been doctored.

instructional league *n.* A special league for the youngest and least experienced professional players.

insurance **1.** *n.* The addition of runs to an existing lead to create a lead that the opposition will probably not be able to surmount.
2. *adj.* Applied to good player who does not start but can be called on to do a good job of filling in for a regular.
3. *n.* DEPTH. A pool of capable reserve players.

insurance run. *n.* Any run that is made by a team already ahead in a game.

intensity. *n.* Modern term for a player or team with concentration and determination. "This year, I'm feeling good. I have that intensity again and that hunger." (Tom Herr, quoted in the *St. Petersburg Times*, March 27, 1987)

intentional pass/intentional walk *n.* Walking a batter on purpose by deliberately throwing four balls outside the strike zone; almost always a decision made by the manager. This action is usually taken for one of three reasons: (1) to avoid pitching to a particularly good or hot hitter; (2) to get to a right-handed batter if the pitcher is right-handed or to get to a left-handed batter if the pitcher is left-handed; (3) to fill first base if it is unoccupied, with runners on second and/or third setting up a force situation to enhance the chance for a double play.

A batter cannot legally hit a ball if he is outside the batter's box, so there is no chance of one of these balls being hit unless the pitcher accidentally throws it in or close to the strike zone. Dizzy Dean on this subject: "I never did like to give an intentional pass. I always figured that I was just about as good as the hitter comin up there and I figgered that I could get anybody out and I hated to put those men on base because when you put them on there, they are not in the dugout and that's where I would rather have them settin." Compare this to the bewildering definition given by a British fan after first seeing the 1986 World Series, which was telecast on Britain's Channel 4: "That means he's deliberately given unplayable to force him to settle for a first-base advance." (*New York Times*, October 27, 1986)
1ST 1898. (*New York Tribune*, April 24; EJN)

intercept *v.* To make the cut-off.

interference *n.* Hindering the course of play. Generally it refers to an action that impedes a player on the opposing team, although umpires, coaches, managers and spectators can be responsible. For instance, interference is called if an umpire is hit by a batted ball or if a fan reaches out of the stands to touch a live ball. The *Official Baseball Rules* breaks interference down into four categories: defensive, offensive, umpire's and spectator's. It adds, "On any interference the ball is dead."

Penalties are awarded in some cases. If a runner interferes with a fielder trying to make a play, the runner is out.

Compare with *obstruction*.

interference at first base *n.* Specific case of interference in which the runner collides with the first baseman. If it occurs with the first baseman receiving the throw in fair territory, the runner is out. If the collision occurs in foul territory, however, the runner is given first base.

interim manager *n.* Individual picked to fill a team's managerial position on a short-term basis while a long-term, permanent manager is being sought. An interim manager is usually hired from the ranks of a team's coaching staff when the manager is fired during the course of a season.

interleague play *n.* Game between teams in different leagues. Major league interleague play is restricted to exhibition games, the All-Star game and the World Series.

intermission *n.* The period between games of a double-header, usually 20 minutes.

International League Triple-A-level minor league, with franchises on the eastern seaboard and Ohio. As of this writing the teams were the Columbus Yankees, Pawtucket Red Sox, Richmond Braves, Rochester Red Wings, Syracuse Chiefs, Tidewater (Virginia) Tides, Toledo Mud Hens and Maine Guides.

International Softball Congress Federation of men's fast pitch softball teams based in Anaheim Hills, California. Founded in 1946 in a merger of the International Softball League and the National Softball Congress.

intestinal fortitude *n* Courage; guts. Created as a gentle way of saying guts. This euphemistic way of saying "guts" may not have started in baseball, but it has commonly been used to describe individual action in baseball.

in the bag *adj.* Safely won.

in the field *adj.* To be in defensive position.

in the groove **1.** *adj.* A pitch through the center of the strike zone; one that is easy to hit. **1ST** 1912. (*New York Tribune,* October 6; EJN) **2.** *adj.* Describing a player who is consistently performing well. **3.** *adj.* Describing a team that is winning a high percentage of its games.

in the hole **1.** *adj.* Describing the player on the batting team who, waiting in the dugout, is next to enter the *on deck circle;* the third player in the sequence of "at bat, on deck and in the hole." **ETY** See at bat, on deck, in the hold, for the etymology of "in the hole." **USE** From the nautical hold, which, according

to Joanna Carver Colcord in her book *Sea Language Comes Ashore,* was originally "hole" and became "hold" through what she terms "a mistaken etymology." Baseball turned it back to hole, although the common nautical pronunciation of hold is hole. **2.** *adj.* Said of a batter when behind in the count, or of a pitcher when behind in the count (behind by at least two pitches: 2-0, 3-0, 3-0). **3.** *adj.* Any gap between two fielders, but it is most commonly applied to the area deep and to the right of the shortstop's normal position. For the shortstop (or the second baseman) to go in the hole, field the ball and throw the runner out is considered to be one of the finer and more difficult defense plays in the game.

in the soup *adj.* In trouble, at a disadvantage.

in the well *adj.* Describing a fly ball hit to an adept outfielder.

intra-squad game *n.* A game played between members of the same team; commonly played during the early days of spring training.

invisible man *n./arch.* Sportswriter, but only when things are going well for the team and nothing negative is being written.

IP Standard abbreviation for innings pitched.

iron arm *n.* Limb attached to a pitcher who is able to pitch effectively for long periods of time.

iron armed pitcher *n.* Mechanical pitching machine; IRON MIKE.

iron bat *n.* A batter who is able to hit the ball consistently for distance is said to wield one of these.

iron doughnut *n.* DOUGHNUT.

iron glove *n.* Sloppy fielding; prone to errors. "All-iron glove team." (*USA Today* headline for a June 6, 1986, list of leading errormakers) Charlie Hough has been widely quoted on Texas Ranger teammate Pete Incaviglia: "He has a glove contract with U.S. Steel."

iron man **1.** *n.* A pitcher who works without seeming to tire or lose concentration. The "iron" in this case refers to the durability of a pitcher who can pitch as often as the needs of the rotation dictate.

In *Ball Four,* Jim Bouton says that the proper

Iron man. Joseph McGinnity.   *National Baseball Library, Cooperstown, N.Y.*

form of address for a player so gifted is, "Give me some steel, baby."

2. *n./obs.* A pitcher who pitches two complete games back to back. "Iron Man" Joe McGinnity of the New York Giants was one of the first players to earn the nickname. On three occasions in one month during the 1903 season he won both games of a doubleheader. McGinnity wore the title well as evidenced by a headline from the *Police Gazette* in the mid-1920s: " 'Iron Man' McGinnity Still Pitching at Fifty-Four." McGinnity was part owner and manager of the Dubuque, Iowa, club of the Mississippi Valley League but also part of the regular pitching rotation.

3. *n.* Any player who is tough, not easily injured and seldom, if ever, misses a game. "The Iron Man" and "The Iron Horse" were two of Lou Gehrig's nicknames earned while playing 2,130

consecutive games. "Ironman HoJo gets a day off." (New York *Daily News* headline, August 13, 1987)

4. *n./arch.* The price of admission.

ETY   Joseph McBride points out in *High and Inside*, "Silver dollars were once called 'iron men,' and $1 was formerly a common price for a general-admission ticket." The term showed up often in T. A. Dorgan's cartoons: "You know papa left me two million iron men and I must spend it some way." (*San Francisco Examiner,* August 22, 1911; PT)

iron mike   *n.* Generic name for all mechanized pitching devices used in batting practice.

Although mechanical pitching devices have been in existence since the late 19th century, it was not until the Brooklyn Dodgers used one in their spring training camp just after World War II that they became accepted. They are as fast as their warm-blooded counterparts and have improved over the years, but they still lack the cleverness and deceptive ability of humans.

ETY/1ST   1950. In the April 17 issue of *Time* there is an article about a highly publicized game between Wake Forest and North Carolina entitled "Iron Mike." In the game both teams batted against the machine. "Wake Forest College, which calls its apparatus 'Iron Mike' got eleven hits (three of them homers), and waited out Iron Mike for two walks."

irregulars   **1.** *n.* Generic name for a ragtag team of amateur baseball or softball players put together to play a team that regularly plays together. They are often given special compensatory opportunities to score. An item in the company newsletter of the Foster Manufacturing Co. of Wilton, Maine, tells of a formula for Irregular scoring that: ". . . allows 7 runs for each run scored by a player over 35 years of age, and 7½ runs for each run scored by a player 35 years old who is also overweight 35 or more pounds." (September 1972)

2. *n.* Players who are normally found on the bench; those who are not regular starters.

I-70 Series   The 1985 all-Missouri World Series between the St. Louis Cardinals and the Kansas City Royals, their two cities linked by Interstate 70.

issue a pass   *v.* To walk a batter.

"It ain't over, 'til it's over"   Aphorism that summarizes baseball's ability to go down to the last moment of play. It is also Yogi Berra's most famous line, which has become a baseball axiom. "Yogi's line gets better and better," was the reaction of John McNamara to the late-inning heroics on display during the 1986 AL playoffs. (*Cleveland Plain Dealer*, October 16, 1986)

EXT   Widely applied to the world at large.

"it's only a game"   Ritualized reassurance to those who have lost a game that it is, in fact, not the end of the world. It is commonly given to youngsters. It is deemed a "famous speech by parents in a station wagon on way home" by Marian Edelman Borden in her article, "Terms for Parents of Little Leaguers."

ivory   **1.** *n.* One or more skilled ball players who are considered a valuable commodity.

"Cuba which long has developed 'ivory' for the American market, has splendid representatives in Conrado Marrero, Sandy Consuegra and Minnie Minoso." (Fred G. Lieb, "Baseball—the UN that Belongs to Us," *Baseball Magazine*, August 1953)

1ST   1913. "IVORY—A natural growth found in the bush league jungle, and polished up in the major league." (definition by J. E. Sherwood, *Baseball* magazine, September)

2. *n.* A high-priced rookie.

USE   The link between the hard, white matter and baseball players is that both are valuable commodities.

ivory-headed   *adj./arch.* Dumb. As recently as 1947, one guide (*New Baseball Rules and Decisions* by Martin Rothan) explained that this was said of "a player who doesn't act quick, makes the wrong play, does not use his brains . . ."

ETY   One is hard pressed to find a connection between ivory and dumbness; however, pure conjecture might link this use of the term to the denseness of ivory.

ivory tip/ivory top   *n./arch.* A dumb player or person.

Ivory tops and ivory tips were equally dumb. "To be dubbed a bonehead in a fashionable New York club, one has to have an ivory-tip of surpassing solidity." (*Munsey's Magazine*, July 1913; PT)

ivory hunter   *n.* SCOUT. "The baseball scouts, who call themselves ivory hunters, met the other night . . . to honor John J. (Patty) Cottrell voted Pro Scout of the Year." (Art Rosenbaum, *San Francisco Chronicle*, February 15, 1974; PT)

1ST   1915 "You'll pick up diamond tiaras just about as often as you will pitchers who are undiscovered wonders. Any ivory hunter will tell you that." (Gilbert Patten, *Covering the Look-in Corner*; DS)

EXT   Archaic student slang for a corporate recruiter who visits college campuses.

IW   Standard scorecard abbreviation for intentional walk.

J

jab *v.* To hit the ball for a short distance.
1ST 1920. (*Spalding's Official Base Ball Guide;* EJN)

jack/jack one *v.* To hit a ball a great distance.

jack a pitcher *v.* For a manager to remove a pitcher from the game.
1ST 1931. (*New York World,* February 25; EJN)

Jackie Robinson Award Since 1987, the official name for the Rookie of the Year Award, named for the man who was the first Rookie of the Year (1947).

Jack Murphy Stadium Located in San Diego, California, the home grounds of the National League San Diego Padres. It was named for the late Jack Murphy, sports editor of the *San Diego Union,* who had been instrumental in getting the city both the Padres and the football San Diego Chargers. The official name of the ballpark is the San Diego/Jack Murphy Stadium, but it is seldom addressed by its full name.

jackpot *n.* See *grand slam.*

jackrabbit **1.** *n.* Baseball that seems to carry farther than most regular balls. The term comes back into use every time the number of home runs hit rises dramatically, prompting calls of a "lively" ball: "Rumors go the rounds that the manufacturers are still experimenting with the ball in hope of eliminating much of the jackrabbit." (*New York Press,* January 28, 1931) In a reference to the liveliness of the balls, Bobby Cox, Atlanta GM, was quoted in the *New York Post,* June 29, 1987: "I was watching the game on TV the other day and it was amazing the way the Cardinal outfielders were running out there. Jackrabbits. Jackrabbits all over the place." **2.** *n.* A speedy ballplayer.
1ST 1912. (*New York Tribune,* September 11; EJN)

jake/jaker **1.** *v.* To loaf or to stall.
2. *n.* Player who is often out of the lineup because of a real or imagined ailment; player

Jaker. Managers Garland "Jake" Stahl of the Red Sox (left) and John McGraw of the Giants pose for the traditional handshake before the 1912 World Series. *National Baseball Library, Cooperstown, N.Y.*

who will not exert himself; one given to loafing or stalling.
USE A serious charge. "Do you want to know what they were saying about James Rodney [J.R.] Richard even three days ago?" wrote Art Spander in the *San Francisco Examiner* after Richard was found to have a potentially fatal blood clot. "They were saying that he was 'jacking,' that he could have played but didn't want to, that he was letting down his teammates." (August 1, 1980; PT)
1ST 1927. "The conversation of players is studded with slang expressions of their own coining and, for the most part, unfamiliar even to close followers of the game. The term 'jake' applied by Combs to Lazzeri, means one who stalls, and the derivation of it is the name of the one-time first-baseman of the Red Sox, Jake Stahl."—*New York Sun,* July 18, 1927, Frank

Graham's "Talking about Baseball" column. Graham also recorded the Combs-Lazzeri conversation in which he heard it:

"'I never thought you'd be a 'jake,'" remarked Combs.

"'I'm not a 'jake,'" replied Lazzeri. 'Hug just told me Koenig was going to play shortstop and Morehart second base. What could I do?'")

ETY As already stated, the term derives from Garland "Jake" Stahl who caught, played first and managed American League teams from 1903 through 1913. There is universal agreement on this point; however, there is some dispute as to why. One theory, favored by the *Sporting News,* Hy Turkin and others, says that Stahl was an aggressive player with a lot of hustle whose trip to eponymity came about because his name was pronounced "stall." Thomas P. Shea in his book of baseball names insists that when Stahl played for the Red Sox he refused to play first base because of a bad foot and that is where the loafing connection was made.

jam 1. *n.* A difficult situation. Usually it is said that a pitcher is "in" a jam when the opposing team is in a position to score.
2. *v.* JAM THE BATTER.
3. *n./arch.* RALLY. According to the glossary of baseball terms in the *Giant Book of Sports* (1948), "When the 'jam is on,' a rally is under way."

jammer *n.* A fastball on the fists; a fastball or slider that moves in on the batter.

jam shot *n.* Brushback or knockdown pitch.

jam the bases *v.* Load the bases.

jam the batter *v.* To throw the ball close to the batter making it hard for him to hit successfully, and keeping him off balance; to throw inside. The intention is not to hit the batter, but rather make him a lot less effective by forcing him to hit with the lower end of his bat.

Japanese liner *n./arch.* Term for a TEXAS LEAGUER in the Pacific Coast League.

jar one/jar the pitcher *v.* To bat a ball hard.
1ST 1908. (*Baseball* magazine, December; EJN)

Jarry Park/Parc Jarry Located in Montreal, the capital of the Canadian province of Quebec; the original home of the Montreal Expos. Situated on Rue Jarry, the ballpark housed the Expos from 1969 to 1976.

Jawn Titus *n./arch.* A spectacular catch; CIRCUS CATCH.
1ST 1917. (*American* magazine, 1917; EJN)
ETY Edward J. Nichols said of this term, "Derivation uncertain, but may refer to a player named [John] Titus, who was once a Philadelphia National League player and who may have been known for making sensational catches."

jaw the ump *v.* To argue with the umpire over a call.
1ST 1898. (*New York Tribune,* June 16; EJN)

jay *n./arch.* Derogatory term for an amateur player.

jeep *n./arch.* Small, fast player in the immediate post-World War II era.

jellyball *n.* GREASE BALL.

jelly bean *n./arch.* Raw recruit.

jerk a pitcher *v.* JACK A PITCHER.

jersey *n.* A long-sleeved pullover that may be worn under a player's uniform shirt.

Jesse James *n.* A player's term for UMPIRE, because of what he robs from them. Before there were three umpires for each game, it was common to refer to the two umps as "Jesse and Frank" or "the James Brothers."

Jesse James single *n.* Hit that is allowed when a batted ball hits the umpire.

Jim Dandy *n.* A admirable person, thing or feat; a prime example.
1ST 1887. The term, which the Oxford English Dictionary traces back to 1887 (in a non-baseball context), shows up quickly in baseball writing. In fact, Gerald Cohen has written that his work on the baseball columns of the *New York World* ". . . provides the startling indication that *jim-dandy* either arose in baseball speech or was spread into standard English by it." His earliest published example from the June 19, 1887, *World:* "The Giants gave the local patrons of the game a couple of surprises during the past week, and whereas on Wednesday night they were proclaimed 'Jim Dandy' players, they were on Thursday declared to be 'no good.'"

jineger/jinnegar *n./arch.* Vigor. May have derived from ginger, vinegar or combination of the two.

Jints *n.* Colloquialism for the Giants when they were in New York City. To call the Giants the Jints was to use a friendly nickname, akin to calling the Brooklyn Dodgers "Dem Bums."

jinx   1. *n.* A run of bad luck.
2. *v.* To create bad luck. "Most of them think a change in hotels would surely 'jinx' or hoodoo them." ("Big League Superstitions," *Literary Digest,* May 9, 1914; PT)
This is a 20th-century word that was so strongly associated with the game of baseball that it appears as baseball slang—rather than general slang—as late as 1927 (so identified by V. Samuels in *American Speech,* February 1927). In 1908 John B. Foster defined it as "another name for a ball player's superstitious ideas."
ETY/1ST   1912. Alfred H. Holt came up with an explanation in his 1936 *Phrase and Word Origins* that links the use of the term in baseball (the *Oxford English Dictionary* cites a 1912 usage by Christy Mathewson) for "a hoodoo of some sort" and the wrynecked woodpecker or *jynx,* which was associated with charms and spells; according to Holt "that particular bird was sometimes used to cast charms." In his *Why You Say It,* Webb Garrison tells more of the bird: "Medieval scholars considered it to have special links with occult forces. So jynx feathers were widely used in making 'philtres, allurements, baits and enticements' for the lovelorn. Jumping the Atlantic, the name of the wizard's bird [of preference] became linked with voodoo and other forms of black magic—hence, any symbol of bad luck is known as a jinx."
EXT   Bad luck in all realms.

jock   1. *n.* Term for an athlete, short for jockstrap.
2. *v.* To overpower. "We were getting jocked, and by the sixth inning, I realized that we were going through an awful lot of pitchers." (Bill Lee, *The Wrong Stuff;* CDP)

jockey   1. *n.* A player who bedevils or "rides" the opposition. Sometimes called a bench jockey because the heckler often comes from the dugout where he also rides the bench or the pine. Defined by William Morris in his 1957 *It's Easy to Increase Your Vocabulary* as, "A loud voiced, often sharp-witted player who continuously ridicules the opposing players with well-timed references to their real or supposed inadequacies of antecedents."
2. *v.* To heckle the opposition and/or the umpires. A report on an amateur game that ended in a brawl contained this telling line: "But wild-

ness occasioned by constant jockeying from the Portola bench, provided Gentile's downfall." (*San Francisco Examiner,* January 20, 1951; PT)
1ST   1927. (*New York Sun,* July 18; EJN)
ETY   An obvious and neat play on the word "ride," a point that is made in explanations of the term when it was still new. For example, Frank J. Frisch writing about "The Gas House Gang" in the June 4, 1936, *Saturday Evening Post:* "It was bitterly fought and there was much jockeying between the benches. A jockey is a player who verbally rides the opposition from the dugout, and we had some great ones on our side."

jockstrap   *n.* See athletic supporter.
1ST   1919. "You can enjoy perfect comfort and freedom. Schnoter's Suspensories and Jock Straps have gained their widespread popularity by quality, wear, fit and low price. (*The Billboard,* Cincinnati, December 20; PT)

jock-strap sniffing   *n.* Derogatory term for a sportswriter's quest for a story or good quote on an otherwise slow day. In *The Jocks,* Leonard Shecter says it refers to the fact that some sportswriters "must go to the clubhouse and elicit clever quotes from dull men." (CDP)

Joe Bush   *n.* A college ballplayer, especially one who shows his lack of experience.

joe college   *n.* An individual who typifies the enthusiasm of collegiate athletics.
ETY   In his 1932 *American Speech* article on college slang ("Johns Hopkins Jargon"), J. L. Kuethe wrote that "joe" was a "term used to designate anyone whose real name is unknown. When used with a place or profession 'Joe' indicates a perfect example of the type connected with that place or profession. Thus 'Joe College' is the perfect specimen of the college man." (June)

Joe Cronin Award   Annual award for "distinguished achievement" by an American League player.

Joe Quote   *n.* Player who talks a lot, especially to the press; a motormouth.

john anderson, a/John Anderson   *n.* Term for the particular boner committed when a runner attempts to steal an occupied base. It has been passed down from John Anderson who, while playing for the New York Highlanders in 1904, pulled a john anderson with the bases loaded.

Joe College. Two members of the Princeton University baseball team of 1901. *Prints and Phtoographs Division, the Library of Congress*

John Anderson. John Joseph Anderson as he looked in 1916. *National Baseball Library, Cooperstown, N.Y.*

John fan *n./arch.* Typical male enthusiast.

Johnson & Johnson **1.** *n.* Name for a player who commonly has adhesive tape showing.
2. *n.* Player who is accident prone or easily hurt.
1ST 1937. (New York *Daily News*, September 5; EJN)
ETY Named for the manufacturer of bandages and surgical dressings.

Jonah *n.* This word had great significance in the baseball world of the 1880s and 1890s according to research conducted by Gerald Cohen and published in the April 1, 1986, *Comments on Etymology.* Cohen found three variations:
1. *v./arch.* To bring bad luck. "It is a well-known fact that a cross-eyed man will Jonah the squarest ballgame that was ever played." (*The World*, August 28, 1888)
2. *n./arch.* One who brings bad luck. In one of the examples collected by Cohen, the Jonahs

are a group of beautiful women who rattle the players on the field.

3. *n./arch.* One who suffers bad luck.

EXT   This is a reference to the Jonah of the Bible who, before he was thrown to the whale that devoured him, had brought the wrath of God down on his ship. The term has had a long history in nautical talk. In *Salty Words* Robert Hendrickson noted, "A *Jonah* still means a bringer of bad luck who spoils the plans of others. The phrase is so popular that it has even become a verb, 'Don't jonah me!' "

jonrun   *n.* Home run. See pochismo.

journey   *n.* A baseball game.

journeyman   *n.* A veteran ballplayer who is reliable but not a star; consistent rather than colorful. Because it contains the word journey, it is often applied to those who have played for several clubs.

joy spot/joy zone   *n.* The best part of the bat with which to hit the ball; the "sweet spot."

judy   *n.* PUNCH HITTER, a play on "punch and judy."

jug/jughandle/jug   handle/jug   handle curve   *n.* A curve with a big break; a broad arc.
ETY/1ST   1920. Edward J. Nichols reports: "The term was given as a nickname to John Morrison, Pittsburgh National League Club pitcher in 1920–1921, because of his sharp-breaking curve." (Nichols' sources were the October 1932 *Baseball Magazine* and the August 4, 1937, *Pittsburgh Post Gazette*.)

juggle   *v.* To mishandle a batted or thrown ball. While a fielder may juggle a ball without dropping it, the act may consume enough time to allow a runner to be safe who otherwise would not have been.
1ST   1873. (*New York Herald*, September 13; EJN)

jugs gun   *n.* Radar device used to measure the velocity of a pitcher's delivery.

juice   *v.* To hit the ball with great power for distance; to crush the ball.

juice ball/juiced ball   *n.* Ball with extra carrying power; jackrabbit ball.

jump   1.   *n.* A base runner's lead, such as getting a good jump on the pitcher; his first step.
2. *n.* The move that a fielder makes toward the

Jughandle. John Dewey Morrison who was also known as "Jughandle Johnny." *National Baseball Library, Cooperstown, N.Y.*

ball on the crack of the bat. A bad fielder is often said to have a poor or lousy jump.
3. *v.* For a batted ball to take off with an extra spurt. "I know the way the ball can jump off my bat. Seems like one at-bat I'll have it, and the next two or three it might be gone." (Jack Clark quoted in the *St. Louis Post-Dispatch*, May 29, 1987)
4. *n.* The hopping motion on a good fastball as it crosses the plate.
5. *v.* To leave the team without permission.
6. *v./arch.* To break one's contract. In the early days of this century such players were labeled "contract jumpers."

jumper   *n.* A player who has left a team, without permission, to play elsewhere or engage in another line of work. After Sal Maglie had left the New York Giants to play in the Mexican League, he returned to the National League team. Commenting on Maglie's return, Giants' Manager Leo Durocher later wrote, "I'll play an elephant if he can do the job, so why shouldn't I play a jumper." (from Durocher's autobiography, *Nice Guys Finish Last;* CDP)

jumping jack   *n.* Player who shows off; grandstander.

jump on/jump on it   1. *v.* To hit the ball hard.
2. *v.* To take control of the game.

jump on the ball   *v.* To move on the sound of the ball making contact with the bat—applicable to base runners and fielders alike.

jump on the fast one, the   *n.* Hopping motion on a good fast ball.
   The phrase is eloquently explained in Hugh S. Fullerton's *Baseball Primer,* which appeared in the June 1912 *American Magazine:* "Sometimes pitchers throw much faster than at others, and on such days they 'have the jump on the fast one' which means that the ball, revolving rapidly, piles up a mound of compressed air and actually jumps over it, rising sometimes, it seems, an inch or two during its sudden leap before resuming its way to the plate."

June bug   *n.* Rookie who is sent back down to the Minor Leagues by early summer.
1ST   1950. "*June Bug.* Recruit who is on his way back to the minor leagues by June." (Sam Nisinson, *A Handy Illustrated Guide to Baseball;* DS)

June swoon   *n.* Term for a team that gets off to a good start in the spring months and falls apart after Memorial Day. It has been applied to several teams, but it has been most closely associated with the San Francisco Giants since the franchise was moved there from New York in 1958. Tom Weir of *USA Today* pointed out in a May 29, 1986, column that since moving to San Francisco the team had a composite record of 373-405 in the month of June (not good, not awful). He added, "If the Giants of the Mays-McCovey-Marichal era hadn't always been so hot in April and May—387-256 from 1958-71, the supposed swoon never would have been coined."

junior circuit   *n.* Term for the American League, because it came into being when the National League was 15 years old. The term is still used but much less commonly than it was before World War II.
SEE   *senior circuit.*

Junior World Series   See Little World Series.

junk   *n.* A term for the slower, softer pitches, which rely on erratic and deceptive movement,

as opposed to the standard fastballs and curveballs. Burt Dunne's definition in *The Folger Dictionary of Baseball:* "Slowly-thrown balls for which hitter must supply his own power . . ."
   Something of a misnomer, junk can be as effective as the faster stuff. "An old Cuban named Conrado Marrero has buried American League under a load of 'junk.'" (subheading to a *Life* profile of Marrero, June 11, 1951; PT)
1ST   1949. "Haefner, noted for his knuckle ball said he didn't use much 'junk.'" (Associated Press dispatch on one-hitter thrown by Mickey Haefner of the Washington Senators, May 11; PT)

junk baller/junk man/junk pitcher   *n.* A pitcher who relies on off-speed pitches and trickery rather than the fastball.
USE   Despite how it sounds, the term carries with it a certain admiration. Hoyt Wilhelm, Doyle Alexander and Stu Miller have been noted as junk men. It was said of Oriole Miller that he had three speeds: slow, slower and slowest.
1ST   Eddie Lopat of the White Sox (1944–1947) and Yankees (1948–1955) was a junk specialist who may have been the first pitcher to attract this label.

Jupe Pluvius/J. Pluvius   *n./arch.* Rain that interrupts or mars a game.
1ST   1868. (*New York Herald,* August 13; EJN)
ETY   From the ancient incantation to Jupiter Pluvius, with Pluvius being an ancient epithet for Jupiter as rainmaker.

Junkballer. New York Yankee coach Ed Lopat. *Courtesy of the New York Yankees*

K

K 1. *n.* The symbol for strikeout in baseball, which by extension is also used as a synonym for strike out.

"It's undeniable that Dr. K is a great moniker for Dwight Gooden, and so are the K banners that unfurl from the cheap seats in Shea Stadium every time he puts the Kibosh on an opposing batter." (*Washington Post*, May 4, 1986; article by Michael Olmert on the symbol K)

The K has long been a staple of headlines for the simple reason that it takes up much less space then the word "strikeout"—"Feller Setting 'K' Record" (*San Francisco Call-Bulletin*, June 5, 1946; PT).

ETY There are two theories as to how K came to stand for strikeout.

When Henry Chadwick invented a scoring system in 1861 he came up with a series of letter symbols: A for a putout at first base, B at second, C at third. F was a caught flyball, S for a sacrifice and, because he had already used F, L was for a batter who had fouled out. He used L because it was the last letter of foul. He picked K for struck out and later (1883) explained the decision: "it was the prominent letter of the word strike, as far as remembering the word was concerned."

Over time Chadwick's system was superseded by elements of other scoring systems, but the K remained.

The second version is much the same story but says that it was created by M. J. Kelly of the *New York Herald* and not Chadwick.

The symbol was given new prominence with the nicknaming of strikeout pitcher Dwight Gooden as Dr. K.

2. *v.* To strike out, as in, he was K'd.

Я (backward K) Standard scorecard symbol for a strikeout on a called strike.

kalsomine *v./arch.* To hold scoreless, to whitewash.

ETY "[S]o called because calcimine—which some creative misspeller long ago turned into 'kalsomine'—is a type of whitewash, and 'whitewash' is a synonym for 'shut out,'" explains Patrick Ercolano in his book on baseball language, *Fungoes, Floaters and Fork Balls*.

kangaroo *n.* Runner who leaps or takes high strides.

kangaroo ball *n.* RABBIT BALL. "Salt Lake was using a kangaroo ball and the theory was soberly propounded that singles went for homers because the air was thin." (Westbrook Pegler, *San Francisco Call-Bulletin*, May 14, 1958; PT)

kangaroo cave *n./arch.* Section of the grandstand reserved for sportswriters.
1ST 1908. (*New York Evening Journal*, August 21; EJN)

kangaroo court *n.* A clubhouse session during which a senior player assesses guilt and fines for errors and omissions on the field. "For the chief justice of the Red Sox Kangaroo Kourt, nothing else would do." (*Cleveland Plain Dealer*, October 17, 1986, article on Don Baylor by Paul Hoynes)

ETY The term has a long history as an irregular or mock court, such as one convened by prisoners in a jail. They are characterized by a disregard of normal court procedure. In his book on animals in language, *The Animal Things We Say*, Darryl Lyman states that the expression apparently stems from the jumping of the kangaroo and the fact that, "the principles of law and justice are disregarded or perverted (that is, 'jumped' over)" in such a court.

In *A Hog on Ice*, Charles Earle Funk guesses that the term may refer to the idea that the earliest kangaroo courts (about the time of the 1849 Gold Rush) were convened to try "jumpers"—that is, those who stole the mining claims of others.

kangaroo hops See 'ROO HOPS.

Kansas City Athletics The name of the American League's franchise in Kansas City, Missouri, from 1955 through the 1967 season. It had come from Philadelphia and moved on to Oakland, California.

Kansas City Royals The name of the American League's Western Division franchise located in Kansas City, Missouri. A 1969 expansion club, the royal in the team's name is an allusion to American Royal Parade, a major event in the livestock world. The name was selected from entries, submitted in a contest held among the fans.

KC Scorecard notation for a called strikeout.

K corner *n.* The left-field corner of the upper deck at Shea Stadium where fans hung cardboard Ks over the railing every time Dwight Gooden got a strikeout. The custom of counting Ks started in the 1985 season.

keep both hands on the ball *v.* Instruction given to softball pitchers who legally must have both hands in front of the body and on the ball before delivering the ball.

keep him honest *v.* Instruction to pitcher to throw strikes. The idea here is that if the batter is to reach base, he should earn it with a hit rather than a walk.

keep one's head in the locker *v.* To have little or nothing to say; to lack the ability to communicate.

Kentucky Wonder *n./arch.* BEAN BALL.
1ST 1943. ". . . such a pitch is known as a *bean ball, Kentucky wonder,* or *duster.*" (Franklin P. Huddle, "Baseball Jargon," *American Speech,* April)

key *n.* A signal given to a player that reveals the pattern of a subsequent signal.

keystone **1.** *n.* Second base.
2. *adj.* Describing defense or fielding up the middle of the infield.
" 'Yeah, kid—you're the keystone tenant. But holding onto it depends on how well you do." (from "A Case of Double Vision" by Ed Conrow, *Ellery Queen's Mystery Magazine,* October 1986)
ETY It is often claimed that this term is a play on the fact that many important (or key) plays involve second base—that it is the key to many defensive plays. Hy Turkin posits a minority opinion in his 1955 *Baseball Almanac:* "Viewed from the plate, second base seems to be the middle of the arch formed by the basepaths. In architecture, a keystone is the tapering stone at the crown of an arch."
Since these two explanations are complementary, they may both have been a factor in the creation of the term.

keystone bag/keystone cushion/keystone sack *n.* Second base.

USE Long regarded as synonyms for sportswriters tired of repeating the words "second base." This telling definition by R. E. Sherwood appeared in the September 1913 *Baseball* magazine:
> KEYSTONE SACK—A term used by baseball writers who are paid by the word, to designate second base. Generally believed to be stone from the number of runners who limp after sliding into it.

1ST 1907 (keystone sack). (*New York Evening Journal,* April 8; EJN)

keystone combination *n.* The shortstop and second baseman, collectively.

keystoner *n./arch.* Second baseman.

kick **1.** *n.* An element of the pitcher's windup that takes place when he lowers his arms, raises one leg and strides toward home plate.
2. *v.* To protest the decision of the umpire; to complain.
1ST 1885. (*Chicago Inter Ocean,* May 23; EJN)

kick away a game *v./arch.* To lose a game through ineptitude and blundering; to boot one.
1ST 1918. (*Spalding's Official Base Ball Guide:* EJN)

kickball *n.* A variation of baseball, using a large rubber ball (approximately 10 inches in diameter) in which one bats with one's foot and outs are made when a runner is tagged or hit with the ball. John Thorndike explained further in an article on backyard games in the August 1984 *Country Journal:* "Five can play on a side, or eight or ten. The pitcher rolls the ball toward the kicker, who may wait through any number of rolls for a good pitch. The rest of the rules are like baseball, save that the runner is out when hit with the ball, as well as when forced at a base." The game is a popular elementary school recess game.

kick it out *v.* To make sure that a ball rolling on the foul side of the first or third base line stays foul and does not become fair by rolling into fair territory. A defensive player ensures this by kicking the ball.

kick one *v.* To commit an error; to boot one.
Not restricted to players: "Because the umpire kicked one, Ryan leads off the third rather than ending the second." (Brent Mussberger on CBS radio during the 1986 National League Playoff series between the Mets and Astros,

after an umpire had called a man out at first who was clearly safe)

1ST 1916. (Ring Lardner, *You Know Me Al;* EJN)

ETY A play on the error that takes place when the player boots the ball as he tries to field it.

kicks *n.* Spikes or cleats.

kid See "hiya kid."

kill **1.** *v.* To put out.
2. *n.* A put out; a double play is sometimes called a double killing.

kill the ball *v.* To swing at a pitch with great ferocity. The term is usually used facetiously since "killing" the ball usually leaves the batter off balance and the ball untouched.

One of the commonest bits of advice given to youngsters learning the game is: "Don't try to kill the ball."

1ST 1896. (*Frank Merriwell's Schooldays;* EJN)

kill the rally *v.* To end a scoring opportunity, such as getting the third out with the bases loaded.

"Kill the umpire" Ritualistic response to a perceived bad call by the umpire.

kindergartners *n./arch.* ROOKIES.
1ST 1917. (*New York Times,* October 4; EJN)

Kiner's Korner The name for an area created to increase home run production at Forbes Field in Pittsburgh. By erecting a chicken wire fence inside the scoreboard as a new wall, home run balls did not have to be hit as far. It was originally called *Greenberg Gardens* to accommodate slugger Hank Greenberg, but was renamed for Pittsburgh's prodigious home run hitter Ralph Kiner in 1948.

King and His Court, the A barnstorming softball team of four players lead by Eddie Feigner, a pitcher who founded the team in 1946. Feigner has pitched more than 500 no-hitters during his career.

Kingdome Since 1977, the home grounds of the Seattle Mariners in King County, Washington. It is known for foul balls that have gone up and not come down and fair balls that bounce off speakers.

king of swat *n.* Nickname applied to Babe Ruth, but also to other sluggers.

kiss *v.* To hit the ball hard. Edward J. Nichols says it is a play on "smack."
1ST 1912. (*New York Tribune,* September 5; EJN)

"kiss it goodbye" Salutation for a home run made famous by Pittsburgh Pirates announcer Bob Prince.

kitchen *n.* The area of a batter's torso inside or at the edge of the high and inside portion of the strike zone. A fastball coming into that area—"pitchin' in the kitchen," "gettin' in his kitchen," "cheese for your kitchen" etc.—is especially tough, if not impossible, to hit.

The term is often used in more elaborate metaphors: "He got in his kitchen and broke a few dishes." The term may also be father to others of a culinary nature, such as comes to eat for a ball that moves in on a batter.

kittenball/kitten ball *n.* One of the early names for softball. After Chicago, Minneapolis was the second city to embrace the new game created in Chicago in 1887. It was introduced in Minneapolis in 1895 by Lt. Lewis Rober of Fire Company #11 as a form of exercise. The first team took the Kittens as their nickname and set up a small diamond in the vacant lot next to the station. The game soon took off in Minneapolis and, in honor of the first team, was called kitten ball.

Klem's line *n.* Practice originated by Bill Klem, the major league umpire, when he drew a line on the ground during an altercation. Any player or manager who crossed that line was ejected from the game. "Klem's line is a symbol applicable not only to player-umpire relationships, but to player-fan and player-player relationships as well. For an umpire or another player will take a surprising amount of abuse if the proper cliches are used and the matter doesn't drag on too long." (Tristram Potter Coffin, *The Old Ball Game,* 1971)

knee-knocker *n.* A low pitch intended to hit or come extremely close to a batter's legs.

Knickerbocker Rules The first codification of a game that could be termed baseball in the modern sense. The present rules of the game evolved from the Knickerbocker Rules. The basic set of 20 rules was first adopted by Alexander J. Cartwright and a band of New Yorkers on September 23, 1845, the same day on which they gave themselves the name Knickerbockers.

Klem's line. Bill Klem is one of five umpires inducted into baseball's Hall of Fame. *National Baseball Library, Cooperstown, N.Y.*

1st. Members must strictly observe the time agreed upon for exercise, and be punctual in their attendance.

2nd. When assembled for exercise, the President, or in his absence, the Vice-President, shall appoint an Umpire, who shall keep the game in a book provided for that purpose, and note all violations of the By-Laws and Rules during the time of exercise.

3rd. The presiding officer shall designate two members as Captains, who shall retire and make the match to be played, observing at the same time that the players opposite to each other should be as nearly equal as possible, the choice of sides to then be tossed for, and the first in hand to be decided in like manner.

4th. The bases shall be from "home" to second base, forty-two paces; from first to third base, forty-two paces, equidistant.

5th. No stump match shall be played on a regular day of exercise.

6th. If there should not be a sufficient number of members of the Club present at the time agreed upon to commence exercise, gentlemen not members may be chosen in to make up the match, which shall not be broken up to take in members that may afterwards appear; but in all cases, members shall have the preference, when present, at the making of a match.

7th. If members appear after the game is commenced, they may be chosen in if mutually agreed upon.

8th. The game to consist of twenty-one counts, or aces; but at the conclusion an equal number of hands must be played.

9th. The ball must be pitched, not thrown, for the bat.

10th. A ball knocked out of the field, or outside the range of the first and third base, is foul.

11th. Three balls being struck at and missed and the last one caught, is a hand out; if not caught is considered fair, and the striker bound to run.

12th. If a ball be struck, or tipped, and caught, either flying or on the first bound, it is a hand out.

13th. A player running the bases shall be out, if the ball is in the hands of an adversary on the base, or the runner is touched with it before he makes his base; it being understood, however, that in no instance is a ball to be thrown at him.

14th. A player running who shall prevent an adversary from catching or getting the ball before making his base, is a hand out.

15th. Three hands out, all out.

16th. Players must take their strike in regular turn.

17th. All disputes and differences relative to the game, to be decided by the Umpire, from which there is no appeal.

18th. No ace or base can be made on a foul strike.

19th. A runner cannot be put out in making one base, when a ball is made on the pitcher.

20th. But one base allowed when a ball bounds out of the field when struck.

An additional rule was adopted at the Club's fourth annual meeting (April 1, 1848), which stated that the player running to first base is

Knickerbocker Rules. Currier and Ives print of the first game—the "Grand Match for the Championship"—at the Elysian Fields, Hoboken, New Jersey, June 19, 1846. The Knickerbockers lost the game to the New York Nine, 23 to 1. *National Baseball Library, Cooperstown, N.Y.*

out without being touched with the ball if the fielder on first is holding the ball.

The rules were amended and expanded in 1854.

Knights of Swat   *n.* Home run hitters.
1ST   1910. (*Baseball* magazine, April; EJN)

knob   *n.* The rounded projection at the end of the bat handle that helps keep the bat from slipping out of the batter's hands.

knock   **1.** *v.* To hit the ball.
1ST   1866. (Constitution and By-Laws of the Olympic Base Ball Club, Philadelphia; EJN)
2. *n./arch.* A batted ball; a base hit.
1ST   1885. (*Chicago Inter Ocean*, May 13; EJN)

knockdown/knockdown pitch   *v.* A vicious pitch that forces the batter to drop to the ground to avoid getting hit.
1ST   1962. "There's the brushback, and there's the knockdown pitch." (*Saturday Evening Post*, June 30; DS)

knock out/knock out of the box   *v.* For a team of individual's successful hitting to cause the removal of an opposing pitcher.

ETY   These terms have obvious antecedents in prizefighting.
EXT   To defeat or diminish.

knock the ball over the fence   *v.* To hit a home run.
EXT   Used as metaphor for success in other fields.

In 1967, for instance, Lyndon B. Johnson said, "They booed Ted Williams, too, remember? They'll say about me I knocked the ball over the fence—but they don't like the way that he stands at the plate." (*New York Times*, May 30, 1968)

knock the cover off the ball   *v.* To hit the ball with great force. The most popular of the series of "knock" phrases—knock the blood out of it, knock the juice out of it, knock the cover loose etc.
1ST   1873. (*New York Herald*, August 10; EJN)

knot/knot the count   *v.* To even the score.
1ST   1915. (*Baseball* magazine, December; EJN)

knothole club/knothole gang   **1.** *n./arch.* Collectively, young fans who try to see the game without paying admission

Knothole gang. Commissioner Kenesaw Mountain Landis at the knothole, along with two younger associates. Though obviously staged, the picture has a certain charm. *National Baseball Library, Cooperstown, N.Y.*

2. *n.* In the days just prior to World War II some teams created knothole clubs and gangs as promotional efforts. Typically, youngsters would get a card that would enable them to get discounted or free tickets to games and the right to attend special clinics.

It is generally agreed that the first to do this was Branch Rickey, as general manager of the St. Louis Cardinals in the 1920s–1930s. As the Dodgers left Brooklyn in 1957 it was pointed out that, since 1940, the team had shepherded 2,256,000 youngsters into Ebbets Field on free Knothole Club passes.

However, there is a claim made for Abner Powell, innovative owner of the New Orleans Pelicans. A very detailed profile of Powell in his biographical file at the National Baseball Library in Cooperstown—by Marshall K. McClelland, it appeared undated in the *Pacific Stars and Stripes*—contains this account: "Early in 1889, Abner gathered together the youngsters of New Orleans and organized the first 'Knot Hole Gang.' As long as the kids observed strict rules of personal behavior both inside and outside the park, Abner permitted them to see a free game or two each week the Pelicans were at home."

Before each game, when the Dodgers were still in Brooklyn, there was a television show hosted by Happy Felton called "The Knot Hole Gang" on which three sandlot players appeared. As Mel Allen and Frank Graham, Jr., explained in *It Takes Heart:* "The boys were asked to pitch or field grounders and fly balls, and the one judged best was allowed to return to the show on the following day and interview the Brooklyn player of his choice." (1959; CDP) **ETY** From the image, favored by cartoonists and illustrators, of youngsters watching the game through a knothole in a wooden fence.

knothole customer *n.* One who found a way to see the game without paying. Under the heading, "Curing a Knot-Hole Customer," the August 1, 1929, *Sporting News* tells of an adult, watching a Laurel, Miss., game through a knothole, who gets a broken nose when an outfielder slams into the fence.

knothole day *n.* A day, usually a Saturday, when the knothouse club was able to get into the ballpark free or at a reduced rate.

knubber *n.* A lucky hit that squirts through the infield; a scratch hit. Sometimes written as nubber.
1ST 1937. (New York *Daily News*, January 17; EJN)

knuckle *n./arch.* Abbreviated version of knuckleball.
1ST 1913. "There was 'the hook,' 'the knuckle' . . . and so many others that there seemed to be no end to them." (J. W. Duffield, *Bert Wilson's Fadeaway;* DS)

knuckleball/knuckle ball/knuckler *n.* A slowly pitched ball that is thrown with little or no spin so that it will dance, bob, wobble and dip unpredictably or, as Jimmy Cannon once put it, "A curveball that doesn't give a damn." Because the ball does not rotate and is moving slowly, it is more directly affected by air currents and breezes. It is gripped against the fingertips, fingernails or knuckles, hence the name, and thrown without twisting the hand or wrist. The pitch can be devilishly hard to hit and not at all easy to catch (hence not a great pitch to use when runners are in scoring position). Bob Uecker once said that the best way

Knothole customers. Free seats created for the opening game of the 1914 World Series in Philadelphia.   *Prints and Photographs Division, the Library of Congress*

for a catcher to handle the pitch was to wait for it to stop rolling and then pick it up.

Eddie Cicotte is thought to have been the first major league player to specialize in throwing it (ca. 1908). Others have been Emil "Dutch" Leonard, Hoyt Wilhelm and Phil Niekro. **1ST**   1906. (*Baseball* magazine, July; EJN)

knuckleballer; knuckle baller/knuckles
n. A pitcher whose main pitch is a knuckleball.

Knuckleball. Eddie Fisher demonstrates the traditional knuckleball grip (1968). *Courtesy of the Cleveland Indians*

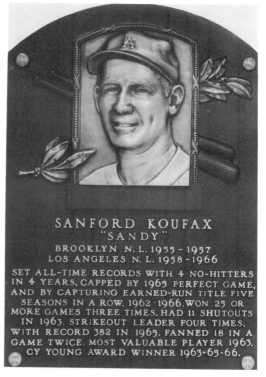

SANFORD KOUFAX
"SANDY"
BROOKLYN N.L. 1955-1957
LOS ANGELES N.L. 1958-1966
SET ALL-TIME RECORDS WITH 4 NO-HITTERS IN 4 YEARS, CAPPED BY 1965 PERFECT GAME, AND BY CAPTURING EARNED-RUN TITLE FIVE SEASONS IN A ROW, 1962-1966. WON 25 OR MORE GAMES THREE TIMES, HAD 11 SHUTOUTS IN 1963. STRIKEOUT LEADER FOUR TIMES, WITH RECORD 382 IN 1965. FANNED 18 IN A GAME TWICE. MOST VALUABLE PLAYER 1963. CY YOUNG AWARD WINNER 1963-65-66.

Koufaxian. Sandy Koufax's Hall of Fame plaque. *National Baseball Library, Cooperstown, N.Y.*

knuckleballing   *adj.* Describing a knuckle-baller.

knuckle curve   *n.* A curve thrown from a knuckleball grip, which causes the ball to drop sharply just before it reaches the batter. A blend of knuckleball and curveball.

knuckler   *n.* KNUCKLEBALL.

Koufaxian   *adj.* In the manner of Sandy Koufax; of masterful pitching.

"Ken Dixon, who might need a Koufaxian final three weeks to oust any of the top four starters, has looked sharp." (*The Baltimore Sun,* March 16, 1986)

KP duty   *n.* See *furlough.*

krank   *n./arch.* Fan, usually crank. Also, the title of Thomas W. Lawson's 1888 pamphlet on baseball slang (fully titled, *The Krank, His Language and What It Means*).
SEE   *crank.*

kranklet   *n.* Female krank.

KS   **1.** Scorecard notation for a swinging strikeout.
2. A sometimes cheer, chanted—kay ess, kay ess etc.—when a pitcher fans a batter.

K 2–3   Scorecard notation for a strikeout in which the catcher drops the third strike and must throw the ball to first base for a force to get the batter out.

KY's   *n.* Strikeouts attributed to pitches with balls doctored with KY lubricant.

"Gaylord Perry, a nonentity at twenty-seven, discovered Vaseline, K-Y vaginal jelly, and hitter hydrophobia (spitter on the brain), and has won 296 games (so far)." (Thomas Boswell in *How Life Imitates the World Series*)

L

L Standard abbreviation for loss.

label **1.** *n.* On a bat, the printed or—in the case of wooden bats—branded portion of the bat head that contains the manufacturer's name. **2.** *v/arch.* To bat a ball, to mark (label) the ball.

label for four *v.* To hit a home run.

lace/lace one *v.* To hit the ball hard. **1ST** 1888. "Lace it out." (caption used in Thomas W. Lawson's *The Krank;* DS)

ladies' day *n.* A promotional event offering free or reduced admission to the ball park. **ETY/1ST** 1883. In an attempt to lure more women to the ballpark, various clubs experimented with the idea as early as 1883. "Thursday is 'ladies day' at Columbus. On other days they must pay." (*Sporting Life*, April 29, 1883; DS) Also: "At the baseball game between the Portlands and the Lewistons on the afternoon of the 4th, ladies will be admitted to the grounds free." (*Portland* [Maine] *Daily Advertiser*, July 3, 1884; PT)

But the custom is said to have first taken hold with the Cincinnati Red Stockings in the latter part of the 1880s. Club owner Aaron Stern

Ladies' day. Ad for ladies' day in the *Boston Herald* (July 23, 1902). *National Baseball Library, Cooperstown, N.Y.*

noted that the number of women in the stands increased significantly when a handsome pitcher named Tony "Count" Mellane was on the mound. Early in 1889 Stern announced that Mellane would pitch each Monday and all women would be admitted free providing they were accompanied by a paying male escort. This became a regular attraction and soon spread to other clubs.

Some early promotions of this nature required that the women have a male escort. This resulted in crowds of women waiting outside the ballpark for men to take them through the turnstiles.

The custom was given a boost in the days after World War II when owners used ladies' days to attract customers to their ballparks. **EXT** In *Listening to America*, Stuart Berg Flexner points out that the term predated baseball and was used to designate a day when men could bring women to their clubs. He finds it used as early as 1787: "George Washington recorded the term in his diary that year, noting that a club at which he dined had a 'ladies' day' every other Saturday."

La Lob *n.* Invented and named by Dave LaRoche of the New York Yankees, a trick pitch that slowly floats toward home plate with a high-arching trajectory. Writing in the *Wall Street Journal* on October 5, 1982, Frederick C. Klein described it as "the sort of pitch you throw to your seven-year-old son in your backyard." Klein was recalling two "La Lob" confrontations between LaRoche and Brewers slugger Gorman Thomas. Late in the '81 season Thomas struck out swinging at the pitch. They met again on June 30, 1982, and LaRoche threw seven of them consecutively. Five were fouled off, one was taken for a ball and the last one was lashed into left field for a hit. "When he reached first base," Klein reported, "he raised his fists over his head, Rocky style."

lam/lambaste *v.* To bat a ball hard.

lamb **1.** *n.* Youngster; an innocent victim. According to Herbert Simons in his 1943 article on baseball slang, Ted Williams used this term

240

La Lob. New York Yankee pitcher Dave LaRoche (1982).   *Courtesy of the New York Yankees*

so frequently that he became known as "The Lamb."
2. *n.* Pitcher who is easy to hit, more commonly referred to as a cousin.

laminate   *v.* To hit the ball extremely hard.
1ST   1914. " 'Murder it, Ted, old man!' " " 'Laminate it!' " (*Lefty o' the Blue Stockings* by Gilbert Patten; DS)

lamp   *v.* To look at. "Lamp the girl in row 22." (John Hall in "How's Your Baseball Lingo?" *Baseball Digest*, December 1973)

lamps   *n.* Eyes.

land on one   *v.* To bat a ball hard.
1ST   1905 (*Sporting Life,* October 7; EJN)

larceny   *n.* Base stealing.

laredo   See throwing laredo

larrup   *v.* To hit a baseball with force. One of Lou Gehrig's many nicknames was "Larruppin' Lou."
1ST   1887. (*Chicago Inter Ocean,* May 10; EJN)
ETY   Colloquialism among the Irish dating back to at least the early 19th century. It means to beat, thrash or flog and is said to be a corruption of the nautical term "lee rope." The earliest example listed in the Oxford English Dictionary dates to 1823.

larruper   *n.* Powerful hitter.
1ST   1908. (*New York Evening Journal,* August 26; EJN)

lash   *v.* To hit a ball hard.
1ST   1917. (*New York Times,* October 8; EJN)

lash a grounder   *v.* To hit a ball that moves fast and hard along the ground.

last   *v.* For a pitcher to remain in the game; for instance, to last for six innings.
1ST   1902. (*Sporting Life,* July 5; EJN)

late foot   *n.* A winning or hitting streak toward the end of the season. Usually stated as, "showing late foot."

late inning   *adj.* Toward the end of the game.
EXT   Late in any realm. "Late-Inning Hardball in the House." (*Washington Post* headline, December 28, 1987)

late-inning pressure situation   *n.* Term for an at bat with a runner on base in the seventh inning or later with the batter's team down by three or fewer runs (four with the bases loaded). There is actually a statistic for this. In 1986, *USA Today* reported that Tim Raines had a career batting average of .340 in such situations.

late innings   *n.* Traditionally, the 7th, 8th and 9th innings of a game.

late season pick-up/late season acquisition   *n.* Player signed after the All-Star break, often one seen as valuable to a pennant drive.

latest line   *n.* A gambling tool featuring a list of odds favoring or disfavoring teams before a given day's games. Latest lines are published in many newspapers and their prime function is to aid betting.

lather   *v.* To hit.
1ST   1934. Listed in a group of baseball terms in *Journalism Quarterly.* (DS)

laugher   *n.* A game with a lopsided score; an easy win. " 'When Lee Lacy hits three home runs and drives in six runs, you figure the game is going to be a laugher,' manager Earl Weaver said, 'But at one point, it sure wasn't.' " (*USA Today,* June 9, 1986)

launching pad   *n.* Stadium from which many home runs emanate. After the Baltimore Orioles set a single-month home run hitting record in May 1987, Coach Frank Robinson said of

Memorial Stadium, "It's a launching pad." (UPI dispatch, June 2, 1987) Atlanta's Fulton County Stadium has long enjoyed the nickname "the launching pad."

lawn mower   *n.* A hard-hit ground ball.
1ST   1891 (*Chicago Herald*, May 7; EJN)

lawyer   1. *n.* A player who talks a lot in the clubhouse.
2. *n.* A player, coach or manager who tends to contest umpires' decisions.

lay an egg   *v.* To fail to score.
SEE   goose egg.

laydown   *adj.* The manner in which a bunt is executed; a soft tap of the ball with the bat.

lay down a ball/lay it down/lay one down   *v.* To bunt.
1ST   1909 (lay one down). (*New York Evening Journal*, June 17; EJN)

"lay it in"/"lay it in there"   *v.* Encouragement to a pitcher to throw a strike.

lay-off   *n.* A period of inactivity; applied to both players and teams.
1ST   1912. (*New York Tribune*, October 7; EJN)

lay the wood on   *v.* To hit the baseball.

lazy   1. *adj.* Describing a ball without great velocity such as a lazy pop-up.
1ST   1932. (*Baseball* magazine, October; EJN)
2. *n./arch.* A drooper; a TEXAS LEAGUER.

LCS   Abbreviation for League Championship Series.

lead   1. *n.* The distance a base runner stands from the bag he occupies when the ball is pitched. The runner must try to take a lead that gives him an advantage for reaching the next base safely while still allowing him the option of getting back to base before the pitcher or catcher can pick him off.
1ST   1896. (*Frank Merriwell's School Days;* EJN)
2. *n.* The advantage in runs scored of one team over another.
3. *v.* During a game, to have scored more runs than the opposing team.
4. *v.* For a team or individual to be ahead in a particular statistical category. For instance, a team in first place leads other teams in the standings. The player with the most home runs is leading in the chase for the home run crown.

lead bat   *n.* A bat that has been weighted down with lead or other metal. Swung in the on deck circle, the purpose of such a bat is to make one's regular bat seem lighter and easier to swing.

leader card   *n.* Baseball card collecting term for cards that depict the players who lead their respective league or division in a particular statistical category during the previous season. An example would be a card with the caption "N. League 1966 Home Run Leaders" along with photos of Hank Aaron, Richie Allen and Willie Mays.

leading lady   1. *n.* The lead base runner. To say "get the leading lady" means to force out the runner furthest along the base path.
2. *n.* The first batter up in an inning.

leadoff/lead-off   1. *v.* To be the first batter in the batting order or in an inning.
1ST   1874. (*New York Sun*, July 3; EJN)
2. *n.* LEAD-OFF BATTER.
1ST   1935. "Lead-off—First batsman at bat at the beginning of an inning." (Ralph H. Barbour, *How to Play Better Baseball;* DS)

lead-off batter/lead-off hitter/lead-off man
1. *n.* The first player in the batting order. Because this batter comes to bat more than any other player on the team, the position is normally reserved for a top player, ideally one with a high on-base average and with the ability to steal bases.
    Tim Raines has been described by Dave Schiber of the *St. Petersburg Times* as "a walking definition of the ideal leadoff hitter." A list of other prime examples would have to include Maury Wills, Lou Brock and Ricky Henderson.
1ST   1910. (*Baseball* magazine, April; EJN)
2. *n.* The first batter for a team in an inning.

lead runner   *n.* When more than one runner is on base, the one farthest along the base path.

league   *n.* A group of teams or clubs that employ a common set of rules and regulations as they play against one another. A league uses a prearranged schedule of games to decide on a championship from among its members.

League Championship Series   *n.* Games between the winners of the eastern and western divisions to determine a champion. Since 1969 when the two major leagues were broken down into eastern and western divisions, each league has held a series between its divisions to determine a champion or pennant winner. Currently the winner of the championship series in each league is decided through a best-of-seven formula.

league president *n.* Person charged with responsibility for the day to day activities of the teams in a given league.

The *Official Baseball Rules* specify that it is the job of the league president to enforce the rules of the game, resolve rules disputes and determine the resolution of any protested games. This officer is also empowered to fine and suspend players, coaches, managers and umpires for rules violations.

leaguer *n.* One identified with a particular league: major-leaguer, Little-Leaguer etc.

lean *v.* To take a lead toward the next base; position assumed for stealing, as in, "He's leaning toward second with stealing on his mind." To be picked-off while taking such a lead is to be caught "leaning the wrong way."

lean against it/lean on it *v.* To bat a ball hard.
1ST 1907 (lean against it). (*New York Evening Journal,* April 25; EJN)

leaping lena *n.* See Texas Leaguer.

leather **1.** *n.* Baseball glove or gloves.
"We told Teufel, 'Way to get leather on it,' " Johnson said, smiling, "He just got the wrong leather."—Davey Johnson on Tim Teufel's errors during the 1986 World Series. (*Washington Post,* October 25, 1986)
2. *n.* Fielding. A game containing a number of stellar defensive plays is said to be "full of leather."
3. *n./arch.* The baseball, a reference to its cowhide cover. From this meaning has come such outdated slang as "leather-hunting" for attempting to get a hit.
1ST 1883. (*Chicago Inter Ocean,* June 6; EJN)
4. *v./arch.* To hit the ball; to leather one.

leather man/leather player *n.* A good defensive player; one who is likely to be known for his fielding rather than hitting prowess.
1ST 1937 (leather man). (New York *Daily News,* January 21; EJN)

leave/leave men on base/leave on base *v.* To end an inning with one or more runners unable to score.

left-center *n.* Area of the playing field between center and left field.

left field **1.** *n.* The left side of the outfield as viewed from home plate.
2. *n.* The defensive position itself; "Who's playing left field?"
1ST 1854. (Knickerbocker Rules)
EXT **1.** *n.* Things that are unusual, unexpected or irrational are deemed to have come out of or from left field.
2. *n.* The political left. "Canadian businessmen last week were playing host to two more trade missions out of far left field. In Canada searching for business were one team of sales-minded Russians and another of inscrutable Hong Kong traders acting as agents for their neighbors, the Communist Chinese." (*Time,* January 20, 1961)

left fielder *n.* The defensive player in left field.
1ST 1883. (*Sporting Life,* May 20; EJN)

left-handed *adj.* Describing a player who favors the left-hand, it applies to one who respectively, pitches or throws with left side of the body. It also refers to a left-handed batter who swings from the left but faces the pitcher with the right side of the body.

Traditionally, the left-handed player has had to overcome a certain amount of prejudice. In a 1956 column on left-handed infielders, columnist E. V. Durling actually wrote: "Right handers are steadier than left handers. They steady an infield. The southpaws are usually temperamental and easily rattled. They are also inclined to fancy 'show off' playing such as overdoing the one hand catch." (*San Francisco Examiner,* September 17, 1956; PT)

left-handed batter *n.* Player who bats from the right-hand side—i.e., the first base side—of the plate. Left-handed batters have several advantages. Because they stand on the first base side of the field, they have a natural, one step headstart on the base path as they complete their swing. Also, since batters tend to have an advantage over pitchers throwing from the opposite side of the body, left-handed batters tend to have an advantage because there are many more right-handed pitchers. Because of these advantages, many batters have learned to bat left-handed while still throwing with their right hand.

left-hander *n.* A left-handed player. In practice, the term is usually used to describe pitchers who throw with their left hand. While there are a number of left-handed pitchers,

left-handedness is something of an obstacle at certain positions, especially third base. For instance, in 1986 after playing five innings of a game at third base, the *Washington Post* said of New York Yankee first baseman Don Mattingly, "[he] is believed to be just the 11th left-hander to play third base in the major leagues since 1900 . . ."
1ST 1879. (*Spirit of the Times,* August 23; EJN)

leftie/lefty   *n.* A left-handed player; one who throws with the left hand.
1ST 1886. "In last Wednesday's game Nashville presented her left-handed battery, Earle and Brynan, to offset our 'lefty' battery." (*Sporting Life,* April 7, 1886; DS)
EXT   Slang for a leftist, especially during the 1950s. "In your June 2 editorial re the Oppenheimer case, you describe Dr. Albert Einstein as a 'dedicated international lefty.' " (letter to the editors of the *San Francisco News,* June 7, 1954; PT)

left on base   *adj.* The number of runners remaining on base at the end of a half inning. As a statistic, the collective number of runners left on base during a game or a number of games is a barometer of a team's overall inability to score. This is commonly abbreviated as LOB.
1ST 1858. (Chadwick Scrapbooks; EJN)

left out   *n.* A common nickname for the left fielder at the amateur level. It refers to the fact that the ball is seldom hit to left field at the non-professional level, where batters tend to push the ball to the right.

left patrol   *n.* LEFT FIELDER.

legal   *adj.* That which is in accord with the official rules of the game.

legal game   *n.* A game is legal and deemed complete if it lasts five innings, or 4½ with the home team in the lead, before being officially called by the umpire because of rain, darkness or other condition that warrants the halt of play.

legger   *n.* LEG HITTER.

leg hit   *n.* A single accomplished by the speed of the runner rather than the hit itself. A key ingredient of a leg hit is that, while the ball has been properly fielded without error, the runner outraces the ball to the base.

Leg hitter. Lloyd "Little Poison" Waner, who was a terror when it came to getting to first base on slap hits. *National Baseball Library, Cooperstown, N.Y.*

leg hitter   *n.* A fast player who can often beat out infield taps. This can, to some degree, compensate for being a weak hitter. ". . . the National League decided to make official the practice of rolling infields after five innings . . . it brought no joy to leg hitters who sometimes beat out 'groundskeeper singles' on balls which strike errant pebbles." (*San Francisco News,* December 8, 1953)
Lloyd "Little Poison" Waner of the Pittsburgh Pirates set a record for singles, with 198 of them in 1927. He accomplished this with a number of leg hits.
1ST 1937. (*The Sporting News Record Book;* EJN)

leg-in-the-face   *adj.* Of a pitcher's high leg delivery.

"Leg it!"   *v./obs.* A common 19th-century call from the grandstand, meaning "Run!"

leg it out   *v.* For a batter or runner to arrive safely at a base ahead of the ball.

legs cut out from under it   *adj.* Description of a well-hit ball that falls short of its destination because it has been hampered by the wind.

lemon   *n./arch.* A player of poor ability, especially one of whom much was expected.
1ST   1910. (*Baseball* magazine, May; EJN)

lemon in the grapefruit belt   *n./arch.* Rookie who flops during spring training.

Lena Blackburn Rubbing Mud   See rubbing mud.

let him know you're out there   *v.* Throw a pitch close to a batter's body.

letter-high   *adj.* Description of a pitched ball that comes in across the chest at the level of the letters spelling out the name or initials of the player's club.
1ST   1927. (WMAQ-Chicago broadcast; EJN)

letter mailer   *n.* Casey Stengel's own term for a player who stayed out late at night. It presumably stems from the time-honored excuse of curfew-breakers who have been caught returning at a later hour; "Gee, I only went out to mail a letter."

letters   *n.* The approximate top of the strike zone which is in line with the name of the club as it is written across the player's jersey.

let up   *v.* To throw a slow ball after a fast one using the same motion.

letup/letup ball/letup pitch   *n.* A pitch that is used to confuse the batter because it comes after a fastball and has less speed. "Then he fed me a high change of pace, a let-up ball you might call it. I swung as hard as I had the day before. But this time I missed." (Harry "Cookie" Lavagetto in *I'll Never Forget the Day;* PT)

lick   **1.** *n.* A time at bat; clubs with a final three outs are getting "last licks."
1ST   1883. (*Sporting Life,* May 6; EJN)
2. *n./arch.* A safe hit.
1ST   1860. (Chadwick Scrapbooks; EJN)
3. *v.* To beat decisively.

licorice   *n./arch.* Vigor or energy.
ETY   Edward J. Nichols has noted that the origin of this could be the licorice candy once used by pitchers to get a better grip on the ball.
1ST   1907. (*New York Evening Journal,* April 12; EJN)

lid is off   The season has begun.

lidlifter   **1.** *n.* Opening Day.
2. *n.* First game of a doubleheader.

Lifer. Manager John J. McGraw (left) with Christy Mathewson. McGraw has been typified as the quintessential baseball lifer.   *National Baseball Library, Cooperstown, N.Y.*

life   **1.** *n.* Another chance for the batter or the batting team, such as that granted when a fly foul ball is dropped.
1ST   1868. "Howe had a life given him by Schaffer muffing his fly in right field." (Chadwick Scrapbooks; DS)
2. *n.* Base on balls.

life-and-limb strike   *n.* Term found in Ron Luciano's *The Umpire Strikes Back.* In the book he says he called such a strike once despite the fact it was an obvious ball, "because if I had called it ball three the fans would've come over the fence." (CDP)

lifer   *n.* Term for a man who starts as a player and spends the rest of his working life as a baseball manager, coach or executive. Famous examples include Casey Stengel, John McGraw, Connie Mack and Earl Weaver.

lift a pitcher   *v.* To remove a pitcher from the game.
1ST   1914. (*New York Tribune,* October 1; EJN)

light ball   *n.* A fastball thrown in such a manner that it feels light to the catcher.

lighted frolic   *n./arch.* A night game under the lights in the 1930s and 1940s when such games were still a novelty.

limit   *n.* The number of players that are allowed to be on a club's active roster at various points in the season. The number of players allowed from a date one month after the regular season begins until September first is 24. This maximum had been 25 for some time, but team owners dropped the number to 24 in 1986.

Linda Ronstadt   *n.* Term first spotted and described by Dave Scheiber in the *St. Petersburg Times* for March 5, 1987: "Good fastballs enjoy an updated alias as well. They're called a Linda Ronstadt. No, the sultry singer was never known for her pitching prowess, but she did record the tune *Blue Bayou.* And baseball linguists soon turned that into *Blew by you*—as in what that sizzling fastball just did."

Scott Ostler reported in the *Los Angeles Times* in 1986 that this is also known as a *Louisiana,* in a more distant reference to the same Ronstadt remake of Roy Orbison's hit record, *Blue Bayou.*

line   **1.** *v.* To hit a ball along a straight path; to get a line drive.
1ST   1892. (*Brooklyn Daily Eagle,* August 1; EJN)
2. *v.* To mark the field.
3. *n.* The foul or base line.
1ST   1866. (Constitution and By-Laws of the Olympic Ball Club of Philadelphia; EJN)

linea   *n.* Line drive in Spanish.

line ball   *n./arch.* A ball that travels a straight line; a line drive.
1ST   1866. (*New York Herald,* July 7; EJN)

line drive   *n.* A solidly batted ball that approximately parallels the ground during its flight rather than arching in the manner of a fly ball.

Line drives has a number of nicknames, including blue darter, clothes line and frozen rope.
1st   1895. (*New York Press,* July 4; EJN)

line drive to the catcher   A swinging strikeout.

line-hit/line-hit ball   *n.* A hard-hit ball that moves close to the ground. "Jack Strobe cleaned the bases with a long line-hit." (Christy Mathewson, *First Base Faulkner;* DS)
1ST   1880. (*New York Herald,* August 20; EJN)

line hitter   *n.* A batter who makes a habit of hitting line drives.
1ST   1932. (*Baseball* magazine, October; EJN)

line-hugger   *n./adj.* A ball that follows the first or third base line.

line out   *v.* To hit a line drive that is caught for an out.

liner   *n.* line drive.
1ST   1883. (*Sporting Life,* April 15; EJN)

lines   *n.* The various boundary marks on and around the playing field.

line score   *n.* An inning by inning account of a game, recording hits, runs and errors. This is what is commonly displayed on scoreboards in the ballpark.

lineup/line-up   *n.* The nine players composing a batting order and the defense on any given day at any given point in the game. It is always presented at the beginning of the game with the players in their proper batting order. The batting order is an integral element of the lineup.
1ST   1905. (*Sporting Life,* October 7; EJN)
EXT   Any listing of events or participants.

lineup card   *n.* A list of the starting players, which is presented to the Umpire in Chief by a representative of each team at the beginning of each game.

liniment   *n./arch.* The worst; anything that is very bad or very poor.

little ball   **1.** *n.* Fastball, because it is hard to see as it comes in toward the batter.
2. *n.* Bunting as opposed to swinging away (big ball). "Manager Gene Mauch used the squeeze bunt—'little ball' is his expression for it—earlier in the season because the Angels were not scoring many runs." (*New York Times,* October 18, 1982)

little bo-bo   *n./arch.* Manager's favorite player.

Little Eva   *n.* A player who performs well even though he is obviously tired and suffering from a hangover.
1ST   1937. (New York *Daily News,* September 5; EJN)
ETY   This term comes from the innocent Little Eva of *Uncle Tom's Cabin* who is the exact opposite of the dissipated ballplayer dragging himself onto the field and showing the effects of the previous night's revelry.

Little League. The official logo. *Courtesy of Little League Baseball*

Little League   1. *n.* A vast, organized network of baseball for boys and girls 8 to 12 years of age; started in 1939 in Williamsport, Pennsylvania when Carl E. Stotz began it with three teams. Although the rules are basically the same as those observed by adult organizations, the physical dimensions of the field are smaller. The Little League field is two-thirds the size of a major league field, which, means, for instance, that bases are 60 feet rather than 90 feet apart.

Little League is highly structured and provides a path for play right up to and including the Little League World Series, which is held annually in Williamsport. Although created for boys only, a 1974 court order included girls in the Little League program for the first time; by 1987 3,000 were participating.

A number of major league players first played in Little League, the first of whom was Joey Jay who went on to play for the Cincinnati Reds. **2.** *n.* The term is used generically to describe baseball at the preteen level.

Baseball at this level has its own set of pet phrases and cliches.

In their book *Laughing and Crying With Little League,* Cath and Loren Broadus list 12 cliches needed to establish an adult as a veteran Little League fan. The full dozen:
1. It only takes one!
2. Way to look—good eye!
3. That's getting a piece of it.
4. Way to hang!
5. Get mean with the stick!
6. That's looking it over!
7. He can't hit!
8. He's looking for a ball!
9. That's OK. You've got two more!
10. Easy out!
11. You can do it!
12. Choke up!

The Broaduses remind us that many of these are cruel cliches and that number 10, for example, is a reminder that the batter is a poor player. They point out, "Most adults would panic if someone announced at the PTA meeting, 'She is a lousy lover,' and the crowd started chanting it as they stared at the victim."

Little League elbow/Little League shoulder   *n.* Medical names for the childhood injuries that can result from the stress of continually trying to throw a baseball hard.

Little Miracle of Coogan's bluff   The miraculous finish to the New York Giants' 1954 season in which the team took the pennant and swept the Cleveland Indians in the World Series four games to none. This should not be confused with the *Miracle of Coogan's Bluff* which took place in 1951.

Little World Series   Term for the championship playoff games in the AAA level of the Minor Leagues.

live   *adj.* Term applied to a pitch that hops, floats or otherwise deviates from a straight trajectory. "Actually, the terms 'live' and 'dead' have been applied to baseballs for more than 100 years." (Rawlings executive quoted in *USA Weekend,* July 10, 1987)

live arm   *n.* Attribute of a pitcher with a good fastball.

live ball   1. *n.* One that is in play.
2. *n.* A ball that is, or is believed to be, inherently livelier and therefore will go farther when hit.
1ST 1914 (second meaning). "At that time 'live' balls were used, that is, balls which had a good bit of rubber in them." (*Outing* magazine, January; DS)

live bat   *n.* Said to be in the hands of a batter who is in the midst of a hot streak.

lively ball   1. *n.* Any baseball that *seems* to have more zip and distance in it than others

because of the way it has been manufactured. The lively ball is often described as one that seems to jump right off the bat on its way to a long voyage. RABBIT BALL.
1ST   1870 (*New York Herald,* June 10; EJN)
2. *n.* Specifically, the ball used during a specific season when a number of players, managers and coaches insist that baseballs have more life to them. A recent lively ball year was 1987.

living in a mustard jar   Applied to a hot dog; a showoff.

loaded   *adj.* Bases full.

load of coal/load of garbage   *n.* Change of pace; slow, soft pitches.

load the ball/load up the ball   *v.* To doctor the baseball by adding a foreign substance such as saliva or hair oil. "Pitchers will load up by putting stuff on their eyebrows, in their hair, on the hair on their chest, on their wrists, all over." (Billy Martin, in *Billyball*)

load the bases/load the sacks   **1.** *v.* To fill the bases with runners (as applied to the offensive team).
2. *v.* To allow the bases to be filled (as applied to the defensive team).

lob   **1.** *n.* A soft throw or toss that is required, for example, when the ball is passed between two fielders who are only a few yards from each other.
2. *v.* To make a soft throw.
1ST   1911. (*Baseball* magazine, October; EJN)

LOB   Standard scorecard or box score abbreviation for left on base.

lobby sitter   *n.* Player who hangs out in hotel lobbies between games on road trips.

lobster net/lobster trap   *n.* ORANGE CRATE.

local World Series   *n.* Term used for a World Championship pitting two nearby teams against each other, such as the New York Yankees vs. the New York Giants (1936–37), St. Louis Browns vs. St. Louis Cardinals (1944), or the Chicago White Sox vs. the Chicago Cubs (1906).

locate a pitcher   *v.* To get hits off a pitcher.

locate the plate   *v.* To throw pitches in the strike zone; to have good control.
1ST   1899. (*Frank Merriwell's Double Shot;* EJN)

location   *n.* A pitcher's ability to place the ball. Good location is putting the ball just where you want it.
  In his essay decrying modern baseballese, Russell Baker recalled a line he heard on television, which was, "Ryan has good velocity and excellent location." After noting that the line sounded like something that happened in a physics lab, he translates the line into traditional baseballese, "Ryan is throwing smoke and nicking the corners."
USE   In his article on jargon encountered in 1982's spring training (*The Sporting News,* March 6, 1982), Joe Goddard reported that location, "Seems to have replaced control, much as 'velocity' has replaced 'speed.' It's because some real estate agent became a pitcher, speculates Kansas City relief ace Dan Quisenberry."

lock   *n.* A certainty; a sure bet. "St. Louis manager Whitey Herzog figures the Cardinals are a lock to steal 200 bases for the seventh year in a row, tying them with 1909–1915 Detroit Tigers for the second longest streak in history." (*St. Petersburg Times,* March 6, 1988)
1ST   1958. "We haven't had a 20-game winner since pitcher Ewell Blackwell in '47 and this guy [pitcher Bob Purkey] looks like a lock now. Not because he's won eight already, but because of the way he's pitching." (*New York Post,* June 11; cited in Harold Wentworth and Stuart Berg Flexner's *Dictionary of American Slang*)
ETY   Wentworth and Flexner trace it to the wrestling term "mortal lock" for a deadly hold that cannot be broken.

locust hitter   *n.* A weak batter, so-called because of the poor quality of locust wood. In other words, the batter is so weak that it seems as if he is using a bat of locust.
1ST   1907. (*Lajoie's Official Base Ball Guide;* EJN)

loft/loft one   *v.* To hit a high fly ball.
1ST   1915. (*Baseball* magazine, December; EJN)

log   *n.* BAT.

lollipop/lollypop   *n.* A soft pitch or weak throw. It is usually used to describe a pitch that is extremely easy to hit, a lollypop curve, for instance; like a lollipop held out in front of the batter. "No . . . he hasn't got the fast ball anymore . . . he throws lollypops, and dew drops them in there." (Russ Hodges, Giants broadcast, September 15, 1963; PT)

long ball 1. *n.* A home run, pure and simple. 2. *n.* A batted ball that travels a considerable distance, usually deep in the outfield or over the fence. Clearly implied by the term is a ball that will require an extraordinary catch or go for extra bases. Jim Brosnan makes his own addition to the definition of this term, "Often used as a nickname for catchers who signal for too many bad pitches."

long-ball hitter *n.* Home run hitter. **EXT** By extension, any dramatic performer. "And the fact that he is a long-ball hitter gives him extraordinary and exciting appeal." (Joe Williams on boxer Rocky Marciano, *San Francisco News*, September 25, 1952; PT)

long bat *n./arch.* A hot streak at the plate.

long bench *n.* A superior collection of substitute players. This term appears to have started in football and jumped to baseball.

long catch *n.* Exercise sometimes used by pitchers to strengthen their arms; involves throwing the ball a much greater distance than that between the pitcher's mound and home plate. For instance, a report on Yankee pitcher Ron Guidry at the beginning of 1988's spring training said that he had ". . . increased his activity of playing long catch in the outfield from 130 to about 150 feet." (*Newsday,* March 27, 1988)

long count *n.* FULL COUNT.

long distance orator *n./arch.* Player who argues from a long range.

long, loud out *n.* A powerfully-hit ball that comes close to going for a home run but that is caught on the fly for an out.

long man *n.* Relief pitcher who is expected to be able to work effectively for longer than three innings in the middle of the game. Some pitchers make this their specialty and major league bullpens contain at least one such specialist.

long relief/long relief man/long reliever *n.* See long man. "The problem for a long-relief man is that he doesn't want to tire himself out before a game in which he may pitch eight innings." (Jim Bouton in *Ball Four;* CDP)

long side *n.* The left-hand portion of the infield from which throws to first base are the longest.

long strike *n.* A powerfully hit foul ball; one that goes a long distance. **1ST** 1937. (*The Sporting News Record Book;* EJN)

long summer *n.* The purgatory for teams low in the standings whose seasons seem like they will never end. Typically, a very sloppy early season loss will occasion the line, "This could be a long summer."

long tater *n.* A well-hit home run. An expression said to have begun in the old Negro Leagues as "long potatoes."

look 1. *v.* For the pitcher to check on a runner before delivering the ball; an action taken to deter the runner from stealing or taking too long a lead. 2. *n.* The pitcher's glance, which is made at the runner. 3. *v.* For a fielder with the ball to hold a runner during a play by glancing in his direction rather than throwing the ball.

look/look at *v.* For the batter to let a pitched ball go by without swinging at it; to take a pitch.

looker *n.* Batter who patiently waits for the right pitch to hit.

look for *v.* To come to the plate anticipating a certain pitch or sequence of pitches. To look for a walk is to anticipate balls.

looking *n.* Letting a pitched ball go for a called strike. Usually phrased as "caught looking."

look them over/look 'em over 1. *v.* For a batter to wait for a good ball to hit even if it means taking a called strike or two. **1ST** 1937. (*Sporting News Record Book;* EJN) 2. Instruction shouted to the batter to encourage patience.

look the runner back *v.* For a pitcher to control a runner's lead by staring at him. The clear implication of the stare is that if the runner continues to lead, he will be thrown out.

"Looooo" A cheer that commonly accompanied plate appearances by batters named Lou or Lew, such as that accorded Lou Piniella at Yankee Stadium. It is notable because the uninitiated often mistook the cheer for the popular pinstriper as a boo. Also, "Mooooooookie" (for Mookie Wilson), "Dewwwwwwwwy" (Dwight Evans) etc.

loop   1. *n.* A baseball league or conference. A league president is often referred to as a "loop prexy."
2. *v.* To hit a high arching ball.

looper   *n.* A fly ball that falls in for a hit.
1ST   1937. (*Sporting News Record Book;* EJN)

loose   1. *adj.* Descriptive of a ball that is not under the control of a defensive player.
2. *adj.* Descriptive of a fluid, easy swing of the bat. "One of the loosest—and most productive—swings in the Pacific Coast League belongs to San Diego's swivel-jointed outfielder, Harry Simpson." (*San Francisco Call-Bulletin,* August 17, 1950; PT)
3. *adj.* A general good attitude and easy approach toward the game. A team that is winning is often described as loose.

loose-as-a-goose/ loose-as-ashes/ loosey-goosey   *adj.* A player who is completely relaxed on the field; one whose moves are easy, graceful and seemingly effortless.

loose fielding   *n.* Poor defense.
This underscores a paradox of baseball talk: it is good for hitters to be loose, but fielders should be tight. A tight infield is one through which no ground balls escape.
1ST   1861. (*New York Sunday Mercury,* October 2; EJN)

loosen a batter/loosen him up   *v.* To throw a beanball or a knockdown pitch to, presumably, loosen him from the plate.
1ST   1937. (*Baseball* magazine, January 11; EJN)

loosener   *n.* A pitch thrown at to loosen a batter.
1ST   1932. (*Baseball* magazine, October; EJN)

Lord Charles   *n.* An appreciative name for a superb curveball, which elevates the term *Uncle Charlie* to a regal level.
ETY   Created to describe Dwight Gooden's curveball. The curveball is often called *Uncle Charlie;* however, at some point in the 1985 season, somebody obviously felt that Gooden's majestic curve required a nickname with more dignity.

Los Angeles Angels   Expansion team joined the American League in 1962. When the team moved from Chavez Ravine in Los Angeles (a.k.a. Dodger Stadium) to Anaheim in 1965, it changed its name to the California Angels.

Los Angeles Dodgers   The name of the National League's Western Division franchise located in Los Angeles, California. The team began as the Brooklyn Dodgers and moved to Los Angeles in 1958. The original reference to trolley-dodging Brooklynites seemed out of place here, but some pointed out that Los Angeles pedestrians had to be adroit automobile dodgers.

Los Angeles Memorial Coliseum   Home grounds of the Los Angeles Dodgers from the beginning of the 1958 season until the end of the 1961 season.

lose   1. *v.* The opposite of "to win"; to allow the other team to score more runs.
2. *v.* To allow a weak hitter to hit safely. A pitcher will say, "I lost him."

lose a baseball/lose one   *v.* To hit a home run out of the park.
"Pete Rose has just lost a baseball in Philadelphia." (Cleveland broadcaster Herb Score, September 18, 1982)

lose a fly   *v.* To misjudge or lose sight of a fly ball, such as a ball that is lost in the sun or in the lights.
1ST   1902. (*Sporting Life,* July 5; EJN)

lose a step   *v.* To slow down. A player well into his 30s will often be said to have "lost a step or two."

losing pitcher   *n.* The pitcher who is charged by the official scorer with the loss of a game because he is responsible for the base runner who scores the opposition's winning run. No matter how many pitchers are involved in a losing effort, only one pitcher can be charged with responsibility for the other team's winning runs.

loss   1. *n.* A defeat.
2. *n.* That which is credited against a losing pitcher and is counted both in his single season and career record. In giving such a statistic, the losses always appear after the number of wins: a season record of 18–8 means 18 wins and 8 losses.

loss column   *n.* See all-important loss column.

lot   1. *n.* BALLPARK.
1ST   1866. (Constitution and By-Laws of the Olympic Baseball Club of Philadelphia; EJN)
2. *n.* Short for sandlot.
1ST   1908 (*Baseball* magazine, July; EJN)

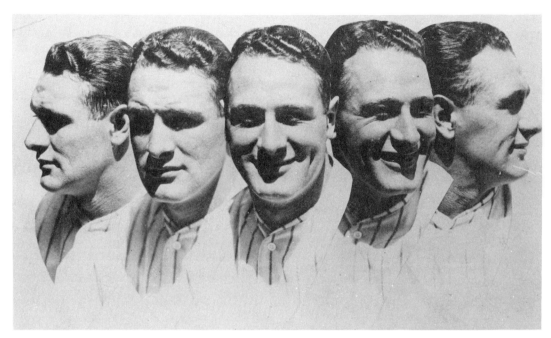

Lou Gehrig's Disease. Gehrig as he looked in his prime. These are stills from a short film in which he is called "The Crown Prince of Swat."   *National Baseball Library, Cooperstown, N.Y.*

loud foul   *n.* A foul ball hit for a long distance, usually close to the foul pole.

Lou Gehrig's disease   *n.* Popular name for amyotrophic lateral sclerosis (ALS), the fatal paralytic disease that claimed the life of Hall of Famer Lou Gehrig. The term has long been applied to all sufferers of the disease, and has done much to increase public awareness of the affliction.
EXT/1ST   1941. The term "Gehrig's Disease" had come into use even before the player succumbed to it. One of its first uses in print came in an Associated Press story on the day of Gehrig's funeral, June 4, 1941, by Harold C. McKinley. That story, which ran in the *Washington Evening Star* of that date under the headline "Science Helpless Treating It, Is Ignorant Even of Cause of 'Gehrig's Disease,' " said that the disease had already been "popularly termed" Gehrig's Disease.

Louisiana   *n.* LINDA RONSTADT.

Louisville Slugger   *n.* Trade name of a bat manufactured by the Hillerich and Bradsby Co., originally of Louisville, Kentucky, but now based in nearby Jeffersonville, Indiana.

low/low ball/low pitch   *n.* A ball that is pitched to a point somewhere at or below the batter's knees. Unless swung at by the batter, a low pitch is a ball.
1ST   1867. (*New York Herald*, July 3; EJN)

low-ball hitter   *n.* Batter known for the ability to hit successfully pitches delivered low, in or below the strike zone.

low bridge/low bridge the batter   *v.* For the pitcher to brush the batter back from the plate; to cause him to bend back as if he were going under a low bridge.
   In relative terms, to low bridge is inches away from beaning. From an 1949 interview with Ferris Fain:
   Q. Much beanballing up there this year?
   A. Once in a while they "low bridge" you, but no real shooting. (*San Francisco Examiner*, August 3; PT)
1ST   1937. (NBC World Series broadcast, Red Barber, October 6; EJN)
ETY   From the days of the canal boat. "The boat moved so slowly that the passengers had fairly long conversations with people walking along the canal bank. Now and then the boat would pass under a bridge. If it were dangerously low the captain or helmsman would yell 'Low Bridge' and the passengers would duck their heads." (*The Way Our People Lived*, by W. E. Woodward, 1944; PT)

Lowdermilk. Grover Cleveland "Slim" Lowdermilk. *National Baseball Library, Cooperstown, N.Y.*

It is also alluded to in a popular American folk song:

Low bridge, ev'ry body down!
Low bridge, for we're going through a town,
And you'll always know your neighbor,
You'll always know your pal,
If you ever navigated on the Erie Canal.
(refrain to "The Erie Canal"; *The American Songbag*, by Carl Sandburg, 1927)

Lowdermilk *n./arch.* Eponymous term for a pitcher given to wildness. From Grover Cleveland Lowdermilk whose lackluster pitching (he had a career record of 21-39 between 1909 and 1920) was characterized by legendary wildness. Lowdermilk attracted some new attention in the mid-1980s when the value of his 1912 baseball card hit $1,200.

lower half *n.* The bottom half of an inning.

low lead *n.* A fastball, one with "good gas"; a heater.

low pitch *n.* Ball thrown to the bottom portion of or to beneath the strike zone.

EXT Crooked deal. "The major sure swings at low pitches! He'll trust a stranger with a face that would set off a bank alarm!" (cartoon, *Our Boarding House,* June 13, 1956; PT)

lucky seventh *n./arch.* The bottom, or home, half of the seventh inning, which was once regarded as lucky.
1ST 1890. (*New York Press,* July 11; EJN)
ETY Edward J. Nichols suggests that it was probably named from the idea of the lucky 7 as known in the game of dice. However, broadcaster Lindsay Nelson reported (NBC-radio, July 20, 1963) that it can be traced back to John Gibson Clarkson, a major league pitcher from 1884–1887, who created the idea when he noted that the highly successful National League team in Chicago won many games by scoring runs in the 7th inning. (PT)

So common was the belief that the 7th inning was a time for big scoring that in 1934 Ford Frick, then head of the National League service bureau, did a statistical analysis of 100 games to see if there was anything to it. He determined that the 7th ranked as the 6th most prolific inning and that the most runs were scored in the first. (*The Sporting News,* September 13, 1934)

lug the bunting *v.* To win the pennant.

lumber 1. *n.* Bat, or bats. "Ready with their 'lumber' preparatory to opening a big five-game series against the Giants tomorrow . . . are the 'big three' sluggers of the Pittsburgh Pirates." (*San Francisco Call-Bulletin* photo caption, May 3, 1958)
2. *n.* A lineup or a portion of a lineup filled with good hitters, such as the Pittsburgh Pirates' "Lumber Company" of the 1970s, composed of Dave Parker, Willie Stargell, Al Oliver and Manny Sanguillen.

lumber man *n.* A player who is primarily a hitter; not a leather man.

lumber yard/lumberyard 1. *n.* The rack of bats in front of the dugout or hung from the dugout wall.
2. *n.* Figurative source of talented batters. "You can shake a tree and a thousand guys who can field will drop out. But it's harder to find guys from the lumber yard. Dave Winfield doesn't make $1.5 million because he's a good defensive outfielder." (Kansas City Royals' DH Hal McRae, quoted in the *San Francisco Examiner,* May 22, 1981; PT)

lumps   *n.* Hard hitting against a pitcher. A pitcher getting back into the rotation after an injury will often remark that he will take his lumps until he is in the groove again.
1ST   1937. (*New York Times*, October 8; EJN)

lunch hooks   *n.* Hands; see dinner tongs.

lunge   *v.* An erratic move made by a batter trying to get at a ball in front of the plate. It is usually the result of the batter misjudging the speed or trajectory of the pitch.

M

mace *n./arch.* The BAT.
1ST 1928. (*New York Times*, October 7; EJN)

machine *n.* A team; specifically, one that works smoothly, precisely and with good teamwork. A case in point was Cincinnati's "Big Red Machine" of the 1970s.
1ST 1908. (*Baseball* magazine, November; EJN)

mackerel *n.* See dead fish.
ETY From the old saying "dead as a mackerel," which is how it appears when compared to the fastball.

Mackmen Nickname for the Philadelphia Athletics during the years that Connie Mack was in charge (1901–1950).

Mackmen. He was born Cornelius Alexander Mc-Gillicuddy, but everyone knew him as Connie Mack. He managed for 53 years, all but four of which were for the Philadelphia Athletics. *Courtesy of the Cleveland Indians*

maestro *n./arch.* MANAGER, usually applied to one who insists on running the team right down to minor details.

maggot *n./arch.* A club owner.
ETY In the *American Language: Supplement II*, H. L. Mencken lists it as a piece of baseball slang and says that it is an apparent play on the word magnate.

magic number *n.* The combination of wins and losses that add up to a championship for a first place team. More exactly, the total number of games that the leading team in a division or league must win and/or the second place team must lose in order to clinch the championship for the leader. If, for example, the Phillies' magic number is six with the Mets in second place any combination of Phillies wins and Mets losses adding up to six gives the championship to the Phillies.

To determine the magic number, you combine the second place team's wins and number of games remaining. From this total subtract the leading team's number of wins. The difference plus one equals the magic number.

The magic number comes into play at the end of a season to dramatize the end of the pennant race and is often featured in headlines. "Red Sox Win, 2–0; Cut Magic Number to One." (*Buffalo News* headline for September 28, 1986) When a team is eliminated, the term is sometimes used facetiously. A September 13, 1960, headline in the *San Francisco Chronicle*, carried as the Giants were removed from contention, read: " 'Magic Number' for S.F. is 1961." (PT) The term and the concept are clearly modern, according to the research of Peter Tamony dating back to the 1940s—perhaps, a bit earlier.

magic wand *n./arch.* The bat of a player who is getting a number of lucky hits.

magic word *n.* A word or phrase, usually obscene, that, when uttered to an umpire, almost certainly provokes the speaker's ejection from the game.

magnate   *n.* Team owner or stockholder.
1ST   1905. (*Sporting Life,* October 7; EJN)

mailbox baseball   *n.* An act of vandalism in which rural mailboxes are struck from a moving car by a person swinging a baseball bat. It is a federal offense. A scene in the film *Stand By Me,* in which the game is played from the open window of a 1949 Ford, may have given the practice ill-deserved publicity.

major company   *n./arch.* Major Leagues.
1ST   1902. (*Sporting Life,* July 12; EJN)

major league   **1.** *n.* One of the two leagues, the American and the National, that constitute the Major Leagues.
2. *adj.* Referring to a level of play or behavior that is at the level of the Major Leagues. A college or minor league player may be said, for example, to have a "major league arm."
EXT   Anything imposing and of the highest level, whether it be a major league client or a major league headache.

Major League Baseball Players Association   The labor union of major league baseball players.

major leaguer   *n.* A major league baseball player.
1ST   1908. (*Baseball* magazine, December; EJN)

Major Leagues   The highest level of professional baseball, comprising the National and American leagues. Each of these two leagues is broken down into an Eastern and Western division.

Major League Scouting Bureau   A service group founded in 1968 to offer free-lance scouting for a fee to any team. The El Toro, California, group has about 50 scouts who are members.

majors, the   *n.* The Major Leagues, for short.
1ST   1911. (*Baseball* magazine, October; EJN)
EXT   The top level of competition.

make a right turn   *v.* Good fielding, a reference to the fact that a man who has been put out turns right at first base on his way back to the dugout.

"make it be good"   *v./arch.* This was once a common instruction to batters. Hugh S. Fullerton in his 1912 *Primer* gave this the definition, "The war cry of coaches and the order of

managers to the batter when the opposing pitcher shows signs of wildness, the meaning being that the batter is not to hit the ball unless it is a perfect strike, whether or not he hits."
1ST   1912 (as above from Hugh Fullerton).

make it too good   *v.* To throw a pitch that is easy for the batter to hit. This usually results when a pitcher has to throw the ball in the strike zone, as on a round of 3–0.

make-up game   *n.* A game that has been rescheduled or a previously scheduled game that has been rained out or cancelled for any one of a number of reasons.

making vitamins   *v.* Committing errors. Reported by Tom Gill of Davis, California: "San Francisco Giants catcher-turned-third baseman Bob Brenly was being interviewed by Giants' broadcaster Phil Stone, who chided him for making an error by bobbling a ground ball.
   " 'Well, ever since they switched me to third base, I've really been making vitamins out there, Phil.'
   "Stone, quizzically, 'Making vitamins?'
   "Brenly, self-assuredly: 'Yeah . . . one-a-day.' "
   (On September 14, 1986, several days after explaining "making vitamins," Brenly became the first major league player since 1901 to make four errors in one inning.)
ETY   From the name of a popular One-A-Day vitamin product.

man, the   *n.* MANAGER.

manage   *v.* To act as a manager.

manager   *n.* The person who has been given the job of running the team. Traditionally, the manager determines the lineup and batting order, makes substitutions and plans the game strategy. The professional manager is hired by the owner or owners of the club.
1ST   1880. (*New York Herald,* July 12; EJN)

M&M Boys   Roger Maris and Mickey Mantle when they played together for the New York Yankees (1960–1966).
   "Now, you can relive through Mickey's eyes the glory days of the New York Yankees: The 'M&M Boys' chasing the Babe's home-run crown . . ." (cover copy of the paperback edition of *The Mick* by Mickey Mantle, with Herb Gluek)
ETY   This nickname was clearly inspired by the name of the popular M&M chocolate candy.

Manager. Hall of Famer Frank Robinson in his managerial debut with the Cleveland Indians (1975). *Courtesy of the Cleveland Indians*

man from outer space *n.* Player whose feats are extraordinary.

manicurist *n.* GROUNDSKEEPER.

man in the middle *n.* Runner caught in a rundown on the base path.

man on the firing line *n.* The pitcher.

man overboard *n.* A runner who has run or slid past a base. See furlough (ETY).

marathon *n.* A long, extra-inning baseball game.

marble **1.** *n./arch.* The BALL.
2. *n./obs.* HOME PLATE. Before it was made of rubber homeplate was commonly a marble slab. The rubber plate replaced the marble plate in 1887 according to Patrick Ercolano in *Fungoes, Floaters and Fastballs.*

marked ball *n.* A ball that has been scratched, cut or scuffed to make it move oddly when pitched.

marker *n./arch.* A RUN.
1ST 1922. (*Baseball Cyclopedia;* EJN)

mascot **1.** *n.* Historically speaking, a youngster, often the bat boy, who takes care of the equipment, does odd chores and is commonly felt to bring luck to the team. Many team photos of the late 19th century show a uniformed boy indentified as the mascot (examples on file at the Library of Congress show a mascot as early as the 1888 St. Louis Browns).

In *High and Inside,* H. Allen Smith explains the traditional linking of mascots and bat boys in baseball, ". . . it's all right to have him around for good luck, but the little twerp oughta do some work too."
2. *n.* An animal or costumed figure used to characterize and bring luck to a team. Such mascots are almost always given names. It has been written on several occasions that the custom of the animal mascot in America may have started in college football. "The first football mascot, so far as anyone can now recall, was Handsome Dan, a bulldog who belonged to a member of the Yale class of 1892." (*Sports Illustrated,* November 5, 1956) However, in his research on the term, Gerald Cohen has found this from the May 25, 1887, *New York World:* "It was Pittsburgh's first victory from the Giants, and the ever-happy Galvin's smile increased in magnitude. The Skye-terrier mascot was left at the hotel." (*Comments on Etymology,* February 1, 1987)
1ST 1887. (*Chicago Inter Ocean,* April 10; EJN)
ETY The direct American origin of the term came in 1880 with the importation of the French comic opera, *La Mascotte.* When looking before that date there are two theories: (1) that it derives from a Provençal word, *masco,* for sorceress or (2) that it comes from *masque,* for one who is covered or concealed, which in provincial France was applied to a child born with a caul. The caul was believed to bring luck.

From whatever source, the notion of the mascot was quickly accepted in some quarters. "Firm believers in both mascots and hoodoos are to be found among sporting men, and also among theatrical people. 'Getting a hunch' is an alternative expression for 'getting a tip' and it springs from the fact that hunchbacks, if properly approached, are a sure source of luck." (*The Illustrated American,* May 24, 1980; PT)

Some American mascots were important figures. "Sharing honors with [Connie] Mack in bringing three world's titles to Philadelphia in four years was the little hunchbacked mascot, Louis Van Zelst. A kindly, good-natured boy,

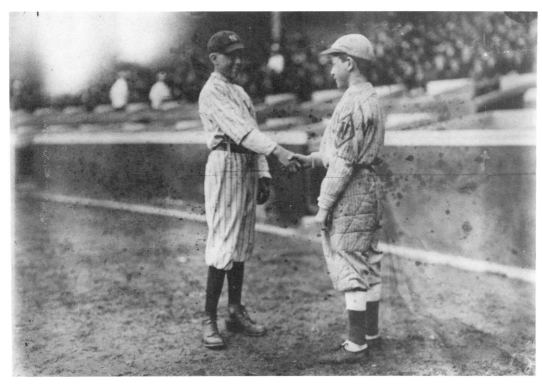

Mascot. Disarming image of the New York Yankee and Washington Senator mascots (c. 1919), from the Bain Collection at the Library of Congress.   *Prints and Photographs Division, the Library of Congress*

he had come to Mack in 1909 and said he was lucky and indeed he was. Nothing but good luck followed in his wake." (*Connie Mack, Grand Old Man of Baseball* by Frederick C. Lieb, 1945; PT)

mask   *n.* Protective facial gear worn by the catcher and home plate umpire.
1ST   1887. (*Harpers Weekly*, September 10; EJN)

mask and mitten work/mask and mit work/ mask work   *n./arch.* The position of catcher.
1ST   1908 (mask and mitten). (*Baseball* magazine, November; EJN)

mask man   Catcher.
1ST   1905. (*Sporting Life*, October 7; EJN)

Massachusetts game   *n.* An early baseball variation played on a box-shaped rather than a diamond-shaped field, with a distance of 60 feet between the bases. It was played in New England from the early 1800s until the time of the Civil War, after which the "New York" version of the game (based on the *Knickerbocker Rules*) began to take hold.

The game, also known as either the New England Game or the Boston Game employed four-foot-high wooden stakes for bases and allowed for an out when a runner, not on base, was hit with the ball thrown by a defensive player. Two rules that emphasize the game's distance from the modern game of baseball are these:

In playing all match games, when one is out, the side shall be considered out.

In playing, all match games, seventy-five tallies [runs] shall constitute the game, the making of which by either Club, that Club shall be judged the winner.

massage/massage one   *v.* To bat a ball.
1ST   1932. (*Baseball* magazine, October; EJN)

mass hits   *v./arch.* As a team, to collect many hits within a short period, usually an inning.
1ST   1915. (*Baseball* magazine, December; EJN)

master fly   *n.* HOME RUN.
1ST   1987. "Wow, that sure was some master fly." (*St. Petersburg Times*, March 5)

master mind   *n.* Manager. Sometimes this term is applied with a hint of cynicism, such as in this definition, which appeared in the 1938 *Baseball Scrap Book:* "Manager who wants to do the thinking for the entire team." The term was often applied to long-time Yankee manager John McGraw during his managing years.
1ST   1920. (*New York Times,* October 5; EJN)

matador   *n.* A timid infielder; specifically, one who positions his body like a bullfighter to avoid being hit by the ball when fielding it.

matching   *n.* Baseball card flipping game in which a card is dropped and it is up to the second player to match it to keep both cards. If the first player's card lands with the photo side up (heads) the second player must flip heads also or lose both cards. The printed back of the card in this game is regarded as tails.

material   *n.* Players, especially recruits.
1ST   1905. (*Sporting Life,* October 7; EJN)

matinee   **1.** *n.* An afternoon game.
2. *n.* Specifically, the afternoon game that was once traditionally played on the same day as a morning game. Such games were once common on holidays like July 4th and Labor Day.

   Although there were no hard and fast rules for this, such same-day games were not usually regarded as doubleheaders and one had to pay separate admissions to each game.
1ST   1898. (*New York Tribune,* June 19; EJN)

mattress   *n.* CHEST PROTECTOR worn by catchers and home plate umpires.
1ST   1908. (*Baseball* magazine, July; EJN)

maul a pitcher   *v.* To get many hits.

maul one/maul the offerings   *v.* To successfully hit for a long distance the balls thrown by a pitcher.
1ST   1910. (*American* magazine, July; EJN)

McGrawism   *n.* An action or strategy characterized by rough, anything-goes baseball, suggested by the play and managerial style of John J. McGraw. For instance, the hit-and-run play, which he is given credit for engineering.

meal ticket/mealticket   *n.* A club's winningest and most effective pitcher. Dizzy Dean once called Ned Garver of the St. Louis Browns a "mealticket" because, "He keeps 'em eatin regular." (DD) But the player most closely tied to the term was Carl Hubbell, who was known as "King Carl, the Meal Ticket" not only because

McGrawism. John McGraw as a New York Giant (c. 1904). *National Baseball Library, Cooperstown, N.Y.*

he kept food on his manager's table, but also because of his reliability between 1933 and 1937, when he won 115 games.
1ST   1905. (*Sporting Life,* October 7; EJN)
ETY   The term had several slang meanings before it attached itself to Hubbell. However, all of the meanings—ranging from a hobo who carries another hobo's food or food money to a woman supporting a panderer or pimp—refer to a valued asset. Another common application is to a prizefighter who is his manager's meal ticket: "A meal ticket is a valuable asset, but one punch can make it null and void." (headline, *San Francisco Call,* March 14, 1914; PT)
EXT   Any person or object that brings success.

measure bats   *v./arch.* To meet and play another team.
1ST   1880. (*New York Herald,* July 16; EJN)

meat   **1.** *n.* The thickest part of the bat.
2. *n.* The strongest hitters in the middle of the lineup; the meat of the batting order.
3. *n.* The hitter's limbs and body. To "take one on the meat" is to be hit by a pitched ball.
4. *n.* A ballplayer.

meatball   **1.** *n.* An easy-to-hit pitch that comes right down the middle of the plate.

Mealticket. "King Carl" Hubbell in 1932.   *National Baseball Library, Cooperstown, N.Y.*

2. *n.* A pitch that is properly met with the bat for a hit, a clear refashioning of "meet the ball," as in the plaintive cry of the Little League coach, "Just meet the ball."

meat hand   1. *n.* A fielder's gloveless throwing hand; the one with which players are loath to field hard-hit balls. So-called because a ball caught in this hand hits flesh rather than leather. "When I was sixteen, I went to work for the Green & Twichell shoe factory. I remember in that summer we chipped in and bought a glove for two dollars. It was made of buckskin and had no fingers. It was used in turn by one player after another, since it was common property. Up to that time we had played with our 'meat' hands, and the catcher caught the pitcher's offerings on the first bounce." (Connie Mack in *The Saturday Evening Post,* April 4, 1936; PT)
1ST   1912. (*American* magazine, June; EJN)
2. *n.* The hand closest to the knob of the bat when the batter grips the bat.

mechanical pitching machine   *n.* See iron mike.

mechanics   *n.* The basic skills and timing of a pitcher. "I wasn't hurting," Oriole relief pitcher Don Aase told Richard Justice of the *Washington Post* (February 20, 1988), "but my mechanics were all messed up. Because of that, I was trying to compensate by over-throwing . . ."

media guide   *n.* A highly detailed and richly statistical annual guidebook to a club and its individual players, which is prepared by the club and released during the spring for the use of the working press during the course of the season. They are also sold to the public.

Because they contain so many numbers and statistics, they often include minor errors, which are occasionally brought to light. "Media guide gaffs keep game light" was a May 13, 1986, *USA Today* headline for a story on players who gain 100 pounds or a foot in height with the publication of the guide.

meet the ball   *v.* To swing the bat while the ball is still out in front of the plate so that the two objects meet at a point that is likely to result in a hit. To take a less than full swing.
1ST   1905. (*Sporting Life,* September 9; EJN)

Memorial Stadium   Located in Baltimore, Maryland, the home grounds of the Baltimore Orioles.

Mendoza line   1. *n.* Figurative boundary in the batting averages between those batters hitting above and below .215. It is named for shortstop Mario Mendoza whose career (1974–

Mendoza line. Mario Mendoza with the Texas Rangers (1981).   *Courtesy of the Texas Rangers*

82) batting average for the Pirates, Mariners and Rangers was .215.

2. *n.* It also has a slightly different meaning according to other sources, including the September 13, 1982, *Sports Illustrated*. "When a struggling hitter pulls his average above .200, he has crossed the Mendoza Line."

ETY Coinage of the term has been credited to George Brett, who has been quoted in the book *Rotisserie League Baseball* as saying, "The first thing I look for in the Sunday papers is who is below the Mendoza line."

USE This is clearly an emerging term that can have two slightly different meanings (.215 *vs.* .200), so it is important to make sure others understand which Mendoza line is being referred to. However, it seems like the .200 line is used more commonly than the .215 version.

men in blue *n.* UMPIRES, who are also known as the boys in blue.

mental error *n.* A mistake made because the player is preoccupied, forgetful or distracted. A classic mental error occurs when, with a man on first, an infielder throws to first base for a putout when he should have thrown to second for the force and a possible double play.

merkle *n./arch.* a boner, named for Fred Merkle.

Merkle's boner The running error that cost the National League Championship of 1908. **SEE** Discussed in detail under *boner*.

merry circle *n.* The trip around the bases.

merry go round *n.* Describing when, with two outs, the bases loaded, and a full count on the batter, all the runners take off on the pitch.

message pitch *n.* A pitch thrown close to the batter, which is intended to convey this message: "Don't crowd the plate."

Mets theory *n.* A theory that says when the New York Mets win the stock market falls, and when they lose it goes up. The Mets theory is one of many tongue-in-cheek barometers, including the length of women's hemlines and the winner of the Super Bowl, which tie success or failure of the stock market to events and trends in popular culture. Explained in full in the September 23, 1985, *Forbes*, the theory was severely damaged in 1986 when the Mets and the Dow Jones average were both in top form.

Mexican standoff *n.* A contest or confrontation with no result, but from which one es-

capes; such as when a pitcher comes out of a game with no decision.

ETY This entry appears in *Western Words, A Dictionary of the Range, Cow Camp and Trail* by Ramon F. Adams:

> *Mexican standoff* Getting away alive from any serious difficulty. The Mexican has never had the reputation, among the cowboys, for being a sticker in a fight. They claim that, if he does not win quickly in a gun battle or if he finds much opposition, he leaves in a hurry.

1ST 1891. " 'Monk' Cline, who got a Mexican stand-off from Dave Rowe has signed with Louisville." (*Sporting Times*, September 19, 1891; DS)

michaelangelo *n.* A pitcher able to paint a masterpiece from the mound.

Mickey Finn *n./arch.* Edward J. Nichols reports: "A printed schedule of league games for a season; named for a former news reporter who became the first expert modern schedule maker."
1ST 1906. (*Sporting Life*, March 10; EJN)

middle **1.** *n./adj.* The center of the plate, as opposed to the corners.
2. *n./adj.* The middle of the playing field, such as a ball hit to center field.

middle cushion/middle sack/middle station *n./arch.* Second base.
1ST 1910 (middle station). (*Baseball* magazine, April; EJN)

middle defense *n.* Collectively, a team's catcher, shortstop, second baseman and center fielder.

middle gardener *n.* Center fielder.

middle innings *n.* Generally, the 4th, 5th and 6th innings of a baseball game.

middle relief *n.* An pitching assignment that begins sometime in the middle innings of the game. Commonly it ends with short relief, which is another pitcher who is brought in during the late innings.

middle reliever *n.* Pitcher situated between a starter and stopper.

midsummer classic *n.* The All-Star game, as opposed to the World Series, which is the fall classic.

midway/midway station *n.* SECOND BASE.
1ST 1906. (*Sporting Life*, March 10; EJN)

mile wide *adj.* Describing a wild pitch or throw.

Millennium Plan A radical 1887 plan advanced by Francis C. Richter of *The Sporting Life* of Philadelphia to rid the professional game of labor unrest, escalating salaries and other problems and result in 1,000 years of peace and harmony. The main feature of the plan called for the equalization of the playing strength among the clubs in any professional league by pooling players and distributing them "impartially." It had many other points, including salary caps, reservation of minor league players by leagues rather than clubs, and a reserve corps of extra players to be used by teams as they were needed during the season. It created much interest at the time and was discussed for several years, but never seriously interested the players or the club owners.

Miller-Brown System or Miller-Brown Relief Pitching Grading System A grading system for ranking pitchers; specifically a measuring rod for middle relievers devised by Ray Miller, when he was Baltimore Orioles pitching coach, and Bob Brown, Oriole publicist. It was brought to public attention in an April 1986 article that first appeared in the *Hartford Courant.*

Because middle relief pitchers don't usually earn wins, losses or saves, the statistics are ineffective measures of their abilities. The Miller-Brown system grants one point for a hold, two for a victory and three for a save. One can also get two points for a hold in which three or more scoreless innings are pitched with the score tied or with the team ahead by no more than two runs. One point is subtracted for a squander and two for a loss. A special two-point squander can be awarded when the pitcher allows an opponent to tie or go ahead by three or more runs. No more than three points can be accumulated in one game and a reliever can be granted a combination score: hold and victory, hold and loss, hold and squander, squander and save, squander and loss, squander and victory.

millionaires' club *n.* Group of players whose annual salaries are in the seven-figure realm. At the beginning of the 1988 season, the *New York Times* reported that 73 players on Opening Day rosters and disabled lists were in the club, compared to 57 at the beginning of the 1987 season.

million ticket year *n.* A milestone in the course of a season, which occurs when and if a team sells its millionth ticket. The ability to sell over a million tickets is considered a sign of a healthy franchise. Several teams have posted three-million-or-more ticket records.

Milwaukee Braves National League team, in Wisconsin, from the time the team ceased being the Boston Braves in 1952 and until it became the Atlanta Braves in 1966.

Milwaukee Brewers The name of the American League's Eastern Division franchise based in Milwaukee, Wisconsin. Once a National League team (1878 only) and a long-time AAA Western team, the Brewers reentered the Major Leagues in 1970 when the Seattle Pilots, an American League expansion team from 1969, moved to Milwaukee the following year. Natural name in a city that has long regarded itself as America's beer capital. The team is sometimes affectionately referred to as the "Brew Crew."

mini *n.* A baseball card that is smaller than the traditional 3½ by 2½ inches.

minimum scale *n.* The lowest salary a league can offer a player.

Minnesota Twins The name of the American League's Western Division franchise based in Minneapolis, Minnesota. Named for the twin cities of Minneapolis and St. Paul, the team was the original Washington Senators franchise, which moved to Minnesota in 1960 where they were to begin as the Twin City Twins; but before opening day 1961, owner Calvin Griffith decided to name them for the whole state.

minnion *n.* Uglier than a *mullion* according to Scott Ostler in his 1986 *Los Angeles Times* article on baseball "lingo."

minor league Any professional United States or Canadian league other than the two Major Leagues: These are the training ground for the Major Leagues and are classified on the basis of the general ability and experience of the players. From the highest level down, the Minor Leagues are classified AAA, AA, A and Rookie. There are 16 Minor Leagues today, which are far fewer than in the past when there were as many as 60 such leagues including those at levels B, C and D. The system of letters was established not only to show the level of play and skill but also the size of the city or

town where the team was located. D-class teams, for instance, used to play in towns with less than 150,000 population.
1ST 1884. (*DeWitt's Official Base Ball Guide*; EJN)
EXT Anything not at the highest level, such as a minor league actor.

minors *n.* The professional leagues below the Major Leagues, which are sponsored, controlled and sometimes owned by big league teams. Currently there are three levels of minor league baseball: AAA, AA and A. "I'd rather go to lunch with my ex-wife's attorney than stay in the minors." (Dave Collins on being brought up from the minors, July 1987)
1ST 1908. (*New York Evening Journal*, March 5; EJN)

Miracle Braves The 1914 Boston Braves, so-called because they won the pennant after coming from last place in July (winning 61 of their last 77 games.) The miracle was complete when they beat the Philadelphia Athletics in the World Series.

Miracle Game, the Name given to the no-hit, no-run game pitched by Bob Feller of the Cleveland Indians on Opening Day of the 1940 season.

miracle man *n.* Manager who achieves success with a reputedly poor team.
1ST 1914. (*New York Tribune*, September 30; EJN)

Miracle Mets Nickname of the 1969 New York Mets who won not only the pennant but also the World Series. In their debut season, 1962, they finished with a 40–120 record.

Miracle of Coogan's Bluff The 1951 New York Giants pennant drive, which ended with Bobby Thomson's pennant-clinching "shot heard round the world"—arguably the most famous home run in the history of the game. The home run won a best-of-three series for the National League championship after the regular season had ended in a tie between the Giants and the Brooklyn Dodgers.

miscue *n.* An error.
1ST 1902. (*Sporting Life*, July 5; EJN)
ETY Edward J. Nichols has traced the term to the game of billiards in which a cue stick and cue ball figure prominently.

misjudge *v.* For a fielder to end up too far in front, behind or to the side of a fly ball.

misplay 1. *v.* To handle the ball badly.
2. *n.* Error.

miss a base/miss the bag *v.* For a runner to advance past a base without touching it. If this lack of contact with the base is noted by the fielding team, the pitcher who gets the ball at the end of the play throws to a fielder who touches the base in an appeal play.

mistake by the lake Cleveland, Ohio, nickname that has sometimes been applied to the perennially striving Cleveland Indians.

mistake hitter *n.* A batter who is fooled by a pitch, but is quick to learn from his mistake.

Mr. Baseball For decades, this is what they called Connie Mack. In recent years it has been used in a self-deprecating manner by Bob Uecker.

Mr. Cub Ernie Banks, for many years the Cubs' "franchise" player.

Mr. Guess Umpire.

Mr. Kodak According to Joe Goddard in *The Sporting News* for March 6, 1982, "A hitter who fakes his time getting into the box, allowing photographers time to focus on him."

Mr. Mustard See *hot dog*.

Mr. October Reggie Jackson, for his playoff and World Series homer heroics in the 1970s.

mit *n./arch.* A variant spelling of mitt, used, for instance, in John B. Foster's 1908 glossary of baseball terms.

mitt 1. *n.* The special gloves used by catchers and first basemen. It has long been said that this stems from the mitten-like shape of both gloves, which have two sections: one for the thumb and one for the other four fingers.
2. *n.* Any fielder's glove.
USE There may be an element of localism involved in calling baseball gloves mitts. In the author's boyhood neighborhood in Yonkers, New York, everything was a mitt while gloves were for boxing and sledding. However, some simply use the word interchangeably with glove, as this headline and subheadline from the *Miami Herald* (April 5, 1986) would attest:
Mizuno mitts make their mark: Japanese gloves become popular with major leagues
3. *n.* A players hand.

mix it up/mix up *v.* To throw an assortment of pitches at various speeds to various

Mr. October. Reggie Jackson as a California Angel. *Courtesy of the California Angels*

locations in and around the strike zone. It is used to confuse and deceive the batter.
1ST 1895. (*New York Press,* July 11; EJN)

modern *adj.* In baseball this has a most particular meaning: after 1900. It is used to make a distinction between this century and the last and is used in the phrase "modern era," which excludes anything before 1900.

moistball/moist ball *n.* SPITBALL.
1ST 1917. (*New York Times,* April 1; EJN)

Molly Putz *n.* Name for player who performs badly on the field. In *Ball Four,* Jim Bouton says that in response to a poor field performance "a lot of managers say their players look like Molly Putz out there." (CDP)

money bags/moneybags *n.* Any highly-paid player, especially one who makes more than most of his teammates.

money pitch **1.** *n.* A pitcher's most effective pitch.
2. *n.* Pitch thrown for a strikeout in a key situation in a game.

money player **1.** *n.* Traditionally, one who is at his best when the most is at stake; for instance, one who shines when a club is making

a drive for first place in the standings. Also, one given to winning games.
1ST 1922. (*Baseball Cyclopedia;* EJN)
2. *n.* In the wake of higher and higher salaries, the term has inevitably been used to describe players who make a great deal of money. Joseph McBride points out in his *High and Inside:* "The term was frequently used in the 1970s to refer to Reggie Jackson and his fellow Yankees, a collection of prima donnas known as 'The Best Team Money Could Buy.' "

monkeys *n./arch.* Poor batters, so-called according to Edward J. Nichols because they make monkeys of themselves in their futile attempts to get a hit.
1ST 1888. (*New York Press,* June 3; EJN)

monkey suit *n.* Uniform.

monster shot *n.* Home run of major proportions.

Montreal Expos The name of the National League's Eastern Division franchise in Montreal, Quebec, Canada. An expansion team that came into being with the 1968 season, it was the first major league team to locate in Canada. The team was named for the popular World's Fair, Expo '67.

moon shot *n.* Home run. A space age term, it took on new meaning in 1986 when a statistician determined that slugger Mike Schmidt hit best under a full moon.

mop up/mop-up man *n.* A relief pitcher who commonly enters a game when the outcome of the game is no longer in doubt, usually when the pitcher's team is far behind. The term is a clear play on the idea of mopping up the mess created by the earlier pitcher or pitchers. A team's top reliever is seldom if ever used as a mop-up man.
1ST 1937. (*Philadelphia Record,* August 28; EJN)

moriarity *n./arch.* A blind swing at the ball. Named for George Moriarity, an infielder (1903–1916) who was widely known for swinging without looking at the ball.
1ST 1914. "I tried to slip the fast one over on him and he shut his eyes and took a Moriarity at it—that's all." (*Colliers,* August 1, 1914; DS)

morning glory *n.* A hitter who shines early in the season but then cools off; a spring hitter; commonly applied to rookies off to a hot start.
ETY The folkname for a flowering vine that only opens its flowers in the morning. In *Good*

Florida·Blues .·. *Swing Time in Spring Time*

Morning glory. Cartoon, with one of the great morning glory lines put into a telegram. *National Baseball Library, Cooperstown, N.Y.*

Words to You, John Ciardi points out that it began showing up in the 19th century as American sports slang for an athlete who begins brilliantly but becomes lackluster in short order.
EXT Anyone whose performance lags over time. Ciardi's example: "The official flower for the fiftieth wedding anniversary should be the morning glory."

morning journal *n.* A bat made of inferior wood, often said to have the effectiveness of a rolled-up newspaper.

moss *n.* Player's hair.

Most Valuable Player (MVP) 1. Player deemed to have made the greatest contribution to a team in his league. Since 1931, the annual award given to one player in each league by the Baseball Writers Association of America. It honors the player voted most outstanding. Earlier MVP awards were given in each league before it was institutionalized by the Baseball Writers. The first American League MVP was George Sisler of the Browns in 1922 and the first National League winner was Dazzy Vance of the Brooklyn Dodgers in 1924.

Currently, the MVP is picked by a vote of two writers from each of the 26 major league cities. Each writer votes for 10 players in descending order, with each first place vote worth 14 points, nine points for second place and one less point down to 10th, which is worth one.

Giving all of this a bit of cynical and jaded perspective, the late Jimmy Cannon described the MVP as, "A guy on the club that wins the pennant." (In fact, many MVP's have come from pennant-winning teams, but this is added proof of the value of the MVP.)
2. A term for an honor voted to players at most levels of the game, including the Major Leagues, which also has such honors as World Series Most Valuable Player.

motion *n.* The pitcher's movement during his delivery to home plate.

Burt Dunne points out in the his *Folger's Dictionary of Baseball:* "Hitting at a pitcher's 'motion' means batter was bewildered by arm action and swung at 'motion' instead of ball."

motor *v.* To run at top speed.

motormouth *n.* A player who talks all the time.

mound 1. *n.* The elevated dirt area where the pitcher is situated. It should be no higher than 10 inches at its peak according to the current official rules. The pitcher's plate or rubber is set in the ground on top of the mound.
1ST 1907. (*New York Evening Journal*, May 4; EJN)
2. *adj.* A synonym for pitching, as in "mound assignment," "mound duel," "mound duty," "mound statesman," "mound mainstay," and, as applied to a relief pitcher in the *Orlando Sentinel* (February 26, 1988), "mound savior."
USE The extent to which the word mound has become part of the patter of baseballese was driven home in Frank Sullivan's "The Cliché Expert Testifies on Baseball" in the August 27, 1949, *New Yorker*. As with other articles of this type, the gist of it is an interview with cliche expert Mr. Arbuthnot. After explaining moundsman, mound assignment and mound nominee, the expert is asked what the pitcher on the other team is called?

A. He is the mound adversary, or mound opponent, or the mound nominee. That makes them rival hurlers, or twirlers. They face each other and have a mound duel, or pitcher's battle.
Q. Who wins?

A. The mound victor wins, and as a result he is a mound ace, or an ace moundsman. He excels on the mound, or stars on it. He and the other moundsmen on his team are the mound corps.

mound conference *n.* Meeting at the pitcher's mound between the pitcher and the manager, the pitching coach or one or more infielders.

What goes on during these meetings? Pitcher Vic Raschi addressed this issue in a 1949 article and pointed out that most conferences were held either to slow down a pitcher who was working too fast or to relieve tension. "Once in a World Series game," Raschi wrote, "the immortal first baseman, Lou Gehrig, walked over to the great Red Ruffing and asked him what town he was in." (*San Francisco News,* July 6, 1949; PT)

moundsman *n.* PITCHER.
1ST 1914. "This information will be received with loud, ringing cheers by that eminent moundsman, Thomas Aloysius Kernohan." (*Colliers,* August 1, 1914; DS)

mount *v.* To ride an opponent, a synonym for jockey.

move **1.** *n.* The action, speed and deception of a pitcher when throwing to first from a set position. A pitcher may be said to have a great or poor move to first.
2. *v.* To advance a runner.
3. *v.* To trade a player or to send a player to the minors; to remove.
4. *v.* To be able to place a pitched ball to various locations; to be able to move the ball around. One pitch may be "high and away," the next "down and in."

move-around fielder *n.* "One who covers more than the average amount of territory; a fielder with a wide range," according to H. G. Salsinger in the April 1945 *Baseball Digest.*

move in the fences *v.* To re-configure a ball park to make it easier to hit home runs.

movement *n.* Characteristic of a pitched ball that deviates vertically or horizontally as it approaches and crosses the plate; a measure of deception.

move the ball around *v.* To pitch at an ever-varying target.

"I felt like I was throwing the ball well and moving it around today." (Roger Clemens, quoted in the *Washington Post,* August 31, 1986)

move up **1.** *v.* To advance a base.
2. *v.* To hit a ball that advances a base runner along the basepath.

moving around the box Describing a batter who employs several different stances during one plate appearance.

mow down/mow them down *v.* For a pitcher to retire a series of batters.
1ST 1891. (*Chicago Herald,* May 5; EJN)

moxie **1.** *n.* Nerve and skill used in playing the game. "A player's guts or know-how shown in a game," according to Frank Graham and Dick Hyman in *Baseball Wit and Wisdom.* Usually couched in a phrase like "lots of moxie" or "the old moxie."
2. *n.* General pluck and mettle on or off the field.

"Love him or hate him—as club owners did Monday in Chicago on an 8–18 minority ratio in refusing to review Bowie Kuhn's contract—but no one can help admiring the moxie of the guy." (This AP dispatch, November 3, 1982, appeared in the *Gloucester County* [New Jersey] *Times* under the headline: "You had to admire the moxie of Kuhn.")
3. *n.* The power that makes a fastball good and hard. In a column on the use of the term moxie in baseball, Edmund A. MacDonald reported in the *Lewiston Daily Sun* (July 12, 1986) that a catcher would say to a pitcher: "Put some Moxie on it!"
ETY/1ST 1908. There is no questioning the fact that the term comes from a drink or tonic that was created and named in 1876 by Dr. Augustin Thompson and marketed as a "nerve tonic" and "nerve food." The link between Moxie and one's nerves led to the obvious "nerve and skill" meaning of the word. In their *Dictionary of Word and Phrase Origins,* William and Mary Morris write, "One theory is that the original *Moxie* was so bitter that you had to have plenty of courage to drink the stuff." Frank N. Potter of Newport News, Virginia, author of *The Moxie Mystique* and *The Book of Moxie,* has disputed this claim, insisting that it is a simple play on the word nerve in Moxie Nerve Food. Writing in *The Book of Moxie* he says, "How do I know that I'm right about the derivation of 'moxie?' Well, before World War I, when I was a kid in Massachusetts, we always said, 'You're full of

Athletes and Business Men

DRINK ... **MOXIE** in order to

Eat Better, Sleep Better and Feel Better

IT'S JUST AS GOOD FOR
THE WHOLE FAMILY

Apollinaris

A Twentieth Century Baseball Score Book
═══FREE═══

This score book is pocket size bound in Linen Cloth containing score sheets for **50** games, and instructions for scoring a ball game. Send us **$1.50** for one-year subscription to the **Baseball Magazine** and we will send you this handsome book **Free** in time to **Score the First Game.**

| A Year Subscription to THE BASEBALL MAGAZINE ... $1.50 One Copy of the TWENTIETH CENTURY SCORE BOOK .. .50 Total .... $2.00 | ALL FOR $1.50 | THE BASEBALL MAGAZINE, 88 Broad St., Boston, Mass. Enclosed find $1.50 for which please send me the BASEBALL MAGAZINE for one year and a copy of the TWENTIETH CENTURY SCORE BOOK FREE and postpaid as per your offer. Name........................ Street........................ City.......... State.......... |

Patronize our advertisers. We guarantee every purchase.

Moxie. This advertisement appeared in the first issue of *Baseball Magazine,* which came out in May 1908. *National Baseball Library, Cooperstown, N.Y.*

Moxie'—never 'You've got moxie.' It's as simple as that." But Potter does not dispute the power of the early formula. He has written that the early tonic, "got up into you nose like horse radish and made you snort."

The question is how did it move to baseball? Several possible explanations present themselves.

Moxie expert Frank N. Potter responded to this question in a letter of December 12, 1986: "Moxie's being peddled in ball parks, especially in Boston, could have had something to do with the matter . . ."

Q. David Bowers of Wolfeboro, New Hampshire, the author of the 760-page *Moxie Encyclopedia,* offered these thoughts in a letter of November 25, 1986: "In general, the word moxie in a generic sense apparently began in a big way in the 1920s. The Moxie Company scrapbooks contain a number of news articles with sports (in particular) references to use of the term at that time. Moxie was used to describe an athlete who had a combination of

skill, energy, and enthusiasm—and this is the way it is still used today. The generic word moxie seems to imply a special spirit or quality . . . Interestingly, the Moxie Company encouraged the generic use of the name. They issued a number of advertisements and even large metal signs bearing the inscription THE DRINK THAT MADE THE NAME FAMOUS—a reference to Moxie, the beverage, making moxie, the generic word, well known."

Significantly, there is an ad for Moxie in the very first issue of *Baseball* magazine, which came out 1908.

As for the origin of the original term as it was applied to the drink, there are a number of theories. These were mentioned in an article entitled "The Moxie Man" by Ambra Watkins, which appeared in the program for the 5th Annual Moxie Festival held in Lisbon Falls, Maine, on July 8th and 9th, 1988. The article was about Frank "Mr. Moxie" Anicetti, the creator of the festival and a leading collector of Moxiana, and it reported that he had been researching the origin of moxie. The possibilities suggested by Anicetti: (1.) it comes from an Indian word meaning "dark water" (the color of the drink is almost black); (2.) it was taken from a Moxie Lake north of the Rangely Mountains in Maine; (3.) it began with a man named Captain Moonsey or a Maine Indian chief named Moxus.

M's *n.* The SEATTLE MARINERS, for short.

muckle *n./arch.* Muscle, power. A playful corruption of the word "muscle."
1ST 1862. (*New York Sunday Mercury*, July 13; EJN)

mud ball *n.* A ball that has been doctored by rubbing mud into its seams so that it will behave unnaturally. (This is not to be confused with the legal process in which pitchers "rub up" balls with mud before the game.)
EXT A dirty allegation. "He has lost his fast ball, he has lost his curve ball. All he's got left is his mud ball."—political candidate, after hearing a last-minute charge that he had Ku Klux Klan backing. (*Time*, September 2, 1946; PT)

mud field *n.* Condition of grounds after rain.

Mudville The mythical town represented by Casey and his teammates in the poem, *Casey at the Bat.*

By extension, Mudville has become the name for any town whose team comes up short. When the 1986 World Series was over, the *Boston Globe* ran this headline, "The Mets Take It, 8–5 . . . and Boston is Mudville Once Again." (October 28, 1986)

muff/muffed ball/muffed fly   **1.** *v.* To drop a grounder or fly ball.
2. *n.* An ERROR.
Henry Chadwick: "A fielder is said to 'muff' a ball when he fails to pick it up neatly, or to hold it long enough to make it a fair catch. Muffed balls are rated as errors of fielding and count against a batsman when he makes bases on them."
1ST   1869 (as a verb). (*DeWitt's Official Baseball Guide;* EJN)
ETY   In the December 1937 *American Speech,* J. Louis Kuethe discusses the baseball glossary that appears in Mrs. John A. Logan's *The Home Manual: Everybody's guide in social, domestic, and business life* (1889) and says, "Nearly all of the terms given in this list are still in use. A possible explanation of the verb *to muff* appears from the spelling of the noun form of the word as given in Mrs. Logan's *Manual; muffin.* Cf. *Drop it like a hot cake.*"
EXT   Any kind of error. "Too often cops bring in good cases only to have district attorneys muff them in court." (*Murder at the Met* by David Black; CDP) The term also seems to apply in the case of intentional errors or missed shots. In *Wise Guy: Life in a Mafia Family,* by Nicholas Pileggi, a fixer tells about how schemes are mounted to make a basketball game pay off. "For instance, if the bookmakers or the Vegas odds-makers said the line was Boston by ten, our players had to muff enough shots to make sure they won by less than the bookies' ten points. That way they'd win their games and we'd win the bets." (CDP)

muffer/muffin   *n./arch.* An unskilled or ineffective player; baseball's equivalent of golf's duffer.
1ST   1864. (*Brooklyn Daily Eagle,* September 1; EJN)
ETY   Here is how "muffins" were defined by Henry Chadwick: "This is the title of a class of ball players who are both practically and theoretically unacquainted with the game. Some 'muffins,' however know something about how the game should be played, but cannot practically exemplify their theory. 'Muffins' rank the lowest in the grade of the nines of a club, the list including first and second nine players, amateurs, and, lastly 'muffins.'"

muffery   *n.* Bad or sloppy defensive play.
1ST   1883. ". . . the last inning was commenced and the Athletics got another streak of muffery . . ." (*Sporting Life,* April 15; DS)

mug a ball   *v.* To make a fielding misplay.
1ST   1874. (*Chicago Inter Ocean,* July 16; EJN)

mullion   *n.* An ugly or unattractive person, male or female.
USE   In a 1979 article on baseball slang, Mike Gonring of the *Milwaukee Journal* termed it the "most famous" word in baseball, adding that a mullion might also be overweight ("having tonnage") or old ("having mileage"). Scott Ostler in his 1986 *Los Angeles Times* article on baseball lingo seemed to concur: "Ballplayers might sit around the dugout or bullpen and select their major league all-mullion team." At another point in the article, Ostler reports: "One player told me that he once had a teammate named Buckethead, who was also a mullion, and thus was referred to as Muckethead."

Murderer's Row   **1.** *n.* Nickname for the heart of the 1927 New York Yankee batting order, which included Babe Ruth (this was his 60 home run season), Lou Gehrig (47 homers), Earl Combs (who led the league in hits, singles and triples), Tony Lazerri and Bob Meusel. The team, which won 110 games, did not have one weak batter.
2. *n.* A term used for any cluster of good batters on a team who are "murder" on opposing pitchers. The label has been used several times, over the years, but it has yet to stick with any team but the 1927 Yankees. In 1936, for instance, several New York sportswriters tried to tag the heart of the Yankee order "Murderer's Row #2" or the "Homicide Squad". Also, on the eve of dropping three in a row to the Dodgers in 1963, New York sportswriter Harry Grayson did an article on San Francisco batters, which he entitled, "Giants Make Murderers' Row Look Like Hitless Wonders!" (*San Francisco Call-Bulletin,* May 14, 1963; PT)
ETY/1ST   1858. According to Bill Bryson in his April 1948 *Baseball Digest* article entitled "Why We Say It," the writer who first called the Ruth-Gehrig-Meusel-Lazzeri combo Murderers' Row, ". . . probably drew praise from his boss for a fresh, vibrant phrase." He then

Murderer's Row. The heart of the Yankees order in 1927 (left to right): Lou Gehrig, Earl Combs, Tony Lazzeri and Babe Ruth.   *National Baseball Library, Cooperstown, N.Y.*

points out, "Well, it had been used in a New York newspaper's account of a game a few years before that—about seventy years in fact. The 1858 writer got it from the name given the isolated row of cells containing dangerous criminals in the Tombs prison in New York." Edward J. Nichols concurs, pointing out in his dissertation that there is a clipping in Henry Chadwick's Scrapbook from 1858 in which it is applied to a lineup of power hitters. Society of American Baseball Research (SABR) founder and baseball historian L. Robert David has found that the term was also used in describing the 1919 New York Yankees.

EXT   Usually carrying sinister overtones, it has been applied to "heavy hitters" outside of baseball. During the Presidential campaign of 1952, for example, Adlai Stevenson attacked Eisenhower for being backed by a "Murderers' Row of reactionaries." (*San Francisco Chronicle*, October 5, 1952; PT)

murder smart stuff   *v.* To hit a pitcher's trick pitch, or as it was put in the 1948 *Giant Book of Sport*, hitting "the one he depends upon to fool the batters."

Murph/Murphy/Murphy money   *n.* Spring-training spending money and/or money given to players for meals while on the road.

ETY   A number of explanations have been given for this term but it is clear that one is conclusive. When the question of where this term came from was brought up in the sports pages of the *San Francisco Chronicle*, Peter Tamony brought together information that was published in Art Rosenbaum's April 12, 1972, column. In 1946, a Boston lawyer named Robert Murphy tried to organize a player's union, which was called the American Baseball Guild. He advocated a number of points, including a pension plan for players, minimum salaries, expense money and more. Murphy then decided to take a stand with the Pittsburgh Pirates, where he said that 95% of the team carried Guild cards. In *The Baseball Story*, Frederick G. Lieb explained what happened next: "There was considerable feeling when William Benswanger, Pirate president, and his attorney refused to negotiate with Murphy, and a players' strike was voted down before a Pirate-Brooklyn game June 5. Murphy then called for strike before a Pittsburgh-New York game two days later. With the stands full of fans, the players locked manager Frisch, coaches Wagner, Davis and Bissonette, and organizer Murphy out of the clubhouse, and took their strike ballot. It was 20 to 16 in favor of the strike, but as two-thirds vote was required, Murphy's strike request was turned down."

The union quickly fell apart, but the owners were eager to block any further efforts by Murphy (and defections by players to the Mexican League) and made a number of concessions by the time of the 1946 All-Star game. They included a $5,000 salary minimum, a pension fund, and money for expenses on the road and for the period of spring training, or, as it was then dubbed, "Murphy money."

mush bags *n.* Old, worn baseballs used in batting practice.

mushball/mushmelon 1. *n.* Nickname for SOFTBALL. "Swede Pierson Makes Hit With Mushball Moguls; Loses 10 to 4." (headline in *San Francisco News,* April 19, 1940; PT)
2. *n.* Nickname for the softball itself.

mussy ball *n./arch.* A blunder-filled game; a sloppy contest.

Mustache Gang Nickname for the Oakland A's of the early 1970s.

mustard 1. *n.* Velocity. A good fastball is one with a lot of mustard.
2. *n.* A fastball.

mustard man *n.* See hot dog.

must have hit an air pocket *v.* A common excuse for a misjudged fly ball.

MVP Abbreviation for most valuable player, commonly used to refer to the *Most Valuable Player Award.*
"Clemens is MVP in AL." (November 19, 1986, headline to AP story in *Washington Post*)
EXT A key performer in any field.

"my pitch" *n.* Batter's favorite pitch; the one he hits most effectively.

mystifier *n.* CURVEBALL.
1ST 1910. (*Baseball* magazine, April; EJN)

N

nab *v.* To throw or tag a runner out, especially when he is trying for extra bases.

nail **1.** *v.* To throw a runner out, especially when he is attempting to steal or pick up an extra base on a play.
1ST 1888. (*New York Press,* April 19; EJN)
2. *n.* A good throw; one that nails the runner.
3. *v.* To hit the ball with force.
1ST 1895. "He tried to nail the ball hard, but he only fanned and went back to the bench." (Herbert Bellwood, *The Rivals of Riverwood;* DS)
4. *n.* A forceful hit.
5. *n.* A rookie or player with temporary status. Leonard Shecter's 1963 "Baseball Spoken Here" explains this usage of the term: " 'They gave me a nail' is often the complaint of a rookie who has just joined the team. There aren't enough lockers so he's asked to hang his clothes on a nail. It also means the clubhouse man doesn't expect him to be around long."

nail biter *n.* Close game.

nails **1.** *n.* Generic nickname for a player who is tough—tough as nails. "At the plate, all twitches and fidgets was Backman's best friend, Len Dykstra. Nails, the Mets call him. Or Pest." (John Feinstein, *Washington Post,* October 12, 1986)
2. *n.* A team that has turned tough. "The Seattle Mariners have been nails in the late innings because of a strong bullpen and rallying ability. They have won or tied twelve games in the ninth inning." (*San Francisco Examiner,* June 3, 1982)

"Na, Na, Na, Na" Fans' victory song from a 1969 song of farewell titled "Na, Na, Hey, Hey, Kiss Him Goodbye" by the rock group "The Steam." It was picked up by Comiskey Park organist Nancy Faust in 1977 and first became popular in Chicago.

National Anthem Since World War II, this has been played at all major league games.

National Baseball Hall of Fame and Museum The official museum of baseball located in Cooperstown, New York, which was established in 1939.

National Baseball Library The baseball research library and archives within the Hall of Fame complex in Cooperstown.

National Commission The board that comprised the three commissioners who governed baseball from 1903 to 1921, when, in the wake of the *Black Sox* scandal Judge Kenesaw Mountain Landis was given sole power over the game.

National Game, the *n.* Name given to baseball at the end of the Civil War when it became the most widely played and popular American game. Typically it was described in words like these: "The game of base ball has now become beyond question the leading feature of the outdoor sports of the United States, and to account for its present truly proud position, there are many and sufficient reasons." (*American Pastimes,* Charles A. Peverelly, 1866)
1ST 1865. (*New York Herald,* July 8; EJN)

National League Major league founded on February 2, 1876, under the leadership of businessman William A. Hulbert of Chicago. The teams that were charter members were Boston, Chicago, Cincinnati, Hartford, Louisville, New York, Philadelphia and St. Louis. The original league represented four western and four eastern cities and was set up with clear rules and policies, including standard player contracts, a code of conduct and a prohibition on the sale of intoxicants in parks under the league's jurisdiction.

National League President See League President.

National League style Real and imagined distinctions exist between the style of play and officiating in the National and American Leagues. For one, the NL is commonly portrayed as the league with the running game as opposed to the AL, which is supposedly a haven for power hitters.

National Game. The original caption of this U.S. War Relocation Authority photograph: "Manzanar, Calif. April, 1942. Boys starting a ball game soon after their arrival at Manzanar, a War Relocation Authority center for the evacuees of Japanese ancestry from certain West Coast areas." *Prints and Photographs Division, the Library of Congress*

Another credo is that a lower strike zone and the lack of a designated hitter in the National League further separate the two circuits.

national pastime *n.* A term commonly applied to baseball in the United States. First used in 1857, it eventually overshadowed other names such as national game and national sport. One of the most fastinating uses of the term appeared on the editorial page of the *New York Times* in 1881: "There is really reason to believe that baseball is gradually dying out in this country. It has been openly announced by an athletic authority that what was once called the national game is being steadily superceded by cricket . . ." (The full version of this premature obituary for baseball appears in H. Allen Smith's *Low and Inside*.) An equally misdirected claim appeared in the *Century* magazine in 1872: "During these years the quiet and social home game of croquet has been steadily gaining ground, and to-day its devotees, not without justice, claim for it the distinction of the true and only 'National Game' of America."
1ST 1857. A letter on file in the National Baseball Library from Fred Ivor-Campbell of Warren, Rhode Island, pinpoints what must be the earliest reference. It appears in the January 31 *Spirit of the Times* in an article on the very first convention of baseball clubs: "Base ball has been known in the Northern States as far back as the memory of the oldest inhabitant reacheth, and must be regarded as a national pastime, the same as cricket is by the British."

Nats Nickname for the Washington Senators, especially during the years (1939–1957) when the team was known as the Nationals.

natural, the/a *n.* Player who seems to have been born with—rather than acquired—the ability to excel at the game. "Canseco's 'The Natural.' " (*Boston Herald* headline referring to Jose Canseco, September 3, 1986)
It is also the title of a highly regarded novel by Bernard Malamud and a motion picture based on the novel.

natural hitter *n.* An easy-swinging and effective batter with a good eye for the strike zone.
1ST 1910. (*American* magazine, July; EJN)

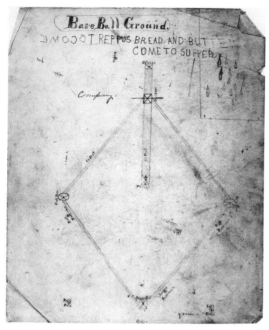

National pastime. Pencil Drawing of baseball diamond in one of Woodrow Wilson's schoolbooks. *Prints and Photographs Division, the Library of Congress*

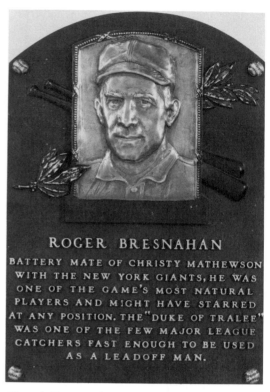

ROGER BRESNAHAN

BATTERY MATE OF CHRISTY MATHEWSON
WITH THE NEW YORK GIANTS, HE WAS
ONE OF THE GAME'S MOST NATURAL
PLAYERS AND MIGHT HAVE STARRED
AT ANY POSITION. THE "DUKE OF TRALEE"
WAS ONE OF THE FEW MAJOR LEAGUE
CATCHERS FAST ENOUGH TO BE USED
AS A LEADOFF MAN.

Natural. This man fit the description so well that he is described as such on his Hall of Fame plaque. *National Baseball Library, Cooperstown, N.Y.*

natural stuff *n.* Hopping fastballs and sharp curves as opposed to trick pitches such as the screwball and knuckleball.

near beer pitcher *n.* Pitcher who commonly works himself into a three ball and two strike count.
ETY "Coined by Aaron Robinson, a New York Yankee catcher during the 1940s," writes Patrick Ercolano in *Fungoes, Floaters and Fast Balls*, his book on baseball terms. ". . . the term alludes to near beer, a weakened type of brew that contains only 3.2 percent alcohol and is sometimes also called '3.2 beer.' "

necessities *n.* A word given a special baseball context in April 1987 when it was used to summarize what blacks were accused of lacking and why they were not being given jobs as managers and general managers. It was given this context by Al Campanis of the Los Angeles Dodgers when he was asked by newsman Ted Koppel if there was a prejudice against blacks in managerial positions. Campanis' reply: "No, I don't believe it's prejudice. I truly believe that they may not have some of the necessities to be, let's say, a field manager or perhaps a general manager."

The word "necessities" became an immediate verbal symbol for prejudice and racism within baseball. Campanis apologized, the Dodgers asked him to resign and—for a time at least—the issue of blacks in baseball management was brought into focus. At the time, black former pitcher Jim "Mudcat" Grant said, "Maybe Al, in a backward way, did us a favor by bringing this out."

Ned in the third reader *n.* Casey Stengel's own description of a dumb player. Another bit of Stengelese involving the hapless Ned was "Ned standin' up in class," which was used to describe a dumb player ruining a play.

need a basket *v.* To field a batted or thrown ball poorly.
1ST 1907. (*New York Evening Journal*, April 27; EJN)

Negro Leagues   Two groups of six black teams that belonged to the Negro American League and Negro National League. When the color bar was finally lifted in 1947 the Negro Leagues began to falter as their stars started signing contracts with major league clubs. With the induction of Roy Dandridge in 1987, eleven negro league players are in the Hall of Fame. The first league, the Negro National League, was founded in 1920. The Negro American League started in 1937 and lasted longest, until 1960.

neighborhood play   *n.* A force play in which the runner is called out because the defensive player with the ball is close enough to touch the base—or in the right neighborhood. Rudy Martzke explained this term in the October 15, 1986, *USA Today,* after it had been used without explanation in the telecast of a National League playoff game: "a shortstop or second baseman is 'in the neighborhood'—but doesn't touch—second base, because he's avoiding an incoming slide. An out, at umpire's discretion." Also known as vicinity play.

nervous breakdown   *n.* SCREWBALL.
ETY   This is an obvious play on the neurotic nature of the human screwball.

new ballgame   *n.* A term used to describe a situation in which a game turns around quickly, for example when one side suddenly overtakes the previous leader by scoring a lot of runs. It underscores the point that no game can be taken for granted.
  "It must also be remembered that baseball not only gave to the language the phrase 'it's a new ball game,' but implements it every day." (Shirley Povich in *The Washington Post,* October 10, 1986)
EXT   Any new start. "New Year is new ballgame for cable." (*USA Today* headline, December 29, 1986)
  A variation on this term is "whole new ballgame," which gives the concept greater emphasis. In *The Dictionary of Cliches,* James Rogers uses a passage from a 1971 issue of *The New Yorker* to illustrate: "If this were to happen [Chinese entry into the Vietnam War], some official of our government would no doubt announce that we were in a 'whole new ballgame,' which would mean that none of the policies or promises made in the past were

binding any longer, including the prohibition against the use of nuclear weapons."

new breed   *n./arch.* Name used by New York *Daily News* sportswriter Dick Young to describe the rabid Mets fans during the franchise's early years. In *The Summer Game,* Roger Angell called them "perversely loyal," adding that their loyalty was in part "engendered by a hatred for the kind of cold-blooded success typified by Mr. O'Malley and by the owners of the New York Yankees."

New England Game   *n.* MASSACHU-SETTS GAME.

New York game   *n.* The precursor to modern baseball, which most closely resembles it. It was played in and around New York beginning in the 1840s and codified in the Knickerbocker Rules and contrasts with the Massachusetts game. **SEE**   *Knickerbocker Rules.*

New York Giants   Long-time National League franchise that began as the Metropolitans in 1883, were next known as the Gothams and became known as the Giants about 1885. They were named by manager Jim Mutrie who called them, "My big fellows! My giants!" within earshot of sportswriters. When they left for San Francisco in 1958, they kept the name.

New York Mets   The name of the National League's Eastern Division franchise in New York City. When this expansion team opened in New York in 1962 it used a shortened version of Metropolitan, the name of the team that arrived in New York in 1883 and later became known as the Giants.
  The new team got off to a shaky start, but won the World Series in 1969. This occasioned sportswriter Jack Lang's famous line, "They said man would walk on the moon before the Mets won a championship. Man barely won the race."
SEE   *Amazing Mets, Amazin's.*

New York Yankees   The name of the American League's Eastern Division franchise in New York City. Originally known as the Highlanders after they arrived in 1903 (they were the old Baltimore Orioles) and later the Hilltoppers, the team began to be called the Yankees in the press, allegedly because it fit the headlines better, and the name stuck. Originally a name for New Englander, it became a term for any Northerner during the Civil War and for any American during World War II.

Also known by a number of other names, including "Bronx Bombers," "Yanks" and "The Bronx Zoo."

Of all the major league teams, it is the one most commonly associated with big bucks, and big egos. Sportswriter Red Smith once pointed out that rooting for the Yankees was like rooting for US Steel.

next stop Peoria   Said of a player who is in a slump, committing a lot of errors or otherwise on the skids. It is a reference to a St. Louis Cardinals minor league team that, under owner Branch Rickey, became baseball's equivalent of Podunk.

"Nice guys finish last."   Famous quote attributed to Leo Durocher during the late 1940s when he was managing the Brooklyn Dodgers. Durocher was proud of the fact that it had gotten him into *Bartlett's Quotations*—between John Betjeman and Wystan Hugh Auden—and named his 1975 autobiography *Nice Guys Finish Last*. In the book he says he directed the remark against the Giants in front of several newsmen: "Walker, Cooper, Mize, Marshall, Kerr, Gordon, Thompson. Take a look at them. All nice guys. They'll finish last. Nice Guys. Finish Last."

nick a pitcher   *v.* To get hits off a pitcher. **1ST**   1912. (*New York Tribune*, September 29; EJN)

nickel/nickel curve   *n.* A derogatory term for a slow curveball; a "cheap shot"; a slider. (Jim Brosnan said that this was what the slider was called by old time ballplayers "who didn't have to hit against it.") **1ST**   1932. (*Baseball* magazine, October; EJN)

nickelbrick/nickel rock   *n.* An extremely cheap baseball of the type once commonly found in five-and-dime stores. Originally, they sold for a nickel (at a time when a regulation ball might cost a dollar or more). In a 1978 essay in the *San Francisco Examiner and Chronicle* (August 20) on the nickelbrick, Le Pacini wrote, "In my era, however, they went for twenty-five to thirty-five cents, and if you got a rare fifty-center you were kicked out of the neighborhood for showboating." He pointed out that the ball lacked a certain quality ("It was the only ball ever invented that windows broke"),

and when hit hard would not unravel, but actually disintegrate.

Nickel Series   Nickname for World Series between New York teams in the days when it cost a nickel to ride the subway.

nightcap/night cap   **1.** *n.* The second game of a doubleheader, so called because they are usually played late in the afternoon or early in the evening. **1ST**   1917. (*New York Times*, October 5; EJN) **2.** *n./arch.* Uncommon. "The ninth inning in a baseball game," according to Maurice H. Weseen in his 1934 *Dictionary of American Slang*. **ETY**   Since the early 19th century, the name for the last drink of the night before retiring.

night club tan   *n.* Used to describe a player who looks pale or washed out, according to a 1959 *Baseball Digest* article on "fieldese."

night game   *n.* Game played under bright artificial lights in the evening. The night game was once a novelty of the electric age, but now most major league games are played "under the lights." All major league parks are equipped for night games.

An indication of the extent to which baseball has become a nighttime game is the fact that up until 1970 all World Series games were played in the daytime. In 1985 Kansas City and St. Louis engaged in the first all-night World Series. Between the fifth game of the 1984 Series and the sixth game of the 1987 Series there was not one daylight game. The last major league park to become equipped for night baseball was Wrigley Field, which hosted its first night game against the Philadelphia Phillies on August 8, 1988. **ETY**   A number of claims exist as to when the first night game was played. The earliest night game identified by the staff at the National Baseball Library is a September 2, 1880, non-professional game at Hull, Massachusetts, between two department store teams. The lighting was poor and many errors were made. The first professional night game was a minor league exhibition game in Lynn, Massachusetts, on June 24, 1927. The first major league night game was played on May 24, 1935, at Crosley Field in Cincinnati.

Nile Valley League   *n./arch.* A term in use around the turn of the century for the mythical

Night game. The first night game was played at Ebbets Field in Brooklyn on June 15, 1938. Cincinnati pitcher Johnny Vander Meer beat the Dodgers on a no-hitter that night. *National Baseball Library, Cooperstown, N.Y.*

realm where the most spectacular feats in the game were performed. Hugh S. Fullerton said of it in his 1912 "Baseball Primer": "Whenever a player tells some extraordinary yarn concerning a play the other players instantly inquire if it happened in the Nile Valley league."
1ST 1912. (Hugh Fullerton, as above)

nine *n.* A baseball team. The term was coined because there are nine players in the starting lineup.
USE Despite the fact that there are actually 10 players on teams using a designated hitter, they are still referred to as nines.
1ST 1860. (Minutes of the Knickerbocker Baseball Club; EJN)

"nine guys named Robinson" A remarkable all-star team could be fielded with Robinsons (beginning with Jackie, Frank and Brooks). The phrase originated with Earl Weaver's response to a question about the challenge of managing: "I don't welcome any challenge. I'd rather have nine guys named Robinson."

nine miles *n.* Dugout exaggeration for a ball hit for a long distance.

90 feet away *n.* A reference to the distance between bases, which is commonly used in tight moments when a runner is on third and the lead or a tie score is only "90 feet away."

ninth inning finish *n.* Stirring finale in which one team takes the game in the last inning.

nip **1.** *v.* To retire a base runner on a close play.
1ST 1868. (Chadwick Scrapbooks; EJN)
2. *v.* To defeat an opponent.

NL Abbreviation for National League.

NLCS Abbreviation for National League Championship Series.

no book *n.* Lack of information on the habits and weaknesses of a particular player, manager or team.
SEE *book.*

Nine. This tobacco wrapper uses the "First Nine" to refer to the original Cincinnati Red Stockings, the team that played its first 70 games without a loss (but with one tie). *Prints and Photographs Division, the Library of Congress*

nod   1. *n.* The manager's decision to start a particular pitcher. It implies some deliberation on the part of the manager, such as when it is reported that a particular pitcher has gotten the nod for opening day.
2. *n.* The decision to bring in a particular relief pitcher.
ETY   From the head gesture—or nod—for "yes."
USE   Invariably termed "the nod," as in a pitcher looking for his first nod of the season.

no-decision   *n.* A game in which a pitcher appears but is not credited with a win, loss or save. "When a pitcher fails four straight times to win his 20th game—twice throwing complete games and once allowing only one run and six hits over nine innings for a no-decision—he might reasonably be forgiven some overt expression of frustration." (Ron Fimrite in a 1987 *Sports Illustrated* article on Oakland Athletics pitcher Dave Stewart)

no-hit   1. *adj.* Refers to a game or a part of a game during which the pitcher gives up no hits.
2. *v.* To not allow a hit. "Orioles Are No-Hit By Brewers' Nieves." (*Washington Post*, April 16, 1987)

no hit game   *n.* NO-HITTER.
1ST   1905. (*Sporting Life*, September 2; EJN)

no hit, no run   *adj.* Descriptive of a game in which the pitcher allows no hits and no runs score. It is used to distinguish such a performance from one in which there are no hits but in which one or more runs score without the benefit of a hit (such as when four batters are walked in an inning).
1ST   1909. (*Baseball* magazine, March; EJN)

no-hitter   1. *n.* A game in which a single pitcher does not throw a single hit to the opposition.
2. *n.* A game in which more than one pitcher from a team does not allow the opposition a single hit.
SEE   *perfect game.*

no hitter jinx   *n.* An old superstition that if one speaks of a no-hit game while it is in progress it will come to an end, i.e., a player will get a hit.
   It seems that Red Barber was the first to defy the jinx from the broadcast booth. Jack Mann of the *Washington Star* wrote of this in a profile of Barber, which appeared on July 31, 1981: "He did it in Bill Bevens' game against the Dodgers in the 1947 World Series, and again in Don Larsen's perfect game of 1956. But the first time was in the first night game ever played in Ebbets Field, in June 1938, when Johnny Vander Meer was in the midst of his second-straight no-hitter."

non-affiliated club   *n.* Minor league team that is not tied to a major league sponsor.

nonchalotted   *v.* Dizzy Deanism for "A play made with great ease or indifference."
ETY   It is a creative corruption of the word nonchalant recast as a verb.

nonfan   *n.* Person who does not follow the game. See also *fan.*
1ST   1913. "And if you, a nonfan, ask *why* . . . you need go no further than a fundamental of American character to understand." (*Technical World*, issue 19, 1913; DS)

No-hitter. These five pitchers had nine no-hitters between them (left to right): Carl Erskine (2), Bob Lemon (1), Allie Reynolds (2), Bob Feller (3) and Virgil "Fire" Trucks (1).   *Courtesy of the Cleveland Indians*

non-roster   *adj.* Refers to a player who has been invited for a tryout without being put on the team's official roster. Non-roster players are common in spring training.

"The 23-year-old left-hander, who spent most of 1985 with Class A St. Petersburg, is in the Cards camp as a non-roster invitee." (article on Greg Mathews in the *St. Petersburg Times*, March 10, 1985)

"No Pepper Games"   Common sign prohibiting such activity in major and minor league ballparks.
SEE   *pepper game.*

northpaw   *n.* Right-handed pitcher, a seldom-used companion term for southpaw. Its main use comes in questions such as, "If a left-handed pitcher is a southpaw, is a right-handed pitcher a northpaw?"
1ST   1922. (*Baseball Cyclopedia;* EJN)
SEE   *southpaw.*

no sweat   To accomplish something with ease. "No Sweat as Pierce Nabs 6–3 Win for '5–0' Perfect," (*San Francisco News-Call Bulletin* headline, May 16, 1962; PT)
ETY   Military slang for a sure or easy task, originating during the Korean War. "Our own Air Force, or flyboys, are credited with 'no sweat,' meaning no trouble at all . . ." (*New York Times* magazine, June 5, 1955)

note-book pitcher   *n./arch.* One who keeps records of batters and the most effective pitches to throw against them.
1ST   1922. (*Baseball Cyclopedia;* EJN)

not get to first base   See first base.

nothing ball   *n.* Ball without speed or anything "on it." See nuthin' ball.
1ST   1937. (*New York Herald Tribune*, October 3; EJN)

nothing but his glove/nothing but the stitches   To pitch ineffectively; to be unable to curve or otherwise give one's pitching a deceptive motion. The idea being that the only advantage the pitcher has is his glove or the stitches on the ball.

1ST 1911 (nothing but his glove). (*American magazine*, May; EJN)

nothing on the ball   *n.* Said of a pitcher who is pitching ineffectively.

1ST 1912. (*New York Tribune* October 10; EJN)
SEE   *on the ball.*

not in it   Out of contention in the pennant race.

1ST 1891. "Baseball vernacular has invaded the church. The crank who created a sensation in the N.Y. Cathedral last Sunday morning by shouting to Archbishop Corrigan: 'Out of my way, Pontius Pilate! I am the Lord's annointed and you are not in it with me.' has evidently been feeding on the slop." (*Sporting News*, October 3, 1891; DS)

not much on the ball   See nothing on the ball.

EXT   Said of a person who is not very bright.

nub   **1.** *n.* A sore finger from a batted or thrown ball.

2. *v.* To hit a slow bouncing ball that stays in the infield.

1ST 1937. (*The Sporting News Record Book;* EJN)

nubber   *n.* Weak hit that bounces into the infield; a tiny hit that behaves like a bunt. See knubber.

nuclear fission ball   *n.* A ball that is hit powerfully and directly at a fielder or the pitcher. It is an exaggerated extension of atom ball, which is a play on words of at 'em ball.

nudist pitch   *n.* Nothing ball—one with nothing on it.

numbering   *n.* System in which numbers are used to identify players. The numbers are put on the backs of the players' uniforms and sometimes on the front. Although not required by the rules, the practice has long been universal among major league teams.

ETY   The first team to number its players was the '29 Yankees. The numbers correspond to each player's usual spot in the batting order, which is why Babe Ruth wore 3 and Lou Gehrig 4.

number 1   *n.* Fastball, so-called because the catcher's traditional signal for the pitch is a single finger pointed down.

numbers   *n.* Statistical record; for instance, a player with a good record is sometimes said to have "impressive numbers."

number 3   *n.* Catcher's signal to the pitcher with three fingers pointing down. Writes William G. Brandt in his 1932 article on baseballese, "[It] can be almost anything, screwball, fork-ball, knuckleball, slop-ball, squib, dipsy-dew."

number 2   *n.* CURVEBALL, so-called because the catcher's traditional signal for the pitch is two fingers pointed down.

nuthin' ball   *n.* Slowly pitched ball that is easy to hit because it does not move deceptively; a definition that Dizzy Dean once amplified by adding ". . . like I was throwin' when I hurt my arm." Pitchers on the decline have been termed "nothin' ballers."

O

O *n.* The letter O, which is used in preference to the word zero in baseball expressions like, "He was O for four at the plate today" (i.e., he had no hits in four at bats).

oak BAT.
1ST 1909. (*New York Call,* August 13; EJN)

Oakland-Alameda County Coliseum
Home for the Oakland Athletics in Oakland, California, since the team's arrival from Kansas City in 1968.

Oakland A's/Oakland Athletics The name of the American League's Western Division franchise in Oakland, California. Once located in Philadelphia (1901–1954), then Kansas City (1955–1967) and now in Oakland (since 1968), the team has been both the A's and Athletics depending on the moment. For instance, in 1987 the Oakland A's officially reverted to the Athletics, a name that was first used for an amateur Philadelphia team in 1860.

OB Common abbreviation for organized baseball.
1ST 1915. (*Baseball* magazine, December; EJN)

obstruction/obstruction play *n.* Bodily interference, usually when a fielder interferes with a runner. For instance, if a fielder is on the base line and is not awaiting a batted ball and collides with a runner, obstruction is ruled. If the umpire determines that the runner would have been safe at the next base without the obstruction he is awarded that base.

OF Common abbreviation for outfield.

off **1.** *adj.* Ineffective; off one's game.
1ST 1890. (*New York Post,* May 13; EJN)
2. *adj.* At the expense of the pitcher. For example, the team scored two runs off him in the third inning.

off base *adj./n.* In a position to be put out.
EXT Out of line; working from the wrong premise. "He doesn't, in his mind's eye, see a union or the labor movement as an impersonal entity or as an institution. He sees it as a bunch of people. And as long as he keeps seeing it

that way, he won't get too far off base." (article on George Meany, *Saturday Evening Post,* November 20, 1943; PT)

Not to be confused with off one's base which has come to refer to a person who is mentally unbalanced.

offense **1.** *n.* The team at bat.
2. *n.* The array of tactics used by the team at bat. Such maneuvers as the use of pinch hitters and runners, bunts, and hit-and-run plays are part of the team's offense.

offer/offer at *v.* To swing at a pitched ball.
1ST 1896. (*Frank Merriwell's Schooldays;* EJN)

offering *n.* A pitched ball.
1ST 1910. (*Baseball* magazine, December; EJN)

off field *n.* OPPOSITE FIELD.

official at bat *n.* A time at bat that is entered in the official record of the game and used as the basis for batting statistics. Four types of plate appearance are not counted as official at bats. Those are: when the batter is awarded a base on balls, is hit by a pitched ball, is awarded first because of interference or obstruction, or hits a sacrifice bunt or sacrifice fly.

official distances *n.* Those field measurements stipulated by the official rules of the game. The most important refer to the distance between the bases (90 feet) and between the pitcher's rubber and home plate (60 feet, 6 inches).

official game *n.* Any game, which is not tied, that completed 4½ innings with the home team in the lead or 5 innings with the visitors leading. The concept comes into play when a game is stopped for rain, darkness or other reason. If a game is not an official game, it must be played over from the start or, in the case of a curfew or light failure, from the point at which play was supended.

official scorer *n.* Individual whose responsibility is to observe the game, interpret the action taking place and, using the *Official Baseball Rules,* enter the events and rules of the game into the report of the game. The scorer also makes judgment calls, including whether or not a particular play should be recorded as a hit or an error. In the case of an error in which more than one player is involved, the scorer must also determine who should be credited with the error. The scorer also determines such things as passed balls, wild pitches and earned runs.

In the Major Leagues, the official scorer is a local reporter who has been so designated by the league president. It is common for a group of reporters to score on an alternating basis. During the World Series, there are three official scorers.
1ST 1902. (*Sporting Life,* July 5; EJN)

off one's base   See off base.
EXT While off base and off one's base are synonymous in the context of the game of baseball, they part company as general metaphors. OFF BASE means to be out of line or incorrect; but *off one's base* means to be mentally unbalanced or crazy. Charles Earle Funk found it in use as far back as 1883 when it appeared in George W. Peck's *His Pa:* "The boy knew the failing, and made up his mind to demonstrate to the old man that he was rapidly getting off his base."

off-season/off season   1. *n./adj.* The time of year from the day after the last day of the World Series in October to the first day of spring training in February, when baseball is not played; or what George F. Will has called, ". . . the interminable cultural drought of the off-season." (*Washington Post,* March 29, 1984)
2. *n.* A bad season for a player or a team.

off-season baseball   *n.* Professional baseball played outside the continental United States during the winter months. Some major and minor league players from the United States play in these leagues for conditioning and experience.

off-side pitcher   *n.* LEFT-HANDER.

off-speed   *adj.* Baseballese for slow. "I've always had pretty good offspeed stuff." (Roger Clemens in the *Boston Globe,* June 27, 1986)

off-speed pitch   *n.* All-purpose term for any pitch that is thrown at less than full velocity: curves, sliders, knuckleballs, forkballs and their many variations.

off-stride   1. *adj.* Said of a batter who steps into the ball—strides—before it reaches the plate. Common to batters anxious to get a hit.
2. *adj.* A term describing the state of a pitcher who has been taken out of the game with his team behind, only to watch it rally and save him from being credited with a loss.

off the hook   *adj.* Out of a jam. For instance, a pitcher who gives up five runs in the first inning is said to be off the hook when his team racks up six in the second.

off the Interstate   *adj.* Batting over .100, a reference to Route I-95 and other Interstate highways with numbers under 100.

off the schneid   *adj.* See schneid.

off the table   *adj.* Description of a curveball or other breaking pitch that dips precipitously. A pitch that is said to appear as if it were rolling down a table and then suddenly drops off.

ohfer/oh-fer   1. *n.* A game or series of games in which a batter fails to collect a hit; a shutout at the plate. If a batter goes hitless in four plate appearances, usually it is described as O for 4.
2. *n.* Second-rate player. ". . . the players in the pin stripes didn't look like Yankees. They looked like the AAA farm club of the Kansas City Athletics. A bunch of oh-fers." (*San Francisco Examiner,* August 1, 1966; PT)
ETY Word created from "Oh for," as one would say when speaking of an 0 for 4 game.

"Oh, for the long one!"   Broadcaster Harry Caray's pet call when he is encouraging a player to hit a home run.

old, the   *adj.* For reasons that are unclear, baseball dotes on the adjective old in common phrases like the old ballgame, the old ballpark, the old college try, the old clutch etc. This was noted in 1927 by Frank Graham in a July 18 *New York Sun* article: "The fondness for the word 'old' on the part of men who in most cases are so young is as strange as it is pronounced. Invariably, it is the 'old army game,' the 'old life,' the 'old pepper,' and the 'old ball game.' " In the 1945 article, "Jargon of the field," H. G. Salsinger notes that players generally prefix their favorite nickname for the ball (apple, pill etc.) with the adjective "old."

old army game   *n.* Style of play that is straightforward and does not rely on strategy.
1ST 1927. (*New York Sun,* July 18; EJN)

ETY   The etymology of this term has proven most elusive. It is also confusing because the term has a contrary meaning in slang outside of baseball. In their *Dictionary of American Slang* Harold Wentworth and Stuart Berg Flexner define it as, "Any swindle; any unfair or crooked gambling game or bet."

old-cat   *n*. Pickup game.

old college try, the   *n*. A wild and desperate attempt to make a play. Sometimes the term carries a hint of showboating. In *Babe Ruth's Own Book of Baseball* the definition for "giving it the old college try" is, "playing to the grandstand or making strenuous effort to field a ball that obviously cannot be handled."

In a column that appeared in the *Columbus* (Ohio) *Citizen* on November 26, 1927 (and was quoted in the April 1930 *American Speech*), Billy Evans gives this explanation of the term:

"Well, I gave it the old college try."

That is a term often used in big league baseball, when some player keeps on going after a fly ball, usually in foul territory, with the odds about ten to one he would never reach it. Teammates of such a player often beat him to it by shouting in unison with the thought of humor uppermost:

"Well, kid, you certainly gave it the old college try," as he falls short of making the catch.

On other occasions, when some player does something that a professional player might not ordinarily attempt, such as colliding with a fielder who had the ball ready to touch him out, in the hope that he might make him drop the ball, regardless of the danger he was courting, someone is sure to say, often ironically, if the speaker happens to be one of the players in the field:

"That's the old college spirit."

Old Oriole. The 1894 Baltimore Orioles. Front row (left to right): Jack Boyle, John McGraw, Willie Keeler, and Charlie Pond. Middle row: Steve Brodie, Bill Huffer, Joe Kelly, Ned Hanlon, Wilbert Robinson, Hughie Jennings, Heimie Reitz. Top row: Joe Quinn, Sadie McMahon, Charles Esper, George Memming, Frank Powerman, Bill Clark and Jimmy Donnelly.   *National Baseball Library, Cooperstown, N.Y.*

Old Timers' Day. Early Wynn (left) and Satchel Paige share pitching chores at an Old Timers' Day game in Cleveland (1963).   *Courtesy of the Cleveland Indians*

EXT   The term was quickly applied to any strenuous effort with limited chances of success.

old folks   *n.* Traditional nickname for the oldest player on the team.

old man   *n.* MANAGER. "What hurt most was that he had always looked up to the Old Man, like a son would regard his own father." (Mickey Mantle on Casey Stengel in *The Mick;* CDP)
1ST   1946. See the *brass* entry for the original appearance of this term.

oldoriole   *n./arch.* A player who stays in the game despite injuries. The term derives from the reputation for toughness and relentlessness of the Baltimore Orioles of the 19th century. "If he gets spiked or hit on the head or upset by a base-runner and laughs it off, he's an 'Oldoriole.' " (William G. Brandt on baseballese, *Baseball* magazine, October 1934)

Old Pluvy   *n.* See Jupiter Pluvius.

old poison pen   *n.* See poison pen.

Old Sal   Name for the underhanded, upward curving or "jump" ball thrown by "Iron Man" Joe McGinnity.
1ST   1908. (*New York Evening Journal*, March 5; EJN)

old timers   *n.* Retired players; players of a previous baseball generation. This term replaced "old stylers," which is what they were commonly called in the last century.
1ST   1905. (*Sporting Life*, October 7; EJN)

Old Timers' Day   Special promotional ceremony at which retired players are honored and play a short game before the regular game takes place.

old timers' game   *n.* Game played by retired players on Old Timers' Day.

Olympic Stadium. Built for the 1976 Olympics, it has also been called "the Big O." *Courtesy of the Montreal Expos*

ole rubber belly *n.* Common nickname for a player with a bulging waistline.

olive in his throat *adj.* Term describing a choking player. See choke.

Olympic Stadium/Stade Olympique Home grounds of the Montreal Expos since Opening Day, 1977. Olympic Stadium is the first park in baseball history with a retractable roof.

on **1.** *adj.* Occupying a base; on base.
1ST 1907. (*New York Evening Journal,* April 30, EJN)
2. *adj.* In good playing form. As opposed to off.

on-base percentage *n.* Statistic used to illustrate a batter's overall effectiveness at getting on base. It is computed by dividing the number of times the batter reaches base (not including by error) by his number of plate appearances and carrying the quotient to three decimal places. The number is particularly important in determining the effectiveness of a lead-off batter whose job it is—more than any other player—to get on base.

on deck *n./adj.* Position of the next batter after the batter at the plate. The on-deck batter stands or kneels at a point between the dugout and the plate. In an effort to speed up the game, in the 1960s it became a rule that the player following the man at bat had to be in on the deck circle and could not wait in the dugout.
1ST 1881. (*New York Herald,* August 23; EJN)
SEE See entry for *at bat, on deck, in the hold* for a full discussion of the etymology of this term.
EXT The next to have a turn; for example, a barber might say that a customer next in line for a haircut is on deck. Despite the nautical origin of deck, the use of "on deck" for next originated in baseball.

on-deck circle *n.* A circular space set in foul territory where the batter following the player at bat waits his turn. These circles are five feet in diameter and there is one in front of each team's dugout. Among other things, it provides a space where the on-deck batter can take practice swings. In the *Official Rules of Baseball,* it is called the "next batter's box," which therefore gives it an official name.

one-armed man   *n.* Fielder who makes one-handed catches.

one away   *n.* One out for the team at bat.

one-bagger   *n.* See single.

one-ball hitter   *n.* A batter who is at his best—or, at least not bothered—when there are two strikes against him.

one-cushion shot   *n.* A batted ball that caroms off the wall, like a billiard or pool ball. They are the bane of most outfielders who find such hits hard to deal with.

One Eye Jim Bats   *n.* Baseball variation. James S. Hanna describes in *What Life Was Like When I Was a Kid* (1973) how the game was played in his Galveston, Texas, neighborhood:

> As we grew older, baseball consumed much of our time, and if there were not enough to make up two full teams we played a variation called One Eye Jim Bats. This might well have been called progressive baseball, for each prospective player shouted the position he wanted to start at, the number one spot, of course, being "batter" which was usually won by the biggest and loudest boy, with "catch," "pitch," "first," "second" etc. following in rapid order. If the batter succeeded in making a base hit, all players advanced to the next highest position, the catcher now becoming batter, the pitcher becoming catcher and so on. If the batter made a home run he was privileged to bat again; if he were put out, all players advanced and the ex-batter started at the bottom at third base. It was a good game and afforded everyone some experience in playing all positions. (CDP)

one for the book   *n.* An odd or freakish play that presumably deserves to be noted in one of baseball's record books.
1ST   1932. (*Baseball* magazine, October; EJN)

one-handed catcher   *n.* Catcher who keeps his throwing hand behind his back when receiving the pitch to protect it from foul tips and other occupational hazards.

one-hole cat   *n.* ONE OLD CAT.

one-hopper   *n.* Batted ball that takes one bounce.

100 games   *n.* Highly significant count in either the win or loss column. "We could be the first team in history to win 100 games one year and lose 100 the next year." (Whitey Herzog quoted in *USA Today,* July 11, 1986)

162-game schedule   *n.* The number of games each team plays per season in the Major Leagues. A team's complete schedule of regular season games.

one-name guy   *n.* Baseball's equivalent of the household name; a player who is known by his first name or nickname alone. As Tony Kornheiser wrote in the *Washington Post* (October 23, 1987), "When I think of a World Series, the kind of names that come to my mind are Catfish, Yogi, Brooks and Reggie. One-name guys."

one o'clock hitter   *n./arch.* A player who hits well in batting practice and badly during the game. The term is a throwback to the days when games started at 2:00 and batting practice began at 1:00. When starting time was commonly moved back to 3:00, the one o'clock hitter became a two o'clock hitter, and with the advent of night games a six and seven o'clock hitter.

one old cat/one o'cat   *n.* A game that predates baseball and is related to rounders. It is an informal game that is usually played by three children. Rules vary depending on circumstances but a typical game has one base with one player at the plate, one pitching and one in the field. Outs occur when a ball is caught on the fly or there are three strikes. The batter can score on a hit, which enables him to run to the base and return before being put out. The players rotate and each keeps his own score.
1ST   1856. "Just then two of his playmates coming along with a ball, Dick . . . went to join them in a game of 'one-old-cat.' " (*The Juvenile Forget Me Not;* DS)

one-run game   *n.* Contest in which there is a difference of only one run separating the scores of the two teams.

one, two, three   **1.** *n.* Said of a team whose first three batters up in an inning are retired in order.
1ST   1862. (*New York Sunday Mercury,* August 13; EJN)

2. *n.* A practice game in which there are fewer than six fielders on a side. Henry Chadwick described it in the *American Game of Base Ball* as follows: "The field side take their positions and a player takes the bat. When the batsman is put out—unless the ball is caught on the fly, in which case the fielder catching it changes place with the batsman—he takes his position at right field, the catcher takes the bat, the pitcher goes in to catch, and the first baseman takes the pitcher's position, and each of the other fielders advance one step towards the in-field positions. There should be at least four players on the batting side."

onion   *n./arch.* The BALL.
1ST   1917. (*American* magazine, July; EJN)

on the ball   *adj.* Describing a pitcher who is working well. A good pitcher with the ability to deceive batters is said to have a lot on the ball. "Confidence is great stuff but the pitcher must put something else on the ball." (*San Francisco Call*, October 16, 1913; PT)
EXT   1. *adj.* At one's best.
2. *adj.* Bright and alert. The term often appears in the negative, such as: "He's got nothing on the ball" for someone who is dull and incompetent.

on the bound   *adj.* In fielding, to catch a ball as it bounces off the ground.
1ST   1880. (*Brooklyn Daily Eagle*, August 20; EJN)

on the fists   *adj.* An inside pitch that comes close to the batter's hands; a jam. Such a pitch is hit off the bat handle, the part of the bat closest to the batter's hands.

on the fly   *adj.* In the air.
1ST   1859. (Knickerbocker Club correspondence; EJN)

on the hip   *adj.* A term describing a pitcher who has the opposing batters under control.
1ST   1905. (*Sporting Life*, September 2; EJN)

on the label   ON THE TRADEMARK.

on the meat   *adj.* Being hit by a pitched ball; usually stated as, "taking one on the meat."

on the mound   A term describing a pitcher who is currently pitching.

on the nose   *adj.* Squarely; directly. For example, hitting a ball on the nose means to connect with it solidly.
1ST   1883. (*Sporting Life*, May 20; EJN)

on the pine   *adj.* On the bench.

on the road   *adj.* Away from home.

on the trademark   To hit a ball on the thick part of the bat at the point where the manufacturer's insignia is located.
1ST   1898. (*New York Tribune*, June 14; EJN)

open base   *n.* A base not occupied by a runner.
   Sometimes, with fewer than two outs, runners on and first base open, a batter will be walked intentionally to fill first base to improve chances of a force out or double play.

opener   *n.* The first game in a season, series or doubleheader.

Opening Day   *n.* The day on which the regular season begins.
USE   Some writers have been known to capitalize it: "They call it Opening Day, but The Day is more like it." (Jonathan Yardley, *The Washington Post*, April 8, 1985)

open stance   *n.* Batter's position in which the front foot is farther from the plate than the back foot; the front foot is pointed toward third base, for a right-handed batter, or first base, for a left-handed batter.

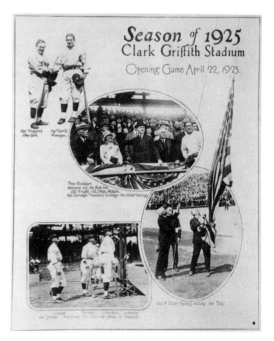

Opening Day. Washington Senators Opening Day as depicted in a Senators program. *Prints and Photographs Division, the Library of Congress*

open the door *v.* To make an error or otherwise grant the opposition an opportunity to score. Walking two batters with two outs would be an example of a team opening the door for the team at bat.

"Open the window, Aunt Minnie, here she comes!" Pittsburgh radio sportscaster Rosey Roswell's trademark salutation for a home run.

opportunity *n.* A team's turn at bat.

opposite field *n.* The side of the playing field that is opposite the side of home plate from which a batter bats. Thus, right field is the opposite field for a right-handed batter, who bats from the left side of home plate. It is called "opposite" because it is the opposite of the direction in which a batter would naturally pull the ball—a right-handed batter naturally pulls his hits to the left and a left-handed batter naturally pulls to the right.

opposite field hitter *n.* A batter who often hits to the side of the field opposite to that he bats from. Opposite field hitting comes from taking a shortened swing, swinging late or swinging at outside pitches.

opposite field-home run *n.* Home run hit to the side of the field opposite to that a batter bats from. Because it is more difficult to hit with power to the opposite field, it is enough of an oddity to merit the lead sentence in a report on a game: "Ernest Riles hit an opposite field-home run to cap a four-run, ninth-inning comeback as Milwaukee completed a three-game sweep of the White Sox." (AP dispatch, March 11, 1986)

option **1.** *n.* The right of a major league team to send a player to the Minor Leagues without putting him on waivers. Under such an arrangement the player is still under contract with the major league team and can be recalled at any time.
2. *v.* To send a player to the minors on the condition that the major league club can reclaim him at the end of the season. This is often stated as "optioned out."
3. *n.* The right of a player to stay with his present team at the end of his contract or to sign with another.
4. *n.* A claim on the future services of a player.
5. *n.* FIELDER'S CHOICE.

option clause *n.* A provision of some players' contracts that allows the club to invoke the terms of an expired contract for an additional season.

option batter *n./obs.* An early name for the designated hitter. The idea had been proposed in the early 1960s and on several other occasions.
The term became immediately obsolete when the concept and term designated hitter were adopted.
"Rules Committee Bars Option Batter for PCL"—*Washington Star* headline for April 1, 1961, on a proposal to test the idea in the Pacific Coast League.

option out *n.* OPTION (2).

orange alert *n.* Description that Oakland A's owner Charles O. Finley used for the orange baseball (the color would be "a little brighter than plain orange" he said) that he tried to have made standard. He pushed the idea hard in 1972.

orange crate *n.* One of several names that attached themselves to the modern glove in which the thumb and forefinger are joined by a deep, wide lacing. "Hank Greenberg, now general manager of the Cleveland Indians, may have pioneered the modern orange crate, or basket glove." (Joe Williams, in his syndicated column for June 4, 1953, *San Francisco News;* PT) The same glove was also dubbed the lobster trap, lobster net etc.

orchard **1.** *n.* OUTFIELD.
2. *n.* BALLPARK.
1ST 1922. (*Baseball Cyclopedia*, EJN)

orchardman *n.* OUTFIELDER. One may also be known as a gardener or pastureworker.

order *n.* Batting order.

order of the can *n.* Mock honor accorded to someone who has been released from a team, i.e., who has been canned.
1ST 1908. (*Baseball* magazine, October; EJN)

organization *n.* The ballclub in its entirety.

organized baseball *n.* Professional baseball—that is, the Major and Minor Leagues as well as the offices that administer them.

oriflamme *n./arch.* The PENNANT.
1ST 1915. (*Baseball* magazine, December; EJN)

ETY This word, borrowed from the French, has become a standard term for a banner or emblem in English. It refers directly to the red banner of St. Denis used as a military banner for the early kings of France. It undoubtedly entered baseball as part of the quest for new synonyms for pennant.

OS Common abbreviation for official scorer.

O's Common nickname for the Baltimore Orioles. Its use is underscored at Memorial Stadium every time the national anthem is sung and the crowd bellows OHHHH! in the line, "Oh say does that star-spangled banner yet wave." The nickname took on a new significance at the beginning of the 1988 season when the Oh became a reference to zero as the club opened with a record-setting loss of 21 straight games.

oscar *n.* Player deserving an award for his feats on the field, from the nickname for the Motion Picture Academy awards statuette.

O'Sullivan sleeper *n./arch.* A daycoach; a passenger rail car on which there are *no* sleeping accommodations.

The original version of this term was *Sullivan sleeper* and O'Sullivan may be a simple misnomer.
1ST 1943. "One phrase obsolete in majors likely will be in vogue again this coming season. That's the 'O'Sullivan sleeper,' the old-timers slang for a day coach." (Herbert Simons, "Do You Speak the Language?" *Baseball* magazine, January)

other thing *n.* Pitcher's second-best pitch. "Vance's sobriquet 'Dazzy' is said to be derived from his own pet name for his 'other thing' used as a co-weapon with his fast ball." (William G. Brandt, *Baseball* magazine, October 1932)

ouija board *n./arch.* The umpire's indicator.
"Check the batteries in your ouija board," was once a common line from a bench jockey on a bad call, according to CB.
ETY From the popular Ouija Board game.

out **1.** *adj.* Not successful in getting on base or advancing to the next base. The status of a batter or base runner who has been retired by the defense. Perhaps, the best definition appears in Zander Hollander's *Baseball Lingo:* "What the game is never over until the last man is."

2. *n.* The act of putting a batter or base runner out of the inning; the official removal of an offensive player.
3. *n.* Unit that defines the length of a half-inning. The half-inning is over after three outs are made on the offense.
1ST 1845. (Knickerbocker Rules)
4. *n.* A putout.
5. *adj.* Away from home plate; the opposite of *in* used in the sense of close.
6. *adj.* Not participating; not in the game.
7. *adj.* Short for "out of play."

outcurve/out curve *n./arch.* A curveball that veers away from the batter. The opposite of incurve.
1ST 1865. (Chadwick Scrapbooks; EJN)

out drop *n./arch.* OUTCURVE.
1ST 1893. (*Harper's Weekly,* July 8; EJN)

outduel *n.* To outpitch. "Fernandez Outduels Dodgers." (*Washington Post* headline, May 30, 1986)

outer garden/outer patch/outer works *n.* The outfield, as opposed to the infield, which is the inner garden.
1ST 1907 (outer garden). (*New York Evening Journal,* April 11; EJN)

outfield **1.** *n.* The playing area beyond the infield perimeter and within the foul lines. Walls or grandstand fences usually set the outside boundaries of the outfield. There is no strictly defined line dividing the infield from the outfield. In the Major Leagues since 1959, the right and left field walls must be at least 325 feet from home plate and the center field wall must be at least 400 feet in all new parks.
1ST 1865. (*New York Herald,* July 11; EJN)
2. *n.* The collective term for the three players playing right, center and left field.
1ST 1888. (*Harper's Weekly,* July 28; EJN)

outfielder *n.* Defensive player positioned in the outfield.
1ST 1883. (*Sporting Life,* May 20; EJN)

outfield throw *n.* A ball thrown to an infielder by an outfielder in an attempt to throw a runner out. In his *Spectator's Guide to Baseball,* Dan Sperling says, "Among baseball's most thrilling plays and impressive sights is an outfielder's throw to a teammate who tags out a runner sliding into base . . . Such a play is baseball theater at its best, as the ball and the runner converge on the base at nearly the same dusty instant, culminating in the umpire's dramatic one-armed gesture signifying 'Out!' "

outfit   *n.* A team.
1ST   1909. (*Baseball* magazine, June; EJN)

outhit   *v.* To get more hits than the opposition.

out in front   *adj.* Swinging at a pitch too soon; ahead of the ball.

outing   *n.* A given game, such as a player's best outing of the season. It tends to be applied to pitchers rather than players who are in the lineup day after day. "If his last two outings are any indication, Dave Steib is back—although in reality the Toronto Blue Jays' five-time all-star pitcher never really left." (Mike Payne in the *St. Petersburg Times,* March 15, 1988)

out in left field/out of left field   1. *adj.* Odd; out of it. Phrase used for that which is a bit off.
ETY   How left field got to be the metaphoric location for oddness has been the subject of no end of speculation. Several have suggested that it comes from the remoteness of left field. But right field is just as remote and, at the lower levels of the game at least, more likely to be populated by an odd player. As Ron Fimrite wrote in an essay on right field: "There was but one position to which the clods, the kids with glasses, the little guys, the sissies, the ones that got good grades, the kids who played with girls, were exiled. That would be right-field, the Siberia of my youth. Right field was the back of the bus, the slow-learners class, the children's department, a sideshow . . . Anyone directed to play right-field would have given anything to 'be out in left-field.' " (*San Francisco Chronicle,* April 28, 1969; PT)
There are two major theories:
1. That it was an insult heaped on kids who were stupid enough to buy left field seats in Yankee Stadium, which for many years would have put them far away from a right fielder named Babe Ruth. This theory was suggested by David Shulman in a letter to William Safire, which appears in Safire's column *I Stand Corrected.* "When I was in my teens, living in the Bronx, we kids were always most anxious to get our seats in the right field where we would be

closest to Babe Ruth, so I suppose anybody in the left field was far out."
2. That it was, in fact, a specific reference to the fact that there was a mental hospital, the Neuropsychiatric Institute, in back of left field in the old, 19th-century West Side Park in Chicago. The most specific description of this appears in a letter by Gerald M. Eisenberg, M.D., of Chicago, also quoted in Safire's *I Stand Corrected.* "In Chicago," wrote Eisenberg, "when someone said that one was 'out in left field,' the implication was that one was behaving like the occupants of the Neuropsychiatric Institute, which was *literally* out in left field." This has been corroborated by researcher Richard Miller of Cincinnati who has been doing research on the Chicago ballparks.
It should also be pointed out that there was a phrase used in the 1930s that was "way out in left field without a glove." According to a United Press International dispatch of April 19, 1937, which carried George Kirksey's by-line, the phrase was not used to describe a player who is out of it but rather one "as proficient at whipping over a smart crack as a sizzling strike." (PT)
EXT   Applied broadly to describe odd, eccentric, unexpected or exceptionally misguided people and ideas in all walks of life.

out in order   *adj.* Situation in which the first three batters coming to the plate in an inning are retired without one of them reaching first base.

outlaw   *n./arch.* A player banned from organized baseball.
A definition that appeared in Hugh S. Fullerton's 1912 "Baseball Primer" shows how widely used the term once was: "The club, league or player who offends against baseball law is punished by being 'outlawed' or blacklisted . . . There are several hundred players on the blacklist at present who cannot play in any clubs belonging to the National Agreement until reinstated by the Commission."
1ST   1906. (*Sporting Life,* February 10; EJN)

out looking   Retired on a called third strike.

out man   *n.* A weak hitter who is a good bet to make an out; an easy out. Pitchers are often out men.

out of form   *adj./arch.* A common 19th-century term for a pitcher who had lost his effectiveness or a batter who was unable to hit the ball.

out of here *adj.* A term used to describe a home run hit out of the park.

out of his hip pocket Apparent source of the ball as the pitcher goes into his windup, turns his back to the batter and delivers.

out of left field *adj.* OUT IN LEFT FIELD.

out of line *adj.* Outside the base lines.

out of order *adj.* BATTING OUT OF TURN.

out of turn *adj.* BATTING OUT OF TURN.

out of play *adj.* A term used to describe a ball that is dead.
SEE DEAD BALL.

out of reach *adj.* Practically unwinnable. For instance, a game in which the score is 9–0 in the 8th inning.

out of the inning *adj.* A term used to desscribe a pitcher who has survived a jam, often thanks to a double play that ends the half inning.

out pitch *n.* The pitch that pitchers depend on to get an out.

outpitch *v.* To pitch a better game than the other pitcher.

outpost *n.* Outfield.
1ST 1902. (*Sporting Life,* July 5; EJN)

outright **1.** *adj.* A term for a transaction between two teams in which a player is obtained for cash alone rather than in a trade or a trade plus cash.
2. *v.* To send a player to the minors after severing all his contractual ties with the major league team. Outrighting a player is the opposite of optioning a player.

outshoot *n./arch.* OUTCURVE.
1ST 1881. (*New York Herald,* July 29; EJN)

outside *adj.* A term for a pitch that is delivered away from the batter on the far side of or beyond the strike zone. One of the reasons that pitchers like it when batters stand away from the plate is that they can throw an outside pitch for a strike that the batter can't reach.
1ST 1908. (*Spalding's Official Base Ball Book;* EJN)

outside baseball *n.* An offensive strategy that depends on powerful hitting rather than skill on the base paths.
SEE *inside baseball.*

outside pivot *n.* a move in which the shortstop brushes second base on the outfield side for the force out as he is throwing to first in the attempt to turn a double play.

outslug *v.* To get more hits than the opposition in high-scoring game.

out swinging *adj.* Retired on a swing and a miss for the third strike.

overhand pitch *n.* A pitch delivered with the arm straight above the shoulder. As underhanded pitches are illegal in baseball and sidearm pitches uncommon, most baseball pitches can be described with this term.

overmanage *v.* For a manager to hamper his team by employing more strategy than is called for. Commonly used when a team gets into trouble after its manager has called on too many relief pitchers.

over-pitch *n./obs.* The error that takes place when the pitcher throws the ball over the head of the batsman and catcher. The term can be traced back to Henry Chadwick.
1ST 1862. (*New York Sunday Mercury,* July 13; EJN)

overpower *v.* To swing with excessive force.

overrun **1.** *v.* To touch a base but then run or slide beyond it to a position where the runner can be tagged out. The runner is allowed to overrun first base, but only if he turns right into foul territory and/or makes no break toward second.
2. *v.* In fielding, to misjudge the course of a batted ball.

overslide *v.* To slide into a base and then to go beyond it to a position where the runner can be tagged out.
1ST 1908. (*Brooklyn Daily Eagle,* May 29; EJN)

overstride *v.* To take too large a step toward the pitcher when swinging the bat; to lunge at the ball.

over the fence/over the garden wall/over the wall *adj.* Describing a ball hit for a home run.

over the top   *adv.* Describing an overhand pitching motion.

overthrow   **1.** *n.* A thrown ball that is too high or too wide and that frequently lands out of play. In cases when the ball is thrown out of play, each base runner is given the base he was heading toward plus one additional base.
2. *v.* For either a pitcher or fielder to throw a ball that is too high or wide.
1ST   1862. (*New York Sunday Mercury,* July 13; EJN)

overtime   *n.* Any inning after the ninth. A borrowing from those sports whose finale is determined by a clock or timer and in which overtime periods are played in the case of a tie at the end of the final period.

own.   *v.* To dominate. A pitcher may own a batter just as a batter may own a pitcher. In his book *Oh, Baby I Love It!* Tim McCarver says that Ty Cobb "owned" pitcher Walter Johnson. Cobb knew that Johnson would not use his blazing fastball to intimidate the batter so Cobb would crowd the plate knowing that he would get a good pitch.

Ozarkisms   *n.* Aphoristic lines attributed to baseball manager Danny Ozark. "Even Napoleon had his Watergate," for example.

P

pace *n.* The rate of speed at which a pitcher works.
1ST 1865. (*New York Herald,* June 29; EJN)

pace-setter *n./adj.* Leading team in a league.

pace the ball *v.* To field the ball without taking an unnecessary step.
ETY Borrowed from horse racing.

Pacific Coast League (PCL) Ten-team AAA minor league with teams in the Western U.S., Western Canada and Hawaii. As of this writing there are PCL teams in Albuquerque, New Mexico; Calgary and Edmonton, Alberta; Hawaii; Las Vegas, Nevada; Phoenix, and Tucson, Arizona; Portland, Oregon; Tacoma, Washington; and Vancouver, British Columbia.

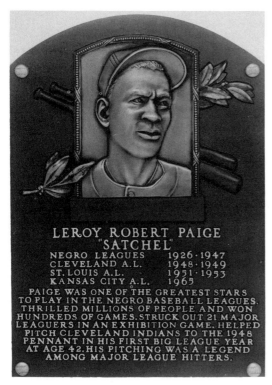

Paige's Rules for Staying Young. Leroy "Satchel" Paige's Hall of Fame plaque. *National Baseball Library, Cooperstown, N.Y.*

pack a punch *v.* To be able to hit the ball with power.

pad *n.* Padded mitt or glove.
1ST 1906. (*Sporting Life,* February 10; EJN)

Pads Nickname for the San Diego Padres, as in "Pads will Pick Pitcher" (*Sporting News* headline for June 6, 1988.)

Paige's Rules for Staying Young A set of guidelines created by Satchel Paige, baseball's "ageless wonder," to explain his longevity as a pitcher.
1. Avoid fried meats which anger up the blood.
2. If your stomach disputes you, lie down and pacify it with cool thoughts.
3. Keep the juices flowing by jangling around gently as you move.
4. Go very lightly on the vices, such as carrying on in society—the social ramble ain't restful.
5. Avoid running at all times.
6. And don't look back. Something might be gaining on you.

paint/paint the black *v.* To throw pitches over the edges of the plate, which appear to be dark or black because of the contrast of the white rubber plate with the surrounding dirt.

Pale Hose *n.* Nickname for the White Sox, who are also sometimes called the noble Pale Hose.

palm ball/palmball *n.* An uncommon off-speed pitch that is thrown with the ball gripped between the pitcher's thumb and palm. The ball is thrown with a pushing motion, making it break in an unpredictable manner. "Palm Ball Helps in No-Hitter"—headline over Associated Press dispatch on Steve Ridzik no-hitter, April 5, 1952. (PT)

pal-ocracy *n.* Vague term for the network of good friends—pals—who supposedly once ran organized baseball.

palomita *n.* Spanish language description for a fly ball. Literally, it means a little dove.

pan *n.* HOME PLATE.
1ST 1891. "These three men make the pitchers put them over the pan day in and day out." (*New York Sporting Times*, May 23, 1891; DS)

pancake **1.** *n.* An old, worn and generally lifeless glove.
2. *n.* A thinly padded glove preferred by some infielders, mostly shortstops and second basemen, who believe it allows them to handle and get rid of the ball more quickly than would be possible with the more thickly padded "bushel basket" glove.

paper mache/paper mashy *adj.* Term for a player who is easily hurt.
ETY Despite some wild spelling deviation, a clear reference to papier-mâché, a light and moldable pulpy paper.

paper team *n.* Team that should be good, but is not; one that looks good "on paper" but not in the field.
1ST 1911. (*Baseball* magazine, October; EJN)

parachute *n.* A pop fly that drops quickly for a hit.

parachute hitters *n.* A team of singles hitters, such as the 1952 Pirates.

parallel stance *n.* Batting stance in which the batter stands with his feet in a line parallel to home plate. Also known as the square stance.

park **1.** *n.* The baseball field and stadium; short for ballpark. "You know, you take your worries to the park and you leave them there." (Humphrey Bogart, in a 1950s promotional ad for baseball)
2. *v.* To hit a home run. The verb figures in a number of expressions describing the long one: to park in the bushes, to park the pill in the bleachers, he parked one in the street etc. "They Really Parked 'Em." (*Newsday* headline, May 12, 1987)

pass **1.** *n.* BASE ON BALLS. Also known as a free pass.
1ST 1902. (*Sporting Life*, September 20; EJN)
2. *v.* To walk a batter.
1ST 1910. (*Baseball* magazine, December; EJN)
3. *n.* A free admission to a game.

pass ball/passed ball *n.* A legally pitched ball that goes past the catcher, allowing a base runner to advance. It differs from a wild pitch in that the official scorer rules that the catcher should have stopped it. If this occurs on the third strike, it is treated as a dropped third strike and the batter may advance to first base. A passed ball is not registered as an error to the catcher.
1ST 1861 (passed ball). (*New York Sunday Mercury*, August 10; EJN)

passing a runner *n.* Rare situation in which a runner illegally passes a teammate on the basepath. When this occurs, the passing man is ruled out.

pasteboards *n./arch.* Tickets.
1ST 1898. (*New York Tribune*, May 13; EJN)

paste one *v.* To bat the ball hard.
1ST 1876. (*Chicago Inter Ocean*, May 6; EJN)

pastime *n.* NATIONAL PASTIME.

pasture *n.* OUTFIELD.
1ST 1891. (*Chicago Inter Ocean*, May 5; EJN)

pastureman/pastureworker *n.* Outfielder.

paternal slump *n.* Poor baseball performance linked to impending fatherhood. "Tigers' Johnson in 'paternal' slump." (*USA Today* headline, August 16, 1984)

paths *n.* BASE PATHS.

patrol *v.* To play a field position. To patrol the pasture is to play the outfield.

Patsy Flaherty pitch *n.* Pitch delivered without a wind-up.
ETY Pete Howe wrote of this in his *San Francisco Examiner* column of May 26, 1957. "Patsy Flaherty was an old-time pitcher in the National League who used the no-wind-up delivery so much it came to be called the 'Patsy Flaherty.' Casey Stengel batted against him and has described his pitching this way: 'Patsy picked up the ball and umpire hollered strike.' " (PT)

pay ball **1.** *n.* Ball delivered when the count is 0–2 (no balls, two strikes).
1ST 1937. (New York *Daily News*, May 2; EJN)
2. Ball that is easy to hit.

payoff pitch *n.* Ball delivered when the count is full (three balls and two strikes). Barring a foul, it is the payoff because the batter must either hit, be walked or strike out with this pitch.

pay-station *n.* HOME PLATE.
1ST 1937. (New York *Daily News*; EJN)

payback pitch *n.* Ball thrown by a pitcher to harm or intimidate a batter in revenge for a real or imagined transgression by him or his team.

PB Standard scorecard and box score abbreviation for passed ball.

pea *n.* Pitched or batted ball that is moving so fast that it appears smaller than it actually is. It is said to look like a pea; also a BB. "Juicier? I know there were a lot of peas out there tonight."—Rocky Colavito on the 1987 model baseball. (*USA Today,* June 30, 1987)
1ST 1910. (*Baseball* magazine, April; EJN)

peacherino *n./arch.* A sensational play or player.
1ST 1908. (*New York Evening Journal,* February 17; EJN)

pebble hit *n.* Hit made with the help of a rock, pebble or other field irregularity, which helps it bounce away from the fielder. "In the old days," said an announcer commenting on a bad hop during the fifth game of the 1952 World Series, "that would have been called a 'pebble hit,' but there are no pebbles on infields now." (October 4, 1952; PT)

pebble hunter/pebble picker *n.* Defensive player, usually an infielder, who hunts for real or imaginary pebbles on which to blame his errors. He will allege that a ball took a bad hop because of a pebble.
1ST 1912. (*American* magazine, June; EJN)
ETY According to Hugh Fullerton in his 1915 "Baseball Primer": "The term arises from the fact that one old-time player was caught carrying pebbles in his pocket to drop on the ground after he fumbled, and then find, claiming each time that the ball struck a pebble and bounded wrong."

Pebble Play An incident, in the 12th inning of the final game of the 1924 World Series between the New York Giants and the Washington Senators, in which a batted ball hopped over a Giant infielder's head, leading to a run that gave the championship to the Senators. It was claimed and verified by members of the Giants that the ball that bounced over Freddy Lindstrom's head did indeed hit a pebble.

pedal music *n./arch.* The stamping of enthusiastic fans.

peddle peruna *v./arch.* To be boastful; to advertise oneself.
ETY Peruna was a patent medicine heavily

Pebble Play. Lindstrom's remarkable record puts the "pebble play" in perspective. *National Baseball Library, Cooperstown, N.Y.*

advertised at the turn of the century. Many gave testimonials in its behalf. In Mark Sullivan's 1933 *Our Times* (1926–35) a Senator from Mississippi gives his testimonial: "For some time I have been a sufferer from catarrah in its most incipient stage. So much so that I became alarmed as to my general health. But hearing of Peruna as a good remedy, I gave it a fair trial, and soon began to improve. I take pleasure in recommending your great natural catarrh cure. Peruna is the best I have ever tried." It was driven from the market by pure food advocates who faulted it for being loaded with whiskey.

peeker *n.* As defined by Burt Dunne: "Pitcher who, with men on, can't resist turning head to watch runners as he is in act of delivery, takes eyes off catcher's target and invariably has bad control."

Pee Wee Baseball Program of play and instruction for boys and girls who are six and seven years of age.

peg 1. *n.* A long, powerful throw, traditionally from the outfield to the infield to make a play. The term tends to be used for accurate throws. "He's had some good pegs from out there. You can't tell him to take it easy." (George Bamberger on Robin Yount as an outfielder, *Tampa Tribune-Times*, March 30, 1986)
1ST 1906. (*Spalding's Official Base Ball Guide;* EJN)
2. *v.* To make such a throw.
1ST 1862. (*New York Sunday Mercury,* July 13; EJN)

Peggy Lee fastball *n.* A fastball that is not that fast and has nothing on it.
ETY The term is used in connection with batters who see the pitch and are reminded of Ms. Lee's sad song, "Is That All There Is?" Attributed widely to pitcher Tug McGraw who specialized in the pitch (his regular fastball minus about 10 miles per hour), but *The Sporting News* cites Dan Quisenberry as father of the term.

pellet *n.* A baseball.
1ST 1907. (*New York Evening Journal,* April 15; EJN)

pen 1. *n.* Defined in Thomas W. Lawson's 1888 *Krank* as, "A row of seats fenced in on all sides in the extreme front of the grandstand."
2. *n.* Bullpen, for short. "After three days in the pen, Whitson's back in the rotation." (headline, Gannett Westchester Newspapers, June 13, 1986)

pennant 1. *n.* The title and honorary consideration given to the team that wins its league championship. It refers to and derives from:
2. *n.* The large triangular commemorative banner given to the champion.
1ST 1879. (*Spirit of the Times,* September 13; EJN)

pennant race *n.* The battle for the championship of the league, especially toward the end of the season when several teams are in contention.
1ST 1880. (*Brooklyn Daily Eagle,* July 25; EJN)

pennant voyage *n.* A baseball season.

'penners *n.* Relief pitchers, denizens of the bullpen. "Nothing, Weaver fears, is beyond the reach of his 'penners.'" (*The Washington Post,* June 5, 1986).

pepper 1. *n.* The ritual of briskly throwing the ball around the infield after a putout.

2. *n.* Vigor and energy.
1ST 1895. (*New York Press,* July 8; EJN)
3. *n.* Fast-paced pregame bunting and fielding drill among small clusters of players playing at close range. One player chops at the ball with a brisk, bunt-like stroke. The batted ball is pitched back to the batter by the man who fields it. "Greatest game in the world for a hitter," wrote Keith Moreland on the subject in a 1987 issue of *Vineline.* "Short pepper is when a batter tries to hit one-hoppers back to the guy throwing to him in pre-game practice."
Many ballparks have NO PEPPER or NO PEPPER GAMES signs stenciled on the infield walls. Because these prohibitory signs are visible on television, the term is known to many who have never seen it played. The ban, dating back to the 1950s, apparently stemmed from the fact that the field was sometimes damaged from pepper play.
1ST 1933. The game was known as "high-low" and perhaps by other names before it became pepper. "Over at the left of the third-base line pepper games are in progress. Six or eight players, glove in hand, line up a yard apart. Thirty feet away stands a batter. He hits the ball with amazing precision . . . Whoever grabs it returns it to the batter as quickly as he can get it out of his hands, only to have it batted back again double quick. This simple game is very popular among training players." ("Rehearsing for Baseball" by Arthur Mann, *American Mercury,* March 1933; PT)
ETY This term would appear to derive from "pep" as well as the "peppy" or "peppery" nature of the game, which in turn appear to be derivatives of pepper, to give the term a circular etymology. Both these adjectives were fairly common in ballpark expressions before World War II. Two examples from Maurice H. Weseen's 1934 *Dictionary of American Slang* are "peppery grasser" (a hit ball that is low and swift) and "peppery pilot" (a lively, aggressive manager of a team).

pepper practice *n.* Period of pepper play before the game.
1ST 1935. "We can suggest nothing more helpful to the young batter than 'pepper practice' in large doses." (Ralph H. Barbour in *How to Play Better Baseball;* DS)

percentage ball/percentage baseball *n.* A strategy in which the game is played with the aid of the law of probabilities. Examples of percentage ball are waiting for hits to bring in

base runners rather than taking chances on the basepaths, or walking a batter to create a force situation. In an earlier time, this was known as inside baseball.
1ST 1932. (*Baseball* magazine, October; EJN)

percentage hit *n.* A fluke hit that nevertheless helps one's batting average.

percentage manager *n.* A manager who makes decisions based on established form, statistics and odds.

percentage patsy. *n.* Player who plays to enhance his individual statistics rather than for the good of the team as a whole.
1ST 1937. (*The Sporting News Record Book;* EJN)

perch *n.* Team's place in the standings.

perfect game *n.* A no-hitter in which no opposing player reaches base. In other words, a game in which a team's pitcher(s) retires all 27 opposing batters in order.

As of this writing, there have only been 12 perfect games in the Major Leagues, with the most famous being the one pitched by Yankee Don Larson against the Brooklyn Dodgers in the 1956 World Series. The first was pitched in 1880 by John Richman of the Worcester team.
1ST 1922. (*Baseball Cyclopedia;* EJN)

perspiration pellet *n./arch.* SPITBALL.
1ST 1907. (*New York Evening Journal,* June 7; EJN)

pest *n.* Fan who always wants something, such as an autographed ball. Pests are nothing new, as this definition from the September 1913 *Baseball* magazine attests:

"PESTS—A grave-yard comedian as funny as a crutch equipped with a megaphone, a pass, and a .44 caliber voice, who tries to address the players by their maiden names. Generally loses both 'goat' and voice in the first inning."

Pete Homer Personification of an umpire who seems to be favoring the home team.

petit larceny *n.* Base stealing. (Pronounced "petty larceny.")

phantom *n.* In baseball memorabilia collecting, an item that was created for an event that did not take place, such as playoff tickets for a team that did not make the playoffs.

phantom double play *n.* A double play in which the out at second base is an illusion. The defensive player making the play at second will elude the sliding runner, cross the bag without

touching it and throw the ball to first. Despite the fact that the rules say that the bag must be touched, many umpires ignore the violation if the ball beats the runner to second base. The reason that umpires do this is to keep players from getting hurt in collisions.
SEE *Neighborhood play.*

phantom hit *n./arch.* Gerald Cohen, in his research on the baseball columns of the New York *World,* defined this as a base on balls.
1ST 1887. ". . . after which Tucker was given a 'phantom hit,' stole second and scored on Griffin's splendid drive to centre field." (*World,* August 11)

phantom infield *n.* A crowd-pleasing pregame drill in which the infield goes through the rigors of infield practice without the benefit of a ball.

phantom tag *n.* A missed tag or a tag from a glove without a ball in it, either one of which is mistakenly credited as a legal tag. Some coaches instruct infielders to discreetly remove the ball from the glove just before the tag to prevent the ball from being jarred loose as the play is made.

phenom/pheenom *n.* A highly-touted rookie; one who gets off to a spectacular start at the beginning of the season or during spring training; an early bloomer.
1ST 1890. Although writer Garry Schumacher is widely credited with coining the term for the Giants' phenom Clint Hartung in the spring of 1947, it regularly shows up in print much earlier. Edward J. Nichols points to three citations before 1900, with the first coming from the July 3, 1890, *New York Press.* Nor was it an uncommon term at the end of the last and the beginning of this century. In *The Tumult and the Shouting,* the legendary sportswriter Grantland Rice recalls a 1904 telegram touting a young "phenom" named Tyrus Raymond Cobb. (CDP)

In *America's National Game* (1911), A. G. Spalding ties the term to a rule change. "The removal of the straight-arm pitching restrictions by the amendment of the rules in 1884 was responsible for the evolution of the 'Phenom.' He came into the game from Keokuk, Kankakee, Kokomo and Kalamazoo. He was heralded always as a 'discovery.' His achievements were 'simply phenomenal.' Once in a great while he 'made good.' Usually he proved to be a flat and unmitigated failure."

Phenom. Pete Incaviglia of the Rangers was one of the crop of rookie phenoms who came up in 1986.   *Courtesy of the Texas Rangers*

ETY   Shortened form of phenomenon or phenomenal player. Phenomenon has had a long and distinguished history as a title for a boxer or racehorse. Peter Tamony has found phenomenons dating back to 1807, when a prizefighter nicknamed the "Israelite Phenomenon" won a 34-round bout in England. In the United States, Tamony found a bay gelding named "Awful" who had a spectacular season in 1838. His backers nicknamed him "The Phenomenon."

Although the shortened form of "phenom" has been used for boxers and other athletes, its early use and primary application has been to ball players. In other words, it is closely linked to baseball.
EXT   Now used for fast-starters in any field. The title of an April 8, 1985, article in *Forbes* on young CEO's was "Pity the poor phenoms."

Philadelphia Athletics   The name was first used in 1859 for an amateur baseball club in Philadelphia. That team turned professional and played with the original American Association through the 1880s. The name lay fallow from 1892 until Connie Mack put an American League team in the city in 1901. The team later moved to Kansas City in 1955 and then to Oakland in 1968.

Philadelphia Phillies   The name of the National League's Eastern Division franchise in Philadelphia, Pennsylvania. The name, which comes from the name of the city, has been in use since 1883, although owner Bob Carpenter tried to rename them the Blue Jays in the 1940s.

Philadelphia triple   *n./arch.* Three consecutive fly ball outs in an inning (ca. 1940s).

Phils   Nickname for the Philadelphia Phillies.

phonographic needle pitch   *n.* Illegal pitch given its odd trajectory by the insertion of a 78 rpm stylus in the seam of the ball. It is described in detail in *The Crooked Pitch* by Martin Quigley, who himself threw the odd pitch in the 1930s.

pianola   *n./arch.* An easy win; a laugher.
ETY   Pianola was the trademarked name of a player piano that was easy to play compared to a regular piano.

Picasso   *n.* CONTROL PITCHER; one who paints the black.

pick/pick 'em/pick it   *v.* To successfully field a ground ball, especially one that is hard to handle. Often used as part of a compliment by one team member to another for a first-rate defensive play: "Good pick," "way to pick it," "he really picked it" etc.

pickle   1. *n.* A runner caught in a rundown between bases, short for "in a pickle."
2. *v.* To bat a ball hard; to pickle one. Edward J. Nichols says: "Named from the idea of 'pickling' in the sense of 'to salt away.' "
1ST   1908. (*New York Evening Journal,* August 20; EJN)
3. *n.* Playground drill or game in which two youngsters stand at bases and throw the ball back and forth, trying to put out a runner.

pickle brine   *n.* Substance given a role in baseball after pitcher Nolan Ryan started the custom of soaking his hands in it to toughen his skin and prevent blisters.

pickoff/pick off   1. *v.* To throw out a base runner who has taken a long lead off the base he is occupying.
1ST   1939. "Then the danger of a throw to first for the pickoff is that the runner has

overrun first not only too far to get back but far enough to make a break for second." (G. S. Cochrane, *Baseball, the Fan's Game;* DS)
2. *n.* See pickoff play.

pickoff play/pick off play   *n.* A play in which either the pitcher or the catcher makes a sudden toss of the ball to an infielder to catch a base runner off base by surprise and tag him out. The play requires careful coordination between the players who are setting up the pick-off.

pickpocket   1. *n.* A signal stealer.
2. *n.* A quick-handed infielder who steals potential hits from batters.

pick-up   1. *n.* A ball caught immediately after it strikes the ground; for example, a first baseman will often make a pick-up on a low throw.
1ST   1875. (*New York Herald*, August 7; EJN)
2. *adj.* Referring to an informal game in which players are divided into two teams just before it begins. Pick-up games are common at the playground and schoolyard level of the game.

pickup-point   *n.* Split second (¹⁵/₁₀₀ of a second according to one estimate) at which the batter can see the ball and decide whether or not to swing at it. Before reaching this point, the ball is an indistinct blur.

pie   *adj./arch.* Easy to beat.
    Gerald Cohen found several examples of this term, apparently derived from "easy as pie." "Those who imagined that the Wolverines would be pie for the pennant-winners yesterday were sadly disappointed." (*New York World*, September 19, 1888)

pie belt   *n./arch.* Nickname for the major league clubs and cities of the Middle West.

piece of iron   1. *n.* Bat made of extra-good wood.
2. *n./arch.* Bat illegally plugged with nails, screws or hardware.

piece of it, getting a/piece of the ball, getting a   *v.* Getting part of the bat on the ball for a foul ball, as in "he got a piece of it." Typically, a batter with two strikes will try to get a piece of a ball to keep from striking out.

pier six   *adj.* A term used to describe a rough and tumble situation such as a brawl between opposing sides or, to quote one news account, "a pier six free-for-all with the Cubs."
ETY   Uncertain, but the use of the term may

have been aided by a 1955 movie entitled "Riot on Pier Six."

pile into a ball   *v.* To hit with great force.

pilfer   *v.* To steal a base.
1ST   1891. (*Chicago Herald*, May 6; EJN)

pill   *n.* Baseball.
1ST   1906. (*Sporting Life*, March 10; EJN)

pillowball   *n.* A softball with a circumference of 16 inches.

pill slinger   *n./arch.* Pitcher.
1ST   1914. " 'Of course, he's some pill slinger,' asserted a stocky, square-shouldered person . . ." (Gilbert Patten, *Brick King, Backstop;* DS)

pilot   1. *n.* Manager, so called because he is at the controls.
2. *v.* To manage.

pinch   1. *n.* A difficult situation, such as being down by a run with only one out to go in a key game; to be in a pinch.
1ST   1902. (*Sporting News*, July 12; EJN)
2. *adj.* Describing a key situation.

pinch hit   1. *v.* To come to the plate and bat in place of the scheduled batter who must then automatically leave the game.
2. *n.* A hit made by a pinch hitter.
1ST   1907. (*Sporting Life*, April 11; EJN)
ETY   In 1892 the permitting of substitutions was added to the rules, and shortly thereafter the term was created by sportswriter Charley Dryden who saw it as a substitution made in "a pinch." The first player to be used in this manner was Johnny Doyle of the Cleveland Spiders, according to Joseph McBride in the book *High and Inside.*
EXT   To substitute or take over for a regular performer. "I'll pinch hit for her while she's on vacation."

pinch hitter   *n.* A replacement sent in during the course of a game to bat for the scheduled batter who must then leave the game. Technically, the pinch hitter can only bat once. If he stays in the game, however, he is no longer a pinch hitter but rather a substitute. The idea at work here goes beyond mere substitution: The pinch hitter is put in expressly because he is more likely to get a hit.
ETY/1ST   1902. The term was used as early as April 26, 1902, in *Sporting Life*. (EJN) Despite this, there have been claims that it did not really enter the language until 1905 when, according

to one account, ". . . [John J.] McGraw engaged Sammy Strang as pinch hitter—the first to fill that role in baseball. By that innovation he gave the words 'pinch hitter' to the English language." ("Genius of the Game," by Bozeman Bulger, *The Saturday Evening Post,* ca. 1930; PT) **EXT** A substitute; an understudy. "Esther Walker went on one night as a 'pinch hitter' at a Winter Garden show in New York and brought down the house." (1920 *Victor Record Catalog;* PT)

pinch-hitting specialist *n.* In some minor leagues, a pinch hitter who is allowed two trips to the plate without the removal of a player from the line-up.

pinch run *v.* To come in as a substitute for a runner who is on base.

pinch runner *n.* A substitute runner sent in for a player who has reached base. Such substitutes are put in because they are much faster than the man on base or because the man on base has been injured during the play. The original runner cannot continue to play in the game.

pine *n.* The bench. To be told to "grab some pine" is to be told to sit on the bench.

pineapple *n.* Minor league player.

pine tar *n.* Sticky, dark pine tree derivative that is rubbed on a batter's hands or bat to create a better grip. It is usually applied by means of a cloth or towel that has been saturated with the substance.

pine tar ball *n.* An illegal pitch in which the ball has been rubbed with pine tar so that it is easier to grip and control. The pine tar is usually placed on the pitcher's glove and transfered to the ball from there. The rule against this "foreign substance" came into play during the third game of the 1988 National League Championship Series when Jay Howell of the Los Angeles Dodgers was ejected from the game and suspended for three days after pine tar was found in his glove.

pine tar bat *n.* Bat that has been rubbed with a pine tar rag to give the batter a better grip.

Pine Tar Game/Pine Tar Incident Infamous 1983 game at Yankee Stadium in which, with two outs in the ninth inning, Kansas City Royals slugger George Brett hit a home run to give the Royals the lead. The umpire ruled that the pine tar on Brett's bat extended beyond the legal limit of 18 inches up the bat handle, nullified the home run, and called Brett out to end the game, giving the Yankees the win. The Royals lodged a protest with the American League president, who eventually ruled in their favor. The home run was restored and the game was later completed with Kansas City ahead with two outs in the top of the ninth.

pine tar towel *n.* A pine tar-soaked cloth that batters rub on their bat handles to provide them with a firmer grip.

ping effect *n.* Term for the distinctive sound of the ball hitting an aluminum bat and the reaction to it, which is commonly negative. "The sound of a ball struck by an aluminum bat is different to different ears, but no one could confuse it with the distinctive crack of an ash bat. In the bat business, that is called the ping effect . . ." (Phil Patton in *Smithsonian* magazine)

pin his ears back *v.* To amass numerous hits against an opposing pitcher.

pin pointer *n.* Pitcher with precise control.

pinstripe *n.* A uniform decoration composed of rows of thin stripes. In a baseball context, it is almost always used to refer to the pinstriped New York Yankees, as in "Pinstripe Potential." (*Albany Times-Union* headline, August 9, 1987) This is true despite the fact that other teams have used pinstripes (the Detroit Tigers, for instance). Both inside and outside the game, they have come to represent power. They have also created their own mythology. According to *USA Today,* the Yankee pinstripes came as a result of Babe Ruth's excessive eating and drinking: "In 1929, Yankees management wanted the slugger to look thinner, so they added pinstripes to the white uniforms to hide his girth." (March 12, 1987) The Yankees, as many photos will attest, had worn pinstripes for many years before 1929, including years in which Ruth was relatively trim.

Pinstriper *n.* A New York Yankee. A profile of Yankee coach and former player Clete Boyer in the *St. Petersburg Times* (February 16, 1988) was simply titled "Pinstriper."

Pioneer League Rookie-class minor league with eight franchises in Billings, Butte, Great Falls, and Helena, Montana; Idaho Falls and

Pocatello, Idaho; Medicine Hat, Alberta (Canada); and Salt Lake City, Utah.

pipe *n.* Throat. A "hot pipe" is a sore throat. This term is part of the odd collection of baseball's renaming of body parts, which also includes *wheels* (legs), *lamps* (eyes) and *hose* (arm).

Pipp *v.* To be replaced due to injury or illness and never regain one's position. See Wally Pipp, after whom the term was created.

pisser and a moaner *n.* Baseballese for a whiner and complainer. "Maris arrived at the Yankees with a somewhat seedy but well-earned reputation as a pisser and a moaner, in baseball parlance, a complainer, a griper." (Leonard Shecter in *The Jocks*; CDP)

pit **1.** *n.* The cellar; the lowest point in the standings.
2. *n./arch.* The dugout.

pitch **1.** *n.* A ball en route to the plate from the pitcher's mound; one delivered to the catcher. The pitch is only one element of the act of pitching. "The fireballer eyes the coiled batsman. Here's the wind-up, the stride, the pitch and the ball explodes on the inside corner of the plate as Lefty lashes out."
1ST 1861. (*New York Sunday Mercury*, August 10; EJN)
2. *v.* To deliver the ball from the pitcher's mound in an attempt to get the batter out, or, under certain circumstances, to advance the batter to first on an intentional walk.
1ST 1845. Knickerbocker Rules #9 stated, "The ball must be pitched and not thrown for the bat." This "pitch" referred to an under the hip toss with an unbent arm. The modern unrestricted delivery would be considered a throw in the original Knickerbocker Rules.
3. *v.* To play the game as a pitcher.
4. *v.* To deliver the ball in a particular way; as in, "He pitched him low and inside."
EXT **1.** To become active; to be part of the action. "Some observers opine that Yankee doughboys will be in there pitching for democracy within the next four weeks."—dispatch from Tokyo quoting a Japanese newspaper, September 21, 1939, *San Francisco Examiner.* (PT) Also, in the sense of "to pitch woo" for "to neck."
2. To present, as in "pitching a new product." Also used as noun meaning presentation, as in "sales pitch."

pitch around/pitch around a batter **1.** *v.* To purposefully refuse to give a batter a good ball to hit. It is a pitching strategy that tends to be employed when first base is open.
2. *v.* To intentionally walk a batter.

pitch baseball cards *v.* FLIP BASEBALL CARDS.

pitch-count *n.* Running tabulation of the number of pitches a pitcher has thrown in a game. The manager and pitching coach watch the pitch-count to keep a pitcher from exhausting himself or his arm. ". . . Davey Johnson said he would've ended Ron Darling's no-hit bid if his pitch-count approached 160." (*New York Post*, June 29, 1987)

pitcher **1.** *n.* The defensive player who starts the game and puts the ball back in play during the game by delivering the ball from the pitcher's mound to the catcher with the batter in position. The primary objective of the pitcher is to put out batters.
1ST !854. (Knickerbocker Rules; EJN)
2. *n.* A term of distinction for a pitcher with great control. "Bob Feller, the former great baseball pitcher, has been quoted as saying that the California Angels' Nolan Ryan was a thrower, not a pitcher. Maybe so. Nevertheless, it's interesting to note that Ryan's fastball has been clocked at 100.9 m.p.h. which is 3 m.p.h. faster than Feller's fastball." (*San Francisco Chronicle*, June 28, 1975; PT)
1ST 1854. (Rules of the Original Knickerbocker Club.)
EXT One who presents—pitches—ideas and policy. Eugene McCarthy used to call Richard Nixon "the same old pitcher." (*San Francisco Chronicle*, August 28, 1968; PT)

pitcher covering first *n.* A common defensive play that takes place when the first baseman must move off the bag to field a batted ball. The pitcher runs to first base to make the putout.

pitcher in the hole *n.* Term used to describe the pitcher when the batter has the advantage.

pitcher of record *n.* The pitcher who is charged with a win or loss of a game, even if he has been removed from the game. A pitcher who has been removed remains the pitcher of record until the score becomes tied or a new lead is established at which point a new pitcher of record is established.

pitcher reader   *n.* Batter who recognizes the upcoming pitch by identifying the pitcher's grip or motion.

pitcher's best friend   *n.* The double play.

pitcher's box   *n.* PITCHER'S MOUND.
1ST   1887. (*Harper's Weekly,* September 10; EJN)

pitcher's duel/pitching duel   **1.** *n.* A low-scoring game in which the quality of the pitching is quite evidently better than the hitting; a game dominated by good pitching.
2. *n.* A contest in which two pitchers throw to the plate without a batter. The pitcher with the least number of walks wins. Such duels tend to be fought at the sandlot level.

pitcher's elbow   *n.* A generic name for ailments that affect the pitching arm due to stress and strain put on tendons, muscles and nerves.

pitcher's mound   *n.* Elevated area in the center of the infield from which the ball is delivered. It is located along the line between home plate and second base. Early Wynn was once asked if he ever threw the ball at a batter's head and he replied: "The pitcher's mound is my office and I don't like my office messed up with a lot of blood." (related by George Will in his syndicated column of August 11, 1986)

pitcher's paradise   *n.* A large park or stadium where it is difficult to hit home runs. The term seems to have been initially applied to Cleveland's Municipal Stadium in the 1940s.

pitcher's plate/pitcher's rubber/pitching rubber   *n.* The rectangular rubber strip or plate on the pitcher's mound on which the pitcher must rest his foot while delivering the ball to the catcher. The added significance of the pitcher's rubber is that the ball is never actually in play until the pitcher, with the ball in hand, steps on the rubber.

pitcher's strike   *n.* Pitched ball that gets a pitcher out of a jam; one that saves him. With the bases loaded and two outs, a pitch that results in a pop fly is regarded as a pitcher's strike.

pitching chart   *n.* A complete, pitch-by-pitch account of a team's pitching in a game. It is used to spot flaws in pitching strategy and technique.

Pitching machine. Cleveland manager Alvin Dark inspects a pitching machine (c. 1969). *Courtesy of the Cleveland Indians*

Tradition has it that the chart is kept by the pitcher who is scheduled to pitch the next day.

pitching coach   *n.* A coach whose job is to work with a team's pitching staff to help them improve their skills and strategy. Among other things, the pitching coach advises the manager on pitching changes during a game.

pitching duel   PITCHER'S DUEL.

pitching machine   *n.* A mechanical device used to throw balls for batting practice.
SEE   *Iron Mike.*

pitching rotation   *n.* A team's regular schedule for starting pitchers.

pitching sequence   *n.* The formulaic mix of pitches that a pitcher throws. Batters try to determine if there is a set sequence and, if there is one, what it is so they can anticipate the pitches to come.

pitching staff   *n.* The total collection of starting and relief pitchers on a club's roster.

pitch of the 1980s   *n.* Term that has been widely applied to the split-fingered fastball.

pitchout   *n.* A defensive move made with a runner on base in which the pitcher deliberately throws the ball high and wide of the strike zone so that the catcher can easily catch the ball and rifle it to a base that a runner may be attempting to steal. The ball is thrown wide to

Pittsburgh Pirates. Composite of 1909 that takes the Pirate nickname to its limit.   *Prints and Photographs Division, the Library of Congress*

keep the batter from swinging at the ball and to give the catcher the best positioning. Used when a steal, squeeze, or a hit and run play is expected, it is a play that must be coordinated carefully between the pitcher, catcher and in-fielder involved. In most cases, either the catcher or the manager calls for the play. "Two rash pitch-outs in the middle of the season deprived the White Sox of their fourth flag and a possible world's title . . ." (*Commy, The Life of Charles A. Comiskey,* by G. W. Axelson, 1919; PT)
1ST   1910. (*American* magazine, July; EJN)
ETY   As Peter Tamony points out in his notes on this term, there are two logical etymologies: (1.) a pitch "outside" the plate and (2.) a pitch calculated to catch the man "out" at second.
EXT   In football, a short lateral pass behind the line of scrimmage is called a pitch-out. This may or may not have been adopted from base-ball, but it did come many years after the term was common in baseball. In *The Polyglot's Lexicon,* Kenneth Versand lists the football meaning as a new one in 1947.

pitch to spots   *v.* To throw to the corners of the strike zone; to mix the locations of pitches purposefully in an attempt to deceive the bat-ter.

pitch with arteries   *n.* "Veteran pitcher who uses head, control and heart," according to Murray Wieman in his 1955 *Baltimore Sun* ar-ticle on baseball slang.

Pittsburgh chopper   *n.* Batted ball that be-comes a hit because it bounces over a fielder's head. Its success depends on a downward-chopping swing and a hard infield. Named by and for the 1960 world-champion Pittsburgh Pirates, who specialized in such hits.
SEE   *Baltimore chop.*

Pittsburgh Pirates   The name of the Na-tional League's Eastern Division franchise in Pittsburgh, Pennsylvania. First called the Al-leghenies in 1886 and then the Innocents, they were dubbed Pirates in 1891 as they attracted—some said "pirated"—players from other teams.

pivot   *n.* The motion of the defensive player covering second base as he touches the bag with one foot and whirls about to get the ball to first for the double play.

pivot foot   **1.** *n.* The foot that one turns on.
2. *n.* The foot used by the pitcher to push off the rubber as he releases the ball. The pivot foot must remain in contact with the rubber

Plate blocker. A rather effective demonstration.   *Courtesy of the Amateur Softball Association of America*

until the ball is released. The pitcher supports himself with the pivot foot as he strides forward with the opposite foot. A pitcher's pivot foot is always on the same side of the body as the arm he pitches with (a right-handed pitcher's pivot foot is always the right one).

pivot man/pivotman   *n.* The relay player at second base during a double play. Second baseman Joe Gordon once put this term in perspective: "Without a good pivotman a double play cannot be made. Without double plays a club will win few close games." (*San Francisco News,* June 29, 1949; PT)

Jackie Robinson wrote in the 1954 *Mutual Baseball Almanac* on the role of the pivot man: "If a second baseman doesn't pivot right, he won't pivot often. He'll be belted, spiked and stepped on, and he won't make double plays. On the double play that starts at shortstop, the second baseman can play two roles. He can be the pivot man. He can be the sitting duck. Myself, I preferred being a pivot man."

place hitter   *n.* Batter with the proven ability to hit the ball to a desired location on the field; one who can place the ball in a predetermined area.

1ST   1928. "The place hitter is the chap who can take a ball which ordinarily he would hit to right, and hit it to left, or vice versa." (G. H. Ruth: *Babe Ruth's Own Book of Baseball;* DS)

plank   *v.* To hit the ball hard, as if whacking it with a plank.

plant one   *v.* To bat the ball.
1ST   1908. (*Brooklyn Daily Eagle,* May 22; EJN)

plaster   *v.* To defeat badly.

plate   **1.** *n.* Short for the home plate; that which must be guarded by the catcher.
2. *adj.* Relating to home plate.
1ST   1869. (*DeWitt's Official Base Ball Guide;* EJN)

plate appearance   *n.* Any appearance at the plate during the course of an official game, including walks and sacrifices.

plate blocker   **1.** *n.* Term for a catcher who tenaciously holds his position in front of home plate during close plays with a baserunner who is trying to score.
2. *n.* Term for a catcher with the ability to prevent wild pitches from getting past; one who protects his pitcher in this manner.

Plate umpire. On top of a close play in softball. *Courtesy of the Amateur Softball Association of America*

plate coverage *n.* The ability of a batter to stay close enough to the plate to deal with all pitches thrown in the strike zone.

"plate jumping" The mock complaint of a wild pitcher that the plate (i.e., the strike zone) will not stand still; that it is jumping around.

plate record *n.* BATTING AVERAGE.

plate shy *adj.* Term for a batter afraid to stand close to the plate.

plate umpire *n.* The umpire stationed behind the catcher at home plate.

platoon *v.* To alternate players at a position or positions to take advantage of each one's strengths. "The Mets even have a bench this year, at last permitting Manager Hodges to do some useful platooning." (Roger Angell in *The Summer Game;* CDP)

platoon player *n.* Player who is alternated with another at one defensive position. Usually platoon players are not among the stars or outstanding players on a team and would like to work themselves out of that role. "Van Slyke making effort to shed platoon player label"— headline for article on Andy Van Slyke in the *St. Petersburg Times,* March 29, 1987.

platoon system *n.* Management style in which players are moved in and out of the lineup depending on the circumstances. "Where Casey relied heavily on the platoon system, Ralph went for the set lineup." (Mickey Mantle in *The Mick;* CDP)

platter *n.* Home plate. The term is a play on the word and image of plate as tableware, the same play that is at work in the term dish and, without pushing too far, in the serving of a pitch.

play **1.** *v.* To participate in a game.
2. *v.* To assume the duties of a particular position; to play third base.
3. *v.* To catch or position oneself for catching a ball; he played it off the wall.
4. *v.* To perform, as in play to the grandstand.
5. *n.* Any action that takes place between pitches, including putouts, errors, stolen bases etc.
6. *n.* Put out, as in the play is at second base.
1ST 1858. (*Brooklyn Daily Times,* June 18; EJN)

playable *adj.* Term for any ball that is not dead; a live ball.

play at the plate *n.* Any play involving the catcher—or an infielder covering home plate for the catcher—and a base runner attempting to score.
USE Because such plays tend to be exciting ones at key moments of the game, the phrase carries with it an extra amount of emotion.

"Play Ball!" **1.** *v.* Command issued by the plate umpire to begin or resume play. Sometimes abbreviated to a simple command of "Play!"
1ST 1901. (*Frank Merriwell's Marvel;* EJN)
2. Words that have become emblematic for any baseball game's beginning, from Opening Day to the World Series Opener.
EXT To cooperate or participate, as in: "If the union will play ball with us on this one, I think we can make the deadline."
One of the more interesting uses of these

words took place in the context of the 1987 Washington Summit meeting between Mikhail H. Gorbachev and Ronald Reagan. According to a *New York Times* report of December 15, 1987, Joe Dimaggio, who had been a guest at the dinner honoring the Gorbachevs, asked President Reagan if he could get the Soviet leader to autograph a baseball for him. Reagan got the autograph personally and according to the *Times,* used the occasion "to tell his guest that the two leaders should 'play ball' with each other."

play-by-play *n.* A running description of a game with all the details. The term is usually applied to the commentary on a game on radio and television, although technically it only applies to printed accounts, now rare, in which each play of the game is reported. *Sports Illustrated* said of longtime broadcaster Red Barber on one occasion, "If Barber didn't invent play-by-play, he came close."
1ST 1912. (*New York Tribune,* October 15; EJN)
EXT Any detailed verbal account, as in: "I had to sit there and listen to his play-by-play of the whole argument."

play by the book *v.* To play in accord with the conventional wisdom of the game.
1ST 1911. (*Book of Baseball;* EJN)

play deep and cut across Way of playing the outfield when the defense anticipates balls being hit deep. "Advice to outfielders from a pitcher who doesn't feel well and expects to be shelled off the mound during the game," according to Jim Brosnan in *The Long Season.*

player development *n.* Modern term for giving a player experience and instruction in the Minor Leagues. "IBM calls it R&D [research and development]. The Dodgers call it 'player development.' " (*Forbes,* April 12, 1982)

player limit *n.* The maximum number of players a team may have on its roster at a given point in the season. In the Major Leagues the number during most of the season is officially 25, but, as of this writing is limited to 24 by agreement among owners. A team's roster may expand to 40 after September 1st so that promising minor leaguers can come up to the parent team for a tryout.

player-manager/playing manager *n.* A manager who is also an active player on the team. Like Pete Rose, who assumed this role for the Cincinnati Reds in 1986, those who fill this position tend to be senior players who concentrate more on managing than playing as they phase themselves out of the regular lineup. Player-managers are no longer as prevalent as they once were in pre-World War II baseball. Other notable player-managers were John McGraw, Connie Mack, Mickey Cochrane, Lou Boudreau, Bucky Harris, and Frank Robinson.

player rep/player representative   *n.* The member of each major league team who has been elected by his teammates as their delegate with the Player's Association.

player running bases   *n./arch.* Base runner. Henry Chadwick defined this term in his 19th-Century *The American Game of Baseball:* "The moment the striker has hit a fair ball he ceases to be 'the striker' and becomes 'a player running the bases.' "

Players' Association   Trade union representing baseball players.

Players' League   Major league created by members of the Brotherhood of Professional Ball Players. It had but one season: 1890. It was created by players frustrated by salary ceilings, fines, the reserve clause and other realities of the existing Major Leagues. Lack of money and organization put the league out of business before Opening Day 1891.

player's manager   *n.* A team manager who commands special respect from players.

player's player   *n.* Player with widespread respect and admiration from other players.

player to be named later   *n.* Phrase commonly used in trades to indicate that the trade will not be completed until one team delivers one more mutually-acceptable player. "Toliver was the 'player to be named later' in a trade last August that also brought shortstop Tom Foley." (*St. Petersburg Times*, April 1, 1986)

playground average/playground numbers   *n.* A high batting average, such as one that could be achieved in a playground league where a strong hitter can overwhelm young pitchers.

playoff/play-off   **1.** *n.* Since 1969, the series of games played between the leading teams of the Eastern and Western Divisions of the American and National Leagues to determine the winners of the pennants, and the partici-

pants in the World Series. The official names for these annual series are the American and National League Championship Series, but they are much more commonly referred to as the playoffs.
2. *n.* A game or series of games played to break a tie in the standings at the end of the regular season. Between 1900 and 1945, there were no playoffs; but there have been several since then. The most famous such contest was the one played between the New York Giants and the Brooklyn Dodgers in 1951. The winner of two out of three playoff games would win the pennant. The Giants won the first, the Dodgers the second and the Giants took the third on what has been widely termed "the most dramatic home run in the history of the game," Bobby Thomson's 9th-inning three-run homer off Ralph Branca.
3. *adj.* Of or pertaining to a playoff game or series; as in, "playoff hopes."
4. *n./obs.* The replaying of a game that originally resulted in a tie.
1ST   1880. (*Chicago Inter-Ocean*, June 7; EJN)

play over one's head   *v.* To perform better than usual or better than expected.

play straight away   *v.* To play in the middle of one's position; not to shade to either side.

play to the grandstand   *v.* To show off; perform.
1ST   1888. "Playing to the Grand-Stand. To accomplish this it is only necessary to smile, strike an attitude, and strike out." (Thomas W. Lawson's *The Krank: His Language and What It Means;* DS)
ETY   In *Heavens to Betsy!*, Charles Earle Funk asserts that the expression is related to the earlier "play to the gallery." He explained, "Originally, it had reference to those actors, expecially in an English theater, who, going over the heads of the near-by, and frequently inattentive, occupants of orchestra seats or stalls, deliberately overacted their roles in seeking to gain the approval of the larger populace in the gallery."
SEE   *grandstand play.*

plenty of wood   *adj.* Said of a team that has a lot of power hitters. The use of wood in this phrase is the equivalent of equating leather with good fielding (as in saying, an infield is full of leather).
1ST   1910. (*American* magazine, July; EJN)

plow-jockey *n./arch.* Country boy, from a time when many players had come into baseball directly from the farm.

plug 1. *v./arch.* To bat a ball hard.
1ST 1900. ("Franks plugged him," *San Francisco Examiner*, August 19; PT)
2. *v./obs.* In some early forms of the game, to put a runner out by hitting him with the ball. Plugging was not allowed by the rules drafted by Alexander Cartwright and the other members of the Knickerbocker Club in 1854.

plugged bat *n.* Bat that has been doctored.

plugger 1. *n.* Fan who roots or "plugs" for his or her team.
2. *n./arch.* A dumb play.

plunk/plunket *n./arch.* BASE HIT.
ETY Gerald Cohen writes, "Both plunk and its diminutive form plunket mean 'base hit' and are of onomatopoetic origin; the ball lands plunk on the ground." Cohen found a number of examples from 1889 in the *New York World*, including this one from October 19: "In a puree of silence that was painful, the Brooklyns came in from the field on the players' bench with nine subdued 'plunks.' "

plunker *n.* See Texas leaguer.
USE An interesting note on this term appears in Herbert Simons' 1943 article, "Do You Speak the Language?": "Curiously, there aren't any Texas Leaguers ever hit in the Texas League. There, low flies that drop safely in the short outfield, too far for the infielders to reach and yet too near for the outfielders to get to, are known as 'plunkers.' "
1ST 1937. (New York *Daily News*, September 5; EJN)

pneumonia ball *n.* Very fast ball, which supposedly passes the batter with such speed that he catches cold from the draught. "Walter Johnson's 'high swift' was admiringly dubbed the pneumonia ball by sluggers who caught cold from the steady draught across their throats and chests." (William G. Brandt, *Baseball* magazine, October 1932)

PO Standard abbreviation for put out.

pochismo *n.* Term for bastardized Spanish and English, which is neither Spanish nor English. The Mexican Academy began crusading against it in 1945, but, according to an article in the October 1945 *American Speech*, could not find suitable equivalents for *jonrun, estraic, jit* and *beisbol* (i.e., homerun, strike, hit and baseball).

pocket *n.* The part of the glove or mitt between the thumb and index finger into which the baseball fits. Although all gloves come with a pocket, a traditional part of the glove breaking-in process has been to reshape and deepen the pocket.

points *n.* Elements of high skill and sophistication. Term defined by Henry Chadwick as a reference to the "special points of play in the game which occur most generally in first class matches"—in other words, those "points" alluded to when someone talks of the "finer points of the game."

poisoned ball *n./arch.* An early 19th century (and, perhaps, earlier) forerunner of baseball, played on a diamond-shaped field. The name shows up occasionally in print, for example in a book published in Paris in 1810, cited in Preston D. Orem's *Baseball (1845–1881) From the Newspaper Accounts.*

poisoned bat *n./arch.* The bat held by a hard hitter.

poison pen *n.* A player's clubhouse term for member of the press, according to Jim Nash of the Atlanta Braves, quoted in the *Sporting News*, April 1, 1972. Sometimes OLD POISON PEN.

poke *v.* To bat the ball; to get a hit.
1ST 1880. (*Chicago Inter Ocean*, May 15; EJN)

poke hitter *n.* Batter whose specialty is placing or pushing balls through infield holes.
"A ball player like Mikes had to be able to run, for he was a poke hitter, a man who pushed singles and doubles where he could get them." (William Brashler, from *The Bingo Long Traveling All Stars and Motor Kings;* CDP)

Polaroid *n.* Player caught looking at a third strike, in the candid vernacular of Reggie Jackson who is also responsible for the term dues collector.

pole 1. *n.* The bat.
2. *v.* To hit with power.
1ST 1905 "At a tight spot in the game Hoffman poled out a vicious liner." (Charles Dryden, *The Athletics of 1905;* DS)

pole the ball *v.* To hit with power.

Polo Grounds. The ballpark in 1887. *Prints and Photographs Division, the Library of Congress*

police the parade grounds *v./arch.* To maintain the park; to groundskeep. See furlough.

polished deception *n.* Term applied to a pitcher who uses style and grace to mask his mechanical weaknesses.

polish off/polish one off *v.* To defeat an opposing team or put out an opposing batter. **1ST** 1871. (*New York Herald,* July 29; EJN)

Polo Grounds Name for four different baseball stadia in New York. The first two were adjoining parks used for the Metropolitans and the Giants in the 1880s. The third and fourth were primarily used by the New York Giants. The final stadium was built when its namesake burned down in 1911; it was used not only by the Giants (1911–1957), but also by the Yankees (1913–1922) and the fledgling New York Mets (1962–1963). As Philip J. Lowrey points out in *Green Cathedrals,* "Demolition started on April 10, 1964, with the wrecking ball that demolished Ebbets Field."

pool cue shot *n.* Batted ball that comes off the end of the bat like a pool or billiard ball being hit by a cue.

pool table *n.* A smooth infield. **1ST** 1937. (New York *Daily News,* January 21; EJN)

pooper *n.* See Texas leaguer.

pop *n.* The extra speed, hop and sound of the most effective fastball; a most desirable characteristic.
"But Clyde admits his fastball doesn't 'pop' like it once did." (*San Francisco Chronicle*, March 14, 1977; PT)
2. *n.* See pop-up.

pop/pop fly/pop-up *n.* A high, batted ball; a high-arching fly ball. A pop fly is usually—or should be—caught by a fielder. "Professional ball players hate to be embarrassed by a simple pop-fly, but in the crazy pattern of Candlestick's cross currents they can't do anything else but suffer and curse under their breath." (*San Francisco Examiner*, April 14, 1966; PT)
1ST 1895. "We've got a strong infield—one that can handle the pops and grounders they are sure to get when Kirk is in the box." (Herbert Bellwood, *The Rivals of Riverwood;* DS)

popcorn *n.* An easily caught fly ball.

pop foul *n.* A short fly ball in foul territory.

pop-off *n.* A player with a mean spirit and a short temper.
1ST 1939. "Pop-off or Rebel: An umpire baiter." (G. S. Cochrane, *Baseball, the Fan's Game;* DS)

pop out *v.* To be retired on a short fly ball.

popper *n.* Pop fly.

popping the ball *v.* Pitching so hard that the ball can be heard popping in the catcher's mitt. "It's good to hear that mitt popping"— heading for the spring training cover story in *USA Today*, February 24, 1987.

poppycock season *n./arch.* The spring training season.

pop-up/pop one up *v.* To bat the ball high into the air over the infield.
1ST 1883. "Ferguson then popped up the ball for a base, sending in the third run of the inning." (*The Sporting Life*, April 15, 1883)

pop-up slide *n.* A maneuver in which a base runner slides into a base and then, in the same fluid movement, pushes himself back up onto his feet. The runner attempts it when he feels that he may have the opportunity to take another base on the play.

porch *n.* Outfield bleacher or grandstand. "If the porch is close to home plate like left field at Fenway Park or right field in Detroit's Tiger Stadium," Tim Horgan wrote in a 1964 article on baseballese, "it's a 'short porch' and hitters 'love' it."

Porkopolis Nickname for Cincinnati that commonly showed up in accounts of teams from that city. So-called since about 1840 because of the meat packing industry there. Edward J. Nichols notes that the name was also used for St. Louis for the same reason.

portsider/port side thrower/port sider/port side slinger etc. *n.* LEFT-HANDER, usually a pitcher. The variations seem limitless and include such forced creations as portpaw, a confusing synonym for southpaw.
ETY Port is left in nautical jargon.

position **1.** *n.* A player's assigned place on a team, both in the field and in the batting order.
1ST 1858. (*Brooklyn Daily Times*, June 18; EJN)
2. *v.* To station oneself at a particular spot defensively, as in, "The outfielders are positioned near the wall with Winfield coming to bat."

positive subtraction See Rickeyism.

postponement *n.* A game that has been delayed and will be resumed on the same day or on a future day. Games are postponed because of bad weather or technical problems. With the exception of games played late in the season, after first place in the standings has been determined, major league games are never cancelled.

postseason *n.* The period after the end of the regular season.

potato *n.* A baseball.

potential tying run *n.* A hitter or runner who, if he succeeds in crossing the plate, will tie the game.

potential winning run *n.* A batter or runner who, if he succeeds in scoring, will win the game.

pot-fly *n.* Obsolete, for pop fly.
1ST 1888. "It looked like an easy pot-fly as it graciously sailed up to me." (Thomas W. Lawson, *The Krank;* DS)

pound a pitcher *v.* To get many hits off a single pitcher.
1ST 1890. (*New York Press*, July 6; EJN)

pound the air *v.* To swing at and miss a pitched ball.
1ST 1908. (*Baseball* magazine, October; EJN)

powder/powder the ball **1.** *v.* To hit the ball with great strength.
2. *n.* Speed with which a pitcher delivers the ball from the mound. "Stuff is still good baseballese for what the pitcher serves, but they like to refer to an excessive amount of speed as 'powder.' Maybe this is a derivative of the term 'fireball.' " (William G. Brandt, from his article on baseballese, *Baseball* magazine, October 1932)

powder puff ball *n.* An illegal pitch in which the ball is covered with resin powder extracted from the rosin bag by the pitcher. It is a doctored ball that confuses the batter because it arrives at the plate trailing a cloud of white dust. As with other similar innovations, Gaylord Perry has been widely credited with the creation of this pitch.

power **1.** *n.* The ability to hit the long ball.
2. *adj.* Describing strength; as in power-hitting or power-pitching.

power alleys *n.* The corridors between the outfielders in left-center and right-center fields. Since this is where the most powerful hitters naturally tend to drive the ball, home run balls more often travel through these paths than to straightaway right, center or left field. In *Ball Four*, Jim Bouton defined power alley as the place "where the sluggers put away knuckleballs that don't knuckle." (CDP)

power game *n.* Play characterized by sluggers who swing for home runs. "Ruth's natural power was responsible for making baseball what it has been ever since—a power game." (Red Barber, The *Christian Science Monitor*, May 23, 1984)

power hitter *n.* Player known for his home run hitting ability. Jimmy Cannon's definition: "A muscular player who strikes out a lot."

powerhouse **1.** *n.* A distance hitter.
2. *n.* A team with a number of home run hitters.
1ST 1937. (World Series Broadcast, Red Barber, October 10; EJN)

power the ball *v.* To hit, pitch or throw the ball with force.

pow wow *n.* A meeting on the playing field, usually involving several players and a coach or manager who convene on the pitcher's mound or at the scene of a disputed play to discuss strategy.

prayer ball *n.* Pitch with nothing on it; one which the pitcher "prays" will not be hit.
There are many variations on this idea, including glove and a prayer. One of the odder examples appears in a 1912 article on player slang, which contains the line, "Christian Science stuff is the only thing you ever get on the ball." (*Sporting Life*, May 18, 1912)

pre-rookie card *n.* Baseball card issued of a player while he is still in the minors before his rookie card is issued.

pre-shower epigram *n.* Roger Angell's tongue in cheek term for the words exchanged on the mound when a manager relieves a pitcher. He introduced it in a 1987 *New Yorker* article on the proliferation of baseball books. He said there were so many being published that he soon expected to see an anthology of pre-shower epigrams.

press box *n.* An area within the stadium reserved for sportswriters and broadcasters. They have evolved from boxed-off wooden areas to the plush, electronics-heavy quarters that in most major league stadiums are located on the mezzanine level behind home plate.
1ST 1892. (*New York Press*, August 13; EJN)

press pin *n.* Colorful identifying pins given to members of the working press during the World Series and other major baseball events. Dating back to the 1911 World Series, they are quite attractive and eagerly sought as collector's items.

pretty **1.** *adj.* Term for an easily injured player.
2. *n.* TISSUE PAPER TOM.

pretzel/pretzel bender *n.* CURVEBALL.
1ST 1908. (*New York Evening Journal*, April 18; EJN)
ETY In the *Language of Sport*, Tim Considine gives this term two derivations: "one from the curved shape of a pretzel, and the other from the fact that a curveball can 'tie a batter up in a knot' like a pretzel."

prima donna *n.* Temperamental player.

principal owner *n.* Title used by George A. Steinbrenner to describe his role with the New York Yankees. "What was left to talk about except the ways in which the principal owner

Press box. At the 1911 World Series in Philadelphia. A letter from Fred Lieb on file in Cooperstown suggests that this photo was taken during a rain delay and that the man in the light-colored coat in the second row is Damon Runyon. *National Baseball Library, Cooperstown, N.Y.*

had degraded the great American game?" (Lewis H. Lapham in *The Washington Post,* April 21, 1984)

pro **1.** *n.* Short for professional. A professional who plays and behaves accordingly. When applied to a player it carries the clear connotation of a man who is experienced and likely to pull through in a pinch.
2. *adj.* Professional as opposed to amateur, as in pro ball.

probable pitcher *n.* Term for the pitcher who is expected to start the next game.

Prohibition Stadium Nickname for Toronto's Exhibition Stadium from 1977 until 1982, the period when beer was banned there.

promoter *n.* Owner or club official who stages events, stunts, and other sideshow attractions and/or gives away free souvenirs to draw crowds. The most famous and flamboyant of the game's promoters was Bill Veeck who at different points in his career owned the St. Louis Browns, Cleveland Indians and Chicago White Sox. Veeck's most famous promotional stunt was using 3-foot 7-inch midget Eddie Gaedel to pinch hit in a 1951 Browns game. Veeck also pioneered promotional notions ranging from exploding scoreboards to free baby sitting.

promotion *n.* An event used to attract people to the ballpark; e.g., Bat Day, Old-Timers' Day, Seat Cushion Night, Fan Appreciation Day, Knothole Day, Senior Citizens' Day, Cap Day, Hot Pants Day, Poster Day, T-Shirt Night, and Nun's Day (which Steve Garvey recalled in his biography as a day on which nuns got in for a dollar to watch the Dodgers play the Cardinals).

Promotion. Bowling Night in Cleveland during the 1963 season. *Courtesy of the Cleveland Indians*

promotions schedule *n.* Schedule distributed by teams that lists the special events and giveaways offered during the season. For instance, the "Orioles 1987 Promotion Schedule" listed no less than 24 special days and nights, including three on which bags were to be given out (Toyota Travel Bag Day, Chase Bank of Maryland Sports Bag Night and Chevron School Tote Bag Day).

prospect *n.* Farmhand or rookie with apparent talent.

The term has been used so widely, that it is regarded with some skepticism. "Prospects," Charlie Finley once said, "are a dime a dozen."

protector *n.* Chest protector for short.
1ST 1908. (*Baseball* magazine, November; EJN)

protect the plate **1.** *v.* To swing at a pitched ball with the intent to foul it off. This usually occurs when, with two strikes in the count, a batter will foul off a pitch that appears headed

for the strike zone but not good enough to hit. Jimmy Cannon once insisted that such protecting was actually, "A series of foul tips by a completely fooled batter who intends to hit every one out of the park."
2. *v.* For catchers, to stand fast and effectively block home plate in anticipation of a close play with a runner trying to score.

protect the runner *v.* To swing at any pitch that is thrown in order to help a runner who is stealing a base or beginning a hit and run or run and hit play. At a minimum the batter is trying to distract the catcher and hamper him from putting the runner out.

protest *n.* A complaint registered against an umpire's call. They fall into two categories: unofficial and official. The rules prohibit unofficial protests, but all major league umpires allow a limited amount of protesting and arguing by players, managers and coaches. Offi-

Promotion. Rocket Day in Cleveland during the 1966 season.   *Courtesy of the Cleveland Indians*

cial protests, on the other hand, can only be filed with the league office on the grounds that the umpire has misinterpreted or misapplied a rule (rather than on a disagreement over an umpire's call on a pitch or base runner). If this protest is upheld, the call is declared invalid and the game may have to be replayed from the point at which the call was made.

An example from recent baseball history occurred as the result of game between the Cardinals and Pirates on June 16, 1986. The game was ended after rain delays of 17 and 22 minutes and the Cardinals who were winning 4–0 were declared the winners. The Pirates appealed on the basis that the game was called too quickly, citing rule 3.10C, which says that the umpire-in-chief must wait at least 75 minutes before calling a game. National League President Chubb Feeney upheld the protest, ruling that the game had to be completed at a later date.

prune   *v.* To trim a team's roster in order to meet the season limit.

prune picker   *n.* Common nickname for a player from California ca. 1950.

psych/psyche/psych out/psyche out   *v.* To gain a real or imagined psychological edge over another player or team, as in the pitcher has his man psyched. This term, like psych up, showed up in many sports at about the same time, ca. 1920.

psycho   *n.* An easily rattled or disturbed player.

psych up/psyche up   *v.* To ready oneself or become readied for a contest.

PTBNL/PTNL   Standard abbreviations for "player to be named later."

public enemy number one   *n.* The CURVEBALL.

pud   *n.* Mitt.
ETY   As pad is also used as slang for a mitt, it is likely that pud is a variation on that term.

puff ball   See Powder Puff Ball.

puff hitter *n.* Weak batter; one without power.
1ST 1909. (Zane Grey's *The Shortstop;* EJN)

Pugball *n.* A form of softball played on a small diamond. Those who played the game were called puggers.

pull *v.* When batting, to hit the ball early in the swing for greater power. A right-handed batter will pull the ball to the left. Pulling is the opposite of hitting to the opposite field.

pull a bone/pull a rock *v.* To err; to pull a boner.
SEE *bone/bone play.*

pull a brenegan *v.* To get hit hard in the hand by the ball.
ETY From Selmar G. Brenegan who played in his one and only game for Pittsburgh in 1914 with no official at bats and a place in the record books as one of the few players with a lifetime .000 batting average in the majors. Brenegan, a catcher, was hit in the hand with the ball and allowed a runner to move from second to third. For reasons unclear, this man whose time in the majors was counted in minutes was remembered in this phrase for years to come.

pull a Casey *v.* CASEY.

pull a pitch *v.* For a catcher to move his mitt quickly after catching the ball to give the illusion that a ball was actually returned in the strike zone. In *The Umpire Strikes Back,* Ron Luciano points out, "This is something umpires really dislike."

pull a pitcher *v.* To remove a pitcher from the game.
1ST 1891. (*Chicago Herald,* May 10; EJN)

pull a rock *v.* To commit a boner.
1ST 1936. (*New York Herald Tribune,* May 21; EJN)

pulled hamstring *n.* A common baseball injury in which the tendons attached to the hollow of the knee are damaged and the back of the thigh is affected.

puller *n.* Player who pulls away from the plate.

pull for *v.* To root for.
1ST 1905. (*Sporting Life,* October 7; EJN)

pull-hitter/pull hitter *n.* A batter who habitually hits a bit early or 'ahead' of the ball. A right-handed batter naturally pulls to the left and a left-handed batter naturally pulls to the right. Thus a pull-hitter mainly hits to the same side of the field on which he stands.

pull off/pull off the bag *v.* To legally lure a runner off the base he occupies.

pull out of the fire *v.* To win a game that appears to be lost.

pull the string *v.* To pitch a slow ball with the same motion as a fastball; to change up. It describes what appears to be a ball attached to and held back by a string.
1ST 1937. (*The Sporting News Record Book;* EJN)
ETY Although this would seem to derive from the idea of a string used to restrain or hold back the ball, in *The Folger Dictionary of Baseball,* Burt Dunne says this is derived from a trick featuring "a trapped badger" in a box overhead. The rookie releases the "badger" by pulling the string, and, says Dunne, "down come refuse—and worse."

pull the switch *v.* To substitute a batter or pitcher for one that bats or pitches from the other side, such as switching a right-handed pitcher for a left-hander.

pummel *v.* To hit a ball hard.
1ST 1922. (*New York Times,* June 5; EJN)

pump **1.** *n.* The element of a pitcher's windup in which he swings his arms back and forward over his head.
2. *v.* For a pitcher to swing his arms back and forward at the beginning of the windup.

Pumpkin Ball *n.* One of a host of names for the game of softball before it became known as softball.

pump out hits *v.* To get many hits.

pump pellet *n./arch.* Spitball.
1ST 1907. (*New York Evening Journal,* June 7; EJN)

pump system *n.* A method of signaling in which the catcher tells the pitcher what he wants with the number of times he moves his fingers—pumps them—rather than with the signal itself.

punch **1.** *n.* Batting power. A team that produces a lot of hits is said to have punch in its lineup.
1ST 1912. (*New York Tribune,* September 6; EJN)
2. *n.* Pitching power.

Punch-and-Judy *adj.* Said of a hitter who tends to hit well-placed but weakly-hit balls for singles; one who chokes up and punches at the ball rather than take full swings.
ETY An embellishment of punch.
1ST 1965. "McCovey didn't hit any cheap one. When he belts a home run, he does it with such authority it seems like an act of God. You can't cry about it. He's not a Punch and Judy belter." (Walter Alston on Willie McCovey, *San Francisco Examiner*, May 3, 1965; PT)

punch drunk *adj./arch.* Said of a player who has become overconfident or arrogant as the result of a string of hits.
ETY A direct borrowing from prizefighting for a boxer who appears stunned or drunk from too many punches; slap happy.

punch hitter *n.* PUNCH-AND-JUDY.

punchout **1.** *n.* STRIKEOUT.
2. *v.* To strike out a batter.

punish the pitcher *v.* To hit hard against a pitcher.
1ST 1867. (*New York Sunday Mercury*, September 7; EJN)

punk/punk hit *n.* Ball that may have seemed well hit, but that quickly drops to the turf.

punk ball *n.* A ball that defies being hit solidly; one that is soft and flabby. "Fellows with unusually strong grips have been able to loosen the cover . . . and thus toss a 'punk' ball." (article on illegal deliveries, *San Francisco News*, July 7, 1938; PT)

punk hitter *n.* Batter who gets on base by beating out poorly hit balls.

punkin **1.** *n.* A ball, especially one that has seen a lot of use.
ETY From the word pumpkin and an apparent reference to a pumpkin's less than perfect roundness.
2. A pitched ball that is easy to hit.

purchase *n.* A transaction in which a professional player is bought for cash rather than being obtained in a trade.

purloin a hassock *v.* To steal a base.

purpose pitch *n.* A pitched ball thrown for the purpose of getting a batter to back away from the plate; usually an inside fastball that can act as a knockdown pitch.
ETY Bob Uecker says that the term was cre-ated by Branch Rickey. If so, it may have originated in the context of Rickey's observation that the purpose of a purpose pitch was to separate a batter's head from his shoulders. Umpire Ron Luciano wrote in his biography, *The Umpire Strikes Back*, that the purpose of the purpose pitch was to remind the batter that the pitched ball is a weapon.

push **1.** *v.* To hit the ball to the opposite field.
2. The forward move made by the pitcher just before the ball is delivered.

push bunt *n.* A swinging bunt in which the batter tries to place, or push, the ball past the pitcher while still keeping it in the shallow portion of the infield.

put a new handle on it Time-tested advice to a player who has just broken his bat.

put away *v.* To put out.
1ST 1881. (*New York Herald*, July 15; EJN)

put fannies in the seats *v.* To be able to attract paying spectators.

put him down *v.* Move a runner from first to second base on a sacrifice, with "down" indicating an advance from one base to another.
1ST 1937. (*The Sporting News Record Book*; EJN)

put him on the train *v.* To trade a player; or term used for a player who has just been traded.

put it over *v.* Command to the pitcher to put the ball in the strike zone. This can come from an opposition batter who wants a good ball to hit or from one of the pitcher's teammates encouraging him to stop throwing bad pitches.
1ST 1901. (*Frank Merriwell's Marvels*; EJN)

put out *v.* To cause someone on the opposite team to be retired from play. A player is credited with the putout when he catches a fly or line drive or when he receives the ball from another fielder for the out at a base.
1ST 1860. (*Beadle's Dime Base Ball Player*; EJN)

putout/put-out **1.** *n.* The elimination of a batter or base runner by a defensive player. The actual putout is credited to the fielder who actually retires the runner by catching the fly, tagging the runner or touching base. Strikeouts are credited to the catcher.

1ST 1869. (*New York Herald,* July 14; EJN) **2.** *v.* To retire a batter or base runner; to create an out.

put some grass in your hat *v.* Advice to an outfielder having trouble catching the ball.

put some mustard on it *v.* To reach back for a little extra velocity on a fast ball.

put something on it *v.* To pitch a ball that will curve, break, float or otherwise behave unnaturally.

put the game in the ice box/put the game on ice *v.* To win a game definitively; to remove any chance of victory from the opposing team.

put the wood on it *v.* To hit the ball solidly. **1ST** 1909. (Zane Grey's *The Shortstop;* EJN)

putty *n.* Injury-prone player.

putty arm *n.* Bad or weak arm.

puzzler *n.* Deceptively pitched ball. **1ST** 1880. (*Chicago Inter Ocean,* June 25; EJN)

Q

"quack, quack" Time-honored call made by players to get the attention of the trainer; a puckish and obvious play on the notion that his healing skills and nostrums are based in quackery.

quail/quail shot *n.* A pop fly that quickly drops in between fielders for a hit. It falls like a dying quail, which is another term for such a hit.

quality starts *n.* Richard Justice explains the term in *The Washington Post* (March 19, 1986): "One of baseball's newest statistics is called 'quality starts' and although it is figured differently by different people, a pitcher is usually credited with one when he pitches at least six innings and allows three runs or fewer."

quantitative quantity See Rickeyism.

quarterback drill *n.* A pregame warmup exercise in which players jog along in a line, throwing and catching the ball over their shoulders. Pitcher commonly use it to sharpen their reflexes.

questionable pitch *n.* A pitched ball that is neither a clear ball or a clear strike and may be ruled as either one by the umpire.

question mark **1.** *n.* A player whose immediate future is uncertain. This can be because of injury, illness or any of a number of other problems.
2. *n.* A rookie or player from another team who is new and untested.

quick bat *adj.* An attribute of a batter who swings the bat fast.

quick hook *n.* A manager's tendency to remove a pitcher from a game at the first sign of trouble.

quick pitch/quick return/quick return pitch *n.* An illegal pitch, which a pitcher hurries off for the sole purpose of catching the batter off balance. It is thrown before the batter takes his position and becomes set in his stance. When detected by the umpire, it is treated as a balk: All base runners are granted a base or, if nobody is on base, the batter is awarded a ball.

R

rabbit *n.* Player with great speed.

rabbit ball **1.** *n.* Ball that is livelier than an ordinary ball; one that jumps like a rabbit and can be hit for distance.

Although the term can be used for a single ball or a small number of them, it is usually applied to the ball in use throughout a particular season. "Has the 1948 horsehide got a rabbit in it?"—question by Jack McDonald, *San Francisco Call-Bulletin,* April 28. (PT)

There have been a number of rabbit balls described through the years. These range from the ball of 1910, which was the first to have a cork center, to the 1987 ball, which was widely alleged to be "juiced up." A few of the other alleged rabbit ball years include 1925, 1950, 1956, 1961, 1969 and 1977.

Over the years players and managers have found many ways of expressing their belief that a ball is a rabbit ball. For instance, in 1969 the International League used a ball from the McGregor-Brunswick Corp. known as the 97. An unnamed player was quoted in the *Sporting News,* "The 97 is the only ball that eats lettuce for breakfast." (May 17, 1969)

2. *n.* Specifically, the modern ball that was introduced in 1920 by the American League and adopted in 1921 by the National. It was brought in to capitalize on the box office potential of the home run. It was presumed that big sluggers like Babe Ruth would draw larger crowds if a livelier ball produced more home runs. Originally, it was said that there was a "rabbit in the ball."

rabbit ears *n.* Originally, an attribute of a player who hears everything; player easily distracted by noise. By evolution and extension, an overly sensitive player or umpire who is especially ready to hear and respond to comments and taunts; one who is easily ridden.

Jim Brosnan gave this definition of the term in the glossary to *The Long Season:* "A physical phenomena that enables a ballplayer or umpire standing in a ball park before a crowd of 50,000 noisy fans to hear his name whispered in the opponent's dugout twenty-five yards away."

rabbitize *v.* To enliven a ball. "If Coast League baseballs aren't rabbitized, as Red Kennealy, the Wilsons man, claims they are not, let us at least say they have been traveling with rare vivacity." (Jack McDonald, *San Francisco Call-Bulletin,* June 6, 1956; PT)

race *n.* The season; the race for the pennant. **1ST** 1880. (*Brooklyn Daily Eagle,* July 26; EJN)

race to the bag *v.* A contest in which a fielder with the ball is trying to beat the runner to a base for the force out.

radio ball *n.* Fastball that can be heard but not seen. **ETY** Attributed to Roy Sievers who in 1955 or 1956 deemed Herb Score's quick strikes to be radio balls. Also attributed to Catfish Metkovitz, who in the early 1950 deemed Max Surkont's fastballs to be radio balls.

raftman *n.* A slow outfielder who appears to be poling a raft rather than running.

The images used to describe slowness on the diamond are often nautical. An example from a 1912 collection of baseball slang: "He couldn't beat a towboat that was tied to the bank." (*Sporting Life,* May 18, 1912)

rag **1.** *v.* To ride or heckle. An alternative term for *bench jockeying.* "Much laughter, too, and not a little ragging of the Indians." (*Catcher Craig* by Christy Mathewson; 1915)

Some recent examples of ragging from an industrial league game in Montgomery County, Maryland:

- To a short player: "Number 20—off your knees."
- To a slow player: "Hey 12, get the piano off your back."

2. *n.* A fielder's glove; his leather.
3. *n./arch.* The pennant.

rag arm. *n.* Disparaging term for a pitcher whose pitches lack speed and deception; one who pitches with nothing on the ball.

ragged fielding *n.* Loose and unreliable defensive play. **1ST** 1885. (*Chicago Inter Ocean,* April 22; EJN)

rag man *n.* Term for a pitcher whose pitching arm sleeve is frayed or loose. This is illegal if detected because it distracts the batter's vision.

rainbow/rainbow curve *n.* A wide, sweeping curveball with a rainbow-like arc; a roundhouse curve. "Scharaldi breaks off a rainbow"—Vin Scully, NBC-TV Game of the Week, Red Sox vs. Royals, May 9, 1987.
1st 1891. (*Chicago Herald,* May 25; EJN)

rain-bringer *n.* High fly.
1ST 1932. (*Baseball* magazine, October; EJN)

rain check/rain-check *n.* The detachable portion of a ticket, which can be used to gain admission to a future game if the game in question is rained out before it becomes a regulation game (4½ or 5 innings, depending on the lead). The custom of giving the ticketholder a rain check became institutionalized in 1890 in the constitution of the National League.

It has long been claimed and often published that the first detachable rain check was issued in 1888 in New Orleans by team owner Abner Powell of the minor league Pelicans.

The 1957 newsstand publication, *Joe Reichler's Book of Baseball Records,* quotes Powell on the discovery. He pointed out that a lot of people were getting into Sportsman's Park, where the Pelicans played, for nothing. In that era of reusable tickets, when there was rain the spectators lined up to pick up a ticket for the next day—reclaiming those that had already been turned in. "Usually," said Powell, "there were more fans in line than there were tickets in the box. All those free riders and fence jumpers joined the line, too. The situation became so acute that, despite weekday crowds of 5,000 and Sunday throngs of 10,000, we were losing money." Powell thought about this for several days in 1889 (according to this account, not 1887 or 1888, as is stated elsewhere) and came up with the raincheck idea.

This claim was heavily publicized in 1953 when Powell died at age 92 in New Orleans and many newspapers carried his obituary. (The Associated Press story said the first Powell rain check was issued in 1887, a year earlier than most other accounts and two years earlier than Joe Reichler's claim.)

The discrepancy may not be all that important because linguistic research conducted by David Shulman points conclusively to earlier use, to wit:

1ST 1884. "Rain checks given out on the St. Louis grounds are good for any succeeding championship game." (*Spalding's Scrapbooks,* vol. IV, July 5, 1884; DS)
EXT 1. *n.* A postponed or deferred acceptance. To ask for a rain check is to decline while asking to be reinvited later. "Sorry we can't make dinner, but we'd love to take a rain check on the invitation."
2. *n.* A coupon guaranteeing a customer the sale price for a future purchase of a sale item that is out of stock.
3. *n.* In criminal slang, a parole.

rain dance *n.* Delaying tactics used when it starts to rain. It is used both by managers losing a game that is not yet official (and will have to be replayed if it is rained out) and by managers winning a game when the required number of innings have been played (and the team will win if the game is called for rain). "You don't think LaSorda's about to go into his rain dance, do you?"—Harry Caray on a WGN telecast of a Dodgers-Cubs game, May 6, 1986, with the Dodgers in the lead.

rain date *n.* The new date for a game that was rained out.

rain delay *n.* The official interruption of a game on account of rain. During such a period play is suspended in the hope that the rain will subside and the game can be resumed.

Despite the fact that games played in domed stadiums are not supposed to suffer such delays, they are not immune. In April 1986 a game was delayed as water poured through a tear in the roof of the Hubert H. Humphrey Metrodome in Minneapolis.

rainmaker *n.* A towering home run; one that seems capable of rupturing a cloud and bringing rain. "It was a rainmaker shot to left," Jon Miller describing Oriole Ken Gerhart's first big league home run on WBAL radio, September 19, 1986.

rain out *v.* To rain on a game hard enough to cause it to be postponed. Usually used in the passive, as in "the Friday night game was rained out."
EXT 1. To rain on any event hard enough to cause its postponement or cancellation.
2. To fail because of some external event or condition.

rainout *n.* A suspended or postponed game.

rain rippler *n./arch.* SPITBALL.

raise ball *n./arch.* A pitched ball that veers upwards as it comes into the plate.

rake in *v.* To catch a batted ball.
1ST 1912. (*New York Tribune*, October 13; EJN)

rally **1** *n.* Several runs scored together or in rapid succession; a scoring surge.
1ST 1858. (Chadwick Scrapbooks; EJN)
2. *n.* Sometimes specifically, a run scoring surge during a half-inning for the offensive team, which causes it to tie or go ahead.
3. *v.* To score heavily.
4. *v.* To make a comeback in a game, or within a season.

rally cap *n.* A cap that has been turned inside out, put on backwards or otherwise oddly displayed by the players on the bench and/or in the bullpen to invoke a rally. The notion became popular during the 1986 season as the New York Mets, Houston Astros and Boston Red Sox, among others, each came up with its own version. The Mets version had the hats worn backwards with the brims turned up, the Astros simply turned the hats inside out and the Red Sox ritual, according to *USA Today*, worked this way: "When the count reaches 2-2 with two out on a Red Sox hitter, the players in the bullpen take their hats off and hold them out, upside down."

rally-killer *n.* That which forestalls or ends a rally, including a double play, timely strikeout or an effective relief pitcher. One statistic published from time to time shows a player's batting average from the seventh inning on, with his team either tied or trailing by a run. A low average in this department is likely to put the glue on the rally killer label. "But Reggie ranked a mere fifth in rally-killing." (*USA Today* on Reggie Jackson's clutch statistics, May 16, 1986)

ram *v.* To hit the ball.

ramicack *v.* To hit the ball.
ETY Origin unknown, but a term that seems to come with its own suggestions—for example, ram and crack.

range *n.* Attribute of a fielder who can reach batted balls. A player with good range is one able to move quickly in front or behind or to either side of his starting position on the field when the ball is hit.

range factor *n.* A defensive statistic combining an individual's putouts and assists. It has been advanced by baseball statistician Bill James as a more accurate method of rating defensive ability than the standard fielding average. Many consider this to be James's most important contribution to baseball resarch.

ranger *n.* Player who covers much ground.

rap **1.** *v.* To hit sharply.
1ST 1888. (*Chicago Inter Ocean*, July 4; EJN)
2. *n.* A batted ball.

raps *n./arch.* A player or a team's turn at bat.
1ST 1898. (*New York Tribune*, May 5; EJN)

raspberry *n.* RAZZBERRY.

rattle **1.** *v.* To distract, usually done by a batter to a pitcher. The batter often rattles the pitcher on purpose as he moves close to the plate, changes batting stance, takes timeouts, takes the bunt position etc.
2. *v.* To disorient or distract a pitcher by getting hits from the balls he pitches.
1ST 1880. (*Brooklyn Daily Eagle*, August 17; EJN)

rattle of tinware *n./arch.* The rumored or threatened release of a player from a club.
1ST 1915. (*Baseball* magazine, December; EJN)
ETY According to Edward J. Nichols, "Named from association with the phrase 'to tie the can on him.' "

rattles *n./arch.* Nervousness; usually referred to as "the rattles."

Rawlings lobotomy *n.* Beanball, so called because Rawlings manufactures the ball and prints its company logo on each one.

razz **1.** *v.* To nag or heckle a player or umpire.
2. *n.* The *razzberry* for short.
ETY See **ETY** for *razzberry*.
EXT To tease or nag in any realm.

razzberry *n.* Sound made by sticking one's tongue between one's pressed lips and blowing loudly. The flatulant sound expresses unequivocal contempt. Also known as a Bronx Cheer.
ETY Commonly believed to be a play on the rasping start of the word raspberry or the sound of a metal rasp. Sometimes spelled raspberry. (After New York Mets Outfielder Darryl Strawberry had been booed in 1986, Marcolm Moran of the *New York Times* asked the inevitable: "How to translate Strawberry's raspberries?")
Charles Earle Funk gives an alternative etymology in his classic *Hog on Ice*. After rejecting

the notion that it comes from the metal rasp he says, "I think that the word should be written 'razzberry,' that it was a humorous extension developed from the slang, 'to razz,' to mock at or make fun of; and that the latter term was originally a contraction of 'to razzle-dazzle,' meaning to bamboozle, banter or deceive." Funk goes on to point out that the first razzle-dazzle was an amusement park ride on which one went in circles merry-go-round style while undulating up and down.

EXT The very same sound and meaning when heard outside the ballpark.

RBI Abbreviation for RUN BATTED IN, one of baseball's most often used initialisms.

USE It is normally spelled out, but sometimes called a ribby. It is usually written as RBI but not always.

Charles Poe has noted from his research that, "There is not, apparently, any standardization concerning the abbreviation for the term 'runs batted in.' " Poe found it written RBIs, RBI, rbi's, RBI's, R.B.I.'s, R.B.I. and rbi.

RBI man *n.* A batter adept at getting hits with teammates on base.

R card *n.* In baseball card collecting, a candy or gum card issued after 1930, the beginning of the "modern" era in baseball cards.

reach *n.* The distance a baseman can stretch his arm without losing contact with the base he is covering.
1ST 1902. (*Sporting Life,* July 11; EJN)

reach back *v.* Said of a pitcher able to summon extra speed or deception to get a strike or an out. "Gooden reaches back and gets something extra"—Johnny Bench commenting on Dwight Gooden during the CBS-Radio broadcast of the National League Playoffs, October 14, 1986.

reaches/reaches base *v.* To get on base; to make it to first base. Often used in the context of an error or walk: "He reaches base on an error."

read *v.* To understand a pitcher's movements so closely that a batter can detect what pitch is about to be delivered.

rebound **1.** *n.* The bounce of the ball off of a wall or fence. To catch a ball after such a bounce is to get it on the rebound.
2. *v.* To bounce off of a wall or fence.

recall *n.* The process of assigning a major league player to a farm club. It is normally understood that the player may be brought back to the parent club on short notice.

receiver *n.* The CATCHER.
1ST 1908. (*Baseball* magazine, August; EJN)

recovery *n.* The retrieving of a ball after it has been momentarily fumbled.
1ST 1880. (*Chicago Inter Ocean,* June 28; EJN)

recruit *n.* New player on a ball club.
USE Seldom used, the term rookie is almost always preferred.

red-ball express *n.* A fastball.
ETY In railroad and trucking jargon red ball describes a fast-moving vehicle that is on schedule. Traditionally, red balls are given priority over slower-moving units.

red-cross walk *n.* Trip to first base after being hit by a pitched ball. From the obvious asociation of the Red Cross and injuries.
1ST 1922. (*Baseball Cyclopedia;* EJN)

red-hot balls *n./arch.* An early term for balls that were hit hard.
1ST 1867. (*New York Sunday Mercury,* September 7; EJN)

red seats *n.* A section in Cincinnati's Riverfront Stadium where only the most spectacular home runs land. Between the time the stadium opened in 1970 through the 1985 season, only 13 home runs landed in these seats. For those familiar with the feat, the measure is applied elsewhere, even in spring training. " 'Red seats,' That was the description attached to Dave Parker's home run blast against the Pittsburgh Pirates in Bradenton the other day." (*The Tampa Tribune-Times,* March 20, 1986)

refuse the ball *v.* For a pitcher to take himself out of the rotation or turn down a relief assignment. "The thing is, I could have refused the ball any one of those days . . . They would never have pressured me if I'd said, 'I can't go out today.' "—Tippy Martinez quoted on his overuse as a reliever for the Baltimore Orioles (*The Washington Post,* February 22, 1987).

regional franchise *n.* Term for a team that draws from a larger area than its name alone suggests. For instance, the Boston Red Sox long ago established themselves as a New England team.

registry station   *n./arch.* HOME PLATE, where balls, strikes and runs are registered.
1ST   1915. "Instead of coming accurately, as usual, into the hands of the catcher waiting at the registry station, the ball struck the dirt a dozen feet from the pan . . ." (Gilbert Patten, *Covering the Look-in Corner;* DS)

regroup   *v.* To attempt to bring a struggling team into line. Milwaukee Brewer manager George Bamberger's definition of the verb was quoted in the *New York Times* on June 18, 1985: "You do that by getting more runs and getting better pitching . . ."

regular/regular player   *n.* Player who routinely starts at the same position.
1ST   1866 (regular player). (Chadwick Scrapbooks; EJN)

regular season   *n.* The period of time during which a championship of the division or league is determined. In the Major Leagues today the term refers to the series of games played to determine the four divisional champions.

regulation game   *n.* Contest played to official completion. A game in which the home team scores more runs in its first eight innings at bat than the opposition scores in its nine innings at bat. Or, in the case of inclement weather or any other event that forces the game to be ended early, five or more equal innings (4½ if the team batting at the bottom of the inning is in the lead).

When a game becomes regulation—or official—individual player performances become part of the record and the rain checks become invalid. A game that does not last for the required 4½ or 5 innings is declared "no game" and must be rescheduled and played from the beginning.

rehabilitation assignment   *n.* A period during which a player is sent to a team playing at a lower level so that he can reestablish his ability.

relay   **1.** *n.* Throwing maneuver in which the ball is taken by a fielder and thrown to another fielder who acts as an intermediary thrower—or relay—for the ball on its way to its final destination. For instance, a ball caught in deep center field would likely be relayed to the second baseman in hopes of getting the ball to third base for a play.

1ST   1908. (*Brooklyn Daily Eagle,* May 21; EJN)
2. *v.* To catch a ball thrown by one player and then throw it to a third.

relay position   *n.* A point from which a ball sent in from the deep outfield can be relayed to the infield.

release   **1.** *v.* To cut or drop a player from a team's roster rather than trade him, sell him or send him to a minor league farm team.
1ST   1880. (*Chicago Inter Ocean,* May 31; EJN)
2. *n.* The discharge of a player—that is, his release from his contract.
1ST   1880. (*New York Herald,* July 5; EJN)
3. *n.* The final position of a motion as the ball leaves a pitcher or fielder's hand.

release point   *n.* The point at which the pitcher lets go of the ball. If the ball is released too early, it will be high; too late, low.

relief/relief duty   **1.** *n.* The replacement of a pitcher who has become ineffective.
2. *n.* A period of work for a substitute pitcher, as in "three innings of relief."
1ST   1909 (relief duty). (*Reach Official Base Ball Guide;* EJN)

relief man   *n.* RELIEF PITCHER.
1ST   1912. (*New York Times,* October 16; EJN)

relief pitcher   **1.** *n.* A substitute pitcher who comes in to take over for the starting pitcher or another relief pitcher.

One of the most dramatic developments in baseball during this century has been the evolution from early in the century of a typical pitching staff, from no regular relief pitcher, to the first few firemen of the 1920s, to the relief staff of today, with three or four pitchers who start every game in the bullpen. With this has come a separate relief culture replete with its own awards, specialties (e.g., "middle relief"), conventional wisdom and body of quotations. Sample: "You can't be thinking about too many things. Relief pitchers have to get into a zone of their own, I just hope I'm stupid enough." (Dan Quiesenberry, *Sports Illustrated,* Sept. 13, 1982)
2. *n.* Pitcher who commonly fills the role of relief pitcher on a team and who seldom, if ever, starts a game.
1ST   1914. (*Harper's Weekly,* May 23; EJN)

relief truck   *n.* The car, golf cart or other vehicle used to ferry relief pitchers in from the bullpen. "That really got me pumped, when I came down the sideline in the relief truck . . ."—Eddie Whitson on being given the Ed-DEEE chant at Yankee Stadium. (*USA Today,* April 28, 1986)

relieve   *v.* To act in the role of a relief pitcher.

reliever   RELIEF PITCHER.

remember Wally Pipp   WALLY PIPP.

rep   *n.* A player's ability; short for reputation.
1ST   1907. (*New York Evening Journal,* April 30; EJN)

repertoire   *n.* A pitcher's assortment of pitches.
1ST   1910. (*American* magazine, June; EJN)

rescue service   *n./arch.* RELIEF.
1ST   1909. (*Reach Official Base Ball Guide;* EJN)

reserve clause   *n.* A traditional provision in a player's contract, before 1974, that bound—or reserved—the player's services for the following season. It gave the club the right to invoke the expired contract for an additional year even if the player and the team had not come to terms on a new contract by a specific date. It amounted to a "perpetual contract" under which the player was the property of the club, which could elect to keep, trade or sell him. Team owners long insisted that this was needed to keep the leagues from being wrecked in bidding wars. Although twice upheld by the Supreme Court (1922 and 1971), it was finally overturned by a series of court decisions at lower levels. Its destruction ushered in the free agent era in baseball.

reserved seats   *n.* Stadium seating accommodations immediately behind the box seats.
   These seats are reserved in the sense that the spectator buys a specific seat defined by row and seat number and can buy or reserve it in advance of the day the game in question is played. These seats are in contrast to general admission or bleacher seats, which are filled on the day of the game by the first person to occupy the seat.

resin bag/resin sack   *n.* See ROSIN BAG.

resin ball   *n.* Illegal pitch that breaks sharply because of resin (rosin) powder on the ball and/or the pitcher's hand.

retire   *v.* To put out a batter or base runner.
ETY   The term is used in both cricket and

rounders from which it appears to have been borrowed.

retired number   *n.* A uniform number no longer available for active players because it has been taken out of circulation—or retired—to honor a key former player or manager on the club who once wore it.

retire the side   *v.* To put down three batters, thereby ending the opposition's turn at bat for that inning.
1ST   1874. (*Chicago Inter Ocean,* July 6; EJN)

retire the side in order   *v.* To put down successively all three batters faced in an inning; a 1-2-3 inning.

retouch   *n.* The act of a runner returning to a base, which he must do after a fly ball has been caught.
2.   *v.* To return to a base to make contact with it.

retread   *n.* Player whose career seems to be nearing its end, but who is given a chance with a new team. Direct borrowing from automotive retreads, which are old tires that are given new life when wrapped in a new tread.

reverse force double play   *n.* A double play in which the first out is a force play while the second is on a runner who is tagged out. The term, which appears in and is defined in the *Official Rules,* is distinguished from a *force double play* in which both putouts are force plays.

revolving   *v./arch.* To jump from a league or a team without regard to one's contract. "This process of switching teams . . . was called 're-volving.' It was against the rules of the assso-ciation, but widely engaged in anyway." (Leonard Shecter, *The Jocks;* CDP)

rhubarb   *n.* A ruckus with the umpire(s); confusion; a fight between players; a stew.
   Dizzy Dean's definition adds, "Most of the fightin' is done with their mouths."
   The most complete definition and explanation of the term appears in H. Allen Smith's 1946 comic novel, *Rhubarb.* The title character is cat, introduced while clawing its way out of a packing crate.
      "Look at the son of a bitch go!" he howled. "That's what I call tearin' up the pea patch! Look at that *rhubarb!*"
      Then and there the cat got his name—perhaps the only printable name he ever

Rhubarb. Brooklyn Dodger manager Leo Durocher leaning into an umpire during one of his many altercations. *National Baseball Library, Cooperstown, N.Y.*

had—derived from a colloquialism insinuated into the Yankee vernacular by Red Barber, the baseball broadcaster. Mr. Barber in turn picked it up from the prose writings of Garry Schumacher and spread it to the far-wandering winds. In Mr. Barber's lexicon a rhubarb was a noisy altercation, a broil, a violent emotional upheaval brought on by epical dispute—such as whether one grown man had touched another grown man on the body with a ball the size of a smallish orange.

Red Barber adds in his book *The Catbird Seat* that Schumacher got the term from Tom Meany, the famous New York sportswriter.

ETY Although there is widespread agreement that Schumacher and Barber first made the term popular in the late 1930s and 1940s, there is no such agreement as to why rhubarb made the leap from the farmyard to the ballpark. There are enough conflicting explanations for a major etymological rhubarb:

1. A popular explanation, which has appeared in a number of places, including the *Reader's Digest* (April 1982), is that the term originated in the early days of radio from the method a director used to create the impression of a menacing, argumentative crowd. To this end, he got a small group of actors to stand together and murmur "rhubarb-rhubarb-rhubarb." From that point on, the story goes, rhubarb has meant a heated dispute.

If there is an immediate problem with this theatrical explanation, it is that the story is never tied to a time, place or person. A variation on this idea, which does tie it, conjecturally, to a person, appeared in the letters column of *The Sporting News* for January 21, 1967. James P. Cruger suggests that it could have come from a German-born baseball man, perhaps Chris Von Der Ahe, legendary owner of the St. Louis Browns, who recalled an old stage trick from his homeland. According to Cruger, German crowd noises were created by actors repeating the word "Rhabarber." In *Good Words to You*, John Ciardi agrees in principle, noting that it probably comes from "theatrical practice in Brit. use since Shakespeare's time, in which the crowd noises are based on the sound of rhu-bar-bar." An equally speculative notion is that it came from the old circus cry of "Hey, rube!" which circus hands supposedly used when there was a fire or when they were being attacked by local toughs.

2. Schumacher recalled having first used the term in 1938 at a Dodgers-Reds game in Cincinnati where he was overheard by Barber who used it on the radio. Red Smith later quoted Schumacher in his column of May 21, 1959, as saying that the word fit because it "suggested an untidy mess, a disheveled tangle of loose ends like the fibers of stewed rhubarb."

3. In his 1955 *Baseball Almanac*, Hy Turkin writes that the expression, "Stems from the old days when rhubarb was used as a purgative and stomach bitter." This fits with an elaborate explanation given by H. Allen Smith, which appeared in the aforementioned 1959 Red Smith column. H. Allen Smith held that in Schumacher's era the boys growing up in the Greenpoint section of Brooklyn were mothered by women who "held firmly to the belief that rhubarb was essential to the good health of their sons,

that several dosages of rhubarb would invigorate them and permit them to fight like bobcats and thus get along in the world." Allen Smith claimed that these youngsters were sent out to play with rhubarb sandwiches, which were often used in fights and it was not uncommon for a boy to find himself with rhubarb in his hair and down his neck. "In time the Greenpoint kids began referring to their happy play as 'rhubarbs'—exclaimed through puffed lips, 'wotta rhubarb.' "

4.   It has often been asserted that it was first used in the barrooms of Brooklyn for a brawl, and a variation on this appears in *The Baseball Catalog* by Dan Schlossberg who claims, "winners of fights in Brooklyn would invariably force the losers to swallow terrible tasting rhubarb tonic."

Red Barber in his book *The Catbird Seat* says that it was in a bar that Tom Meany first picked up the word in 1937 or 1938. It seems that there had been a fight between a Giants fan and a Dodgers fan, which resulted in the Giants' partisan getting shot in the stomach. To quote Barber, "Well, according to the story as I know it, Tom Meany stopped in a tavern the day after this thing happened—I think it was the very place where the shooting had occurred—and the bartender said, 'We had quite a rhubarb last night, Mr. Meany.' . . . Tom told that to Garry [Schumacher] who fell in love with the word."

(In this regard, it seems inevitable that a word like this one should have been created to match Brooklyn's long reputation for offbeat behavior. In *The Cincinnati Reds,* Lee Allen suggests that Brooklyn's reputation for daffiness dated back to June 14, 1870, when the Atlantics of Brooklyn broke the Red Stockings' 130-game winning streak. In the last half of the 11th inning, a Brooklyn fan jumped on the back of a Cincinnati fielder as a fair ball was being picked up. According to Allen, "When order was restored, one Atlantic run had crossed the plate and the tying marker was resting on third. The crowd, of course, promptly went wild, and the spectator responsible for this turn of events was ceremoniously led from the scene by police, the first in a long line of Brooklyn fanatics to be escorted from the premises.")

5.   It is also possible that the term owes something to *rhubarbs,* the next entry.

EXT   Any noisy and/or heated argument is likely to be called a rhubarb. Red Barber has written on the spread of the term: "World War II was the thing that really popularized it—after all, Brooklyn was in every part of the armed forces. I know that it kept popping up in war communiques and dispatches." The link to Brooklyn, however, took a long time to break. A UPI report on a brawl in Havana on October 28, 1957, identified it as "a Brooklyn-style rhubarb." (PT)

rhubarbs   *n./arch.* The sticks.
1ST   1915. "Until I came to Hillsboro I never imagined what the game meant as it's played out in the rhubarbs . . ." (Gilbert Patten, *Covering the Look-in Corner.* DS).

rhythm   *n.* Good tempo, form and consistency in pitching; a most desired characteristic.

ribbie/ribby   *n.* Run batted in. It is the initialism RBI forced into an acronym. Plural: ribbies.
USE   Tends to be spoken rather than written, but does show up in print on occasion. For example, *The Village Voice* on Steve Kemp's Yankee record; ". . . his pre-injury stats project to only 14 homers and 57 ribbies." (October 11, 1983) Willie McCovey was one of the first players to be quoted using ribbies.

When it first began to show up in the early to mid-1960s it fell roughly on some ears. Leonard Shecter called it an "unimaginative word" and added, "It's about as inane as GIDAPS, for grounded into double plays."

rib roaster   *n.* BRUSHBACK PITCH.

Rickeyism   *n.* Name for a series of terms and aphoristic definitions created by the late Branch Rickey, one of the most influential baseball executives of all time, who, among other things, created the farm system while with the St. Louis Cardinals and broke the color line with the Brooklyn Dodgers. For instance, he came up with the line, "Luck is the residue of design," to describe his success with farm teams. Other examples:

Positive Subtraction. The art of improving a team by getting rid of a poor player.

Quantitative Quality. The art of improving a team by signing, or buying, a lot of players who appear to be good; some of them will turn out good.

Rickeyism. Branch Rickey, a front office man who had a revolutionary effect on the game. *National Baseball Library, Cooperstown, N.Y.*

ride *v.* To heckle or deride a player, team or umpire; what bench jockeys do. " 'Any time a new umpire comes to the league,' said Baum, 'the players—that is, the trouble-makers—try to ride him.' " (*San Francisco Bulletin*, March 28, 1913; PT)
1ST 1912. (*New York Tribune*, October 13; EJN)
ETY Conventional explanation is that the term comes from the idea of "riding one's back." Edward J. Nichols adds that it may also be associated with "horse play."

ride blindbaggage *v./arch.* To advance from one base to another through the aid of a batter.
ETY It is an old railroad term for a free ride.
1ST 1920. (*New York Times*, October 8; EJN)

rider of the lonesome pine *n.* A bench-warmer; one who seldom gets in the game.

ride the bench *v.* To sit and wait for one's chance to come into the game as a substitute.

ride the pine *v.* To sit on the bench.

riffle *n.* A hearty swing at the ball.
1ST 1932. "The boys prefer to take 'riffles' this year instead of cuts." (William G. Brandt, *Baseball* magazine, May)

rifle **1.** *n.* A strong arm; a shotgun; usually attached to an outfielder.
2. *v.* To throw the ball quickly and accurately.

rifle shot *n.* Ball that is hit or thrown hard.
1ST 1881. (*New York Herald*, July 26; EJN)

right *n.* Right field for short.
1ST 1883. (*Sporting Life*, May 6; EJN)

right-center *n.* The portion of the outfield between right and center fields.

right down Broadway *adj.* Pitch that is delivered in the middle of the strike zone.

right down the pike/right down the pipe *adj.* A pitch that crosses the center of the strike zone and that tends to be most attractive to the batter.

right field **1.** *n.* The right side of the outfield as viewed from home plate.
1ST 1854. (Knickerbocker Rules; EJN)
2. RIGHT FIELDER.

right fielder *n.* Defensive player who covers the right field portion of the playing area.
1ST 1883. (*Sporting Life*, May 27; EJN)

right-handed **1.** *adj.* With the right hand.
2. *adj.* Pitching from the right-hand side of the body; or batting from the left.

right-hander A player who throws with his right hand, commonly applied to pitchers to distinguish them from left-handers.

right in there pitching *adj. phrase* Describing a pitcher who is working hard from the mound; a compliment. In this phrase the word "pitching" means pitching with intensity or pitching well.
EXT Putting forth one's best effort.

right of way *n.* Reference to the rule that base runners must yield to infielders between the bases. A runner who fails to avoid an infielder can be called out for interference.

right short *n./obs.* A long abandoned position between first and second base for a tenth player. It mainly lives on as an entry in such reference books as *The Dictionary of American English*.

right turn at first base The route taken by a batter who is out on a ground ball or fly. "So for the fourth time, Winfield makes a right turn at first base . . ." (broadcaster Chuck

Thompson during a September 6, 1982, Yankees-Orioles telecast)

righty   *n.* Right-handed player.

rigs   *n./obs.* An early term for baseball uniforms; it came directly from cricket.
1ST   1867. (*Philadelphia Sunday Mercury,* July 14; EJN)

ring the bat   *v.* In softball, to check the size of a bat to make sure it is the officially permitted size. This is done by an umpire passing the bat through a bat ring.

rinky-dinks   *n.* Collective name for those players a who do not get in the game very often.

ripe   *adj./arch.* Said of a player who is ready to perform at the major league level.
1ST   1905. (*Sporting Life,* September 9; EJN)

rip one   *v.* To hit the ball hard for a hit.

rise   *n.* The upward movement a fastball sometimes takes as it approaches the batter.
1ST   1896. (*Frank Merriwell's Schooldays;* EJN)

riseball/riser   *n.* In softball, a pitch that rises as it approaches the plate; usually a fastball that tends to hop as it gets to the plate. "The rise ball," says Loren Walsh in his book *Inside Softball,* "is really the pitch that provides the softball pitcher with a great advantage over the hitter . . . Even when the hitter times the rise ball accurately, he usually hits under the ball and pops it up."

rise-curve   *n.* A softball pitch that combines the rise and the curve. "Many pitchers use the rise-curve as their best strikeout pitch," says Loren Walsh in *Inside Softball.*

Riverfront Stadium   Located in Cincinnati, Ohio, the home grounds of the Cincinnati Reds since 1970.

RO   The letters identifying the model ball supplied to the Major Leagues under contract by Rawlings Sporting Goods.

road   **1.** *n.* Locale of any game not played on a team's home grounds.
2. *adj.* Away; not at home.

road game   *n.* An AWAY GAME.

road grays   *n.* Name for the uniforms that a team wears for its "away" games. They are

RO. Four editions of the RO used in the 1985 season. RO-A (top left) stands for Rawlings Official (ball)-American League; RO-N (top right), Rawlings Official (ball)-National League.   *Courtesy of Rawlings*

sometimes gray but usually drabber than the "home whites."

road secretary   *n.* Member of the front office staff who attends to the team's hotel, transportation and other arrangements while on the road.

road team   *n.* A team that plays well away from its home grounds yet may do poorly at home.
1ST   1905. (*Sporting Life,* September 9; EJN)

road trip   *n.* A series of games played away from a team's home grounds.

roamer   *n.* Fielder, usually an outfielder, who covers a lot of territory.

rob   **1.** *v.* To deprive a batter of a safe hit through skillful or spectacular fielding.
2. *v.* To deprive a batter of a safe hit through skillful or spectacular fielding.
2. *v.* For the umpire to make what appears to be a bad call.
1ST   1905 (both of these meanings). (*Sporting Life,* October 7; EJN)

robber *n.* Derogatory term for an umpire.
1ST 1899. (*Frank Merriwell's Double Shot;* EJN)

Robin Hood league An "outlaw" league, such as the Players' League.
1ST 1922. (*Baseball Cyclopedia;* EJN)

rock **1.** *n.* A dumb play; a boner. Commonly phrased as "pulling a rock."

In his book *Pennant Race,* Jim Brosnan is asked by a young player, what a rock is? He explains, "Any time you do something the manager knows you shouldn't, you pull a 'rock.'" (CDP)
2. *n.* The backward motion of a pitcher as he prepares to deliver the ball.

rocker step *n.* Shifting, sideways motion used by catchers to get positioned for pitches that are low and outside.

rocket *n.* A ball batted high into the air.
1ST 1917. (*New York Times,* October 7; EJN)

rock pile *n.* A rough infield, especially one with more than its share of pebbles, or one that is rock hard.

In his book *The Long Season* a teammate says to Jim Brosnan, "This infield is better than that rockpile in Pittsburgh, isn't it, Bross?"

Rolaids Relief Man Award Annual award given to one relief pitcher in each league by Warner-Lambert Inc., makers of Rolaids Antacid Tablets ("Rolaids spells 100% relief").

Unlike the many awards given on the basis of a vote, this one is determined on a scoring system. Two points are credited to a relief pitcher for a win or a save and one point is deducted for each loss.

role player *n.* A non-starting player who is used during certain specific situations. A player who performs a special role for the team.

roll block/rolling block *n.* When a base runner attempts to disrupt the play of the pivotman at second base by tumbling into the player as a double play is being attempted. The roll block is akin to the similar play in football.

roller *n.* A slow grounder; one that trickles across the field.
1ST 1880. (*Chicago Inter Ocean,* May 14; EJN)

romp *n.* An easy victory; a LAUGHER.
1ST 1907. (*New York Evening Journal,* May 2; EJN)

Rolaids Relief Man Award. The award, replete with fire hat. *Courtesy of American Chicle*

'roo hops *n.* As defined in a *Sports Illustrated* article on international baseball ("Taking 'roo hops in Nerk," July 27, 1981): "The Australians have also made a contribution to the baseball lexicon: Taking a lead off first base is known as taking 'kangaroo hops,' or alternatively, 'roo hops.'"

rook *n.* ROOKIE, for short.

rookie **1.** *n.* A player in his first season; a first year player.
2. More specifically and officially, the *Baseball Blue Book* defines rookie as: (a) a pitcher who has appeared in fewer than 60 major league innings the previous season or (b) a non-pitcher who has appeared in fewer than 30 games the previous season. Furthermore, any player who has been on the roster of a major league team for at least 90 days does not qualify as a rookie the following year.
3. *n.* The term is also used to note a player's first year of eligibility for Hall of Fame voting. Before a player can become eligible he must be out of baseball for at least five years. "One of the largest rookie crops in years—a total of 24 first-time candidates—helps swell the 1988 Hall of Fame ballot to 45 nominees," read the lead

to an article on the 1988 ballot. (*The Sporting News*, December 7, 1987)

4. *adj.* Relating to the first season, such as a rookie manager or a rookie owner.

1ST   1908. (*New York Evening Journal*, August 17; EJN)

ETY   It appears to be a corruption of the word recruit and may have originated as a derisive term for a fresh recruit in the Army, but this is far from certain. It was listed in the 1903 supplement to *Webster's New International Dictionary of the English Language* as soldier's slang for recruit and it was noted that Rudyard Kipling used the word and that its etymology was uncertain. By the time of the first World War, it was in common use. In a review of war slang, *Literary Digest* reported in its March 10, 1917, issue: "*Rookie* is soldiers' slang for a raw recruit. The origin of this meaning has been attributed to the name 'rookery,' given, in former military slang, to the quarters occupied by subalterns in barracks."

In *A Word in Your Ear*, Philip Howard notes that the Falklands War of 1982 revived this term in the U.K. and that the British had to be reminded that it was not an Americanism but, in fact, made its first literary appearance in Kipling's 1892 *Barrack-Room Ballads* in the line, "so 'ark an' 'eed you rookies, which is always grumblin' sore."

Others have suggested:

· A jump from chess where the rook is often the last piece to be used when the game opens.

· A play on the very old slang word rook, to cheat, which was applied to new soldiers on the assumption that they would be easily cheated by con men.

EXT   Although rookie probably existed in military slang first, its American popularity comes from baseball from which it spread to other realms. The citations on the word collected by Merriam-Webster include, among others, rookie cook, rookie Senator, rookie cop, CIA rookie, rookie guard (basketball), rookie goalie, rookie priest, rookie astronaut, rookie fireman, rookie starter, rookie year, rookie actor, rookie quarterback, rookie artist. A recent headline attests to the fact that it is still finding new applications: "Don't pair rookie pilots, warns FAA." (*USA Today*, January 22, 1988)

rookie card   *n.* The first baseball card that depicts a particular player at the minor league

level. In recent years the rookie cards of stars have risen in value much faster than second and third year cards, and must be considered the baseball collecting equivalent of a first edition in book collecting. The lead to an article on Don Mattingly in the *St. Petersburg Times* of March 14, 1987, underscores the extent of the phenomenon: "Don Mattingly seemed amused when told a 3-year-old baseball card picturing him as a rookie was selling for $95. But amusement turned to amazement when he learned people were buying it."

Rookie of the Year   Annual award, given to one rookie in each league by the Baseball Writers Association of America, since 1987 has been officially titled the Jackie Robinson Award. It is based on a vote, which determines the outstanding first year player in each league. The award was first given in 1947 to Jackie Robinson of the Brooklyn Dodgers. For the first two seasons, one player was selected from both leagues.

Rookie of the Year. The first-ever Rookie of the Year (1947); the award now carries Robinson's name. *National Baseball Library, Cooperstown, N.Y.*

EXT Other sports now have "Rookie of the Year" honors. For example, National Hockey League players who have played in "no more than 20 games in the preceding season" are eligible for honors in that sport.
SEE *Jackie Robinson Award.*

rooms *n.* Common generic name for a player's roommate on the road.

room service *adj.* Term describing a pitch or batted ball that comes right to the player in question, a play on the fact that hotel room service will bring food and drink directly to one's room. "Joyner doubled into the right field corner on a room-service fastball." (*The Washington Post,* October 8, 1986)

room service cheeseburger *n.* A fastball right down the middle; a juicy offering.

root *v.* To cheer for or encourage.
ETY/1ST 1887. Although it has been stated often that this term comes from the notion of a fan who is so close to his or her team that he or she is "rooted" to it, Gerald Cohen has come up with another theory. Cohen traces it back to September 1887 when it began showing up with regularity in the baseball columns of the *New York World.* Cohen says: ". . . the basic meaning of *root* is clearly 'to dig,' and rooting can be subdivided into the categories of feet-stamping ('pedal-music'), shouting (chin-music), and hand-clapping. I believe that pedal music may be the key here; we may deal with the imagery of stamping so hard that it is visualized as digging a hole." (*Comments on Etymology,* February 1, 1987)

rooter *n.* A person who cheers for a team or player; a fan.

rope *n.* A line drive, shortened form of frozen rope. "I hit ropes against him"—Lee Lacy on pitcher Danny Darwin. (*The Washington Post,* June 12, 1986) They come in various models including "screaming ropes," extraordinarily hard-hit balls.

rosin bag *n.* A small cloth sack containing and covered with sticky resin or rosin that is kept at the back of the pitcher's mound. Pitchers are legally permitted to rub rosin from the bag onto their hands to dry their hands and improve their grip on the ball. It is illegal to apply rosin to the ball. Sometimes spelled resin.
It is used dramatically by some pitchers or,

as Jerry Howarth described it in his book *Baseball Lite,* it is ". . . constantly being picked up and dropped during the game while occasionally being slammed, kicked, hurled and spat at by angry bilingual pitchers speaking English and Profanity."

roster *n.* A list of the active players on a team at any given moment. The length of the roster is set by league rules and changes during the course of the regular season. During spring training there are no such limits and teams commonly invite roster and non-roster players to report.
1ST 1908. (*New York Evening Journal,* March 3; EJN)

rotation **1.** *n.* The regular order in which a manager will field his starting pitchers. A modern manager likes to leave spring training with his rotation set for, at least, the early weeks of the season. An aspiring starter will try to work his way into the rotation. Commonly, a team has four starters in its rotation.
2. The spin on the ball.

rotator cuff *n.* A supporting and strengthening anatomical structure in the shoulder. A player may strain or tear his rotator cuff while pitching or throwing, an injury that can have a significant effect on a pitcher's career. Don Drysdale once put a torn one in perspective, "A torn rotator cuff is a cancer for a pitcher. And if a pitcher gets a badly torn one, he has to face the facts: It's all over, baby." Significantly, before the term came into general use it was said that a pitcher had blown or blown out his arm.
"Carlton, 41, is coming back from an 1-8 record and a strained rotator cuff last year." (*St. Petersburg Times,* March 7, 1986)

Rotisserie League Baseball Popular armchair baseball game in which participants draft real players for imaginary teams. Players are picked through an open auction in which participants are allowed an amount of cash to purchase 23 players. Standings are determined during the course of the season as the performances of the individuals are added into a collective whole.
ETY The origin of the game and of its name was revealed in a May 14, 1984, article in *Sports Illustrated* by Steve Wulf, who reports that the idea of a statistical baseball league first came up when six baseball enthusiasts met in 1980

Roster. The 1949 Cleveland Indians. *Courtesy of the Cleveland Indians*

at a now-defunct French restaurant in New York called La Rotisserie Francaise.

Rouge Hose Nickname for the BOSTON RED SOX, in the same vein that Pale Hose is a nickname for the Chicago White Sox.

rough up *v.* To score against a pitcher. "Guidry was roughed up for six runs in the first inning, but not once did Piniella get anyone up in the pen." (*New York Post*, August 13, 1987)

round *n./obs.* An INNING.
1ST 1902. (*Sporting Life*, July 5; EJN)
ETY A term borrowed from boxing.

round a base *v.* To run across and touch a base in such a manner that the distance to the next base is minimized.

round arm delivery *n.* An over the shoulder pitching delivery, like that of a cricket bowler.

round ball 1. *n.* ROUNDERS.
2. *n.* Also, facetiously, baseball as opposed to football.

rounders *n.* An ancient British bat and ball game from which baseball is in part derived. It was popular during the 18th and early 19th centuries in Boston, where it was also called goal ball, Indian ball, one old cat, round ball and base ball. A British journalist once wrote that baseball was nothing more than "rounders writ large." There are major differences between baseball and rounders, among which are: rounders has but one base and a runner can be put out by being hit with a thrown ball.

The game exists in several forms including those that are played on an individual basis rather than team against team. Usually, the batter takes a field position when put out and all the other players move up a position.

round heel *n.* A poor player.

roundhouse/roundhouse curve *n.* A sweeping curveball; one that leaves no doubt that it is arching. Though impressive to watch, such a pitch has a trajectory that experienced batters can often spot and thus hit the ball. The same as the jughandle and rainbow curves.

1ST 1910. (*American* magazine, April; EJN)

ETY Probably suggested by the name and shape of the curved track and walls of the railroad structure known as a "roundhouse." Other slang roundhouses include the lavatory on a ship and the full, nothing-held-back swing of the prizefighter. An AP story of September 27, 1938, collected by Peter Tamony begs to be repeated here in part:

> LONDON—Jack Doyle, handsome Irish heavy weight, knocked himself out to-night in the second round of his fight with Eddie Phillips. Letting go with a "roundhouse right," "the Irish thrush" missed an opponent, fell between the ropes and struck his head on the edge of the ring. He still was prone on the floor outside the ropes when the referee finished the count of ten.

round the bases *v.* To trot around the bases, touching each one, after hitting a home run, triple or double.

round trip/round-tripper *n.* A HOME RUN, from the fact that the batter leaves and returns home on the same "ticket."

rout **1.** *n.* A defeat, usually a dramatic one. **2.** *v.* To defeat handily.

route *n.* An entire baseball game, commonly applied to a pitcher when he pitches a full game and is said to have "gone the route" or "gone the whole route."

rover *n.* In softball, the 10th player, who plays at various positions in the field depending on the circumstances; from about 1910 until about 1930 in many softball leagues.

Royals Stadium In Kansas City, Missouri, the home grounds of the American League Kansas City Royals since 1973.

rubber **1.** *n.* The 6-by-24-inch white rubber strip or plate set into and atop the pitcher's mound. While pitching, the pitcher must come

Royals Stadium. This modern stadium features a 322-foot-wide array of fountains and waterfalls that overlook the outfield. *Courtesy of the Kansas City Royals*

in contact with the rubber, which is 60 feet 6 inches from home plate. It is often said that the pitcher "toes the rubber." It is the same size at most levels of baseball, although the Little League rubber is 4 inches by 18 inches.
1ST 1891. (*Chicago Herald,* May 5; EJN)
2. *n.* Home plate. Although this is the only definition given in H. L. Mencken's *American Speech* and elsewhere, the first meaning has completely overwhelmed this one, which must now be considered obsolete.
1ST 1884. (*DeWitt's Official Base Ball Guide;* EJN)

rubber arm *n.* A flexible and strong arm, often applied to that of a relief pitcher who can work often.

Although the term apparently came along later, the all-time rubber arm was attached to "Iron Man" Joe McGinnity of the old New York Giants, who set a career record that will never be broken let alone attempted: He pitched both games of a doubleheader on five separate occasions (winning both games in three of those five double starts).
1ST 1937. (*The Sporting News Record Book;* EJN)

rubber band *n.* Pitcher with a weak arm.

rubber bat *n.* Lucky bat used by player who gets more than his share of fluke or freak hits; from the fanciful notion of a bat that bends and stretches to make contact with the ball.
1ST 1937. (*The Sporting News Record Book;* EJN)

rubber chicken circuit *n.* The winter banquet circuit, sarcastically renamed for the poor quality of its mass-produced main courses.

Under the headline "He'll Duck Rubber Chicken Circuit," Casey Stengel told *The Sporting News:* "I'm 60 years old. I'm too old for that banquet stuff. You get no rest. And, if you don't get rest, how can you keep coming back for such a hard struggle as we've had this year? If you don't feel right, you can't take over a job like this without going batty. And nobody wants to do that." (October 18, 1950)

rubber-coated baseball *n.* Special ball designed for indoor drills and play.

rubber game *n.* The last and deciding game of a series when the previous games have been split. The seventh game of the World Series, for instance.
ETY From the card game bridge, when each side wins one of the first two games, the third and deciding game is called the rubber game. The transfer to baseball makes sense as most regular season series are three games long.

rubbing mud *n.* Mildly abrasive soil that is smeared on baseballs by an umpire to remove their "factory gloss" or shine and make them easier to grip. This procedure dates back many years to a time when tobacco juice or a wad of dirt from the playing field was used. Today both leagues use a special commercial product known as Lena Blackburne Rubbing Mud, named for the Chicago manager who discovered a mud with just the right qualities on the Delaware River near his home in New Jersey. It was introduced to the American League in the late 1930s by Blackburne's friend Connie Mack and adopted by the National League in the 1950s.

rube *n./arch.* Player from the country, or one who appears to be. It was once a very common nickname; more than 25 major league players have been known as Rube, including Edward Rube Waddell, Richard Rube Marquard and Ray Rube Bressler.
ETY General slang for a farmer or country man, which appears to derive from Reuben, a name long-associated with country bumpkins.

rubelet *n./obs.* As defined by Edward J. Nichols, "Any hit obtained from the pitching delivery of Rube Waddell, who made his reputation in the early nineteen hundreds."

rubinoff *n./arch.* Player in need of a haircut.

rub up *v.* To ready or warm up a ball for pitching by rubbing it with some ritualistic intensity.

rug *n.* The infield grass, especially if it is synthetic.

rug rat *n.* Small player, from the slang expression for infant. "Mets don't need baby-sitter for 'rug rats' Dykstra, Backman." (*USA Today* headline, August 14, 1986)

run **1.** *n.* A complete circuit of the bases.
2. *n.* Baseball's only unit of scoring. A run is scored to the team and the individual player after he has touched all bases and arrives home safely.
ETY/1ST 1854. The term comes from cricket and appears in the Rules of the Original Knickerbocker Club.

Rubbing mud. Lena "Slats" Blackburn in 1929.   *National Baseball Library, Cooperstown, N.Y.*

3. *v.* To act as a base runner.
4. *v.* To manage; to run the team.

run-and-hit play   *n.* An offensive tactic in which a base runner is given the green light to steal. As the runner starts with the pitch, the batter eyes the ball in hopes that it is one he can hit. The base runner forces the middle infielder to cover second base thereby giving a hole for the batter to hit into. If the ball is hit safely, the runner will be able to claim, at least, an extra base. If the ball is not swung at or is swung at and missed, the runner finds himself in the midst of a steal, which he may or may not accomplish depending on his speed and the skill of the catcher. It differs from the hit and run play in that the batter chooses whether or not to swing. Or, in other words, he does not have to protect the runner.

runaway game   *n.* Term used in some youth leagues to describe scoring binges of such mag-
nitude that the game is put out of reach. Some leagues have rules concerning such games. From the *Eastern Area Recreation Baseball Leagues Rules— Montgomery County Maryland:* "Limitation on Runaway Games: once the team at bat scores 10 runs in its half of an inning, the sides change regardless of the number of outs at the time."

run batted in   *n.* A run that is caused by a particular batter and that is officially credited to him as part of his record. RBIs are created when a runner scores as the result of a hit, a sacrifice, when the batter is hit by a pitched ball or gets a base on balls. The batter himself is counted in the case of a home run. A bases loaded home run, for instance, is worth four runs batted in to the batter.

The number of RBI a batter accumulates in a season is an important measure of that player's offensive ability at the plate.

rundown/run down   **1.** *v.* To put out a runner who has been caught between two fielders.

This often requires the fielders to throw the ball back and forth several times as the runner tries to avoid being put out.
1ST   1905. (*Sporting Life*, September 2; EJN)
2. *n.* Situation in which a runner caught between bases tries to elude fielders who are trying to tag him out.

rundown play   *n.* Strategic move in which the offensive team allows one runner to get trapped in a rundown while another runner uses the opportunity to steal home.
1ST   1908. (*Spalding Official Base Ball Guide;* EJN)

run for the cycle   See hit for the cycle.

run his ankles hot   *v.* Moved swiftly.

run in   **1.** *v.* To pitch close to the batter's body.
  "On the first pitch, he ran the ball in on me"—Ray Knight describing a Calvin Schiraldi pitch. (*The Washington Post*, October 26, 1986)
2. *n.* A run that has been scored.

run into the box   An illegal movement in softball in which the pitcher delivers the ball while running toward the plate.

run it out   *v.* For a batter to move as quickly as he can on his way to first base even though he is probably going to be thrown out. A batter runs it out on the hope that the defense will commit an error.
1ST   1910. (*American* magazine, April; EJN)

runner   *n.* A player running the bases. A base runner.
1ST   1845. (Knickerbocker Rules)

runners at the corners   *n.* Describing the situation in which runners are at first and third.

runner's interference   *n.* The act of interfering with a fielder or being hit by a batted ball when running the bases. A runner hit by a batted ball is automatically called out by the umpire for interfering with a defensive play and other runners, including the batter, return to the last base touched.

Ruthian. George Herman (Babe) Ruth.   *Prints and Photographs Division, the Library of Congress*

running catch   *n.* Defensive play in which a batted ball is caught on the fly by a swiftly moving fielder.
1ST   1858. (Chadwick Scrapbooks; EJN)

run out   **1.** *v.* To run at maximum speed regardless of where the ball has been batted to. **2.** *n./arch.* Situation in which a runner is caught between bases and put out; see run down.

run out a fly ball   *v.* To run toward first base with full speed and effort despite having hit what appears to be a routine fly ball, i.e., an easy out. The reward for running out a fly ball comes on those occasions when the ball is dropped or missed and the runner gets to take one or more bases.

run out the string   *v.* To wait out the pitcher in hopes of getting a base on balls.

run production   *n.* Scoring.

run-up   *v.* To run a man back and forth on the basepaths; to run down a runner.

runway   *n.* The base paths.
1ST   1922. (*Baseball Cyclopedia;* EJN)

rush seats   *n.* Unreserved general admission or bleacher seats.
ETY   The term, rarely used today, originated in the 19th century when such seats were suddenly opened to the onslaught—or rush—of the crowd as it poured through the gate before a game.

Ruthian   *adj.* Colossal; with great power, from the hitting style and lusty demeanor of Babe Ruth.
   The term has been applied to a number of nouns, including: Ruthian clout, Ruthian smack, Ruthian proportions and Ruthian appetite. It sometimes shows up as Babe Ruthian ". . . a fine Babe Ruthian cameo by Joe Don Baker as the Whammer . . ." *Newsweek* on the movie, *The Natural,* May 28, 1984.

Ryanitis   *n.* Mock disease that, according to *USA Today,* ". . . mysteriously struck hitters on the day they were scheduled to face all-time strikeout leader Nolan Ryan." The symptoms vary, but the result is that batters try to get out of the lineup rather than face Ryan.

S

S/sac Common scorecard and box score abbreviation for sacrifice.

SABR Abbreviation for Society of American Baseball Research, pronounced "saber."

sabermetrician *n.* One who engages in or is a fancier of sabermetrics. A letter soliciting subscribers for *Sabermetric Feview* begins with the salutation, "Dear Sabermetrician."

sabermetrics *n.* The study and mathematical analysis of baseball statistics and records, from the SABR acronym. *Insight* magazine (April 7, 1986) said: "It is a fascinating conglomeration of statistical breakdowns—some basic, others so bizarre and arcane that they almost defy explanation—of baseball's teams and players." The term is closely associated with Bill James who is regarded as the leading sabermetrical scholar of the game.

sac fly *n.* SACRIFICE FLY, for short.

sack *n.* Any base, save for home plate; from the fact that they are filled canvas bags that resemble stuffed sacks.
1ST 1891. (*Chicago Herald,* May 5; EJN)

sacker *n./arch.* A baseman; first-sacker, for example.
1ST 1911. (*Baseball* magazine, October; EJN)

sacrifice 1. *n.* SACRIFICE HIT.
1ST 1880. (*Chicago Inter Ocean,* June 29; EJN)
2. *v.* To make a SACRIFICE HIT.
ETY From the concept of a batter giving himself up for the good of the team by advancing or scoring a teammate.

sacrifice bunt *n.* A bunted ball that gets the batter put out, but advances a runner. Such a sacrifice is not counted as an official at bat.
1ST 1935. "A sacrifice bunt is a bunted ball laid down for a like purpose." (Ralph H. Barbour, *How to Play Better Baseball;* DS)

sacrifice fly *n.* A fair or foul fly ball, specifically one caught for the first or second out, which is hit deep enough to allow a man on base time to tag up and score. It has been typified as a "bunt with muscles."

Such an out does not count as an official at bat for the purposes of computing batting average, but the fact that a runner crosses the plate gives the batter an RBI.
The rule, which does not charge an at bat against the batter who makes the sacrifice fly, was taken away in 1931 and kept out of the game, with the exception of 1939, until 1954 when it returned. By all accounts, it was brought back to help create a few more .300 batters. It was assumed that the rule was worth seven to ten points to a power hitter's batting average.
1ST 1908. The sacrifice fly is introduced. The batter is credited with a sacrifice fly only when a runner scores after the ball has been caught. In his summary history of the rule in the June 1987 *SABR Bulletin* John Kuenster notes that, beginning in 1926, the batter was credited with a sacrifice fly if "any runner advances after the catch."

sacrifice hit/sacrifice play *n.* Either a bunted ball that advances or scores a runner or a fly ball that enables a teammate to tag up and advance or score. The batter makes the sacrifice is out but does not get an official at bat charged against his batting average and he is credited with a run batted in (RBI) if the runner scores. However, if there is more than one man on base and one is put out in the play, the batter is not credited with a sacrifice.
1ST 1881. (*New York Herald,* June 21; EJN)
Another early use of the term is revealing:
"Alike in the field and at bat, a man may do the most effective work in that branch of baseball technically called 'sacrifice play' and yet not receive a word of credit for it at the hands of many of the reporters." (*Sporting Life,* March 3, 1886; DS)

sacrifice hitter *n.* Batter sent to the plate either to sacrifice bunt to allow a base runner to advance or to hit a sacrifice fly to bring in a run.
EXT The term has seen limited use in politics for a candidate who runs for the good of the party and other candidates, but who is likely to lose. "With a 'sacrifice hitter'—another candi-

date involved—they can get the 'right to work' monkey off their backs by supporting him." (*San Francisco Call-Bulletin,* December 17, 1957; PT)

safe   *adj.* Ruling made for a runner who reaches a base without being put out; the opposite of out.

The umpire signifies that a batter is safe by holding his hands down with the palms facing and parallel to the ground.
1ST   1862. (*New York Sunday Mercury,* July 13; EJN)

safe carrier   *n.* A slow runner; one who seems as if he is running with a safe on his back.

safety   *n./arch.* A base hit; a safe hit.
1ST   1907. (*Dick Merriwell's Magnetism;* EJN)

safety set   *n.* Series of baseball cards given out by police and fire departments to promote safety. Almost without exception each card contains the image of a player and a safety tip.

safety squeeze   *n.* A play in which the batter bunts and the runner on third starts or breaks for home if, and *only* if, it looks like a good bunt. It differs from the suicide squeeze in which the runner starts to run as soon as the ball is pitched.

sailer   *n.* A fastball that takes off horizontally—as if it had a sail attached—rather than dropping. In his *Baseball Techniques Illustrated,* Ethan Allen says that it is, "Gripped with the fingers along the seams and released with pressure on the middle finger." Sailers are notoriously hard to control.

St. Louis Browns   The name of the American League franchise in St. Louis, Missouri. The team came from Milwaukee in 1902 and moved to Baltimore in 1954, where it took the traditional Baltimore name of the Orioles. The team spent its life in two ballparks known as Sportsman's Park. It used the latter Sportsman's Park from 1909 to 1953, sharing it for many years with the National League St. Louis Cardinals. Named for the brown trim of the club uniform, many called them the Brownies.

St. Louis Cardinals   The name of the National League's Western Division franchise in St. Louis, Missouri. Once known as the Browns for the color of their stockings, there was a hose change to red in 1899. A woman overheard by a reporter covering the team remarked that the color was a lovely shade of cardinal. This remark appeared in the paper along with the suggestion that the team adopt the name, which it did in that same year, 1900. The cardinal bird was adopted as a symbol for the team.

salami   *n.* Grand slam home run; short for grand slam.
EXT   A pure play on the word slam, which turns it into s(a)lam(i).

salary arm/salary whip/salary wing   *n./arch.* A pitcher's arm, so called because a pitcher earns his salary on the strength and effectiveness of his arm.
1ST   1892. (salary arm). (*New York Press,* August 11; EJN)

Safe. The umpire's signal is unequivocal.   *Courtesy of the Amateur Softball Association of America*

San Diego/Jack Murphy Stadium. A full house in San Diego. *Courtesy of the San Diego Padres*

salary drive *n.* A period of good performance and/or behavior seemingly staged for the benefit of the player's paycheck rather than the benefit of the club. Commonly mounted during the last month of the season so as to improve the player's statistics for salary negotiations and added leverage in arbitration. Former pitcher Jim Palmer defined it as, "A great performance before free agency."
1ST 1904 (salary wing). "The special implication is that Joe McGinnity is more than a mere star if he is capable of teaching a younger rival how to extend the life of his salary wing." (*Everybody's Magazine*, vol. 10, pp. 220–2, DS)

saliva jive *n.* The loading of a spitball.

saliva toss *n./arch.* SPITBALL.
1ST 1920. (*New York Times,* October 10; EJN)

Sally Nickname for the South Atlantic League, a minor league that traditionally supplied many good players to the majors.
1ST 1911. (*Spalding's Official Base Ball Guide;* EJN)

Sammy Vick, do a *v.* As defined in *Babe Ruth's Own Book of Baseball:* "Doing a Sammy Vick—overeating. Sammy Vick was noted for possessing one of the most voracious appetites in the big leagues."

San Diego/Jack Murphy Stadium Official name of JACK MURPHY STADIUM.

San Diego Padres The name of the National League's Western Division franchise in San Diego, California. The team took the Padres nickname from the city's long-established Pacific Coast League team. It was originally adopted because of the city's Spanish heritage and the fact that priests (*padres* in Spanish) established so many early missions in the area.

sandlot *n./adj.* Relating to a class of amateur players, teams and leagues whose games are played on vacant lots, playgrounds, pastures, yards and other such locations. It is a generic term that seldom specifically applies to a sand lot, but rather to a lack of sophistication and organization. It has been said that college baseball, American Legion baseball, Little League Baseball and other organized programs have all but made sandlot baseball obsolete. In 1964 columnist Jack McDonald reported, "Sandlots

Sandlot. Typical sandlot scene on the site of what is now Doubleday Field in Cooperstown, New York.   *Prints and Photographs Division, the Library of Congress*

have virtually dried up as a reservoir for future talent." Some sandlot leagues have survived, however. In a *Boston Globe* article of May 22, 1988, on the beginning of the 59th season of the Boston Park League, John Kelliher, manager of one of the clubs, says, "You might say that our league's longevity is a modern miracle, one of sandlot baseball's very few survivors."

Before about 1960, however, it was hard to pick up a baseball player's biography that did not contain a line on the dust jacket concerning, "his rise from sandlot baseball to the big leagues." For a number of years the Hearst newspapers sponsored its own "sandlot program." In 1965, newspapers in the chain noted that seven graduates of the program were appearing in the Major League All-Star Game.

1ST   1887. "A team called the Joe Gerhardt's of which comedian Pete Daily is pitcher, will tackle the City Island team on the sand lots tomorrow. They will play for a basket of clams." (*New York World,* July 3; from Gerald Cohen's February 1, 1987, article on baseball slang in *Comments on Etymology*)

ETY   Peter Tamony did extensive research on this term, culminating in his article "Sandlot Baseball" in the November 1968 issue of *Western Folklore*. In the article he traces it back to the year 1850 in San Francisco when a cemetery was created from a "triangular piece of land crested by a hill of sand," which is now the site of the Civic Center. Some 5,000 people were interred at the spot between 1850 and 1860. In 1860, the Board of Supervisors ordered the dead moved, had the hill leveled and opened the 17 acres as a park. In 1870 the city demanded the spot for a new City Hall. While the building was going up, the demagogue Denis Kearney led his attacks on Chinese labor here and the name Sand Lot was, as Tamony put it, "cabled all over the English-speaking world." Tamony cited a number of examples in which the term jumped from the name for a specific city lot to a general and extended usage.

The earliest usage Tamony found, which clearly relates to baseball, showed up in the "Base Ball Supplement" to the June 7, 1890, issue of *Breeder and Sportsman:* "why such players are overlooked . . . and 'skates' and 'walters' are kept in the team simply because at one time they were alleged good players by some sand lot critic."

EXT Rough and untutored in other sports and other walks of life. "NFC salvages Pro Bowl triumph with 'sandlot plays.'" (*San Francisco Examiner* headline, February 7, 1983; PT)

Sand Lot Kid Name of a bronze sculpture depicting a barefooted farm boy that stands outside the gates to Doubleday Field in Cooperstown, New York. Since it was put in place in 1939, it has become one of the true icons of the game.

sandlotter *n./arch.* A sandlot player; graduate of the lower realms of the game. In his *Baseball in America*, Robert Smith writes of the growth of baseball in the last century and captures the spirit of the term sandlotter.

This was through the seventies and eighties, when boys began to play the game on the outskirts of every major city, in country pastures, and in public parks. The great camp of Manhattan's west side, the prairies on the edges of fire-gutted

Sandlotter. Men from teams comprising garage workers of Washington, D.C., during World War II. *Prints and Photographs Division, the Library of Congress*

Sandlot Kid. The 1939 sculpture, along with a couple of modern sandlot kids. *National Baseball Library, Cooperstown, N.Y.*

Chicago, the filled grounds on Boston's Back Bay, the wide meadows on Philadelphia's outskirts, the vacant lots in Indianapolis, in Buffalo, in Patterson, the prairies around St. Louis, the back pastures of New England, the flatlands of New Jersey, the windy reaches of Iowa, even the back yards of San Francisco's Telegraph Hill saw baseball diamonds of every size scratched where boys would play the new game.

1ST 1911. (*Baseball* magazine, October; EJN)

sandpaper ball Illegally pitched ball that has been defaced with sandpaper.
1ST 1914. (*New York Tribune*, September 23; EJN)

San Francisco Giants The name of the National League's Western Division franchise in San Francisco, California. The nickname was established by the New York Giants and was carried with the team when it moved to San Francisco in 1958.

sanitaries/sannies *n.* SANITARY SOCKS.

sanitary socks *n.* The long white socks worn by players under the outer stirrup socks. "Underneath you wear long white socks that are called sanitaries." (Jim Bouton, *Ball Four*; CDP)

They are there to prevent blood poisoning in the event that a player is spiked. "Willie McGee sat quietly in front of his Al Lang Stadium locker Friday morning and fiddled with his equipment. First, his long white sanitary socks had to be just so. Then it was time for his cardinal-red stirrup socks to be pulled high and taut. "(Don Banks in the *St. Petersburg Times,* March 28, 1987)

ETY   The term is a direct reference to the fact that these white socks are not dyed, like one's outer socks, and that they would provide a cleaner and more sanitary dressing in the event of a spiking.

USE   This appears to be a term that comes in and out of fashion. In his 1970 book *Behind the Mask,* Bill Freehan tells of Al Kaline calling out for a pair of "undersocks." A younger player asks him what he's talking about and Kaline replies, "You aren't old enough to know. That's what we called sanitary socks in the mid-fifties." (CDP)

SEE ATHLETIC HOSE.

satchelfoot   *n.* Player with large feet requiring large brogans. Reportedly the source of Satchel Paige's nickname, which, according to the June 3, 1940, issue of *Time,* began as "Satchelfoots" in deference to the size 12 shoes.

save   *n.* The credit given to one relief pitcher for ensuring his team's victory by protecting the lead in a given game. In order to get a save the pitcher cannot be taken from the game and must finish it. Even though the starting pitcher receives credit for the win, the save is the formal recognition of the relief pitcher's role in the victory. The save is only awarded to a pitcher who can maintain the team's lead for three innings or longer.

Only one save can be credited in a game. If more than one pitcher qualifies, the official scorer determines which reliever was most effective.

ETY   The save became an officially recognized statistical category in 1969. According to Patrick Ercolano in *Fungoes, Floaters and Fork Balls:* "Chicago sportswriter Jerome Holtzman gets credit for being the main advocate of the save, having long used his newspaper column to promote the stat's official adoption."

save opportunity   *n.* Term used to describe a relief pitching appearance in which the pitcher has the chance to be credited with a save. It is used to give perspective to the save statistic in that two pitchers with 12 saves may have had vastly different save opportunities (say, 14 vs. 24).

sawed-off bat   *n.* A bat shaved flat on the end to reduce air resistance.

saw-off   *v.* To pitch to the inside portion of the strike zone, causing the batter to hit with the bat handle, effectively sawing off the barrel of the bat.

"Say hey!"   Verbal trademark of Hall of Famer Willie Mays, the Say Hey Kid.

"Say it ain't so, Joe."   An oft-heard lament that came to represent the 1919 "Black Sox" scandal in which the World Series was "fixed" to accommodate gamblers. On September 28, 1920, a young boy supposedly walked up to Shoeless Joe Jackson (the most famous player accused in the case) in front of the Cook County Courthouse and delivered the famous line. According to an account of the incident in the *Chicago Herald and Examiner,* Jackson replied, "Yes, kid, I'm afraid it is." The boy was then reported to have said, "Well, I never would've thought it."

As with other elements of baseball lore, there is reason to question the veracity of the quotation and the response to it. David Shulman in a letter published in the May 1, 1988, New York *Daily News* Sunday Magazine writes, "To his dying day, Jackson never admitted guilt in the Black Sox scandal and denied saying anything after he left the Grand Jury room. It is dubious that any newsboy could have approached him then, as he was carefully guarded." Responding to the claim of eyewitnesses, Shulman adds that they were all reporters and, ". . . it is a fact that sometimes reporters contrive their own stories."

EXT   Used broadly as an expression of disbelief or hoped for denial. It was given a brief and specific workout when Senator Joseph Biden of Delaware dropped out of the race for the Democratic nomination for the presidency in 1987. Biden was alleged to have plagiarized the speeches of other politicians. In 1988 the line came into play again when Ben Johnson, the Canadian runner, was stripped of his Olympic gold medal for testing positively for steroid use. This time the cry was, "Say it ain't so, Ben."

SB   Common scorecard and box score abbreviation for stolen base.

WILLIE MAYS

SAN FRANCISCO GIANTS

Say hey. The Say Hey Kid in action and accepting the 1965 National League MVP Award.   *Courtesy of the San Francisco Giants*

scalped field   *n.* A playing surface with little or no turf.

scatter arm   *n.* A pitcher or fielder given to wild pitches and throwing errors.
1ST   1937. (*The Sporting News Record Book;* EJN)

scatter-armed   *adj.* Given to wild throws and bad relays. More often applied to fielders than pitchers.

scatter hits/scatter the hits   *v.* For a pitcher to space the hits he gives up over several innings so that few or no runs are scored.
1ST   1892. (*Chicago Herald,* May 25; EJN)

schedule   *n.* The list of contests that a team will play during a season. Normally, the schedule specifies the date, location and time of day on which games will be played. Each major league team plays 162 regular season games of which half are away and half are at home.

schneid   *n.* A shutout or shutouts for a team or a hitless period for a batter. To be "off the schneid" is to come out of a slump.

ETY   According to Wentworth and Flexner it came originally from the German and Yiddish *schneider* for one who cuts cloth, a tailor. On its way to baseball, it appears to have become a gin rummy term for winning before one's opponent has scored or won any games.

schneider   *v.* To shut out.

schoolboy   *n.* A rookie or new player.

school of slug   *n.* Class of batters who major in long balls.
1ST   1902 (*Sporting Life,* July 12; EJN)

science   *n.* The collective body of strategy and technique accruing to the sport.

scissors glide/scissors slide.   *n.* A slide in which both legs clamp the bag.

scoop   **1.** *n.* A catch of a low batted ball.
1ST   1883. (*Sporting News,* April 15, EJN)
2. *v.* To dig down for a ball hit low.
1ST   1874. (*Chicago Inter Ocean,* July 7; EJN)

scorcher   *n.* A hard-hit, low line drive.

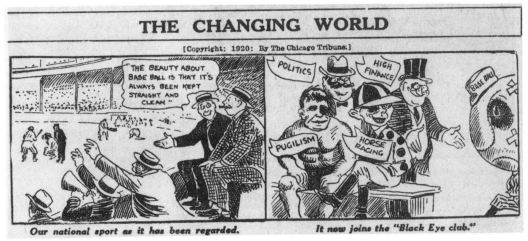

Say it ain't so, Joe. The disillusion of the "Say it ain't so" catchphrase is mirrored in this 1920 *Chicago Tribune* cartoon. *Prints and Photographs Division, the Library of Congress*

scorchers *n./arch.* The bleachers.
1ST 1931. "The term 'scorchers' applies to the bleachers where the fans sit and burn in the sun." (Clifford Harvey, "The Fascinating Language of 'Baseballese,'" *Baseball* magazine, January)

score **1.** *v.* To drive in or safely cross home plate for a run.
2. *n.* The tally in a game, expressed exclusively in runs.
1ST 1858. (*Brooklyn Daily Times,* June 18; EJN, who notes that both of "These terms appear in the account of a game written by Walt Whitman.")
3. *v.* To create a record of a baseball game, including runs, hits, errors and other events.

scoreboard *n.* A signboard erected for the benefit of the specators that, at a minimum, shows each team's inning-by-inning scoring as well as the total number of hits, runs and errors credited to each team.
They appear at every level of the game and range from manually operated wooden structures to elaborate electronic screens replete with special effects and moving images.
1ST 1898. (*New York Tribune,* June 28; EJN)

scorecard/score card **1.** *n.* A card or sheet of paper on which the score of a game is kept using the special shorthand of the game.
1ST 1902. (*Sporting Life,* April 25; EJN)
2. *n.* A magazine-style program sold at the ballpark, which contains ads, articles and other information including a scorecard bound in as its centerspread. It also contains the rosters of both teams witn each player's position and number. The vendors who sell them often have a one-line sales pitch that they shout repeatedly. Ken Abrahams of Al Lang Stadium in St. Petersburg has sold many Cardinals and Mets Grapefruit League scorecards with this simple line: "Get the names and numbers of all the millionaires, just 50 cents."

scorekeeper *n.* Technically the chief umpire who conducts the game and keeps its score. Not to be confused with scorer.

scorer *n.* A person who is given the job of ruling on the quality of play, which will be entered in the official record of a game; usually called the official scorer. The scorer determines the following: errors, base hits, official times at bat, assists, passed balls, wild pitches, stolen bases, earned runs, sacrifice hits, the winning and losing pitcher, and who, if anyone, is credited with a save. In the Major Leagues the scorer is usually a local sports reporter. The rulings of the scorer have no bearing on the score or outcome of the game.
1ST 1902. (*Sporting Life,* April 26; EJN)

scoring *n.* A system of recording the events of a game. It uses its own shorthand, which, for instance, gives every defensive position a number: 1—pitcher; 2—catcher; 3—first base; 4—second base; 5—third base; 6—shortstop; 7—left field; 8—center field; 9—right field. An out is noted by listing all the numbers of the players who touch the ball. A ground ball that is hit to the shortstop who throws it to first base for an out is noted as 6–3. Fly balls are noted by the player who catches the ball.

A strikeout is a K, but if the batter is called out the K is inverted. Base hits are 1B, 2B, 3B and HR.

There are many variations on standard scoring both public and private. Writing about a system he developed, Kenneth Ikenberry noted that he tried to record every nuance of the game up to and including whether or not the pitcher was thinking about his stock portfolio when he threw the hanging curve. "I buy scorebooks of such ancient lineage that they spell baseball as two words on the cover, and I fill them with tiny symbolic letters, arrows, chevrons, circles, stars—the stuff of the cabals. When they are full I throw them in the back of the car." (*Washington Post,* August 7, 1982)

scoring position   *n.* Term for a runner on second or third who should be able to score on any outfield hit. Runners who attempt to steal second are trying to get into scoring position. Having a runner or runners in scoring position is what puts a pitcher in a jam.

scout   **1.** *n.* A person whose job it is to evaluate players at lower levels of the game; a talent scout.
1ST 1905. (*Sporting Life,* September 2; EJN)
2. *n.* A person who observes a team's future opponent and reports on their potential strengths and weaknesses (the same person may scout players and opposing teams).
3. *v.* To act as a scout.
4. *n.* According to Dan Schlossberg in his *Baseball Catalog:* "the original scout—before the Cartwright rules of 1845—was something else. He was a second catcher who played far to the rear of the regular catcher. He grabbed passed balls and wild pitches, and fielded 'hits' that landed near him. (Fouls were then unknown and batters could run on hits behind the plate as well as in front of it.)."

scouting report   *n.* A detailed written evaluation of a player of potential worth to the scout's club.

scratch   *n./obs.* Apparently a term for the batter's box. Gerald Cohen has come up with several examples from the 1880s in the *New York World,* including this from the issue of August

3, 1889: "After two men were out in the first inning of the game between New York and Philadelphia at the new Polo Grounds yesterday afternoon, Capt. Buck Ewing, bat in hand, walked up to the scratch and faced Buffington, the premier pitcher of the Quakers."

scratch/scratch hit/scratch single   *n.* A ball that is not hit solidly but that results, nevertheless, in a hit; a lucky—or fluke—hit, often an infield grounder.
1ST 1876 (scratch). (*Chicago Inter Ocean,* May 1; EJN)

scratch for runs   *v.* To have difficulty scoring.

scratch the diamond   *v.* For the grounds crew to smooth the basepaths. "This is an oldie, brought around by Joe Sewell and it means drag the field," wrote Frank Gibbons in his 1959 *Baseball Digest* article on "fieldese."

scratchy   *adj.* In the nature of scratch hits.

screamer   *n.* A hard-hit ball. "The White Sox tied it in the third, on two singles and an error, and an inning later Tommy Davis pulled a low two-base screamer just inside the bag at third, apparently fossilizing Joe Foy, the young Boston third baseman." (Roger Angell, *The Summer Game;* CDP)

screaming meemie   *n.* A vicious, low line drive.
ETY This is one of those bits of slang that has been applied to a variety of things. Peter Tamony noted that the screaming mimis were the jitters (as in the 1942 film *Balls of Fire* starring Gary Cooper and Barbara Stanwyck). During World War II, it was used as slang for German artillery shells.

screen   **1.** *n.* A wire or net barrier erected in front of spectators to protect them.
1ST 1909. (*Baseball* magazine, December; EJN)
2. *n.* A runner who gets between the ball and the fielder.

screw arm   *n.* The left arm. Left-handed pitchers are occasionally called screw armers.

screwball/screw-ball/screw ball   **1.** *n.* A pitched ball that curves in toward the batter (i.e., toward a right-handed batter when thrown by a right-handed pitcher) rather than away from the batter as most curves do. It is sometimes termed a "reverse-curve," "fadeaway," or scroogie.

The pitch was first made famous by Christy Mathewson—who called it the "fadeaway"—and later revived by Carl Hubbell as the screwball. Hubbell developed three speeds for the pitch.

This exchange occurs in Frank Graham's *McGraw of the Giants:*

"They tell me the reason Cobb got rid of him [Hubbell] is that he thinks the boy will throw his arm out with his screw ball."

McGraw snorted.

"That's a joke," he said. "Screw ball! When Matty was pitching it, they called it a fadeaway—and it never hurt his arm."

Because it is difficult to master, it is not a popular pitch.

1ST   1928. Edward J. Nichols found this term in print and associated with Hubbell as early as October 7, 1928, in the *New York Times.* This was the same year that Hubbell began his long career with the New York Giants (1928–1943). **ETY** George Vecsey interviewed Carl Hubbell and wrote an article on him in the July 9, 1984, *New York Times.* After establishing the fact that Hubbell first threw the pitch in the minors, he concluded, "If the pitch was thrown before Hubbell, it certainly had no mystique until a catcher in Oklahoma City—Hubbell says his name was Earl Walgamot—warmed him up before a game and said: 'That's the screwiest thing I ever saw.' "

2. *n.* A zany player.

3. *adj.* Eccentric; odd. "Giants try to stop screwball errors." (headline in *San Francisco Examiner,* May 16, 1974; PT)

EXT   **1.** *n.* Since the 1930s, an eccentric or nut outside, as well as inside, baseball. An early application: "The spirit of the screwball is neither national nor mortal but transcends time itself, and, like love's fragrant essence, is everywhere." (Nunnaly Johnson's introduction to Stanley Walker's *Mrs. Astor's Horse,* 1935; PT)

2. *adj.* Eccentric, zany or insane. For example, screwball comedy, humorous films featuring madcap plots, old pranks and slapstick.

3. *adj.* Jazz. Crazy, wide-open swing music. "The music of hot bands, on the other hand, is referred to as *swing* or *jive* of which in turn there are several kinds. Accepted meanings vary according to locale, and the terms overlap, but, roughly, the most-used designations, in order of their increasing hotness are *gut-bucket, screwball* and *whacky,* the last being the wildest, most unbridled kind of swing." (Benny Goodman in *The New Yorker,* April 17, 1937)

screwbeenie   *n.* SCRUBEENIE.

screwgie   *n.* SCROOGIE.

screwjack   *n/arch.* Slang for both a player who is notoriously whacky and a player who is notoriously lucky.

scribe   *n.* A sportswriter. In *Babe Ruth's Own Book of Baseball* we are told that they are not just any writers but, "the newspaper men who accompany a big league ball club on the road." **1ST**   1887. (*Base Ball Tribune,* May 23; EJN)

scrimmage   *n.* Informal intra-squad game. The term seems to have been borrowed from football and seems to be applied only at the amateur level. From a report on a high-school team: "The Whalers' first scrimmage of the season will take place at the high school field Saturday when they'll play a doubleheader against a team from Montville, Connecticut." (Steve Sheppard in the *Nantucket Inquirer and Mirror,* April 2, 1987)

scroogie   A screwball pitch. The slang term is also spelled screwgie, as Bill Lee does in his book *The Wrong Stuff:* "Without the benefit of a tape measure, my ego will not permit me to believe that there is any way Luis could hit my screwgie." Although this is the less common spelling, Charles Poe points out, "Since the root word is 'screw' and not 'Scrooge,' it seems to me that Bill Lee's spelling should be the preferred one. 'Scroogie' has a misleadingly Dickensian flavor to it." **1ST**   1953. "Mickey Mantle coined a new word to describe the pitch he hit for [a] home run— 'It was some sort of a scroogie.' [Preacher] Roe confirmed Mantle's description, 'It was a changeup screwball,' the pitcher said." (AP, October 2; from Wentworth and Flexner's *Dictionary of American Slang*)

scrub   *n.* A substitute or member of the "B" or second team. It tends to be used in a derogatory manner.

2. *n.* A term for rounders.

scrubeenie   *n.* A modern variation on scrub or substitute player, which seems a touch more affectionate than the original. "Hell, I wasn't even a regular with the Yankees, I was just a 'scrubeenie' as Phil Linz and Johnny Blanchard and the rest of us substitutes called ourselves, and these racket guys made me feel like I was a star." (Joe Pepitone, *Joe, You Coulda Made Us Proud;* CDP)

1ST 1954. No citation is given, but this term appears in a list of new words for the year 1954 in Kenneth Versand's *Polyglot's Lexicon*.

scrub nine   *n.* A team of rookies and/or substitutes.
1ST 1868. (*New York Herald,* August 11; EJN)

scuffball/scuffed ball   *n.* A ball that has been illegally roughed up—or scuffed—to give it an unnatural trajectory. Pitcher Mike Flanagan once gave this explanation of how the pitch works: "Any time I want four new pitches, I got 'em, because I can make a scuffed ball break in, out, up or down. It's the same principle as one of those flat-sided Wiffle Balls. You hold the ball with the scuffed side opposite to the direction you want it to break. It takes no talent whatsoever. You just throw it like a mediocre fastball. The scuff gives the break." (quoted by Tom Boswell in *How Life Imitates the World Series*)

   "All of this follows the Mets whining about whether Mike Scott's scuffball in the playoffs actually was a scuffball . . ."—*USA Today,* October 24, 1986, from an article on alleged illegalities still being discussed in the post-season. The Mets, who beat the Astros in the playoffs, alleged that Houston pitcher Scott had put marks in the ball which were the size of twenty-five cent pieces.

scuffer   *n.* SCUFFED BALL.

scuffgate   *n.* Controversy involving ball scuffing; surrounding, for instance, the pitching technique of the Astros' Mike Scott during the 1986 National League Championship Series against the Mets.
ETY It is one of many coined terms that play off the Watergate scandal by using the -gate suffix.
SEE *gophergate.*

seagull   *n./arch.* A scratch hit in which the bat is broken.

seams   *n.* The raised, heavy stitching of the baseball. They are used by pitchers to gain added control over the ball. For instance, a pitcher will grip the ball across the seams to help his fastball rise, while a sidearm pitcher will grasp a ball along the seams to help his fastball sink.
USE Although the two pieces of leather covering the ball are actually held together by one continuous *seam,* the stitching is almost always referred to in the plural.

season   *n.* The days from April through October when major league teams play out their regularly scheduled games.
1ST 1880. (*Brooklyn Daily Eagle,* July 22; EJN)

Season of the Rookie   1986, aka *Year of the Rookie.* Writing about it in the *Washington Post,* Tom Boswell explained, "Not since the early '50s have so many splendid kids arrived at once." (October 5, 1986)

season ticket   *n.* A seat, usually a box seat, bought by an individual or corporation for every home game. They are usually bought in groups and the seats carry a nameplate with the owner's name on it. The ticket is only good for the regular season but it usually entitles its owner to an option to buy that seat or one like it for post-season play should the home team make it to the playoffs.

Seattle Mariners   The name of the American League's Western Division Franchise in Seattle, Washington. Formed in 1977, the Mariners were the second American League expansion team to locate in Seattle (after the Pilots in 1969). The name was suggested in a newspaper contest. The team is often referred to as the "M's."

Seattle Pilots   The name of the American League expansion team established in Seattle, Washington, in 1969. It slid into quick bankruptcy and moved to Milwaukee the following year where it survives as the Brewers.

second   *n.* Second base, for short.
1ST 1862. (Chadwick Scrapbooks; EJN)

second base   **1.** *n.* The base 90 feet from first base on the opposite corner of the infield diamond from home plate; the halfway point on the trip around the bases.
1ST 1845. (Knickerbocker Rules)
2. *n.* The defensive position given to the player who normally stands to the first base side of second base.

second baseman   *n.* One of two defensive infield players who cover second base (the other being the shortstop). As seen from the plate, the second baseman is normally positioned to the right of the shortstop and to the left of the first baseman. He normally covers first base on a bunt and is likely to be involved when a ball is being relayed in from the outfield.
1ST 1880. (*New York Herald,* July 12; EJN)

second division   *n.* Originally the last four teams in an eight-team league, or, later, the last five in a 10-team league. However, since 1969, with two divisions in each league, it is used less commonly to refer to the lower four teams.
1ST   1907. (*LaJoie's Official Base Ball Guide;* EJN)

second guess   *v.* To criticize the players or manager either generally or in regard to specific decisions on plays.

second guesser   *n.* One who is habitually criticizing the players and their manager for specific actions.
1ST   1937. (*The Sporting News Record Book;* EJN)

second sacker   *n.* SECOND BASEMAN.
1ST   1911. (*Spalding's Official Base Ball Guide;* EJN)

second season   *n.* Term that was applied, laughingly some said, to the last two months of the 1981 season, which was bifurcated by a 50-day players' strike. It was a 52-game season that began on August 10.

second station   *n.* SECOND BASE.

second story drive   *n.* A long, high drive.

second-string   *n. & adj.* Substitute or relating to being a substitute.
1ST   1912. (*New York Tribune,* September 16; EJN)
ETY   Borrowed from the realm of the bow and arrow. In his *Phrase and Word Origins,* Alfred H. Holt discusses this term under the entry for "two strings to his bow." Holt writes: "The Elizabethans were very fond of this old archery figure for having something in reserve in case of accident. It is not often heard today, but its two children, first-string and second-string, are well known on every athletic field, though almost nobody thinks to pay homage to their sturdy old father."

seed   *n.* Line drive; a pea. It alludes to a batted or thrown balk moving with such speed that it looks small.

seeing-eye ball/seeing-eye job/seeing eye single   *n.* A batted ball that eludes fielders as if it had the power of vision. "Davey Concepcion was the next batter. He broke our hearts with a seeing-eye single up the middle that knotted the game up." (Bill Lee, in *The Wrong Stuff;* CDP)
ETY   From "Seeing Eye," the trademark used

by the trainers of dogs for the blind. The same phrase inspired the next term.
EXT   The metaphor has been adopted in other sports, including football: "Accurate was the kicking of field goal specialist Randy Wersching who was gifted with a seeing-eye foot." (*San Francisco Examiner,* November 2, 1969)

seeing-eye bat   *n.* Implement of a batter in that kind of streak when seemingly routine grounders become hits; a bat that for a period seems to able to connect with every pitched ball for a hit.
1ST   1952. "I got a seeing eye bat, one of those Murine jobs." (*San Francisco Examiner,* July 17; PT)

see the barrels   *v.* To experience a good omen.
ETY   According to the version in Joseph McBride's *High and Inside,* "'Turkey Mike' Donlin of the New York Giants arrived for a game at the Polo Grounds in the early 1900s and noted a wagon load of empty barrels going by. On that day, he got three hits but on the following day he went hitless and blamed this on the fact that he had not seen any barrels before the game. His manager, the crafty John McGraw, hired a wagon loaded with barrels to circle the grounds every day and Donlin went on a hitting spree."

seeya   *n.* A home run.
ETY   Asked about this term in a *Sporting News* article of April 1, 1972, Braves pitcher Jim Nash said, "Yep, that's what you say as it goes out of the park. Seeya!"

sell   *v.* To get a batter to go after a pitch. A pitcher may be said to be having a hard time selling his curveball.

sell out   *v.* To throw a game.
1ST   1874. (*Chicago Inter Ocean,* July 4; EJN)

semi-pro/semi-professional   *n./adj.* The status of a player who is paid to play the game, but who must depend on another occupation to make a living. Sometimes the fee given to such a player is a mere token of $10 or $20.
1ST   1908. (*Spalding's Official Base Ball Guide;* EJN)

semi-swing   *n.* Less than a full cut at the ball.
Complaining about the plethora of home runs hit early in the 1987 season, Angel skipper Gene Mauch commented sarcastically, "Baseball's getting ridiculous. I've never seen such

semi-, semi-, semi-swings, and the ball going out in my life." (AP dispatch in the *Iowa City Press-Citizen,* May 29, 1987)

send   *v.* To order a runner to try to advance to the next base.

send to the rubber   *v.* To put a relief pitcher into the game.

send to the showers   *v.* To replace a pitcher who presumably heads for the clubhouse and a hot shower.

senior circuit   *n.* Traditional nickname for the National League because it is 25 years older than the American League, which is sometimes referred to the junior circuit.

series   *n.* A set of contests between two teams. The term can refer to a regular group of games on the schedule—a three-game series in Cleveland, for example—a post-season play-off or the World Series itself.
1ST   1866. (*New York Herald,* September 7; EJN)

Series, the   Short for the World Series.

Series burnout   1980s term for the problems—injuries, contract disputes, quarrels, etc.—that can accrue to a team after it has been in the World Series.
   "Red Sox Still Smoking From Series Burnout." (Washington *Post* headline, March 24, 1987)

serve/serve it up/serve the cocktail   *v.* To pitch.
USE   Clearly implied is the idea that the pitcher presents the ball to a batter in the way that a waiter serves a meal or a drink. "Dixon Serves 3 Homers Before Orioles Fly Home." (*Washington Post,* April 5, 1987)
1ST   1913 (serve). *Spalding's Official Base Ball Guide;* EJN)
ETY   Edward J. Nichols has identified this as a term borrowed from tennis.

set   **1.** *n.* The motionless position taken by a pitcher before beginning his delivery. A pitcher who holds his arms high above his head is said to have a "high set."
2. *adj.* Established or fixed in place. "Our infield is pretty much set, it's just a matter of who's going to play . . ."—Reds manager Pete Rose on the uncertainty of his lineup. (*USA Today,* January 1, 1987)

set down/set 'em down   *v.* To retire a batter or batters, as in a pitcher "setting down the top of the order."
1ST   1912. (*New York Tribune,* October 17; EJN)

set down in order   *v.* RETIRE IN ORDER.

set himself   *v.* To get in position to throw the ball after fielding it.

set one down   *v.* To retire a single batter.

set pitching position/set position   *n.* The position taken by the pitcher attempting to keep a runner on base. It is a pause in the delivery when the pitcher decides whether to deliver the ball to the plate or to the base occupied by the runner he is trying to hold. The pitcher's pivot foot must be on the rubber in the set position and he must come to a complete stop lest he be charged with a balk.

set tag   *v.* Maneuver in which a man covering a base holds his glove with the ball in it on the ground in front of the bag and waits for the runner to slide into it for an out.

set the table   **1.** *v.* To get on base to start an inning offensively.
SEE   *table setter.*
2. *v.* To put the tying or winning run in scoring position. "The O's have the table set . . ."—Jon Miller during an Orioles vs. Blue Jays game, June 6, 1987.

settle down   *v.* For a pitcher to regain control after several bad pitches.

set up   **1.** *v.* To get to a point in a game at which a short reliever can come in.
2. *v.* To lead a batter into thinking that there is a pattern to the pitching he is getting. This is used to rig—or set up—the batter for a unexpected pitch. "If you are the man with the ball, you are trying to 'set up' the man with the bat, meaning you set up his expectations or thinking and then try to take advantage of any preconceptions he has." (Tom Seaver in the *New York Times,* May 7, 1986)

set up the double-play   *v.* To intentionally walk a batter with first base open and a man on second and/or third. Jim Murray once observed, "Overlooked is the fact that this also sets up the three-run homer."

seven-inning   pitcher/seventh   inning pitcher   *n.* A starting pitcher who regularly

Seventh-inning stretch. President Taft at the ballpark throwing out the first ball. Legend says he inadvertently created the seventh-inning stretch. *National Baseball Library, Cooperstown, N.Y.*

requires relief help after about seven innings of work.

seven o'clock hitter *n.* Same as SIX O'CLOCK HITTER, only one hour later.

seventh-inning stretch *n.* A time-honored baseball custom in which the fans ritualistically stand and stretch before their team comes to bat in the seventh inning. This is done not only to relieve muscles that have begun to stiffen, but also to bring luck to one's team (perhaps from the association of the number 7 with good luck).

The simple ritual has different meanings to different people. Charles Einstein describes his experience in an April 21, 1985, article in the *New York Times:* "My own initial contact with it came in the seventh inning of the first game I ever saw, as a 6-year-old taken to Fenway Park in Boston by my father. 'Did you know I was a magician?' he said. 'Stand up.' I stood up. So did all the other spectators, to the farthest cranny of the bleachers. Two minutes later, his

voice even softer than before, my father said 'Sit down.' Everybody sat."

Einstein added that his grandfather had done this to his father and that, a generation later, he had done it to his own son.

ETY/1ST 1920. The origin of the custom is probably lost in the earliest days of the game. Baseball historian Dan Daniel is quoted in Zander Hollander's *Baseball Lingo* on its origin: "It probably originated as an expression of fatigue and tedium, which seems to explain why the stretch comes late in the game instead of at the halfway point."

The earliest reference that has surfaced appears in an 1869 letter from Harry Wright of the Cincinnati Red Stockings to a friend: "The spectators all arise between halves of the seventh inning, extend their legs and arms and sometimes walk about. In so doing they enjoy the relief afforded by relaxation from a long posture upon hard benches."

The most popular story of its origin is much more colorful. In this version, it was created in 1910 when President William Howard Taft was on a visit to Pittsburgh. According to this story, Taft went to a baseball game and stood up to stretch during the seventh inning. The crowd, thinking the Chief Executive was about to leave, stood up out of respect for the office.

Another story has been published a number of times. This incident occurred in 1882 at Manhattan College in New York City during a game between the college and a semi-pro club called the New York Metropolitans. According to a Manhattan College press release on file at the National Baseball Library in Cooperstown, the inventor of the ritual was Brother Jasper, the school's first Moderator of Athletics and source of the Manhattan "Jaspers" nickname. Quoting now from the college's news release:

Whenever there was a home game, the entire student body marched to the field and stayed in a section of the stands. Brother Jasper, since he was both the coach and the Prefect of Discipline had to watch both the players on the field and the students in the stands. Before each game, he sharply admonished the students not to leave their seats or move about until the game was over and they were ready to return to the college for the evening meal. Then, the good Brother went down to the bench to direct the play of the team . . .

Then, on a hot sticky day in the spring of 1882, Manhattan was playing the Metropolitans . . . The game, it turned out was a long, drawn-out affair.

As the game passed the mid-way mark, Brother Jasper noticed the youngsters in the stands were getting restless and unruly. So as the team came to bat in the seventh inning, he went over to the stand and told his charges to stand, stretch and move about for a minute or two. This eased the tension and unrest, and so Brother Jasper repeated it in the next few games . . . Soon the student body made it a practice "to give it the old seventh inning stretch." Since Manhattan played many of its games in the old Polo Grounds, the seventh inning stretch passed along to the Giant fans and eventually throughout the world of baseball, the unintentional invention of Brother Jasper.

Despite the claims of this story, the term itself may not have come along until much later, Edward J. Nichols traces it back no further than 1920 (*New York Times*, October 10).

SF Common scorecard and boxscore abbreviation for sacrifice fly.

SH Common scorecard and box score abbreviation for sacrifice hit.

shackle *v.* To pitch effectively; to handcuff—or shackle—the batters.

shade *v.* To be defensively positioned slightly—or a shade—toward the side where the batter is expected to hit the ball.

shade in the hole *v.* Instruction to a shortstop to play nearer the third base line or to the second baseman to play closer to the first base line.

shadow/shadow the bag *v.* To remain close to a base for defensive reasons. Also, to remain close to the runner on base.

shadow ball *n.* A crowd-pleasing stunt in which a team plays without the benefit of a ball. It calls for a lot of action, including brilliant leaping catches. Connie Johnson told a reporter from the *Baltimore Sun* that when Satchel Paige played for the Negro league Indianapolis Clowns in 1939 he threw the ball so fast that it seemed like he was playing shadow ball. Johnson recalled saying to himself, "They're not supposed to play 'shadow ball' until the fourth inning. Was Satch playing 'shadow ball' already." (*Sun*, June 27, 1982)

shag/shag flies *v.* To chase and catch fly balls as a part of batting practice. To retrieve foul balls. "Dipsy Ruggles, our first baseman, wore sneakers instead of cleats and was able to shag foul balls over the ledge with the grace of a mountain sheep, but then he would fall down running bases." (John Gould in the *Christian Science Monitor*, April 26, 1985)
1ST 1912. "Gradually, however, I became interested in it. and before long, I was allowed to stand behind the catcher when the Factoryville team was playing, and 'shag' foul balls, or carry the bats or the water." (C. H. Claudy, *The Battle of Baseball;* DS)
ETY This term appears to have begun as "shack," which was a variation on "shake" (as in, to "shake it"), which became shag.
EXT To chase and retrieve, such as shagging golf or tennis balls.

shake off/shake off a sign *v.* For a pitcher to refuse to deliver the type of pitch called for by the catcher; to veto a pitch. So-called because the pitcher commonly shakes his head from side to side to clearly indicate that he will not throw the pitch called for and wants a new signal. Some pitchers shake off a sign with another gesture, such as a move of the glove rather than the head.

1ST 1932. (*Baseball* magazine, October; EJN)

shake the jinx *v.* To win a game after several defeats.

shaky start *n.* A bad beginning for a pitcher.

shallow *adj.* Referring to that portion of the outfield closest to the infield. The opposite of deep.

sharpen one's spikes *v.* To strongly imply that one is preparing to injure another player with the aid of spikes. It can also be defined in the same manner as Hugh Fullerton did in 1912; "The pretense of a player to sharpen the triangular toe and heel plates he wears on his shoes, is to threat to 'cut his way around,' or spike certain antagonists if they attempt to stop or touch him. Chiefly a form of braggadocio, and seldom carried into effect."

sharpshooter **1.** *n.* An effective place hitter; a batter who can put the ball where he wants it to go.

1ST 1912. (*New York Tribune*, September 12, EJN)

2. *n.* A pitcher with good control.

shave *v.* To pitch high and inside; to brush a batter back as if the ball was being used to shave the batter's face. ". . . Tornay walked several steps towards the mound and verbally challenged the statuesque Oakland righthander when he was treated to a 'shave' in the ninth inning." (*San Francisco News*, July 31, 1953; PT)

shave the corners *v.* To pitch to the edges of the strike zone.

she *n.* An injured player, especially one who may be favoring himself.

USE Derogatory remark that somehow equates being or playing injured with femininity.

Shea Stadium Home grounds of the New York Mets since 1964. It is located in Flushing Meadows, Queens. It is named for attorney

Shea Stadium. An aerial view of the New York Mets' home ballpark in Flushing Meadows, Queens. *Courtesy of the New York Mets*

William Shea who headed the special committee that sought to and succeeded in bringing National League baseball back to New York after the city's loss of the Dodgers and Giants in 1958.

sheeny mike   *n./arch.* See Texas leaguer.
USE Sheeny is a highly derogatory term for a Jew. Whether or not, or how, this fits into the etymology of the term is not as important as the fact that it is regarded as highly offensive. Given this, however, one possible etymological link is that sheeny implies, according to Wentworth and Flexner in their *Dictionary of American Slang,* a miser. The hit could be aptly described as miserly. A "cheap" hit.
1ST   1937. (New York *Daily News,* January 31; EJN)

shell/shell off the hill   *v.* To bat so well and so hard that the pitcher must be removed, as if he had been attacked—or shelled—by a barrage of hard-hit baseballs (also known as rockets). "Gooden Rebounds In Scoreless Stint—Makes Up For Shelling"—(headline in the *New York Times,* March 14, 1987).

shellack   *v.* To defeat badly.

shelve   *v.* To take a player out of action; for instance, putting a player on the disabled list. "White Sox Shelve Allen." (*Washington Post* headline, April 22, 1987)

shepherd   *n./arch.* MANAGER.

Shibe Park   Philadelphia major league ballpark from 1909 to 1970. At various times it was home for the American League Athletics and the National League Phillies. It was named for Ben Shibe, a stockholder in the Athletics, and known as Connie Mack Stadium from 1953 to 1970. It was damaged in a 1971 fire and torn down in 1976.

shift   1. *v.* To change fielding position; to move defensive players from their traditional positions in the field to compensate for a batter's proclivities and/or to be in a better position for a double play. Fielders generally shift left for left-handed batters (because they tend to hit in that direction) and vice-versa.
   Occasionally, a radical shift is named for the player the shift is created to defend against, such as the *Williams shift,* employed to stop Ted Williams. A recent example shows up in a *Boston Globe* headline of July 30, 1988, "The Boggs Shift works." In this case the Milwaukee Brew-

ers brought center fielder Robin Yount into the infield to defend against Wade Boggs (then hitting .359) with two runners on base. In this particular instance Boggs struck out.
2. *n.* The act of moving players for defensive reasons, often phrased as "the shift is on."
3. *v.* For the catcher to move in front of the path of the pitched ball so that he will be able to maintain his balance for catching and throwing. In his book *On the Receiving End: The Catcher's Guidebook* Bob Bennett says: "In shifting, the basic idea is to step into the path of the ball. If the ball is thrown to the left, the step should be to the left with the left foot. If the ball is to the right, a step to the right should be taken with the right foot."

shillelagh/shillalah   *n.* The bat as an instrument of power.
1ST   1937 (*Philadelphia Record,* October 11; EJN)
ETY   From the irish fighting club or cudgel.

shinburger   1. *n.* A bruise that is commonly inflicted by a bad hop.
2. *n.* A shot through the pitcher's box that ricochets off his shins.

shine ball   *n.* A ball that the pitcher renders especially smooth by rubbing it hard on his glove or clothing or doctoring it with a foreign substance such as talcum powder. Such shining or polishing, which helps the ball curve when thrown, has been illegal since 1920. Eddie Cicotte is said to have developed the shine ball in 1915 when he discovered that the ball did funny things after he rubbed it to a shine on his uniform.
1st   1917. (*New York Times,* October 6; EJN)
ETY   Gerald Secor Couzens reports in his *Baseball Album:* "probably invented by Dave Darforth in 1915 while pitching for Louisville in the American Association. Oil was used on the field to control the dust problem, and the innovative Danforth discovered that by rubbing the oil-and-dirt-covered ball on his trouser leg the ball became smooth and shiny and hopped when he pitched it."

shin guard   *n.* Piece of protective equipment worn by catchers, home plate umpires and some batters to prevent injury from foul tips and pitches in the dirt. The modern version is a piece of molded plastic, which is strapped to the leg.
1ST   1908. (*Spalding's Base Ball Record;* EJN)

Shin guards. New York Giants catcher Roger Bresnahan. *National Baseball Library, Cooperstown, N.Y.*

ETY   Invented and first donned by New York Giants catcher Roger Bresnahan in 1907.

shin-skimmer   *n.* A hard-hit ground ball.
1ST   1908. (*New York Evening Journal,* August 21; EJN)

SHO   Common scorecard and boxscore abbreviation for shutout.

shoemaker   *n./arch.* A player who is awkward, but not necessarily ineffective, at his position.
ETY   This term has drawn a number of comments along the lines of this one, which appeared in Herbert Simons' 1943 article on baseballeese: "we've always considered that usage a libel against our many friends of the bootmaking profession, who are some of the most polished artisans we know." One can only suggest that the baseball usage might derive from the image of a shoemaker bent over at his workbench. Edward J. Nichols traces it to a player who makes errors and sometimes "boots" the ball.
1ST   1907. (*New York Evening Journal,* May 2; EJN)

shoestring catch   *n.* A catch made by a running fielder just before the ball hits the ground.

Shoestring catch. A spectacular play. *American Softball Association*

It is caught in the vicinity of the player's feet—or shoestrings—and can be quite spectacular to witness. "He took the ball off his shoe-strings and without apparently slackening his pace hurled the sphere on a line to third for an easy double killing." (*National Police Gazette,* January 14, 1928; PT)
1ST   1912. (*New York Tribune,* October 12; EJN)
EXT   A similar catch in other games, such as football.

shoot out   *v.* To rule a player out by pointing to him as if he were being shot with a revolver. This unorthodox signal became the trademark of umpire Ron Luciano who came upon it accidentally during the 1972 season.

   As Luciano points out in his autobiography *The Umpire Strikes Back,* he was having a hard time calling Amos Otis safe in close plays during his first years with the Kansas City Royals. At the start of the 1972 season he consciously worked on calling him safe, but soon found he had overdone it again and was now having a hard time calling him out. Finally, Otis hit into a play in which he was out by a full 15 feet and Luciano was so pleased that he pointed his index finger at him and cocked his thumb. The rest of the Royals began yelling "Shoot him, shoot him!" Luciano realized what he had done and played it to its conclusion. He pretended to shoot him and then as he brought his hand back he blew imaginary smoke away from his index finger and pretended to put his hand in a holster.

short 1. *n.* Short for SHORTSTOP.
1ST 1858. (*Brooklyn Daily Times,* June 18; EJN)
2. *adj.* Relatively close to the plate, such as an infielder playing close—or short—in anticipation of a bunt.

short-arm *adj.* Relating to a throw with the arm close to the body as opposed to a full throw with the arm extended. Short-arm throws are made for short distances, such as between infielders.

shortened game *n.* Term that is given specific meaning in the *Official Baseball Rules;* a game in which the home team is winning and does not need to bat for all or a fraction of its half of the ninth inning. It also refers to any game called by the umpire for whatever reason. If a game is called before it becomes a regulation game, it is declared "No Game" and not considered a shortened game.

shorten up *v.* To move one's hands up on the bat handle in order to get more control on the swing. This is often done when, with two strikes against him, the batter is at a disadvantage.

shortfield/short field *n.* The area between second and third where the shortstop normally plays.
1ST 1854. (Knickerbocker Rules; EJN)

short fielder 1. *n.obs.* See shortstop.
2. *n.* The tenth player in slow-pitch softball. The short fielder is usually positioned in the shallow portion of the outfield.

short fuse *n.* Term for the temperament of an umpire quick to toss a player or manager out of a game.
ETY From the image of an explosive equipped with a fuse that makes it blow up quickly. It is a play linking the human blow-up (temper) with the blow-up of dynamite and other explosives.

short hop 1. *v.* To snatch the ball just as it bounces off the ground. "He short hops it to first for the out."
2. *n.* A batted or thrown ball that hits the ground and is caught low before it can take a sharp, unpredictable bounce.
3. *n.* A ball that seems to die on the first bounce.

short leg *n./arch.* Derogatory term for a player who lets his teammates go after balls that he himself should get.
1ST 1937. (New York *Daily News,* February 14; EJN)

short man 1. SHORT RELIEVER.
2. The infielder who backs up the cut-off man in a relay play. He is there in case of an overthrow.

short park *n.* A stadium with an notably short outfield fence. "Brewers to Cancel Short-Park Solons." (headline in the *San Francisco Chronicle* for August 22, 1975) The article points out that the Milwaukee Brewers had cancelled their agreement with the minor league Sacramento Solons because the short left-field fence at the team's stadium "had impeded the development of many promising young players."

short porch *n.* A right- or left-field wall, barrier or upper deck that is unusually near home plate; a friendly target to a batter.

Term derives from the design of older ballparks, which often featured overhanging roofs that made outfield spectators look like they were sitting on a porch.

short relief *n.* A period of relief pitching, usually two innings or less.

short reliever *n.* A relief pitcher who comes in for a short period of time late in the game, traditionally for two or fewer innings. Because of the brevity of the assignment, a short reliever may appear in several games in a row. Short relievers are specialists who occasionally are called in to face just a few batters in one inning.

short score *n.* Game results that show only the total runs, hits and errors for each team, as opposed to the box score or inning-by-inning tabulation.

shortstop *n.* Infield position that is normally to the left of second base as viewed from home. The shortstop and the second baseman together cover second base. A main element of the shortstop's job is to create double plays. By most accounts, it is the most physically demanding position in the field

1ST 1860. (*Beadle's Dime Base Ball Player;* EJN)

ETY The position was originally that of short fielder, at the time of the Knickerbocker Rules (1854), but gave way to shortstop in the 1860s. It is clearly a blend of short + stop, probably created to better describe the defensive function of the job performed in the short field.

short windup *n.* The abbreviated arm movement a pitcher uses when there is a runner or runners on base. It is condensed to give the runner or runners less time in which to steal.

shot **1.** *n.* An especially hard-hit ball, usually a liner.

1ST 1880. (*New York Herald,* August 20; EJN)

2. *n.* A strong throw.

1ST 1910. (*Baseball* magazine, April; EJN)

shotgun/shotgun arm *n.* A powerful throwing arm.

1ST 1937. (New York *Daily News,* January 17; EJN)

"Shot Heard 'Round the World" The famous home run hit by New York Giant Bobby Thomson on October 3, 1951, to win the pennant in the last inning of the last game of the playoffs against the Brooklyn Dodgers. The incident has also been referred to as the *Miracle at Coogan's Bluff.*

ETY From a line by Ralph Waldo Emerson which he wrote as part of his *Hymn Sung at the Completion of the Concord Monument.* He used it to describe the beginning of the American Revolution:

Here once the embattled farmers stood
And fired the shot heard round the
world.

shove along *n./arch.* Act of stealing a base, as in, he did the shove along.

1ST 1907. (*New York Evening Journal,* May 2; EJN)

shovel *v.* To toss the ball underhanded for a short distance. The motion suggests throwing dirt with a shovel, and it is what the shortstop often does when he throws the ball to the second baseman.

shovel throw *n.* Name for a short, underhanded toss. "The pitcher threw his glove hand up, and took it on the wrist, collapsing in pain; as the ball caromed over to Chambers at first,

who made a backhanded pickup and shovel throw to Wheelock, covering, to nab Samba by a wish." (Michael Schiffer in *Ballpark)*

show, the *n.* The MAJOR LEAGUES.

showboat/show-boat **1.** *v.* To show off.

2. *n.* Player who is clearly playing to the crowd with a fancy style; an exhibitionist. Defined by Fresco Thompson in *Every Diamond Doesn't Sparkle* as, "A player who never catches a ball with two hands that he can catch with one."

In his *Strikeout Story* Bob Feller says, "The term 'showboat' is synonymous with exhibitionism in baseball." (CDP)

1ST 1942. "There will be an all-star team of 'showboats' in the Pacific Coast League. The 'Fancy Dans' are becoming more numerous right along." (*San Francisco News,* July 20, 1942; PT)

ETY An article on "Peanuts" Nyasses in the September 19, 1942, issue of *Liberty* suggests that this well-known black player and baseball clown helped popularize and may have begun this term in the context of baseball. The article explains that Nyasses dubbed himself "the Showboat King of Baseball."

shower *v.* To remove from the game; to send to the showers; to retire to the showers. "Now they'll shower him." (Al Michaels on a pitcher about to removed, ABC, October 12, 1986)

In his 1957 book *How to Watch a Baseball Game,* Fred Schwed, Jr., relates a story, which had been told to him by Charles Einstein, that underscores the extent to which this meaning of shower has become unique to America. "It seems that a number of years ago another reporter took Fred Perry of England, then the best tennis player in the world, to his first American baseball game. Mr. Perry was suspicious of the whole affair, and when in the second inning the losing pitcher was shelled off the mound, and started his lugubrious trudge over second base and the outfield, Perry asked, 'Where is he going?' The reporter said, 'To the showers.' 'It's a hot day,' said Perry, 'I imagine he will feel famously when he comes back.'"

EXT To remove from any activity. Here is an early example alluding to World War I: "No doubt Pershing and Foch has got the game sewed up tight or they would never take a chance and send me to the showers whilst they was more innin's to play." (H. C. Witwer, *A Smile a Minute,* 1919; DS)

Show-Me Series   The 1985 World Series, which pitted the *Kansas City Royals* against the *St. Louis Cardinals*—two teams from Missouri, the Show-Me State. It was also known as the I-70 Series because Kansas city and St. Louis are linked by Interstate 70.

show spikes   *v.* To slide into a base with one spiked foot held high enough to intimidate the man covering.
1ST   1928. (*New York Times*, October 6; EJN)

show up   *v.* To humiliate an opponent; for instance, to steal a base when you are leading by 12 runs. Describing a 1986 fight between the Reds and Giants, Ira Berkow wrote in the *New York Times*, "the fight started after Vince Coleman was first brushed back with a pitch and then hit with a pitch on the foot in the seventh inning. It was apparently intentional. Coleman had stolen second and third in the fifth inning, with the score 10–2, and the Giants felt, according to Roger Craig, that Coleman was trying to 'show up' the Giants—one of the cotton-headed cliches that abound in baseball." (NYT, August 14, 1986)

show your colors   *v.* To display courage.

shut off   *v.* To defeat. To allow the opposing team few or no runs. "Astros Shut Off Braves"—headline in the *Buffalo News*, September 28, 1986.

shut out   *v.* To prevent one's opponents from scoring. It is normally used to describe a pitcher who deprives the other team of scoring any runs.
ETY   A borrowing from horse racing where it has long referred to a bettor who arrives at the window too late to wager a bet and is "shut out."

shutout   **1.** *n.* A game in which the losing team does not score. It is a particular achievement that is credited to the winning pitcher who will begin or add to his season and lifetime shutout total. Shutouts are often described by the number of hits made by the losers, such as a two-hit shutout. In his 21-year career, Washington Senator pitcher Walter Johnson pitched 110 shutouts.
1ST   1889. (*Trenton Times*, July 18; EJN)
2. *v.* To prevent the opposition from scoring.
1ST   1881. (*New York Herald*, July 17; EJN)
3. *adj.* Describing a period in which there are no runs, such as "three innings of shutout relief."

EXT   To prevent scoring in other endeavors, from football to politics.

shut the door   *v.* To pitch exceptionally well in either stopping or preventing a rally. " 'You've got to tip your hat to him,' Nipper said to Saberhagen. 'He threw an outstanding game. He shut the door.' " (*USA Today*, April 17, 1986).

Shuttle Series   The 1986 World Series between the Boston Red Sox and the New York Mets, representing two cities linked by commuter air shuttle routes. Both shuttle operators, Eastern and Pan American, attempted to capitalize on the nickname.

side   *n.* One of the two teams in a game. When a half inning is over, it is common to say that the side has been retired.
1ST   1864. (*Brooklyn Daily Eagle*, September 9; EJN)

sidearm   *adj.* Delivered with the arm at the side of the body; neither overhand nor underhand, but rather off the hip.
1ST   1908. (*Baseball* magazine, June; EJN)

sidearmer/sidewheeler/sidewheel pitcher/ sidewinder   *n.* A pitcher who habitually throws from the sidearm position.
1ST   1910 (sidewheel pitcher). (*Baseball* magazine, December; EJN)

sideline   *v.* To be kept out of a game and literally to be kept outside the foul lines. Players are commonly sidelined with injuries.

side out   *n.* When three men have been retired.

sieve infield   *n.* Poor defensive infield; one with a lot of holes.

sign   **1.** *n.* A secret signal, such as those given by catchers and coaches. Catchers employ them constantly in calling for a specific pitch from the pitcher. Coaches use them to call for offensive plays such as bunts, steals etc. "Giving, getting and carrying out signs win close games. Signs are given by word of mouth and movement." (Joe Cronin, quoted in the July 22, 1940, *San Francisco News*; PT)
1ST   1899. (*Frank Merriwell's Double Shot;* EJN)
2. *v.* To send a signal. "I wanted to give him a spitter but Schalk signs me for the fast one and I give it to him." (Ring Lardner, *You Know Me Al*, 1916)
3. *v.* To put one's signature on a contract.
1ST   1887. (*Base Ball Tribune*, May 23; EJN)

signal   1. *n.* A sign. There are all sorts of signals ranging from the flashing of the catcher's fingers to the tip of a coach's hat to vocal signals.
1ST 1905. (*Sporting Life,* September 2; EJN)
2. *v.* To make a sign or signal.

sign a pass/sign a ticket   *v.* To issue a base on balls.
1ST 1912. (sign a pass). (*New York Tribune,* September 6; EJN)

signing bonus   *n.* An added amount of money given to a player for agreeing to sign a contract with a team.
SEE *bonus.*

sign stealing   *n.* A tactic by which a team spots and deciphers its opponent's signals. For this reason, teams work to keep them as cryptic and confusing as possible. With a runner at second base, the pitcher and catcher usually change signs because the catcher's signs to the pitcher are signs clearly visible to the batting team.
   Some have attached great significance to the practice. "Of all the skills wrapped up in the complex game of big-league baseball, none is practiced with more ingenuity and less publicity than the fine art of diamond larceny. From the days of the old Orioles to Durocher's Giants, sign-stealers have been surreptitiously deciding crucial ball games and winning world championships." (Martin Abramson, *The American Weekly,* June 5, 1955; PT)
   There are many stories that underscore how extensive this practice is. In *The Old Ball Game,* Tristram Potter Coffin insists:
   "The most famous is the one usually told about Charlie Dressen at a now half-forgotten All-Star game. Supposedly the All-Stars were together before the game attempting to come up with a series of signals for the day. Dressen, who was a noted sign-stealer, is [thought] to have said. 'Forget it, I'll give each of you the ones used on your own team.' "
   Coffin points out that there is a moral code at work here. It is fair for a coach, manager or other uniformed participant to steal signs, but not for a member of the staff not in uniform—a "civilian"—to do it.

simulated play-by-play   *n.* A broadcast that apes the live action of a real game. It can occur after the game, be created from telegraph or teletype reporting of a game in progress, or, as

was common during the 1981 baseball strike, be of an imaginary or fantasy game. The process is also used to recreate games from the past.

single   1. *n.* A hit that gets the batter safely to first base; a one-base hit.
1ST 1858. (Chadwick Scrapbooks; EJN)
2. *v.* To make a single.
ETY It is used in cricket, where it originated.

single in a run   *v.* To score a base runner by hitting in a single.

singles hitter   *n.* Player who seldom hits a ball for extra bases.

singleton   *n.* A lone run scored in any inning.

sinker/sinkerball   1. *n.* A pitched ball that drops sharply as it nears the plate; a sinking ball. It is a fast ball that drops because it is delivered with a downward movement and an inward roll of the wrist. Wiley Moore, Yankee relief pitcher for the 1927 championship team, was one of the first sinkerball pitchers.
2. *n.* A batted ball that drops sharply.
1ST 1928. "A sinker—a fly ball that has a back spin which causes it to sink to the ground quickly." (*Babe Ruth's Own Book of Baseball;* DS)

sinkerballer   *n.* Pitcher who is adept at throwing the sinker. Because this pitch drops so sharply, it is nearly impossible to hit it in the air. Sinkerball pitchers are notorious for inducing batters to hit ground balls. "After Floyd Rayford's one-out single, sinkerballer Tommy John got exactly what he wanted." (Gannett Westchester newspapers, July 8, 1986)

sinking fastball   *n.* Pitch that behaves like a sinker but has the velocity of a fastball, often described in terms of its speed, such as "an 89-mph sinking fastball." (*Washington Post,* June 11, 1986)

sinking liner   *n.* A line drive that drops suddenly in mid-flight.

sit on   *v.* To be able to anticipate or wait for a specific pitch.

sitting duck   *n.* A runner who is in a position to be put out by a wide margin by a defensive player. A base runner who attempts to steal on a pitch out is usually a sitting duck.
ETY From the long-established simile used to express an easy shot, "as easy as hitting a sitting duck."

sitting in the catbird seat   In an advantageous position. Fully explained under catbird seat.

6–4–3   *adj*. Describing a double play in which the ball goes from the shortstop (6) to the second baseman (4) to the first baseman (3). It is the most common double play combination.

600 Home Run Club   Imaginary and exclusive club with only three members: Babe Ruth, Hank Aaron and Willie Mays, the only ball players to have hit 600 or more home runs.

six o'clock hitter   *n*. Name for a player who hits well in batting practice, but not during the game that follows batting practice.
ETY   From the fact that batting practice is likely to be in full swing at 6:00 p.m. for a night game beginning at 7:00 or 7:30. When day games were the norm, the six o'clock hitter was likely to be called a two o'clock hitter.

size/size up/size up the batter   *v*. To spot a player's strengths and weaknesses.

sizzle   *v*. To be very hot on the mound, at the plate or as a team. "Leonard's bat still sizzling as Giants topple Cubs 6–2." (*USA Today* headline, April 29, 1987) "Baseball's Boston Red Sox are sizzling like no other Red Sox team has sizzled since '46." (*USA Today*, June 6, 1986)

sizzler   **1.** *n*. A hard, very fast pitch.
1ST   1911. (*Baseball* magazine, October; EJN)
2. *n*. A hard, searing ground ball.
1ST   1908. (*New York Evening Journal*, May 14; EJN)

sked   *n*. Short for printed regular season schedule. Term is used by collectors of baseball cards and other baseball novelties and commonly shows up, for instance, in the magazine *Sports Collectors Digest*.

skillet   *n*. A fielder's glove, especially an unwieldy one or one on the hand of a fielder who doesn't catch very well.

skimmer   *n*. A batted ball that glides across the ground; one that skims the grass.
1ST   1868. "An over-throw of Hatfield allowed Wilkins to seize second; he then stole to third, and ran in on Fisler's 'skimmer' to left field . . ." (Chadwick Scrapbooks; DS)

skin/skin of the infield   *n*. The dirt portion of the infield, which is intentionally kept free of grass or artificial turf.

skin diamond   *n*. An infield devoid of grass.

skip the dew   *v*. To run exceptionally well.
1ST   1937. (New York *Daily News*, February 14; EJN)

skipper   **1.** *n*. Manager, sometimes shortened to "skip."
ETY   From the Dutch *schipper*, which is pronounced skipper; it has a long history as a form of address for the captain or master of a ship.
2. *n*. Grounder.
1ST   1895. "Once more the Riversides seemed trying to see who could make the greatest number of errors, and the way they muffed easy flies, let skippers go through them, and throw wild to bases, was painful to witness." (Herbert Bellwood, *The Rivals of Riverwood;* DS)

skip rope   *v*. To jump up quickly to avoid being hit by a low, inside pitch.

skull   **1.** *v*. To bean or hit a batter in the head with a pitched ball. "Don't skull these boys," says a character to a pitcher in *The Bingo Long Traveling All Stars and Motor Kings*. "You'll kill one of them and we'll never get out of here." (CDP)
2. *n*. A dumb play or an error, usually "to pull a skull."

skuller   *n*. A BATTING HELMET.

skull practice/skull session   *n*. A club meeting where the manager, coaches and players "put their heads together" too discuss strategy before a game.
1ST   1917. (*New York Times*, October 6; EJN)

skunk   **1.** *v*. To SHUT OUT.
2. *n*. Zero. "We beat them three to skunk." (Herbert Simons, "Do You Speak the Language?" *Baseball* magazine, January 1943)
3. *n./arch*. An inning in which a team does not score.
ETY   Term applies in a number of sports and games. It plays an important role in the card game of cribbage, signifying loss by a large margin.

sky/sky a ball/sky one/sky out   *v*. To hit a very high fly ball. "Evans skies to centerfield." (Boston Red Sox broadcast, August 2, 1986)
1ST   1905. (*Montrose* [Pa.] *Independent Republican*, June 30; EJN)

skyer   *n./arch*. A towering fly ball.
1ST   1862. "Manolt was the fifth striker, and he hit a 'skyer' which fell into Abrams' hands

. . ." (Chadwick Scrapbooks: October 12, 1862, *New York Sunday Mercury;* DS)

skyscraper   *n.* A fly ball that goes straight up from the plate and is usually pursued by the catcher in the area between the foul lines and the grandstands. "Fourteen times the Bostons hit what the small boy calls skyscrapers, and fourteen times a pair of big New York hands squeezed the ball." (*New York World,* May 11, 1889; Gerald Cohen) Prior to 1900 there were a number of lesser sky- words that meant the same as skyscraper, including sky rocket, sky chaser, sky searcher and sky ball.
1ST   1866 (skyscraper). (*New York Herald,* June 27; EJN)

slab   *n.* The pitcher's RUBBER. "Rookie on Slab Tonight." (headline, *San Francisco Examiner,* May 6, 1958; PT)
USE   The term has a certain honorific aspect to it. On the eve of the tainted 1919 World Series, Chicago second baseman Eddie Collins was quoted as saying, "Cicotte and Williams are two of the greatest pitchers who ever planted a foot on the slab, and our gang can field and hit."

slab artist/slabman   *n.* Pitcher. "In recent years the 'slab artist' has been given the advantage, and the complaint grows that there is not batting enough." (A. G. Spalding in *America's National Game,* 1911; PT)
1ST   1905. "He was a wonder, and the year following, as a slab artist . . . made an excellent record." "The team developed the league's leading slabman . . ." Both quotes are in the *1905 Official Guide,* National Association of Professional Base Ball Leagues. (DS)

slam   **1.** *v.* To hit with great power.
1ST   1905. (*Sporting Life,* October 7; EJN)
2. *n.* A hard-hit ball.
1ST   1907. (*Reach Official Base Ball Guide;* EJN)
3. *n.* Short for GRAND SLAM. "Bo Jackson's 2 Homers Include Slam, 7 RBI." (headline, *Washington Post,* April 15, 1987)

slant   *n/arch.* Commonly, a curveball, but it may refer to any kind of pitch.
1ST   1902. (*Sporting Life,* July 12; EJN)

slap hit   *n.* Ball that is driven with a quick jab—or slap—of the bat rather than with a full swing. They are characteristically placed just over the heads of the infielders.

slap hitter   *n.* A batter who specialized in slap hits. "Cangelosi is basically a slap hitter,

and he tried to bunt his way on to lead off the first but popped out to McGregor." (*Washington Post,* May 13, 1986)

slapper   **1.** *n.* SLAP HITTER.
2. *n.* An infielder who takes swipes at the ball; one who uses his glove like a fly swatter.

slap tag   *n.* A put out accomplished as an infielder hits the runner with a gloved ball.

slash   *v.* To hit the ball sharply, usually to the opposite field.
1ST   1901. (*Frank Merriwell's Marvel;* EJN)

slaughter   *n.* A decisive defeat.

sleeper rabbit play   *n.* A rare bit of baseball skullduggery that is brought into play with runners on second and third. The man on second, who gets the attention of the catcher, is noticeably slow in returning to his base after the first pitch. He repeats this lazy act until the catcher is lured into throwing to second, at which time the man on second breaks for third and the man on third dashes toward home.
ETY   The play was invented by Tiger George Moriarity in the early 1900s. It would seem that this might be a reversal on the fable of the tortoise and the hare. Unlike the original story in which the rabbit sleeps, allowing the tortoise to win, the baseball play has the rabbit pretending to sleep in order to trip up the opposition.

slice   *v.* To take a late swing at the ball and hit it. A ball sliced by a right-handed batter takes off in the direction of right-field while a lefty will slice a ball that veers towards left.

The opposite of pulling. One who slices habitually is known as a slice hitter or the opposite field hitter.

slicer   *n.* Ball that veers off.

slide   **1.** *v.* To throw oneself along the ground toward a base in order to avoid being tagged out or overrunning a base. Slides are performed either feet first or, more daringly, head first. Contact with the base is made with a hand or a foot, which offers a much smaller target for the defender to tag.
2. *n.* The act of sliding.
1ST   1887. (*Spalding's Official Base Ball Guide;* EJN)

"Slide, Kelly, Slide."   Chant and motto aimed at Mike "King" Kelly, the player widely credited with turning base stealing into an art. It was also a popular song copyrighted in 1889. The phrase tends to emphasize one side of his

Slide, Kelly, Slide. King Kelly in the uniform of the Boston Nationals (c. 1887). *National Baseball Library, Cooperstown, N.Y.*

reputation. He was in fact a remarkable player who Connie Mack later compared to Ty Cobb. The handsome, well-dressed Kelly was the first player to get "important" money (he was paid $5,000 in 1887, when the Boston Nationals bought him for $10,000) and the first to inspire fan adulation—it has been said that he was the first player to be targeted by autograph seekers.

slider/slide ball   **1.** *n.* A modified curveball that is rolled—or slid—out of the hand, rather than spun hard. It has less motion than a pure curve and breaks slightly but sharply just as it is crossing the plate. In other words, it starts out like a fastball and then breaks without warning, like a curve.

It creates a strong illusion, which once caused Willie Stargell to compare hitting a slider to "trying to drink coffee with a fork." Tim McCarver was quoted in the *New York Times* describing Steve Carlton's slider (which he termed the best in baseball): "The tighter you grip the ball, the more spin you can get on it. And with his forearm strength, he could grip it tighter than anyone else. With that tight grip, his slider had a gyroscope-type downward movement that often spun it into the dirt. But the batter and to the umpire it had the illusion of a strike." (June 29, 1986)

"A pitch that is not quite so fast as a good fast ball," wrote Jim Brosnan, "nor curves so much as a good curve ball; but which is easier to throw and control than either of them."

ETY   The origin of the pitch has been obscured by time, but the first pitchers to make a name for themselves throwing the slider worked in the 1930s. They were George "the Bull" Uhle of the Detroit Tigers and George Blaeholder of the St. Louis Browns. The term has been in use since the 1930s, but before then the pitch was known by other names. Two of these were the nickel (or 5 cent) curve and the sailer.

2. A sliding injury in which a patch of skin has been scraped from the leg or thigh. "Many players suffer much from these injuries, often having the skin torn off their limbs in patches four or five inches square," said Hugh Fullerton in his 1912 "Primer."

sliding catch   *n.* Maneuver in which a fielder throws his body on the ground while going after a ball and slides under it.

sliding pad   *n.* A piece of protective equipment worn under a player's pants to prevent injuries while sliding.
1ST   1907. (*Reach Official Base Ball Guide;* EJN)

sliding pit   *n.* The dirt surrounding the bases of fields that have synthetic surfaces.

slingshot   *n.* A strong throwing arm; a shotgun.
1ST   1937. (New York *Daily News,* January 21; EJN)

slip one by   *v.* To get a strike by throwing the ball toward the edges of the strike zone. Bob Uecker's eulogy for one-time American League batting champion (1959) and former Milwaukee Brewers manager Harvey Kuenn, who died in March 1988, contained these lines: "The last couple of years Harvey lived with a 3–2 count on him, but every time they tried to slip one by him on the corner he fouled it off. To get Harvey looking they must have wanted him awful bad . . ." (*St. Petersburg Times,* March 6, 1988)

slippery elm   *n.* substance once used by pitchers to give the ball the same effect as a spitball.
1ST   1908. (*New York Evening Journal,* May 22; EJN)

slip pitch   *n.* A pitched ball that comes toward the plate with diminished velocity and a sudden drop. It is thrown like the palm ball except that the pitcher's fingers are raised above the surface of the ball.

According to research conducted by the National Baseball Library in 1973, Paul Richards brought it into prominence while managing the White Sox and Orioles in the 1950s. Richards claimed he learned it from Fred "Deacon" Jones in the Southern Association in the late 1930s. It was used successfully by Skinny Brown, Dick Hall, Harry Dorish and Jim Wilson.

slobberer   *n.* Artless, clumsy spitball pitcher. In *Me and the Spitter,* Gaylord Perry noted that slobberers not only showed "no respect for a delicate art" but also actually triggered a 1968 rule-change that ended finger-licking on the mound. (CDP)

slo pitch   *n.* SLOW PITCH.

slot   **1.** *n.* A player's position on the team, both in the field and in the batting order.
2. *v.* To be put in a position; for example, a player is slotted second in the batting order.

slow ball   *n.* A pitch delivered with the same motion as a fastball but with much less speed. It is intended to throw off the batter's timing, causing him to swing too soon.
USE   This entirely accurate term has drifted out of fashion and today's slow ball is almost universally referred to as the CHANGE UP.
1ST   1893. (*Harper's Weekly,* July 8; EJN)

slow pitch/slow pitch softball   *n.* One of the two major branches of softball. In this game there are 10 players on each team (including a short fielder) and a hit batter does not get a free base as would be the case in baseball or fast pitch softball. Both bunting and base stealing are illegal in this game. The ball must be pitched underhand at a moderate speed in an arc that peaks above the batter's head.
USE   This is usually spelled slow pitch; however, there are those who use slo-pitch, most notably the United States Slo-Pitch Softball Association.

slud   *v.* To "hit the dirt," in the parlance of the late Dizzy Dean; a past tense for the verb to slide. This may have been the most famous term in Dizzy Dean's lexicon. *Los Angeles Times* columnist Jack Smith wrote in 1975, "I have written to the big dictionary publishers suggesting that the word 'slud' be included in their next editions, and now I am receiving just what they will want to see—public support." Smith

embarked on this campaign after he used the word in a column and some readers had the gall to write in and say that he had made an error. (quoted in the *San Francisco Examiner and Chronicle,* March 23, 1975; PT)

slug   *v.* To bat hard.
1ST   1888. (*Chicago Inter Ocean,* July 6; EJN)
ETY   As early as 1756 this was a slang term for a drink of strong liquor. Not much later it also took on the meaning of a punch or heavy blow, and this passed into baseball usage.

slugfest   *n.* A game characterized by heavy and repeated hitting by one or both teams.
ETY   From the nickname for a boxing match in which offense rather than defense or strategy dominates.

slugger   **1.** *n.* A heavy hitter; one likely to hit the long ball. Sluggers tend to be placed at either the 3rd, 4th or 5th position in the batting order.
USE   The term amounts to an unofficial title and is used with some discretion; there are only a few dozen players in the history of the game who wear it well. A gallery of sluggers appears in Ted Williams' *Science of Hitting,* including: Hack Wilson, Hank Greenberg, Babe Ruth, Lou Gehrig, Ralph Kiner, Mickey Mantle, Roger Maris and Johnny Mize.

Slugger. Kirk Gibson.   *Courtesy of the Detroit Tigers*

1ST   1883. (*Sporting Life,* April 22; EJN)
2. *n.* A heavy bat.
1ST   1901. (*Frank Merriwell's Marvel;* EJN)
3. The Louisville Slugger, for short.
ETY   The term was applied to boxers (alternatively, slogger) before baseball players. A reckless batter in cricket has been known as a slogger for at least 100 years.
EXT   1. *n.* A term of endearment, often applied by an adult to a little kid who is anything but.
2. *n.* A boxer who wins on punches rather than on defense or tactics.

Sluggersville   *n.* Figurative hometown of sluggers.
1ST   1891. "Then he was as frisky as a young colt and a slugger from Sluggersville." (*Sporting Times,* July 11, 1891; DS)

slugging average/slugging percentage   *n.* A statistical representation of a batter's ability to make extra-base hits. It is determined by dividing the player's total times at bat into his total bases. Hence, a batter with a triple, double and a single (6 total bases) in 12 at bats averages .500. During the 1920 season Babe Ruth's slugging average was an astonishing .847 (388 bases in 458 at bats). It would be possible to have a slugging average of over 1.000 if one averaged more than one base per at bat and a slugger who got a home run with every at bat would have a 4.000 slugging percentage.

slugging   contest/slugging   duel/slugging match   *n.* See slugfest.

slugsmith   *n.* Heavy hitter.
1ST   1920. "Good old Rufe, the slugsmith! The crowd was imploring him to bring Tapland home." (Gilbert Patten, *Man on First;* DS)

slump   1. *n.* A period of poor performance. A team is said to be in a slump when it loses games, while an individual may go into a batting, pitching, or even a fielding slump.
2. *n.* A downward trend. In extreme cases, the whole game can be on the skids: "Baseball fell into a slump this week," read a headline in the *Maine Sunday Telegram* for August 10, 1986, after the owners fired arbitrator Tom Roberts (among other things).
   Slumps are also relative. Back in 1956 Jimmy Cannon's definition was: "Any time in the season when the Yankees are leading by less than eight games."

1ST   1895. (*New York Press,* July 1; EJN)
3. *v.* To be in a slump.

slurve   1. *n.* A pitch that slides and curves. It curves more than a slider and is faster than a curveball.
2. *n.* To pitch, relying on the slurve. "Kaat 'Slurves' Yanks." (headline, *San Francisco Examiner,* July 19, 1973; PT)
ETY   A combination of slider + curve = slurve. However, sources for the team vary in specific applications. "Among batsmen of the National League, the favorite pitch of Don Drysdale was known as the 'slurve.' This comprised one part slobber and two parts curve." (Mel Durslag, *San Francisco Examiner,* July 24, 1970; PT)

smack   *v.* To hit the ball hard.

small baseball   *n.* According to Red Barber, this is what Casey Stengel called a "very fast ball." (National Public Radio's "Morning Edition," May 30, 1986)

smash   *v.* To hit a ball powerfully.
1ST   1888. (*New York Press,* April 19; EJN)

smell hit   *arch.* TEXAS LEAGUER.

smoke   1. *n.* Speed in pitching; top velocity; heat. Usually stated as "throwing smoke," it figuratively alludes to a ball that comes in so fast, it leaves a trail of smoke.
   It would appear that this was the source of several baseball nicknames, including that of Smokey Joe Wood, who was also called "Smoke" by the likes of Tris Speaker.
   As Dwight Gooden emerged from a drug rehabilitation center in April 1987 attendants yelled out the windows, "Throw smoke, Dwight." According to the *New York Times,* "In reply, Gooden thrust a fist into the air." (April 30, 1987)
1ST   1912. (*New York Tribune,* September 8; EJN)
2. *v.* To bear down with a fastball— "Smoke him" or "Smoke one by him."

smoker   FASTBALL.
1ST   1914. "That Lewis expected a smoker and had every intention of lacing it out, was perfectly evident from his action." (Gilbert Patten, *Brick King, Backstop;* DS)

smother in leather/smother the ball   *v.* To field the ball effectively; to kill an offensive threat.
1ST   1896. (*Frank Merriwell's Schooldays;* EJN)

snake **1.** *n./arch.* CURVEBALL.
1ST 1906. (*Spalding's Official Base Ball Guide;* EJN)
2. *n.* A pitched ball that changes directions and actually undulates on its way to the plate. Despite turn of the century reports of the snake ball, the experts claimed it never existed. In his 1901 *Book of College Sports,* the great Walter Camp said that it, "exists in the imagination only, unless the ball be blown out of its course by the wind."

snake-bit. *adj.* Unlucky.
ETY In his section of the *Encyclopedia of Sports Talk,* Phil Pepe writes: "Origin is unknown, but since baseball was a game played by country boys who know of such things as snakes, that probably was the derivation. Being bitten by a snake is about as bad luck as one can have."

snap **1.** *v.* To release a curveball.
2. *n.* Characteristic of a curveball as it comes out of the pitcher's hand.

snap throw **1.** *n.* A quick, short toss made with a flick—or snap—of the wrist.
1ST 1896. (*Frank Merriwell's Schooldays;* EJN)
2. *v.* To throw the ball with a flick of the wrist.
3. *n.* The energy of a player or team.
1ST 1890. (*New York Evening Post,* May 5; EJN)

sneaker *n.* A deceptively fast ball. "A pitch that is faster than it appears to be and figuratively sneaks upon the batter," according to H. G. Salsinger in his "Jargon of the Field" article in the August 1945 *Baseball Digest.*

sneakers *n.* Canvas and rubber athletic shoes.
1ST 1909. "He dressed his feet in a pair of rubber soled, canvas shoes—call 'em 'sneakers' now,—and journeyed to Fall River." (*Baseball Magazine,* August 1909; DS)
There are two common theories on how this term originated: (1) from British thieves who found them useful in their work, or (2) from baseball players who found them useful in stealing bases. The shoes themselves predated the name by a number of years; according to a 1987 *Chicago Tribune* article on the subject, "The first sneaker hit the market in 1868, according to historian William Rossi."

sno-cone/snow cone *n.* A catch in which the ball is caught in the top of the glove web-

The Snodgrasss Muff. Fred Snodgrass. *National Baseball Library, Cooperstown, N.Y.*

bing and when held up resembles a scoop of frozen confection in a cone.
SEE *ice cream cone catch.*

The Snodgrass Muff Term for a muff or boner, named for the hapless New York Giant outfielder Fred Snodgrass who dropped a fly ball in the tenth inning of the final game of the 1912 World Series. The Giants had been leading 2-1 but the gaff put the tying run on base and the Red Sox went on to win the game and the Series.

snyder out *v.* To ground out routinely to the second baseman.
This may be a bit of slang primarily used by one team, the Baltimore Orioles, and named for a former player, Russ Snyder, who often snydered out during his Oriole years (1960–1967). The term was used by former third baseman Brooks Robinson on an August 20, 1982, WMAR telecast during which he pointed out that the term was still commonly used by Orioles, even those who were unaware of its background.

SO **1.** Common abbreviation for strikeout.
2. Abbreviation for shutout.

soak *v.* To bat the ball hard. "There is wild demand that 'Shorty, soak 'er home!' " (Charles S. Brooks in *Journeys to Bagdad*)
1ST 1896. (*Frank Merriwell's Schooldays;* EJN)

soaker *n./arch.* Solid hit.
1ST 1895. "You hit a soaker, and I'll bet you've taken some of the sand out of Flood." (Herbert Bellwood, *The Rivals of Riverwood;* DS)

soak the runner *v./obs.* To hit the runner with the ball to put him out; from early variations of the game, such as the Massachusetts version, in which this was a legal way of retiring a base runner.

Society for American Baseball Research Composed of researchers and fans with an interest in the history of the game, it publishes several periodicals and holds both regional meetings and a national convention. It was the brainchild of L. Robert Davids of Washington, DC, who formed it along with 15 other baseball historians at a 1971 meeting in Cooperstown.

sockdolager *n./obs.* Slugger of the game's infancy in the mid-19th century.

socker *n./arch.* SLUGGER.
1ST 1907. (*Lajoie's Official Base Ball Guide;* EJN)

sodfather *n.* Puckish nickname for a head groundskeeper, a punning play on *The Godfather.* When the *Washington Post* carried a profile of Baltimore's Pasquale Santarone, it was headlined "The Sodfather of Memorial Stadium" (April 6, 1983). (Some weeks later the *Post* published a letter from a reader who termed the use of the nickname for an Italian American a "demeaning slur.")

softball 1. *n.* An offshoot of baseball played with a larger, softer ball, which pitchers throw underhand and, depending on the league, throw fast or slow. The field is similar to the baseball diamond but smaller (bases are 60 feet apart).
Fast and slow pitch are played with the same equipment and most of the same rules. The emphasis in fast pitch is on hitting while slow pitch players concentrate on both hitting and fielding. Softball is totally dominated by amateur play.
2. *n.* The ball used to play softball is 12 inches in circumference and weighs 6¼ to 7 ounces. There are variations on the standard ball, including a ball 16 inches in circumference and used in a form of slow pitch. Softball is something of a misnomer as the leather-covered ball is almost as hard as a regular baseball, also known as a hardball.
ETY The game dates back to 1887 when it

Softball. The official logo commemorating softball's 100th anniversary. *Courtesy of the Amateur Softball Association of America*

was created as indoor baseball. It was played under a number of names including kitten and mush ball.
It got a major boost about 1910 when the Playground Society of America acknowledged it as a good game for kids (and suggested the addition of a 10th player known as a *rover*). Its major leap forward occurred in the 1930s after a national tournament at the 1933 Century of Progress Exposition in Chicago. In 1939, *Time* said of the game: "A product of the Depression, softball has grown into a major U.S. mania." (September 26, 1939)
In 1939 the game was brought back indoors when a short-lived attempt was made to promote it as a winter alternative to baseball, organized along the same lines as major league baseball. Under the name National Professional Indoor Baseball League, franchises were sold in New York, Brooklyn, Boston, Cleveland, Chicago, Philadelphia, Cincinnati and St. Louis.
The game has undergone modifications and changes, including the distance from the pitching mound to the plate, which was set at 37 feet 8 inches in 1933, dropped back to 40 feet in 1940 and to 46 feet in 1950.
1ST 1926. The name softball was first applied and approved at a meeting held in Colorado in 1926 that was aimed at establishing a standard set of rules for the state. This explanation for the term was given by Walter L. Hakanson, a leader of the sport in that state, and is reported

in *Softball* by Arthur Noren (A. S. Barnes, New York, 1940). In 1932, at a national meeting in Chicago, the Colorado name was proposed and formally accepted.

It took a while for the term to take hold in the population at large and supersede the many local names for the game. It appears to have spread widely during World War II and shows up in Grosset and Dunlap's 1947 dictionary, *Words: the New Dictionary,* which lists the term in its section on the newest words.

EXT An easy question, such as one asked by a member of a congressional committee of a witness, has become known as a softball. "Practically all of the questions thrown at Carter were softballs that allowed him, in many cases, just to repeat much of his 1976 campaign oratory." (*San Francisco Examiner* article on Jimmy Carter, March 17, 1977) In this regard, see HARD-BALL.

softballer *n.* One who plays softball and/or prefers it to baseball. "But after decades of cavorting like softballers at the company picnic, [the Chicago] Cubs, the Rodney Dangerfields of baseball, finally have earned some respect. (*Newsweek,* September 10, 1984)

softball throw *n.* A track and field event in which individuals compete by throwing a softball for distance.

soft hands *n.* Term for the hands of a fielder who is able to handle the ball with ease and seldom make an error.

softie *n./arch.* Softball player. "Police Softies Defeat Firemen." (headline, *San Francisco News,* August 26, 1937; PT)

soft liner *n.* A line drive without much force behind it.

soldier *n.* Derogatory term for a batter given to keeping his bat on his shoulder.

sold out **1.** *n./adj.* BASES LOADED.
2. Situation in which there are no more seats available for spectators.

solid contact *n.* Getting good wood on the ball.

solo clout/solo jab/solo homer *n.* Solo shot; a home run hit with no runner on base.

solve a pitcher *v.* To begin getting hits from a pitcher, presumably after determining the trajectory and speed of his pitches and the way they are mixed.

1ST 1898. (*New York Tribune,* April 22; EJN)

sophomore jinx *n.* Bad luck or a poor showing in the season after a successful rookie or freshman year. Perhaps the most famous modern example of a player suffering from this condition was Joe Charboneau who was the American League Rookie of the Year at Cleveland in 1980 and was back in the minors in 1981. "Commissioner Kuhn, it can be seen, had a difficult second year in office, and should probably be listed as another victim of the legendary 'sophomore jinx.' " (Roger Angell, *The Summer Game;* CDP)

soupbone/souper **1.** *n./arch.* The pitching arm. "Tim had been a star thrower in his day, but the soupbone had slowed up and he was clinging to his job with his finger-nails, and he was hoping he could bluff his way through another season by putting twenty years of experience and a prayer on every pitch." (*Collier's,* July 19, 1930; PT)
2. *n.* The PITCHER.
1ST 1910. (*American* magazine, April; EJN)
ETY The term seems to have arisen in recognition of the importance of the pitcher's throwing arm, which is to his performance what a soupbone is to a soup.

soupboning *n.* Pitching.

Southern League AA minor league with 10 franchises, in Birmingham, Alabama; Charlotte, North Carolina; Columbus, Georgia; Greenville, South Carolina; Chattanooga, Knoxville and Memphis, Tennessee; and Orlando, Florida.

southpaw/south paw **1.** *n.* A left-handed player, usually a pitcher.
2. *adj.* Of the left-handed. "Southpaw slants," for instance, refers to the pitching style of a left-handed pitcher.
3. *v.* To throw with the left hand. "He hooked up with the Detroit Tigers and he quickly southpawed his way into the baseball headlines." (Bill Stern on Hal Newhouser, in *Favorite Baseball Stories*)
1ST 1885. "Morris and Carroll had never seen the St. Louis team play ball, and as they had always been accustomed to having their opponents hug their bases pretty close, out of respect for Morris' quick throw over to first with that

south-paw of his, they were supremely disgusted by the reckless manner in which the Mound City gang ran the lines on them." (*Sporting Life,* January 14, 1885; DS)

ETY The oft-repeated etymology of this word is that it derives from the "fact" that ballparks were once laid out with home plate to the west which meant that a left-handed pitcher faced the west and threw with his southern limb. This westward orientation kept the sun out of the batter's eyes and out of the eyes of the customers in the more expensive seats behind the plate during an afternoon game.

The story is that it was created by Finley Peter Dunne or Charles Seymour of the *Chicago Herald* and used by them as early as July 1891. However, there is an attestation of its use in 1885 (see above).

H. L. Mencken reported in the *American Language* (Suppl. 2.) that Richard J. Finnigan, publisher of the *Chicago Times,* attributed it to Seymour (d. 1901). As Finnigan put it in a 1945 letter to Mencken: "The pitchers in the old baseball park on the Chicago West Side faced the west and those who pitched left-handed did so with their *southpaws.*"

But does the sun theory work—or did it, before most games were played at night? When Happy Felton mentioned the sun theory on his post-game television show from Ebbets Field in 1951, sportswriter Harry Grayson decided to investigate. In his NEA dispatch for July 12 of that year, Grayson sided with the sun and reported:

"All parks, save one in Lancaster, Pa., are laid out so the sun is not in the batter's eyes. Consequently, the lefthanded pitcher throws from the south side.

"At Stumpf Field, home of the Lancaster Red Roses of the Class B Inter-State League, 25 minutes or so have to be taken out of a late afternoon, or until the sun sinks below the horizon. It is remindful of the English dropping everything for tea in the middle of a cricket match." (*San Francisco News;* PT)

A different theory from Charley Dryden, an early sports writer, has attracted few converts. In this version, an unnamed left-hander from Southpaw, Illinois, tries out for the Cubs at spring training in New Orleans and this inspires the Chicago writers to start calling all portsiders southpaws. The reason why it is hard to muster enthusiasm for this theory is that no maps of Illinois or of any other state reveal a town by the name of Southpaw. Illinois does have a South Pekin and a South Park.

The logical antonym northpaw has been used from time to time for a right-handed pitcher but has never really taken hold.

EXT **1.** *n.* By extension, any left-handed person.

2. *n.* In boxing, a fighter who stands with his right foot and right hand extended and who counterpunches with his left; the left hand itself. "This boxer was Gene Tunney, who had just been whipped by Harry Greb. He was one of the few who discovered what a left hand meant, both offensively and defensively, and worked away hour after hour building up his own southpaw." (*Colliers,* April 12, 1930; PT)

3. *n.* A member of the political left wing. Citations on file at Merriam-Webster indicate that this meaning of the word began showing up in print in 1938. The earliest appearance was in Paul Mallon's "News Behind the News" column in the *Schenectady Gazette* for February 10, 1938: "House southpaws are generally known in the House as the 'mavericks,' not only because Texas Congressman Maury Maverick is the leader but because Webster's new international dictionary defines a maverick as 'a motherless calf.' "

Damon Runyon, Walter Winchell and other newspaper columnists were noted for calling Communists southpaws.

southpaw disease *n.* Name for the common inability of left-handed batters to hit left-handed pitchers.

southpawing *n.* Left-handed pitching.

souvenir *n.* A ball hit into the stands, either a foul ball or home run. Such a ball, kept by a spectator.

Sox *n.* Depending on the context, the Chicago White Sox or the Boston Red Sox.

space cadet *n.* An eccentric; a *flake* who seems to have come from outer space. The name of pitcher Bill Lee is likely to come to mind when the term is used.

ETY The term may have survived from an early television series called "Tom Corbett, Space Cadet."

"Spahn and Sain and pray for rain" Motto of the Boston Braves of the late 1940s. Much of the team's success derived from the abilities of pitchers Warren Spahn and Johnny Sain.

Spahn and Sain and pray for rain. Warren Spahn's Hall of Fame plaque. *National Baseball Library, Cooperstown, N.Y.*

In a 1985 interview with Frederick C. Klein of the *Wall Street Journal* Spahn commented: "It's not so much my pitching people know, but that little poem about me and Johnny Sain with the '48 Braves . . . Guys who were kids 40 years ago learned it as a nursery rhyme. Now they meet me and say, 'Oh, you're *that* Spahn.' I used to think that rhyme was silly, but I guess it's how I'll be remembered. Life's funny, huh?" (WSJ, August 2, 1985)

spaldeen *n.* Name for the hollow, pink rubber ball used in such baseball variations as stickball and stoopball. The name is, to quote Harvey Frommer from his book *Sports Roots*, a "sweetened" form of the name of Alfred Goodwill Spalding, whose company made the spaldeen until 1980. *Newsweek* noted the ball's passing in an October 22, 1984, article, "They were a victim of the trend toward giving boys a place to play where there are no windows . . ."
   The term is deeply embedded in the minds of many. "To this day," writes Leonard Shecter

in *The Jocks,* "when I see 'Spalding' I consider it a misspelling."

spalding *n./arch.* The ball during those periods when it is being manufactured by the A. G. Spalding company.

Spalding Guide *n./arch.* A player whose every move seems posed, as if he were being photographed for the popular *Spalding Base Ball Guides* of yore. The books, published beginning in the 1870s, were illustrated guidebooks featuring records and team profiles.

spangles *n./arch.* Player's uniform.
1ST 1906. (*Sporting Life,* March 3; EJN)

Spanish home run 1. *n./arch.* A ball that is misjudged by a fielder and therefore allows the batter to score, but which, if properly played, might only have gone for a single or double.
2. *n.* By extension, any cheap or easy home run.
SEE *Chinese Home Run.*
ETY This term appears in Franklin P. Huddle's 1943 article "Baseball Jargon" and elsewhere, but no suggestion is made of its origin. Implied, however, is Spanish fielding ineptitude. The expression may have died out as Latin players showed their skill in the field.

spank *v.* To bat the ball sharply.
1ST 1891. (*Chicago Herald,* May 16; EJN)

sparkplug/spark plug *n.* A player or manager with a fiery temper, one with the ability to spark the team.

spasm *n.* An inning. "With the third inning faded into the dim and forgotten past, the fourth spasm in the afternoon's matinee of Dementia Baseballitis hopped into the glare of the calcium glim." (from an article on contemporary baseball slang, *Baseball* magazine, September 1909)
1ST 1907. (*New York Evening Journal,* April 12; EJN)

spear *v.* To catch a ball, usually a liner, with a sudden reach of the arm fully extended, like a spear.
1ST 1902. (*Sporting Life,* July 5; EJN)

special *n./arch.* Texas leaguer, a term once used in the Eastern League (ca. 1933).

special days *n.* Games featuring any of a number of inducements to boost attendance. These range from discounts (Ladies' Day and

$3 Night) to giveaways (Helmet Day and Photo Album Night).

spectator's interference   *n.* A call made by the umpire when he determines that a fan has prevented a fielder from making a play on a batted or thrown ball. When such a determination is made by the umpire the ball is dead and the spectator can expect to be ejected from the ballpark. The umpire will then impose a decision that will attempt to negate the act of interference.

speed   1. *n.* The ability of an individual or a team to run the bases.
2. *n.* The ability to field the ball expeditiously.
3. *n.* The ability to throw the fastball, as in, "his speed is good today."
4. *n.* The velocity with which the ball is thrown.
5. *n.* The velocity with which the bat is swung.
1ST   1897. (*Base Ball Tribune,* September 9; EJN)

speedball   *n.* The fastball
EXT   As with the synonymous "hardballing," "speedballing" is a term used by drug addicts for injecting heroin and cocaine. "The dangers of speedballing: Belushi killed by 'treacherous' combination of drugs, medic says." (headline, *San Francisco Examiner,* March 11, 1982; PT)

speed gun   *n.* An electronic device used to determine the velocity of a pitched baseball.

speed merchant   1. *n.* A particularly fast runner who is likely to steal bases.
1ST   1910. (*Baseball* magazine, May; EJN)
2. *n.* Fastball pitcher.

spellbinder   *n.* A glib, talkative player.

sphere/spheroid   *n.* BASEBALL.
1ST   1874 (spheroid). (*Chicago Inter Ocean,* July 9; EJN)

spike   1. *n.* A metal, rubber or plastic projection on the bottom of a player's shoes to give him greater traction. The term is something of a misnomer for baseball spikes are not sharp and pointed like those which are found on track shoes.
2. *v.* To cut or otherwise injure another player with one's spikes. It commonly occurs when a player is sliding into a base feet first and the defensive player gets in the way. "Nudge him with rubber—don't spike him with steel." (B. F. Goodrich advertisement in *Time* for rubber spikes, April 22, 1940; PT)
1ST   1885. (*Chicago Inter Ocean,* May 17; EJN)

spikes   1. *n.* The array of projections on a player's shoes.
2. *n.* The shoes themselves, which are also called cleats.
1ST   1866. "The uniform [of the Minerva Club of Philadelphia, organized June 10, 1857] consists of gray pants with cord on the side, plaid shirt with rolling collar, leather shoes with spikes, white navy cap trimmed with blue, german-text M on top of cap, and blue silk belt." (C. A. Peverelly, *American Pastimes,* 1866; PT)

spikes high   *adv.* Describing aggressive baserunning tactics. Characteristic of a slide in which a base runner attempts to gain advantage by imperiling the fielder with his spikes.

spikes, to sharpen one's.   *v.* To threaten to harm any fielder in one's way around the bases. Hugh Fullerton says in his 1912 "Primer," "Chiefly a form of braggadocio, and seldom carried into effect."

Legend has it that Ty Cobb was a spike sharpener, but he claimed otherwise. In a 1958 interview he gave at age 71 to *The Saturday Evening Post,* he insisted that it was two other fellows—"neither of them regulars"—who did it to unnerve the Yankees. "These two fellows decided to practice some amateur psychology. So . . . as the Yankees came on the field, the two sat on the bench filing their spikes. Neither of them played in the game. But the press had to have a 'name' to go with the story, so they chose Cobb." (quoted by Prescott Sullivan, *San Francisco Examiner,* June 12, 1958; PT)

spin   1. *n.* The turning of the pitched ball, which keeps it on its intended trajectory. All pitches spin, except for the knuckleball.
2. *v.* To cause the ball to turn as it moves through the air.

spin ball   *n.* Softball.

spin his cap   *v.* To brush back a batter; to intimidate with a high, inside pitch.

spitball/spit ball   1. *n.* A pitch made with a ball that has been spat upon or otherwise moistened, causing it to break more sharply.

It was once legal and used commonly. "The American League, during the early days of the 'spitball' used it so much that Charlie Dryden, angler and scribe, remarked that: 'The American League consists of Ban Johnson, the 'spitball' and the Wabash Railroad.' " (*The Book of Baseball,* 1913; PT)

It was banned in 1920; however, 17 pitchers

Spitball. Grimes threw legal spitballs. *National Baseball Library, Cooperstown, N.Y.*

who were already using it were allowed to continue to do so for the remainder of their playing years under what amounted to a "grandfather clause." The last legal spitball pitcher was Burleigh Grimes who hung up his spikes in 1934 after 19 years in the majors.

The spitball is still thrown despite the fact that the rule against it has been made tougher. For instance, in 1968 a stricter anti-spitball rule was added that prohibited any contact between the pitcher's throwing hand and his mouth. However, the attitude toward the pitch seems to be summed up by one-time pitching coach and manager George Bamberger, as quoted by Tom Boswell in 1987: "A guy who cheats in a friendly game of cards is a cheater. A pro who throws a spitball to support his family is a contender."

Few baseball terms have as many odd and diverse synonyms as the spitball, including: brown spitter, country sinker, aqueous toss, damp sling, Cuban palmball, Cuban forkball, humidity dispenser, wet ball and wet wipe.
2. *v.* To throw the spitball.
EXT In his book *On Language*, William Safire

points out, "Because an old-time baseball pitcher never knew which way his spitball would break, the verb *to spitball* now means 'to speculate.'"
1ST 1905. "There is one way the prevalent 'spit ball' can be neutralized to some extent, and clever batsmen have already figured it out." (*Sporting Life,* May 13; PT)
ETY Hugh Fullerton claims Tom Bond threw the first spitball in New Bedford in 1876 using glycerine, which he carried in his pocket. Most others insist it came later. There are many who have attributed to Elmer Stricklett who started experimenting with it in 1902 and 1903. He brought it to the Dodgers, with whom he pitched from 1905 through 1907.

However, Stricklett himself threw water on this notion. In a 1940 interview he had this to say:

"I never discovered the spitball. In countless magazine articles, radio skits and even in some of the baseball records I've been called the originator of the spitter though I never claimed credit for it. A fellow named Frank Corridon really discovered the spitball.

"Back in 1902 Corridon by chance let a ball leave his pitching hand that was wet with saliva. The ball performed some weird antics en route to the plate . . ." (*San Francisco Call-Bulletin,* July 2, 1940; PT) Corridon told George Hildebrand about it and he passed it along to Stricklett on a train trip.

If Stricklett did not invent the pitch, he certainly developed it, taking it from Corridon (who seldom used it) and turning it into a major weapon in the pitcher's arsenal. And Stricklett may have named it, or at least that is the claim made in G. W. Axelson's 1919 work, *"Commy," The Life of Charles A. Comiskey.* The incident takes place in 1904:

In the Sox camp at Marlin was a pitcher by the name of Elmer Stricklett. He was the opposite to Walsh in build, and yet he handed up a ball to the batters which was unhittable. It took twists and turns in approaching the plate that were against all the laws of gravity. Everybody took a swing at it. Most of them missed it, sometimes by a foot or more. Billy Sullivan, catching, found the ball wet and slippery.

"What's the idea," demanded the backstop, who was not enamored of handling the sphere.

"Oh, that's my way of pitching," explained Stricklett.

"What do you call it?" insisted Sullivan.

"Don't know," was the answer. "I suppose 'spitball' explains it as well as anything."

EXT An act of deception; a dirty trick. "As Joe Biden knows, it would not be the first spitball the Dukakis campaign has thrown." (*National Review,* February 5, 1988; CDP)

spitballer *n.* A pitcher noted for throwing the spitball.

spitter *n.* Another name for SPITBALL; the term had been around for many years, but it was given new prominence with the 1974 publication of Gaylord Perry's audacious, tell-all autobiography, *Me and The Spitter.*
1ST 1908. (*Baseball* magazine, July; EJN)

splendid splinter Nickname that attached itself to Ted Williams—a splendid hitter who was deceptively thin for a power hitter.

splinter squad *n.* Players on the bench.

split a doubleheader *v.* To win one game and lose the other of a doubleheader.

split-fingered fastball *n.* Termed the "Pitch of the 1980s" by Joe Garagiola and others, it has been described as a "fast forkball"—one that is gripped closer to the fingertips and released with a forkball motion. It sinks suddenly as it approaches the plate.

Invented by Roger Craig, it has been used by such pitchers as Bruce Sutter, Mike Scott and Jack Morris. Craig told *Sports Illustrated* that he began teaching the pitch at a boy's camp in 1974.

The extent to which Craig taught his San Francisco Giants the pitch was reflected in the 1987 spring training line that the SF on the players' hats actually stood for split-fingered.

It has created some confusion, as others in the game periodically declare that it is "nothing more than a [fill in the blank]." In *Baseball Lite* Jerry Howarth defines it as, "A pitch five major league pitching coaches call a fork ball, five others call a spitter, six more recognize as a changeup, and ten others won't recognize at all." In his 1987 biography *Billyball,* Billy Martin insists that it is nothing new, just a "variation of the forkball."

split-squad *n.* Exhibition season team composed of regulars and scrubs. They are likely to be fielded in the early days of spring training.

splitter *n.* SPLIT-FINGERED FASTBALL.

Split-fingered fastball. Roger Craig, father of the "Pitch of the 1980s." *Courtesy of the San Francisco Giants*

spoiler *n.* One who gets in the way of a victory or an important personal achievement, such as a batter who gets a hit to break up a no-hitter.

sportscaster *n.* A blend of sports and broadcaster that is used broadly for those who announce baseball and other games on radio and television.

Sportsman's Park The former home grounds for the St. Louis Browns and the St. Louis Cardinals. According to Phillip J. Lowry in the book *Green Cathedrals,* there were four separate stadiums called Sportsman's Park, in St. Louis, all at the same location. The first one was first used for baseball in 1866.

'Spos Shortened name for the Montreal Expos in the tabloids. "Mets 4½ back after Darling dazzles 'Spos." (headline, *New York Post,* August 13, 1987)

spot **1.** *v.* To pitch the ball to a particular part—or spot—of the strike zone. "He's trying to spot everything. The Guidry we know threw everything so hard that he grunted after every pitch." (George Brett on Ron Guidry, *Washington Post,* August 24, 1986)
2. *n.* The location of a pitched ball as it passes through the batter's box. A good spot is one that keeps the batter off balance, such as one

thrown to a corner of the strike zone. "Frustrating Tanana is finding the 'Good Spots'" says a *Sporting News* headline of August 17, 1987 to a story about Detroit Tiger pitcher Frank Tanana.
3. *adj.* Irregular, as in spot pitcher.

spot pitcher   *n.* A pitcher with the ability to place the ball at different points in and around the strike zone.

spot reliever   *n.* A relief pitcher who is used for very short, specific assignments, such as facing two particular batters, finishing an inning etc.

spot starter   **1.** *n.* A pitcher who is not a regular starting pitcher but, rather, is called on to start when the team needs him.
2. *n.* SPOT PITCHER.

spot-throw   *n.* Ball thrown by a fielder to a spot rather than a person.
1ST 1935. "Spot-throw—A throw made to a place rather than a player . . ." (Ralph H. Barbour, *How to Play Better Baseball;* DS)

USE Not to be confused with SPOT PITCHER.

sprayer   *n./arch.* See spitball.

spray hitter   *n.* A batter who is able to place the ball unpredictably all over the field as opposed to one who tends to one portion of the field. Spray hitting can enable a player with limited power to be effective.

spray paint   *v.* To be able to hit to different portions of the field. Larry Whiteside of the *Boston Globe* on Carl Yastrzemski in a 1983 groove: "Yesterday, he drove in five runs with a two-run homer and a bases-loaded double, the kind of spray painting Yaz hasn't done since Jimmy Carter gave up the peanut farm to run for president." (*The Boston Globe,* July 10, 1983)

spring training   *n.* A period of training and exhibition play that begins in late February and ends a day or two before Opening Day. Teams conduct spring training in camps located in Florida or Arizona and play their games in small ballparks in those states.

Spring training. Practicing base stealing at the Cleveland Indians' 1952 camp at Daytona Beach, Florida. *National Baseball Library, Cooperstown, N.Y.*

1ST 1905. (*Sporting Life,* September 9; EJN)
ETY Although teams barnstormed in the South before 1870, Harold Seymour pinpoints that year in *Baseball the Early Years* as the time when the Chicago White Stockings and the Cincinnati Red Stockings started the first formal camps for spring training in New Orleans, Louisiana. The first Florida encampment was made by the Washington club in 1888.
EXT A metaphor for a preliminary event or period that does not count in the final outcome. "Spring training is not very important," was Hubert H. Humphrey's response to questions about the 1968 Presidential primaries. (*New York Times* May 30, 1968)

squab squad *n.* Team of rookies and substitutes.
1ST 1911. "While on the road with the 'squab squad' he slept for two nights in a Pullman berth with his right arm in the hammock, which he had been told was put there for the particular benefit of the baseball players." (C. E. Van Loan, *The Big League;* DS)

squander **1.** *v.* Verb of choice to describe a relief pitcher who comes in with a lead or tie and leaves or ends the game with his team behind.
2. *n.* A demerit counted against a relief pitcher who squanders a lead; as contrasted with a credit for a win, loss, hold or save. See Miller-Brown System.

square around *v.* To attempt to bunt in a move in which the batter turns towards the pitcher and holds his bat parallel to his feet.

square stance. *n.* A batting position in which the batter's feet are parallel to and in line with the pitcher's mound. Also known as a parallel stance.

squawk **1.** *n.* A protest.
2. *v.* To protest.
A section in O. H. Vogel's *Ins and Outs of Baseball* is titled "The Fine Art of the Squawk." He makes this point: "the wise coach or captain seldom protests in the hope that an umpire might change a decision; his objective generally is to cultivate the ground for a better break the next time. This is a definite part of the game, and certainly not illegal or unsporting."

squeaker *n.* A very close game whose outcome is usually decided late in the game by a single hit or run.

squeeze **1.** *n.* SQUEEZE PLAY.
2. *v.* To attempt or make the squeeze play; to attempt to squeeze out a run.
1ST 1908. (*Spalding's Official Base Ball Guide;* EJN)

squeeze bunt/squeeze play *n.* Offensive play in which the batter attempts to score the runner on third base by bunting. The runner sprints with the pitch and the batter bunts the ball into fair territory, attempting to place it so that the fielder cannot get the man out at the plate. It is only attempted with less than two outs. It is also called the suicide squeeze. A variation on the play is the safety squeeze in which the runner waits to see if the bunt is going to be effective.
1ST 1907. (squeeze play). (*Dick Merriwell's Magnetism;* EJN)
ETY Hy Turkin in his *Baseball Almanac* says that it was first used by a couple of Yale men, George Case and Dutch Carter, in a June 16, 1894, game against Princeton. He adds that it was introduced to the Major Leagues by Clark Griffith in 1904. Another version says that Joel Yeager introduced it in Brooklyn in 1898.

squeeze the pitcher *v.* For the plate umpire seemingly to reduce the size of the strike zone.

squib *v.* To bloop or hit the ball without much force, usually off the handle or the end of the bat.

squibber *n.* A blooper or grounder good for a base hit; a scratch hit. Rod Kanehl is quoted in Leonard Shecter's *The Jocks:* "Baseball is a lot like life. The line drives are caught, the squibbers go for base hits. It's an unfair game." (CDP)

squibbs **1.** *n.* Subs; poor players.
1ST 1917. (*Spalding's Official Base Ball Guide;* EJN)
2. *n.* Early version of squibber.

squirrely *adj.* Term for an eccentric player or a flake.
ETY Perhaps a borrowing from car racing where the term has been used for some years to describe a car that is erratic or hard to handle.

SS **1.** Standard abbreviation for shortstop.
2. Common abbreviation for SPLIT SQUAD.

stab and grab *adj.* Describing a defensive move in which a fielder makes a desperate attempt (stab) to catch (grab) the ball. "Pete instinctively lunged to his right, stretching his gloved left hand across his body. It was simply a stab and grab attempt; on a ball that was hit that swiftly, an infielder could do little more than reach and hope it bounced right." (*Relief Pitcher* by Dick Friendlich; CDP)

stair-stuffing *n.* Process in which a pitcher throws a series of higher and higher pitches. The idea is to keep throwing pitches higher in the strike zone until the umpire calls a ball.

stance *n.* The set position taken by the batter in the batter's box when receiving the pitch. Closed, open and square stances are the most commonly referred to.

standing/standings *n.* The ranking of teams in a division based on their won-lost percentages, which also includes the number of games or half-games a team is behind the first place team.
1ST 1881. (*New York Herald,* September 12; EJN)

standing O *n.* Standing ovation.

stand on your ear *v.* To be off balance.

stands **1.** *n.* Seating area, short form of GRANDSTANDS.
1ST 1881. (*New York Press,* June 1; EJN)
2. *n.* The people in the grandstands; fans.
1ST 1907. (*Dick Merriwell's Marvel;* EJN)

stand-up *adj.* Describing a hit on which the batter is able to reach base without sliding— e.g., a stand-up double.

stand-up double/stand-up triple *n.* Hit that does not require the batter to slide into base.

stand-up slide *n.* A short slide into base in which the runner immediately bounces up to a standing position.

stanza *n.* An INNING, which from time to time is also called a canto. This is clearly sportswriter jargon brought in when the word has been used once too often.
1ST 1909. (*New York Evening Journal,* July; EJN)

star **1.** *n.* A player with clear preeminence. There is no official star designation in baseball, but those who are seem able to make it evident.
1ST 1880. (*Brooklyn Daily Eagle,* August 12; EJN)

2. *v.* To assume the role of an outstanding player; to star in a series, for example.

starboard flinger/starboard slinger *n.* A right-handed pitcher. From the nautical term for the right forward side of a boat.
1ST David Shulman traces the former (flinger) to 1913 and Edward J. Nichols the latter (slinger) to 1908.

stare *v.* For a player holding the ball to look at a base runner in such a manner as to convince him that he probably won't be able to take the next base and that he should head back toward the base he is occupying. "Dwight Evans bounced back to the mound, where Darling made the play to first base after staring Rice back to second." (*New York Times,* October 20, 1986)

start *v.* To be in the lineup at the beginning of the game.

starter *n.* Player who begins the game; usually applied to a pitcher to distinguish him from a reliever.
1ST 1912. (*New York Tribune,* October 8; EJN)

starting lineup *n.* The players who begin a game and remain in place until the first substitute is brought into the game.

starting pitcher *n.* The pitcher who starts the game for his team and who cannot be legally replaced until he has finished with his first batter (retired him or put him on base). The only exception to this occurs when the umpire determines that the pitcher has somehow become incapacitated.

starting rotation *n.* ROTATION.

Staten Island sinker *n.* A SPITBALL. Credit for this coinage is generally given to one-time pitching coach and manager George Bamberger.

station *n.* A BASE.
1ST 1860. (*Beadle's Dime Base Ball Player;* EJN)

station keeper *n.* See baseman.
1ST 1914. "This throw was so high that the station keeper was forced to stretch for it." (Gilbert Patten, *Brick King, Backstop;* DS)

stats *n.* Short for statistics. Baseball, the most statistical of sports, is awash in both amateur and professional statisticians. All teams and both major leagues maintain their own statistical records.

Statue of Liberty *n.* Name for a batter who stands at the plate and takes a called third strike.

1ST 1937. (*Pittsburgh Press,* January 11; EJN)

steady a pitcher *v.* To calm a pitcher's nerves; to settle him down, usually by the catcher, a coach or the manager talking to him.

1ST 1914. (*New York Tribune,* October 11; EJN)

steal 1. *n.* A stolen base.
2. *v.* To achieve a stolen base.
1ST 1862. (*New York Sunday Mercury,* July 13; EJN)

steal a base *v.* For a runner to advance safely to the next base by running as the pitcher goes into his delivery.

steal a sign *v.* To sight and decipher a signal between two members of the other team.

steam 1. *n.* The velocity of a pitcher's pitches.
2. *n.* The endurance of a pitcher.
1ST 1896. (*Frank Merriwell's Schooldays;* EJN)

Stengelese *n.* Term coined to describe the vocabulary and implausible brand of double talk spoken by the late manager Casey Stengel. "By talking in the purest jabberwocky he has learned that he can avoid answering questions," wrote Gayle Talbot of the Associated Press in 1954, "and at the same time leave his audience struggling against a mild form of mental paralysis." (*San Francisco Call-Bulletin,* February 1; PT) It is hard to capture—Red Smith once likened it to "picking up quicksilver with boxing gloves"—but here is an example from a 1958 congressional hearing on baseball:

> **Senator Langer:** I want to know whether you intend to keep on monopolizing the world's championship in New York City?
>
> **Mr. Stengel:** Well, I will tell you. I got a little concern yesterday in the first three innings when I saw the three players I had gotten rid of, and I said when I lost nine what am I going to do and when I had a couple of my players I thought so great of that did not do so good up to the sixth inning I was more confused but I finally had to go and call on a young man in Baltimore that we don't own and the Yankees don't own him, and he is doing pretty good, and I would actually have to tell you that I think we are more the Greta Garbo type now from success.
>
> We are being hated, I mean, from the

Stengelese. Casey Stengel's Hall of Fame plaque. *National Baseball Library, Cooperstown, N.Y.*

> ownership and all, we are being hated. Every sport that gets too great or one individual—but if we made 27 cents and it pays to have a winner at home, why would you have a good winner in your own park if you were an owner?
>
> That is the result of baseball. An owner gets most of the money at home and it is up to him and his staff to do better or they ought to be discharged.
>
> **Senator Kefauver:** Thank you very much, Mr. Stengel. We appreciate your presence here. Mr. Mickey Mantle, will you come around? . . . Mr. Mantle, do you have any observations with reference to the applicability of the antitrust laws to baseball?
>
> **Mr. Mantle:** My views are just about the same as Casey's.
>
> (*The Congressional Record,* July 9, 1958)

Stengelese has been applied to others. "Giant manager Tom (Clancy) Sheehan is from the old school of ambiguity in naming names. Clancy's Stengalese often out-Stengels Casey." (Art Rosenbaum, *San Francisco Chronicle*, July 11, 1960; PT)

step in the bucket *v.* To step back or pull away from home plate with one's front foot while batting. A right-handed batter so afflicted will step toward third. Though normally considered poor form as a way of batting, some good batters have gotten away with it. ("You can't hit very well if you step in the bucket," writes Morris Shirts in *Warm Up for Little League Baseball*.) However, most stepping in the bucket occurs when the batter is fooled by an off-speed pitch and shifts his weight and foot in anticipation of a fastball.

step off the rubber *v.* To remove oneself from the act of pitching. A pitcher must have his pivot foot in contact with the rubber while pitching, but he takes his foot off it as the pitch is delivered, to pick off a base runner, to take a time out or to confer with other players or his manager.

step on the plate **1.** *v.* To score. A base runner who touches home plate gains a run for the offensive team.
2. *v.* To commit an infraction. A batter who steps on the plate is out.

step out of the box *v.* To remove oneself from the batter's box. If this is done with the umpire's approval before the pitcher begins his windup, the pitcher must wait until he returns to the box. If the batter steps out after the windup has begun or without approval from the umpire, the pitcher can deliver the ball and it will count as an official pitch and be called a strike or a ball.

steps on his toes Said of a pitcher who cannot field bunts.

step up to the plate *v.* Traditional phrasing for going into the batter's box.

Stetson hitter *n.* Derogatory term for bad hitter; one who hits his hat size.

stick **1.** *n.* The bat. "On our half of the seventh inning Weaver and Schalk got on and I was going up there with a stick when Callahan calls me back and sends Easterly up." (Ring W. Lardner, *You Know Me Al,* 1916)
1ST 1868. (*New York Herald*, August 4; EJN)
2. *n.* The batter's ability at the plate. A player

may be a known as "a good stick," "a weak stick" etc.

Stick, the Nickname for San Francisco's Candlestick Park. It has been called the Stick since it opened in 1960 because, according to local fans, "the wind blew out the Candle." "I can remember one time in the early seventies when the Stick was being expanded for football that he hit one completely out of the park over the scaffolding that was stacked a mile high beyond right field." (Norman Clow on Willie McCovey in the *Anderson Valley* [Cal.] *Advertiser,* April 9, 1986)

stick a fork in him As defined by Frank Gibbons of the *Cleveland Press* in his 1959 *Baseball Digest* article on "fieldese" "It means the man is done for the day. Bushed. Tired. Exhausted." It is based on the culinary practice of sticking a fork in a turkey or roast to determine if it is done.

stickball *n.* A variant game played with a broomstick or similar piece of wood and a rubber ball. It is commonly played on city streets and usually requires an elaborate and very specific set of ground rules along the order of, "The blue Ford is a double if you hit it on the fly, but an out if it hits in on the bounce." Home plate is usually either a manhole cover or a plate chalked on the pavement. A game requires a stick, a ball and at least two players. The distance of a long ball is measured in sewers—generally, passing two sewers is good and three is fantastic. Reminiscing on Willie Mays' custom of playing stickball outside the Polo Grounds in New York, an old-timer told Dave Anderson of the *New York Times* in 1972: "I used to play stickball with Willie up on the hill. He used to hit five sewers." (*San Francisco Chronicle*, May 17, 1972; PT)
  A 1982 *Newsweek* article on the subject says that such stars as Whitey Ford, Willie Mays and Joe Pepitone began as stickballers. Mays expressed his nostalgia for New York in 1959 when he told Jimmy Cannon about the odd customs of San Francisco: "The kids don't play stickball here. The streets are too hilly." (*San Francisco Call-Bulletin*, May 15; PT)

sticker/sticksmith *n./arch.* BATTER.
1ST 1888 (sticker). (*New York Press*, April 7; EJN)

stick it in his ear *v.* Nasty but common advice of the bench jockey to his teammate on the mound to hit the batter in the head. Stronger than "dust him off."

USE Not to be used lightly. From Joe Williams' syndicated column of October 12, 1953: "The Yankees came out of the Series with reduced respect for Jackie Robinson. They claim the Brooklyn star deliberately tried to foment ill feelings when he hung the 'stick-it-in-his-ear' crack on Stengel. Pressed for details, Robinson finally had to admit the information came to him second hand from several players." (PT)

EXT Used impolitely in other walks of life.

stickman *n./arch.* BATTER.
1ST 1914. "But what helped him to this and even more than his natural ability as a stickman, was a cool, indomitable determination . . ." (Gilbert Patten, *Brick King, Backstop;* DS)

stickpin *n.* Batter who chokes up at the bat. A term used by Casey Stengel to the point that it was identified as part of his "private lexicon" in the slang glossary of *Comedians of Baseball Down the Years.*

sticks *n.* Less populous areas of the country where the lower-level teams of the Minor Leagues play; the minors.
1ST 1916. (*You Know Me Al;* EJN)
ETY The term appears to have originated in either baseball or show business as a derogatory reference to the flora of the countryside. It stems from that same urge to label as was behind the terms bush and bush league.

stickwork *n.* Batting ability, as in good stickwork.
1ST 1890. (*New York Press,* July 4; EJN)

"stiff back" Excuse of infielder who does not or cannot bend down to field a grounder.

stinger *n.* A hard-hit ball.
1ST 1868. "He drove a stinger to How, who stopped it, picked it up, and threw it to Gould, making a beautiful play." (Chadwick Scrapbooks; DS)

sting one *v.* To hit the ball sharply.
1ST 1906. (*Sporting Life,* March 10; EJN)

stir a breeze *v.* To strike out.

stitch-ball *n.* SLOW BALL.
1ST 1915. "The second crossed the out-corner and third was Rube's wide, slow, tantilizing 'stitch-ball,' as we call it, for the reason that it came so slow a batter could count the stitches." (Zane Grey, *The Red-Headed Outfield;* DS)

stolen base *n.* A play in which a runner advances safely from one base to the next while the pitcher is in his motion. The success of the play hinges on catching the defensive team off guard. A stolen base is officially credited to the runner and becomes part of his statistical record.
1ST 1889. (*Trenton Times,* July 8; EJN)

stone *adj.* Term describing the inflexible hands and glove of a poor fielder. "It was a brisk game, marvelously enjoyable, and the innings flew by to the accompaniment of hopeful toots on a hundred horns in the stands and a flurry of witticisms in the press rows about Willie Davis's attack of stone hands in Los Angeles." (Roger Angell, *The Boys of Summer;* CDP)

stonewall *n./arch.* An unusually tight infield from which very few batted balls escape. The archetypical stonewall was that of the 1880s Chicago White Stockings, comprising Cap Anson, Fred Pfeffer, Ned Williamson and Tom Burns.
1ST 1888. (*Chicago Inter Ocean,* July 13; EJN)

stool ball *n.* Forerunner of baseball (and cricket). In the book *Bat, Ball and Bishop,* Robert William Henderson traces the game of baseball back to this game.

stoopball *n.* A baseball variation played without a bat. A rubber ball is thrown against a set of steps—or stoop—by the player on offense, while the defense tries to catch the ball on the fly as it comes off the stoop. A ball caught on the fly is an out. Hits and runs are registered by the number of bounces the ball takes or by the distance it flies.

stop *v.* To knock down, slow, smother or otherwise bring a ball under control so that it can be played.
1ST 1864. (*Brooklyn Daily Eagle,* June 3; EJN)

stop at the junk yard Jibe directed at players having trouble holding onto the ball. Example: "I'm stopping at the junk yard on the way home. Want me to pick you up some new hands." (*The Sporting News,* March 6, 1982)

stopper **1.** *n.* A starting pitcher who can be counted on to win a crucial game; a team's top pitcher; one who can stop a losing streak. "Worrell cherishes role as Cards' stopper." (headline in the *St. Petersburg Times,* March 29, 1986)
2. *n.* A relief pitcher who can be counted on to come in and stop the opposition from scoring.

Stolen base. Ty Cobb steals home for the Philadelphia Athletics (1927) against the Boston Red Sox. Catcher Grover Hartley makes a futile attempt of the tag.   *Courtesy of the Cleveland Indians.*

"The 'stoppers,' usually the most dependable on the staff, are apt to get the nod most any time." (Arthur and Milton Richman on the bullpen, *Collier's,* July 9, 1954; PT)

1ST 1948. "I had been known as the 'stopper' for the Sox for a long time and I really had to be on September 13, 1946, in Cleveland, the day we clinched the American League championship." (Tex Hughson, Boston pitcher, quoted in the *San Francisco Examiner,* March 10; PT)

straight as a string *adj.* Fastball without a hop.

straight away *adv.* Pertaining to orthodox defensive positions, which are to neither the right nor left. A center fielder is playing straight away if he is in the center of the outfield in line with the plate and second base.

straight away hitter *n.* A batter who hits the ball toward the area of the strike zone where it is pitched; for example, a right-handed batter will hit an outside pitch to right field and pull the inside pitch to left field.

straight away stance *n.* Stance in which the batter's feet are parallel to home plate.

straighten one out *v.* To hit a line drive.
1ST 1907. (*Harper's Weekly,* October 9; EJN)

strand *v.* To leave one or more runners on base at the end of the team's half inning.

stranded *adj.* LEFT ON BASE.
1ST 1905. (*Sporting Life,* September 2; EJN)

strawberry *n.* A red skin abrasion often produced by a slide into base. It has the look and hue of a strawberry.
1ST 1937. (*Pittsburgh Press,* January 11; EJN)

straw that stirs the drink, the   Phrase that Reggie Jackson once used during his Yankee years to describe where he fit in the metaphoric

Strawberry. To add insult to injury, the base runner is out. *Courtesy of the Amateur Softball Association of America*

scheme of things; in other words, the most important member of the team.

The image was strong enough to inspire many parallels. To quote from a letter to the *Baltimore Sun:* "If there is a drink to be stirred in Baltimore this baseball season, you can bet that Eddie Murray will be the straw that does it." (May 25, 1986)

streak **1.** *n.* An uninterrupted string of accomplishments or failures, such as winning streaks, losing streaks and hitting streaks.

The term is also applied to such things as consecutive-innings streaks, such as Cal Ripken Jr.'s run of 8,243 innings, which ended in September 1987.

Unquestionably, the most famous streak in baseball history was Joe DiMaggio's feat of hitting in 56 consecutive games in 1941. Few have come close to DiMaggio's record. Those who have include Pete Rose, with a streak of 44 in 1978, and Paul Molitor's 1987 run of 39 games.

Both the term and the concept have a high degree of significance. Among other things, they can help give a particular season its character. A key line in United Press International reporter Bill Wolle's summary of the 1978 season: "The season began with a record 13-game winning streak by the Milwaukee Brewers and wound up with San Diego's Benito Santiago fashioning a 34-game hitting streak, a record for rookies and catchers." (*Houston Post,* October 6, 1987; CDP)

Significantly, there is a special section of the *Official Rules* that sets forth the criteria for establishing consecutive hitting streaks, consecutive playing streaks, consecutive playing streaks and consecutive-game hitting streaks. Another major streak was established on September 28, 1988 when Orel Hershiser of the Los Angeles Dodgers pitched the longest string of scoreless innings in the history of the game. Hershiser strung up 59 in a row, besting the 58 scoreless innings put together by Dodger Don Drysdale 20 years earlier.

2. *v.* To be on a streak.

Sensational
JOE DIMAGGIO

Will Seek To Hit Safely In His
49th
Consecutive Game.

Thur. Nite, July 10
AT ST. LOUIS

Browns vs. Yankees
Sportsman's Park--8:30 P. M.

Tickets Now on Sale at Browns Arcade Ticket Office--Phone, CHestnut 7900.

Streak. From 1941, this St. Louis Browns poster turned Joe DiMaggio's hitting streak into a promotional event. *National Baseball Library, Cooperstown, N.Y.*

Stretch. A stretch at third base during Little League World Series action. *Courtesy of Little League Baseball*

streak hitter   *n.* Player known to hit in streaks, which alternate with slumps.

streaky   *adj.* Given to accomplishing things in clusters; for instance, a streaky hitter.
"Streaky Brewers Count Their Blessings in Fans." (*Washington Post* headline, August 27, 1987)

stretch   **1.** *n.* The phase of a pitcher's delivery during which his arms are raised above and behind his head. Its function is to loosen the arm and back muscles.
2. *n.* A modified windup that a pitcher uses with runners on base. It permits him to keep a closer check on the runners and to cut down on the length of time it takes to pitch the ball. It involves stretching the arms above the head, drawing them down slowly and then resting or stopping in the set position to check the runner's lead. It is known as the "stretch position." "I also remember the time I won my first major-league game. It was a shutout against the Washington Senators in which I walked seven guys and gave up seven hits and had to pitch from a stretch position all game." (Jim Bouton, *Ball Four;* CDP)

To go through the stretch without a discernable pause is to commit a balk.
3. *n.* The position taken by a baseman as he keeps one foot on the bag while reaching as far as he can to catch the ball thrown by another fielder. He is stretching to get the ball before the batter touches the base.
4. *v.* To make an extra base on a hit, usually due to fast, bold running, such as that done by runners who can enlarge—or stretch—a double into a triple. To stretch a hit.
1ST 1867. (*New York Tribune,* September 9; EJN)
5. *n.* The late season when divisional races heat up; short for homestretch, which is borrowed from horse racing.
6. *n.* SEVENTH-INNING STRETCH.

stretch drive   *n.* The extra effort of a contending team as it comes into the homestretch of the regular season.

stride   **1.** *v.* To step into and give power to one's swing when batting. Not all batters stride and some of the best have had strides of only a few inches. Daniel E. Jesse reported in his 1939 book, *Baseball:* "Joe DiMaggio, the great young hitting star of the New York Yankees, stands with feet apart and moves the left only a few inches, yet he gets tremendous distance in his drives."
Batters who do not stride are described as flat-footed. To stride to excess, as younger, less experienced players tend to do, is called over-striding.
2. *v.* In pitching, to raise one foot as the ball is about to be delivered.

stride in step with the pitch   *v.* To judge the speed of the pitch exactly and meet the ball squarely; to perfectly time the pitch. "When batters are striding in pace with the pitch the pitcher is in for a drubbing," says H. G. Salsinger in his August 1945, *Baseball Digest* article on "baseball jargon."

striding foot   **1.** *n.* The foot that the batter uses to step into the ball.
2. *n.* That foot with which a fielder or pitcher steps forward to give strength to the throw.

strike   **1.** *n.* A pitched ball that is called as such by the umpire because it is either: (a) swung at and missed, (b) in the strike zone and not swung at or (c) fouled off with less than two strikes against the batter. A batter is out after three strikes. A strike is announced as such by the plate umpire, who also signals it by raising his right hand.
1ST   1845. (Knickerbocker Rules)
2. *n.* A highly accurate throw from the outfield.
EXT   *n.* Something perfectly delivered, such as a "touchdown strike."
3. *n.* A disadvantage or mistake, almost always stated in terms of a strike or strikes against one; for example, "Her attitude is a strike against her." This usage can even be applied to baseball. A headline in the *St. Petersburg Times* for April 2, 1987: "Ueberroth makes it clear: Two drug strikes and you're out."
4. *n.* A work stoppage or walkout by the players. Much was made during the 1981 players' strike of the irony that the word was so important to the game itself. This prompted a reader of *The Sporting News* to redefine other terms in the "letters" section of the July 18, 1981, issue of that newspaper. "For example," wrote Phillip Coe, " 'walk' has been changed to 'walkout' in order to compliment the new definition of 'strike!' " Two of Coe's other redefinitions:
   stealing—what baseball is doing to the fans.
   pop-up—what everything in my stomach wants to do when I think of baseball's predicament.

strikeout   *n.* The act of becoming out or retiring on three strikes. Various rules determine the third strike: (a) an uncaught foul ball does not count as a third strike, but *any* foul bunt after two strikes counts as a third; (b) the third strike must be caught by the catcher, but if it is not, and first base is open, the batter may attempt to take the base.
   In the case of a dropped third strike, the pitcher is credited with a strikeout even if the batter reaches first successfully.
   The number of strikeouts thrown by a pitcher in a game, season or career is a barometer of his effectiveness.
1ST   1862. (*New York Sunday Mercury,* June 29; EJN)

strike out   *v.* To retire from the plate as a result of three strikes.
1ST   1874. (*New York Sun,* July 7; EJN)
EXT   To fail completely.

strikeout artist   *n.* Pitcher who strikes out a lot of batters.

strikeout king   *n.* Pitcher with the most strikeouts during any given season.
2. *n.* Pitcher with the highest total strikeouts in baseball history.
1ST   1922. (*Baseball Cyclopedia;* EJN)

striker   *n./obs.* A batter.
1ST   1845. (Knickerbocker Rules)

strike zone   *n.* The imaginary rectangle over home plate that extends from the batter's knees to his armpits as he assumes his natural stance. The size, of course, depends on the size of the batter.
   A pitch thrown in the strike zone will be called a strike if it is not swung at. One given of the game is that, despite the explicit designation of the rules, the strike zone is in reality a subjective area and its dimensions will vary from umpire to umpire and from league to league. "No pitcher playing today, not even Tommy John," writes Murray Chass in the September 6, 1987, *New York Times*, "can remember when a pitch that went just under a batter's armpits was called a strike. The upper level of the strike zone today is just above the waist." A 1949 rule change lowered the height of the zone from the shoulders to the armpits.
2. *n.* In fast-pitch softball, the strike zone is the same as in baseball; in slowpitch, any space over any part of home plate between the batter's highest shoulder and his knees.

stringbean   *n.* Tall, thin player.

stroke   **1.** *n.* An even, smooth swing, which often results in a hit.
2. *v.* To hit the ball well and with apparent ease.
3. *n./arch.* A batted ball.

stroker   *n.* Batter with a controlled swing; the opposite of a power-hitter who swings from the heels.

stroll *v.* To draw a base on balls.
1ST 1908. (*New York Evening Journal*, September 11; EJN)

'Stros Nickname for the Houston Astros, favored by headline writers who also use 'Spos for the Montreal Expos.

struggle *v.* To be in a slump. A common cliche of the game is to say that a batter is "struggling at the plate."

stuff **1.** *n.* What the pitcher puts on the ball: speed, control, a break or curve. The better the pitcher and the performance in question, the more "stuff" is in evidence.
At the time Hugh Fullerton defined it in 1912, it specifically referred to "English" or the spin on the ball, but the meaning has broadened since.
2. A pitcher's assortment of pitches collectively; his repertoire.
1ST 1905. (*Sporting Life*, September 9; EJN)

stunner *n.* A key hit.
1ST 1868. "Hatfield sends Ho home by a 'stunner' to right field." (Chadwick Scrapbooks; DS)

stunt *n.* An act designed to be different and attract the attention of the fans.
A classic example would be using one player to play all nine positions within a single game. According to an item in the May 29, 1978, *New York Times* this has been done twice: by Bert Campaneris of the Kansas City Athletics in 1965 and Cesar Tovar of the Minnesota Twins in 1968. The *Times* asserted, "These are the only two such stunts in major league history."

stuntman *n.* Honorific name for a reserve or non-starter which implies far greater involvement than the traditional benchwarmer nickname.
ETY It was first applied during the course of the 1988 season by Los Angeles Dodgers manager Tommy Lasorda. It was borrowed from the stuntmen of Hollywood fame and explained by Mickey Hatcher, one of Lasorda's stuntmen, as a proper name for "the doubles, the guys who fill in, the guys who do the dirty work." (*Sporting News*, June 27, 1988.)

styler *n.* A player who always looks good. At bat, a styler looks good before, during and after he swings.

stylin' *v.* Using up time at the plate for grooming; to take time to adjust your batting glove and adjust your uniform. "Some veterans . . . think that the proper reward for a 'stylin' player is a fast ball in the ribs." (Tom Boswell, *Washington Post*, August 30, 1981)

sub *n.* Short for substitute.
1ST 1889. (*Trenton Times*, July 24; EJN)

submarine **1.** *n.* A pitch or throw that is delivered with an underhanded or sidearm motion. Carl Mays, active with the Red Sox, Yankees, Reds and Giants from 1915 through 1929, was famous for the pitch.
1ST 1922. (*Baseball Cyclopedia;* EJN)
2. *v.* To pitch using the submarine delivery.
ETY Derived from the underwater vessel.

submariner *n.* A pitcher who uses the submarine style delivery.

substitute **1.** *n.* Any player not in the original lineup who is brought into the game. Players who have been removed from a game may not return.
USE Although substitute is a legitimate and useful term in baseball, it is usually too general to cover specific situations. The preferred form is to specify the exact role of the substitute (pinch runner, short reliever).
2. *v.* To put a player into a game in progress in any of a number of roles including relief pitcher, pinch hitter, pinch runner or as a replacement for a player who is injured or ill.

suburbs *n.* Destination of the long ball; where monstrous home runs land. The same idea is involved in the expression that a ball has gone downtown.

subway series World Series in which the two opposing clubs could travel between their home grounds by using the New York City subway system.
It traditionally referred to a World Series played between the New York Yankees and the Brooklyn Dodgers (the last one took place in 1956), but today it is most commonly used when a Yankees vs. Mets World Series might be in the offing. Writing on the subject in the *New York Times*, Samuel G. Freedman said, "Subway series is a synonym for civil war." (October 19, 1986)
EXT As other sports have fielded two New York City area teams the term has come to refer figuratively to pairings of the Rangers and Islanders in hockey and the Jets and Giants in football (even though some of these teams are not reached by subway).

Submariner. Kansas City Royals pitcher Dan Quisenberry unleashes another "underhand" pitch. *Courtesy of the Kansas City Royals*

subway slinger *n.* Underhand pitcher; submariner.
ETY From the concept of a subway being under(ground).

sucker *n.* Blooper, especially one that makes the fielders trying to get to it look foolish.
1ST 1868. "Al Reach sent a sucker to right, which gave him first . . ." (Chadwick Scrapbooks; DS)

Suds Series Nickname for the 1982 World Series between the Cardinals and Brewers, representing two teams with ties to beer—suds. The Milwaukee team is named for that city's production of beer and the St. Louis Team is owned by the Busch family, which is the Busch of Anheuser-Busch breweries.

suicide squeeze *n.* SQUEEZE PLAY. This volatile term highlights the gamble involved and stands in contrast to the *safety squeeze*.

sullivan *n./arch.* One who sits up all night; player who will not sleep in a train. For the origin of the term see Sullivan sleeper.

Sullivan sleeper *n./arch.* A railroad daycoach. This is a late-19th-century term, which sometimes showed up as "O'Sullivan sleeper" in later references. In his 1943 article on baseball slang, Herbert Simons brought it up in the context of World War II: "One phrase obsolete in the majors likely will be in vogue again this coming season. That's the 'O'Sullivan sleeper,' the old-timers slang for a day coach."
1ST 1886. "I did not indulge in a Pullman, but took what ball-players call a 'Sullivan sleeper',—that is, I sat up all night in the smoker." (*Lippincott's* magazine, August; DS)
ETY Almost certainly from Ted Sullivan, manager of the Washington Senators, who was notoriously stingy when it came to providing the more expensive sleeping berths. For instance, when he took the team to Florida in 1888 he provided 14 daycoach seats for the 14 players but only seven Pullman berths.

Sultan of Swat Nickname for Babe Ruth.
There have been a number of puckish plays on this title. "A spring season sloth, Horner is the sultan of slow starters," is how Cardinal Bob Horner was described by Roy Cummings of the *Tampa Tribune* (April 3, 1988).
Also, an award named in honor of native Baltimorean, Babe Ruth and given by the Maryland Professional Baseball Players Association.
ETY In *The Armchair Book of Baseball* John

Sultan of Swat. Babe Ruth in 1920 after hitting a then-record third home run in one day (during a doubleheader with the Washington Senators). In the caption to the inset photo, Ruth is quoted as saying he will hit at least 40 home runs by the end of the season. He went on to hit 54 of them.   *Prints and Photographs Division, the Library of Congress*

Thorn traces the title to the Indian state of Swat that once had a sultan or akhond. When the sultan died in 1878 his obituary appeared in the *Times* of London. It inspired Edward Lear to write a ditty called "The Akond of Swat." Thorn says the poem was "surely some sportswriter's inspiration for Ruth's 'title.' " In baseballese, a swat is a long hit—something Ruth specialized in.

Sunday ball   *n.* Baseball played on the Sabbath. Once the most divisive of issues, this was a red flag to those who believed that baseball, especially the professional version, should not take place on the Sabbath.

Sunday best/Sunday pitch   *n.* A pitcher's most effective offering; his out pitch. Correspondingly, a batter may have a Sunday swing. "Well, a pitcher out there, if he's a fast ball pitcher, his best pitch, what we call a Sunday Pitch, would be his fast ball," Dizzy Dean in his 1952 *Dizzy Baseball.*

sun field   *n.* That portion of the playing field where there is the most sun in the fielders' eyes during an afternoon game. To many, the most notorious sun field in baseball is left field at Yankee Stadium, especially the late afternoon sun of October, when the World Series is played. The proliferation of night games has given this term a whiff of nostalgia.

sunglasses   *n.* Dark-tinted eyeglasses used as a protection from the sun; part of the uniform of many players, especially outfielders, during day games. Modern baseball sunglasses differ from other sunglasses in that the lens portion rests against the player's forehead and is flipped down over the eyes as needed.

sun hit   *n.* Batted ball that falls in for a hit because the fielder loses track of it in the sun. **1ST**   1897. (*New York Tribune,* August 9; EJN)

sunshine game, the   *n.* BASEBALL. "It's hard to see how any of this constitutes a menace to the sunshine game." (Roger Angell, *The Summer Game;* CDP)

superscout   *n.* Unofficial title for scout who locates more than his share of talented players. Jim Russo of the Baltimore Orioles, for example.

support   *n.* Fielding aid to the pitcher in disposing of batters.
1ST   1867. (Chadwick Scrapbooks; EJN)

surprise bunt   *n.* A bunt that is attempted when the circumstances of the game do not suggest one.
1ST   1935. "There are two types, the sacrifice bunt and the surprise bunt." (Ralph H. Barbour, *How to Play Better Baseball;* DS)

surveyor   *n.* Player with a good eye at the plate; one who walks a lot, watching as bad balls go by.

suspended game   *n.* A game that has been stopped to be completed at a later date; for instance, one that is still being played at the time a curfew goes into effect.

suspension   **1.** *n.* The temporary stopping of play, for such game-related occurrences as an injured player or dead ball. External causes for a suspension of play primarily come from bad weather.
2. *n.* A period of time during which a player, manager or coach is ordered from the field of play because of a flagrant violation of the rules. Typically, suspension is the punishment for doctoring the bat or ball, refusing to obey the umpire or touching an umpire during an argument. "The Pirates are going so badly that their mascot, the Parrot, was suspended for a game after throwing a Nerf Ball at umpire Brocklander." (Richard Justice in the *Washington Post,* May 3, 1987)

SV   Abbreviation for SAVE.

swang   *v.* According to Dizzy Dean, who had his own patent on the term, "This is what a guy has done after he has took a cut and missed." *Time* magazine once commented on Dean's creative way with the word swing, "The fans also noted, for future reference, that the Arkansas-born announcer conjugates the verb *to swing* as *swing, swanged, swunged.*" (April 24, 1950)

swat   **1.** *v.* To hit the ball with power and for distance.
1ST   1891. (*Chicago Herald,* August 25; EJN)

2. *n.* A long hit, good for extra bases.
USE   Over time, the word swat has been put into a number of other baseball constructions. In his 1934 *Dictionary of American Slang,* Maurice Weseen lists, among others, *swatfest, swat parade, swatsman, swat streak* and *swatter.*
ETY   Term has long signified a knock, hit or hard rub.
EXT   This fascinating item appeared in the July 1948 issue of *American Notes & Queries:*
FLY SWATTER: a term coined by Dr. Samuel J. Crumbine, who in 1904 was appointed head of the Kansas State Board of Health; he was taking a bulletin—on flies as typhoid carriers—to the printer one day, and stopped off to watch a ball game, where he heard "sacrifice fly!" and "swat the ball," etc., and immediately decided to call the bulletin "Swat the fly." Only a few months later a man came to him with an instrument that he wanted to call a "fly bat" and Dr. Crumbine persuaded him to call it a "fly-swatter."

swatsmith   *n.* SWATTER.
1ST   1908. (*New York Evening Journal,* May 5; EJN)

swatstick   *n.* Bat in the hands of a swatsmith.
1ST   1915. "Abruptly, Bob lifted the swat-stick and balanced it in his strong hands, weighing it carefully." (Gilbert Patten, *Courtney of the Center Garden,* DS)

swat team   *n.* Has recently come into play for a team's collection of home run hitters, following the use of the term for quasi-military police units. "Infield 'swat team' adds Leo Hernandez." (*Baltimore Sun* headline, March 31, 1983)

swatter   *n.* SLUGGER.
1ST   1908. (*Spalding's Official Base Ball Guide;* EJN)

sweat ball   *n.* Variation on the spitball.

sweep   *v.* To win all of the games in a series; to make a clean sweep. Fans have been known to wave whisk brooms as they chant "Sweep! Sweep!" as the home team bids to complete a winning series.
2. *v.* The term is also used to describe a team that has won both games of a doubleheader.
3. *n.* A series of wins over time.

sweeping   *n.* A batter's swinging his arms too far from his body. It is a deficiency that detracts from power and accuracy.

sweetheart *n.* A star, especially one who comes through in a pinch.
1ST 1937. (*Fortune* magazine, August; EJN)
USE The term is reserved for those players who are the greatest assets to their clubs although they may not in fact, grab the headlines. Lou Gehrig, Hank Aaron and Mike Schmidt are three who fit the description to a tee.

sweet spot *n.* The place on a bat where the ball can be hit for maximum power; the "joy spot" where one is most likely to hit the ball solidly.

swing **1.** *v.* To move the bat in a full arc in an attempt to hit a pitched ball. A batter who swings and misses is credited with a strike even if the ball is thrown outside the strike zone. This is important when a batter attempts to stop his swing. If the umpire decides that the batter stopped before making a bona fide attempt to meet the ball, it is not considered a swing and the pitch will be ruled a ball.
2. *n.* A cut at the ball; the action of a batter in attempting to hit the ball.

1ST 1905. (*Sporting Life*, October 7; EJN)
EXT To undertake some endeavor is to "take a swing at it."

swing away *v.* To take a full cut at the ball.

swinger **1.** *n.* A batter who takes a full cut at the ball rather than choking up on the bat and simply trying to meet the ball. In the pre-Ruthian year of 1912 Hugh Fullerton wrote: "The 'swinger' is a type of player not wanted in finished ball clubs. They usually are long distance hitters, but uncertain and usually finish with low averages." This opinion does not prevail today.
1ST 1910. (*American* magazine, July; EJN)
2. *n.* A batter who, in the words of Jim Brosnan, ". . . will try to hit any pitch that doesn't hit him."

swing for the fences *v.* To attempt to hit a home run by swinging with maximum force.
EXT To go all out.

swing from the heels *v.* To swing with all of one's power, which involves rocking back on

Sweetheart. Exhibit in Cooperstown devoted to one of the game's sweethearts. *National Baseball Library, Cooperstown, N.Y.*

one's heels for added leverage. It contrasts with a simple, level swing, which is often more effective. "The Pirates, a notorious swing-from-the-heels bunch [five Pirates had 10 or more hits in the Series, a record], seemed to delight in adversity," from a special advertising insert that appeared in *Time* and other magazines just prior to the 1981 Series.

swinging bunt   *n.* A poke at the ball that is effectively a half bunt and half swing. Though sometimes claimed to be intentional, a swinging bunt is commonly the result of a pitch being hit on a checked swing, usually one that is topped and bounces slowly into the infield. It is not scored as a bunt even though it has the characteristic roll of one.

swing late   *v.* To cut at the ball as it is crossing the plate and thus impossible to hit. The bane of the beginner and inexperienced player.

swing like a rusty gate   *v.* To look inept and perform badly at the plate.

swipe a hassock   *v.* Steal a base.

swish   **1.**   *n.* A hard swing of the bat that makes no contact with the ball.
2 *v.* To swing hard and miss.

switch-hit   *v.* To bat from either the right- or left-handed side of the plate, depending on the circumstances of the game.

switch-hitter   *n.* A batter who can and does hit from either side of the plate. Players with this skill tend to bat from the right against left-handed pitchers and vice versa. This ability was rare in earlier decades, and in 1938 syndicated baseball writer Jerry Brondfield wrote: "Switch-hitting appears to be dying out in baseball, bearing out Andy High's contention that the noble athletes, despite lingering ideas to the contrary, can do better by confining their activities to one side of the plate." (*San Francisco News*, July 4; PT)

But more and more players have developed the ability to hit both ways since a switch-hitter named Mickey Mantle first came to both sides of the plate in 1951. Pete Rose, Eddie Murray, Howard Johnson, Tony Fernandez, Tim Raines, Ozzie Smith and Kevin Bass are examples of post-Mantle-era switch-hitters.

The first player to professionally switch-hit, according to a conclusion on file at the National Baseball Library, was Robert V. Ferguson, captain of the Brooklyn Atlantics. He employed the switch on June 14, 1870, when the Atlantics handed the Cincinnati Red Stockings their first defeat.
EXT   Any person who radically alternates his or her orientation. Commonly applied to a person who "swings both ways"—that is, one who is bisexual.

switch-pitch   **1.**   *n.*   Change-of-pace ball. "American Leaguers who had batted against him said he was tough when he kept the ball low, especially his change-up or switch-pitch." (*San Francisco Examiner*, April 10, 1963; PT)
2. *v.* To be able to pitch both right- and left-handed in the same game. An extremely rare ability.

syndicate baseball   *n.* Situation in which one person or a small group working together might have interests in more than one club in a league. It is a bygone evil that was once very real. During the winter of 1898–99, it was announced that much of the Baltimore club, including its manager, would be transferred to Brooklyn by a man who owned the Baltimore team and had a part interest in the Brooklyn club. There had been a falloff in attendance in Baltimore and the talent of the two teams was to be pooled, with Brooklyn getting the best players.

"The respectable public won't stand for 'frame ups,' 'syndicate ball' or a suspicion of crookedness." (*Letters of a Baseball Fan to His Son*, by S. DeWitt; Clough, Chicago, 1910; PT)

synthetic turf   *n.* See artificial grass.

Syracuse Car   *n.* As defined in *Babe Ruth's Own Book of Baseball:* "the Pullman in which the rookies and substitutes ride. Originated with the Giants who used to play an exhibition game in Syracuse each year. Usually the second string men would play the game and their car would be shunted off at Syracuse while the others went off to the next big league town to enjoy a day off."
1ST   1928. In the above quote from *Babe Ruth's Own Book;* DS)

T

T Box score abbreviation for the total time a game has taken.

tab *v.* To select a player, such as tabbing a pitcher to start a game.

tabasco *n.* Vigor.
1ST 1895. (*New York Press,* July 8; EJN)

table is set, the A runner or runners are in scoring position.

table-setter *n.* Player who gets on base and/ or advances others to set up a scoring opportunity.

tag **1.** *v.* To touch a base runner with the ball itself or a glove holding the ball, resulting in an out.

2. *v.* To touch a base with any portion of the body while in possession of the ball.
3. *v.* To hit the ball hard.
1ST 1917. (*American* magazine, July; EJN)
4. *v.* For a runner to touch the bag after a fly has been caught; to TAG UP.

tag out *v.* To put a man out by touching him with the ball when he is off the base.

tag up/tag-up *v.* To touch the base before advancing. With fewer than two outs, a base runner attempting to gain a base or score on a fly ball must tag up the moment the fly is caught, but not a split second earlier. On a reasonably deep fly ball, a runner on third will normally have time to tag up and score.

Tag out. She should have been sliding. *Courtesy of the Amateur Softball Association of America*

tail away *v.* For a pitched ball to move down and away from the batter.

tailender/tail-ender *n.* Team at or near the bottom of the standings.
1ST 1886. "Even the 'coming champions' will have their turns of ill-fortune, while the lives of the 'tail-enders' are awful to contemplate." (*Lippincott's* magazine, August; DS)

tailing fastball *n.* Fastball that moves away from the batter as it approaches the plate.

take *v.* To defeat an opponent.
1ST 1880. (*Chicago Inter Ocean* October 7; EJN)
ETY Edward J. Nichols's assessment: "Named by shortening of the phrase 'take into camp' or 'take the measure of.' "

take/take a pitch/take a strike/take one *v.* To refrain from swinging at a pitched ball; to permit one strike to be thrown before swinging at the ball; to look at a pitch. Batters often do this to get an idea of what a pitcher is throwing. Taking is most common when the count is 3-0. A batter may be told to "take" by his manager, which occasioned Jim Brosnan to give this definition of taking: "a batter being forced to watch a pitch cross the plate that he obviously would have hit out of the ball park if the manager had only permitted him to swing."
1ST 1854. (Knickerbocker Rules; EJN)

take a cut *v.* To swing hard at the ball.
1ST 1932. (*Baseball* magazine, October; EJN)

take a drink *v.* To STRIKE OUT; the presumption being that the batter now has time to go back to the dugout for water.
1ST 1916. (Ring Lardner, *You Know Me Al*; EJN)

take a little off *v.* See TAKE SOMETHING OFF A PITCH.

take a nap *v.* To get picked off base.

take him deep/take him downtown/take him over the wall *v.* To hit a homerun off a pitcher. Correspondingly, a pitcher will say a given batter "took me deep."
USE Often stated in the form of an exhortation.

"Take him out!" Traditional call from the stands for the manager to remove an ineffective player, almost always a pitcher.
1ST 1908. (*Baseball* magazine, December; EJN)

"Take Me Out to the Ballgame" Baseball's unofficial anthem, written by Jack Norworth in 1908. Norworth, who also wrote the hit "Shine on Harvest Moon," was honored with a special day at Ebbets Field in 1940.

take off **1.** *v.* For a pitched ball to suddenly rise or deviate laterally as it nears the plate.
2. *v.* To leave a base in a hurry, such as in an attempted steal.

take one for the team *v.* To allow oneself to be hit by a pitched ball. A batter hit by a pitch is automatically awarded first base.

take one on the meat *v.* To be hit by a pitched ball.

take out *v.* In the process of running the bases, to block or slide into an infielder. It is usually done to disrupt the infielder's throw to another base.

take-out play *n.* Offensive move in which a base runner slides into a fielder in such a way as to attempt to prevent him from making a pivot for a double play.

take sign *n.* A signal from a coach telling a batter not to swing at—to take—the next pitch. Alternative definition from Jimmy Cannon: "How a manager tells a hitter he hasn't any confidence in him."
1ST 1937. (*Philadelphia Record*, October 9; EJN)

take something off a pitch/take something off it *v.* To throw a change-up or slow ball after a fastball or series of fastballs.

take the bat out of his hands **1.** *v.* To keep from hitting, which means either to pitch with great effectiveness or to intentionally walk the batter.
2. *v.* To attempt to steal a base with a good hitter at the plate, thus creating the option to intentionally walk the batter.

take the blood off it *v.* Advice to a player who has just gotten a weak hit, an obvious play on the fact that such hits are sometimes called bleeders.

take the button off his hat *v.* To deck or dust off the batter with a ball that comes close to his head

take the trainer to dinner *v.* Said of a player who is frequently in the trainer's room.

"Take three and sit down": Jeering admonition to a batter, likely to come from the stands or the bench of the opposing team.

take two **1.** *v.* Instruction to allow two strikes to be called in the hopes that the pitcher will issue a walk.
1ST 1909. (*American* magazine, May; EJN)
2. *v.* Instruction to take two bases on a hit.

take two and hit to right Traditional instruction to struggling batter that calls for him to let two pitches go by—take two—and then hit the ball to the right side of the field.

In trying to define this bit of advice in an article in the August 1987 *Vineline*, Keith Moreland could not contain his contempt: "I mean, you're struggling and somebody wants you to *take* two pitches and hit the next one to right-field!"

take your base *v.* Traditional instruction by umpire to batter who has just been given a base on balls or has been hit by a pitch.
1ST 1867. (Chadwick Scrapbooks: EJN)

talesman *n./obs.* OFFICIAL SCORER in some circles in the very early days of the game.

tall grass/tall timber/tall uncut/tall weed *n./arch.* The BUSHES.
1ST 1905 (tall timber). (*Sporting Life*, September 9; EJN)

tally **1.** *n.* a RUN.
1ST 1874. (*Chicago Inter Ocean*, July 21; EJN)
2. *v.* To score a run.

tank town *n./arch.* Small town to old-timers, probably from the fact that a train normally stopped in such a place only to take on water from a water tank.

tap **1.** *n.* A lightly batted ball.
1ST 1901. (*Frank Merriwell's Marvel;* EJN)
2. *v.* To bat without power.

tape job/tape-measure homer/tape-measure job/tape-measure shot *n.* A very long home run; one that calls for measurement. At the major league level the word tape measure is linked to blasts in the vicinity of 500 feet. "Balboni, 29, starred for Eckerd College in 1977 and 1978 and earned the nickname 'Bye, Bye Balboni' in the minor leagues for his tape-measure home runs." (article on Steve Balboni in *St. Petersburg Times*, March 16, 1986)
ETY/1ST 1953. The expression and the custom it refers to date to a spectacular home run

hit by Mickey Mantle off of Washington Senator Chuck Stobbs at Griffith Stadium. Yankee public relations director Red Patterson immediately got up, left the ballpark, found a witness who had seen the ball land and measured the distance to the spot. The total distance was in the neighborhood of 560 feet, one of the longest on record.

tapper *n.* Lightly hit ball. One without power, but perhaps well placed. "Forsch gave up a ground-rule double to Larkin to open the Cincinnati third but Forsch struck out Davis on a high fastball, got Parker on a tapper and Daniels on a bouncer to Clark." (*St. Louis Post-Dispatch,* June 2, 1987)

tapperitis hitter *n./arch.* Batter who hits tappers.

tap-tap *adj.* Describing a close play in which the runner is out; similar to the bang-bang play.

target **1.** *n.* The positioning of the catcher's hands prior to the pitcher's delivery. The catcher places the mitt at the exact point where the ball should be pitched.
2. *n.* By extension, the outstretched catcher's mitt, which the pitcher is trying to hit with the ball.

tarp *n.* Short for tarpaulin. The common name for the covering used to protect the playing field during a downpour. Baseball's oddest tarp incident came in the midst of the 1985 National League Championship Series when Cardinal Vince Coleman was injured by a moving motorized tarp that caught his leg.
ETY From the nautical canvas used to cover hatches.

Tartan Turf *n.* A brand name of artificial turf. "This is a very good hitting ball park. The Tartan Turf permits many balls to skip through the infield and through the outfield as well for extra bases." (Edwin Silberstang on Royals Stadium, in *Playboy's Guide to Baseball Betting;* CDP)

tarzan *n.* "A slovenly, frowzy baseball player," according to Maurice H. Weseen in his 1934 *Dictionary of American Slang.*

tater *n.* A HOME RUN; aka long tater. "I'm a line-drive hitter, and if it happens to be up in the air, then I have a tater." (Lloyd Moseby, quoted in the *St. Petersburg Times*, March 11, 1987)

"Taters," Reggie Jackson has been quoted as

saying on more than one occasion, "that's where the money is."

ETY   Term that may have originated in the old Negro Leagues as "potato" and "long potato" but took on new life when George Scott made a habit of calling them "taters" when he came to the Red Sox in 1966. One observer wrote in 1971 that the term "will probably die when he is given his final release." Scott last played in 1978 but the term is still in use—with variations, like tater trot for home run tally. "Their tater trot has been led by the 27 . . . of lefthander Bell." (*New York Post*, June 29, 1987)

tattooed man   *n.* Pitcher who has been hit hard; who has been tattooed by batted balls.

TB   Common abbreviation for total bases.

T-ball/tee-ball   *n.* Game, played mostly by very young children, that features a stationary tee at home plate. Batters attempt to hit a rubber ball placed on top of the adjustable tee.

TC   *n.* Insignia for "Twin Cities" that appeared on the Minnesota Twins' caps until 1987 when it was replaced by an M for Minnesota. The TC insignia was moved to the Twins' uniform sleeve. Outside the Minneapolis-St. Paul area, the TC initials have left fans guessing.

T-card   *n.* Tobacco card in baseball card collecting circles. Most of the early baseball cards were issued with tobacco.

teacher   *n.* MANAGER.
1ST   1917. (*New York Times*, October 6; EJN)

teacup end   *n.* Describing a bat that has been scooped-out at the top. A Japanese innovation, cupped bats have been legal in the Major Leagues since the 1971 meeting of the Playing Rules Committee. The concave shape allows the bat weight to be shaved by an ounce or so over the same bat with a convex end. Some believe that the cup creates a vacuum, which allows the batter to get extra speed in his swing, but this was disputed when the Committee legalized the bat with the conclusion that, "the driving power is not accentuated, and batter does not have an advantage."

team   1. *n.* The nine players in a game—10 when the designated hitter is allowed.
2. *n.* The entire uninformed congregation of a baseball club, including players, coaches and the manager.
1ST   1868. (*New York Herald*, July, 24; EJN)

T-card. T-cards of Philadelphia's National League club (1887) for Old Judge cigarettes. *Prints and Photographs Division, the Library of Congress*

team rules   *n.* Regulations that obtain at a particular ballpark and for a particular team. Paul I. Fagan, who owned the minor league San Francisco Seals from 1945 to 1963, is an example of an owner who made a number of them. His obituary recounted that: "Fagan banned billboard ads and insisted players shave before games, quit swearing, and [quit] chewing tobacco. At one time he even banned the sale of peanuts at the park." AP, December 19, 1960; PT)

tear   *n.* A winning streak for a team; a hot period for an individual. "To be on a tear" is how it is commonly expressed.

teaser   *n.* An especially deceptive pitcher.

tee   *n.* A simple, adjustable device on which a baseball is placed and batted at. See T-ball.

tee off   *v.* To hit one hard, an obvious borrowing from golf where the tee shot is the power shot. Players generally "tee off a pitcher's delivery," which William G. Brandt described in his 1932 article on baseballese as to, "step right up and swing from their ankles instead of crouching carefully and taking a good look before making a pass at anything tossed towards the plate."
1ST   1932. (*Baseball* magazine, October; EJN)

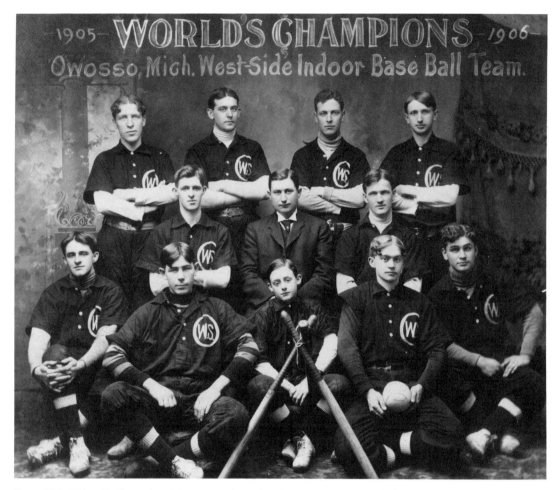

Team. This "World" Championship team strikes a familiar pose. *Prints and Photographs Division, the Library of Congress*

tee party **1.** *n.* Game or portion of a game in which batters get strong hits—tee off—against a pitcher
2. *n.* A batting streak.
1ST 1932. (*Baseball* magazine, October; EJN)

telegraph/telegraph a pitch *v.* For a pitcher to suggest through his mannerisms what kind of pitch he is about to throw. The catcher can also telegraph a pitch by giving an identifiable sign to the pitcher.
1ST 1916. (*American* magazine, August; EJN)

Temple Cup A post-season best of seven series played from 1894 through 1897 and again in 1900 between the two top teams in the National League. Named for William C. Temple who once owned the Pittsburgh Pirates.

tenant *n.* BASE RUNNER.

ten cent beer night BEER NIGHT.

10-five man *n.* Major league player who has been in the majors for 10 years and with the same team for five. The significance of the term is that 10-five players are allowed to veto trades involving them. For instance, it was noted that Mike Flanagan could have vetoed his trade from the Baltimore Orioles to the Toronto Blue Jays late in the 1987 season because of his 10-five status.

tenney *n./arch.* A padded glove around the turn of the century. According to Joseph McBride in *High and Inside*, it referred to Fred Tenney, a famous fielder, and his fat, circular glove.

10 o'clock hitter *n.* Player who hits well during morning practice sessions, but who is a poor hitter during the game.

ten run rule *n.* In some amateur leagues a game is stopped and a winner declared after seven innings if one team is 10 or more runs ahead.

tenth man **1.** *n.* The crowd in the sense that it can help or hinder a team.
2. *n.* An umpire who seems to be favoring one team.
3. *n.* The designated hitter.

territory **1.** *n.* General area for which a fielder is responsible.
2. *n.* Fair or foul ground; a ball is said to land in fair or foul territory.

Texas League AA minor league with eight franchises, in San Antonio, Midland, El Paso and Wichita, Kansas; Little Rock, Arkansas; Jackson, Mississippi; Shreveport, Louisiana; and Tulsa, Oklahoma.

Texas League grip *n.* Nickname for *The Sporting News.* Charley Graham in an interview published just after his death in 1948 discussed the term while recalling the life of a minor league player at the turn of the century: "Our reading matter was *The Sporting News* or the 'Texas League grip.' You wrapped your shirt, collar and underwear in it and that was your suitcase." (*San Francisco News,* August 31, 1948; PT)

Texas Leaguer/Texas League single **1.** *n.* A poorly hit ball that loops meekly over the infield and lands for a hit. H. L. Mencken defines it as, "A pop fly which nevertheless takes the batter to first base."

"Term current everywhere but in Texas League" was part of the definition of the term in the 1933 *Baseball Scrap Book.*

Other names for the same hit include: awful, banjo hit, bleeder, blooper, drooper, humpie, humpback, humpback liner, Japanese liner, Leaping Lena, looper, percentage sinker, plunker, pooper, punker, smell hit, squibber, stinker and sucker.
USE This term is always being tagged as archaic or old-fashioned but, nevertheless, retains its currency. Here is how Damon Runyon used it in 1933: "Cronin, with two and two on him, drops a lucky hit back of third. It is of the variety that used to be called 'Texas Leaguers.'

It is too far back for Critz, and not far enough for Ott to get." (*San Francisco Examiner,* October 7; PT)
1ST 1905. (*Sporting Life,* October 7; EJN)
ETY In his 1912 "Primer," Hugh S. Fullerton says such hits are usually accidental but are sometimes accomplished on purpose "by good batters who merely tap the ball and float it safe." He goes on to say: "The term originated from the fact that Ted Sullivan, the veteran player-manager-magnate had a team in the Texas League that was noted for that kind of batting."

However, Hy Turkin in his *Baseball Almanac* states that the term originated much earlier: "First used to describe the kind of hits that enabled Arthur Sunday, fresh out of the defunct Texas League, to finish with a .398 batting average at Toledo in 1889." This version ends with a quote from a Toledo sportswriter that Sunday had hit another of those "Texas League hits."

Equally common is the version that traces the term to either the major league debut of Ollie Pickering in 1896 or his earlier debut in Houston of the Texas League. There are various versions of the story, but the earliest version (1906) tells of him showing up in Houston where he is given a trial with the team. He gets seven hits in his first seven at bats, all of them bloopers. An unidentified news clipping of April 2, 1906, (on file at the Hall of Fame) says that as word of the feat spread these hits became known as Texas Leaguers, since they had been made in the Texas League.

The Encyclopedia of Sports Talk offers this theory: "So called because before the turn of the century the parks in the Texas League were particularly small." This contrasts dramatically with the theory Bill Brandt proposed on his "Inside Sports" radio show: "In former days, the fences in the Texas baseball parks were away out in the wide open spaces, far from home plate. The outfielders had to play deep, and the consequence was that many short flies went for hits." (September 9, 1946; recorded by PT)

Finally there is the Gulf Stream theory that E. V. Durling set forth in a 1948 column and attributed to Giants infielder Larry Doyle. According to Doyle, "the strong winds from the Gulf Stream greatly affected flyballs in most of the cities of the Texas League. A hard hit fly would seem certain to reach an outfielder and

be too far out for an infielder. Then the wind would stop the ball's progress and cause it to drop for a hit between the outfielder and infielder." (*San Francisco Examiner;* PT)
2. *v./arch.* To bloop the ball.
1ST 1912. "If you can't shoot 'em, Texas League 'em." (*Sporting Life,* May 18.)

Texas Rangers   The name of the American League Western Division franchise in Arlington, Texas. The team was once the expansion Washington Senators (1961–1971) before moving to Texas where it was named for the state's most famous law-enforcement group.

"That one'll bring rain."   Expression sometimes used to describe a very high fly ball.

the   *article* Word that has had a peculiar role in baseball. As explained by Leonard Shecter in his June 1963 *Baseball Digest* article, "Baseball Spoken Here": " 'The' is the most used word in baseball. No one knows why, but one does not simply say, 'He is a good hitter.' The expression is: 'He's got THE good bat.' One doesn't say anybody is a poor fielder; rather 'He's got THE bad hands.' "

In the lexicon that accompanied the article, Shecter included such examples as: "He's got the tools" and "He's got the good wheels."

The Book   **1.** *n.* Information on the strengths and weaknesses of players on the opposing team. Usually expressed as "to have the book on" a player.
2. *n.* Collection of assumptions and percentages used to make decisions—that is, if one goes by the book.

theft   *n.* Stolen base.

"they ought to pay their way into the ball parks"   Long-established taunt made by pitchers about outfielders and by outfielders about pitchers.

"they show movies on a flight like that"   Comment for a booming home run ball.
1ST 1983. (Tom Marr about a John Lowenstein home run, WTOP, August 28; reported by Joseph C. Goulden)

thimble   *n.* A small glove.

think tank   *n.* The brain; contents of a player's or manager's cap.
1ST 1909. "But 'Blondy' Moeller got things twisted in his think tank and allowed the ball

to ooze through his dinner tongs . . ." (Edward M. Thierry, "Slang of the Sporting Writers," *Baseball* magazine, September)
EXT   Many years after its original use as baseball slang this term became general slang for brain and then for a policy research institute, such as the Rand Corporation.

third/third base   **1.** *n.* The base located to the left side of home plate which is three quarters of the way around the bases on the way to scoring a run.
2. *n.* Position played by third baseman.
1ST   1854 (third base). (Knickerbocker Rules; EJN)

third base coach   *n.* Uniformed coach who stands in the coaching box adjacent to third base. He normally decides whether a base runner should stop at third or head home, and commonly gives signals to the batter.

third baseman   *n.* Defensive player who covers third base.
EXT   A blackjack term for the player on the left-hand side of the table who is the last player to be able to ask for a hit. (*Scientific Blackjack and Complete Casino Guide* by Donald I. Collyer, 1966)

third sacker   *n.* THIRD BASEMAN.

third strike dropped   *n.* DROPPED THIRD STRIKE.

30-30 club   *n.* Select group of 30-30 guys collectively.

30-30 guy   *n.* A player who has hit 30 home runs and stolen 30 bases in the same season. " 'We talk a lot about 30-30 guys,' Orioles General Manager Hank Peters said, 'They don't come along too often. This guy has a chance.' " (article on Ken Gerhart, *Washington Post,* March 22, 1987)

Thomas Edison   *n./arch.* Pitcher who is continually experimenting with new pitches.

thread the needle   *v.* To pitch with skill and precision; to keep the batter from hitting he ball.

threat   **1.** *n.* Team likely to contend for first place.
2. *n.* Player likely to hit or steal.

three and two.   *n.* Three balls and two strikes on the batter. Unless the batter fouls it off, the next pitch will determine if the batter is out or gets on base. See full count.

1ST   1908. (*Baseball* magazine, July; EJN)

three-bagger   *n.* TRIPLE.

three-base hit   *n.* Triple. In his 1947 "Rookie Diction-err-y," Milton Richman defined it as, "The poke invented to test your wind."

1ST   1879. (*Spirit of the Times*, August 23; EJN)

three blind mice   *n.* Before the fourth umpire was added to the crew, a phrase used to heckle the umpires as they came out of the dugout. One oft-told tale had Leo Durocher leading thousands of fans in greeting the umpiring crew, on the day after a series of disputed calls, with: "Three blind mice, See how they come!"

At Ebbets Field a zany band of musicians known as the Dodger Symphony used to play "Three Blind Mice" when the umps came out. It has since been picked up by ballpark organists who have been known to play a few bars of the song after a disputed call. In 1985 an organist for the Class A Clearwater Phillies was ejected from the stadium for playing the song.

three-decker   *n.* Towering home run capable of landing in the real or imagined third and uppermost deck of a large stadium.

Three-Eye League/Three-I League   *n./arch.* Minor league composed of teams from Illinois, Iowa and Indiana. Used in a derogatory manner when talking of the ineptness of minor league players.

1ST   1902 (.300 class). (*Sporting Life*, July 5; EJN)

three foot lines   *n.* The lines marking the last half of the distance to first base.

.300 Class/.300 Hitter/.300 Man   *n.* Term for a player whose batting average is .300. It is a term of high distinction, as an average above, or even close to, .300 is remarkable in any league.

1ST   1902 (.300 class). (*Sporting Life*, July 5; EJN)

300th victory   *n.* Major mark of accomplishment for a pitcher. "Well I sent Gaylord Perry a telegram early last week about his 300th victory." (Early Wynn in the *New York Times*, May 4, 1982)

three old cat   *n.* Variant form of baseball.

three-quarters delivery   *n.* Pitch that is thrown with the arm in between the sidearm and overhead deliveries.

3RH + WPG = WINS   Formula advocated by Earl Weaver, which translates to "three-run homers plus well-pitched games equal victories." (*The Baltimore Sun*, May 25, 1986)

Three Rivers Stadium   Located in Pittsburgh, Pennsylvania, the home grounds of the Pittsburgh Pirates since 1970. It takes its name from the fact that it is located at the point where the Ohio, Allegheny and Monongahela Rivers converge. It was once known as "The House that Clemente Built," for Hall of Fame right fielder Roberto Clemente.

three-sacker   *n.* Triple.

1ST   1870. "Barnes hit a three-sacker, bringing Deming in." (*The Yale Courant*, October 5; DS)

3-6 game   *n.* Contest in which three players produce six of a team's hits. A large number of these will make a team successful over the long run.

3-6-3   *adj.* Term used to distinguish a double play in which the ball goes from the first baseman, to the shortstop, back to the first baseman.

three up, three down   *n./adj.* Said of an inning in which three batters are retired in order.

throat cutter   *n.* A knockdown pitch.

throttle   *v.* To defeat an opponent.

through the hole   *prep. phrase* Ball that is hit through the space between the shortstop and third baseman.

1ST   1935. "A batsman hitting past an unguarded area of the infield is said to hit 'through the hole.'" (Ralph H. Barbour, *How to Play Better Baseball;* DS)

through the slot   *prep. phrase* Over home plate.

through the wickets   *prep. phrase* Batted ball that goes between the legs—wickets—of a fielder, often the pitcher's.

throw   **1.** *v.* The act of throwing as distinguished by the rules of baseball from the act of pitching. As defined in the rules, a pitch is a ball delivered to the batter by the pitcher while a throw covers all other deliveries by one player to another. Hence, a pitcher throws to first base but pitches to the batter.

1ST   1845. "The ball must be pitched, and not thrown, for the bat." (Knickerbocker Rules)

2. *v.* To use a pitcher, as in "He's great but I can't throw him every game."
3. *v.* To deliver the ball.

throw a game   *v.* To deliberately let the other team win.
1ST   1874. (*New York Herald,* September 10; EJN)
ETY   A horse racing term as early as 1868; to throw a race.

throw a glove   *v.* To attempt to stop a batted or thrown ball by throwing a glove at it. There is no penalty for this action if the glove misses the ball, but if it hits a batted ball the batter is granted three bases (two, on a thrown ball).

throw a rainbow   *v.* Arching trajectory of a throw from the outfield, which resembles the arch of a rainbow more than the straight line of a rifle shot. Such pegs favor runners.

throw a runner out/throw out   *v.* To make a throw to a base where the runner is either tagged or forced out by the man covering.

throw away a game/throw a game away   *v.* To lose a game by poor pitching or poor throwing.
1ST   1902. (*Sporting Life,* July 12; EJN)

throw darts   *v.* To pitch with great control.

throw-down   *n./arch.* Throw from the catcher to player covering second base.
1ST   1916. "Smith made the other [error] when he fumbled Sam's throw-down and let the runners steal second." (Christy Mathewson, *First Base Faulkner;* DS)

thrower   *n.* Pitcher without finesse; one who relies on speed and power as opposed to deceptive pitching. "The thing that disturbs me is when they're drafting pitchers, they're really not drafting pitchers. They're drafting throwers. They want somebody who throws 90 to 95 miles an hour. I feel I'm a pitcher. I throw 86 to 88, and my ball moves." (college pitcher Mike Loynd, quoted in the *New York Times,* June 1, 1986)

throw ground balls   *v.* To pitch balls that tend to yield grounders.

"throw his glove in the box"   Said of a pitcher who has another team so completely dominated that all he has to do is to throw his glove in the box to win.
1ST   1916. (Ring Lardner, *You Know Me Al;* EJN)

throw Laredo   *v.* To throw underhanded.
ETY   It appears in the book *Rotisserie League Baseball* where it is explained geographically. "The term is derived from the fact that Laredo is in the lower left-hand corner of Texas, which is where Ken Tekulve and Dan Quisenberry seem to be throwing from."

throw out   **1.** *v.* To put a runner out because of a good throw or relay.
1ST   1880. (*Brooklyn Daily Eagle,* October 10; EJN)
2. For an umpire to eject a player from the game.
1ST   1937. (*New York Times,* August 22; EJN)

throw out the first ball   *v.* To toss a ball from the stands as part of a pregame ceremony. Traditionally, a political figure throws out the FIRST BALL of the season.

thumb/thumb out   *v.* For an umpire to banish a player, manager or coach from the playing field or the bench for the remainder of the game. Umpires often make a gesture of ejection with the thumb raised. "Bobo Given Thumb"—headline on the ejection of "Bobo" Newsome, *San Francisco Call-Bulletin,* August 29, 1949. (PT)
1ST   1937. (*New York Times;* EJN)

thumber   *n.* A slow pitched ball that seems to slide off the thumb.
1ST   1910. (*American* magazine, June; EJN)

thumbing   *n.* An ejection. "He was tossed out of an opening day game for the first time in his long career which includes few 'thumbings' from umpires on any day." (on the removal of minor league manager Joe Gordon, *San Francisco News,* April 1, 1952; PT)

thumb on   *v.* To reach base solely by hitting a ball on the bat handle, close to the thumb.

thumb one   *v.* To hit a pop fly ball with the handle of the bat.

thump   **1.** *v.* To hit the ball.
2. *v.* To defeat.
3. *n.* A batted ball.

thunder round   *n.* Batting practice finale in which the batters try to hit the ball out of the park. "Mike Young is the Thunder Round champion." (Richard Justice in the *Washington Post,* April 4, 1986)

ticket/ticket to first   *n.* A BASE ON BALLS.

ticket to the minors   *n.* A demotion to a lower level of the game.

tickie-hitter   *n.* Batter who "ticks"—or makes only partial contact with—the ball rather than hitting it with good wood.

tie   1. *n.* A contest in which the game is called and ruled official, with each team having scored the same number of runs. Ties are increasingly uncommon as the level of play rises. The only time the term tends to show up in a major league context is in an exhibition game, such as the 1988 Hall of Fame game in Cooperstown, which yielded this *USA Today* headline, "Cubs, Indians tie 1-1 in Fame game" (August 2, 1988) **2.** *n.* Series, road trip or other stretch of games in which a team wins and loses the same number of games. "There is an old saying that you play to tie on the road and win at home." (*Changing Pitches,* by Steve Kluger; CDP)

Tiger Stadium   In Detroit, Michigan, the home grounds of the American League Detroit Tigers since 1912. It was saved in 1974 when then-owner John Fetzer chose not to move the Tigers to the Pontiac Silverdome. Before becoming Tiger Stadium, it was known as Navin Field and Briggs Stadium.

tighten up   *v.* To become more effective. **1ST**   1910. (*New York Tribune,* July 5; EJN)

tight pitch   *n.* A pitch thrown close to the batter.

timber   *n.* the bat. **1ST**   1868. (*New York Herald,* September 27; EJN)

time/time called/time out   *n.* A temporary suspension of play called by the umpire. It can be initiated by the umpire or called in response to a request by a player, manager or coach.

When a player is injured, time cannot be called until the umpire considers the play to be over. For instance, if two fielders collide while attempting to catch a fly ball, another player

Tiger Stadium. Even the center field bleachers are sold out.   *Courtesy of the Detroit Tigers*

Tinker to Evers to Chance. The three, as shown in a composite created when they were elected to the Hall of Fame in 1946. The picture, however, places them (l. to r.) as Evers to Chance to Tinker.   *National Baseball Library, Cooperstown, N.Y.*

must retrieve the ball and it must be returned to the pitcher before time can be called and the ball deemed dead.

time at bat   AT BAT.

time of game   *n.* The length of the game expressed in hours and minutes.

time the pitch   *v.* The ability of a batter to judge the speed of a pitched ball and time the swing of his bat so that it makes contact with the ball.

timothy trimmer   *n.* DAISY CUTTER.
1ST   1869. (*New York Tribune*, September 16; EJN)

Tinker to Evers to Chance   A reference to the early-20th-century double play combination of Cubs shortstop Joe Tinker, second baseman Johny Evers and first baseman Frank Chance, which has become synonymous with precision teamwork.
    Franklin P. Adams brought added fame to the combination and his poem contained one of the most repeated lines in American light verse:
        These are the saddest of possible words:
        "Tinker to Evers to Chance"
ETY/1ST   1902. From Frank Graham's *Baseball Extra:*
        On September 15, 1902 at the old West Side Park in Chicago, where the Cubs were playing the Cincinnati Reds, a for-

gotten scorer set down on the sheet before him:
        "Double play: Tinker to Evers to Chance."
    He didn't know it, but he was linking on paper for the first time in that fashion the names of a double-play combination which, if not the greatest of all time, certainly was the most colorful . . .
    The fame of the combination got a gigantic boost in 1910 when columnist Franklin P. Adams featured them in the poem "Baseball's Sad Lexicon."

tip   1. *v.* To make incomplete contact with the ball.
2. *n.* A ball that has barely made contact with the bat; one that glances off the bat.
1ST   1845. (Knickerbocker Rules)

tip-foul   *n./arch.* TIP.
1ST   1874. (*Chicago Inter Ocean*, July 7; EJN)

tipped bat   *n.* Situation in which the catcher brings his mitt into contact with the swinging bat of the man at the plate. A tipped bat can result in the umpire awarding the batter first base.

tires   *n.* Feet. A player who cannot get moving quickly is said to have "two flat tires."
SEE   *wheels.*

tissue-paper Tom   *n./arch.* An athlete who is easily injured.

1ST 1937. (New York *Daily News,* January 17; EJN)
SEE *paper mache.*

titanic *n./arch.* A sinking liner, from the name of the famous ocean liner that went down on its maiden voyage.

titans *n.* Traditional term for teams that "clash in the Fall Classic," i.e., the World Series.

titty-high *adj.* A pitched ball that comes in at chest level.
USE A note in Edward J. Nichols's 1939 dissertation puts this term in historic context: "The term is obviously not likely to appear in print, but its common use has been attested for the writer by an interview with Honus Wagner, long one of the greatest players in the game."

tobacco card *n.* T-CARD.

tobasco tap *n.* A hard hit ball, from the hot and spicy tabasco sauce.
1ST 1907. (*New York Evening Journal,* April 30; EJN)

toe *v.* See toe the rubber.

toehold/toe hold *n.* In a batter's stance, a firm position close to the plate that a batter effects by digging in with his spikes.
1ST 1912. "Get a toe-hold and make the best of it." (*Sporting Life,* May 18)

toe plate *n.* Extra piece of leather on the pitcher's pivot foot shoe that protects the shoe as it is dragged across the mound.

toe the rubber/toe the slab *v.* To prepare to pitch. To make a legal delivery to home plate a pitcher must have his foot in contact with the rubber.
1ST 1901 (both terms). (*Frank Merriwell's Marvel;* EJN)

tomahawk/tommy-hawk *v.* To take a high chop at the ball with a bat.

tomato *n.* A BASEBALL.

tonk *n.* Home run.
ETY A article in the July 7, 1974, *Sporting News,* indicates that this term was associated with Roger Maris.

too hot to handle *adj.* A hard-batted ball that eludes capture.
1ST 1932. (*Baseball* magazine, October; EJN)

tools 1. *n.* A player's abilities; his specific talents. "Your tools—let's break that out. You

have speed, movement, placement. I never had speed. I have movement and placement. If you have two of the three you can be outstanding. If you have all three, you're Sandy Koufax." (Tommy John, quoted in the *New York Times,* September 11, 1983)
2. *n./arch.* Physical strength and size. This usage seems to have been eclipsed by the first. In 1963 the shift in the term's meaning was put in context by Leonard Shecter in his *Baseball Digest* article on baseball slang: " 'He's got the tools' means he's big enough, now if he only had some talent. Today it would mean that the player had talent, but, perhaps, was not big enough."

tools of ignorance *n.* The catcher's paraphernalia: shinguards, chest protector, helmet, mask and mitt.
1ST 1937. (New York *Daily News,* January 17; EJN)
ETY The term is based on the notion that catching is a grueling, painful job that a smart player would try to avoid. Hy Turkin insists in his *Baseball Almanac* that the term was, "Coined

Tools of ignorance. Sandlot player donning catcher's equipment. Photo taken by Russell Lee in May 1940. *Prints and Photographs Division, the Library of Congress*

by Muddy Ruel, a college graduate and a law-yer, in disgust at his catching chores."

A conflicting attribution appeared in Charles C. Meloy's article, "Diamond Jargon," in the August 1939 *Baseball* magazine: "The ballplay-ers love phrases that are pungent and redolent with meaning. Thus, Bill Dickey, Yankee catcher, coined a phrase that was greeted with whoops of joy and at once included in the language. Brooding over the fate that made him a catcher on a blazing July day, Bill spoke of the catcher's armor as 'the tools of ignorance.' "

toothpick *n.* The baseball bat.

too true *adj.* Said of a pitcher who cannot get the ball over the corners; who can only throw over the heart of the plate.

top **1.** *n.* The first half of an inning; it is followed by the bottom half.
2. *v.* To bat the ball on the upper half, which usually results in a grounder.
3. *v.* To win.
4. *n.* The first batter or batters in a team's batting order.

topflight *adj.* First rate.
1ST 1939. "Because, when the heat is on in a close race, the championship club is the team which holds its own with the topflight teams and annihilates the lesser clubs." (G. S. Coch-rane, *Baseball, the Fans' Game;* DS)

topnotcher/top notcher *n./arch.* First-class player or game. "In the major leagues there are three classes of players designated in the picturesque language of the game as 'bushers,' 'bone-heads' and 'topnotchers.' " (H. S. Fuller-ton in the September 11, 1909, *Collier's*)
1ST 1891. "Heretofore two games per week was about the limit for first class work with him, but he can reel off three top notchers now without bad effects." (*Sporting Times,* July 25, 1891; DS)

top of the order *n.* The first batter or bat-ters in a team's batting order.

Toronto Blue Jays The name of the Amer-ican League's Eastern Division franchise in To-ronto, Ontario, Canada. The team took its name from more than 4,000 submitted by potential fans. Not one, but 154 picked Blue Jays, a bird common to Southern Canada.

torpedo **1.** *n.* Runner who knocks down or attempts to knock down the infielder covering

second base in an attempt to break up a double play.
2. *v.* To attempt or effect a knockdown of the second baseman.

toss **1.** *n.* A short, soft throw, usually under-handed.
1ST 1881. (*New York Herald,* August 13; EJN)
2. *v.* To throw a short distance.

toss out *v.* To throw out a base runner.
1ST 1920. (*Spalding's Official Base Ball Guide;* EJN)

toss up *adj./n.* Term used to describe a game or series between equally matched teams; one whose outcome could as easily be determined by the flip—or toss up—of a coin.
1ST 1891. (*Harper's Weekly,* April 18; EJN)

total average (TA) *n.* A ratio between the number of bases a player gets for his team and the number of outs he makes. The statistic was advocated by writer Tom Boswell who has termed himself its "proprietor and purveyor." A Boswellian rule of thumb is that any player with a TA over .900 will end up in Cooperstown and any with a TA below .500 should not be allowed on a major league field unless he is a top-flight shortstop. His summary of it: "This simple stat . . . cleanly combines the virtues of batting average, slugging average, on-base per-centage and stolen-base proficiency." (*Washing-ton Post,* February 17, 1983)

total bases *n.* The total number of bases credited to a batter and created by base hits. It is a means of computing a player's worth as a batter, in which one base is credited for a single, two for a double, three for a triple and four for a home run. It was created as an alternative accounting to the batting average in which all hits count as one.

total chances. *n.* The sum of a player's field-ing opportunities. Specifically, it is arrived at by totaling putouts, assists and errors.

touch *v.* As defined in the *Official Baseball Rules,* "To touch a player or umpire is to touch any part of his body, his clothing or his equip-ment." The term has a bearing on altercations with umpires.

touch/touch a pitcher/touch up/touch up a pitcher *v.* Get a hit or hits off a pitcher, as in "He was touched up for two runs."
1ST 1887. (*Chicago Inter Ocean,* May 9; EJN)

Town ball. Vale, Oregon, team standing at attention as the chief justice of the United States gives the pledge of allegiance over the radio. The Russell Lee photograph was taken the summer before America's entrance into World War II.   *Prints and Photographs Division, the Library of Congress*

touch all bases   *v.* To make sure that contact is made with each bag on one's way around the base paths.
EXT   1. To cover a large variety of things; to explore all avenues. "Reagan and press: Touching all bases." (USA *Today* headline, February 12, 1986)
2. Also, to touch base(s) is to make contact with, as in, "I'll touch base with you in the morning."

tough out   *n.* A batter who is not easily retired. Tough outs are usually players who can hit as well as attract walks.

tourist   *n.* Player who performs on several different teams.

towel   *n.* A rare but dramatic means of showing displeasure with an umpire's decision is throwing a towel onto the field from the dugout. Burt Dunne reported in his 1958 dictionary: "Umpire usually interprets towel as white flag—symbol of personal cowardice—and may even clean bench."

ETY   Throwing in the towel has long been the means by which a boxer's handlers surrender for him in a prizefight. By extension, to surrender or quit any activity or pursuit, usually in defeat.

town ball   1. *n./obs.* Another name for the baseball forerunner also known as the Massachusetts game or the New England game.
2. *n.* TOWN TEAM BASEBALL.

town team baseball   *n.* Competition at the level at which villages, towns and small cities field a team, usually featuring players of various ages; for instance, the Pine Tree League in Maine.

TP   Common abbreviation for triple play.

track it down   *v.* To pursue and catch an outfield fly ball

trade   1. *v.* To exchange and/or sell players between clubs.

1ST   1911. (*Book of Base Ball;* EJN)
2. *n.* The exchange of such players.

trade bait   *n.* Player or players useful in attracting trade offers from other teams.

trademark   *n.* The printed or embossed manufacturer's logo and name that appears on the barrel of a bat.

trading block   *n.* Status of a player being offered for trade or sale.

trading deadline   *n.* The last moment at which two teams are allowed to trade players. The concept is fast losing all meaning as teams now use WAIVERS to trade at almost any time. As recently as the 1970s, the deadline for interleague trading was at midnight on the final day of the winter meetings, the early December get-together of team and league officials.

traffic cop   **1.** *n.* Third-base coach.
2. *n.* Ball that is "difficult to handle," like a traffic cop.

tragic number   *n.* The magic number, as seen from the perspective of the team about to be eliminated from contention.

trail   *v.* To be behind in runs.

trainer   *n.* One member or more of a team's staff who tends to minor injuries, weight, exercise, aches and other matters of the players' physical well-being.

training camp   *n.* Place where a team goes to prepare itself for the regular season.
1ST   1906. (*Sporting Life,* March 3; EJN)

training trip   *n.* Exhibition games played on the road in preparation for the regular season. Such trips were common before World War II.
1ST   1910. (*Baseball* magazine, May; EJN)

transfer   *v.* To move a franchise from one city to another.

trap   **1.** *v.* To field a ball on a short hop rather than catch it on the fly. An alert outfielder will usually do all that he can to catch the fly.
2. *v.* To catch a runner on the base paths between two fielders.
1ST   1863. (Chadwick Scrapbooks; EJN)

trap a ball   *v./obs.* To deliberately drop an infield fly with less than two outs and runners at second and third. The ball is muffed to trick the runners into advancing and getting thrown

Trainer. This 1887 baseball card depicts a trainer working on Harry Lyons of the Philadelphia Phillies. *Prints and Photographs Division, the Library of Congress*

out. Now illegal and impossible because of the infield fly rule.
1ST   1892. (*Chicago Herald,* May 16; EJN)

trapped ball   *n.* A batted ball that is ruled to have been caught near the ground or after it has hit the ground or fence. Sometimes fielders tend to make it look as if trapped balls are fly balls.

trapped runner   *n.* An offensive player caught between the bases.

trapper/trapper's mitt   *n.* Name for modern, shovel-like first baseman's glove, composed of three large sections—one for the thumb, one for the fingers and the one in the middle that serves as a pocket.

trap play   *n.* Defensive maneuver in which a batted ball is short-hopped. "You know, one of the toughest plays for an umpire is the trap play in the outfield." (Ron Luciano in *The Um-pire Strikes Back;* CDP)

trash bag   *n.* Term created to describe the flabby plastic "walls" at the Metrodome in Minneapolis, which appear to have the characteristics of a mammoth trash can liner. A player catching a ball off this surface is said to "play the trash bag."

traveling secretary   *n.* Member of a club's staff who is charged with road arrangements, including hotel accommodations and airplane and bus charters.

trial   *n.* A period in which a player from a lower level is given a chance to succeed at a higher level.
1ST   1902. (*Sporting Life,* September 20; EJN)

tribe   **1.** *n.* Any baseball team.
2. *n.* Common alternative nickname for a team whose primary nickname relates to Indians, especially the Cleveland Indians. "Most members of the Cleveland press corps and the Tribe's front office would not be so ambiguous as Dark." (Pat Jordan in *The Suitors of Spring;* CDP)
USE   When applied to the Indians or any other specific team the name is usually capitalized.

trickle in   *v.* To score by making one base at a time.

trickler   *n.* A slow grounder.
1ST   1922. (*New York Times,* June 2; EJN)

trimmer   *n.* Ball hit along the ground; one that trims the grass.
1ST   1870. (*New York Herald,* June 19; EJN)

trip/trip to the plate   *n.* A turn at bat.
USE   Almost always used retrospectively, as in, "One hit in three trips to the plate."

triple   **1.** *n.* A hit that allows the batter to reach third base safely. Joe Garagiola once said that Willie Mays's glove was where triples went to die.
1ST   1880. (*New York Press,* June 3; EJN)
2. *v.* To hit a three-base hit.

triple bagger/triplet   TRIPLE.
1ST   1880 (triple bagger). (*Chicago Inter Ocean,* June 29; EJN)

Triple Crown   Rare distinction by which a batter ends the season leading his league in batting average and number of RBI's and home runs. The only players to win more than once

Tribe. A loyal Cleveland Indians fan. Bat Day at Cleveland's Municipal Stadium, July 3, 1976. *Courtesy of the Cleveland Indians*

are Rogers Hornsby (1922 and 1925) and Ted Williams (1942 and 1947).

triple double   *n.* Term for a player's achievement of leading his league in doubles for three consecutive years. It came into play in late 1986 when Don Mattingly was bidding to repeat Tris Speaker's triple double of 1920–1922.
ETY   Borrowed from basketball where it means to post double-digit numbers in three statistical categories in a single game.

triple header   *n.* Three games in a row on the same date between the same two clubs.

triple play   *n.* A situation in which there are three successive putouts on one play.
   Though rare today—many ardent fans have never seen one—in 1912 Hugh Fullerton could write, "There are records of eight triple plays made by one man unassisted, and about twenty triple plays are made in each league every season." However, a modern player, Brooks Robinson, holds the record for hitting into the most triple plays—three times.
1ST   1869. (*DeWitt's Official Base Ball Guide;* EJN)
EXT   A sexual encounter involving three peo-

Triple play. Bill Wambsganss pictured with his three 1920 Triple Play victims (left to right): Pete Kilduff, Clarence Mitchell and Otto Miller. Wambsganss caught Mitchell's line drive for the first out, stepped on second base before Kilduff could get back to the bag for the second out and then tagged Mitchell who was running from first. In the same game, Cleveland outfielder Elmer Smith connected for the first grand slam home run ever hit in a World Series game. *Prints and Photographs Division, the Library of Congress*

ple; for instance, a March 1968 ad for an X-rated film in the *San Francisco Chronicle* features Bianca, Mona and Sylvia in *Triple Play.*

triple steal   *n.* A play in which three base runners simultaneously steal the next base.

triple threat   *n.* Unofficial title for pitchers who, in one season, post 20 wins, 200 or more strikeouts and maintain an earned run average of less than 3.00.

triple up   *v.* To make the third out in a triple play.

trolley dodgers   Nickname for the Brooklyn Dodgers.

trolley league   *n./obs.* Minor or bush league, specifically one made up of teams close enough together to be reached by interurban trolley cars.
1ST   1899. (*Frank Merriwell's Double Shot;* EJN)

trounce   *v.* To defeat soundly.

truck horse   *n./arch.* A particularly slow base runner.

true blue brew crew   Nickname for the blue-uniformed Milwaukee Brewers.

tryout   *n.* TRIAL.
1ST   1905. (*Sporting Life,* September 2; EJN)

tumble bug   1.   *n.* An acrobatic player given to crashing and diving in the field.
2.   *n.* A grandstand player.
1ST   1932. (*Baseball* magazine, October; EJN)

tunneler   *n.* A player who takes on managerial airs and begins giving other players orders.

turkey   *n./obs.* Home plate. Also, home turkey.
1ST   1889. ". . . and Gore travelled . . . around to third . . . Tiernan . . . slammed a tall and ornamental fly into left field for two bases, bringing Gore across the turkey." (*New York World,* July 13; Gerald Cohen)
ETY   This 19th-century term showed up repeatedly in Gerald Cohen's research into baseball slang in the *New York World.* He speculates as to its origin: "Might we perhaps deal with the 19th century home plate likened in shape

to a turkey plate? Then: *turkey plate > turkey;* and by blending *turkey + home plate > home turkey.*"

turn   1. *n.* TURN AT BAT.
1ST   1863. (Chadwick Scrapbooks; EJN)
2. *n.* A pitcher's time to pitch in the normal rotation.
1ST   1905. (*Sporting Life,* September 9; EJN)

turn a double play/turn it   *v.* To execute a defensive play in which two offensive players are put out in continuous action.

turn around a fastball   *v.* To pull a fastball.

turn at bat   *n.* The period from when a player enters the batter's box until he is either out or becomes a base runner. A player's opportunity to bat the ball.

turn away   *v.* To retire a side without allowing it to score.

turn in   *v.* To complete, as in, "He turns in another fine performance."

turn it into a souvenir   *v.* Hit a home run.

turn on the big guns   *v.* To use the best players, especially pitchers.

turn on the current/turn on the heat   *v.* To play well and with intensity.

turn-over hitter   *n./arch.* SWITCH HITTER.
1ST   1928. (*New York Times,* October 7; EJN)

turnstile   *n.* Device for counting spectators as they enter the ballpark.

turnstile count   *n.* Total attendance at a ballpark.
1ST   1902. (*Murname's Official Base Ball Guide;* EJN)

Turnstile. Young fans coming through the turnstiles in Cleveland on this particular day get free baseballs.   *Courtesy of the Cleveland Indians*

turnstiler   *n./arch.* Spectator.
1ST   1932. (*All Sports Record Book;* EJN)

turn the ball over   *v.* To throw the ball and turn one's hand over the top of the ball in the process; specifically, to throw the screwball. From the fact that the ball has been turned to give it a reverse spin.

tweener/'tweener   *adj.* Said of a ball that goes between two outfielders or between two infielders, for example, the second baseman and the shortstop, for a hit. When he was denying his ability as a power hitter, Vada Pinson was once asked to account for the doubles and triples he was hitting. "Oh," he replied, "those were just 'tweener' hits, those that light between outfielders." (*San Francisco Call-Bulletin,* May 16, 1959; PT)

24-man roster   *n.* The list and number of players allowed on a major league team as of 1986, down from the old limit of 25. The reason for this cut was purely economic—cost cutting, to be more specific—and was, by all accounts, a detriment to a team's ability to make strategic moves in the late innings of a game. "The new 24-man roster limit claimed another victim Tuesday when the Chicago Cubs released veteran pinch-hitter Richie Hebner, who came up in 1968." (USA *Today,* April 2, 1986)

20-game winner   *n.* Pitcher who has won 20 or more games in a single season. Winning 20 games in a season is a common standard of excellence for pitchers.

20-second count/20-second rule   *n.* The rule that allows the pitcher 20 seconds between pitches when there is nobody on base and no time outs are called. With a runner or runners on base, there is no time limit.

twilight ball   *n.* One of the many names for the game of softball before it became universally known as softball.

twilight baseball   *n.* A game played too late for a day game and a bit early for a night game. An Acme wire photo of June 15, 1942, contains this caption:
    "TWILIGHT BASEBALL. The Brooklyn Dodgers inaugurated a modified form of night baseball at Ebbets Field . . . The game which started in the daylight at 7:00 PM, and finished under the arc-lights two hours later, drew a crowd of 15,157 fans." (Cleveland Public Library Photo Collection)

twilight-night   TWI-NIGHT DOUBLE-HEADER.

twin bill   *n.* DOUBLEHEADER.

twi-night doubleheader/twi-nighter   *n.* Two games on the same date with the first starting in the late afternoon, usually about 5:30 p.m., and the second being played at night under the lights. A blend of the words twilight and night.
1ST   1949. The term shows up in the context of baseball in Parke Cummings' *Dictionary of Sports.* Research conducted by Mamie Meredith at the University of Nebraska and on file in the Tamony collection reveals that the term may actually date back to the World War II period.

twin killing   *n.* DOUBLE PLAY.
1ST   1937. (*Philadelphia Record,* August 24; EJN)

twirl   *v./arch.* To pitch.
1ST   1883. (Sporting Life, June 3; EJN)
ETY   From the fact that a pitcher winds up—or twirls his arm—before delivering the ball.

twirler   *n.* Pitcher. "Asa Brainard . . . was one of the first great twirlers." (Alfred H. Spink, *The National Game;* 1910)
1ST   1883. (*Sporting Life,* April 15; EJN)

two-bagger   *n.* DOUBLE.
EXT   A double victory; a repeat success. "Brown 'Two-Bagger' Brings in $132,000,000." (*San Francisco Call-Bulletin,* May 27, 1959; PT)

two-base error   *n.* Misplay that allows a batter or base runner to take two bases.
1ST   1917. (*New York Times,* October 9; EJN)

two-base hit/two baser/two-cushion shot/ two-sacker   *n.* See *double.*
1ST   1874 (two-base hit). (*New York Sun,* July 24; EJN)

two class   *adj./arch.* Highly select group of pitchers who are able to keep their earned run average below 2.0.
1ST   1922. (*Spalding's Official Base Ball Guide;* EJN)

two fingers only   *adj.* Said of a pitcher whose only deceptive pitch is the curveball. It alludes to the traditional catcher's signal for a curveball: two fingers.
1ST   1912. (*American* magazine, June; EJN)

two-hopper   *n.* Batted ball that bounces twice before it is fielded. "If he can't get the ball up

Tygers. Ty Cobb's Hall of Fame Plaque. *National Baseball Library, Cooperstown, N.Y.*

he's going to hit a two-hopper to the second baseman." (Bill Lee, *The Wrong Stuff;* CDP)

two league *n./arch.* A league that plays many doubleheaders.

two-o'clock hitter *n./arch.* Player who hits well in batting practice, but bats poorly in the game. It dates back to a time when most games began at 3:00 p.m. As most games are now played at night, the term is seldom used today. **1ST** 1937. (*Sporting News Record Book;* EJN)

two-ply killing *n.* DOUBLE PLAY.
1ST 1920. (*Spalding's Official Base Ball Guide;* EJN)

two-seamer **1.** *n.* A type of home run described by Joe Goddard in an article on spring training jargon in the March 6, 1982, *Sporting News.* "One of those duck-hook jobs that barely gets over the fence. It's not awesome. The ball sinks a little and the hitter gets on top of the ball, only getting his bat on two seams."

two time a pitch *v.* To take an extra step forward to swing at an especially slow-pitched ball.

Tygers Nickname for the Detroit Tigers when Ty Cobb was on the roster.

U

ukulele hitter *n.* A batter who hits weak groundballs to the infielders; generally a poor hitter.

ukulele umpire *n.* Third-base umpire.

ump *n.* Umpire for short; "Playoff umps not chosen blindly." (*USA Today* headline, October 7, 1986)
1ST 1888. (*New York Press,* June 3; EJN)

umpire **1.** *n.* An official who is on the field during the game as a judge of play; baseball's third party adjudicator.

There are four umpires at a major league game (one at home and one at each base) and an additional two during postseason play (one down each foul line). The plate umpire is the umpire-in-chief while the others are field umpires. The umpires are responsible for a number of individual calls during the course of a game, from the initial instruction of "Play ball" through the announcement of the last out. They determine, among other things, if a given pitch is a ball or strike, if a given base runner is safe or out and if the ball is in play or dead.
2. *v.* To act as a judge or umpire.
1ST 1845. (Knickerbocker Rules)
ETY From the Middle English *nomper* or *noumper* for an extra person brought in when two individuals disagreed. The Middle English word, in turn, derives from the old French word *nompair* meaning not paired (hence, ideally suited to act as the third party to arbitrate a dispute). Umpires are also employed in cricket, field hockey, badminton, polo, tennis, table tennis and volleyball. John Ciardi notes in *Good Words to You* that the term was "nonced" in Middle English—the letter n was dropped from the word and attached itself to the article. This is the same process (also known as nunnation) that transformed a napron into an apron.

umpire-baiter *n.* Manager or player who is known for bickering with the umpires, perhaps with an eye to getting the benefit of close calls in the future.
1ST 1902. (*Sporting Life,* October 4; EJN)

umpire-in-chief *n.* The umpire positioned behind the plate when there are two or more umpires assigned to a game. He is the official in charge of the game and the only person with the authority to declare a forfeit. He makes all decisions regarding the batter, which includes calling balls, strikes and foul balls.

umpire's interference *n.* Called when an umpire touches a fair ball before it gets to a fielder or when an umpire hinders a play, such as by impeding or preventing a catcher from stopping a stolen base. The result of umpire interference depends on the circumstance. A pitched or thrown ball that hits the umpire is in play, but if the plate umpire interferes with the catcher's throw, the runners may not advance. If a batted ball hits an umpire after it has bounded over or past the pitcher, the ball is dead.

umpiring *n.* The art of judging a game. "Anybody can see high and low," says Durwood Merrill, American League umpire, on calling balls and strikes, "It is 'in and out' that is umpiring." (George Will column, *Washington Post,* March 29, 1987)

umpiring motions/umpiring signals *n.* A simple set of hand and arm movements an umpire uses to indicate calls. Along the base paths, a thumbs-up signal means that the runner is out while an emphatic horizontal crossing of the hands with the palms down indicates the runner is safe. At the plate, the right arm is raised for a strike while the left arm is raised for a ball.

ump's broom *n.* Common whisk broom used by the plate umpire to clean off home plate so that it is clearly visible. Before the turn of the century umpires swept the plate with a long-handled house broom and then tossed the broom toward the visitors' bench.

In 1904 a Chicago Cub named Jack McCarthy was running from third base to home when he stepped on the umpire's broom and seriously injured his ankle. With this the National League president issued an order banning the long-handled brooms and requiring that umps carry brooms small enough to put in their pockets. The American League adopted the rule a year or two later.

unassisted   *adj.* Without help. Specifically, to make a putout without the help of a teammate. An example is the unassisted double play in which one player is credited with two outs. The rarest of all is the unassisted triple play, which, at last count, has happened eight times in the history of the Major Leagues.
1ST   1884. (*DeWitt's Official Baseball Guide;* EJN)

unbutton your shirt   *v.* To take a good swing at the ball. Based on the idea that a player might want to loosen his shirt for maximum freedom in swinging.

Uncle Charlie   *n.* Curveball. "To the lefties, fork balls away make you break your back lunging. Fast balls hard and in get your respect and a few sweeping curves can remind you of what a real Uncle Charlie looks like." (Tom Boswell, *The Washington Post*, May 18, 1987)
ETY   The origin of this term is elusive, but the two words—uncle and charlie—may onomatopoetically suggest a curve.

Uncle Charlie's got him   Phrase describing a player who can't hit the curveball.
1ST   1952. "When she [Laraine Day, wife of Leo Durocher] fastens her eye on a batter and says, 'Uncle Charlie's got him,' she means simply he can't hit curve balls.' " (*Collier's* magazine article quoted in the May 1952 *Word Study;* PT)

unconditional release   *n.* The discharge of a player who is still paid under the terms of his contract but is free to offer his services to another club. It is also the elimination—firing—of a player or roster candidate who has no contract with the team.
1ST   1897. (*New York Tribune*, July 22; EJN)

uncork   *v.* To throw explosively, like a champagne cork coming out of a bottle.
1ST   It is sometimes used facetiously. "G. P. rared back and uncorked a throw that landed about four feet in front of him." (account of a game in Boonville, California, Anderson Valley *Advertiser*, June 11, 1986)

underhand   *adj.* Term for a throw or pitch made with the hand below the elbow; one that begins below the belt. Underhanded pitching is illegal in baseball and mandatory in softball. Infielders in both games often throw underhanded on close plays because there is not enough time to get positioned for an overhanded throw.
1ST   1866. (*Base Ball Players Book of Reference;* EJN)

underslung delivery   *n.* A submarine pitch. "Carl Mays, Yankee pitcher of the 'underslung' delivery, was waived out of the American League." (*National Police Gazette*, December 22, 1923; PT)

under the big top   *prep. phrase* In the majors.

under the lights   *prep. phrase* Phrase used to describe a night game.

undress him   *v.* To slide into a catcher with such force that, literally, at least one piece of his equipment is jarred loose—a shin-guard loosened or a chest protector knocked out of place.
   The term is also used in the figurative sense for any hard slide into the catcher as if the slamming was enough to tear his equipment off.

undress somebody   *v.* To hit the ball hard.

unearned run   *n.* Run that is scored because of an error, catcher interference or following an error on a play that would have ended the inning. The significance of unearned runs is that they are not charged against a pitcher in computing his earned run average (ERA). "The Tigers got an unearned run in the second inning when Darrell Evans walked, reached third and scored when Buckner dropped Doug Baker's grounder at first base." (*New York Times*, April 11, 1986)
1ST   1879. (*Spirit of the Times*, August 23; EJN)

unhittable   *adj.* Term for pitched ball that is very hard to hit.

uni/unie   *n.* Short for uniform. "The uni change may be second only to the managerial change in front-office strategy." (*Village Voice*, October 7, 1986)

uniform   *n.* A team's official costume. Major league teams have two different uniforms: one for home games and another for those played on the road.

Union Association   A major league that barely lasted but one season: 1884. It was

Underhand. All eyes are on the ball.   *Courtesy of the Amateur Softball Association of America*

BASE BALL.
The Captain of our Nine.

Uniform. A drawing from 1872 in the collection of the New York Public Library demonstrates the extent to which baseball uniforms have changed.   *Courtesy of the New York Public Library*

founded on the premise that the reserve clause was invalid. As a result, the new league announced that it would openly and freely contract with players from established teams. The existing teams fought back by luring their players to return, and before the first season was over the upstart league was in shambles.

union hours   *n.* A nine-inning ballgame.

United States Slo-Pitch Softball Association   Group based in Petersburg, Virginia, that promotes the slow pitch version of amateur softball.

United States Stickball League   Organization dedicated to the promotion of the version of baseball played with a broomstick and lightweight rubber ball. Among other things, it features a Hall of Fame and a speaker's bureau. It is located in Far Rockaway, New York.

unleash a barrage   *v.* To get many hits in succession.

unpack the bat bag   *v.* To start hitting effectively.
1ST   1917. (*New York Times,* April 2; EJN)

unsportsmanlike conduct   *n.* Catchall term for fighting, swearing and other actions that are likely to get a player, manager or coach ejected from a game. The *Official Baseball Rules* are quite specific about what constitutes unsportsmanlike conduct; it includes inciting, or trying to incite, a demonstration by spectators.

up   **1.** *n.* AT BAT, which can be applied to an individual or a team, as in "Batter up."
EXT   Taking or in a position to take one's turn: "The keynote speaker is up next."
2. *prep.* Brought from a minor league team to the parent club.
3. *adj.* High, as in a pitch that is high in the strike zone.

up-and-down   *adj.* Describing a player who finds himself being sent back and forth between the majors and minors.

update set   *n.* Special series of supplemental baseball cards issued at the end of the season to represent rookies and players who were traded after the regular set of cards was printed.

up in air/up in the air   *adj.* Unnerved or excited. In his 1912 "Primer," Hugh Fullerton wrote, "A term used to describe the condition of a pitcher who loses his courage or presence of mind at critical stages of a contest."
1ST   1898. (*New York Tribune,* May 31; EJN)

up in his neck   Term applied to someone who does not come through in the pinch. According to the 1937 *Sporting News Record Book,* such a player is said to "have it up in his neck."

uppercut   *n.* Upward batting stroke that commonly yields fly balls. Generally regarded as a flaw.
ETY   A boxing term for a punch that comes up from the waist toward the head of an opponent.

upper deck   *n.* The top level of the grandstands.

upper half   *n.* The first or top half of an inning.

uprising   *n.* A batting rally.

upstairs   **1.** *adv.* To or on the upper grandstands; to or on any tier of seats above those at ground level. Most commonly used to describe the destination of pop foul balls: "He fouled one upstairs."
2. *adj.* Term for a pitched ball that is high.

up the chute/up the shaft/up the silo   *adv.* Said of any ball that is hit straight up.

up the middle   **1.** *adv.* Around and over second base. A ball that is hit straight up the center of the playing field is said to be up the middle.
2. *n.* The players at home (the catcher), second base and center field collectively. A team is said to be weak or strong up the middle.

use the whole field   *v.* To hit to all locations; to be able to place the ball.

utility/utility man/utility player   *n.* A substitute who can play any one of several positions as needed. "He used to be Dave Concepcion, All-Star shortstop. Now he's Dave Concepcion, utility man." (*St. Petersburg Times,* March 24, 1987)

There is much room for word play with this group of terms. "They ought to change our name to the Cleveland Light Company," Indian infielder Lou Camilli once punned. "We don't have anything but utilitymen."
1ST   1868. (Chadwick Scrapbooks; EJN)

V

vacuum cleaner   *n.* Excellent fielder; a Hoover.

Valhalla   In the pumped-up prose of early-20th-century sportswriting, the place where baseball greats go after death. "Years of pain, torture and misery finally came to an end for one-legged Joe Tinker, who on his sixty-eighth birthday decided it was time to join his teammates in Valhalla." (Bill Stern in his *Favorite Baseball Stories*) The image was boosted when Lou Gehrig was buried at Kensico Cemetery in Valhalla, New York.
ETY   From the banqueting hall of the gods and the dwelling place of slain warriors in Norse mythology.

Van Heusen   *n./arch.* A day at the plate without a hit; a collar. Often, "a big Van Heusen."
ETY   From the name of the collar and shirt maker.

Variable Chance Deviation Theory
Mock-scientific notion invented and named by pitcher Jim Palmer. Its premise is that a little wildness on the mound can be an asset; or, if you aim for the middle of the plate, you might hit the corners.

varsity   **1.** *n.* The first or senior team competing for a school, college or university.
2. *adj.* Pertaining to first-level athletes.
ETY   According to Richard D. Mallery in *Our American Language* it comes from the shortening and 19th-century pronunciation of uni*versity.*

Vaseline ball   *n.* Variation on the illegal spitball that is fueled by the famous petroleum product. The application of the Vaseline is facilitated by the fact that it can be used as a hair dressing and easily get on a pitcher's fingers when he is fussing with or tugging at his hat.
1ST   1964. Although one must assume that the Vaseline ball was thrown secretly for years before this date, the pitch was announced as new in the May 16, 1964, *Sporting News* by Arno Goethel who had originally written about it in the *St. Paul Pioneer Press.* "In a conversation that sounded more like a commercial for hair dressing, a member of the Twins pitching staff said that the trickier twirlers around the American League have come up with a new illegal delivery," he wrote. "It's called the Vaseline ball and rapidly is replacing its predecessor the spitball."

vaya   *adj.* Spanish for "gone" and a popular way of describing the destination of a home run.

velocity   *n.* The speed of a pitch; that which determines a good fast ball.
USE   Velocity and location have become modern terms for what used to be called speed and control.
SEE   location for further comment.

verbal signals   *n.* Signs expressed in coded expressions and words.

vest-pocket catch   *n.* A high fly ball caught with the glove close to the body at, or just above, the waist.

vet   *n.* Short for veteran.

veteran   *n.* An experienced professional baseball player.
1ST   1880. (*New York Herald*, August 23; EJN)

Veterans Committee   *n.* A group of Hall of Famers empowered to elect members to the Baseball Hall of Fame who have eluded or failed to appear on the normal ballot of the Baseball Writers Association of America. Candidates include managers, executives, umpires and former players. The players include those from the Negro Leagues and those major league players who have been overlooked or passed over by the BBWAA election.

Veterans Stadium   Home grounds of the National League Philadelphia Phillies since Opening Day, 1971. It is also known affectionately as "the Vet."

vicinity play   *n.* See *neighborhood play.*

vines   *n.* Street clothes.

violinist   *n.* Hitter with an especially smooth swing.

visiting team/visitors, the   *n.* The traveling club; the visiting team always comes up to bat in the top of the inning.

voice   *n.* Announcer; person at the microphone.

Voodoo ball   *n.* Nickname for baseballs assembled and stitched in Haiti.

vultch   *n.* A save by a relief pitcher.
ETY   According to Tim Considine in his *Lan-*

guage of Sport: "From the word 'vulture.' In the 1960s, pitchers likened relievers, who came into well pitched games in the late innings and got credit for saves and sometimes wins, to vultures, figuratively picking over the bones of starting pitchers."

vulture   *n.* A relief pitcher. Reliever Phil Reagan was nicknamed "the Vulture" by his Los Angeles Dodger teammates.

vulture-bait   *n.* Pitcher with a dead arm.

W

W Common abbreviation for win(s). "Schmidt counting Ws not HRs." (headline in *USA Today*, April 17, 1987)

wabble *v./arch.* To lose control of the ball while pitching.

Wacks Museum, The Nickname for Ebbets Field.

waft *v.* To hit one hard, usually referring to a home run. "Hank Aaron has wafted nineteen . . ." (Roger Angell in *The Summer Game;* CDP)

Wagner card The most valuable baseball card of all. It dates from 1909 and carries the likeness of Honus Wagner and has fetched $25,000 in mint condition.

The extreme rarity of this card stems from the fact that Wagner was opposed to smoking and the card was issued by Sweet Caporal cigarettes. When Wagner found that he was depicted on a tobacco premium he demanded that his image be taken out of circulation. Only a handful are known to exist.

wagon spoke *n.* BAT.

wagon-tongue *n.* BAT.

waist ball *n.* A pitched ball that comes in at the batter's waist.
1ST 1908. (*Baseball* magazine, June; EJN)

waister *n.* WAIST BALL.
1ST 1914. "After the high balls came 'waisters' and then low ones . . ." (Christy Mathewson, *Pitcher Pollock;* DS)

waiter **1.** *n.* A batter who attempts to get on base by waiting for a base on balls.
2. *n.* Batter who swings only at good balls.
3. *n.* Batter who swings late.

wait him out/wait out *v.* To make the pitcher keep throwing; to stay in the batter's box until the pitcher throws the kind of pitch one wants. Accomplishing this feat often means fouling off a number of pitches. "They wait you out in the series. You've got to put it over the plate or else." (*San Francisco Call-Bulletin,* October 12, 1949; PT)
1ST 1908. (*American* magazine, August; EJN)

wait on a pitch *v.* WAIT HIM OUT.

wait 'til next year/wait until next year The plaintive motto of fans whose team has once again fallen short of expectations. The refrain was long associated with the Brooklyn Dodgers and their fans. It achieved its greatest play in those years (1941, 1947, 1949, 1952, 1953 and 1956) when the Dodgers lost to the New York Yankees in the World Series. Among other things, it was the name of a book written by Jackie Robinson.

It is now applied to other teams. "There is no light in the Old North Church tonight. Boston is dark and despairing, waiting, as always, until next year." (Tony Kornheiser, *The Washington Post,* October 28, 1986)
1ST 1941. This is the year in which it first achieved prominent display as a headline in the *Brooklyn Eagle,* after the Dodgers were beaten by the Yankees in the World Series.
EXT The line has been used as a battle cry in a host of areas and situations.

waiver(s) *n.* A major league team's abandonment of the right to purchase the contract of a another team's player for a stipulated price. It amounts to a system by which all the teams in a league have a chance to bid on a player about to be released to the minors. Before a player can be released, waivers must be granted by all of the other big league teams, in reverse order of their standings. If the rights to that player are claimed (not waived) by one of those teams, he must be sold at a standard waiver price. The team offering the player can decide to retain him at this point.
1ST 1908. (*New York Evening Journal,* February 26; EJN)

walk **1.** *n.* Base on balls. The taking of first base by a batter to whom four balls have been pitched. "There is no defense against a walk," is Joe Garagiola's oft-quoted remark on the subject.
1ST 1866. (*New York Herald,* August 28; EJN)
2. *v.* To move to first base after the fourth ball.
3. *v.* To force in a run by issuing a base on

balls with the bases loaded. For example, "He walked in the winning run."

walker   *n.* Batter who receives many bases on balls.
1ST   1911. (*Spalding's Official Base Ball Guide;* EJN)

walkfest   *n.* A game or part of a game in which there is an unusual number of bases on balls.

walking man   *n.* WALKER.

walkover   *n.* An easy victory.
1ST   1881. (*New York Herald,* September 24; EJN)

walk the ball park   *v.* To issue many bases-on-balls; to pitch a walkfest.

walk year   *n.* The last year of a player's contract, with the player becoming a free agent the next season. Increasingly, players are being traded—or, at least, offered in trade—during their walk year so that the club can get some value from them before they are lost to the open market.

wall   *n.* The outfield fence. A ball hit over the wall is a home run.

Wall, the   The 37-foot-tall left field wall in Fenway Park. "The Wall is the most unique aspect of the park with the most distinct personality in baseball, with apologies to Wrigley Field." (Jim Henneman in the *Baltimore Evening Sun*)

wallop   **1.** *v.* To hit the ball with great power.
1ST   1908. (*New York Evening Journal,* February 25; EJN)
2. *v.* To thrash an opponent.
1ST   1888. (*New York Press,* April 7; EJN)
3. *n.* A hard-hit ball.
ETY   Pre-baseball slang: to beat or thrash.

Wally Pipp   *n.* A player who takes himself out of the lineup; one who makes a bad move, especially one associated with illness or injury. Often stated as "Remember Wally Pipp," when a player takes himself out of the lineup.
ETY   Pipp was the Yankee who, according to a story told a million times, got a headache on June 1, 1925, took himself out of the lineup and was replaced by Lou Gehrig, who went on to play in a record 2,130 consecutive games.
    However, there is another version to the story. In *My Luke and I,* Eleanor Gehrig, Lou's wife,

Wally Pipp. Walter Clement Pipp, who went on to play in Cincinnati after losing his job to Lou Gehrig in New York. *National Baseball Library, Cooperstown, N.Y.*

reports: "They said that Pipp had a headache and couldn't make it that day. The real thing was that Pipp was slowing down and hadn't been hitting, so he just decided that a day's relaxation at the racetrack might help his state of mind and his bankroll. So Wally went to the racetrack that June 2 and Lou Gehrig went to first base." (CDP)
    Pipp's name still carries a strong image. "Traber was still hitting when Murray got hurt, so he got the call. After a week or so, his Oriole mates began calling Murray 'Wally Pipp' . . ." (*Boston Globe* profile of Jim Traber, August 10, 1986)

Wally World   Where Wally Joyner's home-runs land in Anaheim Stadium. The name comes from a place made famous in the comedy movie, *National Lampoon's Summer Vacation,* and the fact that Disneyland is also in Anaheim.

wami   *n./arch.* A curse. "The breaks have been on us ever since the bell rang. Got a wami I guess."—player using baseballese in William G. Brandt's October 1932 article in *Baseball* magazine. Wami appears to have evolved into WHAMMY.

wand   *n.* BAT.
1ST   1910. (*New York Tribune,* July 2; EJN)

war club   *n.* BAT.

warm the bench/warm the pine   *v.* To sit on the bench. "He is too valuable a player to warm the pine, no matter who is serving the cocktails." (Bill Croum, *Fort Worth Star Telegram,* 1934)
1ST   1907. (*Dick Merriwell's Magnetism;* EJN)

warm up/warm-up   **1.** *v.* To throw the ball in practice before the game begins.
1ST   1883. (*Chicago Inter Ocean,* June 27; EJN)
2. *n.* A pregame routine for stretching and limbering up the body.

warm-up jacket   *n.* Windbreaker used by players as they warm up or sit on the bench. To prevent their arms from getting cold, pitchers tend to wear them any time they are not actually on the mound or in the batter's box.

warm-up pitch   *n.* Pitch allowed before an inning begins, or one of the pitches that a relief pitcher is allowed to make from the mound before the batter steps into the batter's box. Between innings, pitchers are allowed eight warm-up pitches.

warm-up swing   *n.* Preliminary swing taken by a batter before the ball is pitched.

warning path/warning track   *n.* A wide track that encircles the outfield just inside the fence. Its purpose is to protect outfielders from crashing into the wall as they back up to catch a ball. With his eyes fixed on the ball, a player knows he is nearing the wall as he senses the granular texture of the warning track with his feet.
According to a *New York Times* article of July 19, 1982, the tracks were conceived of when Pete Reiser of the Brooklyn Dodgers was seriously hurt in 1947 after he crashed into the outfield wall at Ebbets Field. In 1948 the Dodgers covered the walls with foam rubber and, soon after, warning tracks began to appear. The first parks to use them were Wrigley Field in Chicago, Braves Field in Boston and Philadelphia's Shibe Park. Reiser suffered seven concussions and *five* skull fractures during his career. After his death in 1981, Byron Rosen of *The Washington Post* wrote of padding and warning tracks and concluded, "And if such protection had been provided in his day, Harold Patrick [Pete] (born March 17, 1919) Reiser

might be in baseball's Hall of Fame." (October 27)

warning-track power   *n.* The ability of a batter with enough strength to hit a ball to the warning track but not enough to hit a home run. A player with warning-track power is useful when a sacrifice fly ball is called for.

Washington Senators   Since 1886 the name for the American League franchise in Washington, D.C., which was also known as the Nationals at several times in its history. The franchise moved to Minneapolis at the end of the 1960 season and became the Minnesota Twins. An expansion team named the Senators came to the city in 1961 and then moved to Texas after the 1971 season and became the Texas Rangers.
Their nicknames included the "Nats," "Griffs" (after Clark Griffith) and "Solons," and they were the target of the old line on Washington, "First in war, first in peace and last in the American League."

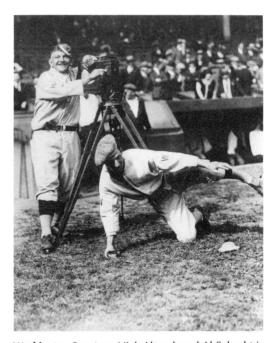

Washington Senators. Nick Altrock and Al Schacht in Washington Senators uniforms. These men gave clown performances for the Senators and were used by the club to fill seats. This photo was taken in 1924 when Altrock had but a single at bat for the team and Schacht was no longer on the roster. *National Baseball Library, Cooperstown, N.Y.*

waste/waste a pitch/waste one   *v.* To deliberately throw a ball out of the strike zone. To throw a waste pitch.
1ST   1909 (waste). (*Baseball* magazine, December; EJN)

waste hits   *v.* To make safe hits that do not help in the scoring of runs.
1ST   1902. (*Sporting Life*, September 13; EJN)

waste pitch   *n.* A pitch that is wasted; one thrown out of the strike zone on purpose, usually with an 0 and 2 count on the batter. This pitch is commonly thrown in an attempt to get the batter to swing at a bad pitch, to head off a steal by giving the catcher a high pitch on which to make the play on a base runner, or to prevent a hit and run play by making the pitch unhittable.

waster   *n.* A pitcher who habitually tries to get batters to swing at bad balls.
1ST   1909. (*American* magazine, May; EJN)

watch your lips   *v.* Line used to warn players of a bumpy or rough infield, one on which the ball is likely to take a bad hop. A phrase of the late 1980s, it may be a play on the popular "read my lips" and "watch my lips" cliches.

wave, the   *n.* A fans' activity in which spectators in sections of the grandstand rise to their feet in sequence, giving the appearance of an undulating wave.
USE   Decried by many purists. "One more reason seeing a game at Wrigley Field is a special experience: According to Cubs publicist Ned Coletti, Cubs fans have never done the wave." (*USA Today*, May 29, 1987)

wave howdy/wave howdy-do   *v.* For a fielder to let a hard-hit ball pass rather than risk injury.

wave on   *v.* For a coach to signal a runner to continue to the next base.

wax   *v.* To hit a pitcher hard.
USE   Term seems to be used almost exclusively in reference to pitchers. Scott McGregor, when asked how Don Mattingly struck him, replied, "All over the place. He just waxes you and goes home."

wax pack   *n.* Baseball cards wrapped in a package of wax paper, as opposed to a cello pack, which holds cards in cellophane.

weaken   *v.* To lose one's pitching effectiveness over the course of a game.
1ST   1905. (*Sporting News*, September 2; EJN)

Wax pack. An assortment of collectibles.   *Courtesy of Fleer*

weak end of the batting order   *n.* The last batters in the batting order. They usually hold this position because they are the least effective hitters and are likely to get one less at bat in a game than those at the top of the order.
1ST   1899. (*Frank Merriwell's Double Shot,* EJN)

weak grounder   *n.* Powerless batted ball that infielders are never supposed to miss.
EXT   Figuratively, something that one should not misplay. "With big Ed Pauley ducking pop bottles, and Harry Truman's Missouri infield bobbling weak grounders, the President's critics were ready to boo almost anyone he sent in." (*Time,* March 11, 1946; PT)

weakness   *n.* Area in or around the strike zone that a batter has trouble with.

weapon   *n.* BAT.

wear a size 3/wear a size 4 etc   *v.* To go without a hit for the stated number (3, 4 etc.) of at bats in a game. It is a play on the term collar, for a hitless performance.

wear out the wood   *v.* To ride the bench.
1ST   1916. (Ring Lardner, *You Know Me Al;* EJN)

wear the horns   *v.* To be the GOAT.

Weaverism   *n.* Any one of the multitude of pronouncements on winning baseball games uttered by Earl Weaver over the years. For instance, "The way to win is with pitching and three-run homers" and "The hit and run is the worst and dumbest play in baseball." A few Weaverisms are saved for the nature of the game itself: "This ain't a football game. We do this every day."

webbing   *n.* The array of laces and leather panels that connect the thumb and finger sections of a glove or mitt.

weigh in   *v.* To contribute to the outcome, such as weighing in with a triple.

went the other way   *v.* Hit to the opposite field.

Western Division   The two portions of the American and National Leagues that are grouped around cities in the Western United States and have their own standings throughout the regular season. The winners of these divisions face the winners of each league's Eastern Divisions in their League Championship Series.

Webbing. The web of a modern glove is a dominant feature. These feature the basket weave.   *Courtesy of Rawlings*

western swing   *n.* A road trip through the Western states by an Eastern or Midwestern club.

wet grounds   *n.* A playing field deemed unfit for play because of rainwater on the ground.
1ST   1912. (*New York Tribune,* September 19; EJN)

wet one/wet pitch   *n.* SPITBALL.

whack   *v.* To hit the ball.
1ST   1905. (*Sporting Life;* EJN)

whale   *v.* To bat a ball hard.
1ST   1905. (*Sporting Life,* September 9; EJN)

whale belly   *n.* Overweight player.

whammy   *n.* A jinx.
   "Nearly every player in the game engages in some little practice which he believes will bring him good luck or put the whammy on the other fellow." (*American Legion Monthly,* February 1937,

from an article by Jim Hurley entitled "Putting the Whammy on 'Em")
   Dizzy Dean's definition: "Hoo-doo. That's what ol' Diz used to have on all them batters in the national league when I was the world champion player." (DD)
ETY   From WAMI.

whang   To hit the ball hard.
1ST   1883. "A new ball was put in as the old one had ripped, and Lewis whanged it nicely to center field." (*Sporting Life,* April 15, 1883)

whangdoodle   *n./obs.* A good play or hit.
1ST   1902. (*Sporting Life,* October 4; EJN)

wheel and deal   *v.* For a pitcher to wind up and throw.

wheelhouse   *n.* The area of a player's hitting strength; the path of a batter's best swing. A pitcher tries not to "hang one in the batter's wheelhouse." To do so is to invite disaster: "Dixon put a fastball in Moore's wheelhouse in the eighth inning of a 3-3 game and dared Moore to hit it." (*The Washington Post,* June 7, 1987)
1ST   1959. "It just seems he's not seeing 'em the way he used to. Take today, for instance. He had a couple that came right into the wheelhouse—the kind he used to knock out of sight—and he fouled 'em off." (Bill Rigney on Orlando Cepeda's slump, *San Francisco Chronicle,* May 11, 1959; PT)
ETY   Peter Tamony suggested that it was probably ". . . because the batters 'wheel' at the ball . . . take good, level 'roundhouse' swings . . . such wheels probably suggested the word association, 'wheelhouse.'"

wheels   *n.* A player's legs; a "bad wheel" is a leg injury while a "flat wheel" or "flat tire" is a bad foot.

wheels came off, the   Describing a situation in which a lead is evaporating or the other team starts to pile on the runs.

Wheeze Kids   Nickname for the 1983 Phillies whose roster included several older players; a clear play on the Phillies' *Whiz Kids* team of 1950.

"When does the balloon go up?"   Traditional greeting for a player who shows up overweight, for instance, on the first day of spring training.

whiff   **1.** *v.* For a pitcher to strike out a batter. "I whiffed eight men in five innings in Frisco yesterday and could of done better than that if I had cut loose." (Ring W. Lardner, *You Know Me Al,* 1916; PT)
2. *v.* For a batter to strike out. "Mickey Mantle tied the New York Yankees' club strikeout record today when he whiffed for the 111th time this season." (UPI dispatch, September 3, 1958; PT)
3. *v.* To swing at a pitch without touching the ball.
4. *n.* A strikeout.
EXT   To fail.

whip   **1.** *n.* The throwing arm.
1ST   1905. (*Sporting Life,* October 7; EJN)
2. *n.* A quick throw.
3. *v.* To throw the ball fast.

whisker trimmer   *n.* Inside pitch.
1ST   1914. ". . . the pitcher sneaked over a fast 'whisker trimmer,' catching the batter napping . . ." (Gilbert Patten, *Brick King, Backstop;* DS)

whisperette   *n.* A batted ball with little power.
1ST   1909. (*New York Evening Journal,* July 1; EJN)

whistler   **1.** *n.* Fastball.
1ST   1915. "'And that's pitchin' 'em!' came from Granton as the whistler spanked into the pocket of his mitt." (Gilbert Patten, *Covering the Look-in Corner;* DS)
2. *n.* Batted ball that moves with great speed, such as a whistler down the third base line.

White Elephants   Nickname for the old Philadelphia Athletics. The nickname derived from a comment made by John McGraw early in the 1902 season. He said that the owner of the Philadelphia team had a white elephant on his hands. The Athletics went on to win the pennant and the McGraw insult was turned into a nickname and a team symbol.

white lines   *n.* The confines of the game itself; both literally and figuratively falls into fair territory.
USE   Implied in this term is baseball isolationism. A quote from the February 27, 1987, *Sports Illustrated* underscores the point: "At the conclusion of every baseball storm—be it a strike or rash of drug busts or the latest contract hassle—players and executives fall back on that

Whip. Tug McGraw of the Phillies. *Courtesy of the Philadelphia Phillies.*

White Elephants. Outfielder Bill Tuttle models the elephant patch that was worn by the Athletics after the team moved to Kansas City in 1955. It disappeared in the early 1960s but then reemerged on the sleeves of the 1988 Oakland A's, who wore green elephants on the road and white at home. *(Kansas City Athletics Publicity Photo—Author's Collection.)*

old bromide: 'All that really matters is what goes on between the white lines.' "

whites *n.* See *home whites.*

whitewash **1.** *v.* To shut a team out.
2. *n.* A win in which the loser is scoreless.
1ST 1851. (*Short Oxford Dictionary;* EJN)
ETY It is easy to see how this might derive from both the obliterating quality of the white stain and the laundered purity of a pitcher's shutout.

whittle away a lead/whittle a lead *v.* To catch up with an opponent who is ahead in a game.
1ST 1912. (*New York Tribune,* September 29; EJN)

whittler *n.* A pitcher who throws the ball just outside the strike zone and lures the batter into swinging at bad pitches. "A good whittler," said Charles C. Meloy in his 1939 article, "Diamond Jargon": "can drive a batter screwy in no time with his tantalizing offerings that aren't quite good enough."
Defined by Babe Ruth in *Babe Ruth's Own*

Book of Baseball as ". . . a pitcher who mixes up balls with strikes and carries a batter along to a two-two or three-two count before making him hit."

1ST 1928. David Schulman finds this and the next term first in *Babe Ruth's Own Book of Baseball.*

whittling *n.* A term describing pitchers who try to fool batters with balls just off the corner of the plate.

whiz chuck *n./arch.* A swiftly pitched ball.
1ST 1908. (*New York Evening Journal,* August 21; EJN)

Whiz Kids Nickname for the 1950 Philadelphia Phillies who took the National League pennant with a starting lineup of players all under the age of 30.

whole ball of wax *n.* The pennant and/or world championship.

ETY From general slang term that emerged in the 1950s for the whole thing, the whole deal. Peter Tamony toyed with the notion that this started out as "the whole bailiwick."

whole new ballgame NEW BALLGAME.

"Who's on first?" Name of the famous radio and motion picture comedy skit by Bud Abbott and Lou Costello in which confusion reigns because the man on first is named "Who," the man on second named "What" and "I Don't Know" is on third.

wicket(s) *n.* Player's legs, specifically when a ball passes through them. Such a ball is commonly said to have gone through the wicket or wickets. "That's a goal, right through the wicket into the outfield." (Joe Garagiola on NBC television)
ETY The wicket is a prime piece of equipment in both croquet and cricket. Because the

Who's on first? Although the classic routine was made famous on radio Bud Abbott (left) and Lou Costello (right) did include it in a film from which this still is taken. *National Baseball Library, Cooperstown, N.Y.*

cricket ball cannot go through the wicket in that game and the croquet ball is supposed to go through the croquet wicket, the latter is most certainly the inspiration for the baseball usage.

wide   **1.** *adj.* Off target; far to one side or the other of a base or, in the case of a pitch, home plate.
2. *n.* A ball thrown wide of the plate.

wide ball/wide one   *n.* A ball pitched outside the plate and normally too far out for the batter to hit.

wield a wicked bat   *v.* To bat well.

Wiffle Ball   Trade name for a hollow, perforated plastic ball with which it is easy to make trick pitches ("the curvingist ball in the world"). A Connecticut man named Dave Mullany invented it in 1953, and more than a million of the balls have been sold since then.

wig-wag   *n.* Signal.
1ST   1917. (*New York Times*, October 9; EJN)

wig-wagger   Coach.

wild   **1.** *adj.* Lacking consistent accuracy. A pitcher who is wild is likely to be quickly removed from a game.
2. *adj.* Describing a ball that is thrown or pitched far from its intended target.
1ST   1883. (*Sporting Life*, May 20; EJN)

wild pitch   *n.* Any pitched ball that is so high, wide or low that the catcher cannot control or block it with ordinary effort and, as a result, it rolls to the backstop and a base runner advances. The distinction between a wild pitch and a passed ball—a misplay charged to the catcher in which a base runner advances on a pitch that should have been caught—is one that is made by the official scorer. A wild pitch is charged against the pitcher only if there is a runner on base who advances.
1ST   1880. (*Chicago Inter Ocean,* June 28; EJN)
EXT   A careless statement or action. "At midweek the Republican campaign was bolstered by an innovation—the 'truth squad'—a team of senators who trailed whistle-stopping Harry Truman to field what they denounced as his wild pitches." (*Life,* October 13, 1952)

wild-pitch   *v.* To pitch a ball without control and be charged with a wild pitch.

wild throw   *n.* A ball thrown by a fielder that is outside the reach of the man he is throwing

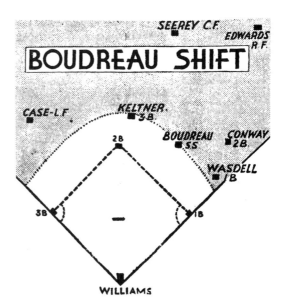

Williams Shift. A newspaper diagram of the shift—here termed the Boudreau Shift.   *National Baseball Library, Cooperstown, N.Y.*

to and allows a runner or runners to advance.
1ST   1861. (*New York Sunday Mercury*, October 2; EJN)

Williamsburg   The right field bullpen area at Fenway Park when Ted Williams was using it as a target for line drives.

Williams shift   A strategical defensive move created in 1946 to deal with the particular pull-hitting strength of Boston's powerful hitter, Ted Williams. The Cleveland Indians pioneered the technique, moving playing-manager Lou Boudreau from his usual shortstop position to a location just to the right of second base. For this reason, it was also more commonly known at the time as the Boudreau shift. During the 1946 World Series, the St. Louis Cardinals borrowed the strategy and moved shortstop Marty Marion to the right of second base and then loaded the right side of the infield with second base and then loaded the right side of the infield with second baseman Al Schoendienst and first baseman Stan Musial.

William Tell   An easy bounding ball; see big bill.
ETY   From the legendary archer who shot an apple off his son's head with an arrow. It is used in the context of baseball because the ball so-described bounces head high or close to it—

as if it could knock an apple off the fielder's head.

willow   *n.* A BAT, despite the fact that ash has long been the wood of choice.
1ST 1871. (*New York Herald,* September 2; EJN)

Wilson Pickett   A rather elaborate pun on the name of rock musician Wilson Pickett that has been applied to sharp infielders who use their trademarked Wilson gloves to make sharp, skillful defensive plays—they *pick it.* The term was used by John Hall in the December 1973 *Baseball Digest* to underscore the complexity of baseball lingo. Among others, Bill Buckner gave this name to his glove.

wilted lily   *n.* Batter who lets his bat droop as he awaits the pitch.

win   1. *v.* To defeat an opponent.
2. *n.* A victory.
USE   As recently as 1934 this particular use of a verb as a noun was noted as an oddity of American sports writing by J. Willard Ridings in *Journalism Quarterly,* December 1934)
1ST 1905. (*Sporting Life,* September 2; EJN)

wind-blown home run   *n.* Ball that goes over the fence with the real or imagined help of the wind.

wind is holding it up   Said of a batted ball that flies into the wind and not only is prevented from going for a home run, but also is easier for the fielder to reach because the wind holds it back.

windmill/windmill pitch   *n.* Common softball pitch and unorthodox baseball pitch in which the pitcher makes a full vertical circle with his arm before delivering the ball.

wind pad   *n.* Chest protector worn by catchers and plate umpires.
1ST 1905. "Each had a mask and a mitt, but the wind pad was common property worn on alternative days." (Charles Dryden, *The Athletics of 1905;* DS)

wind paddist/windpaddist   *n.* Catcher.

wind up   *v.* To go into a windup motion before delivering a pitch.

windup   *n.* The preliminary action of the pitcher prior to pitching the ball, which involves taking a step back from the rubber, raising one's hands together over one's head (the wind up) and then stepping forward to deliver the ball. Along with the stretch, it is one of the two legal pitching deliveries.
    With a runner or runners on base, the pitcher will usually pitch from the stretch rather than a windup for the simple reason that it is easier for a base runner to steal during a time-consuming windup.
1ST 1906. (*Lajoie's Official Base Ball Guide;* EJN)

windup position   *n.* Stance taken by the pitcher when he faces the batter with his pivot foot touching the pitcher's mound.

wing   1. *n.* The throwing arm. "Talk about pitchers with a good wing!" (article in *Yankees* magazine on Kevin Quirk, August 31, 1981)
2. *v.* To throw the ball.

wing a base runner   *v.* To put out a runner by throwing the ball to the base in front of him.
1ST 1908. (*Spalding's Official Base Ball Guide;* EJN)

wing a batter   *v.* To hit the batter with a pitched ball.
1ST 1914. (*New York Tribune,* October 11; EJN)

wings   *n.* Irregularities on the surface of the ball created when a pitcher uses his fingernails to illegally raise a piece of the cover.

wingy ball   *n./arch.* Ball with a rough, loose cover.

wink-out   *v.* To go berserk and attack someone or something, such as a water cooler or the clubhouse wall. In *The Wrong Stuff,* Bill Lee notes that once in a while two players will wink-out at the same time and attack each other. He adds puckishly that this is called a "twin wink-out, better known as a twinkie." (CDP)

win/loss record or **won/lost record**   *n.* The record of a club or pitcher stated with the number of wins followed by the number of losses.

winning pitcher   *n.* Pitcher given official credit for his team's victory. It can be the starting pitcher or a reliever who comes in with his team tied or behind and wins the game. A starting pitcher must complete at least five complete innings to be so credited.

winning streak   *n.* Consecutive victories by a team as an individual pitcher.
1ST 1897. (*New York Tribune,* August 3; EJN)

winter ball   *n.* Organized off-season play for major and minor leaguers desiring added experience. Winter ball is played in the Venezuelan League, Dominican League, Mexican Pacific League and Puerto Rican League. "Havens looked great in winter ball. Course, they'll chase the breaking ball in the dirt in Puerto Rico." (Earl Weaver on Brad Havens, *Washington Post,* February 9, 1986)

winter league   *n.* Any of the several leagues outside the United States where baseball is played during the off-season.

winter meetings   *n.* December get-togethers in a warm locale at which the brass from various teams convene. Among other items on the agenda, the minor league player draft is held, trades are made and various matters, including team expansion, are discussed.

The relative importance of these meetings has declined with the decline of rigid trading deadlines. Until the 1970s the deadline for interleague trading was the final night of the winter meetings. *USA Today* columnist Hal Bodley pointed out in his report on the 1987 meetings, "Since 1985 there has been virtually no deadline. With waivers, teams can trade virtually at any time."

wire cage   *n./arch.* Catcher's mask.
1ST   1908. (*New York Evening Journal,* August 26; EJN)

wish ball   *n.* A pitch that is thrown with the hope that the batter doesn't hit it. A speciality of pitchers who have "lost their stuff."

wobble   *v.* To falter or lose one's pitching effectiveness.
1ST   1912. (*New York Tribune,* September 11; EJN)

wolf   *v.* For a spectator to heckle and complain.
1ST   1902. (*Sporting Life,* July 12; EJN)

wolves   *n.* Spectators who constantly heckle a player or a team.
1ST   1932. "Even our wolves have quit us."— dejected player in William G. Brandt's article on baseballese in *Baseball* magazine.

won-lost percentage   *n.* Number expressed to the nearest thousandth that shows a team's relative standing in its league or division. It is created by dividing the total number of wins into the total number of official games played.

wood   *n.* The bat, as in he "got some good wood on that one."

wood carrier   *n.* Batter who often strikes out; one who carries his bat to and from the plate.
1ST   1932. "The day Ed gets a drink of water for every at bat he's just a 'wood-carrier' instead of an 'apple-crasher.' " (William G. Brandt in his article on baseballese in *Baseball* magazine)

wooden indian   **1.** *n.* A batter who does not swing at the ball; one who waits on the pitcher. **2.** *n.* A coach who does not give a signal to a man running down the baselines.
SEE   *Statue of Liberty.*

wood man/woodman   *n.* Skilled batsman.

woodpile/wood pile   *n.* Row of bats such as in a rack or laid out in a row in front of the dugout.
1ST   1917. (*American* magazine, August; EJN)

wood player   *n.* A good hitter who can not field; the opposite of a leather man.
1ST   1937. (*Sporting News Record Book;* EJN)

woods   *n.* The BUSHES.
1ST   1902. (*Sporting Life,* July 12; EJN)

word sign   *n.* A signal that is passed along verbally, perhaps encoded in a seemingly meaningless bit of chatter.

work   **1.** *v.* To pitch. **2.** *v.* To take part in a game. **3.** *v.* To umpire.

work a pitcher for a pass   *v.* To be issued a base on balls.
1ST   1902. (*Sporting Life,* April 26; EJN)

work on a batter   *v.* To try to get a batter out.
1ST   1899. (*Frank Merriwell's Double Shot;* EJN)

work the corners   *v.* To pitch to the edges of the strike zone.
1ST   1901. (*Frank Merriwell's Marvel;* EJN)

work the count   *v.* To attempt to get the count in one's favor by taking pitches, fouling off potential strikes etc.

work up   *v.* Another name for ROUNDERS.

World Series   *n.* Series of games played in October between American and National League pennant winners to decide the "World Championship." The first team to win four games is

World Series. View of the first World Series at the old Huntington Avenue Baseball Grounds in Boston (1903). The photo, presumably taken from a balloon, shows fans swarming onto the field after the game. Today the site is covered by buildings of Northeastern University.   *National Baseball Library, Cooperstown, N.Y.*

the champion. The first modern World Series took place in 1903, but before then the name had been attached to other championship contests.

1ST   1884. First "World's Championship Series" held in New York, according to research conducted by the National Baseball Library. Edward J. Nichols finds the term World Series in the 1887 *Spalding Official Base Ball Guide*.

EXT   The term has been applied to high-level contests in other sports, games and activities, for example the World Series of Poker.

World Series Ring   *n.* Prize given to the players, manager and coaches of the team that wins the World Series.

world's largest saloon   *n.* A nickname for Dodger Stadium in Los Angeles, California. "People in the concession business refer to Dodger Stadium as 'the world's largest saloon,' " says Howard Cosell in *I Never Played the Game*. (CDP)

World's Serious   *n.* Facetious name for World Series that pokes fun at the self-importance surrounding the event.

worm burner   *n.* Batted ball that moves across the ground hard and fast.

wounded duck   *n.* A Texas Leaguer or blooper that drops like a duck shot in flight; a dying quail.

WP   Standard score card and box score abbreviation for wild pitch.

wrapper   *n.* Cellophane or wax paper enclosures for baseball cards, that have become collectible in their own right.

wrecking crew   *n.* Group of heavy hitters. "The 1932 Yankees . . . a great wrecking crew," said Vin Scully on the August 30, 1986, Game of the Week.

Wrigley Field   Home grounds of the Chicago Cubs since 1916. Located at the corner of

Clark and Addison on Chicago's North Side. Noted for day baseball (until 1988 when lights were installed), natural grass and, since 1937, an outfield wall of Boston ivy. A ground rule double is granted when the ball sticks in the ivy. Named for long-time owner William Wrigley, Jr.

Wrigleyville   *n.* Nickname for Wrigley Field, Chicago. The day after the first night game was started there, the lead sentence in an Associated Press report read, "Wrigleyville looked no different Tuesday." (*Bangor Daily News,* August 10, 1988)

wrinkle   *n.* A curveball with little break; the break itself.
1ST   1908. (*New York Evening Journal,* May 24; EJN)

wrist hitter   *n.* Batter who gets added power from a quick, timely turn of the wrists rather than relying on pure body strength.

write out a pass   *v.* To issue a base on balls.
1ST   1910. (*New York Tribune,* July 13; EJN)

wrong armer/wrong sider   *n./arch.* LEFT-HANDED PITCHER.

wrong-field   See OPPOSITE FIELD.

wrong turn   *n.* A move to the left of the first base by the base runner, which comes up in the context of an umpire's ruling that a runner has made a move toward second base on an overrun of first base and can therefore be tagged out. It is legal to overrun first base as long as a "wrong turn" is not made.

WUNY   Wait [Un]'til Next Year, as an acronym.

X

X **1.** Symbol used in standings to indicate that a team has clinched its division title.
2. Symbol used in box scores to indicate something out of the ordinary, an extraordinary play or occurrence.

X-ray test *n.* Use of X-ray equipment to examine baseball bats for possible corking. The test was first employed when the bat used by New York Met Howard Johnson to hit his 27th home run of the 1987 season was impounded and X-rayed. According to the official results the test did not reveal cork or other foreign substance.

(This is not the first time the X-ray machine made baseball headlines. According to Jerry Howarth the day after Dizzy Dean was beaned, a headline read, "X-rays of Dean's head show nothing.")

Y

yack attack *n.* Cluster of YAKKERS.

"ya gotta believe" Slogan of and for the 1973 New York Mets, a team that was in last place on August 30 of that year but still managed to win the National League pennant. The rallying cry was originated by Mets' pitcher Tug McGraw.

yakker *n.* A sharp-breaking curveball. The term also shows up as a hard fastball. "Eckersley had the world's greatest vernacular. He knew more words that weren't in the dictionary than ones that were. If he threw a 'yakker for your coolu' it meant you were going to get nailed in the ass with a fastball." (Bill Lee in *The Wrong Stuff*; CDP)
ETY See *yellow hammer*.

Yallerhammer *n.* YELLOW HAMMER.

yan See YANNIGAN.

yank a pitcher *v.* To remove a pitcher from a game.
1ST 1914. (*Lippincott's* magazine, September; EJN)

Yankee Doodle game *n.* BASEBALL; the national pastime.
1ST 1902. (*Sporting Life*, April 26; EJN)

Yankee-Doodle hitter *n.* A weak hitter.

Yankee hater *n.* Term for those with a long-standing pinstripe aversion. "We hated the Yankees, of course, the whole country did." (Pete Hamill in *The Washington Post*, March 9, 1981)

Yankee Stadium Home of the New York Yankees since 1923. It is also known as the "House that Ruth Built" because of Babe Ruth's immense and immediate popularity. It went through a major renovation between the end of the 1973 season and the opening of the 1976 season. The Yankees played at Shea Stadium during the rebuilding.

yannigan *n.* A recruit; a player on the second team in a spring training camp game. The opposite of a regular. "The Yannigans hooked it on to the Regulars in great style this afternoon. Yannigans 9; Regulars 5." (*San Francisco Examiner*, March 24, 1912; PT)
1ST 1906. (*Sporting Life*, February 10; EJN) This was the year the term got national publicity when, according to *The Bill James Historical Abstract*, Brooklyn held a benefit game for the survivors of the San Francisco earthquake. It pitted the Regulars against the Yannigans. The Yannigans won.
ETY The term appears in other slang contexts; for instance, the "yannigan bags" which lumberjacks, prospectors and others used to carry their clothing. Joseph McBride says that the baseball term derived from the carpetbag, and was a reference to the disreputability of rookies and subs. McBride adds, "According to Lee Allen, Jerry Denny, a third baseman for Providence in 1884, was responsible for dumping the name 'yannigan' on rookies."

There is no clear link between this term and a word in another language or an earlier form of English or an English dialect (for instance, no word close to yannigan appears in J. S. Farmer and W. E. Henley's *Historical Dictionary of Slang*). One writer has suggested it as a word born in American lumber camps. James Stevens writes in his article on "Logger Talk" in the December 1925 *American Speech*, "Like such old terms as 'cross-cut,' 'bitted,' 'yannigan,' and 'snubline' they had the ringing life of the timber in them."

yardball *n.* A HOME RUN.
1ST 1986. "Today, you go to the suburbs, just go deep or leave the yard. A home run is sometimes also referred to as a yardbird."—from a Scripps Howard News Service article of September 17, reporting on current player terms used and heard by R. J. Reynolds of the Pittsburgh Pirates.

Year of the Asterisk Season of 1981, which was interrupted and disoriented by a player's strike. See asterisk.

Year of the Family Season of 1986, proclaimed by the commissioner. Teams took ac-

Yankee Stadium. The "House that Ruth Built." *Courtesy of the New York Yankees*

tion to appeal to the family trade; for instance, the Pittsburgh Pirates opened special sections where the sale of beer was prohibited.

Year of the Rookie   1986. "Canseco, Joyner, Incaviglia, Worrell, Bonds, Eichorn. The fresh names and faces that stamped the 1986 baseball season 'The Year of the Rookie' are growing more familiar and famous each day." (*St. Petersburg Times*, March 22, 1987)
SEE   *Class of '25.*

yellow error/yellow game/yellow misplay/ yellow work   *n.* Inexcusably bad play.
1ST   1890. (yellow game). (*New York Press*, July 6; EJN)

yellow hammer   *n.* The CURVEBALL. "Watching the ballgame today someone broke off a real good curve and I said, 'That was a real yellow hammer.'" (Jim Bouton in *Ball Four;* CDP)
ETY   Almost every reference made to this term in print notes that the person uttering the term has no idea where it came from or how it became a name for a curveball.

Only a few have even hazarded a guess, even a wild one. "Don't ask me where it came from," said Steve Garvey, a language major at Michi-

gan State, in *Baseball Digest.* "Maybe it started with a Chinese right-hander."

Two recent books on baseball terminology assert that it came from the name of a bird. Both Mike Whiteford and Patrick Ercolano claim it is named after a type of woodpecker (the yellow-shafted flicker) that travels in an undulating manner resembling a curveball. Both men also maintain that *yakker* derives from yawker, a kind of woodpecker.

yodeler   *n.* Third base coach, especially a noisy one who may be trying to unnerve the pitcher.
1ST   1937. (*Sporting News Record Book;* EJN)

Yogiism/Yogism   *n.* One of a series of aphorisms and comments issued by Lawrence Peter "Yogi" Berra. Some are gaffs, but many of them contain their own special logic. A very small sampling:

· On a player's permission to steal: "He can run anytime he wants. I'm giving him the red light."

· On whether he would make a good manager: "I've been playing for 18 years, and you can observe a lot by watching."

· On putting on a Houston Astros uniform: "It doesn't make any difference. Besides, I can't look at myself."

Yogism. Yogi Berra as a coach with the Houston Astros (1986). *Courtesy of the Houston Astros*

- On how many slices he wanted to have his pizza cut into: "Better make it four, I don't think I can eat eight."
- On Johnny Bench breaking one of his records: "I always thought the record would stand until it was broken."
- On Yogiisms: "I really didn't say everything I said."
- On winning: "You can't win all the time. There are guys out there who are better than you are."

"You Can't Steal First" Expression signifying that baseball has its precise limits. It is also practical advice in that it is the one base you must earn and cannot steal whether it be from home or from second base.
ETY An old baseball cliche with a fascinating history. The season after a game in which Herman "Germany" Schaefer stole second base and then went back and stole first base to disrupt the pitcher's concentration, Rule 7.08(i) was created to prevent stealing first.

"You Can't Win 'Em All" Someone else undoubtedly said it earlier, but it has attached itself to a Boston Pitcher named Clifton G.

Curtis who said, "Oh well. You can't win 'em all," after losing his 23rd game in a row over the seasons of 1910–1911.

It has also been associated with manager Connie Mack who reportedly uttered it after losing 117 games in the 1916 season.
EXT This phrase long ago generalized to other sports and endeavors. It is often invoked as understatement after a severe defeat or series of defeats.

"You could look it up!" Particular verbal punctuation used by Casey Stengel to let listeners know that he was not merely making things up and that the point he was making was doubtlessly written down somewhere.

"youneverknow" Joaquin Andujar's "favorite English word," which has attached itself to baseball. Its meaning is summed up in this story about Don Sutton, which appeared in the April 2, 1986, *USA Today:*
    " 'Hey,' he yells to some of his California Angels teammates across the room, 'what's the one word that sums up baseball perfectly?'
    "No one knows the magic word, so Sutton, quoting Joaquin Andujar, gleefully provides it for them: 'Youneverknow.' "
ETY All of this stems from a quote attributed to Andujar when he was with the Houston Astros: "There is one word in America that says it all, and that one word is, 'You never know.' "

young hopeful *n.* A newly acquired player with promise.

youth baseball *n.* Collective term for various national and local programs for boys and girls under 18 years of age who play baseball as part of an organized team and league. Babe Ruth Baseball and Little League are two of many participants. An interesting use of the term was found on coupons attached to meat sold under the Oscar Mayer label in 1987; they stated that "for every coupon redeemed, Oscar Mayer will donate 5¢ to youth baseball, up to $1 million . . . to help kids in communities like yours." (CDP)

youth movement *n.* Name given to the process of releasing old players and bringing highly-promising rookies up from the minors. "First baseman Bill Buckner, who has more than 2,500 major-league hits and one unforgettable World Series error, was waived Thursday as part of the Boston Red Sox' youth movement." (*Lewiston* [Maine] *Daily Sun,* July 24, 1987)

Z

zackyzooky *n.* As defined by Mike Gonring of the *Milwaukee Journal* in the June 1979 *Baseball Digest:* "Peculiar to the Brewers, meaning the minor leagues. Derived, somehow, from Sacramento, where the Brewers used to have a Triple A club. You don't want to be sent . . . to Zackyzooky."

Zamboni *n.* Trade name for a machine used to clean Astroturf and other artificial playing surfaces. The original Zamboni was used to resurface the ice on hockey rinks.
ETY Named for Frank Zamboni, who introduced his ice-resurfacing machine in 1947. On Zamboni's death in July of 1988 at age 87 the *Boston Herald* (July 30) reported that he had been an ice supplier who was forced out of that business in the 1930s by the growth of mechanical refrigeration. He invented his first machine after he opened a skating rink and discovered that it took five men 90 minutes each night to create a new layer of ice.

zebra *n.* A very fast outfielder (not to be confused with the zebra of football, who is a referee).

zigzagger *n.* A curveball or erratic throw.
1ST 1915. "Keith swung his right arm in a wide sweep, balancing himself on his right foot, and shot over a zigzagger which Manny missed by inches." (Gilbert Patten, *Courtney of the Center Garden;* DS)

zimmerman *n./arch.* A bonehead play, along the lines of Merkle's Boner, but here it refers to a case in which a fielder supposedly chased a runner home instead of beating him with the ball. Prescott Sullivan tried to exonerate the man behind the eponym in his *San Francisco Examiner* column of May 8, 1957, pointing out that it is misused. "Heinie Zimmerman, an infielder for the New York Giants, did chase Eddie Collins across the plate in a World Series game but the numbskull wasn't his. Zimmerman had to chase Collins because home plate was left uncovered and there was nobody he could throw the ball to." (PT)

zip **1.** *v.* To shutout. "Tigers Zip Yanks in 10 Innings, 1-0, for Morris' 20th." (headline, *The Buffalo News*, September 28, 1986)
2. *v.* To move with the sound and character of the fastball. "I gave them nothing but fast ones but they sure were fast ones and you could hear them zip." (Ring W. Lardner, *You Know Me Al*)
3. *n.* Speed

Zurdo *n.* Spanish nickname for lefty.

AFTERWORD

". . . a certain ancient game, played with a ball, hath come up again, yet already are all mouths filled with the phrases that describe its parts and movement; insomuch, indeed, that the ears of the sober and such as would busy themselves with weightier matter are racked with the clack of the same till they do ache with anguish."

—Mark Twain's "An Extract from Methuselah's Diary."

It goes without saying that this book is already out of date and has been for many months. There is no shame in this because the same can be said about virtually any book that attempts to capture an element of a living language.

However, one must always strive for currency and comprehensiveness, and it is with this in mind that the author announces here that he is most interested in hearing from the readers of this book as they encounter new terms. I am, of course, also interested in hearing of errors, omissions, alternative theories on the origins of terms, and earlier dating of a term's earliest appearance in print. Such correspondence will be acknowledged immediately and consulted for future editions of this dictionary. I can be reached directly at Box 80, Garrett Park, MD 20896–0080.

BIBLIOGRAPHY

I. An annotated collection of works that are specifically related to baseball terminology in whole or in part.

Allen, Ethan, *Baseball Play and Strategy*. Ronald Press, New York, 1969. (Both this book and the next two by Allen contain excellent glossaries.)

———, *Baseball: Major League Technique and Tactics*. MacMillan, New York, 1953.

———, *Baseball Techniques Illustrated*. A. S. Barnes, New York, 1951.

Archibald, Joe, *Baseball Talk for Beginners*. Julian Messner, New York, 1969.

Baker, Russell, "Come Back, Dizzy," *The New York Times*, October 9, 1979. (Essay in which Baker takes the position that the language of baseball was becoming arid and lifeless.)

Barber, Red and Creamer, Robert, *Rhubarb in the Catbird Seat*. Doubleday, Garden City, N.Y., 1968. (Barber explains his role in the origin and spread of several key terms, including the two in the title.)

Berrey, Lester V. and Van Den Bark, Melvin, *The American Thesaurus of Slang*. Thomas Y. Crowell, New York, 1942. (Extensive section on baseball slang. Essential.)

Birtwell, Roger, "Three R's Taught in Diamond Lingo," *Baseball Digest*, September 1948.

Borden, Marian Edelman, "Terms for Parents of Little Leaguers," *New York Times* [undated clipping].

Brandt, William G., "That Unrecognized Language—Baseballese," *Baseball*, October 1932. (An extremely valuable article in which the author distinguishes play jargon, baseballese, from the baseball slang encountered in pulp fiction. He also makes the point that baseballese is precise and economical; comparable to the verbal shorthand of surgeons.)

Brosnan, Jim, *The Long Season*. Dell, New York, 1961. (This book, which Jimmy Cannon termed "the greatest baseball book ever written," opens with a glossary of words and phrases heard by the player/author during the 1959 season. It is a key to the player jargon of the time.)

Bryson, Bill, "Why We Say It," *Baseball Digest*, April 1948.

Cannon, Jimmy, "Sport Page Dictionary," *Baseball Digest*, November-December 1956. (Certainly the best set of comic baseball terms ever defined in one book. Samples: "*Clubhouse boy* A man who is a valet for a lot of boys" and "*Rabid fan* A guy who screams for fair play after he heaves a bottle at the umpire.")

Chadwick, Henry, *Technical Terms of Baseball*. American Sports Publishing Co., New York, 1897. (Because the British-born Chadwick was responsible for naming or renaming a number of elements of baseball—e.g., he replaced "striker" with "batter"—this small booklet is particularly important.)

Cochrane, Gordon S., *Baseball: The Fan's Game*. Funk and Wagnalls Company, New York, 1939.

Coffin, Tristram Potter, *The Old Ball Game: Baseball in Folklore and Fiction*. Herder and Herder, New York, 1971. (An extremely valuable overall reference. Contains a key chapter on "Baseball Talk.")

Cohen, Gerald, "Old baseball columns as a repository of slang; reading through *The World*," *Comments on Etymology*, April 1/15, 1986, Part II; *Comments on Etymology*, February 1/15, 1987. (Important commentary on 19th-century baseball slang as well as offering several fascinating discoveries; e.g., an account of the first ground rule double.)

Cold Spring Publishers, *1957 Baseball Schedules*. (A giveaway from the East River Savings Bank of New York City containing "Baseball Terms to Know.")

Considine, Tim, *The Language of Sport*. Facts On File, New York, 1982.

Couzens, Gerald Secor, *A Baseball Album*. Lippincott and Crowell, New York, 1980. (Book with a most useful glossary.)

Cummings, Parke, *The Dictionary of Baseball*. A. S. Barnes, New York, 1950.

Dean, Jerome H. "Dizzy," *Dizzy Baseball: A Gay and Amusing Glossary of Baseball Terms Used by Radio Broadcasters, with Explanations to Aid the*

Uninitiated. Greenberg, New York, 1952.
———, *The Dizzy Dean Dictionary.* Falstaff Brewing Company, St. Louis, 1943 and 1949.

Dunne, Bert, *Folger's Dictionary of Baseball.* Folger's Coffee and Stark-Rath Printing Co., San Francisco, 1958. (Solid booklet collection that mixes official terms with the slang of the period. Many terms appear here that do not appear elsewhere. This is a particularly hard reference to find, but several copies appear in the Tamony collection.)

Ercolano, Patrick, *Fungoes, Floaters and Fork Balls: A Colorful Baseball Dictionary.* Prentice-Hall, Englewood Cliffs, N.J., 1987.

Falletta, Joe, "Here's a Look at Some Baseball Jargon of the 80's," *Baseball Digest,* December 1983.

Farine, Michael. "Coming to Terms with Baseball Lingo," *The Potomac Almanac,* April 22, 1987.

Flexner, Stuart Berg, *Listening to America.* Simon and Schuster, New York, 1982. (Contains a lively and most useful chapter on baseball language and how it has changed through the years.)

Foster, John B., "Glossary of Base Ball Terms," an appendix to *Collier's New Dictionary of the English Language.* P. F. Collier & Son, New York, 1908. (An important and often overlooked glossary written by the editor of the Spalding baseball record and guide books of the time. The note that Peter Tamony attached to his copy of this work: "Filed to show small number of terms thought to be peculiar to this field of sport in its early period.")

Frank, Lawrence, *Playing Hardball. The Dynamics of Baseball Folk Speech.* Peter Lang, New York, 1984. (Based on the author's years playing for the semi-pro Novato Knicks of Novato, California; it is a study of the language on the field itself.)

Frommer, Harvey, *Sports Lingo.* Atheneum, New York, 1979.
———, *Sports Roots.* Atheneum, New York, 1979.

Fullerton, Hugh S., "The Baseball Primer," *The American Magazine,* June 1912. (An extremely important glossary in which certain terms are defined in print for the first time.)

Gast, Carol R., *Skill on the Diamond.* Douglas Publishing Co., Omaha, 1953.

Gibbons, Frank, "Handy Guide to 'Fieldese!'" *Baseball Digest,* May 1959.

Gibbs, C. M., "Gibberish," *The Baltimore Sun,* January 1, 1935.

Goddard, Joe, "Hoover, Mr. Kodak, Salami, Yakker," *The Sporting News,* March 6, 1982.

Gonring, Mike, "Baseball Still Has Its Own Special Lingo," *Baseball Digest,* June 1979.

Grieve, Curley, "Baseball Slang Growing Fast," *San Francisco Examiner,* March 11, 1937.

Hall, John, "How's Your Baseball Lingo?" *Baseball Digest,* December 1973.

Hartt, Rollin Lynde, "The National Game," *The Atlantic,* August 1908.

Harvey, W. Clifford, "The Fascinating Language of Baseballese," *Baseball,* January 1931.

Heck, Henry J., "Baseball Terminology," *American Speech,* April 1930.

Holiday, Editors of, "Baseball Words," *Holiday,* March 1955.

Hollander, Zander, *Baseball Lingo.* W. W. Norton, New York, 1967.

Horgan, Tim, "Smoke Over the Short Porch," *Baseball Digest,* June 1964.

Howarth, Jerry, *Baseball Lite.* Protocol Books, Toronto, 1986. (A book of funny definitions that really is funny.)

Huddle, Franklin P., "Baseball Jargon," *American Speech,* April 1943.

Joyce, Joan and Anquillare, John, *Winning Softball.* Henry Regnery, Chicago, 1975. (Contains a glossary of softball terms.)

Kiernan, John. "The Sportsman's Lexicon," *Saturday Review of Literature,* July 22, 1933.

Lawson, Thomas W., *The Krank: His Language and What It Means.* Rand Avary Co., Boston, 1888. (The first attempt to put baseball slang in one volume, this small book is now dated and very rare, but it is essential to any attempt at deciphering the baseball slang of the 19th century.)

Lee, Gretchen, "In Sporting Parlance," *American Speech,* April 1926. (An inventory of baseball terminology of the '20s.)

Levinson, Bill, "My Wife's Own Dictionary of Baseball," *San Francisco Examiner,* September 6, 1959. (Comic baseball glossary—better than most.)

Lieb, Frederick G., "How the Big League Clubs Got Their Nick Names," *Baseball,* February 1922.

Lindop, Al, "The Names of Summer," *The Indianapolis Star,* April 5, 1981.

Lipsyte, Robert, "Sportspeak Without Tears," *The New York Times,* May 30, 1968.

Literary Digest, Editors of, "Peril of the Baseball Lingo," *Literary Digest,* September 6, 1913.

Litwhiler, Danny, *The Glossary of International Baseball Terms.* The United States Baseball Federation, Hamilton Square, N.J., 1961. (Terms in Italian, Spanish, Dutch and English.)

Logan, Mrs. John A., *The Home Manual. Everybody's Guide in Social, Domestic and Business Life.* H. J. Smith and Co., Philadelphia, 1889. (This book contains everything from rules of etiquette to recipes for such things as toast water and tamarind whey, but it also contains a very early and ambitious glossary of baseball terms prepared by George A. Stackhouse, described as an authority on baseball. Commenting on this glossary in the December 1937 issue of *American Speech,* J. Louis Kueth of the Johns Hopkins University Library wrote, "Nearly all of the terms given in this list are still in use.")

Lukas, J. Anthony, "How Mel Allen Started A Lifelong Love Affair," *New York Times* magazine, September 12, 1971.

Masin, Herman L., "Diamond Definitions You Won't Find in the Dictionary," *Baseball Digest,* June 1959.

McBride, Joseph, *The Complete Guide to Baseball Slang.* Warner Books, New York, 1980.

McDonald, Jack, "Sandwiches and Flies," *San Francisco Examiner,* April 11, 1966.

McGlone, Joe, column in the *Providence* (Rhode Island) *Evening Bulletin,* August 2, 1946.

Meloy, Charles C., "Diamond Jargon," *Baseball,* August 1939.

Merriam-Webster, Editors of, *Webster's Sports Dictionary.* G. and C. Merriam and Co., Springfield, Massachusetts, 1976.

Miller, John H., "The Jargon of the Diamond," *Baseball,* October 1916.

Minshew, Wayne, "Dugout Lingo Has a Flavor of Its Own," *Baseball Digest,* June 1972.

———, "Players' Lexicon Unique Like Tweener, Chin Music," *The Sporting News,* April 1, 1972.

Moreland, Keith, "Talkin' Baseball Is What Makes It Quite Interesting," *Vineline,* August 1987. (Excellent glossary written from the players' standpoint.)

Murnane, T. H., *How to Umpire, How to Captain a Team, How to Manage a Team, How to Coach, How to Organize a League, How to Score, and the Technical Terms of Base Ball;* Spalding Athletic Library. American Sports Publishing Co., New York, 1915. (Six special and detailed glossaries [pitching terms, umpiring terms etc.] make this an especially important source.)

The Nation, Editors of, "English and Baseball," *The Nation,* August 21, 1913.

Nichols, Edward J., *Historical Dictionary of Baseball Terminology.* University Microfilms, Ann Arbor, 1939.

Nugent, William Henry, "The Sports Section," *The American Mercury,* March 1929. (Shows the seldom-acknowledged influence of Pierce Egan, an English writer of the early 19th century, who Nugent deems "the father of newspaper sports slang.")

Ostler, Scott, "Baseball Lingo Throws Curve for Dudes Trying to Stay Hip," *Binghamton* (New York) *Press and Sun Bulletin,* May 4, 1986.

Paley, Steve, "In There Pitching For Arms Control," *New York Times,* September 6, 1987.

Parrott, Harold, "Bewildering Are Slang Terms Used in Talk of Baseball Players," *Brooklyn Eagle,* August 9, 1936.

Powers, Jimmy, "Dugout Slang," New York *Daily News,* January 12, 1937.

Reichler, Joe, *Joe Reichler's Great Book of Baseball Records,* No. 2. Dell, New York, 1957.

Remmers, Mary, *Ducks on the Pond: A Lexicon of Little League Lingo.* Austin, Texas, Shoal Creek Publishers, 1981.

Richman, Milton, "Rookie Diction-err-y," *Baseball Digest,* May 1947.

Ridings, J. Willard, "Use of Slang in Newspaper Sports Writing," *Journalism Quarterly,* December 1934.

Rose, Howard N., *A Thesaurus of Slang.* Macmillan, New York, 1934.

Rosenbaum, Art, "Sports Terms Have Enriched Our Language," *San Francisco Examiner,* July 30, 1985.

Rothan, Martin, *New Baseball Rules and Decisions Book.* Baseball Decisions Co., Lexington, Kentucky, 1947.

Rush, Red, "Red Rush's Dictionary of Baseball Slang," *San Francisco Examiner,* August 12, 1979.

Ruth, George Herman, *Babe Ruth's Own Book of Baseball.* G. P. Putnams, New York, 1928. (Contains a glossary with bygone bits of slang that do not appear elsewhere. Peter Tamony noted in his file on baseball terms that the text of the book is also useful, "for usage of practically all words and terms used in the play of the game of baseball.")

Ryan, Calvin T., "Sports Writers' Semantics," *Word Study*, February 1952.

Safire, William, *I Stand Corrected.* Times Books, New York, 1984. (Key section on "out in left field," pp. 232–235.)

———, *What's the Good Word?* Avon, New York 1983. (Very important section on the word "fungo," pp. 69–75.)

Salak, John S., *Dictionary of American Sports.* Philosophical Library, New York, 1961.

Salsinger, H. G., "Dugout Dictionary," *Baseball Digest*, January–February 1957.

———, "Jargon of the Field," *Baseball Digest*, August 1945.

Samuels, V., "Baseball Slang," *American Speech*, February 1927. (Published as a letter, it amends Gretchen Lee's "In Sporting Parlance.")

Sargent, Lester L., "Novel Baseball Inventions," *Baseball*, March 1914.

Scheiber, Dave, "Talk Like a Fan," *St. Petersburg Times*, March 5, 1987. (Solid report on the slang heard during spring training.)

Schlossberg, Dan, *The Baseball Book of Why.* Jonathan David Publishers, Middle Village, New York, 1984.

———, *The Baseball Catalog.* Jonathan David Publishers, Middle Village, New York, 1980.

Scholl, Richard, *The Running Press Glossary of Baseball Language.* Running Press, Philadelphia, 1977.

Schoor, Gene, ed., *The Giant Book of Sports.* Garden City Publishing Co., Garden City, New York, 1948. (Useful, slangy section entitled "Familiar Terms Connected with Baseball.")

Schwed, Fred Jr., *How to Watch a Baseball Game*, Harper and Row, N.Y., 1957. (Fascinating chapter on baseball semantics.)

Scripps Howard News Service, "Reynolds Guide to Baseball Jive," September 17, 1986.

Shea, Thomas P., *Baseball Nicknames.* Gates-Vincent Publications, Hingham, Massachusetts, 1946.

Shecter, Leonard, "Baseball Spoken Here," *Baseball Digest*, June 1963.

Sherwood, R. E., "Breezy Bits of Baseball Humor," *Baseball*, September 1913. (Comic treatment of pre-World War I baseball slang.)

Shirts, Morris A., *Warm Up for Little League Baseball.* Pocket Books, New York, 1971, 1976.

(Contains a good, small glossary with certain terms that do not appear elsewhere.)

Shulman, David, "Baseball's Bright Lexicon," *American Speech*, February 1951.

Simons, Herbert, "Do You Speak the Language?" *Baseball,* January 1943.

———, "Here's Some More Slang," *Baseball,* April 1943.

Smith, Chester L., "Diamond Slang Goes G.I.," *Baseball Digest*, May 1946. (The only reference on the influence of the slang and terminology of the Second World War on baseball slang that I could find.)

Smith, Ken, "How They Express Themselves," *Baseball*, August 1939.

Smith, Red, "Sportspeak and Stuff," *The New York Times*, July 1, 1981.

Spector, Robert Donald, "Baseball, Inside Out and Upside Down," *American Speech*, December 1956.

———, "Compound Words in Baseball," *American Speech*, May 1955.

———, "Little Words in the Big League," *Word Study*, May 1955.

Sperling, Dan, *A Spectator's Guide to Baseball.* Avon, New York, 1983.

Spink, C. C. & Son, *The Sporting News Record Book.* St. Louis, 1933 and 1937 editions. (Both contain important sections on the game in slang.)

Spink, C. C. Johnson, "Sports in Our Language," *The Sporting News*, June 10, 1978.

Spink, J. G. Taylor, Lieb, Fred, Biederman, Les and Burnes, Bob, *Comedians of Baseball Down the Years.* Charles C. Spink and Son, St. Louis, 1958. (Contents include a rich and very important slang dictionary.)

Sporting Life, Editors of, "Many Gems of Slang Heard on Ball Field," *Sporting Life*, May 18, 1912.

Sullivan, Frank, "The Cliche Expert Testifies on Baseball," *The New Yorker*, August 27, 1949.

Tamony, Peter, "Baseball," *Newsletter and Wasp*, April 14, 1939.

———, "Baseball and Its Fans," *Words*, March 1939.

———, "Break," *Newsletter and Wasp*, October 6, 1939.

———, "Championship of the World," *Newsletter and Wasp*, October 13 and 20, 1939.

———, "Dick Smith," *Newsletter and Wasp*, September 15, 1939.

———, "Downtown: A Baseball Nickname," *Comments on Etymology*, May 1, 1983.

———, "Fungo and Bingo Again," *American Speech*, October 1937.

———, "Sandlot Baseball," *Western Folklore*, October 1968.

Thierry, Edward M., Slang of the Sporting Writers," *Baseball*, September 1909.

Thompson, Fresco, *Every Diamond Doesn't Sparkle*. David McKay, New York, 1964. (Contains a very useful glossary of diamond argot, including a handful of slang terms that are not found in other compilations.)

Turkin, Hy, *The Baseball Almanac*. A. S. Barnes, New York, 1955. (Particularly interesting glossary because he attributes a number of slang coinages to particular players.)

Vidmer, Richard, "Down in Front: Native Tongue," *New York Herald Tribune*, June 7, 1941.

Vogel, O. H. (Otts), *Ins and Outs of Baseball*. C. V. Mosby, St. Louis, 1952.

Walker, Henry, *Illustrated Baseball Dictionary for Young People*. Prentice-Hall, Englewood Cliffs, New Jersey, 1970.

Walsh, Edward R., "Baseballese: Truth Stranger Than Diction," *USAir* (inflight magazine), September 1982.

West, Harwell E., *The Baseball Scrap Book*. Diamond Publishing Co., Chicago, 1938. (Good section on baseball slang on the eve of World War II.)

Whiteford, Mike, *How to Talk Baseball*. Dembner Books, New York, 1983. (Fascinating and insightful work, but one that must be watched for its attribution of coinages, which in several cases are made to terms and phrases that were already well-established.)

Winchell, Walter, "On Broadway," *San Francisco Call-Bulletin*, May 4, 1933.

Wolpow, Edward R., "Baseballese," *Word Ways*, August 1983. (A very small but revealing article on the troubles the editors of *Webster's Second New International Dictionary* had in classifying baseball terms. Wolpow points out that there are many inconsistencies in tabbing terms "ordinary" vs. cant, slang or colloquialism.)

II. Works on baseball and sports that were especially useful in providing examples and insights into baseball terminology. Many more books were consulted.

Andreano, Ralph, *No Joy in Mudville: The Dilemma of Major League Baseball*. Schenkman, Cambridge, Massachusetts, 1965.

Angell, Roger, *Five Seasons*. Simon and Schuster, New York, 1977.

———, *Late Innings*. Simon and Schuster, New York, 1982.

———, *The Summer Game*. Popular Library, New York, 1972.

Asinof, Eliot, *Eight Men Out*. Ace, New York, 1963.

Bancroft, Jessie H. and Pulvermacher, William Dean, *Handbook of Athletic Games*. Macmillan, New York, 1917.

Barber, Red, *1947—When All Hell Broke Loose in Baseball*. Doubleday, Garden City, New York, 1982.

Bennett, Bob, *On the Receiving End: The Catcher's Guidebook*. Mid-Cal, Fresno, California, 1982.

Blackwell's Durham Tobacco Co., *The Bull Durham Baseball Guide*, vol. 2. New York, 1911.

Boswell, Thomas, *How Life Imitates the World Series*. Doubleday, Garden City, New York, 1982.

Bouton, Jim, *Ball Four*. World, Cleveland, 1970.

Brashler, William, *The Bingo Long Traveling All Stars and Motor Kings*. Harper and Row, New York, 1973.

Brosnan, Jim, *The Long Season*. Harper and Row, New York, 1960.

———, *Pennant Race*. Harper and Row, New York, 1962.

Chadwick, Henry, *DeWitt's Base-Ball Guide for 1874*. Robert M. DeWitt, New York, 1874.

Clark, Steve, *The Complete Book of Baseball Cards*. Grosset & Dunlap, New York, 1976.

Conner, Anthony J., *Baseball for the Love of It*. Macmillan, New York, 1982.

Creamer, Robert W., *Babe . . . the Legend Comes to Life*. Simon and Schuster, New York, 1974.

———, *Stengel: His Life and Times*. Simon and Schuster, New York, 1984.

Crepeau, Richard C., *Baseball: America's Diamond Mind, 1919–1941*. University of Central Florida, Orlando, Fla., 1980.

Dolan, Edward F., Jr., *Calling the Play*. Atheneum, New York, 1982.

Einstein, Charles, *The Fireside Book of Baseball*. Simon and Schuster, New York, all three volumes 1956, 1958 and 1968.

Evans, Billy, *Simplified Base Ball Rules*. Billy Evans, (no location), 1923 edition.

Freehan, Bill, *Behind the Mask*. World, Cleveland, 1970.

Frick, Ford C., *Games, Asterisks, and People.* Crown, New York, 1973.

Friendlich, Dick, *Relief Pitcher.* Scholastic Book Services, New York, 1966.

Frommer, Harvey, *New York City Baseball.* Macmillan, New York, 1980.

———, *Rickey and Robinson.* Macmillan, New York, 1982.

Garagiola, Joe, *Baseball Is a Funny Game.* Bantam, New York, 1962.

Gardner, Martin, *The Annotated Casey at the Bat.* Bramhall House, New York, 1967.

Graham, Frank, *Baseball Extra.* A. S. Barnes, New York, 1954.

Graham, Frank and Hyman, Dick, *Baseball Wit: and Wisdom.* David McKay, New York, 1962.

Grey, Zane, *The Shortstop.* Grosset and Dunlap, New York, 1937 (reprint of 1909 original).

Jordan, Pat, *The Suitors of Spring.* Dodd, Mead, New York, 1973.

Kahn, Roger, *A Season in the Sun.* Harper and Row, New York, 1977.

———, *Good Enough to Dream.* Doubleday, Garden City, New York, 1985.

———, *The Boys of Summer.* Harper & Row, New York, 1972.

Koppett, Leonard, *A Thinking Man's Guide to Baseball.* Dutton, New York, 1967.

Lardner, Ring, *You Know Me Al.* World Publishing Company, Cleveland, 1945 (reprint of 1914 ed.).

Lee, Bill, with Dick Lally, *The Wrong Stuff.* Viking, New York, 1986.

Lomax, Stan and Stanley, Dave, *A Treasury of Baseball Humor.* Lantern Press, New York, 1950.

Lowry, Phillip J., *Green Cathedrals.* Society for American Baseball Research, Cooperstown, New York, 1986.

Lyle, Sparky and Golenbock, Peter, *The Bronx Zoo.* Crown, New York, 1979.

McCarver, Tim, *Oh, Baby, I Love It.* Dell, New York, 1988.

Maikovich, Andrew J., *Sports Quotations.* McFarland, Jefferson, North Carolina, 1984.

Marazzi, Rich, *The Rules and Lore of Baseball.* Stein and Day, New York, 1980.

Mathewson, Christy, *Catcher Craig.* Grosset and Dunlap, New York, 1915.

Mead, William B., *Even the Browns.* Contemporary Books, Chicago, 1978.

Mitchell, Jerry, *The Amazing Mets.* Grosset & Dunlap, New York, 1970.

Murray, Jim, *The Best of Jim Murray.* Doubleday, Garden City, New York, 1965.

Nelson, Kevin, *Baseball's Greatest Quotes.* Fireside Books/Simon and Schuster, New York, 1982.

Offit, Sidney (editor), *The Best of Baseball.* Putnam, New York, 1956.

Peterson, Harold, *The Man Who Invented Baseball.* Scribners, New York, 1973.

Quigley, Martin, *The Crooked Pitch: The Curveball in American Baseball History.* Algonquin Books, Chapel Hill, North Carolina, 1984.

Reichler, Joseph L. (editor), *The Baseball Encyclopedia.* Macmillan, New York, 1969, "revised, updated and expanded" edition through 1985.

Rice, Grantland, *The Tumult and the Shouting: My Life in Sport.* A. S. Barnes, New York, 1954.

Richter, Francis C., *The Millennium Plan of Sporting Life.* Sporting Life Publishing Co., Philadelphia, 1888.

Ritter, Lawrence S., *The Glory of Their Times.* Macmillan, New York, 1966.

Robinson, Jackie with Dexter, Charles, *Baseball Has Done It.* Lippincott, Philadelphia, 1964.

Schiffer, Michael, *Ballpark.* Signet, New York, 1982.

Smith, H. Allen, *Low and Inside.* Doubleday, Garden City, New York, 1949.

Smith, Myron J., *Baseball: A Comprehensive Bibliography.* McFarland and Co., Jefferson, North Carolina, 1986.

Smith, Robert, *Baseball.* Simon and Schuster, New York, 1947.

Stern, Bill, *Favorite Baseball Stories.* Pocket Books, New York, 1949.

United States Congress, House of Representatives, Committee on the Judiciary, *Organized Baseball.* GPO, Washington, D.C., 1952.

Veeck, Bill, with Linn, Ed, *Veeck—As in Wreck.* New American Library, New York, 1962.

Vogel, O. H., *Ins and Outs of Baseball.* C. V. Mosby, St. Louis, 1952.

Waggoner, Glen (editor), *Rotisserie League Baseball.* Bantam, New York, 1984.

Wallop, Douglas, *Baseball: An Informal History.* Norton, New York, 1969.

———, *The Year the Yankees Lost the Pennant.* Norton, New York, 1954.

Williams, Ted, with John Underwood, *The Science of Hitting.* Simon and Schuster, New York, 1970.

Wills, Maury, with Don Freeman, *How to Steal a Pennant.* Putnam, New York, 1976.

III. Works on words and language and general works that were especially useful in the preparation of this dictionary.

Ciardi, John, *A Browser's Dictionary.* Harper and Row, New York, 1980.

————, *A Second Browser's Dictionary.* Harper and Row, New York, 1983.

————, *Good Words to You.* Harper and Row, New York, 1987.

Colcard, Joanna Carver. *Sea Language Comes Ashore.* Cornell Maritime Press, New York, 1945.

Evans, Bergen, *Comfortable Words.* New York, Random House, 1962.

Farmer, John S., *Americanisms.* Thomas Poulter and Sons, London, 1889; republished by Gale Research Co., Detroit, 1976.

Farmer, John S. and Henley, W. E., *Slang and Its Analogues.* Arno Press, New York, 1970; reprint of the original multi-volume series of 1890–1904.

Funk, Charles Earle, *Heavens to Betsy!* Harper, New York, 1955.

Hendrickson, Robert, *The Facts On File Encyclopedia of Word and Phrase Origins.* Facts On File, New York, 1987.

————, *Salty Words.* Hearst Marine Books, New York, 1984.

Holt, Alfred H., *Phrase and Word Origins.* Dover, New York, 1961.

Howard, Philip, *A Word in Your Ear.* Oxford University Press, New York, 1983.

Mallery, Richard D., *Our American Language.* Halcyon House, New York, 1947.

Marckwardt, Albert H., *American English.* Oxford University Press,, New York, 1958.

Mathews, Mitford M., *Americanisms.* Chicago: University of Chicago Press, 1966.

Morris, William and Morris, Mary, *Morris Dictionary of Word and Phrase Origins.* Harper and Row, New York, 1977.

Partridge, Eric, *A Dictionary of Catch Phrases.* Stein and Day, New York, 1977.

————, *A Dictionary of Slang and Unconventional English;* 8th edition, edited by Paul Beale. Routledge & Kegan Paul, London, 1984.

Plunkett, E. R., *Folk Names and Trade Diseases.* Stamford, Connecticut, Barrett, 1978.

Rogers, James, *The Dictionary of Cliches.* Facts On File, New York, 1985.

Shipley, Joseph T., *Dictionary of Word Origins.* Philosophical Library, New York, 1945.

Smith, Logan Piersall, *Words and Idioms.* Constable, London, 1925.

Sullivan, Mark, *Pre-War America,* vol. III of *Our Times.* Scribner, New York, 1930.

Vallins, G. H., *The Making and Meaning of Words.* Adam and Charles Black, London, 1949.

Versand, Kenneth, *Polyglot's Lexicon 1943–1966.* Links Books, New York, 1973.

Weingarten, Joseph A., *An American Dictionary of Slang.* Privately published; New York, 1954.

Wentworth, Harold and Flexner, Stuart Berg, *Dictionary of American Slang.* Thomas Y. Crowell, New York, 1960.